CRIME
AND JUSTICE

Volume III

THE CRIMINAL IN CONFINEMENT

CRIME AND JUSTICE

edited by Leon Radzinowicz and Marvin E. Wolfgang

Volume I   THE CRIMINAL IN SOCIETY

Volume II   THE CRIMINAL IN THE ARMS OF THE LAW

Volume III   THE CRIMINAL IN CONFINEMENT

CRIME

AND JUSTICE

Volume III

THE CRIMINAL IN CONFINEMENT

EDITED BY

Leon Radzinowicz and Marvin E. Wolfgang

Basic Books, Inc., Publishers

NEW YORK / LONDON

Preface

Until quite recently criminology was taught through the medium of textbooks, each the work of one or two authors at most. In their heyday such volumes could present a comprehensive, if somewhat simplified, view of all the important aspects of the subject. Some of them are remarkable achievements of their kind.

In contrast to these textbooks stands the casebook. It was only a few years ago that this teaching device, already so familiar in the neighboring fields of criminal law and sociology, as indeed in the whole field of legal disciplines and social sciences, was introduced into criminology. Since then, however, it has rapidly overhauled the textbook as a pedagogical tool and collections have multiplied.

Three circumstances at least have fostered the change. The first is the composite character of criminology. Because it derives so many of its principles, its methods and its theories from those of other disciplines, and because it covers such diverse kinds of inquiry, it is often to the specialist that we must look for the leading statement of a particular problem, the new challenge to an established assumption. Second, criminology has been so active in the past few years, penetrating into so many fresh areas, that it is no longer possible for a single author to do full justice to the whole. Third, important criminological material is so widely scattered, and in such disparate places, that it is often difficult for students to spot and lay hands upon it, or to discern its place in the scheme of things. The best of it can be brought together and made easily available only by the process of catholic exploration, followed by arduous sifting, that goes to the making of a collection such as this.

Though some overlapping is unavoidable, each collection of reading material has its characteristic flavor reflecting the personality, the experience, the judgment and the approach of those who have compiled it. This particular selection emphasizes above all the interaction of several aspects of criminological study. It traces the major trends in crime, in criminal justice, and in correctional practice, so as to bring out the ways in which they affect each other. It does not, however, take in the side of criminology concerned with the individuality of the offender and with his criminal behavior as a manifestation of his biological or psychological makeup.

A collection of material does not offer a rigid scheme for teaching. On the contrary, it provides a reservoir of material from which the teacher can select and re-select. The Introductions, in which we have been assisted by Miss Joan F. S. King, give a general guide to contents and continuities throughout.

We anticipate that these volumes will be used by law schools in the teaching of criminal law and the administration of justice. They should prove of value in new courses and special seminars on the social and behavioral sciences. They should also provide pertinent material for police academies, correctional training centers and sentencing institutes. And hopefully these essays will interest laymen who would like to learn more about problems of crime in contemporary society.

This selection was compiled when Professor Marvin Wolfgang was a Visiting Fellow at the Cambridge Institute. During this period we worked in collaboration, drawing upon the resources of the Institute and on our respective experiences of teaching at Columbia Law School and at Philadelphia. We both found it rewarding enough to respond to the suggestion of Mr. William L. Gum, an editor at Basic Books, that it should be published. We are grateful to him for all the good advice he gave us during its final preparation.

Throughout this collection we have adopted the attitude that our authors should be allowed to speak for themselves; therefore we have reduced our editing to the strict minimum. We should like to express our thanks for their courtesy in making this enterprise possible.

The material has been divided into three volumes: the first concerned with crime as a part of society, the second with that part of the social response to crime embodied in the official law-enforcement agencies, the third with the treatment of convicted offenders.

(Vol. I)

This volume, *The Criminal in Society,* sets the scene. It raises questions about the nature of deviance, of which crime is often regarded as only one aspect; about the proper scope of the criminal law; about the true shape and trends of crime; about social disharmonies that may be responsible for crime in general and for juvenile delinquency in particular.

(Vol. II)

This volume, *The Criminal in the Arms of the Law,* looks at the enforcement of criminal justice. It weighs the evidence relative to how far the actual performance of the police or of the courts defeats their stated ends, how far they discriminate against certain classes, how far they threaten the liberties they are designed to protect, and how far they themselves are in need of fundamental re-appraisal.

(Vol. III)

This volume, *The Criminal in Confinement,* explores the correctional system not in terms of its official objectives but of its actual effects and effectiveness.

challenges over-simplified assumptions about the results of probation or parole supervision. It examines critically some of the outstanding correctional experiments of recent years. And it also examines critically the experimental methods and statistical tools of criminology itself.

LEON RADZINOWICZ   MARVIN E. WOLFGANG

Contents

C. EXPERIMENTAL STUDIES

Part III

IDENTIFYING AND PREDICTING OFFENDERS

CRIME

AND JUSTICE

Volume III

THE CRIMINAL IN
CONFINEMENT

Introduction

This volume is concerned with the effects and the effectiveness of the penal system. It questions whether the treatment of convicted offenders reduces the likelihood that they will offend again and whether it is possible to forestall criminal careers by early identification of the children who risk beginning such careers. As in previous volumes, the main approach is empirical. Attention is focused not only on what is intended but on what actually happens, whether intended or not. Some of the effects of conviction and imprisonment, for example, may prove to be very different from those intended. On the other hand some of the assumptions about the value and results of penal measures may fail to stand up to objective testing.

The first section weighs the consequences that flow from the criminal's loss of status and of rights, in the community and still more in prison. To some extent deprivations are inevitable consequences of loss of trust and restrictions on liberty. To some extent they are deliberately imposed, perhaps on the general ground that they are necessary for public protection or because it is held that the criminal should be worse off than the poorest of honest citizens, or that the law-abiding must be satisfied and deterred by the knowledge that lawbreakers are likely to be permanently stigmatized. On one hand is the traditional emphasis on the need to mark out the criminal and warn others against him, on the other the modern stress upon restoring him to the community and helping him put the past behind him. How far, if at all, are statutory provisions for curtailing prisoners' rights still necessary? How far, if at all, could the law go in restoring the reputation of offenders who are genuinely rehabilitated? How far, if at all, do the deprivations implicit in imprisonment hamper or help them become more responsible and accept legitimate values?

The second section turns to the question of whether the penal system achieves the purposes for which it was designed? Penal measures are assumed to be protective, deterrent or reformative, or all three: this, as was seen in the previous volume, is the main justification for imposing them. But are current methods of treatment effective in any of these terms? Would offenders do just as well or badly without them? Do experiments in new methods show promise of greater success? Even when the wider questions of general deterrence are set on one side, an enquiry is concentrated upon whether individuals are prevented from offending again, investigations are full of pitfalls, findings by no means easy to interpret. In criminology, as in other social sciences, the possibility of controlled experiment is very limited, and those attempted are seldom immune from criticism. Most studies must rely upon statistical devices alone to take account of the fact that different offenders have very different risks of conviction at the outset, and such decrees are not yet fully developed.

Attempts to identify children who are likely to become persistent offenders are described in the final section. Are there distinctive elements in personality, in family backgrounds, in social setting, which would enable such children to be picked out at an early age, even before they had become launched on a delinquent career? The problems of methodology are discussed in some detail, but in this context they are not the only problems. In dealing with convicted offenders, the question of identification has been settled, a measure of stigmatization is inevitable, some kind of decision has to be made, some kind of treatment (if only a warning) imposed. In dealing preventively with young children, on the other hand, there is at most a likelihood of delinquency rather than a certainty, there is the danger that selection for treatment will impose a stigma that could otherwise be avoided, there is the doubt as to whether measures designed to help them or their families will be acceptable without the legal necessity of intervention. Here, even more than at the other end of the scale, good intentions and assumptions about results are not enough. Unintended effects have also to be taken into account.

Conviction for a crime, still more a sentence of imprisonment, may in itself undermine family cohesion and security, destroy the offender's prospects, result in loss of employment and assets, all quite apart from any deliberate legal measures to curtail his rights. A majority of those who commit crimes as youths outgrow criminality in their twenties. But they may never be able to outgrow their criminal records. This can be a serious handicap in rehabilitation: there is still truth in the old adage, "Give a dog a bad name and hang him." If a man finds his legitimate aspirations blocked by a past he has tried to put behind him he may be tempted to think that he has little to lose in returning to crime. A good name is, after all, one of the strongest inducements to keep the law. On the other hand, both employers and society have the right to protect themselves against the threat of recidivism. Nor can legislation alone prevent the ferreting out of a man's previous criminal record even after many years of good behavior: this is a matter of educating public opinion and also a part of the larger question of the storing and dissemination of personal information about individuals. The Report of the Canadian Committee on Corrections suggests, however, that legislation should permit the automatic nullification of convictions for minor offenses after a few years, and the discretionary nullification of more serious convictions if an offender could demonstrate continued good behavior over a longer period. All sorts of difficulties are raised by these proposals, but they draw attention to the undiscriminating permanency of some of the results of conviction.

Instances in which many states and countries have imposed specific disabilities on those convicted of offences are discussed by Rubin and by Damaska. Usually such disabilities are additional to the sentence imposed by the court and automatic in their application. They may relate to property, to employment, to marital status or parental rights, to jury service, political activity, public office, the right to vote, even to citizenship. Can such measures be justified in terms of public protection, of deterrence? Do they reduce the chances of rehabilitation and reintegration? Should they ever be permanent? Should they ever be automatic?

Rather similar questions arise in relation to the rights of prisoners. Vogelman refers to the constitutional and practical reasons for the reluctance of courts to intervene in this sphere. Such reluctance has not disappeared, but he traces the more recent trend, in some courts at least, toward the idea that, since the prisoner has not forfeited all his rights as a citizen, it is the duty of the court to respond to appeals and to see that a balance is maintained between these rights and the needs of prison discipline. Some rights are lost as a necessary consequence of a sectence of confinement, or are incompatible with the reasonable rules of an institution. But what rules are unreasonable or unnecessarily restrictive? And what of cases where the institution breaks its own rules? What principles should govern restrictions of such basic liberties as freedom of speech, religious observance, access to legal advice and to the courts? What limits should be set to contacts with the world outside? Again, as well as the constitutional issues, there is often the conflict between the need for protection and the need for rehabilitation. And there is also a practical problem, similar to that raised in the previous volume, of how facilities for appeal could be extended without overwhelming the courts.

Status depends not only upon rights but upon responsibilities. The degradation of the prisoner flows not merely from the loss of rights but from loss of responsibility, of participation in the decisions that shape his environment. It is this that underlies the considerations in the Task Force Report on Corrections, of schemes to allow prisoners a part in the running of penal institutions. These range from the short-lived attempts at self-government to very limited representation on committees concerned with recreation. Can such participation contribute to improving conditions and relationships within a prison, to restoring self-respect and responsibility to prisoners? Or will committees that are given any real power inevitably come to be dominated and exploited by corrupt cliques?

The prisoner's loss of status, his sense of vulnerability and helplessness, can severely hamper efforts to rehabilitate him. He may defend himself either by denying his need of help, or by putting the whole responsibility for his "cure" upon the authorities. Mathieson examines these reactions from the point of view of a psychiatrist, but similar responses are likely to be encountered by psychologists and social workers. Indeed, they focus some of the basic conflicts of the penal system, and especially the conflict between individualization on one hand and equality, justice, order on the other. Because imprisonment is a punishment there is the expectation that it will be impartially applied: if it is not, there will be complaints of unfairness. Because individualization is justified on the ground that it contributes to rehabilitation, failure to demonstrate success produces complaints of inefficiency. The fact that psychotherapy tends to be intangible, both in its methods and effects, adds to the suspicion with which it is viewed by prisoners and often also by prison staff. Moreover, whatever may be hoped of treatment measures, they have to be seen against the only too obvious deprivations involved in imprisonment. Mathieson found that although a somewhat higher proportion of men expected to be helped by their period of imprisonment in an institution geared to treatment than in a conventional prison, well over half of those in both institutions expected their incarceration to do them more harm than good.

The major deprivations experienced by prisoners are analyzed by Sykes. Loss of liberty, loss of outside links, moral rejection, deprivation of material amenities, sexual frustration and thus partial loss of identity, loss of autonomy and choice, the threats implied in forced intimacy with other criminals —all these are seen as undermining adult status, as reducing the prisoner to the dependence of a child. Sykes and Messinger go on to suggest that, in direct response to these deprivations, the inmates maintain their own social code, a code designed above all to reassert their autonomy and manliness. If they cannot control what is done to them, they can at least control their own reactions: they can cultivate opposition to the staff and the values upheld by the institution, they can develop loyalty to each other. It is not claimed that such a code, any more than the criminal or delinquent codes discussed in earlier volumes, commands complete loyalty. On the contrary, some prisoners adopt, or have assigned to them, roles which contradict particular tenets. One way of combatting specific deprivations is to accept exploitation by certain "merchants," the feminine role of certain homosexuals. But in so far as an inmate society accepts a degree of mutual loyalty it can mitigate the total insecurity of a "war of all against all," and can reduce the pains of imprisonment.

Wheeler, comparing prisons in Scandinavia and the United States, challenges any idea that the nature of prison culture is the same everywhere and that it can be explained simply in terms of response to the deprivations that imprisonment brings. He contends that the kind of society from which the prisoners come will also help decide the degree of cohesion and the values of inmate society. In Norway, where there is more isolation and introspection, less emphasis on toughness, less tendency to measure status by material possessions, less preoccupation with protest and opposition to authority, there are corresponding differences in the attitudes of prisoners. They show little cohesion, little violence, only vestiges of an inmate code, and that not enforced. Shorter sentences and more segregation may contribute to this, but it is suggested that the prisoners, there as in America, are reflecting the society from which they are drawn.

The danger that prisons will be dominated by the most criminal elements among the prisoners often gives cause for concern. It is they, after all, who are likely to have the longest experience of the penal system: the longest sentences, the least chance of parole. They know the ropes best, have the greatest investment in the prison community, and will often be the least scrupulous, the most violent, the most committed to criminal values. The inquiry reported by Schrag confirms that, in a large mixed prison, it is such men as these who are likely to be preferred as leaders. It also, however, brings out the fact that particular categories of offenders, taken separately, tend to choose leaders of their own types. Hence the argument for smaller institutions, for dealing with such groups as first offenders, short-term prisoners, the well behaved, separately from the more hardened or long-term men. Yet here also there is the need for balance, the danger of going to extremes. If all the most difficult prisoners are segregated for long periods, as they were at Alcatraz, the situation may become intolerable to themselves and to the staff.

The awareness that imprisonment can be both debilitating and corrupting goes back at least to John Howard. The idea is not confined to penal reformers and criminologists: the popular conception of the ex-prisoner as dangerous, untrustworthy, different, rests not only on the knowledge that he has committed crime but upon the fact that he has undergone imprisonment. Clemmer's analysis of the processes of "prisonization" distinguishes the debilitating from the more directly corrupting effects of a penal institution. Few who are incarcerated for any length of time escape the dependence, the loss of self-responsibility, which are common adaptations, common dangers of institutional life; but not all are equally involved in the sharing of antisocial attitudes and activities. Criminal learning, when it occurs, affects prisoners in different ways, at different speeds and at different stages of their prison careers. The nature of a man's links with the outside world, his own record and attitudes, as well as the position he occupies and the contacts he makes in prison, will affect this aspect of his response.

Wheeler carries this further, looking not only at response in prison but at response after release. He distinguishes between the prisoner who adapts superficially and temporarily to the standards of the prison subculture, as a means of making his life tolerable while he is inside, and the prisoner who really absorbs them as part of himself and retains them after he is freed. It is the offender of the second type who would be expected to demonstrate increased dependence or criminality by recidivism, and it is this kind of offender who gives support to the argument that rehabilitation after release will require another deep change of attitude. But is he typical of the majority? After examining a number of important criminological studies of prison subcultures and prison regimes, Wheeler finds little to support the assumption that effects are lasting, once allowance has been made for the different types of offender committed to different institutions. Admittedly, there have so far been few direct studies of the relationship between changes of attitude during the course of imprisonment and subsequent recidivism. But on the evidence so far Wheeler concludes that changes are usually superficial and temporary rather than fundamental or permanent.

Garabedian considers in more detail the patterns of individual involvement during sentence with the values of prison staff on one hand and of the prison subculture on the other. He confirms the general tendency for prisoners to be most deeply involved with their fellows in the middle of their sentences, least so at the beginning and end. He finds differences in the degree, and even the direction, of change for those carrying different roles, though for all but the "outlaws" there is a move back toward noncriminal values as freedom approaches. It is suggested that the timing and content of rehabilitation programs should be geared to these differences, and that for most prisoners they have the best chance of success in the last phase of imprisonment. On the other hand, this last phase may produce over-optimistic expectations, and disappointment after release may contribute to recidivism.

Accurate assessment of the extent of homosexual behavior in either men's or women's prisons is extremely difficult, though no more so than assessment of the real extent of sexual offenses in the community at large. In one sense it is a problem that has to be faced by all one-sex institutions. But it is exacerbated by the totally closed nature of many prisons, by the fact that prisoners have no legal means of securing their own discharge or transfer, and above all by the fact that a community of criminals will include an unnaturally high proportion of the violent and the sexually abnormal.

The report on homosexual assaults in prison included here concentrates on cases in male prisons where threats, force, or some form of blackmail have been employed, especially against youths. The research in a women's prison, on the other hand, is concerned with the more diffuse effects produced by suspicion of homosexual attachments, with the strain and tension, for staff as well as prisoners, involved in attempting to discourage them.

Homosexual behavior and homosexual preoccupations are, like prison subcultures, responses to the deprivations involved in imprisonment: unintended side-effects that tend to corrupt in the short run, even if not more permanently. It is necessary to understand the way they develop, whom they affect, when and how, if precautions are to be taken to counteract them and to protect the more innocent from their worst effects. Defensive as well as constructive measures have to take full account of the nature of prison communities and of human responses to the unnatural conditions under which they exist.

At first sight demands that criminology should test and demonstrate the effectiveness of the penal system seem eminently reasonable. So long as it could be assumed that retribution was an end in itself there was no necessity to measure results; but the modern stress upon the protection of society, the prevention of crime, as the only basic justification of punishment makes the question of whether these ends are being achieved inescapable. Again, this is a scientific and technical age: in the material sphere, instruments and even drugs can be designed to accomplish complicated tasks with efficiency and precision, results can be measured and predicted. When criminal statistics were first introduced it was thought that they would become the basis of similar accuracy in penal legislation: that they would, in themselves, tell the ruler the effects of his laws and guide him as to their future direction.

Such hopes were doomed to swift disappointment. Crime is deeply interwoven with the whole fabric of society, with its structure and its values. Its extent, its distribution, its nature and its trends, will change as society changes. Compared with this deep underswell, the penal system can have only a subsidiary effect. This is not to deny that it is a vital instrument of control, but to accept that any attempt to test its effectiveness must take into account the other changes that are going on all around it. These changes are swift, complex, profound and not always recognized or understood.

The discussion by Andenaes in Volume II indicated some of the problems of assessing effectiveness in terms of general deterrence. Until recently, almost all criminologists have turned instead to examining the effects of penal measures upon individual offenders. These form the theme of the extracts collected here. Such inquiries are in line with the modern stress upon rehabilitation as the aim of penal treatment; many of them have been concerned with experiments designed to discover more powerful methods of changing delinquent attitudes. Moreover, they have seemed to offer a more manageable field of study than the broader and vaguer subject of general deterrence; the researcher is dealing with identified offenders, available for study in institutions or under supervision and the subject of official records.

Yet even on this basis, assessment of the effectiveness of punishment and treatment has proved much less straightforward than it might appear at first sight. It is still necessary to take account of the changing social and criminal conditions from which offenders come and to which they return. Allowance must be made for the different initial probabilities of reconviction for offenders of different ages, sexes, records, offenses. Samples of offenders, criteria of success and failure, vary widely between researchers, making the greatest caution essential in comparing their results, even where this is possible at all. Very seldom has an investigation carried out at one time or in one area been repeated elsewhere to discover how far generalization can be justified. Nevertheless, recognition of past shortcomings exerts its own pressure toward more systematic research in future.

Hood analyzes and illustrates both the pitfalls and the possibilities. What should be the criteria of "success"? What are the limitations of studies which confine themselves to a single form of treatment? Which offenders are the worst risks? Under what conditions can valid comparisons be made between different forms of treatment? Quite apart from more subtle considerations it is obvious that a great deal needs to be done at the most basic level of all, in securing more adequate and accurate information about offenders. And alongside this is the problem of improving the techniques of research.

The effectiveness of different kinds of treatment in the penal system cannot be compared without reference to the considerations which guide courts in sentencing. Courts may differ in their sentencing practices, but they all take account of the element of risk. In deciding between discharge, probation or imprisonment, for example, they will tend, in general, to favor discharge for those they think least likely to offend again, imprisonment for those most likely, probation for those who may need supervision to keep out of trouble. Hence, quite apart from any subsequent treatment, discharge starts out with the highest proportion of those thought likely to "succeed," prison with the highest proportion of those thought likely to fail. Even when the aftermath of sentences is compared in terms of offenders with similar crimes, ages, records, there are social and personal factors which may have influenced the courts in choosing one sentence rather than another and which may also have a bearing upon prospects of recidivism. The excerpt from the English analysis of recidivism rates following various sentences both takes account of the more objective differences between offenders and acknowledges that other differences, relevant alike to the courts' decisions and to subsequent recidivism, may have been left out of account.

Similar considerations apply to subsequent administrative decisions to allocate offenders to particular forms of treatment. In the normal way it will be the "good risks" who are sent to open prisons, or who make the best relationships and maintain contact on probation. Therefore it cannot be assumed without further investigation that superior success rates are due to the type of institution or supervision: they may simply be attributable to a superior clientele. This is yet another illustration of the impossibility of examining one part of the system of criminal justice in isolation from the rest.

If similar offenders could be allocated at random to one kind of treatment or another these difficulties would be overcome. There are, however, two major obstacles: the sense of justice, especially typified by the courts; and faith in clinical judgments about the needs of individuals, especially pronounced among those responsible for carrying out treatment. Neither of these principles give place lightly to the requirements of scientific investigation. The Provo experiment achieved a very modified form of random sentencing; the Californian Community Treatment Project achieved random allocation among a certain class of persistent delinquents; but these are exceptions. Most attempts to test the effectiveness of treatment have to depend upon *ex post facto* comparison of individuals or groups of offenders who have been dealt with in different ways.

For this it is necessary to take account of the different risks of reconviction on the basis of the statistical probabilities. The English study already mentioned is a comparatively simple example of this. It is known that young offenders have a higher risk of reconviction than adults, men than women, recidivists than first offenders: assessment of results of treatment must therefore take account of these differences. Prediction studies involve a much more elaborate search for factors which have been statistically related to recidivism in the past and which can be combined to forecast the risks of recidivism for different groups of offenders in the future. These will usually include such things as age and the past criminal record, but they can also take account of other social and personal factors. Prediction techniques in this sense have been applied not only to assessing the risks of recidivism in treatment research, but to parole decisions and to attempts to identify potential delinquents amongst children. Discussion of the technical and ethical issues they raise has accordingly been left to the last section.

Hood notes that, in general terms, research into treatment so far has shown little difference in effectiveness between different measures, once allowance has been made for the different reconviction risks of the offenders. He quotes Shoham's dictum that "success and failure are more related to the offender's personality than to the type or severity of the sentence he receives." There is no evidence that prolonged detention or training is more successful than short, or probation more successful than fines, or imprisonment more successful than either. Neither the deterrent nor the rehabilitative approach can derive much comfort from the findings, though it becomes clear that many of the better risk offenders could be dealt with by simpler methods, such as discharge or fine, without fear of increasing their reconviction rates.

Bailey reaches similar conclusions after his evaluation of empirical researches. Studies have been becoming more rigorous and systematic, but they have failed to demonstrate the effectiveness of the types of treatment investigated. He and Hood suggest four reasons. Perhaps reformative treatment is ineffective as such, or ineffective if attempted in the context of crime and punishment. Perhaps treatment could be effective but is not really being carried out in practice. Perhaps treatment is based upon false theories about crime and criminals. Perhaps certain kinds of treatment are successful for some kinds of offender, damaging for others: research methods may still be too crude to distinguish these groups.

Is this last explanation feasible? Do different types of offender react differently to the same treatment so that the effects, both good and bad, are masked when they are considered as a whole? As Hood points out, if there are grounds to believe such differences exist, there is a strong incentive, both for researchers and practitioners, to try to develop typologies of offenders which are genuinely relevant to treatment, and types of treatment which are genuinely relevant to the needs of particular kinds of offender. What kinds of people will respond best to discipline, fines, group treatment, individual therapy, casework, limited supervision? Can new forms of treatment be devised to meet the needs of those who respond to none of these?

This approach, too, brings its own problems. Useful typologies of offenders are not easy to devise: ideally they should be objective so that they can be consistently applied by different people. But many personality differences cannot yet be measured in this way. The facts that few people fit neatly into groups, that their attitudes change, that in taking account of one set of differences it is necessary to ignore many others, all contribute to the difficulty of establishing reliable and relevant typologies of offenders. Typologies of treatment are even less developed. If one kind of treatment proves more successful than others for a particular kind of offender, what element in the treatment is responsible? This difficulty is apparent even when some particular aspect of a regime, like group counselling in prisons, is selected for study. It is much more apparent when institutional and community regimes are contrasted. Are differences in these cases to be attributed to the dichotomy between detention and liberty or to that between conventional and experimental treatment methods? Even the simplest kind of treatment has many components, deliberate and accidental, conscious and unconscious.

The prevention of recidivism, the effectiveness of penal measures, are not solely academic issues. The results of research, and the inferences drawn from them, have political as well as scientific repercussions. Both Ward and Glaser discuss the implications of negative findings from this point of view. Support for research into treatment has owed much to public concern about rising crime and violence. There is a temptation for governments and even researchers to hold out hopes that criminological investigation will demonstrate the effectiveness of established penal measures or of cherished innovations. Ward suggests that the emphasis should rather be upon the inadequacy of existing methods and the need to work out new ones. Glaser considers the devices employed to suppress or delay publication of discouraging findings. It may be argued that they are as yet no more than tentative or that the conditions under which the research was carried out have already changed and that it would be misleading to publish it without bringing it up to date. It is hinted that researchers themselves contribute unconsciously to the suppression of their findings by publishing them in terms incomprehensible to those who work in the penal system. Perhaps there is some excuse both for politicians and criminologists. Research is still in its infancy, findings are still tentative, the information on which they are based is often inadequate, the methods of handling it often crude. If results are not to be misleading they must be hedged with caveats and qualifications. Even then they can easily lead to a chain of over-simplifications and unwarranted generalizations which can prematurely affect public opinion or political decisions. While suppression of results is anathema to the scientist and a bar to any real progress in research, there is great need to give adequate warning to others of the limitations of research findings at this stage.

The pieces of research included under the heading of *"ex post facto* studies" are all concerned with established methods of treating offenders and with attempts to test some of the common assumptions about them.

The popular belief that once a man has been sent to prison he is likely to go back there provides one theme of Glaser's inquiry. He demonstrates the fallacies on which it is based, estimating the proportion returning to prison at nearer one in three than the two in three usually quoted. Incidentally he points out that the proportion varies greatly between different states, invalidating generalizations, and that these variations depend not only on differences in criminality but on differences at all stages of law enforcement. The use of a single reconviction or return to prison as the criterion of failure can be misleading in another way: reformation is not necessarily an all or nothing matter. Criminal careers can be dropped and resumed, perhaps at long and unpredictable intervals. Almost all ex-prisoners have had periods in honest occupations and may become reformed later in life after a criminal career. This qualification applies, of course, to the measurement of recidivism after any form of treatment. But it can be argued that it is of particular importance in assessing the response of persistent offenders who may be less likely to make a clean break with crime on discharge. If they are going to reform, they may do so only after several relapses; if they make a fresh start at once, they may be particularly tempted to slip back when things become difficult.

Even though the rates of recidivism among those sent to prison may have been exaggerated it remains true that imprisonment is very expensive in terms of suffering, of waste of human resources and of money. As was seen in Volume II, it has been urged that it should yield place to probation or other noncustodial methods as the primary means of dealing with offenders. This makes it the more important to examine in some detail the claims for the success of probation. Sparks, England, Babst and Mannering, Scarpitti and Stephenson, take up this question from various angles, but certain themes emerge from them all.

If the common picture of the results of imprisonment is too pessimistic, that of the results of probation may be too rosy. Success rates of ninety per cent are sometimes claimed. Two groups of factors have been suggested as accounting for this: one relates to the basis on which the success of probation has been assessed, the other to the selection of offenders for probation.

The comparison of the results of probation with those of institutional treatment presents several difficulties. Failure on probation is sometimes defined as revocation of the order, sometimes as a further offense during probation, sometimes as a breach of conditions (whether an offense or not). The period over which success or failure is measured may be the currency of the order, or a certain number of years after the order expires, or both. To include breaches of conditions as well as actual offenses, and to include the period of treatment as well as the first years free of supervision, is to subject probation to a severer test than imprisonment, since the results of prison treatment are assessed in terms of recidivism, often (as in Glaser's study) of actual reimprisonment after release. On the other hand, to ignore the probation period and measure only subsequent behavior allows probation, as Scarpitti and Stephenson point out, to "get rid of its worst risks" before the measurement of results begins. In practice the most satisfactory approach seems to be to include both periods, since the aim of probation is to prevent recidivism both during and after the order. But when comparison is made with the behavior of those sent to institutions it must be remembered that probationers have a longer period at risk, some of it before any treatment can take effect.

Even on this strict basis, it is evident that successes for probation are much higher than those for many penal institutions, especially institutions for juvenile offenders. Is this because probation gets much better risks, offenders more likely to respond? If courts have regard to the principles of sentencing this should be so: the gravity of the offense and record, the danger of further crime, the likelihood of response to probation, are all factors which they should take into account in selecting probation.

Comparisons, such as those made by Babst and Mannering and by Scarpitti and Stephenson, indicate that the worse the record the higher the proportion of offenders sent to institutions, the lower the proportion put on probation. They also indicate that those with more stable backgrounds and personalities are likelier to receive probation. In this sense the probationers can be said not only to have less initial risk of another offense but to be more likely to respond to treatment.

Two questions arise. Is probation being used in cases where no further offense is likely in any case and no supervision really required? The finding of Wilkins that, for similar offenders, there was little difference in response to prison, fine or probation, and the fact that many probationers succeed with no more than nominal supervision, suggests that fine or discharge might be equally effective (as well as more economical) in some cases; the difficulty, of course, is to distinguish at the outset which these cases are. On the other hand, what of the argument that courts have up to now been too cautious in the use of probation, that they should extend it to more difficult cases rather than rely so heavily upon institutions? The finding by Wilkins could be quoted to support this also, and so could the conclusions reached by Mueller and by Roberts and Secker in California that considerably more offenders could be released on probation or immediate parole without serious risk to the community. Again, it must be remembered that there are great differences in the discretion allowed courts in the use of probation and in the extent to which individual courts employ it. It may well be that areas following a comparatively restrictive policy could safely reduce imprisonment in favor of probation. When all this is said, however, account must be taken of the fact that probation depends heavily upon the co-operation of the offender. If it is used for more difficult cases it will find it harder to make and maintain contact or achieve improvement in their attitudes or behavior. This might reduce public support for probation. Yet to say that to bring in more difficult offenders would reduce success is, in one sense, to beg the question: the important thing is not to demonstrate that a particular treatment has a high proportion of successes but to ensure that difficult offenders get the kind of treatment most likely to rehabilitate them, and protect the public for the future. On one hand it is no good passing over to probation cases it cannot handle. On the other there is little evidence that institutions can handle many of them any better. Obviously there are some who must be incarcerated in the interests of example or public protection. But there are others who give rise to the question of whether probation could be strengthened. Could closer supervision or the combination of other measures with probation, make its impact more powerful?

Sparks finds little evidence from studies so far made that greater frequency of contact would increase the potency of supervision: the best risks seem to succeed, the worst to fail, regardless of whether their supervision is intensive or merely nominal, though the middle risks may show some response to extra attention. However, even the most intensive supervision in these experiments involved less than seven meetings a month: considerably more than that could well be needed to provide the support and stimulus required in the difficult cases. Experiments like the Community Treatment Project or Provo involved almost daily contacts, with hours of intensive treatment.

Another possible way of strengthening the impact of probation might be to combine with it some explicitly punitive measure. In some jurisdictions a fine or a preliminary period of detention can form part of the order. In England it is possible for an attendance center order (involving deprivation of leisure) to be run parallel with a probation order, though not for the same offense. McClintock's study however, gives no encouragement to the idea that the combination of probation and a punitive measure increases success. If anything the indications are the other way.

The experimental studies included in this selection entailed much greater diversification of treatment in the open. Yet they too can be seen as potential extensions of probation. They are all concerned with alternatives to conventional institutional sentences, with finding means of giving intensive treatment to persistent offenders without removing them from the community. They demonstrate that the choice is not simply between prison or reformatory on one hand and probation in its present form on the other. An important trend in future development involves new measures halfway between the two. From the point of view of the criminologists concerned with "effectiveness," the degree of liberty, or restriction of liberty, needs to be considered as one among the many elements in treatment.

It is impossible to study the results of parole without reference to the results of imprisonment that went before it or to the policies which lie behind decisions to grant it. Administrative decisions are as important here as sentencing decisions in considering probation.

The Task Force Report on Parole and After-Care reveals great variations between states, with parole for all prisoners at one extreme and for only ten per cent at the other. Because of this, as Glaser and O'Leary point out, it is meaningless to compare "success-rates." The characteristics linked with revocation of parole are the same as those linked with recidivism in any circumstances: it is the younger men, with the longest criminal records and the most experience of the penal system, who are likeliest to fail. Property offenders are the most likely to violate parole and to repeat their previous crimes in doing so. Violent offenders, those who have committed homicide or rape, are least likely to break parole or to commit the same offenses again. To some extent public fears about parole are unjustified: it is not true that violent offenders carry a high risk on parole, or that the majority of those who break parole are progressing to more serious crimes. Of parole, as of probation, it may well be said that the great variations in its use, together with the evidence of research, reveal that it could be employed more freely without increasing the risks to the public. Moreover the fact has to be faced that a decision to refuse parole, like a decision to refuse probation, on the grounds that a further offense may be committed, will normally do no more than postpone the danger. There are cases where it is necessary to continue detention as the only means of prevention, but the advantages of doing this have to be weighed against the disadvantages of the offender's eventual release with no supervision at all.

All this is not to ignore the wider considerations that court or parole board may have to take into account: questions of general deterrence and of upholding the law. But it is to emphasize the need, in attempts to rehabilitate individual offenders and protect the public from them, to look at the whole sequence of their treatment rather than a single stage in isolation.

It is easy to point out practical and theoretical objections to current penal methods, more difficult to demonstrate that new regimes are feasible or will have any greater success. The experimental studies which conclude the central section of this volume were designed to test certain sociological or psychological theories about more appropriate and effective ways of treating persistent young offenders. The experimental methods are compared with conventional measures: sometimes with ordinary probation, sometimes with ordinary institutional treatment.

Most of them start from sociological theories about delinquent subcultures, assuming that if it is group-values that support and encourage delinquency it is group-values that must be changed. The group should not only be the primary object of treatment, but the primary means of treatment as well. This approach is contrasted with various measures of individual therapy, education or training in institutions, the emphasis upon individual treatment in probation. Nevertheless another feature of all these measures is the avoidance of institutionalization: contact with the community, work in the community, treatment in the community, are contrasted with incarceration. A third element is the belief that delinquents are ambivalent in their attitudes and values, and that they can be brought, through their own anxieties, through mutual pressures or through leadership with which they can identify to question their delinquent standards and to work out legitimate standards instead.

Accounts of the Provo experiment include a very explicit statement of the hypotheses it was designed to test, though they are less explicit as to how some of the objectives and methods could be reconciled in practice. Groups were used both in discussion and in action, pressures came both from within the groups and from the community. The hope of comparing results with those of a closed institution was disappointed, since the judge concerned was willing to allocate very few boys to a reformatory. The comparison between the experimental group and the control group of probationers showed a very marked improvement in both on the previous rate of probation success. In the absence of other information as to what might account for this, it seems that an intensification or diversification of methods, rather than the principle of group treatment as such, must be held responsible for the improvement.

The Highfields Project also pinned its faith mainly upon group treatment and interaction between the boys, though apparently with more direct guidance from the staff. The period of intensive treatment was shorter (only four months and not dependent upon the boy's progress), but unlike the Provo boys those at Highfields were resident during this stage. Though the Highfield boys were on probation, their results were not compared with those of other probationers but with those of boys with similar records sent to a local reformatory. Allocation to Highfields was selective rather than random. The findings were disappointing, in that there was little evidence of change in attitudes or personalities and the general failure rate was as high for Highfields as for the reformatory. Though the few Negroes sent to Highfields did better than those at the reformatory, it was held that this was probably because they learned for the first time that white boys had similar problems to theirs: if Highfields were flooded with Negroes this advantage would be lost. But it could be claimed that Highfields demonstrated that short-term institutional treatment was no less effective than long.

The Community Treatment Project is much bolder in its sweep than either the Provo or the Highfields experiments, and it comes nearer to a genuinely random allocation of offenders as between treatment in an institution and treatment in the open. It does not, however, carry this on to include random allocation to the various methods of treatment available in the community: the type of supervision, the use of group or individual therapy, of education or training, of short-term detention as a measure of discipline or control, are tailored to the needs of the delinquents. Hence the real comparison lies between institutional and community treatment rather than between different approaches within these frameworks.

Taking the offenders as a whole, it appears that, after two years, less than four out of ten of the experimental group had had their parole revoked, as against over six out of ten of those dealt with in an institution. Distinguishing between different subtypes, it is claimed that treatment in the community has been demonstrated to be significantly superior for three kinds of adolescent: for neurotics who act out their emotional problems in delinquency; for the "easily led"; and for those who conform to a group of delinquent peers. So far the only type for whom the institution has been shown to be more effective consists of fairly normal youths who have adopted delinquent values as a way of life and who need to learn explicitly that crime does not pay.

These findings are not unchallenged. Sparks questions the allocation of offenders to subtypes by subjective judgments in the absence of appropriate objective tests. It is admitted that differences in the enforcement of parole revocation may account for at least part of the difference in success-rates. It is also admitted that a longer follow-up period will be necessary before it is possible to assess the comparative effectiveness of the new measures in checking the development of criminal careers. Neither success nor cost can be realistically compared except on this long-term basis. Nevertheless, the experiment has already demonstrated the possibility of carrying out flexible and varied programs of treatment for persistent young offenders outside institutions without serious risk to the community, and it has encouraged further ventures in this direction.

Since it has proved so difficult to bring about any change in the attitudes and behavior of confirmed offenders, would it not be more effective to tackle the problem a stage further back, in the poor and disorganized city neighborhood, in the gang of young people with delinquent values? The Midcity Project described by Miller made contact with existing groups through detached workers and at the same time tried to mobilize community resources to help them. The view of delinquency as a group phenomenon, requiring group treatment, was again put to the test: though a few cases were referred for individual therapy, the central aim was to change the attitudes of groups as a whole. Much attention was also paid to the hypothesis that delinquency among such groups is a response to lack of legitimate opportunities: the workers succeeded in opening up new avenues to achievement, both in work and leisure. A third suggestion has been that youths in this kind of area become delinquent because they lack adequate adult "role models": the workers were able to win their respect, trust and admiration and to offer them such models. Yet the impact of all these endeavors was negligible. Except for an improvement in behavior at school (also noted in the Provo experiment) there was no improvement in general behavior and attitudes nor in illegal behavior or the number of court appearances. It appears that it is possible to make strong personal contacts, to stimulate legitimate activities, to open up opportunities, to provide example and leadership, all without effect so far as criminality is concerned. And though the community program was less fully developed, and therefore less fully tested, the results throw doubt on the usefulness of this approach also as a method of combatting adolescent delinquency, however valuable it may be in its own right.

Is it possible to go further back still, to identify the potential delinquent, the future persistent criminal, before his attitudes harden, before social and family deficiencies or the processes of law enforcement leave their mark upon him? In other words, is it possible, as the Gluecks claim, to predict and to prevent persistent delinquency while children are still very young?

It is clear that the problem of prediction, as such, is not peculiar to endeavors to forestall delinquency in children, though it involves special difficulties in that sphere. Within the system of criminal justice attempts to predict future criminality are commonplace and inevitable. The police may consider the likelihood that an offense will be repeated in deciding between caution or arrest; the courts will consider it in deciding between discharge, probation or prison; parole boards will consider it in granting or withholding parole. The more the administration of justice is individualized, the more attention is paid to the future protection of the public rather than to retribution for the past, the more inevitable it becomes that decisions will be based upon predictions, implicit if not explicit, of an offender's future behavior.

Behind all these predictions, lies experience of the ways that offenders with different backgrounds and characteristics have reacted in the past. Prediction studies attempt to select, summarize and organize this material in a

more objective way. The characteristics selected as "predictors" are not necessarily "causes" of crime, nor do studies attempt to take account of all the
factors that may be associated with criminality. A few criminologists hope
that successful prediction studies may throw light upon causation or prevention. But the primary purposes are practical, the primary questions are
whether prediction tables are workable and whether they work as reliable
means of estimating the probabilities of future criminal behavior.

As Wilkins points out, however, prediction studies cannot be regarded as
deterministic. On the contrary, the whole basis of such studies is the calculation of probabilities, not of certainties.

Gottfriedson surveys the whole panorama of prediction in criminology, relating it to scientific objections on one hand, social objectives on the other.
He considers the purposes for which it has been used, the kinds of factor selected as predictors in different fields, the definition of criteria of "success,"
the stages in the construction and validation of a prediction table. Referring
to evidence that "statistical prediction devices have generally proved more
accurate than clinical judgments," he nevertheless points out that their greater
precision is linked with a narrower range, and calls for "a less competitive,
more collaborative attack," to improve both practical decisions and predictive
devices.

As has been suggested, the prediction of delinquency among children
raises special problems of method and policy. These are of such importance
that five of the extracts are focused upon them: the articles by the Gluecks
themselves and by Craig and Glick, describe and defend the Glueck Social
Prediction Table and its subsequent application in New York; the articles by
Kahn, by Ward and by Hirschi and Selvin, as well as a section of that by
Gottfriedson, criticize not only the methodology of the study, but the claim
that it has been validated and that it could and should be put to practical use
in the prevention of delinquency.

On one hand it is claimed that the Table has been shown to work, in that
eighty-five per cent of those predicted as future delinquents among samples of
New York and Washington schoolchildren subsequently turned out to be so.
On the other hand it is objected, first that the original sample on which the
study was based was not representative of any normal population of children,
since half of it was made up of persistent delinquents, the other half of non-
delinquent "controls." It is objected, second, that the Gluecks did not handle
their data with the special care necessitated by the fact that their sample was
unrepresentative. It is objected, third, that it did not in fact work in New
York: that it over-predicted to such an extent that it had to be drastically
modified, making it a new prediction study rather than a demonstration of the
validity of the original. It is objected, fourth, that even the new table is less
accurate than claimed: that for practical purposes account needs to be taken
not only of the "correct" but of the "incorrect" predictions. What of the children predicted as delinquent who did not become so, and those predicted as
non-delinquent who did? Finally, it is objected that the criterion of delin-

quency was vague and variable: some of those classified as delinquents in New York were not officially recognized as delinquents at all.

The legal and social arguments have been equally heated. The Gluecks start from the premise that, if potential delinquents could be identified young enough, their criminal or anti-social tendencies could and should be checked, mainly through guidance given to their parents. Kahn leads the attack on this position. First, to act upon the mere probability of future delinquency would mean stigmatizing children before their time: far from preventing delinquency, this could become a "self-fulfilling prophecy," making it more certain. Second, even if the Social Prediction Table were validated, it could never give more than probabilities: some of those marked out as potential delinquents might never become so, but the stigma might well damage them in other ways. Third, there is no basis in criminal law for intervention at such an early stage, and it cannot be justified as necessary to protect the public. Fourth, there is no evidence that early intervention does any good: though some of the children in New York and Washington studies were given treatment, no information has been published about its effects. It seems doubtful, indeed, whether parents with the damaging, non-affectionate or over-protective attitudes deplored by the Gluecks would willingly accept the information that their small children were "potential delinquents," still less cooperate by altering their own behavior.

The other major application of prediction tables in criminology has been to parole. Here the technical problems, in particular those of "sampling," have been less severe and some of the tables constructed have been shown to work in predicting the risks of reconviction or recall. The extract by Gottfriedson, Ballard, Mannering and Babst describes how such a study was carried through and validated.

Not only are there fewer technical difficulties in constructing this kind of prediction table, there are also fewer legal, social or ethical difficulties about using it in practice. Those involved are known offenders about whom an administrative decision has to be taken. Moreover one of the accepted grounds for refusal of parole is the likelihood of a further offense. In some prison systems, prediction tables have been admitted, at least in theory, among the sources of information to be taken into account in reaching decisions. They have also proved useful in experiments in parole supervision enabling risks to reconviction to be taken into account with some precision. Even in parole, however, prediction tables have never been accepted as the sole guide to decisions. Apart from anything else, though risk is an important element in the decision to release it is not the only one.

This is even more apparent in sentencing. So far the courts have not used prediction tables even in a supplementary way. Gottfriedson considers some of the reasons for this. In the long run the greatest help they give in sentencing may be indirect rather than direct. In so far as they make it possible to divide offenders more accurately into risk-categories they can facilitate the comparison of the effects of different kinds of treatment.

It is clear that much remains to be done in criminology. It is essential to extend and refine understanding of the social processes linked with trends in crime and its control; it is essential to explore more thoroughly the processes of control itself; it is essential to improve the information and methods that form the basis of studies of criminal careers and of the impact of penal treatment. And both in the planning of research and in drawing inferences from its findings it is essential to keep in mind the picture as a whole: no detail, however significant, can be properly understood in isolation.

Part I

DEPRIVATION OF LIBERTY

A

THE STATUS OF PRISONERS

1: Loss and Curtailment of Rights /
Sol Rubin

A. Civil Rights Lost by Operation of Law

§ 1. CIVIL RIGHTS LOST BY CRIMINALS GENERALLY

Under our law a person's rights are supreme and may be taken away only by due process of law. Accordingly it is a basic tenet of the penal laws (under which rights may be taken away) that they are to be strictly construed. Some barbarous punishments formerly imposed on persons charged with or convicted of crime are no longer allowed. The punishments may be only those allowed by law: imprisonment—deprivation of the right to liberty; fine —deprivation of the right of property; death—deprivation of the right to life; and certain others which our civilization accepts and our codes impose.

The foregoing losses of rights, or punishments, are imposed individually, more or less selectively, by a judge or, less often, a jury. But conviction of crime entails the loss of other rights even though the deprivation is not mentioned in the sentence. A common truism of correctional philosophy is that the penal law and correctional treatment have two consistent purposes— treatment of the offender and protection of the public. Another common truism is that the treatment of the offender should be individualized—that is, it should be appropriate for *him*. If the sentence—the form of treatment—is to be individualized, it cannot be *automatic*. But although the civil rights lost upon conviction of crime are of the same order as the right to liberty (which can be expressly taken away by sentence to imprisonment), property (which can be expressly taken away by sentence to fine), and life (which can be expressly taken away by sentence to death), they are lost *automatically,* for neither the judge nor an administrative board exercises any discretion about the loss of these civil rights. Automatic loss of rights can be justified only if it

serves some universally useful purpose in rehabilitating the defendant or protecting the public. Whether it does so or not is considered below.

§ 2. PROPERTY RIGHTS, CIVIL RIGHTS, STATUS

The rights affected by conviction or imprisonment [1] fall roughly into three
classes: property, civil liberties, and status.

Property rights are in general secure, except as limited by the statutes. In
the absence of statute the convict may take, hold, and dispose of property by
will, deed, or other methods.[2] The statute may establish the prisoner's property rights [3] as well as limit them. In several states it provides for appointment of trustees or a committee to care for the prisoner's property until his
release.[4] A parolee may be subject to some of the same disabilities.[5] In twen-
ty-seven states forfeiture of public office and of any position of trust is a
consequence of conviction and sentence to imprisonment for felony or an infamous crime.[6] Sometimes the result is automatic,[7] sometimes a matter of
administrative decision.[8]

The loss of the right to vote is a statutory penalty for conviction of felony
in three-fourths of the states.[9] It is doubtful that any state permits a prisoner
to vote.[10] In almost all states a person convicted of a felony is allowed to testify, although the conviction may generally be used to destroy the credibility
of his testimony.[11] In half a dozen states conviction is a statutory disqualification for jury duty.[12]

Conviction of felony or sentence to imprisonment is a ground for divorce
under the statutes of most states.[13] In several of these states commitment is a
ground only if a certain minimum term is imposed.[14] In the absence of statute
the conviction is not a ground for divorce,[15] and except in the few states
where the statute refers to a conviction in any state, the conviction is ground
for divorce only in the state of judgment.[16]

Where civil rights are suspended under the statute, the right to sue is denied,[17] although a prisoner may be sued and has a right to defend himself.[18]
Hence imprisonment is generally, by statute, a disability that tolls the statute
of limitations.[19] Execution of an insured for crime does not prevent the enforcement of an insurance policy on his life.[20]

The status of a convicted person entails its own legal and social strictures.
Often no punishment is imposed on a defendant—sentence is suspended
without conditions, and, as we shall observe, often such a disposition does
not carry any loss of civil rights, whereas punishment in addition to the conviction does.[21] But even the person whose sentence is suspended has the status of having been convicted of crime. He may be required to confess the fact
under oath in a variety of judicial and administrative proceedings, and he
may be penalized for it in different situations.[22] Under the New York law he
loses some of his natural rights as a parent: consent to adoption is not required of a parent who has been deprived of civil rights.[23]

The status of citizenship may be involved on conviction. Citizenship or nationality can be lost only in accordance with federal law.[24] The United States

Code Annotated [25] provides that conviction by a court martial on a charge of desertion in time of war from the military or naval service of the United States, or conviction on a charge of treason or attempting to overthrow or bear arms against the United States, results in loss of citizenship.[26]

With few exceptions, the criminal statutes of the United States do not provide for forfeiture of civil rights on conviction.[27] In general, each jurisdiction governs the loss of rights of its citizens, and only with respect to rights granted by it.[28] However, a state may nevertheless by law take away rights from its citizens upon conviction by the United States or another state.[29] State policies differ on the point,[30] and remedial action is needed.[31]

§ 3. CIVIL DEATH

Seventeen states provide by statute that a defendant sentenced to a life term (or, in some states, sentenced to death) is deemed civilly dead, a status carrying with it disabilities generally greater than those that follow a lesser sentence.[32] In seven states the statutes provide that the property of the civilly dead convict shall be distributed as though he were naturally dead.[33] The statute may provide that civil death dissolves his marriage, as would a natural death [34] (although his obligation to support wife and child does not cease).[35] His children are subject to adoption as though he were actually dead.[36]

§ 4. RETENTION OF CIVIL RIGHTS UPON CONVICTION

Some act of positive law is necessary in order for the convicted defendant to lose rights; in general, therefore, a right not lost by statutory provision is retained.[37] The rule has important effects in limiting not only the kinds of rights lost but also the application of the statutes governing the loss of rights. Some rights are generally lost upon mere conviction—for example, the right to vote.[38] But other rights may be retained if sentence is suspended instead of executed—for example, a ground for divorce from a convicted person does not exist if the conviction is not followed by imprisonment.[39] As might be expected, this is often the result of strict interpretation of the statute, and in fact basically is always dependent on an interpretation of statute. The interpretation, however, often (but not in every jurisdiction) leans heavily toward sustaining rights.

Legally—and even more, socially—the defendant's status worsens from conviction to suspended sentence to commitment, and perhaps improves with parole.[40] Even at the risk of doing violence to statutes which provide for deprivation of rights upon conviction, the courts have frequently held that conviction followed by a suspended sentence or probation does not have this effect.[41] It would appear that if the conviction is not absolute because of a pending appeal, the loss of rights should not follow.[42] Until a term of imprisonment is begun, the convicted defendant may manage his property and make contracts.[43] A prisoner who escapes from a penitentiary is not constructively within it while he is at large.[44]

The strict construction of the statutes is illustrated also in the holdings that where the statute speaks of "prisons" or "penitentiaries," a commitment to a reformatory,[45] or to a penitentiary of another jurisdiction,[46] does not entail loss of rights, even though a felony is involved.

§ 5. EVALUATING THE STATUTES

A glance at the origin of the loss of rights of offenders should help us evaluate the present applicability of usefulness of the deprivation. Under the ancient common law a sentence for felony placed the offender in a state of attainder by operation of law. Attainder had three principal incidents—forfeiture of property, corruption of blood, and extinction of civil rights, called "civil death." The blood of the attainted person was deemed to be corrupted, so that he could not transmit his estate to his heirs.[47] The early common law incident of civil death attached in circumstances where the legal status reflected the actual condition. It attached to persons entering religious orders or abjuring, or being banished from, the realm. In the law of sanctuary a criminal escaped punishment on condition of taking an oath of abjuration and leaving the realm forever.[48]

Under modern law the common law incidents of conviction are swept away. The constitutions commonly forbid corruption of blood and forfeiture on conviction. These old incidents of conviction no longer have any meaning, because the feudal economic relationships on which they were based have vanished.[49] But there has been little change or progress in the law since the states were established. In today's world it is hard to justify the statutes depriving offenders of civil rights. Although Blackstone mentioned deterrence, crime was not deterred by the deprivation of rights. The rules had an economic and social origin; they did not arise from the incidence of crime. No one today suggests that deprivation of rights is a deterrent to crime.[50] The better evidence is that states with few such statutes are not beset with crimes by reason of the lack.[51] As we have seen, although some rights (e. g., the right to vote) are commonly lost, a sizable number of states do not deprive the offender of rights. In fact, an old Michigan supreme court decision declared the forfeiture of any civil rights to be a violation of the constitutional prohibition of cruel and unusual punishment,[52] but it seems not to have been followed.

Should a prisoner retain the right to sue? [53] It is hard to see why he should not. If sued, he may sue. A limit on suits does not give the public greater protection. In fact, since almost every prisoner is released sooner or later, allowing suits would put his affairs in better order on release and hence would assist his rehabilitation. Furthermore, due process requires that he be granted habeas corpus and other remedies as a prisoner, and yet other suits may be denied.

Should public office or a position of trust be automatically forfeited upon imprisonment? [54] We need not stop to debate the question of whether one who commits a serious crime should hold high and responsible public office. The more practical question concerns ordinary public employment, public office on a lower level. The task of rehabilitating the offender includes the important problem of suitable and steady employment. Correctional authorities make special efforts to persuade private employers to employ former offenders,[55] but the state would be in a stronger position if it set the example itself. Often it does, many jurisdictions having no automatic barrier based on conviction.[56] The automatic barrier seems illogical, inconsistent, and destructive. Rules requiring automatic forfeiture of positions of trust [57] are of the same order as barriers to public or private employment and have no greater justification.

Should the right to vote be retained by a convicted person? Some states permit it; most do not.[58] A full discussion of the subject would refer to the value of voters in a democracy, the value of voting to citizens, and the general requirements for voters. The point we stress here is the one most relevant to correction: allowing a convicted person to vote does not injure the state, and it supports his rehabilitation by giving him a greater feeling of restoration as a full-fledged citizen. To a *prisoner,* the right to vote would be even more important than to the person in the community who has been convicted, for he has few activities indeed that place him in touch with the world outside, and the lack of contact is destructive of morale and personal confidence.

Should a person who has been convicted be disqualified for jury duty? Few statutes include the disqualification,[59] which, apparently, is not needed.

Should conviction of felony and sentence to imprisonment be a ground for divorce? [60] The ground, it is worth noting, is based on a "practical" rather than a moral consideration, for it is not the conviction of crime but rather the imprisonment that establishes the ground for divorce. Yet most prisoners, even those in a state prison, actually serve two years or less, either through termination of sentence, good-time allowance, parole, or clemency. To make such imprisonment a ground for divorce is a harsh provision without parallel in the law of divorce.

Should a person convicted of treason or desertion lose his citizenship? [61] Treason and desertion are quite different offenses. The traitor rejects his country; the deserter does not. Loss of citizenship is a natural punishment for treason, but not for desertion, which is not different in its nature from other ordinary crimes that do not involve loss of citizenship.

Should certain punishments (a life term, or a sentence to death) carry the range of disabilities and loss of rights consequent on "civil death"? [62] Of all the laws depriving offenders of civil rights, this one is the most obvious throwback, now thoroughly outmoded and without value. If a life term meant incarceration until death, the rule might be debated. But it does not. Most life-term prisoners are eligible for parole just as other prisoners are, and, in practice, many obtain parole.[63] In any event any prisoner—including one sentenced to death—may be released by pardon [64] or may have his sentence commuted and thus be eligible for parole.

§ 6. LIMITED KNOWLEDGE OF RIGHTS LOST

Despite the statutes providing for loss of civil rights of offenders and despite the considerable case law on the subject, the particular rights lost, the point at which they are lost, and the problems of restoring them are obscure both to convicted persons and to officials. Frequently the statutes refer generally to suspension of "civil rights" without specifying which rights are involved. As a result, "it is impossible," says one authority, "to state with certainty just what civil rights are lost by convicts generally. The statutes in the various states do not undertake to define in any inclusive manner the effect of criminal conviction upon civil and political status. Neither has any serious attempt at critical research into this neglected field of law ever been made. Since the statutory provisions in their present form are not sufficiently definitive to settle the matter of the civil and political status of convicted persons and since variations in their wording and differences in judicial interpretation have led to widely divergent results, this phase of the law becomes one of confusion and uncertainty." [65] As a step toward removing this uncertainty, the 1956 National Conference on Parole adopted the following standard: "In each jurisdiction the appropriate authorities should make a study of the laws and practices regarding loss and restoration of rights. The extent of loss may vary according to whether it occurs upon suspension of sentence, probation or commitment. A policy should be adopted whereby the appropriate agency interprets his status to the offender. This agency would be the court or probation staff, the institutional authorities, or the parole service." [66]

B. Civil Rights Lost by Administrative or Judicial Discretion

§ 7. PROFESSIONAL LICENSES

Loss of a professional license may result from a conviction, not by the sentencing process but by a later decision, and typically not by the judge but by administrative officials or agencies.

Within the general police power the state legislature may regulate the issuance of licenses of various kinds. Thus it requires a person seeking to practice law or other professions to meet certain conditions. Many statutes authorize the disbarment of an attorney who is convicted of a felony or a misdemeanor which involves moral turpitude. A court may exercise summary jurisdiction in dealing with misconduct by an attorney and may suspend or disbar him.[67] Not every crime justifies disbarment.[68]

Statutes establishing administrative boards to regulate the issuance and revocation of licenses to practice medicine have been enacted in all the states. Generally the authority is placed in a public board; in some jurisdictions it is conferred on medical societies.[69] Although under the statutes conviction of crime, particularly one involving moral turpitude, is usually regarded as sufficient ground for revocation of a license,[70] the statutes are not uniform in making revocation mandatory; some require a hearing and give the board discretion on the decision.

The other professions are similarly regulated.[71]

§ 8. BUSINESS, INDUSTRIAL, AND PERSONAL LICENSES

Statutes regulate the right to practice a trade or conduct a business, and issuance of personal licenses regulating certain rights of citizens, such as a license to possess a weapon, to drive, or to fish. Eligibility for any of these rights and licenses may be affected by a criminal record.[72] The statutes, which vary from state to state, authorize administrative boards to deny to persons with a criminal record licenses to sell or deal in liquor or beer; practice beauty culture or barbering; engage in nursing or real estate; serve as private detective, special policeman, undertaker, embalmer, notary public, insurance adjuster, etc.; and in some states, to conduct gambling activities.[73] A man with a record may be barred from certain industries.[74]

§ 9. PUBLIC EMPLOYMENT; ENLISTMENT

A person with a record of a criminal conviction is more often than not denied public employment. The denial arises sometimes from constitutional provision, more often from statutory provision,[75] but mainly from administrative rule or the exercise of administrative discretion.[76] If based on rule the administrative decision may exclude any person with a record of crime, or a crime involving moral turpitude, or specific crimes such as habitual drunkenness or drug addiction. Sometimes the record excludes the applicant from certain employments, particularly police or correctional positions, related positions (motor vehicle inspector, probation officer, conservation officer), and those in which the employee regularly handles money. Sometimes particular offenses are bars to particular positions.

Although the policy varies somewhat from time to time, in general the United States military services refuse or strictly condition the enlistment of persons with a criminal record.[77]

§ 10. RESTRICTIONS BY LAW ENFORCEMENT
AND CORRECTIONAL AGENCIES

As a practical matter, usually not as a consequence of any legal provisions, the police exercise a certain surveillance over persons known to have been convicted. However, in some jurisdictions the person who has been convicted is limited in his rights by being required to register with the police in the local community where he resides. The requirement is usually found in local ordinances, not in a state statute.[78]

The correctional agencies (probation, prison, parole administration) of course exercise control over persons who have been convicted, and this is their function. The ways in which they limit the civil rights of offenders in the course of exercising that control and the wisdom of these limitations are examined briefly below.

The person on probation or parole is subject to "conditions" or rules of release. We have referred to these in detail, and have observed that some of the routinely adopted rules may well be burdensome and obstructive to rehabilitation, rather than helpful. Most of the conditions are limitations on civil rights—the probationer and parolee may be prevented from marrying, from obtaining a license to drive, from changing his residence (without permission), etc. Similarly the inmate of a penal institution is limited in the exercise of civil rights which have at best a questionable relationship to a rehabilitative program. We are referring not to disciplinary action, such as isolation or forfeiture of good-time allowance, but to certain routine limitations which in most institutions apply to every prisoner. His right to read is severely limited in practice; so is his right to write. He is limited in the control of his money. The number of letters he may send and receive and the classes of persons to whom he may write and from whom he may receive mail are limited, and his correspondence is subject to censorship. He is severely limited as to those who may visit him, the frequency of their visits, and the manner of visiting.[79]

§ 11. SHOULD CRIMINALS RECEIVE LICENSES?

The administrative agencies are not—or should not be—imposing penal sanctions (the function of the courts); rather, they are determining rights or privileges under general governing policies. The very fact that a variety of administrative agencies have the discretion to grant or deny a license to a convicted person implies that the applicable test is the test of the agency's function.

If the administrative agency's function is to determine the qualifications of applicants for licenses or privileges, what weight should they give or be authorized to give to a record of a criminal conviction? Should a person convicted of a sex offense or embezzlement be denied a license to drive an automobile? For this particular license the offense which almost always serves as a barrier is one related to the use of the license, such as driving while intoxicated.

Should an engineer or accountant lose his engineer's or accountant's license if he has been convicted of driving while intoxicated, or of negligent manslaughter by auto, or of assault? To obtain the answer we must ask, first, is the public endangered by the grant of that license to such a person; second, does the conviction have any bearing on the person's qualification to perform his work? As stated above, the administrative agency's function is to pass on the person's qualifications, not to impose penal sanctions. A license should be granted where, on the basis of reasonable test or proper qualification, the applicant is proved competent to perform the duties and responsibilities of the license. If the criminal conviction is relevant, it should be weighed; if irrelevant, it should not.[80]

Another consideration is the protection of the public morals. Should a convicted burglar be permitted to practice medicine? If the conviction occurs at sixteen, should it bar a professional career? A great variety of employments

—barbering, driving a taxicab, etc.—require licenses. Public morals do not appear to be protected by arbitrarily barring such licenses to persons convicted of crime. Furthermore, the legal barriers are not consistently applied. Persons managing companies rendering vital services are not barred by reason of criminal conviction, and the corporate franchises are customarily not lost, even where the conviction is a violation involving the basic function of the business or service (e. g., fraudulent advertising by an advertising agency or a company; adulteration of food by a food products corporation).

§ 12. SHOULD CRIMINALS BE ELIGIBLE FOR PUBLIC EMPLOYMENT?

Almost half the states, and the United States, do not bar public employment to persons with a criminal conviction.[81] However, even in these jurisdictions the convicted person may be barred by administrative action. In most of the states where public employment of convicted persons is permitted, the number hired is extremely low. The administrative decision is generally made by the examining and certifying agency, rather than the employing department. By policy in many of these jurisdictions, former offenders are never hired for such positions as police officer, prison guard, and liquor control agent. Particular kinds of offenses are often barriers to the same kinds of positions. In some jurisdictions a recent offense and certain offenses—habitual drunkenness, bribery to secure appointment, and others—are considered barriers to any position.[82]

The survey from which these findings were extracted revealed the virtually unanimous view of personnel directors that each case should be treated on its merits—that is, by viewing the candidate in relation to the job and by viewing the conviction not as a barrier by itself but in the light of what it tells about the qualifications of the applicant for the job. Most stressed that government must share with private employers the responsibility for the rehabilitation of former offenders. Several listed positive policies of government in employment of offenders, including counseling, setting aside a percentage or number of jobs for them, and applying special procedures to qualify such candidates.

A policy of attempting to rehabilitate offenders would obviously be served by a statute which did not prevent public employment of offenders. Under such a statute attention must be turned to the examining and qualifying officers and the employing departments. Administration can defeat as well as support a policy of employment on the basis of individual merit. Many public personnel administrators are personally opposed to hiring offenders in general or certain classes of offenders. Needed, therefore, are administrative rules that establish a positive policy of employment of persons with a criminal record, where employment is feasible.

Should men with a criminal record be eligible for enlistment in the armed forces? Although the policy has varied from time to time, ordinarily being more liberal in wartime, those with a criminal record are usually barred. The

problem is similar to that of employment by public agencies, and we suggest
the same remedy. A liberal policy in accepting enlistment of offenders was
amply sustained in World War II.[83]

§ 13. EVALUATING RESTRICTIONS BY LAW ENFORCEMENT AND CORRECTIONAL AGENCIES

We have observed that certain restrictions on the civil rights of offenders
are imposed by local statute (criminal registration ordinances), or by the
more or less formal rules of administrative policy (probation and parole conditions of release; prison regulations) [84]—that is, they are not related to the
needs of an individual case. That such blanket policies have disappointing results is not surprising. The survey referred to above [85] points out that the ordinances requiring police registration hamper individualized supervision by
probation and parole services. Few of the statutes provide that persons on
parole or probation, or persons who have completed parole and probation
successfully, need not register. Often the harassment and additional stigma
conflict with the rehabilitative aims of the correctional services. The practice
of divulging registration information to employers has an adverse effect on
the efforts of registrants to obtain employment. The registration ordinance is
a means of harassment, and some of the officers who deemed it useful said it
was useful *because* it permitted harassment. But many police officers thought
the statute not helpful because it did not assist in the detection or prevention
of crime. Finally, such a statute may be questioned as to its constitutionality
(as a burden on the right to movement, among other things).[86]

§ 14. RESTRICTIONS RESULTING FROM ARREST WITHOUT CONVICTION

The statutes that provide for automatic loss of rights upon conviction or
imprisonment are clearly inapplicable to arrest. However, loss of certain
rights may result, upon administrative discretion, from mere arrest which
does not eventuate in a conviction. The authorizing statutes are characteristically vague. For example, the licensing and employment statutes refer not
only to convictions (as the occasion for denial), but (sometimes) to "disgrace-
ful conduct" or similar language. Under these provisions a record of an arrest
may be a ground for denying a license or a job.

The correctional agencies also act upon arrests which do not ripen into
convictions. An arrest may be referred to in a pre-sentence investigation (unless, as in Massachusetts, the statute forbids reference to arrest not followed
by conviction). Also, probation and parole are in practice frequently revoked following arrest of the probationer or parolee, even where the arrest is
followed by discharge.

The rationale of this administrative behavior is that the ground is not
merely the arrest, but the underlying behavior upon which the arrest was
based, behavior which could have been the basis for the administrative action
without arrest. There, however, the administrative and legal reasoning is sub-

ject to some question. While behavior without arrest could not be questioned, discharge following arrest is itself proof of failure to establish the behavior, and as such could well be considered a reply to the charge of misbehavior.

The remedy for the unfair loss of civil rights upon mere arrest must be found, in part at least, in specific legislation.

§ 15. DEPORTATION FOR CRIME

A criminal conviction may be the occasion for a special loss of a right by an alien. The United States Attorney General may deport an alien who was convicted of a crime which involved moral turpitude and which was committed prior to entry; an alien who has been imprisoned for a term of a year or more for such a crime within five years of entry; and an alien who has been convicted twice for such crimes at any time after entry.[87] From the point of view of correctional policy, two points should be considered. The first is that there should be no grant of administrative discretion—in this instance, authority to deport for crime—without adequate controls to assure equal treatment.[88] The second is the disproportionate severity of the punishment.

Is special, derogatory punishment needed to deter crime by aliens—that is, are aliens more criminal than the general native population? Although the statistics are not an absolute guide, they indicate that immigrants are less criminal, although their first born—citizens—are more criminal. A review of the studies concluded that "this problem resolves itself into one of cultural nonassimilation and social maladjustment, affected to some degree by pure prejudice and differential treatment, rather than to any inherent criminal tendencies residing in any specific foreign group or combination of groups." Rather than enhancing the morale of aliens, the existing penalties depress it.

A distinction should be made between aliens who are in the country wrongfully (and for whom deportation, although a hardship, is a legal restoration to a preexisting status) and those whose original entry was lawful. For the latter the punishment for a crime is not the same as the one imposed on the nonalien who has committed the same act. It is a worse penalty than loss of citizenship, and we have seen how seldom citizenship is forfeited. It is, in fact, a form of transportation as punishment of crime, a penalty proscribed as cruel and unusual. Finally, still from the correctional point of view, conviction of crime does not render anyone—an alien as well as a citizen—hopelessly unfit.

NOTES

1. In some cases rights are not lost upon suspension of sentence, or upon less than a specified imprisonment. Nor are they always lost permanently. Under some provisions the loss of rights is related to particular crimes. Because these laws are in derogation of liberty they are strictly construed. Defendant not disfranchised pending appeal from conviction; State ex rel. Heartsill v. County Election Board, 326 P.2d 782 (Okl.1958). Life imprisonment sentence in federal court does not constitute civil death under Cali-

fornia statute referring to imprisonment in state prison, Hayashi v. Lorenz, 42 Cal.2d 848, 271 P.2d 18 (1954); similar holding. *In re Anonymous,* 175 N.Y.S.2d 282 (1958). Civil death statute does not automatically terminate a marriage under law providing that conviction of felony shall be ground for divorce; Villalon v. Bowen, 70 Nev. 456, 273 P.2d 409 (1954). One under sentence of death is not civilly dead under statute providing for civil death in life imprisonment; Gray v. Stewart, 70 Kan. 429, 78 P. 852 (1904). See Federal Probation Officers Association, A Compilation of State and Federal Statutes Relating to Civil Rights of Persons Convicted of Crime (1960).

2. State Board of Charities and Corrections v. Hays, 190 Ky. 147, 227 S.W. 282 (1920); Haynes v. Peterson, 125 Va. 730, 100 S.E. 471, 6 A.L.R. 1456 (1919).

3. Arizona, California, Idaho, Montana, North Dakota, Oklahoma, Utah. Citation of statutes on this point and most of the others in this section is from Widdifield, The State Convict (1952), a doctoral thesis on file at the Yale law library. A summary of much of the problem dealt with in this chapter is also contained in Tappan, The Legal Rights of Prisoners, Annals, May 1954, p. 99, and Tappan, Loss and Restoration of Civil Rights, in National Probation and Parole Association Yearbook (1952), p. 97.

4. Kansas, Missouri, New York, North Carolina, Rhode Island, Virginia, West Virginia (Widdifield, *op. cit. supra* note 3).

5. Rosman v. Cuevas, 176 Cal. App.2d 867, 1 Cal. Rptr. 485 (1959), parolee may not be held to contract to purchase car.

6. Arizona, California, Colorado, Florida, Idaho, Illinois, Iowa, Missouri, Montana, Nebraska, Nevada, New Hampshire, New Jersey, New York, North Dakota, Ohio, Oklahoma, Oregon, Pennsylvania, Rhode Island, South Dakota, Tennessee, Utah, Virginia, Washington, Wyoming (3). What constitutes infamous crime or one involving moral turpitude constituting disqualification to hold public office, 52 A.L.R.2d 1314 (1955).

7. *Infra* § 17.

8. *Infra* § 18.

9. Alabama, Arkansas, California (but see *infra* note 118), Colorado, Connecticut, Florida, Georgia, Idaho, Illinois, Indiana, Kentucky, Louisiana, Maryland, Minnesota, Mississippi, Missouri, Montana, Nebraska, Nevada, New Hampshire, New Jersey, New Mexico, New York, North Carolina, Ohio, Oklahoma, Oregon, Rhode Island, South Carolina, Tennessee, Texas, Utah, Virginia, Washington, West Virginia, Wisconsin, Wyoming—Widdifield, *op. cit. supra note* 3. Some statutes distinguish between civil and political rights; the Texas Penal Code, art. 52, defines political rights as holding office, serving on juries, and voting. See also State v. Collins, 69 Wash. 268, 124 P. 903 (1912). Oregon—civil rights regarded as suspended, but political rights lost (Or.Rev.Stats. § 421.110).

10. Correspondence. Arizona, Pennsylvania, Vermont—residence for voting not lost when in prison; Widdifield, *op. cit. supra* note 3.

11. *Ibid.* If the convict is not allowed to appear in person, depositions are taken in prison, in Arkansas, Maine, Missouri, Montana, New Mexico, Oregon, South Dakota, Tennessee, Texas. In Kentucky, Pennsylvania, and South Dakota, the conviction, if for perjury, disqualifies as a witness. *Ibid.* See Note, Conviction of Perjury as a Disqualification of a Witness in the State of Washington, 21 Wash.L.Rev. 172 (1946).

12. Illinois, Missouri, Montana, Nebraska, Ohio, Wyoming; Widdifield, *op. cit. supra* note 3.

13. Alabama, Arizona, Arkansas, California, Colorado, Connecticut, Delaware, Georgia, Indiana, Iowa, Kansas, Kentucky, Michigan, Minnesota, Mississippi, Missouri, Montana, Nebraska, Nevada, New Hampshire, New Mexico, North Dakota, Ohio, Oklahoma, Oregon, Rhode Island, South Dakota, Tennessee, Texas, Utah, Vermont, Virginia, Washington, West Virginia, Wisconsin, Wyoming; *Ibid.* Heindl, Divorce upon Conviction for Crime, 27 Chi.-Kent. L.Rev. 189 (1949). Ploscowe, The Truth about Divorce 265 (1955) states that the laws of all except six states list conviction of a felony or imprisonment as a cause for divorce.

14. The minimum term must be at least two years in Alabama, Delaware, and Georgia, and three years in Michigan, Vermont, and Wisconsin, Heindl, *op. cit. supra* note 13.

15. Am.Jur. Divorce and Separation § 41 (1957).

16. *Id.* § 47. See *infra* note 47.

17. Lipschultz v. State, 192 Misc. 70, 78 N.Y.S.2d 731 (1948); Hayes v. State, 50 N.Y.S.2d 492 (1944); *Cf.* Hill v. Gentry, 280 F.2d 88 (C.A.1960), certiorari denied 364 U.S. 875, 81 S.Ct. 119, 5 L.Ed.2d 96.

18. State ex rel. Page v. Hollingsworth, 117 Fla. 288, 157 So. 887 (1934); Hayes v. State, *supra* note 17. Some states specifically provide for service on the prisoner; in state prisons—Alabama, Arizona, Maine, Massachusetts, Michigan, Mississippi, Nevada, Tennessee; in county prisons—California, Idaho, Montana, Utah. In Page v. Hollingsworth, *supra,* suit was permitted against the prisoner where he was not personally served. Am.Jur. Prisons and Prisoners § 39 (1942). The prisoner does not have a right to compel prison authorities to produce him in court as a defending party (although he may be available as a witness); State ex rel. Gladden v. Sloper, 209 Or. 346, 306 P.2d 418 (1957); People v. Lawrence, 295 P.2d 4, 140 Cal.App.2d 133 (1956); Edgerly v. Kennelly, 215 F.2d 420 (C.A.Ill.1954), certiorari denied 348 U.S. 938, 75 S.Ct. 359, 99 L.Ed. 735; People v. Cook, 97 Cal.App.2d 284, 217 P.2d 498 (1950). Am.Jur. Death § 9. A judgment against a prisoner may be enforced by garnishee process against his debtor, and his property is subject to payment of his debts; *id.* § 10.

19. Arizona, California, Colorado, Idaho, Illinois, Indiana, Kansas, Maine, Massachusetts, Michigan, Minnesota, Mississippi, Montana, Nebraska, New Mexico, New York, North Carolina, Ohio, Oklahoma, Oregon, Pennsylvania, Rhode Island, South Carolina, South Dakota, Texas, Utah, Vermont, Washington, Wisconsin, Wyoming (3).

20. Fields v. Metropolitan Life Insurance Co., 147 Tenn. 464, 249 S.W. 798, 30 A.L.R. 1250 (1922), annot. p. 1255 (some holdings *contra*).

21. *Infra* § 4.

22. *Infra* § 7.

23. Domestic Relations Law § 111. The right is not restored upon parole; In re Adoption of O'Daniel, 128 N.Y.S.2d 351 (Surr. 1953).

24. The extent of such statutes may be limited. The Expatriation Act of 1954, 68 Stat. 1146, providing for forfeiture of citizenship upon conviction of the antisubversion statute (18 U.S.C.A. §§ 2383–2385), "as applied to native-born citizens . . . is of dubious constitutionality"—Wachtell, Annual Survey of American Law: Criminal Law and Enforcement, 30 N.Y.U.L.Rev. 112 (1955), p. 118; Kiyokuro Okimura v. Acheson, 99 F. Supp. 587 (D.C.Haw.1951), vacated for further findings of fact, 342 U.S. 899, 72 S.Ct. 293, 96 L.Ed. 674 (1952), reaffirmed upon findings, 111 F. Supp. 303 (D.C.Haw.1952).

25. Tit. 8 § 801 (g–h).

26. A partial list of the federal rights of citizenship includes the right to hold federal office, to the care and protection of the federal government when on the high seas or within the jurisdiction of a foreign government, to transact any business with the government, to come to the seat of government, to have access to the courts of justice and government institutions, to have free access to seaports, to use navigable waters of the United States, to travel from state to state. Crandall v. Nevada, 6 Wall. 35, 43–44; The Slaughter House Cases, 16 Wall. 36, 79; Edwards v. California, 314 U.S. 160, 62 S.Ct. 164, 86 L.Ed. 119 (1941), concurring opinion of Mr. Justice Jackson. See Holtzoff, Loss of Civil Rights by Conviction of Crime, Fed.Prob., April–June 1942, p. 19; and Gathings, Loss of Citizenship and Civil Rights for Conviction of Crime, 43 Am.Pol.Sci.Rev. 1228 (1949). Furthermore, a state may by law deprive a person of rights if he does not have federal citizenship, the common example being the right to public employment.

27. Holtzoff, Gathings, *op. cit. supra* note 27.

28. Gathings, *op. cit. supra* note 27. Wilson v. King, 59 Ark. 32, 26 S.W. 18 (1894)—conviction in one state does not affect right to maintain action in another. Am.Jur.Prisons §§ 38–40 (1942).

29. Gathings, *op. cit. supra* note 27.

30. See 86 A.L.R. 297 (1933) (holding office); 79 A.L.R. 38 (1931) (disbarment of attorney).

31. The 1956 National Conference on Parole recognized this situation in adopting the following statement: "Because the law varies from state to state, and a convicted person may reside at different times in several states, his status with respect to the rights he has lost or retained will vary from one state to another and will frequently be quite unclear. It is recommended that this problem be referred to the Council of State Governments for consideration of needed action, whether in the form of a proposed interstate agreement, or uniform legislation, or other clarification of law on the status of convicted offenders." Parole in Principle and Practice 138 (1957).

32. Alabama, Arizona, California (and person sentenced to death, during period in which death penalty not executed), Idaho, Kansas, Maine (life imprisonment or death sentence), Minnesota, Missouri, Montana, New Hampshire (death sentence), New York, North Dakota, Oklahoma, Oregon, Rhode Island, Utah, Vermont—Widdifield, *op. cit. supra* note 3. In the absence of statute conviction and sentence for crime do not result in civil death—Frazer v. Fulcher, 17 Ohio 260 (1848); Cannon v. Windsor, 1 Houst. 143 (Del.1855); Kenyon v. Saunders, 18 R.I. 590, 30 A. 470 (1894); Willingham v. King, 23 Fla. 478, 2 So. 851 (1887); Dade Coal Co. v. Haslett, 83 Ga. 549, 10 S.E. 435 (1889); Commonwealth v. Clemmer, 190 Pa. 202, 42 A. 675 (1899); Hine v. Simon, 95 Okl. 86, 218 P. 1072 (1923)—cited Widdifield at 166. Construction of statutes, *supra* note 1. See Attorney General's Survey 279 (1939).

33. Alabama, Kansas, Maine, Missouri, New Hampshire, Rhode Island, Vermont; Widdifield, *op. cit. supra* note 10. In several states the prisoner's property is not distributed immediately upon civil death, but the statutes provide for the appointment of trustees or committees to take charge for the benefit of the convict, his family, and creditors—New York, North Carolina, South Carolina, Texas, Virginia, West Virginia; *ibid*.

34. Maine, Michigan, New Hampshire, New York. In Rhode Island and Vermont the marriage is dissolved, but a decree must be entered; *ibid*. Civil death statute interpreted as not automatically terminating marriage, Villanon v. Bowen, 70 Nev. 456, 273 P.2d 409 (1954). Am.Jur. Death § 6 (1938).

35. In re Lindewall's Will, 287 N.Y. 347, 39 N.E.2d 907 (1942).

36. Wright v. Price, 226 Ala. 468, 147 So. 675 (1933). And see text *supra* at note 31.

37. *Supra* note 2 and text; note 15 and text; note 33. In re Donnelly, 125 Cal. 417, 58 P. 61 (1898). As to the right to sue where there are no statutes suspending civil rights, convicts can sue; Hardin v. Dodd, 176 Ga. 119, 167 S.E. 277 (1932); Bosteder v. Duling, 115 Neb. 557, 213 N.W. 809 (1927); Kenyon v. Saunders, 18 R.I. 590, 30 A. 470 (1894); Scott v. Scott, 192 Ga. 370, 15 S.E.2d 416 (1947); unless the statute provides for suit by warden (Tennessee), or a trustee (Kansas), or committee (West Virginia).

38. *Supra* § 2.

39. *Supra* note 22 and text. See 2 Attorney General's Survey of Release Procedures 345 *et seq.* (1939). And see *supra* ch. 6 § 4 for consideration of the proper ground for the holding. Idaho Code § 18–310, after providing for suspension of rights upon imprisonment, adds that all civil rights that are not political may be exercised during parole or probation.

40. Since the parolee is responsible for his daily living, of course he exercises many rights not exercised by the man in prison; in fact, he is free of restraint except as the specified conditions of release restrict him, and these conditions may be broad or narrow; see *supra* ch. 15, § 8. To treat the parolee as a prisoner is to push the concept that

he is serving his term outside prison walls to an unrealistic interpretation inconsistent with the purposes of parole. But this is done in some situations; see cases cited *supra* notes 12, 31. Compare Idaho Code provision cited *supra* note 40.

41. People v. Fabian, 192 N.Y. 443, 85 N.E. 672 (1908). See 30 Colum.L.Rev. 1045, 1046; 36 A.L.R.2d 1238 (1953). *Contra,* People v. Andrae, 295 Ill. 445, 129 N.E. 178 (1920); Opinions Atty.Gen.Ill.1933, 277; discussed 2 U. S. Attorney General's Survey of Release Procedures 348 (1939).

42. Am.Jur. Death § 44 (1938).

43. Martin v. Long, 92 W.Va. 624, 115 S.E. 791 (1923).

44. State v. Griffith, 88 W.Va. 582, 107 S.E. 302 (1921).

45. People v. Yurkiates, 404 Ill. 157, 88 N.E.2d 458 (1949); Foster v. State, 205 Misc. 736, 129 N.Y.S.2d 418 (1954). Generally, see Note, 26 Geo.L.J. 1051 (1938).

46. Hayashi v. Lorenz et al., 42 Cal.2d 848, 271 P.2d 18 (1954).

47. Am.Jur. Criminal Law § 506 (1938). *Id.,* Prisons and Prisoners § 39 cites Blackstone as giving the reason for the rule of forfeiture that it affected the prisoner's family, and his sense of duty to them as well as his dread of punishment would tend to deter him from crime.

48. Am.Jur. Death § 3 (1938).

49. "The effect of corruption of blood was that descent could not be traced through a person whose blood was corrupted. Also his real property escheated to the lord of the fee or to the king. The personal property of a traitor or felon was forfeited not by his attainder but by his conviction. These incidents of treason and felony have their source in the feudal theory that property, especially landed property of a superior lord, was held upon the condition of discharging duties attaching to it, and was forfeited by the breach of these conditions. . . . They were abolished [in 1870]." Stephen, A History of the Criminal Law of England 487–88 (1883).

50. Widdifield, Tappan, *op. cit. supra* note 3.

51. "In Michigan a person loses no civil rights upon conviction of a criminal offense, or upon sentence following conviction. . . . We have, of course, observed that the problem exists with some of the parolees we have supervised for other states, and we have felt that we were fortunate to be free of this added complexity. In our opinion, to cause convicted offenders to lose their civil rights is to add to the degradation or stigma that they already feel, and complicates further their readjustment." Gus Harrison, director, Department of Corrections, correspondence with author.

52. Robison v. Miner and Haug, 68 Mich. 549, 563, 37 N.W. 21 (1888). "It is safe to say that throughout the United States any fine or forfeiture is unusual which has not some limitation of value, and any punishment is unusual which forfeits any civil rights. Duelling and conviction on an impeachment are the only two things in most states which involve civil incapacities of a public nature, and both of these are provided for by the constitution. Disability to transact business is almost or quite unheard of in this country."

53. *Supra* § 2.

54. *Ibid.*

55. *Infra* § 22.

56. *Infra* § 9.

57. *Supra* § 2.

58. *Supra* § 2. In practice, of course, electors are generally not queried on the point.

59. *Supra* § 2.

60. *Supra* § 2.

61. *Supra* § 2.

62. *Supra* § 3.

63. National Prisoner Statistics, 1960, tables 58–106.

64. Note, Civil Death Statutes—Medieval Fiction in a Modern World, 50 Harv.L. Rev. 968 (1937).

65. Attorney General's Survey of Release Procedures 345, 352 (1939): "It seems desirable that probationers should always be carefully instructed as to their civil status from the very outset of supervision. Otherwise misunderstandings are likely to arise which will have an unfortunate effect upon the attitude of the probationer. Unfortunately, in the present confusion of the law not even judges are qualified to offer such instructions." Widdifield, *op. cit. supra* note 3, at 174: "The principal difficulty is that where rights are suspended by a blanket suspension statute, the civil rights of a convict are usually in doubt because of the exceptions that may be allowed such as the right to sue or to transfer property."

66. National Conference on Parole, Parole in Principle and Practice 137 (1957).

67. Am.Jur. Attorneys at Law § 279 (1936). C.J.S. Attorney and Client §§ 18–20 (1937). This authority of the court is subject to legislative regulation, which usually exercises it by placing supervision of attorneys in the hands of the court, specifying the general criteria of punishment; *id.,* § 251.

68. Am.Jur. Attorneys § 12 (1936).

69. Am.Jur. Physicians and Surgeons §§ 19, 41, 42 (1942).

70. *Id.,* § 55.

71. *Id.,* Drugs and Druggists; Licenses § 9 *et seq.*

72. In one unusual case, the deprivation of right was held in violation of the constitutional prohibition against cruel and unusual punishment.

73. Persons who have been convicted of crime may not receive a license under the New Jersey raffles licensing law; N.J.S.A. 5:8–52.

74. See *infra* § 22.

75. *Supra* § 5.

76. By constitutional provision—*e. g.,* Louisiana; by statute—*e. g.,* Massachusetts.

77. Felons are not acceptable for employment; youthful offenders or juvenile delinquents may enlist, if waiver granted by major commanders, which authority may be delegated to recruiting main station commanders; Code of Federal Regulations, tit. 32, pt. 571.2(f) (5) (b).

78. Note, Criminal Registration Ordinances: Police Control over Potential Recidivist, 103 U.Pa.L.Rev. 60 (1954). Florida Stats. ch. 57–19 requires registration of felons when entering any county; Nevada has a similar statute (Nevada Rev.Stats. § 207.080). Local registration ordinances invalid if state legislation has preempted the field; Abbott v. Los Angeles, 53 Cal.2d 674, 3 Cal.Rptr. 158 (1960). Registration of sex and narcotics offenders is often required; see *supra* ch. 11, § 14.

79. American Correctional Association, Handbook on the Inmate's Relationships with Persons from Outside the Adult Correctional Institution (1953). And see *supra* ch. 8.

80. License to practice medicine was suspended where there was a conviction of failing to produce documents subpoenaed by a congressional committee; Barsky v. Board of Regents, 347 U.S. 442, 74 S.Ct. 650, 98 L.Ed. 829 (1953). Conviction of violating Internal Revenue Code, filing false and fraudulent income tax return, does not necessarily involve moral turpitude, under California statute authorizing summary disbarment of attorneys convicted of felony involving moral turpitude; referred to the governors of the state bar for hearing as to whether the particular offense involved moral turpitude; In re Hallihan, 43 Cal.2d 243, 272 P.2d 768 (1954) disbarment was subsequently ordered. Needless to say, lawyers and doctors guilty of such offenses as adultery and tax evasion (almost always not prosecuted criminally) continue to practice. Which way public protection?

81. *Supra* note 13.

82. Wise, Public Employment of Persons with a Criminal Record, 6 NPPA J. 197, 198 (1960).

83. During World War II 8,313 federal probationers entered military service; 61 were known to have received dishonorable discharges during the period 1940 through 1946 (Fed.Prob., June 1950, p. 39). See New York State Division of Parole, New York's Parolees Fight for Their Country (1946).

84. *Supra* § 13.

85. *Supra* note 84. See also Wilson, McPhee and Magleby, Are Criminal Registration Laws Sound? 4 NPPA J. 271 (1958).

86. American Correctional Association, *op. cit. supra* note 81. An ordinance was held a violation of due process where it required a felon to register with the municipal police, as to defendant who had no knowledge of the duty to register and there was no proof of the probability of such knowledge; Lambert v. California, 355 U.S. 225, 78 S.Ct. 240, 2 L.Ed.2d 228 (1957), modification and rehearing denied 355 U.S. 937, 78 S.Ct. 410, 2 L.Ed.2d 419 (1958).

87. U.S. Code Ann. tit. 8, § 1251. The statute is strictly construed; where sentence of imprisonment was suspended, defendant held not subject to deportation; Holzapfel v. Wyrsch, 157 F.Supp. 43 (D.C.N.J. 1957), affirmed 259 F.2d 890 (C.A. 1958).

88. National Commission on Law Observance and Enforcement, Report on the Enforcement of the Deportation Laws of the United States (Report No. 5, 1931), p. 101; Note, The Attorney-General and Aliens: Unlimited Discretion and the Right to Fair Treatment, 60 Yale L.J. 152 (1951).

2: Consequences of Conviction in Various Countries / *Mirjan R. Damaska*

Consequences of Conviction Affecting Citizenship and Political Rights

The consequences of conviction affecting citizenship will be taken up first, because it is citizenship which represents the basis upon which all political rights are superimposed.[1] Next we will deal with the possible loss of political rights—those rights which enable a person to participate in public affairs.[2] Consequently we will not only deal with various electoral and voting disqualifications, but also with various restrictions on the freedom of public expression, freedom of assembly, etc.

A. EFFECTS REGARDING CITIZENSHIP

Very few countries surveyed *explicitly* provide that conviction of certain offenses entails loss of citizenship. Until the reform years beginning in 1958, Soviet law contained an expatriation statute. Included in all criminal codes of the constituent republics was the measure of "designating the convict as an enemy of the toilers," which implied stripping of citizenship and even expulsion from the country. This punishment was, however, limited to the most serious offenses considered to endanger the security of the state, and was hardly

From Mirjan R. Damaska, "Adverse Legal Consequences of Conviction and Their Removal: A Comparative Study," *Journal of Criminal Law, Criminology and Police Science* 59:3 (1968): 356–359.

ever used in practice; the new Soviet criminal legislation contains no such expatriation statute. Some countries still *explicitly* provide for the punishment
of loss of nationality to others than natural-born citizens. They apply only to
persons who acquired citizenship through naturalization or some other legal
device. This, for instance, is the case under the *French* Code on Citizenship
of 1945, which contains a provision whereby citizens, other than natural-
born, may forfeit their nationality, *inter alia,* in case of conviction of an offense against the "internal or external security of the state." Similarly, by
Spanish law,[3] naturalized citizens convicted of some offenses of treasonable
nature and various offenses against international law may suffer loss of citizenship. Treasonable conduct, coupled with failure to return to the country
and stand trial, may cause a naturalized *Canadian* citizen to lose his citizenship (Citizenship Act, as amended in 1958).

Perusal of various nationality laws reveals, however, that the number of
countries in which the state has the power to strip convicts of their citizenship may be much larger. Many nationality laws, in speaking of grounds leading to the forfeiture of nationality, use language so broad that they obviously
cover convictions of criminal offenses. Analysis of all these laws falls, however, outside of the scope of this study.

In this connection, it should perhaps be noted that a few nationality laws
explicitly prohibit deprivation of citizenship following conviction of a criminal offense. An example of this rare provision is the *Yugoslav* law on citizenship of 1945, which allows the stripping of one's nationality only if the
citizen resides outside the country, damages his homeland, and acquires another nationality; conviction of a criminal offense per se will not suffice.[4]

On the other side of the coin, conviction may operate as a legal impediment to the *acquisition* of *citizenship* by way of naturalization. If used dis-
criminately, this particular effect of conviction appears understandable and
justifiable. But here again, few countries expressly refer to conviction as an
impediment to naturalization (*France* and *Norway*). Most jurisdictions use
broad formulas in describing prerequisites to the granting of naturalization,
and such formulas, no doubt, cover conviction of at least those offenses
which involve moral turpitude. An illustration in point is the *West German*
Statute on Federal and States' Citizenship of 1913 (§18) which requires as a
prerequisite to naturalization, "blameless life." Soviet law, in this area, is less
restrictive than most others in that it provides practically no impediments to
naturalization usually inserted in contemporary nationality laws.[5]

B. EFFECTS REGARDING THE RIGHT TO VOTE

Although this disqualification is one of the most commonly found in contemporary legal systems, its scope is somewhat ambiguous. Most civil-law
(legislative) enactments simply refer to the loss of the right to vote, without
amplification. As a rule, the disqualification is broadly construed so as to
encompass not only voting for electoral purposes (parliamentary, municipal
or local), but also voting in plebiscites, referenda and the like. Marginally,

with respect to voting in various aspects of public life (school boards), the demarcation line is not clear. In *West Germany,* the right to vote is understood as relating only to the right to elect; this disqualification however, is coupled with another—"voting in matters for public concern" (§34 *West German* P.C.). The clarity is somewhat greater in countries like *Canada, Greece* and *Israel,* which enacted specific electoral laws for different elections and inserted disqualifications therein.

Loss of the right to vote is invariably found in countries which still include the sweeping penalty of loss of civil (civic or honorary) rights in their catalogues of punishments. In most of these countries, the disqualification attaches to certain sentences either by *operation of law,* or as a result of a *mandatory decision* on the part of the *judge.*[6]

Disenfranchisement sometimes attaches to conviction of specific offenses, sometimes mandatorily, at other times in the discretion of the judge. Thus, for instance, in *Norway,* the judge may deprive the convict of the right to vote only upon conviction of particular offenses and with the further proviso that this disqualification be required in the public interest.[7] Similar provisions are found in the *Ethiopian* Penal Code.[8]

In many countries, the disqualification from voting is only temporary (unless, of course, the life sentence is involved).[9] In others, the disqualification may often be permanent (e.g., *France*).[10] The disqualification takes effect on the day the sentence becomes final, but the time spent serving one's sentence does not count as part of the period during which the disqualification is imposed (e.g., *Norway, Switzerland* and *West Germany*).

Some countries provide for loss of the right to vote only while the convict is *imprisoned*. The disqualification, in other words, does not outlive the execution of the sentence. This limited disqualification is found in *Japan* (unless the crime involves electoral fraud), *Spain,*[11] *England* (Forfeiture Act of 1870), and various *Canadian* jurisdictions (e.g., the Ontario Election Act). As will soon appear, the practical consequences of this system approach the one in countries which have discarded all voting disqualification.

The usual justification for the loss of the right to vote as a consequence of conviction is that anti-social elements should not partake in the political life of a country. This *raison d'être* of the disqualification was challenged in *Sweden* as early as the thirties. Although the weight of argument on this matter depends on the particular circumstances of a given country (such as the actual meaning and importance of the right to vote), it still may be of interest to present briefly the *Swedish* argument against the voting disqualification. The mere desire to attach legal stigma on a convict is in itself no sufficient justification for voting disqualifications. What other considerations may be used in its support? The ratio of convicts to the total voting populace is so negligible that convicts are not likely to materially affect the outcome of elections. On the other hand, voting disqualifications soon become a matter of common knowledge (particularly in small townships and rural areas), the result in reactions impeding the reintegration of the former convict into the community.

Following this line of reasoning, the *Swedes* abolished voting disqualifications as early as 1936; *Denmark* followed in 1951.

Independently of this Scandinavian movement, voting disqualifications were discarded by the *Soviets* in 1958, and *Yugoslavia* in 1959. The *Yugoslav* law, however, suspends the exercise of voting rights of prisoners during the execution of sentence.[12] Of the countries surveyed, no voting disqualifications exist in *India* and *Israel*.[13]

C. EFFECTS REGARDING THE RIGHT TO BE ELECTED

As a rule, disqualification to be elected receives treatment parallel to the disqualification to vote. In fact, the "right to vote" in many civil law countries is understood to include the so-called "active" and "passive" right to vote, the latter taken to mean the right to be elected. It is probably only for purposes of clarity or perhaps because "poenalia sunt restringenda," that statutes refer, often redundantly, to the right to be elected besides the right to vote. Consequently, what has been said regarding the right to vote applies to the present disqualification. The reader, however, may be curious about the *Swedish* argument in support of the former convict's right to be elected. While it seems plausible that the convict in exercising his right to vote will probably not affect political life, the former convict elected to an office may. Here, the *Swedes* rely on the voters. It seems very likely, they say, that the former conviction will become an issue during the campaign and the voters will not be misinformed about the candidate. If they nevertheless choose to elect him, it is felt that the legislature should not interfere with their choice.[14]

The fact that in a few countries the former convict suffers no electoral disqualifications should not be taken to mean that he can be elected to any office or position. While retaining his general elective capacity, he may be shackled with various occupational disqualifications.[15]

D. DISQUALIFICATIONS FROM POSITIONS OF INFLUENCE

If political rights are taken to mean rights enabling one to partake in the public life of the country, then many occupational disqualifications should concern us here. This is the case with the disqualification to hold *public office*, found in various forms in almost all countries. The concept of public office is, of course, quite elusive and differs from country to country. But, whatever the meaning of public office, at least *some* public offices are considered distinctly political.

Other occupational disqualifications, such as prohibition from managerial and leading positions in the press and publishing activity, disqualification from leading positions in the trade unions and political parties,[16] are relevant here, but they are inextricably bound up with various other occupational disqualifications, and their proper situs is among them.

E. THE BAR TO PUBLIC APPEARANCE

The bar to public appearance imposed on a convict may be motivated by political as well as non-political reasons. The lawmaker, for instance, may decide to attach such a disability as a consequence of the abuse of mass media for obscene purposes. However, because of the potential the measure has in the way of preventing a person from influencing public life in any way, we will deal with this disability in the present context.

The bar to public appearance exists in *Yugoslav* law, and consists of the prohibition from publishing in the press, appearing on the radio and television, or speaking at public gatherings. The bar can take two legal forms. It may be provided by statute as a collateral consequence of certain convictions,[17] and in that case takes effect by operation of law,[18] or it may be imposed upon conviction by the judge if, in the court's opinion, public appearance has been misused in committing a crime.[19] Since the disability imposed by the judge is classified not as a penalty but rather as a security measure, it is justified only as a means of preventing recidivism and, in both its forms, is temporary.

F. OTHER DISABILITIES AFFECTING POLITICAL RIGHTS

Some jurisdictions limit the disabilities affecting the convict's participation in political life to those voting disqualifications and occupational restrictions specifically delineated by the legislator. In addition to, or in place of, specific disabilities, other jurisdictions have enacted a broad provision depriving the convict of all "political rights." Such a sweeping formula has been found in the penal codes of *Italy*,[20] *Portugal*,[21] *West Germany*,[22] and, with a slightly different wording, in *Colombia*.[23] The scope of this prohibitive formula is quite ambiguous and the Commentaries, great repositories of law in civil law countries, are unenlightening.[24] No illuminating cases arising under the relevant provisions are known to this author. Many questions remain unanswered—probably in view of the delicate nature of the subject. Can the convict join or form a political party? Can he express his views on political matters on any mass media, etc.? The relationship of at least some of the imaginable disqualifications to the constitutions of the respective countries is not altogether clear.

NOTES

1. The term "citizenship" is not used in the strict technical meaning it often has in civil law legal literature, where it is opposed to "nationality." See 1 PLANIOL & RIPERT, TRAITÉ ELÉMENTAIRE DE DROIT CIVIL (12 ed.) Partie 2, Chapitre 3, § 1, no. 425.

2. We avoid speaking of participation in "political life" and preferred the term "public affairs" because some legal systems use disqualifications going beyond the domain of political life proper.

3. Art. 34, Criminal Code.

4. Leaving aside other considerations, let us note only one, often deplored, possible consequence of expatriation laws. Unless the expatriated person has already acquired another nationality, he becomes a stateless person—a status most countries pledged to keep down to a minimum. See the preamble to the 1930 Hague Convention on Citizenship.

5. Compare Lepeshkin, KURS SOVETSKOGO GOSUDARSTVENNOGO PRAVA 467 (Moscow, 1961).

6. *Argentina* (art. 19, P.C.); *Colombia* (art. 56, P.C.); *Finland* (chapter 2, art. 14, P.C.); *France* (art. 34, P.C.); *Greece* (art. 63, P.C.); *Luxembourg* (art. 31, P.C.); *Monaco* (art. 35, P.C.); *Poland* (art. 54, P.C.); *South Korea* (art. 43, P.C.); *Switzerland* (art. 52, Federal Code) and *West Germany* (§32 P.C.). Automatic disenfranchisement is also found in *Canada* (Crim. Code, section 654[1]), although the punishment of loss of civil rights does not exist there.

7. Art. 31, P.C.

8. Art. 122, P.C.

9. *Holland, Norway, Poland, Portugal, Switzerland* and *West Germany*.

10. Art. 34.

11. Arts. 35, 37, 39 P.C.

12. Art. 55a, P.C.

13. A separate problem is the *opportunity* of prisoners undergoing punishments in an institution to exercise their right to vote. Many electoral laws require electors to vote only at the polling place at which they are registered, and prisoners are excluded from voting unless they can cast their ballot by proxy. To change this, the Committee of Ministers of the Council of Europe recommended in 1962 that prisoners be afforded the opportunity to vote by whatever legal expedient seems appropriate. See Resolution (64)2 on electoral, civil and social rights of prisoners.

14. Compare Strahl, *Les conséquences de la condemnation pénale, Rapport Général, Presenté au VIIème Congrés International de Droit Pénal,* 28 RIDP 573 (1957).

15. On this point, *Swedish* law is unique; as will appear later, there are practically no occupational disqualifications in that country.

16. Such disqualifications can be found in the famous article 123 of the *Belgian* Penal Code before its repeal in the wake of the de Becker case. They also appear among the numerous disqualifications entailed in the so-called "national degradation" provided by a *French* decree of 1944 for the crime of "national indignity." For details see Donnedieu de Vabres, *Traité de droit criminel et de législation pénale comparée* 368, Paris (1947).

17. Art. 37a, C.C.

18. It is interesting, however, to note that so far not a single statute has provided this kind of disability and it remains only a legislative possibility. This is not surprising if the legislator's motive is revealed. The legislative purpose of article 37a, providing many other consequences of conviction besides the one we consider here, was that of *limiting* the power to lay down disabilities flowing from conviction. Before the amendment adding art. 37a, disabilities were provided by a host of bodies (municipal and local regulations, charters of enterprises, etc.). Now, the legislator has the *monopoly* in laying down collateral consequences of conviction.

19. Art. 61c, C.C.

20. Art. 28.

21. Arts. 60, 61.

22. Sec. 34.

23. Art. 42.

24. Compare, for instance, Schönke & Schröder, STRAFGESETZBUCH (12th ed., München, Berlin, 1965). Comment explanatory of § 34.

3: Significance of Criminal Records and Recognition of Rehabilitation / *Report of the Canadian Committee on Corrections*

Criminal Records

When they become public knowledge, records of criminal conviction greatly handicap rehabilitation and thus threaten to destroy the correctional process. In the Committee's view, it follows, then, that convictions should be recorded only for offences dangerous enough to society to override the harm they do to the offender. Accordingly, a way should be open to the courts to deal with minor offenders without registering a formal conviction. There is no federal provision for this in Canada at present. Other countries have introduced such reforms as discharge without conviction and probation without conviction. The Committee evaluated and made recommendations on these procedures in Chapter 11 of this report.

Availability

The public has relatively little trouble learning that a man has been convicted of a criminal offence. Among other organizations, credit firms, bonding companies and employment agencies have such information, and it is available to a wider public through court records.

The Committee deplores this widespread dissemination, which can be needlessly harmful to an offender, whether he is just out of prison or has abided by the law for many years. It is our opinion that official criminal records should be available only to organizations requiring them for court, police or correctional purposes. We are aware, however, that there are methods, apart from access to official records, of finding out if a man has been convicted of a criminal offence. Legislation, therefore, is likely to be an incomplete safeguard in this area. Continuing public education is necessary to discourage such methods as questioning a man's neighbors about his past.

The Committee is aware that many of the legal disabilities arising from a

From *"Toward Unity: Criminal Justice and Corrections," The Report of the Canadian Committee on Corrections* (Ottawa; The Queen's Printer, 1969), pp. 407–412.

criminal record relate to property and civil rights, and are therefore under the jurisdiction of the provinces. It is also evident that there are far more records of convictions for offences created by provincial legislation than for offences created by federal legislation. We urge the initiation of discussions between the federal government and the provinces to consider the effect of our recommendations dealing with recognition of rehabilitation on matters under provincial control.

International Travel and Immigration

To allow rehabilitated former offenders normal freedom of movement from country to country would, of course, require international agreement. A Canadian tourist with a criminal record may find his record little handicap in travelling to a country where a visa is not required, but immigration is almost certain to be barred. The United States Government, for example, is not prepared to accept for immigration purposes an ordinary pardon granted under the Criminal Code.

This problem can be solved only by reciprocal agreements between nations establishing international standards for rehabilitation and ensuring their recognition.

Different considerations apply to major offences, which the Committee, for practical purposes, defines as those classified by the criminal law as indictable. Because some of the criminals most dangerous to society are among those convicted of indictable offences, care must be taken to ensure that recognition of rehabilitation is not granted prematurely. Yet if, as this Committee believes, society's best long-term protection is rehabilitation, the need for such recognition is most urgent for those who must overcome the stigma of conviction for a major offence.

The Committee's view is that the most effective safeguard against an unjustified recognition of rehabilitation is a full hearing with the onus of proof placed on the applicant. We have considered suggesting that a court conduct this hearing, but the judiciary is already carrying a heavy workload, and furthermore, does not have adequate resources to assist it in making the necessary assessment of the offender. The National Parole Board, as this Committee sees it reconstituted, would seem the more practical choice. It would have the field staff and the experience.

The Committee, therefore, recommends:

(a) that criminal records resulting from conviction for indictable offences be annulled after a successful hearing before the National Parole Board, the hearing to take place on application of the offender at any time following a crime-free period of five years from the end of sentence;
(b) that "end of sentence" be taken to mean the same for nullifying records resulting from conviction for indictable offences as for records resulting from summary conviction.

Employment

One of the most debilitating social consequences of a criminal record is the difficulty of finding employment. An ex-offender, to have any chance at all, must be able to make a legitimate living for himself and his family. This can revive his self-respect and give him a feeling of belonging to the law-abiding community. It also gives him an opportunity to make friends—most likely fellow workers—who have no connection with his past life.

Yet society must have the right to protect itself against the threat of recidivism. An employer's reluctance, for example, to entrust funds to someone who has been convicted of embezzlement is a fact that must be recognized. This further underscores the need for a five-year wait and a full hearing before the National Parole Board before nullifying records for indictable offences.

Even so, nullifying alone is not enough for an ex-offender confronted with a job application form which asks: "Have you ever been convicted of a criminal offence?" What is needed is legislation that would be of practical assistance in getting him past this first stage in the employment process and into a personal interview. This legislation should provide that the National Parole Board, once satisfied that the applicant is worthy of the risk, issue him a certificate of good behavior and recommend to the Executive that he is a proper person to be granted a pardon. The pardon should state that "the conviction shall be deemed to have been vacated." An ex-offender, faced with the question, "Have you ever been convicted of a criminal offence?" could then reply: "Yes, but I hold a certificate of good behavior from the National Parole Board." If pardoned, he could reply: "Yes, but I hold a pardon which vacates my conviction."

The Committee, therefore, recommends:

(a) that a person, who has applied to the National Parole Board at any time after five crime-free years from the end of sentence for an indictable offence and who has satisfied the Parole Board after a full hearing that he has been of good behavior, be granted a certificate of good behavior;

(b) that the National Parole Board issue this certificate and accompany it with a recommendation to the Executive that the holder is a proper person to be granted a pardon, which shall state that the conviction shall be deemed to have been vacated;

(c) that, in the case of indictable offences, the two above steps be taken in addition to nullifying the record;

(d) that "end of sentence" be taken to mean the same for a certificate of good behavior and a recommendation for pardon as for nullifying.

The Committee makes this recommendation after carefully considering an alternate procedure: that the National Parole Board issue successful applicants a certificate of rehabilitation which would provide that "the conviction shall be deemed to have been vacated." It was suggested that an ex-offender could then reply, "No," to the question, "Have you ever been convicted of a criminal offence?" and be asserting a legal fact.

After strong representations from consultants, the Committee has rejected this alternative on at least three grounds. First, that the term "certificate of rehabilitation" suggests a guarantee by the Government that the holder is re-habilitated and will commit no further crime. Second, that to reply, "No," to the question, "Have you ever been convicted of a criminal offence?" would be legally correct but morally ambiguous. Third, that the question could be rephrased in such a way as to induce an ex-offender to disclose a vacated conviction.

The Committee realizes that legislation cannot solve all the problems an ex-offender encounters in his efforts to find employment. For example, job applications present particular difficulties for those who have served a prison term. Blanks in insurance stamps, social security and hospitalization pay-ments and lack of references all suggest time spent in prison. Continuing pub-lic education would be necessary to supplement legislative change.

In the Committee's view, society's right to be protected against crime and the threat of crime demands that an offender demonstrate his rehabilitation by leading a crime-free life in the community for an appropriate number of years. Only when society is satisfied that he is worthy of the risk would it be prepared to annul his conviction. But what of the intervening years? An of-fender who is sincerely trying to rehabilitate himself ought not to be demoral-ized by running into his record at practically every turn. There are many other aspects of rehabilitation which this Committee has dealt with in other parts of this report.

Recognition of Rehabilitation

When an offender has shown over an appropriate number of years that he wants to lead a crime-free life and is capable of it, there should be a procedure to ease, as much as possible, the legal disabilities and social stigma of a criminal record. In such cases legislation should provide for nullifying his record, granting him a certificate of good behaviour and recommending him for a pardon which would vacate his conviction. The chance, thus given, to start again with a clean record would provide additional and strong motivation to earn this new status and, once earned, not to risk it by further crime.

All three parts of this provision need not apply to minor convictions. Con-sider, for example, the man who once made a mistake—say, taking a car without the owner's consent (joyriding) as a teen-age prank—and finds him-self years later embarrassed publicly and professionally and perhaps unable to be bonded or transferred to another country. The hardship in such cases is ob-vious, but it would be effectively alleviated by nullifying the record alone. There would be no necessity further to recognize rehabilitation by a certifi-cate of good behaviour and a pardon.

By nullifying, the Committee does not mean physical destruction. It would be both impractical and unwise to attempt, in effect, to erase all trace of a criminal record. Such information is widely disseminated and kept on file by governmental and private agencies, some of which—newspapers, for example —could not be expected to destroy their records. Nor, of course, could the police be expected, in cases of public necessity, to do without the proper and indispensable intelligence that criminal records provide. Further, a criminal conviction will be remembered and memory cannot be obliterated.

By nullifying, the Committee means that official criminal records should not be available to the court, where they affect sentence, or the public, where they affect many aspects of an ex-offender's life, including employment. The record of an offender whose rehabilitation has been recognized should be placed in past records and sealed. The effect should be that, for the purposes of the court and the public, the conviction never occurred. The Committee also feels there should be an onus on the police to show cause that an annulled record they require is of sufficient public importance to justify releasing it to them. Such cause should be shown to the satisfaction of the Solicitor General or the appropriate provincial minister of justice or attorney general.

To indicate more precisely the Committee's views as to the effect of the annulment or vacating of a criminal conviction, the Committee recommends that, save as provided in this report with respect to the investigation of crime and subject to the safeguards and restrictions specified, a conviction which has been annulled or vacated shall be deemed never to have taken place in respect of all matters over which Parliament has jurisdiction and in particular and without limiting the generality of the foregoing shall be deemed never to have taken place:

(i) for the purpose of any criminal proceeding or other proceeding over which Parliament has jurisdiction;
(ii) in relation to the cross-examination of a witness in any proceeding over which Parliament has jurisdiction;
(iii) in relation to any provision in an act of Parliament by virtue of which a person who has been convicted is disqualified from holding any office or performing any public function;
(iv) for the purpose of employment in any branch of the public service of Canada.

Summary Conviction Offences

The Committee considers it feasible for the purposes of nullifying to separate offences into minor and major on the basis of their danger to society. We define a minor offence as one punishable on summary conviction. Because the consequences of a criminal record for such convictions are out of proportion to the gravity of the offence, nullifying should be automatic after an appropriate crime-free period. In the Committee's opinion, neither a hearing nor a document recognizing rehabilitation nor a pardon is necessary.

The Committee, therefore, recommends:

(a) that criminal records resulting from summary conviction be annulled automatically after a crime-free period of two years from the end of a sentence;
(b) that "end of a sentence" be taken to mean, in the case of a fine or other punishment not involving probation or prison, from the date of conviction; in the case of probation, from the end of the probation period; in the case of prison, from the end of the prison sentence; in the case of parole, from the end of the parole period;
(c) that an annulled record of summary conviction not be activated in the event of any later conviction, which would be dealt with as a first offence.

The Committee feels that, as experience is accumulated, consideration might be given to broadening this category to include certain other offences.

4: Prison Restrictions—Prisoner Rights /

Richard P. Vogelman

The old retributive view of penology was to a large extent based upon the idea that a person convicted of a crime was an "outlaw" without legally protected rights. Gradually, however, as a result of nineteenth-century humanitarian influences, corrective treatment, reform and rehabilitation came to be regarded as more desirable principles of penology. Along with this change in attitude came much needed reform in the treatment of prisoners initiated by the prison system administrators.[1]

Courts, on the other hand, concerned themselves mainly with protecting the rights of persons accused of a crime rather than with defining the rights of those already convicted. The determination of prisoner rights was generally left to the administrative discretion of prison officials.[2] The judicial basis for affording this wide administrative discretion was the belief that the courts were without power to supervise prison administration or interfere with the ordinary rules and regulations of penal institutions.[3] This "hands-off" doc-

From Richard P. Vogelman, "Prison Restrictions—Prisoner Rights," *Journal of Criminal Law, Criminology and Police Science* 59:3 (1968): 386–396.

trine continues to be applied by a majority of courts today, and may be given particular emphasis when federal courts are called upon to review complaints of state inmates.[4]

Generally, if a court adheres to the "hands-off" doctrine the allegations contained in a prisoner's petition will not be examined, and as a result, no inquiry will be made to determine whether the asserted claims warrant relief. Two related bases appear to underlie this doctrine. One is the separation of powers principle of government. It is argued that the judiciary should not interfere with the executive function of prison administration.[5] The second is the fear that judicial review of administrative decisions will seriously interfere with the ability of prison officials to carry out the objectives of the penal system.[6] As one commentator has pointed out, however, neither of these rationale constitutes a satisfactory basis for denying a prisoner judicial review of administrative action.[7] The mere delegation of authority to the executive does not immunize its acts from review by the judiciary. Furthermore, the detrimental effects of such review on the penal purposes of restraint, deterrence, and rehabilitation, or on the maintenance of an orderly prison, are much exaggerated—if not completely untenable.

During the past twenty-five years, a number of courts have recognized that the "hands-off" doctrine is not a satisfactory principle in prisoner litigation, and a trend has been noted away from it.[8] Perhaps the leading statement indicative of this trend was made in dictum by the Court of Appeals for the Sixth Circuit in *Coffin v. Reichard*.[9] The court stated: "A prisoner retains all the rights of an ordinary citizen except those expressly, or by necessary implication, taken from him by law."[10] If the courts are prepared to face the task of defining what rights are taken away by "necessary implication" rather than leave it wholly within the discretion of administrative officials, they will of necessity have to strike a balance between prisoner and prison interests. This comment will examine the rights that are ascribed to prisoners today and the practical problems encountered in managing a prison; additionally, some suggestions on how the conflicting interests might be partially resolved will be made. Three areas will be considered: freedom of speech, freedom of religious practice, and the right of access to the courts.

Freedom of Speech

The right of prisoners to communicate with the outside world, essentially through use of the mails and conversation with visitors, is subject to restrictions. Prison regulations usually provide for an approved mailing list consisting of the names of persons with whom a prisoner may correspond. In *Fussa v. Taylor*,[11] a prisoner received permission to write to his common-law wife who was incarcerated at the state reformatory for female prisoners. Upon receipt at the state reformatory, the letter was confiscated and returned along with a note to the petitioner's warden. In the note, the reformatory superintendent stated that he found no constructive elements in the relationship of the two inmates and did not approve of their corresponding. As a result, petitioner's warden cancelled his mailing privilege with this woman. In upholding the action taken by the warden, the court held that such a restriction was an ordinary mail regulation within penitentiary rules, and being such, the court would not interfere with the administration of it.

Prison rules may also specify what persons are allowed to visit the prisoner. In *Abamine v. Murphy,*[12] a prisoner in a maximum security jail was not allowed a visit from his wife who at that time was free on bail, awaiting trial on theft charges. A prison rule provided that any person who had been released from the jail could not visit an inmate within thirty days of such release. The prisoner contended that the rule was cruel and unusual punishment when applied to deny him the right of a visit from his wife. The court, after listing the security reasons given by the warden for the rule, held it to be a reasonable regulation and that the courts should not hamper officials by interfering with long established practices of a reasonable nature. Significantly, the court reached the issue of reasonableness rather than rely entirely, as in the *Fussa* case, upon administrative discretion.

It would appear that from a practical standpoint, approved mailing and visitor lists are necessary for several reasons. Since certain correspondents and visitors would be more likely to attempt to formulate escape plans, send or give the prisoner contraband or be partners in an illegal business, they must be kept from the approved lists. Ex-convicts, for example, may be inclined to give the prisoner information about the physical layout or routine of the jail. Also, there may be a likelihood that if an old business partner was involved with the prisoner in an illegal business he would try to obtain information concerning such business from the inmate during the latter's incarceration.

Prison approved mailing lists are also considered necessary because of censorship requirements. Mail censorship is justified by officials because it facilitates interception of escape plans, narcotics or any other contraband. In addition, censorship provides a means of assuring that inmates are not controlling or otherwise participating in an illegal business or other scheme. Since censorship and confiscation of the mails are thus essential for effective prison management, the volume of mail to be screened must be kept within the capacity of a limited prison staff. This is accomplished by limiting the number of persons with whom a prisoner may correspond.

In dealing with mail censorship controversies, courts generally allow a high degree of discretion to prison officials,[13] as exemplified by the leading case of *Numer v. Miller.*[14] There the prisoner complained that his right of free speech had been abridged and that he was denied access to educational facilities which were afforded all other fellow inmates. The basis for petitioner's complaint was the warden's refusal to allow him to mail lesson sheets required of an English extension course. The prisoner's first assignment had been to state his reasons for taking the course; his response was that he intended upon his release to write a book which would expose the brutality of prison authorities. As a result of this answer the warden said the prisoner would not be allowed to continue with the course unless he changed his objectives. This the petitioner would not do so the privilege was taken away. The court refused to give any relief to the prisoner and stated that supervision of such disciplinary action was not within the province of the court. Furthermore, it said, a prisoner who abuses a privilege is not in a position to complain if that privilege is taken from him.

Although discretionary prison censorship and confiscation have been upheld in many other cases, courts will not permit either where the correspondence concerns only the prisoner's legal affairs and is addressed to the courts.[15] This freedom from censorship was further extended by the court in *Brabson v. Wilkins* [16] to legally related letters addressed to the prisoner's attorney or to the United States Attorney General.

Prisoners occasionally claim the right to communicate with the outside world through the publication of manuscripts written during incarceration or in furtherance of a legitimate business purpose. Generally, however, the courts do not recognize such a right. In *United States v. Maas,*[17] the court issued a preliminary injunction prohibiting the publication of a prisoner written manuscript. The court held that the manuscript did not conform with the policy of prison rules regulating such matters.

In *Stroud v. Swope,*[18] the issue was whether the petitioner was entitled to carry on business affairs regarding efforts to secure publication of books he had written while in prison. He claimed he had the right to reasonable correspondence in furtherance of his business enterprise. As in *Maas,* the court rejected the argument that it should decide the question of reasonableness, stating that the burden of supervision may not be imposed upon or assumed by the courts. Furthermore, the court reasoned, supervision of the treatment and discipline of prisoners is not a judicial function; the role of the court is solely to deliver from imprisonment those who are illegally confined.

A major practical reason advanced for restricting correspondence in furtherance of a business interest is the fear of continued illegal activity under the guise of a legitimate business. Such correspondence may be a potential source of financial strength for corrupting guards and it would unreasonably increase the volume of mail subject to censorship. Regarding prisoner manuscripts, there is fear expressed by some that writing about past crimes or abusive treatment by prison officials may reinforce criminal behavior or increase resentment and make rehabilitation more difficult.[19]

Considering the various restrictions placed upon a prisoner's freedom of communication with the outside world, it is not surprising to find severe restraints placed upon speech between fellow inmates.[20] In *Fulwood v. Clemmer,*[21] Black Muslim inmates held a meeting in the prison recreation yard at which several members of the group preached racial Muslim doctrines in a sufficiently loud voice to be heard by other non-Muslim white and Negro inmates. The court held that the Black Muslim "preachers" could be punished for this because the language was offensive, insulting and disruptive enough to engender those feelings in non-Muslims which tend to menace order. The court's approach indicates that the basic reason for suppressing oral intercourse between inmates is the necessity of maintaining discipline, order, and security within the penal institution.

Although the practical reasons advanced for limiting a prisoner's absolute freedom of speech appear to deserve considerable weight, the value of free speech to prisoners must also be taken into account.[22] One of the values which has been advanced is the prisoner's need to have an outlet for expression. Since writing and speech are two of the few expressive outlets a confined person may practically be able to enjoy, stifling them may seriously affect the basic human desire and need of individual fulfillment. A second value of free speech is the role which it plays in affording society the opportunity to evaluate and judge how well prison administrators are discharging their function and duties. Furthermore, free speech may indicate prisoner attitude—the knowledge of which may be useful to prison officials in detecting potential security breaches early enough to prevent their actual occurrence. Prisoner attitude is also useful as an indicator of progress or problems in rehabilitation programs.

The difficult task which the courts face is balancing the values of prisoner free speech with prison administrative considerations. In doing so, one of the fundamental principles which should be observed is that any arbitrary or discriminatory rules or regulations are unconstitutional. It may be assumed that very few prison rules will fall into this category, so that on their face the purposes of the restrictions will appear valid. A court should not, however, cease inquiry at this point. It has been suggested that a regulation may still be invalid if a reasonable alternative which involves less deprivation of the prisoner's freedom of speech is available to accomplish the same purpose.[23] For example, a court may find that restricting all prisoner group discussion serves the purpose of maintaining prison security and discipline. Further inquiry may show, however, that reasonable alternatives are available to accomplish the same purpose; for instance, group discussions in a meeting room under guard supervision. Total deprivation would constitute an unnecessary and unreasonable, and unconstitutional, denial of the prisoners' rights.

It is suggested that prison officials should be required to show that not only a valid purpose for restraint exists, but also that such purpose is being accomplished with a minimum deprivation of free speech.

Consideration should also be given to allowing limited business correspondence. Any wealth derived in conducting an enterprise could be paid directly to the inmate's family or held until his release. In this way, the prisoner would not have the feared financial strength to corrupt prison guards. Furthermore, the volume of mail could simply be restricted within reasonable limits. It would seem that allowing the prisoner to carry on a legitimate business, publish books, or patent inventions [24] would reduce family hardships created by imprisonment and might have some rehabilitory effects on the inmate. Prohibiting all such activity may not be the most reasonable alternative.

Freedom of Religion

There has been a considerable amount of litigation in recent years concerning the prisoner's right to practice his religion. A large proportion of this has resulted from the growth of the Black Muslim faith, with its beliefs and practices radically different from those of Christianity or Judaism.

A distinction is drawn in the prison environment,[25] as in the outside world,[26] between freedom to believe, which is absolute, and freedom to exercise one's belief, which may be subject to certain limitations. These limitations are those necessary for the protection and security of the remainder of society, whether it be the prison society or the freemen's society.

In *McBride v. McCorkle*,[27] a Catholic prisoner confined in a segregated wing of the prison alleged that the warden's refusal to allow him, in the free exercise of his religious beliefs, to attend Mass with other Catholic prisoners for a period of two years was cruel and unusual punishment. A chaplain was available, however, to all segregated inmates such as the petitioner. The court, in denying any relief, said that the social interest of depriving petitioner the opportunity to attend Mass with the rest of the prison population is the necessity to preserve order and discipline in the prison. A prisoner is privileged to worship God to the extent his conduct in prison permits. The court went on to state that it was not for it to review the practical judgment of the authorities based on prison experience.

In a similar case, *United States ex rel. Cliggett v. Pate*,[28] a prisoner in the prison segregation unit was not allowed to worship with his fellow inmates in a corporate body. The court held this not to be discrimination against the prisoner's belief because for security reasons all those in segregation were equally denied such right.

Relief has also been denied a prisoner who was prevented from obtaining Bible study aids offered by the Watch Tower Society,[29] and similarly, no relief was given a prisoner who was forbidden to take an Arabic grammar book, for his religious education, into the prison recreation yard.[30] In both cases, the courts relied on the "hands-off" doctrine. Such actions, it was stated, were matters of prison discipline entrusted to prison officials.

When considering the religious freedom of Black Muslims, the first inquiry has been whether Muslim practices are recognized for legal purposes as constituting a "religion." [31] Although a few courts have denied them such status,[32] recognition is generally given to the existence of a Black Muslim religion.[33] In *Fulwood v. Clemmer*,[34] the court said that a religion calls for belief in a supreme being controlling the destiny of man and that the Black Muslims meet this test by their belief in Allah.

Before discussing to what extent Black Muslim religious practices may be prohibited, it may be useful to explore the administrative problems created by the doctrines of the religion itself.[35] Very basic to the Black Muslim religion is an inexorable hatred of the white race and the closely related doctrine of Negro race supremacy. As a manifestation of these teachings, some Muslim practitioners feel that in time the Negroes will have their own segregated section of the United States. The expression of these beliefs by spoken word, publications and actions may create an extremely volatile prison atmosphere. Friction may develop between Muslims and other white or non-Muslim Negro members of the prison community. This friction may in turn create the spark for a disturbance or even a full-blown prison riot.

Because Negro prisoners often feel they are imprisoned by "white man's justice," the Black Muslim religion breeds especially well in the prison environment and produces many Muslim leaders and ministers. A problem arises when incarcerated members of the Muslim faith claim the right to receive ministration from their leaders or ministers. Prison officials must decide how to resolve the conflict between the principle of equal treatment of religions and prison rules prohibiting inmates from having any contact with former convicts who frequently fall within this classification.[36]

The basic issue confronting the courts is, to what extent do the Black Muslims have a right to practice their religion. The answer to that question may be dependent, however, upon the answer to another: do Black Muslims have the same right to practice their religion at *all,* as do members of other faiths? The answers which courts have given to this latter question range from allowing the total deprivation of Muslims' religious privileges to holding invalid any deprivation of such privileges if given to other faiths.

Total deprivation is exemplified in the California case of *In re Ferguson.*[37] There a Black Muslim prisoner complained of religious discrimination. He alleged Muslims were not allowed a place of worship, religious meetings were broken up, purchase and possession of the Muslim Bible and other religious literature were prohibited and religious leaders were not allowed to visit the prisoners. The prison officials admitted to the discrimination but argued that prison discipline justified it. The court agreed saying that it was no abuse of discretionary power for officials to manage the prison system and to base restrictions on the potentially serious dangers to prison security which the Black Muslim practices involve.

A similar result upholding total deprivation of Muslim practice was reached by a United States District Court for the District of Kansas in *Jones v. Willingham.*[38] In that case, a Black Muslim inmate alleged that he was being deprived of religious privileges accorded adherents of other religious faiths—the right to assemble for worship, to receive religious instruction, and to receive Muslim literature. After discussing the Black Muslim doctrines and the disciplinary problems created by them the court concluded that the warden's actions based upon his observations and prison experience were not arbitrary, capricious or unlawful. The court also noted that the warden ". . . not only was fully justified in imposing on the plaintiff and others professing

Muslim beliefs the restrictions of which the plaintiff now complains, but it was his duty to so act." [39]

Other courts appear to take a middle position by allowing partial deprivation of Black Muslim's privileges. In *Cooke v. Tramburg*,[40] the New Jersey Supreme Court upheld the Board of Managers' prohibition of Muslim religious services. The court held such a restraint to be reasonable in light of the disciplinary problems which such an assembly of Muslims might create. Although relief was thus denied with regard to this one privilege deprivation, the court took cognizance of the fact that Black Muslims were allowed other liberties in the exercise of their religious beliefs. Purchase and possession of their Qu'ran were permitted; they were permitted to gather in the exercise yard up to six in number to discuss their religion; and they could readily communicate with Muslim ministers.

In *Childs v. Pegelow*,[41] another case of partial deprivation, Muslim prisoners sought to compel the warden to recognize their special fasting practices during the month of Ramadan. The warden had agreed to comply with their dietary restrictions and to serve their meals before sunrise and after sunset. The prisoners complained, however, that in carrying out this agreement prison officials did not determine sunset by the traditional Muslim manner.[42] The complaint was dismissed as not presenting a justiciable issue. The court said that the petitioner was merely seeking to enforce an agreement of special privilege, not a constitutionally or legally protected right. The granting of such a privilege was clearly a routine matter of internal prison administration with which the court would not interfere. The reference to "special privilege" might infer that "ordinary" religious privileges would be afforded different treatment by this court. There was no indication by the court that all Muslim privileges may lawfully be denied but only that those of a "special" or "peculiar" nature could be so treated.

A third position regarding the equal rights of Black Muslims is taken by other courts. These courts hold any deprivation of religious privileges invalid if it appears that corresponding privileges are given other faiths. Cases in this category are generally based on either of two rationale. One is that if prison administrators promulgate rules of religious non-discrimination, the court will require the prison personnel to adhere to them. The second rationale is based upon equal protection of the law, and is independent of the existence of administrative rules or proclamations.

The first of these rationale was the basis for two District of Columbia cases. In *Fulwood v. Clemmer*,[43] Black Muslim prisoners complained of not being given facilities and rights on an equal basis with members of other religions. The court held that to allow some religious groups to hold services at public expense while denying that right to Black Muslims was religious discrimination in violation of an order of the prison commissioners to make facilities available without regard to race or religion. Similarly, since the Department of Correction purchased religious medals for Catholics, Protestants, and Jews with public funds it was held that medals must also be made available to Muslims in order to comply with the commissioners' regulation.

In *Sewell v. Pegelow*,[44] prisoners professing the Black Muslim faith alleged that they were discriminated against solely because of their religious beliefs. They complained of being denied the right to wear religious medals, to communicate with religious advisors, to recite prayers, and to receive publications. The court held that the complaints stated enough to require a hearing, and remanded the case to the district court. A cause of action was stated because this was not an attack upon disciplinary measures nor bare conclusory allegations of a denial of constitutional rights; it was an extensively detailed specification of deprivations and hardships inflicted by personnel where there had been no apparent infraction of any prison rules. It was, therefore, unlike cases where the courts had declined to interfere because of disciplinary measures imposed under the authority of normal regulations of the institution. On a second appeal, the court dismissed the case after consideration of a letter from counsel for both parties which set forth the policy Order of the District of Columbia Government Regarding Non-discrimination, and which specified with particularity the rights Black Muslims were to have to enable them to practice their religion on an equal basis with members of other faiths.

The second basis for holding invalid any deprivation of Muslims' religious privileges—equal protection without regard to administrative action—is exemplified in *State ex rel. Tate v. Cubbage*.[45] In that case the court held it to be a denial of equal protection of the laws to deny Black Muslims equal facilities for religious services and to forbid them to wear religious medals on the same basis as other faiths. Significantly, the court rejected the argument that equal protection was qualified by the clear and present danger test; the right to equal protection was held to be "almost" an absolute right, although the exact significance of "almost" was not indicated.

It should be noted that in the *Sewell* case, although the second appeal was dismissed on the basis of assurances contained in the administrative policy order, the court appeared ready even without such a policy order to hold invalid any deprivation of Muslim privileges if corresponding rights were given other faiths. It is probable, therefore, that the *Sewell* court would follow the *Cubbage* decision if a similar situation arose.

As seen by the preceding cases, courts have differed greatly in their solution to the Black Muslim religion problem. As in all other areas of prisoners' rights, however, arbitrary or discriminatory regulations based solely on a prisoner's religion and its teachings should not be permitted. Such discrimination was allowed by a lower court in *Cooper v. Pate*.[46] The prisoner alleged that because of religious discrimination he was not permitted to purchase a copy of the "Koran." The court upon taking judicial notice of certain social studies of the Black Muslim movement found the religion dangerous and threatening to prison security in general. As a result, relief was denied. The United States Supreme Court reversed in a per curiam opinion, stating that a cause of action was shown on the authority of the *Sewell* case.[47]

Perhaps the test framed by the court in *Brown v. McGinnis* [48] represents the most equitable balancing of interests when dealing with freedom to practice religion. In reply to the contention that restrictions on religious practices were valid merely because of the potential dangers inherent in the Muslim faith the court said: "Although potential dangers if realized may justify curtailment or withdrawal of petitioner's qualified rights, mere speculation . . . is insufficient. . . ." [49] There appears to be no valid reason to deny any religion equal protection of the laws, even if it is feared that its members might abuse its rights in the indefinite future. On the other hand, prison officials should not have to wait for a breach in discipline and order if such a breach is imminent and if it is practically speaking realized. It must be remembered that religious practice is not absolute but is always subject to the overriding interests of society. So long as officials have a reasonable basis for taking away the qualified privilege, this cannot be considered discriminatory nor violative of prisoners' constitutional rights.

Access to the Courts

It has been stated: "A right of access to the courts is one of the rights a prisoner clearly retains." [50] A denial or undue restriction of reasonable access is a denial of due process.[51] As was indicated previously in connection with the prisoner's freedom of speech, mail addressed to the courts or to the United States Attorney General is not subject to prison censorship or confiscation.[52] In *Ex Parte Hull*,[53] where a prison official refused to mail an inmate's habeas corpus petition, the United States Supreme Court said:

The state and its officials may not abridge or impair petitioner's right to apply to a federal court for a writ of habeas corpus. Whether a petition for writ of habeas corpus addressed to a federal court is properly drawn and what allegations it must contain are questions for the court alone to determine.[54]

In connection with the prisoner's right to mail his petition to the proper officials, it has also been held that prison officials may not punish inmates for making false statements of deprivations until there has been a court adjudication of the allegations on the merits.[55] To allow such punishment would be to permit prison officials, against whom the complaints are directed, to be the judge and jury as to the truth of the allegations.

There may be, however, certain limitations on a prisoner's right of access to the courts when his purpose is not to complain of an unlawful restriction of his rights. One such restriction is that an inmate may be denied the right to institute civil proceedings involving his affairs prior to conviction.[56] Another is that a prisoner may not be permitted to sue prison officials for damages during his incarceration arising out of alleged injuries due to mistreatment or prison negligence.[57]

Even though the prisoner has free access to the courts to complain of what he believes to be unlawful deprivations, exercising this right is often conditioned upon the means available to him to prepare the necessary papers. A number of difficulties involving this right to prepare have faced inmates in the past. The prison may be unable to provide many law books and delay may be encountered in the use of those it is able to provide.[58] For security reasons, a prisoner may only be allowed to obtain a limited supply of legal materials from approved sources,[59] may not be allowed to keep legal materials in his cell,[60] and in many instances is not permitted to receive help from another prisoner in preparing.[61] A prisoner may also be restrained in efforts to obtain the help of counsel even though he is financially capable of paying for such assistance.[62]

In recent years, however, greater recognition has been given to the fact that the right to prepare is basic to any realistic free access to the courts. In *Bailleaux v. Holmes*,[63] the court was aware that prison authorities must be able to maintain effective discipline, but it stated that "this end could not be achieved by stifling the study of law, where such study is necessary to the effective utilization of a basic right." [64] In that case, prisoners had alleged that they had to engage in their own legal work because they could not afford an attorney. On subsequent appeal, the decision was reversed, but the reason for reversal was the appellate court's finding that the prisoners *did* have reasonable access to the courts, and not a repudiation of the basic proposition quoted from the district court's opinion.

Even where the right to study law and to have access to legal materials is recognized, a distinction may be drawn between the genuine need of such material in order to present a claim and access merely to engage in a "fishing expedition." In *Roberts v. Pepersack*,[65] the court stated:

> The right to petition or correspond with the court does not include the right to be furnished with an extensive collection of legal materials. Such a collection will encourage "fishing expeditions" in which an inmate seeks out cases where the allegations may receive favorable consideration and adopts those allegations as his own.[66]

The court indicated that all a prisoner need do is set forth his allegations, even if not in terms of constitutional deprivations, and the court will frame them properly for him. Exactly how the distinction between "fishing expeditions" and genuine need is to be determined is not clear. It may depend upon whether the alleged right appears to have any reasonable foundation.

If a prisoner is able to obtain legal materials and is in the process of preparing his petition, he will usually desire to keep such materials in his cell in order to assemble the document ultimately to be transmitted to the court. In *In re Schoengarth*,[67] the court said that a prisoner has this right. It held that reasonable access to the courts includes the right of a prisoner to possess in his cell the legal materials which he desires to include in his petition while it is being put into a mailable form.

Merely having access to law books and other legal material, however, is not enough. Prisoners may need some form of personal assistance, but such assistance will usually be difficult to obtain. Allowing prisoners to help each other in preparing petitions is generally forbidden by prison regulations. In one federal district court case, however, such a state regulation was held invalid, and a prisoner was given the right to receive aid from a fellow inmate.[68] The court said that a state prison regulation forbidding prisoners from preparing habeas corpus petitions for other inmates interfered with the federal statutory right of prisoners, incapable of acting for themselves, to have someone act on their behalf.

The right of an inmate to consult with an attorney has also been recognized. In the case of *In re Allison*,[69] the court held a prisoner to have the right to consult privately with his counsel at reasonable times in preparation for trial and during the pendency of an appeal. As previously indicated, the prisoner has this same right of communication when carried on through the use of the mails.[70]

Probably the foremost practical problems to be considered when evaluating a prisoner's right of access to the courts is that of spurious claims and the amount of litigation which prisoners generate. An inmate may feel that he is entitled to contest every rule and regulation he dislikes. Moreover, because he is in prison he may have a substantial amount of time available in which to contrive various allegations of unlawful deprivations. The burden on the courts will be very great if they must hear every claim that a disgruntled prisoner thinks warrants relief. For these reasons courts are hesitant about enlarging the inmate's means of research and preparation, and often rely upon the "fishing expedition" distinction in order to avoid doing so.

Furthermore, prisons are confronted with the problem that they are ordinarily unable financially to provide what prisoners would consider adequate legal research facilities. It must also be kept in mind that a person is not sent to prison to obtain a legal education, and, as a consequence, cannot expect to have made available to him a complete set of even one state's statutes or decisions. Moreover, even if the prison were able and willing to provide research tools for their inmates, "jailhouse lawyers" might be created. Such prisoners might exchange legal advice or other legal services for favors from "client" inmates. In addition, such novices might be inclined to misconstrue the law and thus create disciplinary problems with those prisoners who were advised that they were being deprived of their legal rights.

Although these practical considerations advanced for some limitations on a prisoner's access to the courts cannot be ignored, it must be constantly kept in mind that the right of a prisoner to have his complaint heard is probably the most important of all his rights. Without free access to the courts, all other recognized prisoner rights have no effective means of protection. This was aptly stated by the court in *Coleman v. Peyton*.[71] It said " [Access to the courts] is a precious right, and its administratively unfettered exercise may be of incalculable importance in the protection of rights even more precious." [72]

While it is true that prisoners may bring spurious and unmerited claims before the court, this is a problem inherent in a free legal system. Many unfounded claims are also brought by citizens outside of jail, but it is not thought that as a result of this access to the legal process should be restricted. Similar reasoning may be applied to prisoners with equal validity. Closely related to this spurious claim problem is the familiar "flood of litigation" argument. An adequate response to it, however, was stated in *United States ex rel Marcial v. Fay,*[73] "We must not play fast and loose with basic constitutional rights in the interest of administrative efficiency." [74]

Even with a generally recognized right of access to the courts, it must be remembered that for indigent prisoners this right is meaningless without adequate means to engage in their own legal preparation. This does not mean that extensive legal resources should or must be furnished or that reasonable restrictions may not be placed on their use. What it does seem to require is that no restriction should be placed upon the means of preparation meant only to discourage or totally prevent petitioning the courts for relief. An example of such a restriction would be denying a prisoner the use of the prison library as a punishment for the exercise of a right he feels he has and wants to establish through adjudication. Any such restriction in the right of access to the courts cannot be considered a reasonable incident of punishment.

Providing an indigent prisoner with the means of preparation is not the only way, however, to preserve his right of access to the courts. An effective alternative would be to provide him with court appointed counsel. Since the complaining prisoner is not an accused in a criminal prosecution, but is rather the plaintiff in a civil action, it is clear he has no federal constitutional right to assigned counsel under the Sixth Amendment to the United States Constitution [75] or under similar state constitutional provisions.[76] But it is suggested that by giving an inmate such a right by statute or otherwise his need for an adequate means of self-preparation would no longer exist, and the problems of the prison in providing those means would be solved.

Conclusion

Although the "hands-off" doctrine has not been abandoned, it is apparent from this brief survey of prisoners' rights that at least some of the courts are facing the difficult task of balancing the interests of inmates against the practical considerations involved in effectively operating a penal institution.[77] While such balancing may be considered by some to be a court invasion into prison administration, it must be remembered that, presumably, this interference will be only to the extent necessary to protect constitutional rights. The courts are capable of perceiving what regulations are reasonably necessary in a particular prison and should accept the responsibility of judicially defining what rights a prisoner retains when lawfully incarcerated rather than leave it to administrative discretion.

Some would probably argue, also, that judicial determination of prisoner complaints places too great a burden upon the courts because many of the allegations will turn out to be undeserving of relief. This argument is not without merit, but it does not justify leaving prisoners at the sole mercy of prison officials to fashion rules and regulations as they please.

A compromise solution may be to establish by statute some form of quasi-judicial or administrative review procedure where a complaining inmate could take his claim in the first instance. The courts would then merely serve in an appellate capacity in reviewing such agency's decisions when one party was unsatisfied with the resolution. To assure fair and impartial treatment of prisoners such an agency would preferably be an arm of the court and under its direction rather than under the auspices of the prison system. Hearings could be held in the various prisons at designated times in a "circuit riding" fashion. State agencies under state court supervision would travel to state penal institutions, and federal agencies under similar federal supervision would hear complaints of inmates in United States prisons. In this way prisoners would not have to be absent from their institutions nor would there be any incentive for them to bring a complaint merely to get out of jail for a hearing.

Although the exact procedure put into effect may not be as proposed, the point remains that some form of judicial or prison administered review system would be desirable. It would hopefully allow for the fair adjudication of prisoner complaints without, at the same time, overburdening the courts. Without a doubt any completely adequate means for the protection of prisoners' rights will be expensive, but a truly civilized society must bear the additional cost in order to protect the fundamental personal rights of *all* its members.

NOTES

1. Tappan, *The Legal Rights of Prisoners,* 293 ANNALS 99 (1954).
2. *Id.*
3. Banning v. Looney, 213 F.2d 771 (10th Cir.), *cert. denied,* 348 U.S. 859 (1954); *In re* Taylor, 187 F.2d 852 (9th Cir.), *cert. denied,* 341 U.S. 955 (1951); Stroud v. Swope, 187 F.2d 850 (9th Cir.), *cert. denied,* 342 U.S. 829 (1951); Numer v. Miller, 165 F.2d 986 (9th Cir. 1948); Fussa v. Taylor, 168 F. Supp. 302 (M.D. Pa. 1958); Commonwealth *ex rel.* Smith v. Banmiller, 194 Pa. Super. 566, 168 A.2d 793 (1962); Cooke v. Tramburg, 43 N.J. 514, 205 A.2d 889 (1964).
4. *See e.g.,* Walker v. Pate, 356 F.2d 502 (7th Cir.), *cert. denied,* 384 U.S. 966 (1966), at 504 where the court said:

In the event that inmates of state prisons within the Seventh Circuit persist in bringing actions in the federal courts in which the complaints are based upon various matters concerning the rules and regulations in effect in those prisons, and such matters are brought to this court on appeal, it is likely, in the ordinary case, that this court will dispose of the appeal either by a per curiam opinion or by an order.

5. Powell v. Hunter, 172 F.2d 330, 331 (10th Cir. 1949).
6. Sigmon v. United States, 110 F. Supp. 906 (W.D. Va. 1953); *See generally* cases cited in note 3 *supra.*
7. For a full critique of the rationale behind the "hands-off" doctrine see Comment, *Beyond the Kin of the Courts: A Critique of Judicial Refusal to Review the Complaints of Convicts,* 72 YALE L.J. 506 (1963).

8. Note, *Constitutional Rights of Prisoners: The Developing Law*, 110 U. OF PA. L. REV. 985 (1962).

9. 143 F.2d 443 (6th Cir. 1944), *cert. denied*, 325 U.S. 887 (1945).

10. *Id.* at 445.

11. 168 F. Supp. 302 (M.D. Pa. 1958).

12. 108 Cal. App.2d 294, 238 P.2d 606 (1951).

13. Courts have also upheld the monitoring of conversations between visitors and prisoners. *See e.g.* People v. Morgan, 197 Cal. App.2d 90, 16 Cal. Rptr. 818 (1961), *cert. denied*, 370 U.S. 965 (1962).

14. 165 F.2d 986 (9th Cir. 1948).

15. Spires v. Dowd, 271 F.2d 659 (7th Cir. 1959); United States *ex rel.* Vraniak v. Randolph, 161 F. Supp. 553 (E.D. Ill.), *aff'd*, 261 F.2d 234 (7th Cir. 1958), *cert. denied*, 359 U.S. 949 (1959); Brabson v. Wilkins, 45 Misc.2d 286, 256 N.Y.S.2d 693 (Sup. Ct. 1965).

16. 45 Misc.2d 286, 256 N.Y.S.2d 693 (Sup. Ct. 1965).

17. Civil Action No. 1219–'66, D.D.C., May 24, 1966.

18. 187 F.2d 850 (9th Cir.), *cert. denied*, 342 U.S. 829 (1951).

19. Note, *The Right of Expression in Prison*, 40 S. CAL. L. REV. 407 (1967).

20. A requirement of complete silence, however, such as in the "Auburn System" of penology which developed in New York in 1821, probably would be unconstitutional today as cruel and unusual punishment. *See* Lewis, THE DEVELOPMENT OF AMERICAN PRISONS AND PRISON CUSTOMS 1776–1845, at 86–87 (1922).

21. 206 F. Supp. 370 (D.D.C. 1962).

22. Note, *The Right of Expression in Prison, supra* note 19.

23. *Id.*

24. A prisoner was denied the right to obtain a patent on his invention during his incarceration in United States v. Ragan, 213 F.2d 294 (7th Cir.), *cert. denied*, 348 U.S. 846 (1954).

25. Banks v. Havener, 234 F. Supp. 27 (E.D. Va. 1964); *In re* Ferguson, 55 Cal.2d 663, 361 P.2d 417, 12 Cal. Rptr. 753, *cert. denied*, 368 U.S. 864 (1962).

26. Cantwell v. Connecticut, 310 U.S. 296 (1940).

27. 44 N.J. Super. 468, 130 A.2d 881 (App. Div. 1957).

28. 229 F. Supp. 818 (1964).

29. Kelly v. Dowd, 140 F.2d 81 (7th Cir. 1944).

30. Wright v. Walkins, 26 Misc.2d 1090, 210 N.Y.S.2d 309 (Sup. Ct. 1961).

31. The practices of Black Muslims have the appearance of a religion. The Muslims have their own bible, priests, temples, parochial schools, dietary laws, and are granted tax exemptions on an equal footing with other churches and parochial schools by state and municipal governments. Comment, *Black Muslims in Prison: of Muslim Rites and Constitutional Rights*, 62 COLUM. L. REV. 1488, 1490 (1962).

32. *In re* Ferguson, 55 Cal.2d 663, 361 P.2d 417, 12 Cal. Rptr. 753, *cert. denied*, 368 U.S. 864 (1961).

33. Sewell v. Pegelow, 291 F.2d 196 (4th Cir. 1961), *appeal dismissed per stipulation*, 304 F.2d 670 (4th Cir. 1962) (without predjudice); Pierce v. La Vallee, 293 F.2d 233 (2d Cir. 1961), *dismissed*, 212 F. Supp. 865 (N.D.N.Y. 1962), *dismissal aff'd*, 319 F.2d 844 (2d Cir. 1963); Fulwood v. Clemmer, 206 F. Supp. 370 (D.D.C. 1962); Brown v. Mc Ginnis, 10 N.Y.2d 531, 180 N.E.2d 791, 225 N.Y.S.2d 497 (1962).

34. 206 F. Supp. 370 (D.D.C. 1962).

35. *See* LINCOLN, THE BLACK MUSLIMS IN AMERICA (1962).

36. Note, *Suits by Black Muslim Prisoners to Enforce Religious Rights-Obstacles to a Hearing on the Merits*, 20 RUTGERS L. REV. 528 (1966).

37. 55 Cal.2d 663, 361 P.2d 417, 12 Cal. Rptr. 753, *cert. denied*, 368 U.S. 864 (1961).

38. 248 F. Supp. 791 (D. Kan. 1965).

39. *Id.* at 794.

40. 43 N.J. 514, 205 A.2d 889 (1964).

41. 321 F.2d 487 (4th Cir. 1963), *cert. denied*, 376 U.S. 932 (1964).

42. The Black Muslim method of determining daylight hours for fasting during the month of Ramadan is by inspection of a black and a white thread held in the air. If no difference can be detected the hours of darkness have commenced. The prison officials, instead of using this test, relied upon Naval Observatory time.

43. 206 F. Supp. 370 (D.D.C. 1962).

44. 291 F.2d 196 (4th Cir. 1961), *appeal dismissed per stipulation,* 304 F.2d 670 (4th Cir. 1962) (without prejudice).

45. 210 A.2d 555 (Del. Super. Ct. 1965).

46. 324 F.2d 165 (7th Cir. 1963), *rev'd per curiam,* 378 U.S. 546 (1964).

47. Cooper v. Pate, 378 U.S. 546 (1964). This case may be distinguished from Jones v. Willingham, *Supra* Note 38, in that the latter case was based upon specific disciplinary problems within the warden's experience and not merely upon judicial notice in general.

48. 10 N.Y.2d 531, 180 N.E.2d 791, 225 N.Y.S.2d 497 (1962).

49. *Id.* at 793.

50. Coleman v. Peyton, 362 F.2d 905, 907 (4th Cir. 1966), *Accord, Ex Parte* Hull, 312 U.S. 546 (1941); Kirby v. Thomas, 336 F.2d 462 (6th Cir. 1964); Warfield v. Raymond, 195 Md. 711, 71 A.2d 870 (1950).

51. Hymes v. Dickson, 232 F. Supp. 796 (N.D.Cal. 1964); Bailleaux v. Holmes, 177 F. Supp. 361 (D. Ore. 1959), *rev'd sub nom.,* Hatfield v. Bailleaux, 290 F.2d 632 (9th Cir.), *cert. denied* 368 U.S. 862 (1961).

52. *See* text accompanying notes 15 and 16 *supra.*

53. 312 U.S. 546 (1941).

54. *Id.* at 549.

55. Fulwood v. Clemmer, 206 F. Supp. 370 (D.D.C. 1962); *In re* Riddle, 57 Cal.2d 848, 372 P.2d 304, 22 Cal. Rptr. 472 (1962).

56. Harell v. State, 17 Misc.2d 950, 188 N.Y.S.2d 683 (Ct.Cl. 1959).

57. Tabor v. Harwick, 224 F.2d 526 (5th Cir. 1955). It has been held, however, that a prisoner may sue under the Federal Civil Rights Act even if civil suits by prisoners are prohibited by the state. McCollum v. Mayfield, 130 F. Supp. 112 (N.D. Cal. 1955). *See generally* 21 Am. Jur.2d *Criminal Law* §621 (1965); 18 C. J. S. *Convicts* §7 (1939).

58. Bailleaux v. Holmes, 177 F. Supp. 361 (D. Ore. 1959), *rev'd sub nom.,* Hatfield v. Bailleaux, 290 F.2d 632 (9th Cir.), *cert. denied,* 368 U.S. 862 (1961).

59. *Id.* at 365.

60. Hatfield v. Bailleaux, 290 F.2d 632 (9th Cir.), *cert. denied,* 358 U.S. 862 (1961).

61. Wilson v. Dixon, 251 F.2d 338 (9th Cir.), *cert. denied,* 358 U.S. 856 (1958).

62. Bailleaux v. Holmes, 177 F. Supp. 361 (D. Ore. 1959), *rev'd sub nom.,* Hatfield v. Bailleaux, 290 F.2d 632 (9th Cir.), *cert. denied,* 368 U.S. 862 (1961).

63. *Id.*

64. *Id.* at 361.

65. 256 F. Supp. 415 (D. Md. 1966).

66. *Id.* at 433.

67. 57 Cal. Rptr. 600, 425 P.2d 200 (Sup. Ct. 1967).

68. Johnson v. Avery, 252 F. Supp. 783 (M.D. Tenn. 1966).

69. 57 Cal. Rptr. 593, 425 P.2d 193 (Sup. Ct. 1967).

70. *See* text accompanying note 16 *supra.*

71. 362 F.2d 905 (4th Cir. 1966).

72. *Id.* at 907.

73. 247 F.2d 662, *cert. denied,* 355 U.S. 915 (2d Cir. 1957).

74. *Id.* at 669.

75. "In all criminal prosecution, the accused shall enjoy the right . . . to have the

Assistance of Counsel for his defense." U. S. CONST. amend. VI; Dorsey v. Gill, 148 F.2d 857 (D.C. Cir.), *cert. denied,* 325 U.S. 890 (1945).

76. People *ex rel.* Ross v. Ragen, 391 Ill. 419, 63 N.E.2d 874 (1945).

77. This need of balancing interest was recognized in United States *ex rel.* Yaris v. Shaughnessy, 112 F. Supp. 143 (N.D.N.Y. 1953) at 144 where the court said:

It is hard to believe that persons . . . convicted of crime are at the mercy of the executive department and yet it is unthinkable that the judiciary should take over the operation of the . . . prisons. There must be some middle ground between these extremes.

5: Inmate Participation in Prison Management / *President's Commission on Law Enforcement and Administration of Justice*

Shared Decision-Making

A fascinating aspect of the history of American correctional institutions consists of the attempts made to formalize inmate-staff cooperation by establishing inmate "governments" to direct a large part of institution operations. Such attempts began in the late 19th and early 20th centuries in private training schools which were organized as "Junior Republics," with elected inmate legislatures, courts, and "police." In the first quarter of the present century, Thomas M. Osborne established inmate governments at the Auburn and Sing Sing Prisons in New York and at the Naval Prison at Portsmouth, N.H. They were copied in several state prisons elsewhere in the eastern United States. Staff, of course, always had ultimate authority and veto power over inmate government actions.

Many of these inmate self-governments were remarkably successful at first, maintaining secure, orderly, and efficient institutions, but almost all were eliminated before long. Sometimes their demise came primarily because all the prison staff were politically appointed, and the political party or faction out of power made the "mollycoddling" of prisoners by inmate self-government a political issue, exaggerating its harmful consequences and obscuring its accomplishments and prospects. In several instances, however, self-govern-

From U.S. President's Commission on Law Enforcement and Administration of Justice, *Task Force Report: Corrections* (Washington, D.C., U.S. Government Printing Office, 1967), pp. 49–50.

ment failed because a clique of corrupt inmates gained key positions in the governmental structure and exploited or abused the other inmates. In a few cases the self-government was terminated by vote of those governed.

Formal efforts to involve inmates in the management of institutions now occur at only a minority of prisons.[1] No tabulations are available on their frequency in training schools. In any case, this involvement is never a systematic effort to maximize self-government, as were the enterprises of pre-World War I days. It consists, instead, of "inmate advisory councils" that are somewhat comparable to student councils in high schools and colleges. Often they are given primary responsibility for organizing inmate recreation and cultural activities—athletic contests, talent shows, art exhibits, and writing contests rather than actually advising on problems intimately connected with institution management.

Opposition of most prison officials to advisory or governing functions by inmate groups stems from scattered episodes of abuse by such groups. Sometimes inmate cliques have controlled elections to councils or have put pressure on those elected to reduce their orientation to staff objectives. Frequently, advisory groups are oriented primarily to articulating and exaggerating inmate complaints and presenting staff with their demands, without addressing the merits of the complaints objectively or responsibly appraising the difficulties involved in trying to meet the demands. On some occasions, inmate councils have been blamed for riots or lesser disturbances.

Nevertheless, some institution officials report that inmate advisory groups are highly useful. In these cases there generally have been some conditions in the election process that assured a diversity of inmate representation, and there has been more stress on delegating responsibility to the inmate groups than on soliciting unrestricted advice. This delegation takes such forms as giving the inmate group the task of organizing safety and sanitation campaigns or contests, mutual aid funds, and participation in blood donation or other civic activities, in addition to organizing recreational affairs. Some prison administrations maximize the distribution of inmate influence on these diverse activities, yet reduce concentration of inmate power, by organizing a separate inmate committee for each project rather than assigning them all to a single institution council.

In a few institutions there have been experiments with joint staff and inmate committees to deal with important areas of mutual concern, such as food service, housekeeping, and safety. In these cases, and also when inmate councils have been encouraged to advise on these matters, the inmates have sometimes been given all of the relevant information for management in these problem areas, including the financial data on costs and appropriations.

As a consequence, in many cases, inmates have organized campaigns against waste or have made suggestions which were valuable in improving conditions for the comfort and safety of all concerned.

From a rehabilitation standpoint, such inmate involvement with staff is not so important for its practical contribution to the efficiency of institution management as for its social function in bringing inmates and staff into collaborative interaction. Inmate involvement in institution management groups can thus be still another mechanism, in addition to those already described, for reducing the extent to which prison social structure alienates inmates from noncriminal persons and increases their identification with other offenders.

NOTE

[1] I. E. Baker, "Inmate Self-Government," Journal of Criminal Law, Criminology and Police Science, 55:39–47 (March 1964).

6: The Inmates' Perception of Treatment /
Thomas Mathieson

1. Introduction

In large measure, the inmates' stress on injustices of treatment in the institution implies ideas about what is a morally correct way of handling offenders. Little is then implied about the selection of means to reach given goals. That is, little is implied about efficiency in handling inmates.

However, to some degree the ideas inmates formulate about justice and injustice are couched in terms of efficiency. That is, just handling according to unequivocal and clear rules is thought to be the best way in which to make inmates work steadily, behave in an orderly way, and so on. In so far as this is the case, staff members are arraigned not only for being immoral, but also for being inefficient. And, again, the inmates strike tellingly: staff members do not in all cases act completely efficiently, and a critique of this is often difficult to face.

But there is another aspect of efficiency that is equally, or more, important from the point of view of inmates. The inmates have been examined by psychiatrists, and many claim that they have been "promised" treatment or help by the court. At the same time, they clearly realize that recidivism from the institution is high, and that the treatment experts, when judged by this criterion, are by no means always successful. The inmates often present the staff with this discrepancy, explicitly criticizing them for not adhering to, not managing to adhere to, or not wanting to adhere to established principles of efficiency.

From Thomas Mathieson, *Defences of the Weak* (London: Tavistock Publications Ltd., 1965), Chapter 9, pp. 166–178.

Inmates do not always use words like "just" and "unjust." They also stress other moral principles that have the comparison function, in this case of indicating that the staff rehabilitation programme is not efficient. In the present chapter we shall deal with this aspect of censoriousness and discuss some of the functions it may have.

2. Models of Efficiency

A variety of views implying ideas about the efficiency of the institution's rehabilitation programme are voiced by inmates. We shall attempt to classify them under three major headings. However, it should be noted that relatively few instances may be classed within only one of the categories that are outlined. For one thing, it is possible that for some inmates our categories represent stages of development as incarceration proceeds. For another, many inmates vacillate a great deal in their views of the rehabilitation programme. The categories presented here are constructed types, though we shall present examples and excerpts from interviews as we proceed.

The first category does not really imply censoriousness in our sense, because it is not based on consensus with senior staff members on the rehabilitation programme of the institution. It is presented by way of introduction, and because it is a reaction that quite a few inmates show at one time or another.

(A) THE PHILOSOPHY OF FREE WILL
AND THE NEGATION OF TREATMENT

Mention must be made of the rather widespread belief in what may be called "the philosophy of free will." This philosophy essentially says that the only thing that can help an inmate is his own personal will to get over his problems. The philosophy of free will is regularly associated with the view that treatment or help from others is unnecessary. The following excerpt is quite typical of this view:

Either you have to tell yourself that you're going to change, or you don't change. There is no point in any help. I have told the doctors that I don't need any help; either I change because I want to, or I don't change.

Adherence to this philosophy obviously has a very complex psychological background. In part it appears to stem from an unwillingness to define oneself as mentally ill. To the inmate, physical illness implies the possibility of not having to fulfil everyday role-expectations. However, it is important that not having to fulfil normal expectations is perceived as a consequence of the physical illness. To the inmate, "admitting" *mental* illness (as one inmate expressed it) easily implies that the lack of fulfilment is a part of the illness itself.

But the inmate who claims that he can change only through his own will and that treatment staff should more or less disappear from the scene does not argue that the treatment staff is deviating from established principles. Rather, he negates the established norms and values. It is the next category of reactions that brings the inmate into cultural consensus with staff members.

(B) THE PHILOSOPHY OF DETERMINISM
AND THE STRESS ON SOMATIC MEDICINE

Even the inmate who appears to be a strong advocate of the philosophy of free will has from time to time to face the fact that recidivism is high, and that his own chances of success in later life may be small. This possibility or probability is hard to face. Facing the brutal prediction that probably he will go wrong again, the inmate tends to advocate a philosophy that in an important way contradicts the philosophy of free will. Rather than stating that he is unwilling to change, he claims that he cannot change by himself. This philosophy, which to the inmate in a sense "explains" his plight, is perhaps even more widespread than the philosophy of free will. It is based on the idea that the inmate's poor prognosis is "caused" by something unknown to the inmate himself, though the inmate often has some hypotheses or guesses about what the causes are. From the point of view of the inmate, the causes cannot be changed in any decisive way through his own actions. We may call this "the philosophy of determinism."

The philosophy of determinism is regularly associated with some kind of expectation towards the treatment expert in the direction of requiring that something should be done to remove the cause of the problems. Important in this connection is the notion that "the doctors" should act and cure as ordinary doctors treating somatic illness do. We hypothesize that a link between the philosophy of determinism and this particular notion of treatment is established by the increased salience of what is perceived as illegitimate patriarchalism. The feeling of being unable to change by oneself makes the inmate feel more at the mercy of "the system" and the manipulation of benefits and burdens. In turn, this leads to the view that psychiatrists should act as ordinary and presumably more successful doctors do.

It should be noted that we are not sure *how* prevalent this notion of treatment is. Unlike the inmates' opinions to the effect that staff decisions are unpredictable, that there is a lack of inmate solidarity, that staff decisions are unjust, and that there is a discrepancy between the "promise" of treatment and the staff's actual treatment efforts, inmates' specific claims to the effect that the doctors should behave as "somatic doctors" do not appear as a regular and recurring pattern. The inmates' view of the doctors as "somatic doctors" appears only from time to time. Furthermore, some inmates are more prone than others to stress this image of the treatment experts. For example, drug-addicts are, for obvious reasons, particularly prone to stress that the experts should employ "pills and injections" as "treatment."

For these reasons, the general statements that follow need, even more than those presented elsewhere in this book, to be refined in future research. Our statements about "the inmates' stress on somatic medicine," etc., are admittedly not specific enough.

What do the inmates' expectations of "the doctors" consist of in more detail?

The ordinary practitioner treating somatic illnesses diagnoses his patients according to fairly observable criteria. Furthermore, he prescribes an observable medicine, and on this basis he hopes for recovery. Because of the observable character of methods of treatment, the inmate feels that something is in fact being done. In addition, and most important, this observability of methods makes it possible for the inmate as a layman to some degree to control what is and what is not being done with him, because it makes it possible for him to compare his own fate with the fate of others.

This is not to say that the inmate understands and wants to control the precise scientific nature and effect of medicines or prescriptions. In fact, the methods of the ordinary medical doctor are not only observable ones. They include a strong element of scientific secrecy. The inmate both wants to be able to see what is being done *and* be impressed with scientific strangeness.[1] Lack of success of treatment may probably be acceptable to the inmate as layman if both elements are present. The treatment of cancer and other physical illnesses whose outcome is problematical seems to constitute cases in point.

The following excerpts from interviews are illustrative of some of the above observations:

Drug-addicts and alcoholics and sex and so on need treatment, injections, or what the hell it is.

I am against imprisonment—I think improvements could be made through the use of medicines. That's the correct road.

The psychiatrist as treatment expert is here in a very problematic position. First of all, his methods do not appear to include any strong element of scientific strangeness. The patient is brought into the office, as in cases of somatic illness. But once in the office, pills, injections, etc. are by no means always used. "Talking" takes place in the office. Or inmates gather in a group and "talk" with the psychiatrist. Some inmates seem to ask themselves, Is anything scientific really being done this way? Are not even subordinate guards talking with inmates all the time? And again from the point of view of inmates, the consideration is equally important that the methods at the disposal of psychiatrists are not all clearly observable. Is not then the so-called "individual treatment," referred to so often, simply a rationalization for an unpredictable and very personal régime?

The following excerpt from an interview is illustrative:

[The doctor] must not make any differences between people, that's the most important thing. He must not say that it is "individual treatment" when he coddles some people [and is hard against others] because coddling is not treatment.

In conjunction with this, the results of the treatment are difficult for the inmate to see, except for the negative fact that it very often goes wrong. Here the inmate forces legal standards to the attention of the psychiatrist. The expert is brought into the system precisely to reduce recidivism. Expertise notions about "some improvement" or "greater self-insight" seem to appear irrelevant to many inmates, as long as they are not processes contributing to reduction of recidivism. Lack of obvious success might be accepted if the methods used were always observable and had an element of scientific strangeness. In so far as they do not, lack of obvious success tends to become a liability for the treatment expert: the inmate seems to feel even more strongly that the psychiatrist does little but exert control.

In short, then, the psychiatrist lives in the shadow of the doctor treating somatic illnesses. The psychiatrist lacks the advantages of the latter, in the sense that he cannot as easily "disappear" as the incumbent of an expert role.

The attitudes pointed to here are, or course, not only characteristic of some inmates in correctional institutions. They are probably typical of laymen in general. As in the case of the inmates' ideas about justice, ideas about medical treatment are no doubt to a considerable extent learned outside institutional walls or fences, and brought into the institution. In the institution, they are elicited among other things by the apparently unpredictable and patriarchal régime of treatment experts—almost as an answer to their apparently threatening ways of distributing important rewards, punishments, etc.

Very often it is probably tempting for treatment experts to follow the advice they get from inmates in this respect. What the expert has considered as his efforts at treatment are now criticized as illegitimate distribution. Facing the fact that recidivism is very high, this interpretation is not entirely unconvincing. A reduction of treatment efforts in favour of the employment of sedatives and similar observable means makes the psychiatrist appear to fall into line with the central norms of his profession, which are focused on illness as a somatic disturbance. Furthermore, it reduces the number of conflict situations between inmates and senior staff members, because such methods generally appear more acceptable to the latter than "coddling." Insofar as the psychiatrist gets into line with the norms of the regular medical doctor, the expert is not able to carry out his policy of individualized distribution and what is perceived by inmates as his patriarchal régime appears less personalized and more limited by the clear rules of the expert role. His activities must either be confined to the field of somatic illness, or a rationale for his distribution of rewards, punishments, etc. must be given in terms of clear criteria that resemble those of treatment of somatic illness. At the same time, the system of distribution also appears more legitimate to the inmate.

(C) THE PHILOSOPHY OF DETERMINISM AND THE STRESS ON "PSYCHIATRY"

But despite the stress among inmates on somatic medicine, quite a number of inmates certainly feel that psychiatry somehow differs, and should differ, professionally from other disciplines of medicine.

In the first place, psychiatric treatment is frequently made into a joke, where perceived injustices and staff errors are jokingly called "psychiatric treatment" or "a part of the treatment." But for some inmates the matter is not a joke. As an inmate's sense of inability to change by himself increases, and with it his reliance on the philosophy of determinism, treatment becomes less of a joking matter. So much so, indeed, that there is often an increasing stress on normative expectations towards the treatment expert. Indeed, there is often an increasing stress on expectations that imply some kind of "psychiatric" or "psychological" treatment.

What do inmates in this context expect of a psychiatrist?

First of all, the individual inmate often claims that he does not know what to expect, except that "something" ought to be done for him. The psychiatrist must necessarily agree with the latter part of the claim. It is an established principle in our society and within the prison setting. As two inmates expressed it:

Inmate: They talk about treatment here, but I don't know what that means. I have asked them up there, but then I get the answer that it is up to you.
Interviewer: Did you expect any kind of treatment here?
Inmate: Yes, I expected one would get psychiatric treatment, but that's just something they call it . . .
Interviewer: What kind of treatment should there be, do you think?
Inmate: No, I don't have [any idea] . . . I don't know [anything about] these medical things.

The first inmate was told that it was up to him because the psychiatrist wanted to make him enter a co-operative treatment relationship. But as indicated already, normative expectations directed towards the treatment expert are regularly coupled with a philosophy of determinism. This, of course, reduces the chances of establishing a co-operative relationship between treatment expert and his potential patient.

But more important for our purposes is the following consequence of inmates' persistent questions about what psychiatric treatment really is and arguments that the psychiatrist ought to do something: the treatment expert easily feels he is justifiably criticized because inmates have in fact often been promised "treatment," explicitly (by the court) or implicitly (on account of the psychiatric examination, and simply on account of the presence of psychiatrists in the institution). In turn, in order to face the criticisms, he easily reverts to standard treatment of standard somatic illnesses. In so far as he does this, his ability to manipulate important benefits and burdens according to his policy of individualized distribution is circumscribed.

We suggest that this function of censoriousness on the part of inmates is a latent one, though again the end-result is satisfying from the viewpoint of inmates.

Furthermore, some inmates claim that the psychiatrist as psychiatrist could in fact accomplish miracles, but that he for some reason does not want to:

Inmate 1: [The doctors] say that everybody here is sick, but why don't they build a hospital over there, then . . .

Inmate 2: They can't help that.
Inmate 2: Oh, if the doctors did go in for it, it would result in something.

Even here the inmate argues that the ruler deviates from established principles. Though the expert would clearly say that he is no magician, he would at least claim that, because of his professional training, he is the one who knows best. So even here a certain measure of consensus is established between inmate and expert. And even in this case it does to some degree have a defensive function for inmates. Again, the expert easily reverts to more acceptable and more observable and clearly scientific means. This function of censoriousness appears to be latent.

The views of inmates described in the present section, though having defensive functions for them, cannot be traced as easily as reactions to the inmates' image of the system of distribution.

It should be noted that while inmates do stress somatic medicine as well as the fact that they do not know what psychiatry should be like, these are of course not the only ways in which "treatment" is viewed. For example, inmates often feel that psychiatry may be equated with "sympathy" for the plight of inmates. At times, this feeling is coupled with stress on certain "modern" principles of psychotherapy. As one inmate expressed it:

I expected to find people with white coats in the corridors; I thought there would be group therapy and so on . . . [But] here it's almost like a prison . . . [The doctors] ought to show some understanding, and tell us that they are here to help us as much as they can. If that's wrong, then I'm crazy!

By way of concluding the present section, it may be said that the psychiatrist (or for that matter the psychologist) who attempts to conduct treatment faces a severe problem in connection with the views and reactions of the inmates. As we have noted, when the inmate advocates a philosophy of free will, stressing that recovery "depends on himself," he also fights against contact with treatment personnel. Furthermore, those who claim they want to have some kind of contact with treatment personnel at the same time often appear to advocate a philosophy of determinism. The inmate tends to want either no "input" from the treatment staff or all "input" from the treatment staff. These constellations of philosophies and expectations may in large measure be consequences of particular psychological characteristics of inmates, though we should keep in mind that they may certainly be found in outside society as well.

NOTE

1. The elements of observability and strangeness are also clearly present in the use of magic as a cure of illness. In fact, some inmates have expectations towards the treatment expert that seem to imply that he should be a kind of "magician."

B

THE PRISON COMMUNITY

7: Inmate Social System /
Gresham M. Sykes and
Sheldon L. Messinger

The Prison Society

Despite the number and diversity of prison populations, observers of such groups have reported only one strikingly pervasive value system. This value system of prisoners commonly takes the form of an explicit code, in which brief normative imperatives are held forth as guides for the behavior of the inmate in his relations with fellow prisoners and custodians. The maxims are usually asserted with great vehemence by the inmate population, and violations call forth a diversity of sanctions ranging from ostracism to physical violence.

Examination of many descriptions of prison life suggests that the chief tenets of the inmate code can be classified roughly into five major groups:

(1) There are those maxims that caution: *Don't interfere with inmate interests,* which center of course in serving the least possible time and enjoying the greatest possible number of pleasures and privileges while in prison. The most inflexible directive in this category is concerned with betrayal of a fellow captive to the institutional officials: *Never rat on a con.* In general, no qualification or mitigating circumstance is recognized; and no grievance against another inmate—even though it is justified in the eyes of the inmate population—is to be taken to officials for settlement. Other specifics include: *Don't be nosey; don't have a loose lip; keep off a man's back; don't put a guy on the spot.* In brief and positively put: *Be loyal to your class—the cons.* Prisoners must present a unified front against their guards no matter how much this may cost in terms of personal sacrifice.

From Gresham M. Sykes and Sheldon L. Messinger, "The Inmate Social System," in *Theoretical Studies in the Social Organization of the Prison* (New York: Social Science Research Council Pamphlet No. 15, 1960), pp. 5–11, 14–19. Copyright by the Social Research Council.

(2) There are explicit injunctions to refrain from quarrels or arguments with fellow prisoners: *Don't lose your head.* Emphasis is placed on the curtailment of affect; emotional frictions are to be minimized and the irritants of daily life ignored. Maxims often heard include: *Play it cool* and *do your own time.* As we shall see, there are important distinctions in this category, depending on whether the prisoner has been subjected to legitimate provocation; but in general a definite value is placed on curbing feuds and grudges.

(3) Prisoners assert that inmates should not take advantage of one another by means of force, fraud, or chicanery: *Don't exploit inmates.* This sums up several directives: *Don't break your word; don't steal from the cons; don't sell favors; don't be a racketeer; don't welsh on debts.* More positively, it is argued that inmates should share scarce goods in a balanced reciprocity of "gifts" or "favors," rather than sell to the highest bidder or selfishly monopolize any amenities: *Be right.*

(4) There are rules that have as their central theme the maintenance of self: *Don't weaken.* Dignity and the ability to withstand frustration or threatening situations without complaining or resorting to subservience are widely acclaimed. The prisoner should be able to "take it" and to maintain his integrity in the face of privation. When confronted with wrongfully aggressive behavior, whether of inmates or officials, the prisoner should show courage. Although starting a fight runs counter to the inmate code, retreating from a fight started by someone else is equally reprehensible. Some of these maxims are: *Don't whine; don't cop out* (cry guilty); *don't suck around.* Prescriptively put: *Be tough; be a man.*

(5) Prisoners express a variety of maxims that forbid according prestige or respect to the custodians or the world for which they stand: *Don't be a sucker.* Guards are *hacks* or *screws* and are to be treated with constant suspicion and distrust. In any situation of conflict between officials and prisoners, the former are automatically to be considered in the wrong. Furthermore, inmates should not allow themselves to become committed to the values of hard work and submission to duly constituted authority—values prescribed (if not followed) by *screws*—for thus an inmate would become a *sucker* in a world where the law-abiding are usually hypocrites and the true path to success lies in forming a "connection." The positive maxim is: *Be sharp.*

In the literature on the mores of imprisoned criminals there is no claim that these values are asserted with equal intensity by every member of a prison population; all social systems exhibit disagreements and differing emphases with respect to the values publicly professed by their members. But observers of the prison are largely agreed that the inmate code is outstanding both for the passion with which it is propounded and the almost universal allegiance verbally accorded it.

In the light of this inmate code or system of inmate norms, we can begin to understand the patterns of inmate behavior so frequently reported; for conformity to, or deviation from, the inmate code is the major basis for classifying and describing the social relations of prisoners. As Strong has pointed out, social groups are apt to characterize individuals in terms of crucial "axes of life" (lines of interests, problems, and concerns faced by the groups) and then to attach distinctive names to the resulting roles or types.[1] This process may be discerned in the society of prisoners and its argot for the patterns of behavior or social roles exhibited by inmates; and in these roles the outlines of the prison community as a system of action [2] may be seen.

An inmate who violates the norm proscribing the betrayal of a fellow prisoner is labeled a *rat* or a *squealer* in the vocabulary of the inmate world, and his deviance elicits universal scorn and hatred.[3] Prisoners who exhibit highly aggressive behavior, who quarrel easily and fight without cause, are often referred to as *toughs*. The individual who uses violence deliberately as a means to gain his ends is called a *gorilla;* a prisoner so designated is one who has established a satrapy based on coercion in clear contravention of the rule against exploitation by force. The term *merchant,* or *peddler,* is applied to the inmate who exploits his fellow captives not by force but by manipulation and trickery, and who typically sells or trades goods that are in short supply. If a prisoner shows himself unable to withstand the general rigors of existence in the custodial institution, he may be referred to as a *weakling* or a *weak sister*. If, more specifically, an inmate is unable to endure prolonged deprivation of heterosexual relationships and consequently enters into a homosexual liaison, he will be labeled a *wolf* or a *fag,* depending on whether his role is an active or a passive one.[4] If he continues to plead his case, he may soon be sarcastically known as a *rapo* (from "bum rap") or *innocent*. And if an inmate makes the mistake of allying himself with officialdom by taking on and expressing the values of conformity, he may be called a *square John* and ridiculed accordingly.

However, the individual who has received perhaps the greatest attention in the literature is the one who most nearly fulfills the norms of the society of prisoners, who celebrates the inmate code rather than violates it: the *right guy,* the *real con,* the *real man*—the argot varies, but the role is clear-cut. The *right guy* is the hero of the inmate social system, and his existence gives meaning to the villains, the deviants such as the *rat,* the *tough,* the *gorilla,* and the *merchant*. The *right guy* is the base line, however idealized or infrequent in reality, from which the inmate population takes its bearings. It seems worth while, therefore, to sketch his portrait briefly in the language of the inmates.

A *right guy* is always loyal to his fellow prisoners. He never lets you down no matter how rough things get. He keeps his promises; he's dependable and trustworthy. He isn't nosey about your business and doesn't shoot off his mouth about his own. He doesn't act stuck-up, but he doesn't fall all over himself to make friends either—he has a certain dignity. The *right guy* never interferes with other inmates who are conniving against the officials. He doesn't go around looking for a fight, but he never runs away from one when he is in the right. Anybody who starts a fight with a *right guy* has to be ready to go all the way. What he's got or can get of the extras in the prison—like cigarettes, food stolen from the mess hall, and so on—he shares with his friends. He doesn't take advantage of those who don't have much. He doesn't strong-arm other inmates into punking or fagging for him; instead, he acts like a man.

In his dealings with the prison officials, the *right guy* is unmistakably against them, but he doesn't act foolishly. When he talks about the officials with other inmates, he's sure to say that even the hacks with the best intentions are stupid, incompetent, and not to be trusted; that the worst thing a con can do is give the hacks information—they'll only use it against you when the chips are down. A *right guy* sticks up for his rights, but he doesn't ask for pity: he can take all the lousy screws can hand out and more. He doesn't suck around the officials, and the privileges that he's got are his because he deserves them. Even if the *right guy* doesn't look for trouble with the officials, he'll go to the limit if they push him too far. He realizes that there are just two kinds of people in the world, those in the know and the suckers or squares. Those who are in the know skim it off the top; suckers work.[5]

In summary then, from the studies describing the life of men in prison, two major facts emerge: (1) Inmates give strong verbal support to a system of values that has group cohesion or inmate solidarity as its basic theme. Directly or indirectly, prisoners uphold the ideal of a system of social interaction in which individuals are bound together by ties of mutual aid, loyalty, affection, and respect, and are united firmly in their opposition to the enemy out-group. The man who exemplifies this ideal is accorded high prestige. The opposite of a cohesive inmate social system—a state in which each individual seeks his own advantage without reference to the claims of solidarity—is vociferously condemned. (2) The actual behavior of prisoners ranges from full adherence to the norms of the inmate world to deviance of various types. These behavioral patterns, recognized and labeled by prisoners in the pungent argot of the dispossessed, form a collection of social roles which, with their interrelationships, constitute the inmate social system. We turn now to explanation of the inmate social system and its underlying structure of sentiments.

The isolation of the prisoner from the free community means that he has been rejected by society. His rejection is underscored in some prisons by his shaven head; in almost all, by his uniform and the degradation of no longer having a name but a number. The prisoner is confronted daily with the fact that he has been stripped of his membership in society at large, and now stands condemned as an outcast, an outlaw, a deviant so dangerous that he must be kept behind closely guarded walls and watched both day and night. He has lost the privilege of being *trusted* and his every act is viewed with suspicion by the guards, the surrogates of the conforming social order. Constantly aware of lawful society's disapproval, his picture of himself challenged by frequent reminders of his moral unworthiness, the inmate must find some way to ward off these attacks and avoid their introjection.

In addition, it should be remembered that the offender has been drawn from a society in which personal possessions 'and material achievement are closely linked with concepts of personal worth by numerous cultural definitions. In the prison, however, the inmate finds himself reduced to a level of living near bare subsistence, and whatever physical discomforts this deprivation may entail, it apparently has deeper psychological significance as a basic attack on the prisoner's conception of his own personal adequacy.

No less important, perhaps, is the ego threat that is created by the deprivation of heterosexual relationships. In the tense atmosphere of the prison, with its perversions and constant references to the problems of sexual frustration, even those inmates who do not engage in overt homosexuality suffer acute attacks of anxiety about their own masculinity. These anxieties may arise from a prisoner's unconscious fear of latent homosexual tendencies in himself, which might be activated by his prolonged heterosexual deprivation and the importunity of others; or at a more conscious level he may feel that his masculinity is threatened because he can see himself as a man—in the full sense —only in a world that also contains women. In either case the inmate is confronted with the fact that the celibacy imposed on him by society means more than simple physiological frustration: an essential component of his self-conception, his status as male, is called into question.

Rejected, impoverished, and figuratively castrated, the prisoner must face still further indignity in the extensive social control exercised by the custodians. The many details of the inmate's life, ranging from the hours of sleeping to the route to work and the job itself, are subject to a vast number of regulations made by prison officials. The inmate is stripped of his autonomy; hence, to the other pains of imprisonment we must add the pressure to define himself as weak, helpless, and dependent. Individuals under guard are exposed to the bitter ego threat of losing their identification with the normal adult role.[6]

The remaining significant feature of the inmate's social environment is the presence of other imprisoned criminals. Murderers, rapists, thieves, confidence men, and sexual deviants are the inmate's constant companions, and this enforced intimacy may prove to be disquieting even for the hardened recidivist. As an inmate has said, "The worst thing about prison is you have to live with other prisoners." [7] Crowded into a small area with men who have long records of physical assaults, thievery, and so on (and who may be expected to continue in the path of deviant social behavior in the future), the inmate is deprived of the sense of security that we more or less take for granted in the free community. Although the anxieties created by such a situation do not necessarily involve an attack on the individual's sense of personal worth—as we are using the concept—the problems of self-protection in a society composed exclusively of criminals constitute one of the inadvertent rigors of confinement.

In short, imprisonment "punishes" the offender in a variety of ways extending far beyond the simple fact of incarceration. However just or necessary such punishments may be, their importance for our present analysis lies in the fact that they form a set of harsh social conditions to which the population of prisoners must respond or *adapt itself*. The inmate feels that the deprivations and frustrations of prison life, with their implications for the destruction of his self-esteem, somehow must be alleviated. It is, we suggest, as an answer to this need that the functional significance of the inmate code or system of values exhibited so frequently by men in prison can best be understood.

As we have pointed out, the dominant theme of the inmate code is group cohesion, with a "war of all against all"—in which each man seeks his own gain without considering the rights or claims of others—as the theoretical antipode. But if a war of all against all is likely to make life "solitary, poor, nasty, brutish, and short" for men with freedom, as Hobbes suggested, it is doubly so for men in custody. Even those who are most successful in exploiting their fellow prisoners will find it a dangerous and nerve-racking game, for they cannot escape the company of their victims. No man can assure the safety of either his person or his possessions, and eventually the winner is certain to lose to a more powerful or more skillful exploiter. Furthermore, the victims hold the trump card, since a word to the officials is frequently all that is required to ruin the most dominating figure in the inmate population. A large share of the "extra" goods that enter the inmate social system must do so as the result of illicit conniving against the officials, which often requires lengthy and extensive cooperation and trust; in a state of complete conflict the resources of the system will be diminished. Mutual abhorrence or indifference will feed the emotional frictions arising from interaction under compression. And as rejection by others is a fundamental problem, a state of mutual alienation is worse than useless as a solution to the threats created by the inmate's status as an outcast.

As a population of prisoners moves toward a state of mutual antagonism, then, the many problems of prison life become more acute. On the other hand, *as a population of prisoners moves in the direction of solidarity, as demanded by the inmate code, the pains of imprisonment become less severe.* They cannot be eliminated, it is true, but their consequences at least can be partially neutralized. A cohesive inmate society provides the prisoner with a meaningful social group with which he can identify himself and which will support him in his struggles against his condemners. Thus it permits him to escape at least in part the fearful isolation of the convicted offender. Inmate solidarity, in the form of toleration of the many irritants of life in confinement, helps to solve the problems of personal security posed by the involuntary intimacy of men noteworthy for their seriously antisocial behavior in the past.

Similarly, group cohesion in the form of a reciprocity of favors undermines one of the most potent sources of aggression among prisoners, the drive for personal aggrandizement through exploitation by force and fraud. Furthermore, although goods in scarce supply will remain scarce even if they are shared rather than monopolized, such goods will be distributed more equitably in a social system marked by solidarity, and this may be of profound significance in enabling the prisoner to endure better the psychological burden of impoverishment. A cohesive population of prisoners has another advantage in that it supports a system of shared beliefs that explicitly deny the traditional link between merit and achievement. Material success, according to this system, is a matter of "connections" rather than skill or hard work, and thus the imprisoned criminal is partially freed from the necessity of defining his material want as a sign of personal inadequacy.

Finally, a cohesive inmate social system institutionalizes the value of "dignity" and the ability to "take it" in a number of norms and reinforces these norms with informal social controls. In effect, the prisoner is called on to endure manfully what he cannot avoid. At first glance this might seem to be simply the counsel of despair; but if the elevation of fortitude into a primary virtue is the last refuge of the powerless, it also serves to shift the criteria of the individual's worth from conditions that cannot be altered to his ability to maintain some degree of personal integration; and the latter, at least, can be partially controlled. By creating an ideal of endurance in the face of harsh social conditions, then, the society of prisoners opens a path to the restoration of self-respect and a sense of independence that can exist despite prior criminality, present subjugation, and the free community's denial of the offender's moral worthiness. Significantly, this path to virtue is recognized by the prison officials as well as the prisoners.

One further point should be noted with regard to the emphasis placed on the maintenance of self as defined by the value system of prisoners. Dignity, composure, courage, the ability to "take it" and "hand it out" when necessary —these are the traits affirmed by the inmate code. They are also traits that are commonly defined as masculine by the inmate population. As a consequence, the prisoner finds himself in a situation where he can recapture his male role, not in terms of its sexual aspects, but in terms of behavior that is accepted as a good indicator of virility.

The effectiveness of the inmate code in mitigating the pains of imprisonment depends of course on the extent to which precepts are translated into action. As we have indicated, the demands of the inmate code for loyalty, generosity, disparagement of officials, and so on are most fully exemplified in the behavior of the *right guy*. On the other hand, much noncohesive behavior occurs on the part of the *rat,* the *tough,* the *gorilla,* the *merchant,* and the *weak sister.* The population of prisoners, then, does not exhibit perfect solidarity in practice, in spite of inmates' vehement assertions of group cohesion as a value; but neither is the population of prisoners a warring aggregate. Rather, the inmate social system typically appears to be balanced in an uneasy compromise somewhere between these two extremes. The problems confronting prisoners in the form of social rejection, material deprivation, sexual frustration, and the loss of autonomy and personal security are not completely eliminated. Indeed, even if the norms of the inmate social system were fully carried out by all, the pains of imprisonment would only be lessened; they would not disappear. But the pains of imprisonment are at least relieved by whatever degree of group cohesion is achieved in fact, and this is crucial in understanding the functional significance of the inmate code for inmates.

One further problem remains. Many of the prisoners who deviate from the maxims of the inmate code are precisely those who are most vociferous in their verbal allegiance to it. How can this discrepancy between words and behavior be explained? Much of the answer seems to lie in the fact that almost all inmates have an interest in maintaining cohesive behavior on the part of others, *regardless of the role they play themselves,* and vehement vocal support of the inmate code is a potent means to this end.

There are, of course, prisoners who "believe" in inmate cohesion both for themselves and others. These hold the unity of the group as a high personal value and are ready to demand cohesive behavior from their fellow prisoners. This collectivistic orientation may be due to a thorough identification with the criminal world in opposition to the forces of lawful society, or to a system of values that transcends such divisions. In any case, for these men the inmate code has much of the quality of a religious faith and they approach its tenets as true believers. In a second category are those prisoners who are relatively indifferent to the cohesion of the inmate population as a personal value, but who are quick to assert it as a guide to behavior because in its absence they would be likely to become chronic victims. They are committed to the ideal of inmate solidarity to the extent that they have little or no desire to take advantage of their fellow captives, but they do not go so far as to subscribe to the ideal of self-sacrifice. Their behavior is best described as passive or neutral; they are believers without passion, demanding adherence from others, but not prepared to let excessive piety interfere with more mundane considerations. Third, there are those who loudly acclaim the inmate code and actively violate its injunctions. These men suffer if their number increases, since they begin to face the difficulties of competition; and they are in particular danger if their depredations are reported to the officials. The prisoners who are thus actively alienated from other inmates and yet give lip service to inmate solidarity resemble a manipulative priesthood, savage in their expression of belief but corrupt in practice. In brief, a variety of motivational patterns underlies allegiance to the inmate code, but few inmates can avoid the need to insist publicly on its observance, whatever the discrepancies in their actions.

NOTES

1. Samuel M. Strong, "Social Types in a Minority Group," *American Journal of Sociology,* 48:563–573 (March 1943). Schrag in "Social Types in a Prison Community" notes the relevance of Strong's discussion for examination of the inmate social system.

2. See Schrag, *ibid.,* and Sykes, "Men, Merchants, and Toughs" for discussion of this approach to the prison as a system of action.

3. The argot applied to a particular role varies somewhat from one prison to another, but it is not difficult to find the synonyms in the prisoners' lexicon.

4. The inmate population, with a keen sense of distinctions, draws a line between the *fag,* who plays a passive role in a homosexual relationship because he "likes" it or "wants" to, and a *punk,* who is coerced or bribed into a passive role.

5. We have not attempted to discuss all the prison roles that have been identified in the literature, although we have mentioned most of the major types. Two exceptions, not discussed because they are not distinctive of the prison, are the *fish,* a novitiate, and the *ding,* an erratic behaver. The homosexual world of the prison, especially, deserves fuller treatment; various role types within it have not yet been described.

6. Bruno Bettelheim, "Individual and Mass Behavior in Extreme Situations," *Journal of Abnormal and Social Psychology,* 38:417–452 (October 1943).

7. Gresham M. Sykes, *Crime and Society* (New York: Random House, 1956), p. 109.

8: Leadership among Prison Inmates /
Clarence Schrag

Ineffectiveness of our penal institutions as therapeutic agencies is usually explained in terms of inadequate treatment facilities,[1] inferior qualifications of administrators,[2] or the criminogenic characteristics of inmates.[3] The social climate of the prison and the interpersonal relations among the inmates have received less attention.[4] Failure to investigate more thoroughly the dynamics of interaction among prison inmates may be a serious theoretical and methodological omission in criminological research.[5]

Results of an investigation into inmate interaction in a western state prison are reported in this chapter. Although data were obtained on several kinds of interaction, such as congeniality, antagonism, and leadership, the discussion here is limited to leadership phenomena.

The Problem

The study is chiefly concerned with two problems: (1) How may inmate leaders and their followers be identified? (2) Assuming that leaders and followers are known, how may their interrelations be investigated so as to promote the eventual prediction and control of leadership phenomena?

Conclusive solutions to the above problems would require an experimental answer to the question: Who among the inmates says or does what to whom, and with what effect? However, common sense opinions are such compelling forces in the determination of penal policies that random techniques and experimental controls are rarely tolerated in prison research. We are consequently forced to use non-experimental research procedures which, if interpreted consistently with certain assumptions, may enable us to approximate the results of an experiment.[6]

From Clarence Schrag, "Leadership among Prison Inmates," *American Sociological Review* 19 (1954): 37–42.

Research Procedures

DESIGNATION OF LEADERS AND FOLLOWERS

Data on leadership were obtained from a sociometric schedule which was administered to the residents of Trusty Quarters, a medium custody building within the prison.[7] One hundred and forty-three respondents completed and returned their schedules.[8] Included in the schedules is an item designed to obtain the names of inmate leaders.[9] Responses to this item were validated against the results of an official election in which members of the Inmate's Council were chosen.[10] Results of the election, held one week after the schedules were completed, are in agreement with our sociometric data.[11]

HYPOTHESES TO BE TESTED

Eventual prediction and control of prison leadership require (1) identification of the general characteristics of leaders and (2) knowledge of the kinds of inmates who are most likely to be influenced by certain types of leaders. Accordingly, two sets of hypotheses were in this study submitted to statistical test. The first set is concerned with the question: Are the social and criminal backgrounds of inmate leaders significantly different from those of the other prisoners? Specifically, these hypotheses, stated in null form, assert that leaders are not significantly different from the total Trusty Quarters population with respect to age, ethnic status, occupation, marital status, educational attainment, test intelligence, type of offense, previous criminal record, or institutional adjustment. Rejection of certain of these hypotheses identifies background characteristics that are significantly associated with the status of inmate leader.

The second set of hypotheses is concerned with the question: Do variations in the social and criminal backgrounds of our respondents influence their choices for leaders? Stated in null form, these hypotheses assert that leadership preferences, as indicated by responses to our schedule, are independent of the background factors mentioned above. That is, expressions of preference are expected to be uninfluenced by variations in the backgrounds of our respondents. However, rejection of some of these hypotheses implies that the characteristics of leaders differ significantly according to the characteristics of the respondents by whom they are chosen. Thus, consensus among the prisoners does not occur with respect to their leadership preferences.

Detailed knowledge of the general characteristics of leaders and of the variations in leadership preferences among different groups of inmates should facilitate the prediction and regulation of interpersonal contacts and influences within the prison community. Such information should simplify the control of the prisoner population by means of segregation or special assignments.

PROCEDURES FOR TESTING THE HYPOTHESES

The above hypotheses, when tested by conventional chi-square analysis,[12] may be accepted or rejected within specified degrees of probability. For example, the assertion that leaders do not differ from the rest of the Trusty Quarters prisoners was tested by classifying the two groups of inmates according to the sub-categories of a given characteristic, and then determining the significance of the difference between the two resulting frequency distributions.[13] This procedure was repeated for each of the characteristics on which reliable information was available.

The second set of hypotheses, asserting that leadership preferences are independent of the respondents' characteristics, requires a somewhat more elaborate testing procedure. To illustrate, Table 8–1 presents data on leaders and followers classified according to type of offense. Leaders and the respondents by whom they were chosen are classified with respect to a given characteristic, type of offense, and the resulting data are recorded in a 3 by 3 table. Traits of leaders are plotted in rows and those of followers in columns. Obviously rows equal columns in number, and there are as many of each as there are sub-categories within the characteristic used in classifying the inmates.

Table 8-1

Leaders and Respondents Who Chose
Them Classified by Type of Offense

| | Respondents | | | |
Leaders	Violence	Sex	Property	Totals
Violence	31	20	41	92
Sex	3	12	4	19
Property	7	3	22	32
Totals	41	35	67	143

Cell frequencies in Table 8–1 may easily be compared to a hypothetical model which is based on the assumption that leadership choices are independent of type of offense. This model is constructed by making cell frequencies proportional to the products of their row and column totals. If the hypothesis of independence is tenable, the model should duplicate the cell frequencies in Table 8–1. Large discrepancies between the two sets of frequencies, on the other hand, would require that the hypothesis be rejected.

Significance of the differences between the frequencies observed in Table 8–1 and those of the model may be determined by the usual chi-square test of independence. Chi-square for Table 8–1 rejects the independence hypothesis at the one per cent level of significance. Thus, leadership preferences, according to our data, are significantly related to the crimes for which the respondents were committed to prison.

What, however, is the nature of the relationship between leadership and type of offense? Further analysis of the data brings out several other important facts regarding prison leadership. For example, the most striking disparities between the independence model and Table 8–1 occur along the diagonal of homogeneity. That is, violent offenders [14] are almost exclusive in their preference for leaders who are also violent offenders, while sex offenders prefer sex offenders, and property offenders likewise choose leaders from their own offense category. This tendency for like to choose like is significant at the one per cent level.[15] Furthermore, persons committed for violent or property offenses refrain from choosing sex offenders and, conversely, sex offenders avoid choosing property offenders.[16] Despite these differences in the choice patterns of certain types of offenders, there is nevertheless a significant tendency for persons in all offense categories to select leaders who are committed for crimes of violence. Thus, statistical analysis of Table 8–1 shows that although a certain offense category—crimes of violence—is uniformly related to leader status, important differences occur in the preference patterns of inmates who are classified by the offenses for which they were imprisoned.

Analyses similar to the above were made of the interrelations among leaders and followers classified according to each of the previously mentioned background factors.

Summary of Findings

CHARACTERISTICS OF THE LEADER GROUP

What are the determinants of leadership in a prison community? Comparison of our leaders with the total population suggests that, in general, factors related to criminal career and institutional adjustment are significantly associated with leadership, while social and economic background traits are not. Leaders, as a group, do not differ from the other inmates with respect to age, occupation, educational attainment, ethnic status, marital status, or scores on an intelligence test.[17] However, leaders have served more years in prison, have longer sentences remaining to be served, are more frequently charged with crimes of violence, and are more likely to be repeated offenders.[18] Significantly more leaders than other inmates are officially diagnosed as homosexual, psychoneurotic, or psychopathic.[19] Finally, the institutional adjustments of leaders are marked by a significantly greater number of serious rule infractions, including escape, attempted escape, fighting, and assault.

Infrequently selected as leaders are first offenders, non-violent offenders, or persons with short prison sentences. Most important among the determinants of leadership are criminal maturity, comparatively permanent tenure in the institution, and habits of aggressiveness and violence. It is probable, therefore, that the group identifications of the inmates are generally organized around the activities and interests of the least improvable offenders, and that the values of the prison culture encourage rebellion and non-conformity.

PATTERNS OF PREFERENCE AMONG THE RESPONDENTS

What are the major variations in the leader preferences of our respondents? Choices of certain groups of inmates deviate significantly from the pattern outlined above. Different choice patterns of inmates classified by type of offense have already been mentioned. Other important variations occur with respect to both social and criminal background factors.

First offenders, for example, select leaders who are first offenders.[20] Recidivists do so infrequently. Inmates serving short sentences prefer short-termers, whereas persons serving long sentences very rarely choose short-termers as leaders. Again, inmates with clear conduct records exclude those who have committed serious rule infractions. Conversely, the well-behaved inmates are excluded by the more fractious prisoners. Homosexuals, psychoneurotics, and psychopaths show greater preference for leaders from their own ranks than do the rest of the inmates.

We have already noted that leaders, as a group, do not differ significantly from the other inmates with respect to social background. However, preference patterns are significantly associated with certain social characteristics. Ethnic status is an example. Whites choose whites with rare exceptions, while Negroes tend to choose Negroes. Other ethnic groups scatter their choices throughout the prisoner population. Preferences are also associated with level of intelligence. Superior inmates choose leaders who have superior intelligence, while average and dull inmates choose leaders from their own intelligence classes. On the other hand, no significant differences were observed among respondents classified by age, occupation, education, or marital status.

Data on preference patterns, then, show that respondents, when classified by offense, sentence, previous criminal record, institutional adjustment, ethnic status, or test intelligence, tend to choose leaders who have traits similar to their own. This tendency for like to choose like is statistically significant. It provides the chief source of deviation from the general pattern of leader preference.

IMPORTANCE OF PROPINQUITY

Are leadership preferences related to the physical distances between groups of inmates? Segregation of inmates presumably regulates frequency of contact and thereby facilitates the regimentation of inmate activities. If segregation is effective, its influence should be reflected in the choices of our respondents. To test the effect of segregation, leaders and the respondents who chose them were classified according to whether they (1) reside in same cell,[21] (2) reside in different cells on same tier of building, (3) reside on different tiers of same building, and (4) reside in separate buildings. The data show that degree of physical proximity is an important determinant of leader preference.[22] The probability that a given inmate will be chosen by a certain respondent varies inversely with the physical distance between them. Thus, our findings confirm the utility of segregation as a device for regulating inmate interaction.

Conclusions

Results of this study, of course, cannot be generalized to other institutions until similar investigations are made elsewhere. Tentatively, however, we may conclude that leadership in prison is exercised by the criminally mature inmates who are serving long sentences for crimes of violence.[23] Status of an inmate is ordinarily enhanced by acts of violence within the institution, by homosexuality, or by psychoneurotic or psychopathic behavior. Prison culture is organized around the values of its most persistent and least improvable members. It stimulates aggressive anti-social behavior and minimizes the status of the naïve or accidental offender. Socialization in prison means, for many inmates, the acquisition of the skills and attitudes of the habitual criminal.

Despite the dominance of the violent recidivists, certain groups of inmates direct their leadership choices toward persons who possess characteristics the same as their own. Short-termers, first offenders, persons convicted of non-violent crimes, and inmates who make good institutional adjustments create within the prison society a number of dissentient minorities. These minorities resist, at least to some extent, the dominant influence of the typical leader group. Thus, an effective classification program may segregate these minorities and in this way neutralize the influence of the more mature criminals.

Physical proximity is an important determinant of inmate influence and leadership. The kinds of influences an inmate encounters in prison life are largely determined by his immediate associates, especially his cell partners.

The above considerations clearly challenge the current trend toward construction of massive, multi-purpose prisons. They indicate the desirability of smaller and more specialized institutions. In a heterogeneous prisoner population, the hardened offenders may inevitably rise to positions of leadership. This is true even among the carefully selected Trusty Quarters inmates. It therefore seems likely that mass treatment, with its economy in construction and supervision, provides a misplaced emphasis in contemporary prison administration.

NOTES

1. Harry Elmer Barnes and Negley K. Teeters, *New Horizons in Criminology,* New York: Prentice-Hall, 1951, especially Chapters 22 and 26.

2. Kenyon J. Scudder, *Prisoners Are People,* Garden City, New York: Doubleday and Company, 1952.

3. J. A. Johnson, *Alcatraz Island Prison,* New York: Scribner's, 1949.

4. Most important among the studies of prison social structure are Donald Clemmer, *The Prison Community,* Boston: Christopher Publishing House, 1940; Hans Reimer, "Socialization in the Prison Community," *Proceedings of the American Prison Association* (1937), pp. 151–155; Norman S. Hayner and Ellis Ash, "The Prison as a Community," *American Sociological Review,* 5 (April, 1940), pp. 577–583; Kirson

Weinberg, "Aspects of the Prison's Social Structure," *American Journal of Sociology,* 47 (March, 1942), pp. 717–726.

5. For studies of inmate interaction see J. L. Moreno, *Who Shall Survive?* Washington, D. C.: Nervous and Mental Disease Publishing Company, 1934; and Helen Jennings, *Leadership and Isolation,* New York: Longmans, Green and Company, 1943.

6. Assumptions in science are propositions which, although perhaps capable of proof, are accepted without proof for the purposes at hand. They should be consistent with current theories and empirical evidence. The assumptions required in this study are: (1) Social interaction is a prerequisite for any important influence to be exerted on one inmate by another. (2) Inmates are able and willing to name those of their fellows who influence them. (3) A sociometric test is a reliable device for securing information on inmate influence and interaction. For evidence concerning these assumptions see, for example, Moreno, *op. cit.,* and Jennings, *op. cit.*

7. Trusty Quarters houses inmates adjudged unlikely to escape or commit serious rule infractions. More seriously maladjusted inmates are housed in the Strong Box, a close custody building. The author for several years was Director of Classification at the prison.

8. This is a forty per cent sample of the Trusty Quarters population. No significant differences were observed between the sample and the rest of the inmates on any social or criminal characteristics. Chi-square tests were used at the five per cent level of significance.

9. This item was stated as follows: "Name the inmates now in the institution who are in your opinion best fitted to represent the rest of the inmates by selection for the Council. List your first choice on the line below, then your second choice on the second line." The present analysis is restricted to first choices.

10. The Council, elected annually, consults with the staff on such matters as recreation, inmate welfare, visits, and correspondence privileges.

11. Distributions of sociometric choices and of votes in the election did not differ significantly according to the chi-square test at the five per cent level.

12. Testing procedures were followed as outlined in John F. Kenney, *Mathematics of Statistics,* New York: Van Nostrand, 1939, Vol. II, pp. 168–186.

13. Chi-square test was used at the five per cent level.

14. Violent offenders include, chiefly, cases of murder, assault, or robbery with a weapon.

15. The significance of the departure of any cell or set of cells from the frequencies expected according to the model can be computed by appropriately partitioning the contributions to the chi-square total.

16. This barrier between sex offenders and other inmates is also statistically significant.

17. Differences not significant at five per cent level.

18. Differences are significant at five per cent level.

19. All diagnoses were obtained from official case records.

20. Differences in choice patterns discussed in this section are significant at the five per cent level.

21. Trusty Quarters houses four inmates in each cell.

22. The findings are statistically significant. For example, the ratio of observed to expected choices in the first distance interval is 27 to 1; in the fourth interval, it is 1 to 3.

23. Our findings are generally consistent with those of Clemmer, *op. cit.,* who used a participant observer technique. They do not, however, support the observations of Reimer, *op. cit.*

9: The Process of Prisonization /
Donald Clemmer

Assimilation or Prisonization

When a person or group penetrates and fuses with another group, assimilation may be said to have taken place. The concept is most profitably applied to immigrant groups and perhaps it is not the best term by which to designate similar processes which occur in prison. Assimilation implies that a process of acculturation occurs in one group whose members originally were quite different from those of the group with whom they mix. It implies that the assimilated come to share the sentiments, memories, and traditions of the static group. It is evident that the men who come to prison are not greatly different from the ones already there so far as broad culture influences are concerned: All speak the same language, all have a similar national heritage, all have been stigmatized, and so on. While the differences of regional conditioning are not to be overlooked, it is doubtful if the interactions which lead the professional offender to have a "we-feeling" with the naïve offender from Coalville can be referred to as assimilation—although the processes furnishing the development of such an understanding are similar to it. The term assimilation describes a slow, gradual, more or less unconscious process during which a person learns enough of the culture of a social unit into which he is placed to make him characteristic of it. While we shall continue to use this general meaning, we recognize that in the strictest sense assimilation is not the correct term. So as we use the term Americanization to describe a greater or less degree of the immigrant's integration into the American scheme of life, we may use the term *prisonization* to indicate the taking on in greater or less degree of the folkways, mores, customs, and general culture of the penitentiary. Prisonization is similar to assimilation, and its meaning will become clearer as we proceed.

Every man who enters the penitentiary undergoes prisonization to some extent. The first and most obvious integrative step concerns his status. He becomes at once an anonymous figure in a subordinate group. A number replaces a name. He wears the clothes of the other members of the subordinate group. He is questioned and admonished. He soon learns that the warden is

From Donald Clemmer, *The Prison Community* (New York: Holt, Rinehart & Winston Co., Inc., 1958), pp. 298–304. Copyright 1940, © 1958, 1968 by Donald Clemmer. Reprinted by permission of Holt, Rinehart & Winston, Inc.

all-powerful. He soon learns the ranks, titles, and authority of various officials. And whether he uses the prison slang and argot or not, he comes to know their meanings. Even though a new man may hold himself aloof from other inmates and remain a solitary figure, he finds himself within a few months referring to or thinking of keepers as "screws," the physician as the "croaker" and using the local nicknames to designate persons. He follows the examples already set in wearing his cap. He learns to eat in haste and in obtaining food he imitates the tricks of those near him.

After the new arrival recovers from the effects of the swallowing-up process, he assigns a new meaning to conditions he had previously taken for granted. The fact that food, shelter, clothing, and a work activity had been given him originally made no especial impression. It is only after some weeks or months that there comes to him a new interpretation of these necessities of life. This new conception results from mingling with other men and it places emphasis on the fact that the environment *should* administer to him. This point is intangible and difficult to describe in so far as it is only a subtle and minute change in attitude from the taken-for-granted perception. Exhaustive questioning of hundreds of men reveals that this slight change in attitude is a fundamental step in the process we are calling prisonization. Supplemental to it is the almost universal desire on the part of the man, after a period of some months, to get a good job so, as he says, "I can do my time without any trouble and get out of here." A good job usually means a comfortable job of a more or less isolated kind in which conflicts with other men are not likely to develop. The desire for a comfortable job is not peculiar to the prison community, to be sure, but it seems to be a phase of prisonization in the following way. When men have served time before entering the penitentiary they look the situation over and almost immediately express a desire for a certain kind of work. When strictly first offenders come to prison, however, they seldom express a desire for a particular kind of work, but are willing to do anything and frequently say, "I'll do any kind of work they put me at and you won't have any trouble from me." Within a period of a few months, however, these same men, who had no choice of work, develop preferences and make their desires known. They "wise up," as the inmates say, or, in other words, by association they become prisonized.

In various other ways men new to prison slip into the existing patterns. They learn to gamble or learn new ways to gamble. Some, for the first time in their lives, take to abnormal sex behavior. Many of them learn to distrust and hate the officers, the parole board, and sometimes each other, and they become acquainted with the dogmas and mores existing in the community. But these changes do not occur in every man. However, every man is subject to certain influences which we may call the *universal factors of prisonization*.

Acceptance of an inferior rôle, accumulation of facts concerning the organization of the prison, the development of somewhat new habits of eating, dressing, working, sleeping, the adoption of local language, the recognition that nothing is owed to the environment for the supplying of needs, and the

eventual desire for a good job are aspects of prisonization which are operative for all inmates. It is not these aspects, however, which concern us most
but they are important because of their universality, especially among men
who have served many years. That is, even if no other factor of the prison
culture touches the personality of an inmate of many years residence, the influences of these universal factors are sufficient to make a man characteristic
of the penal community and probably so disrupt his personality that a happy
adjustment in any community becomes next to impossible. On the other hand,
if inmates who are incarcerated for only short periods, such as a year or so,
do not become integrated into the culture except in so far as these universal
factors of prisonization are concerned, they do not seem to be so characteristic of the penal community and are able when released to take up a new
mode of life without much difficulty.

The phases of prisonization which concern us most are the influences
which breed or deepen criminality and antisociality and make the inmate
characteristic of the criminalistic ideology in the prison community. As has
been said, every man feels the influences of what we have called the universal
factors, but not every man becomes prisonized in and by other phases of the
culture. Whether or not complete prisonization takes place depends first on
the man himself, that is, his susceptibility to a culture which depends, we
think, primarily on the type of relationships he had before imprisonment, i.e.,
his personality. A second determinant effecting complete prisonization refers
to the kind and extent of relationships which an inmate has with persons outside the walls. A third determinant refers to whether or not a man becomes
affiliated in prison primary or semi-primary groups and this is related to the
two points already mentioned. Yet a fourth determinant depends simply on
chance, a chance placement in work gang, cellhouse, and with cellmate. A
fifth determinant pertains to whether or not a man accepts the dogmas or
codes of the prison culture. Other determinants depend on age, criminality,
nationality, race, regional conditioning, and every determinant is more or less
interrelated with every other one.

With knowledge of these determinants we can hypothetically construct
schemata of prisonization which may serve to illustrate its extremes. In the
least or lowest degree of prisonization the following factors may be enumerated:

1. A short sentence, thus a brief subjection to the universal factors of prisonization.
2. A fairly stable personality made stable by an adequacy of positive and
   "socialized" relationships during pre-penal life.
3. The continuance of positive relationships with persons outside the walls.
4. Refusal or inability to integrate into a prison primary group or semi-primary group, while yet maintaining a symbiotic balance in relations with
   other men.
5. Refusal to accept blindly the dogmas and codes of the population, and a

willingness, under certain situations, to aid officials, thus making for identification with the free community.

6. A chance placement with a cellmate and workmates who do not possess
   leadership qualities and who are also not completely integrated into the
   prison culture.
7. Refraining from abnormal sex behavior, and excessive gambling, and a
   ready willingness to engage seriously in work and recreative activities.

Other factors no doubt have an influencing force in obstructing the process
of prisonization, but the seven points mentioned seem outstanding.

In the highest or greatest degree of prisonization the following factors may
be enumerated:

1. A sentence of many years, thus a long subjection to the universal factors
   of prisonization.
2. A somewhat unstable personality made unstable by an inadequacy of "socialized" relations before commitment, but possessing, nonetheless, a capacity for strong convictions and a particular kind of loyalty.
3. A dearth of positive relations with persons outside the walls.
4. A readiness and a capacity for integration into a prison-primary group.
5. A blind, or almost blind, acceptance of the dogmas and mores of the primary group and the general penal population.
6. A chance placement with other persons of a similar orientation.
7. A readiness to participate in gambling and abnormal sex behavior.

We can see in these two extremes the degrees with which the prisonization
process operates. No suggestion is intended that a high correlation exists
between either extreme of prisonization and criminality. It is quite possible that the inmate who fails to integrate in the prison culture may
be and may continue to be much more criminalistic than the inmate
who becomes completely prisonized. The trends are probably otherwise, however, as our study of group life suggests. To determine prisonization, every case must be appraised for itself. Of the two degrees presented
in the schemas it is probable that more men approach the complete degree
than the least degree of prisonization, but it is also probable that the majority
of inmates become prisonized in some respects and not in others. It is the
varying degrees of prisonization among the 2,300 men that contribute to the
disassociation which is so common. The culture is made complex, not only by
the constantly changing population, but by these differences in the tempo and
degree of prisonization.

Assimilation, as the concept is customarily applied, is always a slow, gradual process, but prisonization, as we use the term here, is usually slow, but
not necessarily so. The speed with which prisonization occurs depends on the
personality of the man involved, his crime, age, home neighborhood, intelligence, the situation into which he is placed in prison and other less obvious
influences. The process does not necessarily proceed in an orderly or meas-

ured fashion but tends to be irregular. In some cases we have found the process working in a cycle. The amount and speed of prisonization can be judged only by the behavior and attitudes of the men, and these vary from man to man and in the same man from time to time. It is the excessive number of changes in orientation which the men undergo which makes generalizations about the process so difficult.

In the free communities where the daily life of the inhabitants is not controlled in every detail, some authors have reported a natural gravitation to social levels. The matter of chance still remains a factor, of course, in open society but not nearly so much so as in the prison. For example, two associates in a particular crime may enter the prison at the same time. Let us say that their criminality, their intelligence, and their background are more or less the same. Each is interviewed by the deputy warden and assigned to a job. It so happens that a certain office is in need of a porter. Of the two associates the man whom the deputy warden happens to see first may be assigned to that job while the one he interviews last is assigned to the quarry. The inmate who becomes the office porter associates with but four or five other men, none of whom, let us suppose, are basically prisonized. The new porter adapts himself to them and takes up their interests. His speed of prisonization will be slow and he may never become completely integrated into the prison culture. His associate, on the other hand, works in the quarry and mingles with a hundred men. The odds are three to five that he will become integrated into a primary or semi-primary group. When he is admitted into the competitive and personal relationships of informal group life we can be sure that, in spite of some disassociation, he is becoming prisonized and will approach the complete degree.

Even if the two associates were assigned to the same work unit, differences in the tempo of prisonization might result if one, for example, worked shoulder to shoulder with a "complete solitary man," or a "hoosier." Whatever else may be said of the tempo of the process, it is always faster when the contacts are primary, providing the persons contacted in a primary way are themselves integrated beyond the minimal into the prison culture. Other factors, of course, influence the speed of integration. The inmate whose wife divorces him may turn for response and recognition to his immediate associates. When the memories of pre-penal experience cease to be satisfying or practically useful, a barrier to prisonization has been removed.

Some men become prisonized to the highest degree, or to a degree approaching it, but then reject their entire orientation and show, neither by behavior nor attitudes, that any sort of integration has taken place. They slip out of group life. They ignore the codes and dogmas and they fall into a reverie or stupor or become "solitary men." After some months or even years of playing this rôle they may again affiliate with a group and behave as other prisonized inmates do.

Determination of the degree of prisonization and the speed with which it occurs can be learned best through the study of specific cases. The innumerable variables and the methodological difficulties which arise in learning what particular stage of prisonization a man has reached, prohibit the use of quantitative methods. It would be a great help to penology and to parole boards in particular, if the student of prisons could say that inmate so-and-so was prisonized to $x^3 + 9y$ degrees, and such a degree was highly correlated with a specific type of criminality. The day will no doubt come when phenomena of this kind can be measured, but it is not yet here. For the present we must bend our efforts to systems of actuarial prediction, and work for refinements in this line. Actuarial procedures do not ignore criteria of attitudes, but they make no effort as yet to conjure with such abstruse phenomena as prisonization. It is the contention of this writer that parole prediction methods which do not give as much study and attention to a man's rôle in the prison community as is given to his adjustment in the free community cannot be of much utility.

10: Socialization in Correctional Institutions / *Stanton Wheeler*

One of the most obvious but important features of socialization processes is that they take place within a broader social context. The structure of that social context may be expected to have an important effect upon the nature of the socialization process itself. A potential contribution of sociologists to the study of socialization processes, therefore, may be made through the analysis of the settings within which socialization takes place.

Increasingly in modern societies, those settings are large-scale formal organizations. Just as industrialization has brought on the development of massive industrial and business organizations, so has it led to the development of organizations for the processing of people: the school, the university, the mental hospital and prison, as well as a variety of related organizations (Brim & Wheeler, 1966). And increasingly, such organizations are thought of not merely as places to train or contain people, but as sources of fundamental change in their attitudes, beliefs, and conceptions of themselves and their place in society. The prison is one such setting. It differs from more traditional socializing organizations in many ways. But like the school or university, socialization processes do indeed go on there, whether they follow the patterns intended by the prison staff or not.

From Chapter 25, "Socialization in Correctional Institutions," by Stanton Wheeler in *Handbook of Socialization Theory and Research*, David A. Goslin, ed., (N.Y.: Rand McNally & Co., 1969).

It is my purpose in this chapter to examine socialization processes within the prison, with emphasis on the social organization and culture of the prison as it has an impact on socialization, and particularly on the relationship between what an inmate experiences within the prison, and his attachments to the outside world. Although these problems could be discussed in the standard fashion of a review article, I find it easier to get into them through the tracing of the changes that have occurred in my own thinking about socialization processes in the prison over the course of some ten or twelve years during which I have been reading and reflecting on the work of others in this area, and conducting research projects of my own. Over the course of that period of time, I have been forced to modify my own thoughts on the process in response to new data and observations from studies my colleagues and I have conducted, and in response to the ideas generated and developed by others in our field. Very largely, these changes have required moving beyond the immediate experiences to which inmates are exposed in the prison, to the nature of its culture and social organization, and finally to its connection with the external world.

Socialization in a State Reformatory

Until the decade of the 1950's the most serious effort to understand the process of socialization in prison was that of Donald Clemmer (1958). Clemmer was a sociologist with many years of experience behind the walls of prisons and he produced the first book-length study of a prison as a community. Clemmer described the culture and social organization of the prison, and noted that most of the characteristics he found suggested a system distinctly harmful to anything that might be regarded as a process of rehabilitation: The norms and codes of the inmate world appear to be organized in opposition to those of conventional society. He then turned his attention to the process by which inmates become a part of that world. He used the concept of *prisonization* as a summarizing concept revealing the consequences of exposure to inmate society. He defined prisonization as "the taking on, in greater or lesser degree, of the folkways, mores, customs and general culture of the penitentiary." And while he felt that no inmate could remain completely "unprisonized," he devoted a good deal of attention to variables that he thought probably influenced both the speed and the degree of prisonization. Some of these variables reflected the inmates' participation in conventional society. Thus prisonization would be lowest, he felt, for inmates who had positive relationships during pre-penal life and for those who continued their positive relationships with persons outside the walls during the time they were in prison. But the feature that he thought was most important in determining the degree of prisonization was simply the degree of close interpersonal contact that inmates had with other inmates within the institution. Those who became affiliated with inmate primary groups and those whose work and cell assignments placed them in very close contact with other inmates were likely to show the greatest degree of prisonization.

It was possible to put these ideas to a fairly direct empirical test in a survey research study of Washington State Reformatory (Wheeler, 1961b). An attitude measure of attitudinal conformity versus non-conformity to the values of the staff (and presumably, those of the conventional world) was developed to serve as an empirical indicator reflecting Clemmer's concept of prisonization. And although the study utilized a cross-sectional design rather than a panel design in which we could actually trace changes in attitudes over time, we could at least approximate the temporal aspect of imprisonment by comparing inmates who had been in the institution for varying lengths of time in order to test Clemmer's hypothesis that the longer the duration of stay, the more likely one was to become "prisonized."

The result of this analysis provided strong support for Clemmer's hypotheses. There was a general trend toward greater nonconformity to staff values with increase in length of time in the prison. And the trend was much stronger for those inmates who had made many friends in the institution than for those who were relatively isolated.

But one of the interesting features of Clemmer's account is that he had little to say about what happens to inmates as they prepare to leave the institutions. Many of his ideas about the socialization process in prison were drawn from studies of assimilation of ethnic groups into American life, and since by and large those groups were here to stay, the problem of what happens to them as they prepare to return to a former way of life does not arise. Perhaps for this reason, Clemmer's account has much to say about the early stages of imprisonment and about the general effects of being in prison, with no systematic attention devoted to the process of leaving the prison, and particularly to the possibility that the impact of prison culture is short-lived.

These concerns led us to consider the time measure in studies of prisonization in a manner different from that conceived by Clemmer. Very simply, we divided inmates into three groups: those who had been in only a short time, those who had only a short time remaining to serve, and those who were near neither entry nor release. The general results of this analysis suggested important modifications in Clemmer's original hypotheses. While we found a larger percentage of inmates who were strongly opposed to staff norms during the last stage of their confinement than during the first, we also found a U-shaped distribution of high conformity responses over the three time periods: there were fewer than half as many high conformity respondents during the middle phase than during the early and later phases of imprisonment. These findings suggest that while some inmates might become increasingly alienated during the course of their stay, an even larger number may exhibit the process of resocialization to the more conventional values of the outside world. And there was further evidence in support of the latter pattern: The U-shaped pattern of conforming responses was found both for inmates who had developed many friends in the institution and for those who had not, though it was stronger for the former group. It was also found both for first offenders and for recidivists. The clear suggestion from the evidence, then, was that this may well be a systematic feature of response to imprisonment, and not simply a minor deviation from the prisonization theme.

It would be simple enough to add the idea of "anticipatory socialization" to that of prisonization in an effort to make sense of both patterns of data. Indeed, Robert K. Merton (1957) had already written about the process of anticipatory socialization, and in retrospect there was good reason to assume that such a process would operate, even though it had not been formally incorporated into Clemmer's scheme. But while this would have given us two descriptive labels for two different patterns of empirical results, it would not have moved us very far toward understanding the conditions under which one or the other pattern would be expected to occur. In attempting to move toward the latter aim we were forced to ask questions about the nature of the inmate culture itself, and particularly about the sources that give rise to it.

Almost all accounts of close custody prisons in the United States are in agreement on the fundamental qualities of the inmate world in such institutions (Sykes & Messinger, 1960). Very briefly, three features seem most important:

1. There is a normative order defined largely in opposition to the staff and placing great emphasis on loyalty to other inmates.
2. There is a system of informal social differentiation that is reflected in the series of social types or argot roles noted by Sykes (1958), Schrag (1944) and many others. Special labels are assigned to inmates depending on their mode of response to prison life and expressing the quality of their interaction with staff and inmates. The system of informally defined social types gives evidence both of the dominant values of the inmate world— for the pejoratives always apply to those inmates who support the staff or who exploit other inmates for their own benefit—and of the range of subcultures that form within the walls of the institutions.
3. Accounts of everyday life in American prisons point to numerous struggles for power, frequent involvement in illicit activities, and a fair amount of violence behind the walls. Every institution has its share of fist-fights and occasional knifings, with force used as a means of social control. Though it would be easy to exaggerate such matters, it seems clear that the American prison is not a particularly warm, tolerant or congenial cultural setting. Almost every institution finds that it needs, in addition to the unit designed to hold the assault-minded or escape-risk inmates, a special segregation unit to protect some inmates from others who are out to get them.

Why does the prison so typically show these patterns of inmate response? Two conflicting views can be found. One interpretation is along the lines of "cultural diffusion" theories in anthropology. Very briefly, inmate society is what it is because inmates have imported their antagonism toward law and order from the outside world. The single trait held in common by all inmates is participation in criminal activity. The capacity to engage in criminal acts suggests at least some degree of withdrawal of support from conventional values, and indeed can be viewed as indicating an opposition to conventional norms and values. By bringing together in a twenty-four-hour living establishment individuals who have deviated from conventional norms, the prison offers opportunities for mutual reinforcement of criminal values. Those inmates who occupy prominent positions within the inmate hierarchy and who spend the most time in interaction with their fellows should be the ones whose values are most likely to serve as the basis for the organization and culture of inmate life. And these same inmates, we know from other sources, are those who are likely to be most committed to a criminal value system—those who have followed systematic criminal careers, those who are most hostile and aggressive in their expression of opposition to the staff (Schrag, 1954; Wheeler, 1961a). And if the culture is viewed as an outgrowth of the dominant sort of attitudes entering inmates bring with them, it is reasonable to expect a reinforcement process operating throughout the duration of their confinement. This is consistent with the image of correctional institutions as "crime schools" and with a theory that accounts for the socialization processes in prison largely in terms of a concept such as "prisonization." And this is very much the sort of process hinted at by Clemmer, although he very largely took the values of the inmate system for granted, and did not set out to explain them.

An alternative interpretation of the sources for the inmate culture emerged in the years following Clemmer's work, and received its fullest expression in an analysis of the inmate's social system presented by Gresham Sykes and Sheldon Messinger (1960). Instead of viewing inmate culture as a simple expression, and perhaps extension, of the individual values inmates may bring to the prison, Sykes and Messinger saw the inmate culture as a response to the adjustment problems posed by imprisonment itself, with all of its frustrations and deprivations. Among the important deprivations include the low and rejected status of being an inmate, the material and sexual deprivations of imprisonment, the constant social control exercised by the custodians of the prison, and the presence of other offenders who may be perceived as dangerous and threatening. The normative order and the system of social differentiation discussed above can be seen as responses to the series of deprivations. The normative order may reinstate self-esteem by providing a meaningful reference group that will support an inmate's attack on the staff, and it may lessen the dangers of exploitation on the part of other inmates. Further, the system of social differentiation itself reflects the variety of individual adaptations to the deprivations in question. In short, an alternative to the cultural diffusion scheme is a functional theory in which inmate culture is seen as a response to the conditions of imprisonment rather than an extension of the values men bring to prison.

If this interpretation is valid, we might expect that inmate culture would exert its major impact on inmates during the middle of their stay in prison, at the point in time when they are farthest removed from the outside world. And if the inmate value system is a response to the deprivations of imprisonment, it would seem only natural that as men prepare to leave the prison, those deprivations begin to wane in their significance. Thus they move away from adherence to the inmate value system and toward the values of the conventional society to which they are soon returning. Furthermore, the deprivations themselves may be objectively less severe as men approach release, when they are likely to be allowed more freedom within the walls, and somewhat more of the few amenities prison life may offer.

This provides us with a more substantial theoretical underpinning for the empirical finding of a U-shaped socialization and resocialization cycle within the prison. We are left, then, with two different patterns of change over time in the prison, and with two different and conflicting ideas regarding the sources of inmate culture itself, ideas that might possibly explain one or another of the patterns of adjustment to the prison over time.

Social Organization in Scandinavian Prisons [1]

A clear opportunity to further refine and test these ideas would be provided by a setting in which the prisons are relatively much like those found in the United States, with all their accompanying deprivations, but where the culture of the country as a whole is different. If the primary source of inmate culture lies in the deprivations of imprisonment themselves, the same inmate culture should be found wherever the deprivations are present, and should not vary widely with differences in the nature of the criminal and non-criminal world outside the walls. If differences in the external culture are very important, then we should find that despite a relatively uniform pattern of deprivations, inmate life sharply reflects the culture of the world outside the prison.

Some of the prisons in the Scandinavian countries provide a relevant case in point. In what follows, I shall present two different types of evidence from studies of Scandinavian prisons that enable us to elaborate on the themes developed above. The first is based upon a case study of a single institution in Norway, where we have both observational data and survey research data concerning the nature of inmate organization. The second type of evidence consists of survey data from some fifteen prisons spread throughout the Scandinavian countries, institutions which differ in the composition of their inmate population as well as in the nature of the goals and organization of the prisons themselves.

The major institution for normal long-term adult offenders in Norway is the Botsfengslet in Oslo. The prison houses about 200 offenders serving from six months to life, for crimes ranging from simple theft to treason and murder. It is a particularly interesting case for comparative analysis because its design and philosophy are modeled after American institutions based on the Pennsylvania system of prison architecture, and it is quite similar to Trenton prison, where Sykes' observations were made. Prison design was apparently one of the first elements of American culture to penetrate Norway, coming by way of English prison reformers of the early 19th century. Indeed, the deprivations mentioned in most functional accounts, such as the constant presence of guards, lack of women, attacks on self-esteem, and material deprivations, were clearly present at Botsfengslet, and were apparently felt as strongly by men there as they are by American inmates.

The most striking feature of inmate organization in Botsfengslet is the apparent weakness of the normative order and the lack of cohesive bonds. Almost all respondents volunteered that the inmates "lacked cohesion." Intensive interviews with a few of the inmates revealed that there was indeed general agreement regarding a minimal normative order, including the injunction not to rat or inform. But the inmates agreed that even this rule was never enforced by coercive pressures. For example, two inmates offered the same story about a former inmate who upon his release had informed the staff about the presence of narcotics and alcohol in the prison. He did the same thing at another institution, and later was returned to Botsfengslet. There was some talk among the prisoners of doing something to him, but in fact after his return no one made a move to harm him. Other examples were given of a similar unwillingness to sanction inmates for violations of inmate norms.

Neither the interviews nor the survey data gave any evidence of organized opposition to the staff. In the questionnaire, for example, only 15 per cent of the inmates said that other inmates often put pressure on them to work less hard than they otherwise would, and only 9 per cent said that inmates often put pressure on other inmates to oppose the staff. One inmate, perhaps a bit extreme, suggested something of the lack of organization and clear opposition: "If someone unlocked all the cells and opened the front gate, not more than three inmates would take off. Most would run to the guard and ask what was happening."

It is important to note that the lack of organization was not due to any sense of being well-treated and therefore having nothing to fight against. In fact, a larger percentage of inmates in this institution than in any others in Norway and Sweden felt that their stay was going to hurt them. Individually, they indicated no great warmth of feeling for their keepers. But the individual complaints had not led to collective resistance. Rather, they seemed to be an atomized and depressed mass.

A similar deviation from the expected strong inmate culture characterizes the special vocabulary found at Botsfengslet. Unlike the American case, there has been almost no development of nouns with a special meaning to depict an inmate's social role in the prison. Patterns of behavior can be described which are similar to those for which a vocabulary has developed in American prisons, but there is no jargon, no institutional shorthand, to refer to them.

Three exceptions, however, should be noted. There is a word for "rat," and an expression that literally means "noisemaker," referring to the occasional inmate who disturbs both staff and prisoners by talking too much, gossiping, and in general making a verbal nuisance of himself. Also, there are terms referring to the various roles involved in homosexual relations. But for the most part there is only an embryonic development of a special argot describing behavior patterns in the prison.

This may be due in part to the small number of inmates in Norwegian prisons at any one time. In Norway no more than 500 inmates are serving sentences of more than six months, and it may take a much larger base community to support a separate vocabulary. But this explanation seems doubtful, for there definitely are many terms which have special meaning only to prisoners. Most of these, however, refer not to behavioral patterns and social roles, but to the crime committed by the inmate or the nature of his life outside the institution. Thus, there is a special word for offenders who committed indecent acts with children (as there is in the United States), and a clear distinction between those who committed their acts against boys or against girls (unlike the United States). Another expression, meaning "traveler," characterizes those inmates who were nomadic and wandering in their pre-institutional life. Indeed, if any aspect of the typical American behavior pattern is present at Botsfengslet to a strong degree, it is the norms against asking persons about their pre-prison background or their offense—not the norms against ratting or other pro-staff behavior. The special language draws much more from the everyday vocabulary, and more frequently refers to life outside the institution than is the case in American prisons.

Finally, observations on characteristic behavior patterns in the institution reveal more deviations from the typical American case. I know of no way of getting an adequate picture of the amount of illicit activity in Norwegian institutions, but my impression is that the amount of gambling and homosexual activity, and probably the amount of drinking, is less than it is in comparable American institutions. And one fact is clear: there is almost no violence within the walls. Inmates and staff agreed that there had not been as much as a fist-fight between two Botsfengslet inmates for at least nine months preceding my contact with the institution. One inmate remembered a small fight in the short-term jail in which he had served some time before, but apparently this was remembered simply because fights are so unusual. As a Norwegian colleague expressed it: "Our institutions are like Sunday schools compared to yours."

In short, the deprivations usually pointed to may be necessary conditions for the emergence of a strong and resistive inmate value system, but the Norwegian evidence suggests that they are not sufficient. Although the deprivations were present at Botsfengslet, the strong inmate culture was lacking. There are, however, four respects in which this is not a complete test of the functional argument.

First, it may be that *other* deprivations are more important than those usually cited, and that these deprivations vary from country to country. One major difference is length of sentence. The average stay in most American institutions is from two to five years. At Botsfengslet, it is much shorter, averaging slightly more than a year. Only life-termers are likely to be sentenced for more than two or three years. It is possible, then, that the differences in sentence length alone would account for much of the variation in the inmate culture.

A second condition concerns the rate of incarceration in Norway compared to the United States. Probation is used more, the crime rate is lower anyway, and officials are reluctant to give prison sentences if there is any alternative. As a result, a much smaller proportion of the criminal population is institutionalized. It may be that the inmate system fails to receive the type of inmate who is best at organizing and generating group opposition.

Third, the apparent normlessness at Botsfengslet may be partially accounted for by the structural constraints on interaction in the prison. One major way in which Botsfengslet departs from current American patterns is that the inmates there are more isolated. As in the American institutions of the turn of the century, inmates at Botsfengslet are locked in at 5 p.m., at the close of the work-day. They eat in their own cells, rather than in the dining hall. Those who go out in the evening must have a special task or assignment, such as band or a school course. Although inmates work together in the shops (as the American prisoners did after the industrial revolution had penetrated into the prison), the general policy is still against fraternization.

All these features make for a much greater degree of isolation than is found in modern American prisons. Indeed, 43 per cent of the inmate population at Botsfengslet report that they have made no friends among other inmates. The comparable figure for the American prison described above is 10 per cent. Thus the constraints on communication and interaction at Botsfengslet may well prevent formation of a solidary inmate culture.

Fourth, and perhaps most important, although it is possible to show that most of the deprivations in American prisons are also objectively present at Botsfengslet, it is not so easy to know whether they are subjectively defined as deprivations by Norwegian prison inmates. It may well be, for example, that inmates from a society that lacks some of the material abundance of the United States do not experience confinement in the same ways that American inmates do. A warm shelter, a clean bed, and three square meals a day—features that both prison systems provide—may have relatively greater value in Norway, with the result that prison itself is experienced as less depriving. Unfortunately, we do not have evidence on these matters of relative deprivation.

Based solely upon the case study of Botsfengslet, however, the most plausible explanation of the difference between inmate culture in Norway and in the United States is that general features of Norwegian society are imported into the prison, and that they operate largely to offset tendencies toward the formation of a solidary inmate group united in its opposition to the staff. The most important element seems to be the virtual absence, in Norway, of a sub-culture of violence and antagonism. Few offenders use weapons. The police do not carry guns. There are only three or four offenders in the entire country who fit our model of a professional criminal. Younger offenders have not participated extensively in organized delinquent gangs, as have many in this country. Consequently, the thought of using violence as a means of social control simply does not arise. Even the fact that boxing is an important recreational activity in American prisons was surprising and dismaying to the Norwegian inmates. In short, the value American inmates place on being tough, being smart, seeing society in "we-they" terms, is characteristically absent. This in turn would seem to reflect the relatively narrow range of the stratification system, the virtual absence of American-style slums, and the greater homogeneity of Norwegian society.

The relatively greater sense of isolation in Norwegian life, and the related tendency to be more inward-looking, may yield personality components which also work against the formation of social bonds with other inmates. One gets the strong impression that many prisoners, like their counterparts outside, would rather not get deeply enmeshed in an extended social circle. They are more likely to go their own way.

This extended set of observations on a Norwegian prison may seem out of place in a chapter intended to deal generally with problems of socialization in prison communities. They are included here simply to indicate in the clearest possible way how much the cultural environment surrounding the prison is likely to influence the internal life of the institution, and along with it the processes of socialization that go on there.

Botsfengslet was one of fifteen institutions in the Scandinavian countries where we were able to collect systematic survey data relating to inmate culture and social organization. One way to examine further the relationship between influences from outside the prison versus the deprivations from within is to find out which of these possible sources of influence bears the strongest relationship to the formation of an anti-staff culture and set of attitudes among the inmates (Cline & Wheeler, 1968). We developed an index of the degree to which inmates felt that others held attitudes in opposition to those of the staff, an index which could be applied across the fifteen institutions. The range of responses on that index, without presenting the evidence here, indicates clearly that there is a wide variation in the extent to which an anti-staff climate tends to develop in different institutions. It is thus a perpetuation of a stereotype to assume that all prisons are alike.

What is most striking is that the variation in anti-staff culture and attitudes can be accounted for much better by examining the type of inmate that flows into the system than it can by examining the nature of the prison itself. The best single predictor of the anti-staff climate in these fifteen prisons is the median age of their inmates at first arrest. The older the median age of first arrest, the less the climate of the institution is one that is polarized in opposition to the staff ($-.80$). The youth institutions in our sample tend to be the highest in anti-staff climate scores and, of course, they have the institutions where the average age of first arrest is lowest. But even when those institutions are removed, other indicators of the criminal background inmates bring to prison continue to show the strong relationship to the nature of the climate that forms within. For example, if we order the institutions according to the percentage of men who have previously served a sentence in prison, the correlation between that index and the anti-staff climate scores is +.73.

Relationships between anti-staff climate scores and various indexes of deprivation, on the other hand, tend either to be inconsistent or nonexistent. Indeed, the one measure of deprivation that seems consistently related to the kind of attitudinal climate that forms behind the walls is a measure that reflects the extent of *social* deprivation faced by the inmates: the extent to which the institutions keep inmates from contacts with each other, with friends and relatives outside the prisons, and with prison officials. But this is a special kind of deprivation, for while it assuredly is generally discomforting for the inmates, and in that sense is a true "deprivation," it is the kind of deprivation that may well preclude the development of a strong culture of opposition to the staff. For to the extent that inmates are not free to associate with one another, it is clearly difficult for such a culture to emerge. Indeed, the direction of the relationship in our fifteen institutions is just the opposite from what one might anticipate given a simple deprivation model: in these institutions, the greater the degree of social deprivation, the less the extent to which the inmate culture is formed in opposition to the staff ($-.36$).

These data, then, point again to the importance of experiences inmates bring into the prison when they enter as a determinant of the general climate within the institution. But two important qualifications have to be noted. First, there is great danger of generalizing far beyond the particular institutions contained in this study. One qualification concerns the actual range in the nature of the deprivations presented in different prisons. Even though we have institutions that were constructed as long ago as 1859 and as recently as 1959, even though they differ in many aspects of their organization, and even though these differing aspects can be shown to be related systematically to inmate feelings and attitudes on many issues, there remains a basic similarity in the degree to which a prison is likely to be perceived as a depriving experience from the perspective of the inmates. This is perhaps the one basic feature of prisons, and the one that is most difficult to change by altering prison organization, design, and program. And it may take a truly radical departure from traditional patterns if the socialization setting known as the prison is to produce major variations in the patterning of socialization itself. In a later section of this chapter, we turn to some examples of efforts to modify the general pattern of prison life through very intensive kinds of programs. Here I want simply to underscore the fact that our sense of the importance of external rather than internal features of imprisonment may be a limited historical judgment, rooted in the kinds of prisons our Western nations have so far developed.

The second qualification has to do with the nature of the materials them-selves. The kind of survey data reported here is far from the intimate life experiences of individual inmates. When we get closer to those lives, as in autobiographies of individual prisoners, we get a much more dramatic feeling for the meaning of imprisonment in the personal lives of offenders. Whatever else such experiences reveal, they need to be viewed against a background of the general character of the prison. A most important quality of that general character, it appears from the above, is the nature of the ties its members have had with the outside world, and the nature of that outside world itself.

Socialization in an Institution for Juvenile Offenders [2]

A detailed analysis of feelings and experiences of young inmates as they move through their first stay in a correctional institution for juveniles pro-vides the empirical base for the observations that follow. These boys are be-tween 14 and 16 years of age, and they have all been committed to youth institutions in the State of Massachusetts. Our study design called for them to be interviewed at the beginning of their stay in a correctional institution, at a point roughly in the middle, again just before they were released, and after they had been out in the community for three of four months. In this case, because of the panel design, we are in a better position to assert something about the changes the inmates undergo as they experience the correctional system. (For further details, see Baum & Wheeler, 1968.)

Our aim in this study was to attempt to capture the experience of impris-onment through the direct reports of the boys studied. Thus we asked rela-tively simple and straightforward questions in an open-ended fashion, and treated the boys as respondents about the setting rather than as "subjects" in a more traditional sense. The observations here will be limited to describing some central themes that emerge from our interview data and that have direct bearing on the nature of the relationship between the world inside the prison and the world outside.

One of our central lines of questioning concerns whether the boys think their stay in a correctional institution will be helpful or harmful to them in terms of their ability to get along in the world after they get out. After asking about the general direction of their feeling, we probed in detail as to why they felt that way. Somewhat over half of the boys feel that their stay will be helpful to them, and the vast majority of those who feel this way see the help largely in a classic free-will deterence framework. Being put away is helping them, they feel, because it is teaching them a lesson. Institutions are pretty lousy places, and it is very rough being away from home and family. In brief, it is an experience to be avoided and it will help them remain free from crim-inal activity after their release, because they don't want to come back again. They do not feel it is helping them because of the therapeutic qualities of the institutions, the warm and kind character of the staff, the education and trade-training opportunities, or most of the other reasons associated with current correctional philosophies and programs. Indeed, these reasons loom as relatively insignificant in comparison with the general status of being removed from the outside world.

Those who feel the stay will be harmful (and this constitutes a smaller proportion of the respondents) likewise do not attribute the harm to the dynamics of life within the institution, but rather to the way in which the institution is perceived by the outside world. It is not the institution's effect on *them* that they perceive as most important, but rather the effect of their having been there on others. It will harm them because it will make employment opportunities more difficult to find, because it may prevent them from being accepted by the armed services, and for a few, because of the general stigma attached to institutional confinement by community members. There is little mention of such factors as turning bitter while they are in confinement, learning crime from others, and the like. In other words, it is the fact of imprisonment per se that looms as most important, rather than any specific events that happen during confinement.

These are experiences reported by the boys at an early point in their stay. As they move through to the period just before their release, the only major change in response is that those who originally saw the institution as primarily harmful in its effect move to viewing it as neutral. This movement is apparently occasioned by their learning that juvenile records are handled differently from adult criminal records and that they may be able to conceal the fact of confinement from employers and others. Among those who still feel that their stay will help them, there is a slight increase in the number who attribute the help to something specific about institutional programs, but the main thrust of their responses remains the same as before: they don't like being away from home and are motivated to stay out of trouble so that they won't come back.

It could be argued that these are only verbal mouthings and that they only serve to conceal the real dynamics of the socialization process within the institution. Indeed, the boys may be observed to fight and argue vigorously, to jockey for position in the status hierarchy among the boys, to play up to the staff in their presence while verbally attacking them in their absence, and in other ways to be going through the routines we have come to expect from persons in closed institutions. These observations might all be correct, but they would give only a partial indication of the significance of life within the institution for the boys in question. For when we ask them what they spend most of the time thinking about while they are in the institution, even during the middle of their stay, about twice as many report thinking most about the outside world as report thinking about what is going on within the institution. Their minds are likely to be on family, friends, activities they used to enjoy but now can't, and the like. And when asked what are the worst and the best times while they are in, the great majority report that their high points and their low points center around visits and contacts from the outside, rather than around activities within the institution. They are happiest when they get a visit, when they receive letters, when they go on weekend furloughs to their home community. They are lowest when a planned visit does not materialize, or when it is time for a visit to end, or when no one writes.

We might expect these feelings to be strongest among young offenders who are separated from free community life for the first time and whose length of separation is relatively short, and both of these characteristics are present for those we studied. But coupled with the other observations regarding their sense of the impact of the institution on them, these data on juvenile offenders show clearly how life outside the institution has real cognitive and motivational significance for those inside.

It may seem that we have been wandering through the vineyards of several unrelated studies, but a consistent theme appears to emerge from each additional piece of empirical data. There is a hint of the importance of the external world in our earliest finding regarding the "U-shaped curve," for it suggests the ease with which inmates can begin adapting to the world beyond the prison even before they have emerged from behind the walls. The case study of a Norwegian prison pointed clearly to the importance of the culture outside the prison as a determinant of the life that forms within. The survey data from fifteen Scandinavian institutions show the relatively great impact of inmates' prior backgrounds outside the prison, the lesser importance of prison deprivations themselves. Finally, the reports of juvenile offenders give further evidence of the powerful impact of life outside while they are inside. Taken together, these observations force a redirection of interest from life in the inner regions of the prison to the world of experience that lies beyond its boundaries.

Discussion

The concept of socialization, like so many of the concepts in behavioral science, has been subjected to a wide variety of definitions and interpretations. The definition suggested in the introduction to this volume, "the process by which individuals acquire the knowledge, skills and dispositions that enable them to participate as more or less effective members of groups and the society," can be given either a narrow or a broad interpretation. As applied to the prison, for example, it can be taken to refer to the ways in which inmates learn how to manage their lives within the institution at some minimal level of effectiveness. A substantive focus on this concern would lead to an effort to answer the questions: What does an inmate need to know, in addition to what he already knows, that will enable him to make a minimal adjustment to the prison? What skills must he develop that he does not already have? What attitudinal or behavioral dispositions will be needed?

There are abundant documentary materials to suggest that, in terms of these questions, adaptation to the prison is not greatly different from adaptation to any other setting. The inmate will learn from others what the guards expect of him as a routine matter, what the inmates expect, and how he can successfully negotiate between these two conflicting sets of expectations. He may also learn how to achieve those minimum creature comforts that make life tolerable within the institution (Goffman, 1961b). What is learned will depend upon the local culture of the institution in question, and on the degree to which an individual inmate becomes involved in that culture. The chief difference between the prison and many other social settings in this connection is that, as a "total institution," the pains resulting from failure to become socialized are particularly severe for there is literally no escape from the norms and role demands of the setting. As Goffman has pointed out, the prison shares this quality with many other forms of organization, including the ship, the mental hospital, the private boys' school, and the monastery (Goffman, 1961a). But aside from the "total" character of such settings, and the special importance that attaches to getting along, there is not a lot that distinguishes the total institution from other settings where socialization, in this narrow sense, goes on.

A more inclusive view of the socialization process would place less emphasis on problems of surface adjustment, more emphasis on deeper, more fundamental changes. It would emphasize the internalization of norms, rather than overt compliance with the setting in question. It might give less attention to external features of adjustment, more to possible changes in one's basic conception of himself, his sense of worth and dignity. Many who speak of socialization within the prison indeed have these latter qualities in mind. The typical assumption has been that the harsh and dramatic circumstances of imprisonment as a form of human existence are likely to lead to deep-seated and fundamental changes in values, ideologies and personal styles. And the assumption has typically been that these changes will have long-lasting effects. Similarly, when persons have talked about "rehabilitation" or "resocialization" they have been concerned with more than establishing a new surface adaptation to conventional ways of life. They have had in mind some relatively basic reconstruction or reconstitution of one's values, beliefs, and way of life (Studt, Messinger & Wilson, 1968).

It is this broader meaning of socialization that has been implicit in the matters discussed in this chapter. The prison is often viewed as a setting within which fundamental changes in attitudes and values are likely to take place. A growing body of both evidence and thought suggests that this view may be incorrect. Indeed, the central argument of this chapter may be put as follows:

1. Persons do not enter prison motivated to seek a basically new and different vision of themselves.
2. To the extent that they do change, the change is produced as much by the reaction to being confined and separated from the free community as it is by the dynamics of life within the institution.
3. The values and attitudes expressed by prison inmates are shaped in impor-

tant ways by the circumstances to which inmates have been exposed prior to their period of incarceration.

4. In addition to its impact on the values held by entering inmates, the external world influences the kind of culture and social organization that is formed within the prison, and which serves as the social context within which adaptation to imprisonment takes place.

5. As a result of these conditions, whatever impact the experience of imprisonment itself might have on inmates, either positive or negative, is sharply attenuated. *It is the social definition of the prison in society, rather than the social status of the inmate within the prison, that appears to be most relevant for the future life and career of prison inmates.*

6. It follows from all of the above that a full understanding of processes of socialization and resocialization within the prison requires much greater attention than has heretofore been given to the relationship of both the prison and the prisoner to the external world.

The remainder of this chapter will examine other studies of the prison to assess their bearing upon this argument.

Inmates obviously differ in the roles they come to play within the prison, and these differences are related to the backgrounds they bring to prison. Further, such differences have been shown to be related to the way men change as they experience prison life (Garabedian, 1963; Wellford, 1967). But often, the divergent sociocultural backgrounds men bring to the institution are forgotten as analysts attempt to untangle the nature of prison life. This fact is noted clearly in the one report that is most closely related to the argument of this chapter (Irwin & Cressey, 1962). Irwin and Cressey call attention to the existence of three separate subcultures within the prison: a "convict" subculture, whose participants are oriented inward toward the internal life of the prison; a "thief" subculture, whose participants are oriented to the criminal culture outside the prison; and finally, there are prisoners oriented toward the legitimate culture in the broader society. To understand the prison behavior of the second and third types of men, it is crucial to understand the nature of their ties outside the prison. Although Irwin and Cressey make their case by examining individual differences within any one institution, their argument is entirely consistent with our findings on the degree to which inmate life generally reflects broader cultural conditions.

There are several studies of correctional communities that attempt to draw the link between the social organization of the prison and the individual adaptation of the inmates. Most of these studies focus on the nature of the formal authority system. For example, Street, Vinter and Perrow (1966) are able to show that inmates in youth institutions ranged along a continuum from custody and discipline to group and individual treatment responded rather differently to the staff and to their fellow inmates. From their data, they are able to argue effectively that the "solidary opposition" model of inmate culture in prisons does not adequately describe institutions that develop a fairly rich and complex set of treatment goals and programs. Related studies of prison camps by Grusky (1959) and by Berk (1966) point to substantially the same conclusion, as do comparative studies of adult institutions where some are operating within a traditional custodial model and others within a psychiatrically oriented version of the correctional process (Mathiesen, 1965; Wheeler, 1968).

It is clear from all these studies that different patterns of formal organization and structure may produce differences in inmate organization and in attitudes toward the prison experience. But these studies have not gone on to demonstrate the relationship between participation in inmate society and future behavior. Thus, as much as these studies tell us about the different patterns of organization within the prison and potentially different socialization processes, they have not yet shown whether changes occur that are deep and long lasting enough to produce real differences in rates of recidivism.

A number of other studies have examined rates of recidivism for men housed in different types of institutions. This has been part of a long-term series of studies supported by the California Correctional System. And if there is any one conclusion that appears to be safely drawn from those studies, it is that differences in prison organization themselves apparently produce relatively little difference in recidivism rates. Once one takes account of the nature of the inmate population in the different prisons, the institutional differences in recidivism rates tend to disappear. Relatively small effects may be shown for one or another aspect of prison programs, but the overall sense one gets from such studies is that the differences attributable to institutions are small relative to the differences attributable to the prior backgrounds of individual inmates. A recent Danish investigation lends cross-national support to this finding. Larsen (1967–68) has produced one of the few studies that has both recidivism data, and data on inmate attitudes and perspectives toward the institutions. He is able to show that institutions ranging along a treatment-custody dimension do indeed produce differences in the perspectives inmates have with regard to their life within the prison. But, again, once one controls for the differences in type of inmate, there are only small differences in the rates of recidivism among those released from the institutions. Indeed, the one current study in the field of correction that has been successful in demonstrating what appears to be the real impact of an experimental program is a project which compares inmates in traditional institutions with those who remain outside the institutions entirely and are subject to a special and intensive treatment program on the outside (Warren, 1967). And even in this case, it remains unclear whether the results are due to merely not going to prison, to a more lenient recommitment policy for those in the treatment group, or to the effects of the treatment program itself.

Again, it is necessary to interpret these studies with caution, for in many respects the institutions do not offer really radical differences in their form of organization or in the kinds of treatment programs used with inmates. For the most part, it is a matter of providing more of what is already present in a minimum "treatment" model—more psychiatrists per inmate, more counseling facilities, more group therapy, better trade-training programs, and so forth. It may be that a much more radical reorientation of prison organization will be necessary in order to produce institutions that really make a difference. That such a reorientation is difficult to establish is suggested by the experiences of Elliot Studt and her colleagues (Studt et al., 1968).

Glaser's (1964) study of federal institutions provides further data that are relevant to the argument made above. He found a U-shaped pattern of response to prison life quite similar to that described for the State Reformatory, thus again suggesting that the changes that take place during the middle of imprisonment may not remain until the time of release. Further, when inmates in the institutions he studied were questioned regarding the effect of imprisonment on them, the responses were quite similar to those given in the study of juvenile institutions: inmates thought the primary impact of imprisonment was a deterent effect, rather than anything specific about institutional programs, although there were a minority who felt that they benefited from the trade-training program of the federal prison system. And to the extent they felt the institution had a bad effect, they were likely to see it primarily in terms of what it meant to have a "record" when they returned to civilian life.

A final study that has bearing upon our argument is Giallombardo's (1966) recent research in the federal women's prison at Alderson, West Virginia. She too found functional theory wanting as an explanation of the nature of inmate society. She observed that the same general deprivations are present in women's institutions as in men's but that the form of inmate society is radically different. The difference has to do with differences in what inmates bring into the institution as a result of role definitions provided by the broader society:

> The deprivations of imprisonment may provide necessary conditions for the emergence of an inmate system, but our findings clearly indicate that the deprivations of imprisonment in themselves are not sufficient to account for the form that the inmate social culture assumes in the male and female prison communities. Rather, general features of American society with respect to the cultural definition and content of male and female roles are brought into the prison setting and function to determine the direction and focus of the inmate cultural systems (Giallombardo, 1966, p. 187).

Conclusion

The argument presented above is clearly based on partial and fragmentary evidence. Despite the growing number of studies of prison environments over the past score of years, there is still a relative absence of a truly cumulative body of knowledge about the prison as a social environment, and about the changes inmates undergo as they experience imprisonment. On the basis of that partial evidence, we argue that studies of the formal and informal social organization of the prison and its effects on new inmates need to be supplemented by a stronger concern for the relationship between both prison and prisoner and the external world. When such studies are completed, we should be in a better position to assess the relative impact of the external and internal world on the conduct of offenders both during and after imprisonment.

REFERENCES

BAUM, M., & WHEELER, S. Becoming an inmate. In S. Wheeler (Ed.), *Controlling delinquents*. New York: Wiley, 1968.

BERK, B. B. Organizational goals and inmate organization. *American Journal of Sociology*, 1966, 71 (5), 522–534.

BRIM, O. G., JR., & WHEELER, S. *Socialization after childhood*. New York: Wiley, 1966.

CLEMMER, D. *The prison community*. New York: Rinehart & Co., 1958. (First published in 1940.)

CLINE, H. F., & WHEELER, S. The determinants of normative patterns in correctional institutions. In N. Christie (Ed.), *Scandinavian studies in criminology*. Vol. 2. Oslo: Universitetsforlaget, 1968.

GARABEDIAN, P. C. Social roles and processes of socialization in the prison community. *Social Problems*, 1963, 11, 139–152.

GARRITY, D. L. The effect of length of incarceration upon parole adjustment and estimation of optimum sentences; Washington State Correctional Institution. Unpublished doctoral dissertation, Univer. of Washington, 1956.

GIALLOMBARDO, R. *A study of a women's prison*. New York: Wiley, 1966.

GLASER, D. *The effectiveness of a prison and parole system*. Indianapolis: Bobbs-Merrill, 1964.

GOFFMAN, E. On the characteristics of total institutions. In E. Goffman, *Asylums*. New York: Doubleday, 1961. Pp. 1–124. (a)

————. The underlife of a public institution: A study of ways of making out in a mental hospital. In E. Goffman, *Asylums*. New York: Doubleday, 1961. Pp. 171–320. (b)

GRUSKY, O. Organizational goals and the behavior of informal leaders. *American Journal of Sociology*, 1959, 67 (1), 59–67.

IRWIN, J., & CRESSEY, D. R. Thieves, convicts, and the inmate culture. *Social Problems*, 1962, 10 (Fall), 142–155.

LARSEN, F. B. Aspects of a strategy for research in criminology. *Sociologiske Meddelelser: A Danish Sociological Journal*, hoefte 1967/68, 12, serie 1, 25–52.

MATHIESEN, T. *The defense of the weak*. London: Tavistock, 1965.

MERTON, R. K. *Social theory and social structure*. Rev. Ed. Clencoe, Ill.: Free Press, 1957.

SCHRAG, C. C. Social types in a prison community. Unpublished master's thesis, Univer. of Washington, 1944.

————. Leadership among prison inmates. *American Sociological Review*, 1954, 19 (1), 37–42.

STREET, D., VINTER, R. D., & PERROW, C. *Organization for treatment*. New York: Free Press, 1966.

STUDT, E., MESSINGER, S. L., & WILSON, T. P. *C-unit: Search for community in prison*. New York: Russell Sage Foundation, 1968.

SYKES G. M. *The society of captives*. Princeton, N. J.: Princeton Univer. Press, 1958.

————, & MESSINGER, S. L. The inmate social system. In R. A. Cloward, D. R. Cressey, G. H. Grosser, R. McCleery, L. E. Ohlin, G. M. Sykes, & S. L. Messinger (Eds.), *Theoretical studies in social organization of the prison*. New York: Social Science Research Council, 1960. Pp. 11–13.

WARREN, M. Q. The community treatment project after six years. *Bulletin of the California Youth Authority,* 1967.

WELLFORD, C. Factors associated with adoption of the inmate code: A study of normative socialization. *The Journal of Criminal Law, Criminology and Police Science,* 1967, 58 (2), 197–203.

WHEELER, S. Role conflict in correctional communities. In D. R. Cressey (Ed.), *The prison: Studies in institutional organization.* New York: Holt, Rinehart & Winston, 1961. (a)

————. Socialization in correctional communities. *American Sociological Review,* 1961, 26 (5), 697–712. (b)

————. Legal justice and mental health in the care and treatment of deviants. In M. Levitt & B. Rubenstein (Eds.), *Orthopsychiatry and the law.* Detroit: Wayne State Univer. Press, 1968.

NOTES

1. The materials in this section are derived from a broader study of Scandinavian prisons being conducted by Hugh F. Cline and the author. We are indebted to many Scandinavian sociologists, but will not attempt to give full acknowledgment of that help here.

2. The following materials are drawn from a study currently in progress being carried out by Martha Baum, Brendan Maher, Anne Romasco and the author.

11: Social Roles in Prison /
Peter G. Garabedian

Methods and Results: The Adaptive Pattern

The data to be reported were collected from a maximum custody prison in a Western state. At the time of the study there were approximately 1,700 convicted adult felons housed in the institution. To derive an index of socialization, a random sample of 380 inmates and 141 staff members was asked to evaluate a series of five contrived situations referring to life in prison. The five items are as follows:

1. Two inmates, who are planning an escape, ask one of their close friends, Brown, to distract the guard's attention so that they will have a chance to get out of his sight. Brown refuses, stating that he doesn't want anything to do with the plot.

2. Officer Green discovers that officer Black is carrying contraband into the

From Peter G. Garabedian, "Social Roles and Processes of Socialization in the Prison Community," *Social Problems* 11:2 (Fall 1963), 140–152.

institution and is receiving pay from some of the inmates. Green immediately reports all of his information to his supervisor.

3. White, a civilian, is friendly with Lemon, a parolee. White notices that Lemon is getting upset and is talking about pulling some holdups. If Lemon doesn't get help right away he is likely to do something that will result in his return to the institution. White talks to Lemon's parole officer about the whole situation.

4. The parole board is setting a minimum sentence for inmate Gray. Gray was committed for grand larceny. However, the parole board learns that Gray pulled a couple of robberies for which he was never charged. The board therefore decides to give Gray a longer minimum than they otherwise would.

5. Inmate Blue is a cook in a prison camp. The camp superintendent tells Blue that meat is being stolen from the freezer, and since Blue is in the kitchen most of the time, it looks as if Blue is responsible. Later, Blue discovers that officer Jones is actually stealing the meat. Blue immediately goes to the superintendent, and tells him who is stealing the meat.

Both staff members and inmates were asked to state as to whether they approved, disapproved, or neither approved nor disapproved of the action taken in the above situations. Weights of two, one, and zero were assigned to the approve, neutral, and disapprove categories, respectively. The weights were summed over the five items, with possible scores ranging from zero to ten.

The distribution of scores for staff members was skewed in the direction of the upper end of the scale, indicating a high degree of normative consensus. Eighty per cent of the staff obtained scores of eight to ten, and 94 per cent received scores of six to ten. On the other hand, the inmate scores approached a rectangular distribution with a slight tendency for scores to cluster between three and five (40 per cent). Compared with the staff, inmates exhibited considerably less normative consensus with respect to the five hypothetical situations. In this study inmates are classified into two groups: those obtaining scores of six to ten (33 per cent) are defined as conformists, i.e., in normative agreement with staff, while those with lower scores are considered nonconformists.[1]

With the above information it was possible to determine the number and per cent of inmates conforming to staff norms at each of the three institutional career phases. The phases were operationalized in the following manner: inmates located in the early phase were those who had served less than six months on their sentences; those who had served more than six months but who had more than six months remaining to be served were defined as being located in the middle phase; inmates located in the late phase had less than six months remaining to be served.[2] A tabulation of the number and per cent of inmate conformists to staff norms in each of these periods gives some suggestion of the process of socialization as conceptualized within the present temporal framework.

The results of this tabulation, which are presented in Figure 11–1, suggest that the trend is a U-shaped or curvilinear one and provide additional support for the evidence reported by Wheeler in his recent study.[3] Inmates located in the early phase of the institutional career are proportionately twice as likely to conform to staff norms as compared with inmates in the middle period. The trend suggests that there may be a steady absorption of the prison culture between these two phases which is similar to the process of prisonization, but that this process is reversed as the inmate comes to the end of his prison career.

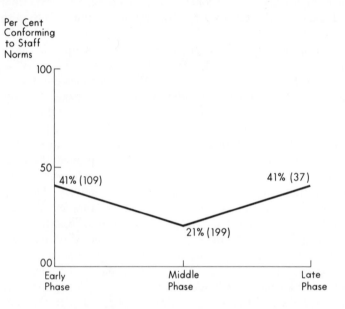

FIGURE 11–1. *Conformity to Staff Norms among Inmates in the Three Career Phases.*

In fact, the data show that the per cent of conformists in this phase is identical to the per cent conforming at the early phase, suggesting a "recovery" or a shedding of some of the effects of the prison culture between the second and final stages of the career. This "recovery" may be due to the anticipation of relinquishing one's present status in favor of a new social position.[4] The *adaptive* pattern of response observed in Figure 11–1 appears to be consistent with the notion that the prison culture has its greatest impact at a point where the inmate is furthest removed from the free community. However, firm empirical support of these data must await panel studies.

The Inmate Social System

Recent discussions of the inmate social system have stressed its problem-solving character by viewing prisoner roles as alternative patterns of adjustment to a variety of focal issues and deprivations imposed by maximum security prisons.[5] Many of these roles are recognized by staff and inmates alike and are frequently identified in terms of the prison argot. The terms *punk* and *peddler* are examples of two roles that inmates may occupy. It should be noted, however, that these roles do not belong to the same set or subsystem. The role of punk belongs in that subsystem which performs the function of coping with sexual deprivations, while the role of peddler belongs in the set dealing with problems of food. In short, there are a variety of role sets in prison and each set is differentiated and integrated around a focal issue or issues. The interrelationships between the various role sets comprise what is known as the inmate social system.[6]

One of the major role sets that exist in many prisons throughout the country consists, in the language of our sample of inmates, of the *square John, right guy, politician, outlaw,* and *ding.* There is an increasing amount of documentation in the literature lending support to the notion that these roles do in fact exist and that they represent alternative modes of adjustment to problems of prison life. Moreover, recent empirical studies have found systematic differences existing in the criminal careers, institutional and post-institutional behavior, and affective attachments of the various role incumbents.[7] These studies have shown that square John incumbents have had little or no systematic involvement in crime, actively participate in staff-sponsored treatment programs and have more than average contact with prison officials. Right guy incumbents, on the other hand, have been found to exhibit a rather extensive career in delinquency and crime, do not become involved in staff-sponsored treatment programs and are relatively isolated from staff contacts. Square Johns identify with conventional norms while right guys are committed to illegitimate standards. Both role types are similar, however, in that they are collectivity-oriented and thus tend to subordinate personal interests in favor of group goals.

Politicians tend to commit relatively sophisticated crimes which involve manipulating the victim by skill and wit. They become actively involved in staff-sponsored programs and have a wide range of contacts both with officials and inmates. Outlaws tend to commit crimes in which the victim is confronted with force. They are isolated from staff and inmate contacts primarily because of their preoccupation with violence and their generally disruptive behavior. Politicians and outlaws are affectively neutral with respect to group norms, but differences in cognitive knowledge of legitimate and illegitimate standards influence the manner in which the neutrality is expressed. Politicians possess a high degree of cognitive knowledge and thus shift their normative perspectives to meet the exigencies of the situation. Outlaws reject both staff and inmate norms outright with little thought or consideration of the consequences. Both types are self-oriented in that personal interests take precedence over group goals.

The term ding is used to identify inmates whose responses to focal issues and deprivations lack the consistency and reliability necessary to be assigned to one of the above roles. However, it is not unusual to find non-violent sex offenses in the backgrounds of dings, and although they tend to become involved in staff-sponsored religious programs they are nevertheless isolated from staff and inmate contacts.[8]

In prison these roles are allocated on the basis of inmates informally observing and assessing the behaviors and verbalizations of a given inmate to a variety of real and contrived situations. The language system of inmates is used, as suggested above, to identify the role incumbent. As the process of allocation is accomplished, the role becomes a major component of the inmate's personality structure. It affects his personal orientation and in most cases attitudes toward self and others are modified or reinforced so as to be consistent with the incumbent's perception of the expectations of other inmates.[9]

Methods and Results: Social Roles and Socialization

The method of identifying incumbents of the five roles described above consisted of the sample of inmates responding to a set of fifteen items included in the questionnaire. The items, which dealt with attitudes toward self, others and philosophy of life, are listed below.

1. You've got to have confidence in yourself if you're going to be successful.
2. I generally feel guilty whenever I do wrong.
3. "Might is right" and "every man for himself" are the main rules of living, regardless of what people say.
4. The biggest criminals are protected by society and rarely get to prison.
5. I worry a lot about unimportant matters.
6. There's a little larceny in everybody, if you're really honest about it.
7. The only criminals I really know are the ones here in the institution.
8. You have to take care of yourself because nobody else is going to take care of you.
9. Inmates can trust me to be honest and loyal in my dealings with them.
10. I am very nervous much of the time.
11. Who you know is more important than what you know, and brains are more important than brawn.
12. Most people try to be law-abiding and true.
13. It makes me sore to have people tell me what to do.
14. Police, judges, prosecutors, and politicians are just as crooked as most of the people they send to prison.
15. Most people are not very friendly towards me.

Each of the above items is assumed to reflect a component of the attitudinal organization of a given role type. Items 1, 6, and 11 are assumed to reflect some of the attitudes of politicians; items 2, 7, and 12 tap square John attitudes; items 3, 8, and 13 refer to outlaw attitudes; items 4, 9, and 14 tap right guy attitudes; and items 5, 10, and 15 are assumed to reflect ding attitudes. In short, for each of the role types there are three items designed to tap attitudes characteristic of a given type.

Inmates responded to the items by checking one of four response categories for each statement: strongly agree, disagree, and strongly disagree. Weights of plus two, plus one, minus one, and minus two were assigned, respectively, to each of the above response categories. The weights for the five sets of three items were then algebraically summed for each inmate. Thus, a given inmate was represented by a set of five scores, with each score having a possible range of plus six to minus six and indicating his status on the five role types mentioned above.

Ideally, the occupant of a given role should endorse (strongly agree or agree) the three items designed to tap his attitudes, and should not endorse the remaining twelve items. That is, an inmate who has been assigned a given role in the prisoner society should exhibit a high positive score with respect to the items characterizing the role type and should exhibit low positive or negative scores on items characterizing the other role types. The highest positive score shown by an inmate on any one set of items determined his classification.[10] On this basis, an empirical typology was constructed classifying 251, or 73 per cent, of the inmate sample as incumbents of one of the five roles. Each of the 251 role types was then located according to career phase and the number of conformists to staff norms tabulated. The results of this tabulation are presented in Table 11-1 and graphically portrayed in Figure 11-2.

Table 11-1
Conformity to Staff Norms Among Role Types in the Three Career Phases

	Per Cent High Conformity					
	Early Phase		Middle Phase		Late Phase	
Role Type	per cent	n*	per cent	n	per cent	n
Square Johns	67	12	30	20	60	5
Right Guys	46	24	8	39	29	7
Politicians	46	26	30	43	33	9
Outlaws	19	16	15	20	00	2
Dings	12	8	22	9	60	5
Total	—	86	—	131	—	28

*In this Table n refers to the bases upon which the percentages are computed. For example, of the 12 square Johns located in the early career phase, 67 per cent are high conformists.

Several observations can be made on the basis of the data reported above. First, not all inmates exhibit the adaptive pattern of response. However, by differentiating the sample according to role type, four distinct trends emerge. The patterns of response for square Johns and right guys appear to be *adaptive* or U-shaped; that is, both types are prisonized and "de-prisonized" as well, the trends being almost identical in form to the distribution of responses shown in Figure 11–1. For both role types the rate of absorption appears to be the same between the early and middle phases, and although the rate of "recovery" is somewhat slower for right guys, both types show definite signs of shedding some of the prisonization effects as measured by the index of conformity to staff norms. The major difference between the two types appears to be one of *degree* rather than *rate* of socialization.[11]

The pattern of response exhibited by the subsample classified as outlaws approximates *prisonization*. That is, the net result of movement through the career phases is to reduce progressively the per cent of conformists among these role types. Although a considerable percentage of outlaws enter prison as deviants, the data suggest that processes operating within prison produce a pattern of adjustment that appears to be consistent with Clemmer's observations on inmate socialization.

The two remaining trends apparent in Table 11–1 and Figure 11–2 appear to conform to patterns of *stable conformity* and *delayed rehabilitation* hypothesized by Wheeler.[12] Politicians tend to conform to staff norms throughout the institutional career, suggesting the relatively slight impact of prison culture on this role type. Although there is a slight dip in the middle phase, proportionately there are as many politicians conforming during this period as there are among the square Johns. Theoretical formulations regarding the pseudo-social orientation of the politician-type appear to be consistent with the pattern of stable conformity shown above.

Dings follow the pattern of delayed rehabilitation, showing a progressive increase in the per cent of conformists and suggesting the operation of social processes that might be therapeutic or reformative for this role type.[13] Again, these findings should be corroborated by panel data observing shifts in attitudes on the part of the same inmates over time.

Further inspection of Table 11–1 and Figure 11–2 reveals that there is less variance in prisoners' responses to the five contrived situations in the middle than during the two extreme periods of confinement, indicating that there may be a higher degree of consensus among inmates during this period and that it tends to be in the direction of nonconformity. Movement of inmates toward common non-conformist definitions of the situation might lead to the inference that they also move in the direction of taking over the role of right guy. If this inference were correct then we should, for example, observe fewer square Johns in the middle than during the early or late periods. But as the percentage distributions in Table 11–2 indicate, this is not the case. There are almost identical proportions of square Johns during each of the three career phases, and the same is true of politicians as well as right guys. Thus, while prisonization might operate to move these types of inmates toward certain common definitions during the middle period, it does not have the effect of crystallizing certain roles and eliminating others. Apparently, then, square Johns who become prisonized retain their status as square Johns within the prisoner group and, moreover, right guys who become "de-prisonized" retain their status as right guys. In short, Table 11–2 suggests that pris-

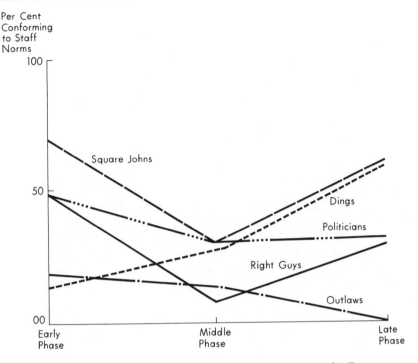

FIGURE 11–2. *Conformity to Staff Norms among Role Types in the Three Career Phases.*

oners are typed early in the institutional career and that shifts in attitude may occur without relinquishing the role.

Finally, Table 11–2 shows that the per cent of outlaws and dings, although stable through the first two periods, becomes unstable in the late career phase. The per cent of outlaws decreases, while there is a proportionate increase in dings. Retention of the outlaw role during the late periods of confinement might be dysfunctional for its occupants and for inmates in general and consequently expectations in this period might be to relinquish this role in favor of other roles. But the relatively stable proportions of square Johns, right guys, and politicians throughout the three career phases suggest that these roles are not available to outlaws, but that the alternatives open to them are either to assume the role of ding or to continue the role of outlaw. The data indicate that many outlaws choose the former alternative since by choosing the latter their mobility out of the institution may be hindered.[14]

Social Roles and Social Processes

At this point the question arises as to the types of social processes that might be operating to produce the various patterns of adjustment observed in Table 11–1 and Figure 11–2. For example, it is surprising to find square Johns ex-

Table 11-2

Location of Role Types in the Three Career Phases

Role Type	Early Phase per cent	N	Middle Phase per cent	N	Late Phase per cent	N
Square Johns	14	12	15	20	18	5
Right Guys	28	24	30	39	25	7
Politicians	30	26	33	43	32	9
Outlaws	19	16	15	20	7	2
Dings	9	8	7	9	18	5
Total	100	86	100	131	100	28

hibiting the U-shaped adaptive pattern of response during incarceration; the trend definitely suggests signs of prisonization as well as "deprisonization." On the basis of recent formulations which have characterized the square John as the pro-social, isolated, non-involved inmate who openly identifies with the prison administration, a pattern of stable conformity would have been predicted for this type. But the drop in square John conformists from 67 to 30 per cent between the early and middle phases does not indicate a stable conformity pattern and suggests that they may not be as isolated as previously assumed, but rather that they become involved to some degree with other inmates.

If square Johns do become involved, it may be an indication of their attempt at resolving role conflict to which most inmates are exposed as they move through correctional institutions. Wheeler, for example, has argued that it is difficult to cultivate and maintain inmate friends while holding conformist attitudes at the same time, since the dominant normative order among prisoners is strongly opposed to that of the staff.[15] And although the conflict may not be perceived during the early stages of confinement, the strain becomes more acute with increasing length of time in prison. Resolution of the strain may be either in the direction of involvement, in which case a shift in value orientation occurs, or in the direction of isolation which makes possible the retention of conformist attitudes.[16] The observed pattern of adjustment for square Johns suggests that *both* social processes are linked to this role but operate at different periods of incarceration. It is likely that isolation may be the dominant process during the early and late stages, but that involvement becomes the operative process in the middle period of confinement.

Evidence gathered in the present study made possible the testing of these and other inferences regarding the processes of involvement and isolation. Inmates were asked to report their relative amount of contact with inmates and with staff members, as compared with the average inmate.[17] Table 11−3 presents the main findings of this measure of inmates' perceptions.

Inspection of the modal percentages in each career phase provides some suggestion of the operation of processes of involvement and isolation for each of the role types. The modal percentages shown for square Johns indicate

that these types report being isolated from staff and inmates during the early
and late phases, but report involvement with *both groups* during the middle
period. This suggests that in spite of square John's conventional value orientations, they may perceive the incompatibility of establishing social bonds
with other inmates and holding conformist attitudes, and that they yield to
the resulting strain. But the adaptation is *not* to become involved solely with
inmates, but with staff *as well as* with inmates. Although this might not be a
completely satisfactory adjustment from the point of view of the inmate normative order, it at least provides a partial solution to the problem, enabling
as it does a degree of involvement with inmates without complete relinquish-
ment of conformist attitudes. However, the involvement with staff members
suggests that the resolution of the conflict is only a partial one and consequently square Johns should continue to experience some degree of strain.

Table 11–3 also shows that if square Johns become involved only with
other inmates, it is likely that they will do so during the early and late periods of incarceration, but not during the middle phase, indicating that the
strains resulting from the conflict situation are not as keenly felt during the
first and third phases. In short, the data suggest that square Johns are not
completely insulated from informal pressures nor are they as unaffiliated with
inmate groups as previously thought.

The modal percentages shown for right guys also indicate isolation in the
early and late phases and a high degree of involvement during the middle pe-

Table 11-3

Social Contacts Among Role Types in the Three Career Phases

	Hi Staff- Hi Inmate		Hi Staff Lo Inmate		Lo Staff- Hi Inmate		Lo Staff- Lo Inmate		Total	
	per cent	N	per cent	N	per cent	N	per cent	N	per cent	N
Square Johns										
Early Phase	25	3	00	—	25	3	50	6	100	12
Middle Phase	50	10	5	1	5	1	40	8	100	20
Late Phase	20	1	00	—	20	1	60	3	100	5
Right Guys										
Early Phase	12	3	4	1	17	4	67	16	100	24
Middle Phase	20	8	10	4	47	18	23	9	100	39
Late Phase	14	1	14	1	14	1	58	4	100	7
Politicians										
Early Phase	8	2	00	—	24	6	68	17	100	25
Middle Phase	35	15	5	2	23	10	37	16	100	43
Late Phase	34	3	00	—	22	2	44	4	100	9
Outlaws										
Early Phase	00	—	00	—	25	4	75	12	100	16
Middle Phase	20	4	5	1	35	7	40	8	100	20
Late Phase	00	—	00	—	00	—	100	2	100	2
Dings										
Early Phase	00	—	00	—	29	2	71	5	100	7
Middle Phase	00	—	00	—	33	3	67	6	100	9
Late Phase	75	3	25	1	00	—	00	—	100	4

riod. The apparent lack of involvement during the first and third stages is perhaps somewhat surprising but it points up the prominent role of isolation even among those prisoners considered to be the leaders and builders of inmate cohesion and solidarity. The per cent of isolated right guys drops sharply between the first two stages, however, as these men become involved with other inmates. Unlike the square Johns, right guys continue to remain isolated from staff contacts. Evidence from other parts of this study shows that on the *formal* level of participation right guys remain isolated from staff contacts in that they do not avail themselves of staff-sponsored therapy and religious programs. Instead, they become intensively involved in "neutral" activities such as sports which tend to promote contacts with inmates but not with prison officials.[18] The net result of this one-sided involvement is likely to be the establishment of close inmate ties along with a marked shift in conformist attitudes (as seen in Figure 11–2 above).[19]

While the majority of politicians perceive themselves as being isolated during the early career phase, this per cent drops sharply in the middle period and continues to be relatively low through the late phase of confinement. Although the modal percentages for the second and third periods also appear in the isolation category, it can be seen that there are almost as many politicians during these same periods who report extensive contacts with *both* staff and inmates. In fact, the per cent involved with both groups rises sharply between the early and middle phases and remains completely stable through the late period. This continued high rate of involvement apparently does not produce any radical attitudinal shift in the direction of non-conformity, however, for as Table 11–1 and Figure 11–2 indicate, the pattern of stable conformity obtains for these role types. Additionally, it can be seen that nearly equal proportions of politicians report having extensive contacts with inmates but not with staff throughout the three confinement periods. Assuming the incompatibility of involvement and conformist attitudes, we would therefore expect that the processes linked with this role generate a high degree of strain among its occupants. The alternative shifting of allegiances from staff members to inmates and vice versa, according to the exigencies of the situation, might be the politicians' attempts at coping with these strains.

The processes associated with the outlaw role are difficult to determine partly because of the small number of cases in the late career phase. And although there are sizeable proportions of outlaws reporting involvement during the middle phase, there is a tendency for these types to be isolated throughout the three confinement periods. Evidence from other parts of this study suggests that outlaws are isolated from inmate activities—legitimate or illegitimate—and that they present the most serious disciplinary problem for prison officials.[20] Perhaps the outlaw should be regarded as a "double failure" in both opportunity structures, and his isolation regarded as a reflection of this fact.[21] Dings, on the other hand, follow a pattern similar to outlaws but with the major difference that during the late period they become involved with both staff and inmates. The fact that Table 11–2 shows an increase in the per cent of dings during the late phase suggests that the social stigma attached to the ding role may have less import during the final period of incarceration, thus enabling these types to become involved in some degree.

Conclusions

The findings reported in this chapter suggest that when aspects of inmate social structure are taken into account a variety of patterns of response to prison life emerges. Consistent with the reports of Clemmer and Wheeler, inmates are socialized in varying degrees and rates, which indicate a differential impact of the prison culture on its participants. The data also suggest that the *point of heaviest impact* varies with the different role types; the early phase being important for dings, the middle period for right guys and square Johns, and the late phase for outlaws.

Evidence on reported contacts provided an indirect test of the social processes that might be linked to the various role types and which might be responsible for the observed patterns of adjustment. From the data presented, it is apparent that the processes of isolation and involvement operate at different periods of confinement. Isolation appears to be the dominant process during the early career phase, even among politicians and right guys, suggesting that the conception of the inmate who becomes highly involved shortly after his arrival to prison may be in need of revision. Additionally, the extensive operation of isolation may have the result of placing definite limits on the degree of solidarity that can develop among inmates.

While the dominant process in the early period appears to be one of isolation, processes of involvement are linked to most of the role types during the middle period. The tendency for inmates to become involved suggests that pressures toward involvement are stronger and more keenly felt at a period when they are furthest removed from the free community. Processes of involvement, however, may take different forms such as with *either* inmates *or* with staff members or with *both* groups. But it is seen that involvement *only* with staff members occurs infrequently even among those types of inmates (square Johns) who might be expected to exhibit this tendency. Apparently there are socially structured conditions in maximum security prisons that function as barriers against the frequent operation of this process while at the same time they promote other forms of involvement. Thus involvement with prison officials generally implies involvement with inmates as well.

The trend for inmates to be isolated during the early period but involved in the middle period, coupled with the fact that inmates move toward common definitions of the situation, provides some empirical support for the "problem-solving" point of view of inmate culture. Sykes and Messinger, for example, have argued that as inmates become solidary the pains of imprisonment are lessened.[22] And although we do not have a measure of perceived deprivations, our data do in fact indicate movement toward consensus (as measured by the index of conformity to staff norms) and that consensus exists despite the lack of movement in the direction of the right guy role.[23]

It should be noted also that the data indicate movement away from a solidary position as the terminal period of confinement approaches. Inmates might become less concerned with deprivations that accompany imprisonment than with anticipated problems to be faced in the free community upon their release. The degree of inmate solidarity, then, is likely to depend not on the number of right guys found in the prisoner population, but rather on the balance than exists between inmates located at the two extremes of the institutional career and those located in the middle periods of confinement.

If inmate solidarity is greatest during the middle period, then institutional treatment programs could perhaps be more strategically located during the pre-release phase of the career, thus increasing the likelihood of their effectiveness. Moreover, specific programs might be geared toward the treatment of certain role types. It is likely that some programs will be more effective for square Johns and right guys, for example, while others will be more effective for politicians and outlaws.[24]

The process of anticipatory socialization, which many inmates apparently undergo prior to release, may be strong enough to "undo" or "override" many of the specific effects incurred during incarceration. On this basis, we would be led to predict a favorable post-institutional prognosis for many parolees. Yet, it is well known that a large proportion of inmates released from correctional institutions return either as parole violators or are convicted on new offenses. A partial answer to this problematic datum may be obtained by investigating the relationship between expectations regarding life on parole and post-institution experiences in the free community.[25] From the data presented, it can be inferred that many inmates aspire to membership in non-membership groups, but that discrepancies exist in the sense that post-institution experiences do not coincide with levels of expectation regarding parole which may be activated and crystallized during the pre-release phase of confinement. Pre-release represents a learning period where expectations are developed regarding future social positions. A variety of socially structured barriers operating in the free community may prevent fulfillment of expectations, thus generating pressures to become involved in continued criminal activity.[26] In short, certain expectations may be dysfunctional for the prospective parolee in light of certain socially structured barriers. The nature of these expectations and socially structured barriers and how they are distributed among inmates, is a problem that merits further investigation.

NOTES

1. The per cent of conformists is computed on N of 345. Of the original sample of 380 inmates, there was a loss of 35 cases, or a shrinkage of approximately 9 per cent. The extent to which the findings to be presented were influenced by the 35 drop-outs is

negligible. See Peter G. Garabedian, *Western Penitentiary: A Study in Social Organization*, unpublished Ph.D. dissertation, University of Washington, 1959, Chapter 2.

2. The questionnaire included two items which made it possible to determine the institutional career phase in which any given inmate was located. The first item, "How long have you been in the penitentiary on your present commitment?" provided a measure of *time served*, while the second item, "How long do you have to serve until your good-time release date?" provided a measure of *time remaining to be served*. The combining of responses to these two items identified the career phase in which inmates were located at the time of the study.

3. Wheeler also found that the U-shaped adaptive pattern held for first termers and recidivists and for those reporting extensive primary group involvement, as well as for inmates who were isolated from primary group contacts.

4. S. F. Nadel, *The Theory of Social Structure*, Glencoe: The Free Press, 1958.

5. For example, see the following works by Clarence Schrag: *Social Types in a Prison Community*, unpublished master's thesis, University of Washington, 1944; "Social Role, Social Position, and Prison Social Structure," *Proceedings of the American Correctional Association, 1959*, New York: American Correctional Association, pp. 178–189; and "Some Foundations for a Theory of Corrections," in Donald R. Cressey, editor, *The Prison: Studies in Institutional Organization and Change*, New York: Holt, Rinehart, and Winston, 1961, pp. 309–358. See also Gresham Sykes, *The Society of Captives*, Princeton: Princeton University Press, 1958, pp. 84–108, and Gresham M. Sykes and Sheldon L. Messinger, "The Inmate Social System," in Richard A. Cloward, Donald R. Cressey, George H. Grosser, Richard McCleery, Lloyd E. Ohlin, Gresham M. Sykes and Sheldon L. Messinger, *Theoretical Studies in Social Organization of the Prison*, New York: Social Science Research Council, 1960, pp. 5–19.

6. Clarence Schrag, "Some Foundations for a Theory of Corrections," in Donald R. Cressey, *op. cit.*, pp. 346–347.

7. *Ibid.*, pp. 346–357. See also Gresham M. Sykes, "Men, Merchants, and Toughs," *Social Problems*, 4 (October, 1956), pp. 130–137.

8. Most studies have neglected an examination of correlates associated with those socially shunned inmates who lack the consistency of response to focal issues necessary to be classified reliably by other inmates. However, possible exceptions to this may be the "ball buster" discussed by Sykes, *op. cit.*, pp. 99–102, and the non-violent sex offender, the "rapo," investigated by Walter T. Martin, *The Religious Attitudes of the Prison Sex Offender*, unpublished master's thesis, University of Washington, 1947. See also, Peter G. Garabedian, "Social Roles in a Correctional Community," unpublished manuscript.

9. For a discussion of the relationship between role and personality, see Talcott Parsons and Edward A. Shils, editors, *Toward a General Theory of Action*, Cambridge: Harvard University Press, 1954, Chapter 4.

10. Inmates whose highest score on any of the five sets of items was three or less were not considered in the classification. The problem of tied scores on two or more sets of items was handled by classifying the inmate in favor of the score which was furthest from the absolute mean of its distribution. The distributions of scores for the five role types showed absolute means of five for the politician items; four for the right guy items; three for the square John items; two for the outlaw items; and one for the ding items.

11. This statement is made on the basis of the data as presented in Table 11–1 and Figure 11–2. It is quite likely, however, that had a large number of observations been made on a panel of inmates over time, square Johns and right guys might exhibit differing rates of socialization.

12. Stanton Wheeler, *op. cit.*, p. 709.

13. The trend exhibited by dings approximates that which might be observed among patients in agitated or disturbed states during the initial stages of commitment in mental hospitals, but who over time show progressive improvement. The pattern of response among outlaws is quite the opposite. They enter prison as non-conformists and become

increasingly so over time. For suggestive material on a related subject, see Erving Goffman, "The Moral Career of the Mental Patient," *Psychiatry,* 22 (May, 1959), pp. 123–142.

14. Since the data from the present study are based on a cross sectional rather than longitudinal design, it is of course possible that the observed percentage distributions in Table 11–2 could be obtained by inmates shifting from one role to another in the various career phases. Thus, firm empirical verification of the findings must await data based on panel studies.

15. Stanton Wheeler, *op. cit.,* pp. 704–705.

16. *Ibid.,* p. 704.

17. The items read as follows: Because of their particular jobs, activities, or interests, some inmates come into contact with other inmates frequently, while others do not. Comparing yourself with the average inmate, do you have more contact with other *inmates* or less contact than average? For staff contacts, the item read as above with the exception that the word *staff* was substituted for the word inmate in the appropriate places. The response categories of *much more* and *somewhat more* were considered high contact, while *somewhat less* and *much less* were considered low contact.

18. Peter G. Garabedian, "Legitimate and Illegitimate Alternatives in the Prison Community," *Sociological Inquiry,* 32 (Spring, 1962), pp. 172–184.

19. To derive reliable statements regarding the interplay between conformity, time and involvement of the various role types, it is, of course, necessary to treat these variables simultaneously. However, because of the small N involved this was not possible in the present analysis. For a discussion of multi-variate analysis, see Paul F. Lazarsfeld and Morris Rosenberg, editors, *The Language of Social Research,* Glencoe: The Free Press, 1955, pp. 111–197.

20. Peter G. Garabedian, *op. cit.,* pp. 178–179.

21. Richard A. Cloward, "Illegitimate Means, Anomie, and Deviant Behavior," *American Sociological Review.* 24 (April 1959), pp. 164–177.

22. Greshman M. Sykes and Sheldon L. Messinger, in Richard A. Cloward *et al., op. cit.,* p. 16.

23. Sykes and Messinger state that "almost all inmates have an interest in maintaining cohesive behavior on the part of others, regardless of the role they play themselves." See *Ibid.,* p. 18.

24. For example, because of socially structured conditions, it is likely that staff-sponsored therapy programs will be available to square Johns and politicians. When therapy activities are sponsored by inmates, on the other hand, they may become available to right guys. On the problem of role conflict, see Lloyd E. Ohlin, *Sociology and the Field of Corrections,* New York: Russell Sage Foundation, 1956, pp. 34–37; and Stanton Wheeler, "Role Conflict in Correctional Communities," in Donald R. Cressey, *op. cit.,* pp. 229–259.

25. Jerome H. Skolnick, "Toward a Developmental Theory of Parole," *American Sociological Review,* 25 (August, 1960), pp. 542–549.

26. Richard A. Cloward, "Social Control in Prison," in Richard A. Cloward *et al., op. cit.,* pp. 30–32.

12: The Pains of Imprisonment /
Gresham M. Sykes

The Deprivation of Liberty

Of all the painful conditions imposed on inmates, none is more immediately obvious than the loss of liberty. The prisoner must live in a world shrunk to thirteen and a half acres and within this restricted area his freedom of movement is further confined by a strict system of passes, the military formations in moving from one point within the institution to another, and the demand that he remain in his cell until given permission to do otherwise. In short, the prisoner's loss of liberty is a double one—first, by confinement to the institution and second, by confinement within the institution.

The mere fact that the individual's movements are restricted, however, is far less serious than the fact that imprisonment means that the inmate is cut off from family, relatives, and friends, not in the self-isolation of the hermit or the misanthrope, but in the involuntary seclusion of the outlaw. It is true that visiting and mailing privileges partially relieve the prisoner's isolation— if he can find someone to visit him or write to him and who will be approved as a visitor or correspondent by the prison officials. Many inmates, however, have found their links with persons in the free community weakening as the months and years pass by. This may explain in part the fact that an examination of the visiting records of a random sample of the inmate population, covering approximately a one-year period, indicated that 41 percent of the prisoners in the New Jersey State Prison had received no visits from the outside world.

It is not difficult to see this isolation as painfully depriving or frustrating in terms of lost emotional relationships, of loneliness and boredom. But what makes this pain of imprisonment bite most deeply is the fact that the confinement of the criminal represents a deliberate, moral rejection of the criminal by the free community. Indeed, as Reckless has pointed out, it is the moral condemnation of the criminal—however it may be symbolized—that converts hurt into punishment, i.e., the just consequence of committing an offense, and it is this condemnation that confronts the inmate by the fact of his seclusion.

Now it is sometimes claimed that many criminals are so alienated from conforming society and so identified with a criminal subculture that the moral

From Gresham M. Sykes, *The Society of Captives: A Study of Maximum Security Prison* (Princeton: Princeton University Press, 1958), pp. 65–78. Copyright © 1958 by Princeton University Press. Reprinted by permission of Princeton University Press.

condemnation, rejection, or disapproval of legitimate society do not touch them; they are, it is said, indifferent to the penal sanctions of the free community, at least as far as the moral stigma of being defined as a criminal is concerned. Possibly this is true for a small number of offenders such as the professional thief described by Sutherland [1] or the psychopathic personality delineated by William and Joan McCord.[2] For the great majority of criminals in prison, however, the evidence suggests that neither alienation from the ranks of the law-abiding nor involvement in a system of criminal value is sufficient to eliminate the threat to the prisoner's ego posed by society's rejection.[3] The signs pointing to the prisoner's degradation are many—the anonymity of a uniform and a number rather than a name, the shaven head,[4] the insistence on gestures of respect and subordination when addressing officials, and so on. The prisoner is never allowed to forget that, by committing a crime, he has foregone his claim to the status of a full-fledged, *trusted* member of society. The status lost by the prisoner is, in fact, similar to what Marshall has called the status of citizenship—that basic acceptance of the individual as a functioning member of the society in which he lives.[5] It is true that in the past the imprisoned criminal literally suffered civil death and that although the doctrines of attainder and corruption of blood were largely abandoned in the 18th and 19th Centuries, the inmate is still stripped of many of his civil rights such as the right to vote, to hold office, to sue in court, and so on.[6] But as important as the loss of these civil rights may be, the loss of that more diffuse status which defines the individual as someone to be trusted or as morally acceptable is the loss which hurts most.

In short, the wall which seals off the criminal, the contaminated man, is a constant threat to the prisoner's self-conception and the threat is continually repeated in the many daily reminders that he must be kept apart from "decent" men. Somehow this rejection or degradation by the free community must be warded off, turned aside, rendered harmless. Somehow the imprisoned criminal must find a device for rejecting his rejectors, if he is to endure psychologically.[7]

The Deprivation of Goods and Services

There are admittedly many problems in attempting to compare the standard of living existing in the free community and the standard of living which is supposed to be the lot of the inmate in prison. How, for example, do we interpret the fact that a covering for the floor of a cell usually consists of a scrap from a discarded blanket and that even this possession is forbidden by the prison authorities? What meaning do we attach to the fact that no inmate owns a common piece of furniture, such as a chair, but only a homemade stool? What is the value of a suit of clothing which is also a convict's uniform with a stripe and a stencilled number? The answers are far from simple although there are a number of prison officials who will argue that some inmates are better off in prison, in strictly material terms, than they could ever hope to be in the rough-and-tumble economic life of the free community. Possibly this is so, but at least it has never been claimed by the inmates that the goods and services provided the prisoner are equal to or better than the goods and services which the prisoner could obtain if he were left to his own devices outside the walls. The average inmate finds himself in a harshly Spartan environment which he defines as painfully depriving.

Now it is true that the prisoner's basic material needs are met—in the sense that he does not go hungry, cold, or wet. He receives adequate medical care and he has the opportunity for exercise. But a standard of living constructed in terms of so many calories per day, so many hours of recreation, so many cubic yards of space per individual, and so on, misses the central point when we are discussing the individual's feeling of deprivation, however useful it may be in setting minimum levels of consumption for the maintenance of health. A standard of living can be hopelessly inadequate, from the individual's viewpoint, because it bores him to death or fails to provide those subtle symbolic overtones which we invest in the world of possessions. And this is the core of the prisoner's problem in the area of goods and services. He wants—or needs, if you will—not just the so-called necessities of life but also the amenities: cigarettes and liquor as well as calories, interesting foods as well as sheer bulk, individual clothing as well as adequate clothing, individual furnishings for his living quarters as well as shelter, privacy as well as space. The "rightfulness" of the prisoner's feeling of deprivation can be questioned. And the objective reality of the prisoner's deprivation—in the sense that he has actually suffered a fall from his economic position in the free community—can be viewed with skepticism, as we have indicated above. But these criticisms are irrelevant to the significant issue, namely that legitimately or illegitimately, rationally or irrationally, the inmate population defines its present material impoverishment as a painful loss.

Now in modern Western culture, material possessions are so large a part of the individual's conception of himself that to be stripped of them is to be attacked at the deepest layers of personality. This is particularly true when poverty cannot be excused as a blind stroke of fate or a universal calamity. Poverty due to one's own mistakes or misdeeds represents an indictment against one's basic value or personal worth and there are few men who can philosophically bear the want caused by their own actions. It is true some prisoners in the New Jersey State Prison attempt to interpret their low position in the scale of goods and services as an effort by the State to exploit them economically. Thus, in the eyes of some inmates, the prisoner is poor not because of an offense which he has committed in the past but because the State is a tyrant which uses its captive criminals as slave labor under the hypocritical guise of reformation. Penology, it is said, is a racket. Their poverty, then, is not punishment as we have used the word before, i.e., the just consequence of criminal behavior; rather, it is an unjust hurt or pain inflicted without legitimate cause. This attitude, however, does not appear to be particularly widespread in the inmate population and the great majority of prisoners must face their privation without the aid of the wronged man's sense of injustice. Furthermore, most prisoners are unable to fortify themselves in their low level of material existence by seeing it as a means to some high or worthy end. They are unable to attach any significant meaning to their need to make it more bearable, such as present pleasures foregone for pleasures in the future, self-sacrifice in the interests of the community, or material asceticism for the purpose of spiritual salvation.

The inmate, then, sees himself as having been made poor by reason of his own acts and without the rationale of compensating benefits. The failure is *his* failure in a world where control and possession of the material environment are commonly taken as sure indicators of a man's worth. It is true that our society, as materialistic as it may be, does not rely exclusively on goods and services as a criterion of an individual's value; and, as we shall see shortly, the inmate population defends itself by stressing alternative or supplementary measures of merit. But impoverishment remains as one of the most bitter attacks on the individual's self-image that our society has to offer and the prisoner cannot ignore the implications of his straitened circumstances.[8] Whatever the discomforts and irritations of the prisoner's Spartan existence may be, he must carry the additional burden of social definitions which equate his material deprivation with personal inadequacy.

The Deprivation of Heterosexual Relationships

Unlike the prisoner in many Latin-American countries, the inmate of the maximum security prison in New Jersey does not enjoy the privilege of so-called conjugal visits. And in those brief times when the prisoner is allowed to see his wife, mistress, or "female friend," the women must sit on one side of a plate glass window and the prisoner on the other, communicating by means of a phone under the scrutiny of a guard. If the inmate, then, is rejected and impoverished by the facts of his imprisonment, he is also figuratively castrated by his involuntary celibacy.

Now a number of writers have suggested that men in prison undergo a reduction of the sexual drive and that the sexual frustrations of prisoners are therefore less than they might appear to be at first glance. The reports of reduced sexual interest have, however, been largely confined to accounts of men imprisoned in concentration camps or similar extreme situations where starvation, torture, and physical exhaustion have reduced life to a simple struggle for survival or left the captive sunk in apathy. But in the American prison these factors are not at work to any significant extent and Linder has noted that the prisoner's access to mass media, pornography circulated among inmates, and similar stimuli serve to keep alive the prisoner's sexual impulses.[9] The same thought is expressed more crudely by the inmates of the New Jersey State Prison in a variety of obscene expressions and it is clear that the lack of heterosexual intercourse is a frustrating experience for the imprisoned criminal and that it is a frustration which weighs heavily and painfully on his mind during his prolonged confinement. There are, of course, some "habitual" homosexuals in the prison—men who were homosexuals before their arrival and who continue their particular form of deviant behavior within the all-male society of the custodial institution. For these inmates, perhaps, the deprivation of heterosexual intercourse cannot be counted as one of the pains of imprisonment. They are few in number, however, and are only too apt to be victimized or raped by aggressive prisoners who have turned to homosexuality as a temporary means of relieving their frustration.

Yet as important as frustration in the sexual sphere may be in physiological terms, the psychological problems created by the lack of heterosexual relationships can be even more serious. A society composed exclusively of men tends to generate anxieties in its members concerning their masculinity regardless of whether or not they are coerced, bribed, or seduced into an overt homosexual liaison. Latent homosexual tendencies may be activated in the individual without being translated into open behavior and yet still arouse strong guilt feelings at either the conscious or unconscious level. In the tense atmosphere of the prison with its known perversions, its importunities of admitted homosexuals, and its constant references to the problems of sexual frustration by guards and inmates alike, there are few prisoners who can escape the fact that an essential component of a man's self-conception—his status of male—is called into question. And if an inmate has in fact engaged in homosexual behavior within the walls, not as a continuation of an habitual pattern but as a rare act of sexual deviance under the intolerable pressure of mounting physical desire, the psychological onslaughts on his ego image will be particularly acute.[10]

In addition to these problems stemming from sexual frustration per se, the deprivation of heterosexual relationships carries with it another threat to the prisoner's image of himself—more diffuse, perhaps, and more difficult to state precisely and yet no less disturbing. The inmate is shut off from the world of women which by its very polarity gives the male world much of its meaning. Like most men, the inmate must search for his identity not simply within himself but also in the picture of himself which he finds reflected in the eyes of others; and since a significant half of his audience is denied him, the inmate's self-image is in danger of becoming half complete, fractured, a monochrome without the hues of reality. The prisoner's looking-glass self, in short—to use Cooley's fine phrase—is only that portion of the prisoner's personality which is recognized or appreciated by men and this partial identity is made hazy by the lack of contrast.

The Deprivation of Autonomy

We have noted before that the inmate suffers from what we have called a loss of autonomy in that he is subjected to a vast body of rules and commands which are designed to control his behavior in minute detail. To the casual ob-

server, however, it might seem that the many areas of life in which self-deter-
mination is withheld, such as the language used in a letter, the hours of
sleeping and eating, or the route to work, are relatively unimportant. Perhaps
it might be argued, as in the case of material deprivation, that the inmate in
prison is not much worse off than the individual in the free community who
is regulated in a great many aspects of his life by the iron fist of custom. It
could even be argued, as some writers have done, that for a number of imprisoned criminals the extensive control of the custodians provides a welcome
escape from freedom and the the prison officials thus supply an external Su-
per-Ego which serves to reduce the anxieties arising from an awareness of deviant impulses. But from the viewpoint of the inmate population, it is
precisely the triviality of much of the officials' control which often proves to
be most galling. Regulation by a bureaucratic staff is felt far differently than
regulation by custom. And even though a few prisoners do welcome the strict
regime of the custodians as a means of checking their own aberrant behavior
which they would like to curb but cannot, most prisoners look on the matter
in a different light. Most prisoners, in fact, express an intense hostility
against their far-reaching dependence on the decisions of their captors and
the restricted ability to make choices must be included among the pains of
imprisonment along with restrictions of physical liberty, the possession of
goods and services, and heterosexual relationships.

Now the loss of autonomy experienced by the inmates of the prison does
not represent a grant of power freely given by the ruled to the rulers for a
limited and specific end. Rather, it is total and it is imposed—and for these
reasons it is less endurable. The nominal objectives of the custodians are not,
in general, the objectives of the prisoners.[11] Yet regardless of whether or not
the inmate population shares some aims with the custodial bureaucracy, the
many regulations and orders of the New Jersey State Prison's official regime
often arouse the prisoner's hostility because they don't "make sense" from the
prisoner's point of view. Indeed, the incomprehensible order or rule is a basic
feature of life in prison. Inmates, for example, are forbidden to take food
from the messhall to their cells. Some prisoners see this as a move designed
to promote cleanliness; others are convinced that the regulation is for the
purpose of preventing inmates from obtaining anything that might be used in
the *sub rosa* system of barter. Most, however, simply see the measure as another irritating, pointless gesture of authoritarianism. Similarly, prisoners are
denied parole but are left in ignorance of the reasons for the decision. Prisoners are informed that the delivery of mail will be delayed—but they are not
told why.

Now some of the inmate population's ignorance might be described as "accidental"; it arises from what we can call the principle of bureaucratic indifference, i.e., events which seem important or vital to those at the bottom of
the heap are viewed with an increasing lack of concern with each step up-
ward. The rules, the commands, the decisions which flow down to those who
are controlled are not accompanied by explanations on the grounds that it

is "impractical" or "too much trouble." Some of the inmate population's ignorance, however, is deliberately fostered by the prison officials in that explanations are often withheld as a matter of calculated policy. Providing explanations carries an implication that those who are ruled have a right to know—and this in turn suggests that if the explanations are not satisfactory, the rule or order will be changed. But this is in direct contradiction to the theoretical power relationship of the inmates and the prison officials. Imprisoned criminals are individuals who are being punished by society and they must be brought to their knees. If the inmate population maintains the right to argue with its captors, it takes on the appearance of an enemy nation with its own sovereignty; and in so doing it raises disturbing questions about the nature of the offender's deviance. The criminal is no longer simply a man who has broken the law; he has become a part of a group with an alternative viewpoint and thus attacks the validity of the law itself. The custodians' refusal to give reasons for many aspects of their regime can be seen in part as an attempt to avoid such an intolerable situation.

The indignation aroused by the "bargaining inmate" or the necessity of justifying the custodial regime is particularly evident during a riot when prisoners have the "impudence" to present a list of demands. In discussing the disturbances at the New Jersey State Prison in the spring of 1952, for example, a newspaper editorial angrily noted that "the storm, like a nightmarish April Fool's dream, has passed, leaving in its wake a partially wrecked State Prison as a debasing monument to the ignominious rage of desperate men."

The important point, however, is that the frustration of the prisoner's ability to make choices and the frequent refusals to provide an explanation for the regulations and commands descending from the bureaucratic staff involve a profound threat to the prisoner's self-image because they reduce the prisoner to the weak, helpless, dependent status of childhood. As Bettelheim has tellingly noted in his comments on the concentration camp, men under guard stand in constant danger of losing their identification with the normal definition of an adult and the imprisoned criminal finds his picture of himself as a self-determinint individual being destroyed by the regime of the custodians.[12] It is possible that this psychological attack is particularly painful in American culture because of the deep-lying insecurities produced by the delays, the conditionality and the uneven progress so often observed in the granting of adulthood. It is also possible that the criminal is frequently an individual who has experienced great difficulty in adjusting himself to figures of authority and who finds the many restraints of prison life particularly threatening in so far as earlier struggles over the establishment of self are reactivated in a more virulent form. But without asserting that Americans in general or criminals in particular are notably ill-equipped to deal with the problems posed by the deprivation of autonomy, the helpless or dependent status of the prisoner clearly represents a serious threat to the prisoner's self-image as a fully accredited member of adult society. And of the many threats which may confront the individual, either in or out of prison, there are few better calculated to arouse acute anxieties than the attempt to reimpose the subservience of youth. Public humiliation, enforced respect and deference, the finality of authoritarian decisions, the demands for a specified course of conduct because, in the judgment of another, it is in the individual's best interest—all are features of childhood's helplessness in the face of a superior adult world. Such things may be both irksome and disturbing for a child, especially if the child envisions himself as having outgrown such servitude. But for the adult who has escaped such helplessness with the passage of years, to be thrust back into childhood's helplessness is even more painful, and the inmate of the prison must somehow find a means of coping with the issue.

The Deprivation of Security

However strange it may appear that society has chosen to reduce the criminality of the offender by forcing him to associate with more than a thousand other criminals for years on end, there is one meaning of this involuntary union which is obvious—the individual prisoner is thrown into prolonged intimacy with other men who in many cases have a long history of violent, aggressive behavior. It is a situation which can prove to be anxiety-provoking even for the hardened recidivist and it is in this light that we can understand the comment of an inmate of the New Jersey State Prison who said, "The worst thing about prison is you have to live with other prisoners."

The fact that the imprisoned criminal sometimes views his fellow prisoners as "vicious" or "dangerous" may seem a trifle unreasonable. Other inmates, after all, are men like himself, bearing the legal stigma of conviction. But even if the individual prisoner believes that he himself is not the sort of person who is likely to attack or exploit weaker and less resourceful fellow captives, he is apt to view others with more suspicion. And if he himself is prepared to commit crimes while in prison, he is likely to feel that many others will be at least equally ready. But for the moment it is enough to point out that regardless of the patterns of mutual aid and support which may flourish in the inmate population, there are a sufficient number of outlaws within this group of outlaws to deprive the average prisoner of that sense of security which comes from living among men who can be reasonably expected to abide by the rules of society. While it is true that every prisoner does not live in the constant fear of being robbed or beaten, the constant companionship of thieves, rapists, murderers, and aggressive homosexuals is far from reassuring.

An important aspect of this disturbingly problematical world is the fact that the inmate is acutely aware that sooner or later he will be "tested"—that someone will "push" him to see how far they can go and that he must be prepared to fight for the safety of his person and his possessions. If he should fail, he will thereafter be an object of contempt, constantly in danger of being attacked by other inmates who view him as an obvious victim, as a man who cannot or will not defend his rights. And yet if he succeeds, he may well become a target for the prisoner who wishes to prove himself, who seeks to enhance his own prestige by defeating the man with a reputation for toughness. Thus both success and failure in defending one's self against the aggressions of fellow captives may serve to provoke fresh attacks and no man stands assured of the future.

The prisoner's loss of security arouses acute anxiety, in short, not just because violent acts of aggression and exploitation occur but also because such behavior constantly calls into question the individual's ability to cope with it, in terms of his own inner resources, his courage, his "nerve." Can he stand up and take it? Will he prove to be tough enough? These uncertainties constitute an ego threat for the individual forced to live in prolonged intimacy with criminals, regardless of the nature or extent of his own criminality; and we can catch a glimpse of this tense and fearful existence in the comment of one prisoner who said, "It takes a pretty good man to be able to stand on an equal plane with a guy that's in for rape, with a guy that's in for murder, with a man who's well respected in the institution because he's a real tough cookie. . . ." His expectations concerning the conforming behavior of others destroyed, unable and unwilling to rely on the officials for protection, uncertain of whether or not today's joke will be tomorrow's bitter insult, the prison inmate can never feel safe. And at a deeper level lies the anxiety about his reactions to this unstable world, for then his manhood will be evaluated in the public view.

NOTES

1. Cf. Edwin H. Sutherland, *The Professional Thief,* Chicago: The University of Chicago Press, 1937.

2. Cf. William and Joan McCord, *Psychopathy and Delinquency,* New York: Grune and Stratton, 1956.

3. For an excellent discussion of the symbolic overtones of imprisonment, see Walter C. Reckless, *The Crime Problem,* New York: Appleton-Century-Crofts, Inc., 1955, pp. 428–429.

4. A Western culture has long placed a peculiar emphasis on shaving the head as a symbol of degradation, ranging from the enraged treatment of collaborators in occupied Europe to the more measured barbering of recruits in the Armed Forces. In the latter case, as in the prison, the nominal purpose has been cleanliness and neatness, but for the person who is shaved the meaning is somewhat different. In the New Jersey State Prison, the prisoner is clipped to the skull on arrival but not thereafter.

5. See T. H. Marshall, *Citizenship and Social Class,* Cambridge, England: The Cambridge University Press, 1950.

6. Paul W. Tappan, "The Legal Rights of Prisoners," *The Annals of the American Academy of Political and Social Science,* Vol. 293, May 1954, pp. 99–111.

7. See Lloyd W. McCorkle and Richard R. Korn, "Resocialization Within Walls." *Ibid.,* pp. 88–98.

8. Mirra Komarovsky's discussion of the psychological implications of unemployment is particularly apposite here, despite the markedly different context, for she notes that economic failure provokes acute anxiety as humiliation cuts away at the individual's

conception of his manhood. He feels useless, undeserving of respect, disorganized, adrift in a society where economic status is a major anchoring point. Cf. Mirra Komarovsky, *The Unemployed Man and His Family*, New York: The Dryden Press, 1940, pp. 74–77.

9. See Robert M. Lindner, "Sex in Prison," *Complex*, Vol. 6, Fall 1951, pp. 5–20.

10. Estimates of the proportion of inmates who engage in homosexuality during their confinement in the prison are apt to vary. In the New Jersey State Prison, however, Wing Guards and Shop Guards examined a random sample of inmates who were well known to them from prolonged observation and identified 35 percent of the men as individuals believed to have engaged in homosexual acts. The judgments of these officials were substantially in agreement with the judgments of a prisoner who possessed an apparently well-founded reputation as an aggressive homosexual deeply involved in patterns of sexual deviance within the institution and who had been convicted of sodomy. But the validity of these judgments remains largely unknown and we present the following conclusions, based on a variety of sources, as provisional at best: First, a fairly large proportion of prisoners engage in homosexual behavior during their period of confinement. Second, for many of those prisoners who do engage in homosexual behavior, their sexual deviance is rare or sporadic rather than chronic. And third, as we have indicated before, much of the homosexuality which does occur in prison is not part of a life pattern existing before and after confinement; rather, it is a response to the peculiar rigors of imprisonment.

11. We have suggested earlier, in our discussion of the defects of prison as a system of power, that the nominal objectives of the officials tend to be compromised as they are translated into the actual routines of day-to-day life. The modus vivendi reached by guards and their prisoners is oriented toward certain goals which are in fact shared by captors and captives. In this limited sense, the control of the prison officials is partly concurred in by the inmates as well as imposed on them from above. We will explore this issue at greater length in the analysis of crisis and equilibrium in the society of captives, but in discussing the pains of imprisonment our attention is focused on the frustrations or threats posed by confinement rather than the devices which meet these frustrations or threats and render them tolerable. Our interest here is in the vectors of the prison's social system—if we may use an analogy from the physical sciences—rather than the resultant.

12. Cf. Bruno Bettelheim, "Individual and Mass Behavior in Extreme Situations," in *Readings in Social Psychology*, edited by T. M. Newcomb and E. L. Hartley, New York: Henry Holt and Company, 1947.

13: Sexual Assaults in Prison /

Report on Sexual Assaults in a Prison System and Sheriff's Vans

Sexual assaults are epidemic in some prison systems.

Virtually every slightly built young man committed by the courts is sexually approached within a day or two after his admission to prison. Many of these young men are overwhelmed and repeatedly "raped" by gangs of inmate aggressors. Others are compelled by the terrible threat of gang rape to seek protection by entering into a "housekeeping" relationship with an individual tormentor. Only the toughest and more hardened young men—and those few so obviously frail that they are immediately locked up for their own protection—escape penetration of their bodies.

After a young man's body has been defiled, his manhood degraded, and his will broken, he is marked as a sexual victim for the duration of his confinement. This mark follows him from institution to institution. He eventually returns to the community ashamed, confused and filled with hatred.

This then is the sexual system existing today in some prisons. It is a system which imposes a cruel, gruesome punishment which is not, and could not be, included in the sentence of the court. Indeed, it is a system under which the least hardened criminals and many later found innocent suffer the most. Since it is a system which exists under the aegis of the court and the community, it is the duty of the court and the community to destroy it.

The sexual system can be destroyed by identifying and eliminating the conditions which foster it. But first, the scope and nature of the system must be understood. That is the function of this chapter.

A. Typical Assaultive Patterns

A few typical examples of sexual assaults convey the enormity of the problem. In an earlier draft of this Report an attempt was made to couch this illustrative material in sociological, medical and legal terminology less offensive than the raw, ugly, and chilling language used by the witnesses and

From Report on Sexual Assaults in a Prison System and Sheriff's Vans, an investigation in a major U.S. City (1968), pp. 17–29.

victims themselves. This approach was abandoned. The incidents are raw, ugly and chilling. Any attempt to prettify so outrageous a situation would be hypocrisy. Here then are a few of the stories, told as they really were.

A witness describes the ordeal of John MacNamara, 24 years, and mentally disturbed:

That was June 11th, I was assigned to "E" Dorm. Right after the light went out I saw this colored male, Cheyenne, I think his last name is Boone. He went over and was talking to this kid and slapped him in the face with a belt. He was saying come on back with us and the kid kept saying I don't want to. After being slapped with the belt he walked back with Cheyenne and another colored fellow named Horse. They were walking him back into "E" Dorm. They were telling him to put his hand down and stop crying so the guard will not know what is going on. I looked up a couple of times they had the kid on the floor. About 12 fellows took turns with him. This went on for about two (2) hours. After this he came back to his bed and he was crying and he stated that they all took turns on me. He laid there for about twenty minutes and Cheyenne came over to the kid's bed and pulled his pants down and got on top of him and raped him again. When he got done Horse did it again and then about four (4) or five (5) others got on him. While one of the guys was on him, raping him, Horse came over and said "Open your mouth and suck on this and don't bite it." He then put his penis in his mouth and made him suck on it. The kid was hollering that he was gagging and Horse stated "You better not bite it or I will kick your teeth out." While they had this kid they also had a kid named William in another section in "E" Dorm. He had his pants off and he was bent over and they were taking turns on him. This was Horse, Cheyenne, and about seven (7) other colored fellows, two (2) of the seven were brothers.

Horace came back and stated "Boy I got two virgins in one night, maybe I should make it three." At this time he was standing over me, I stated what are you looking at and he said "We'll save him for tomorrow night."

George White, 18 years old:

White stated that he has been in prison since March 29, 1968, and that about a week and a half ago, on Thursday he was in "I" block, his cell was number 926. On this date in the morning after breakfast W. called him into his cell, he went into W's cell, Donald R. was in there also. Further that he had owed Williams 4 cartons of cigarettes. W's. said to him that he would have to give the cigarettes back right now or he would have to give them something else. He (White) then started to walk out of the cell and W. pushed him down, W. picked up the window pole, R. picked up a bench and stood blocking the door. R. told him that if he goes to the Guard they are going to get him anyway, there were other men outside the cell.

Further that he walked out of the cell, they were all around him and walked to cell #971 and they pushed him inside. He went over and sat on the toilet seat (clothed). Twin came into the cell, they made him lay down on the floor and Twin pulled his (White's) pants down and made him lay face down. Twin pushed his (White's) legs apart and Twin put his penis into his (White's) rectum, he was on him until he discharged, when he got through, White saw that he was bleeding from the rectum. Then Twin, W., R., and M. told him that if he went to the Guard their boys would get him to "D" block and he was scared then to tell the Guard. Further that he did cry out when Twin did this to him but the Guard wouldn't be able to hear him because the block is long.

White went on to say that the next day after chow (breakfast) W., M., I., and L., got him in cell #972 (J's cell), they told him that everything is cool now as long as he doesn't tell. Further that he had never been in jail before and he was too scared to tell anybody. Then four of them did it to him, they put their penises into his rectum, J. first, I. second, L. third, M. fourth. Twin did not bother him that time. That after they did this he was bleeding and got sick.

That night R. came into his cell and changed with his partner. R. told him that he would have to do it. When the guard came to check the cells, R. turned over so he wouldn't be recognized. After the guard counted and left R. got on top of him, put his penis into his (White's) rectum and discharged.

William Blake, 19 years old:

On Tuesday morning, the first week of June at about 9:30 a.m., I was in my cell #412 on "D" block and I had started to clean up. A tall heavy set fella came into the cell and asked for a mirror and shaving brush and a comb, and that my cell partner said he could borrow. He then said that he had heard something about me concerning homosexual acts. I told him what he had heard was not true. He then started to threaten me if I didn't submit to him. Then I hit him with my fist in his face before he could hit me. Then about three more men came into the cell, and they started to beat me up too. I fought back the best I could and then I fell on the floor and I got kicked in the ribs. Three guys were holding me while the other one tore my pants off; I continued to fight until one of the guys knocked me out. One of the guys was holding me on the floor and had my arm pinned to the floor. And about 7 or 8 guys came into the cell and they took turns sticking their penis up my A—. When they finished they left my cell, and I was still laying on the floor.

B. Frequency of Sexual Assaults

156 sexual assaults during the twenty-six month period June, 1966, to July, 1968, have been documented, and substantiated either through polygraph examination, institutional records, or other corroboration. The following table analyzes by place of occurrence:

	No. of Assaults
Detention Center	81
County Prison	47
House of Correction	21
Sheriff's Vans	7
Total	156

The total of 156 incidents involved assaults on at least 97 different victims by at least 176 different aggressors. Including unidentified victims and aggressors, there may well have been as many as 109 different victims and 276 different aggressors.

The types of assaults were as follows:

Buggery (anal penetration)	82
Sodomy (oral penetration)	19
Attempts and Solicitations with Force or Threats	35
Other Coercive Solicitations to Commit Sexual Acts	20
Total	156

These figures represent only the tip of the iceberg. A number of factors make it possible to document only a tiny fraction of the true total. First, investigators interviewed only 3,304 of the approximately 60,000 persons who passed through the prison system since June, 1966. Ninety-four (94) assaults, exclusive of those reflected in institutional records, were discovered. This suggests that had all 60,000 been interviewed, approximately 20 times 94 or 1,880 additional assaults would have come to light.

Second, almost all of the victims who are still in prison are so terrified of retaliation that they are very reluctant to complain. Third, many of the victims and their families want to avoid the shame and dishonor they feel would be attendant upon disclosure. Finally, many of the victims would not even consider disclosure because they themselves mistrust and are hostile to constituted authority.

Taking these factors into consideration, the present investigators conservatively estimate that the true number of assaults in the last two years was approximately two thousand. One guard put the figure at 250 per year in the Detention Center alone. The superintendent and the wardens agreed that virtually every slightly built young man admitted to the prisons in the past two years was at least approached sexually. They believe that the extent of the assault depended primarily on their individual resistance, except for those inmates who were so obviously incapable of self-defense that the prison could isolate them in one of a small number of maximum security units.

In any event, having established the horrifying number of 156 as an absolute minimum, a controversial estimate of the actual number is unnecessary. The situation is intolerable.

C. The Relationship between Forcible and Consensual Homosexuality

Sexual assaults are a major cause of "consensual" homosexuality in the County Prison System. In many, if not in a majority of cases, both continuing and isolated homosexual relationships originate with a gang rape, or with the ever-present threat and fear of a gang rape.

Typically, an experienced inmate, or the leader of a young man's torment-
ors, will offer protection in return for a "housekeeping arrangement." Many
of these perverse marriages of convenience are consummated annually in the
county prisons.

Similarly, many individual homosexual acts are possible only because of
the fear-charged atmosphere generated by the ease and frequency with which
sexual assaults occur. A threat of rape, express or implied, will cause an already broken or fearful young man to submit without physical resistance.

Some prison officials are too quick to label such activity "consensual."
They should recognize that a youth who parts with his manhood in the face
of otherwise certain torture and ruin acts no more willingly than a merchant
who parts with his money in the face of a gun.

A homosexual act is truly "consensual" only where both parties are motivated by their own desires without force, threat of force, or fear of force.
While it is probably true that in any institution segregated by sex there will
usually be more consensual homosexual activity than in the general population, truly consensual homosexual activity must be sharply distinguished from
those acts which are a by-product of the assaultive pattern, and which could
be eliminated once the assaults were brought under control.

D. Economic Coercion and Homosexuality

Homosexual favors can be purchased with luxuries such as cigarettes, sedatives, stainless steel blades, candy or extra food pilfered from the kitchen. Although theoretically segregated from the general prison population, confirmed
homosexuals known as "sissys," "freaks" or "girls" are readily available as
male prostitutes. Investigators learned of repeated instances where homosexual "security" units were left unguarded by an overextended and sometimes
indifferent staff, and even of some cases where guards unlocked cells housing
homosexuals, or turned their backs, so that certain favored inmates could
have homosexual relations.

In some instances male prostitutes are created by a combination of bribery,
persuasion and the threat of force. Typically, an inexperienced young man
will be "given" cigarettes, candy and other items by another more experienced inmate, who after a few days will demand sexual "repayment." Similarly, an inexperienced inmate will be enticed into large gambling debts and
then told to either "pay or f——." Of course, the initial "voluntary" homosexual act indelibly stamps the victim as a "punk boy," and he is pressed into
prostitution for the remainder of his imprisonment.

The common thread in this category of cases is the employment of economic advantage to obtain sexual advantage. Unfortunately it is virtually impossible to obliterate economic distinctions between inmates. In a prison
economy where a shop-worker earns 15 to 25 cents a day, where more than
half the inmates have no prison job at all, and where most inmates get little or

no help from outside the institution, even a small accumulation of luxuries or money can give an inmate substantial economic leverage.

However, it is the clear duty of prison officials to keep at a minumum the economic power that any inmate might exercise over another. Regrettably, investigators discovered one area where through either gross neglect or indifference, the prison officials completely disregarded this duty. As a result, at least one inmate became so economically powerful that he was able to choose as cellmates a series of young men attractive to him, and sexually subvert each one by bribery.

14: Sexual Tensions in a Woman's Prison/ *David Ward* and *Gene Kassebaum*

Problems in Defining Homosexual Behavior

When we use the term homosexual behavior we are referring to *kissing and fondling of the breasts, manual or oral stimulation of the genitalia and simulation of intercourse between two women.* Our definition of homosexual behavior does *not* include emotional arousal over another woman, or kissing, handholding, or embracing when these actions are not followed by overt sexual behavior. Our definition of homosexuality thus differs slightly from that of Kinsey, Pomeroy, Martin, and Gebhard, who distinguished between erotic responses to other females, physical contact with other females which, at least on the part of one of the partners, is deliberately and consciously intended to be sexual, and activity resulting in an orgasm.[1]

Staff definitions of what constitutes homosexual behavior at Frontera vary considerably as can be seen in the following excerpts from disciplinary reports describing "immorality":

X and Y were lying across X's bed. Y had an arm across X's abdomen.

. . . sitting in living room with legs across X's lap. Had been spoken to before about physical contacts.

. . . was observed walking on sidewalk in front of cottage—arms entwined about the waist of X. Stood in that position for a few moments before parting.

. . . showering in same stall with Y.

They were sitting very close, kissing occasionally and embracing.

From David Ward and Gene Kassebaum, *Women's Prison* (Chicago: Aldine Publishing Company, 1965), pp. 80–93; 98–101. Copyright © 1965 by David A. Ward and Gene G. Kassebaum.

X placed herself in a compromising position which might lead to the commission of immoral acts. Staff found her lying prone on the bed beside Y with her arm around Y.

While checking halls at 7:05 p.m., found X kissing Y on the lips. X was lying on Y's bed. Y was also lying on the bed. There appeared to be no other bodily contact.

I was walking down the hall . . . when my attention was directed to a room occupied by two women, one of whom was bending over the other and kissing her. The woman seated on the bed, leaning way back on it, was X. Bending over her and kissing her so loudly that I could hear the smack of their lips was Y.

X and Y were standing face to face, Y was fondling X with hand low on X's body and faces were together. X had on only a light-weight robe at that time—not fastened—and she had been told early today to dress before she had company.

. . . X and her friend were found back of the bushes . . . X was lounging with her weight on her arms and her legs sprawled out. The upper part of her body was protected from viewers by Y's trunk as she sat beside and facing her. As I came closer X grabbed the front of her blouse and buttoned it. They went to a bench as I came closer but returned to the same spot and same positions as soon as I left the area.

Two girls were lying on the bed—I could not see their heads and shoulders but their legs were entwined one upon the other. The girl next to the wall had her dress above her waist and the other girl was reaching under her slip with her right hand.

One reason for the ambiguity of some of these write-ups is the apparent reluctance of staff members to describe more explicitly the behavior they observed. Another reason is that with the exception of overt sexual contact, there is an area of judgment which must be exercised in deciding what is a violation of institutional rules. Becker has pointed out that what is regarded as deviant depends on more than the behavior itself:

[Deviant behavior] is the product of a process which involves responses of other people to the behavior. The same behavior may be an infraction of the rules at one time and not at another; may be an infraction when committed by one person, but not when committed by another; some rules are broken with impunity, others are not. In short, whether a given act is deviant or not depends in part on the nature of the act (that is, whether or not it violates some rule) and in part on what people do about it.[2]

During the course of the study the staff, in an effort to reduce the incidence of overt behavioral manifestations of homosexuality on the grounds, were told to write disciplinary reports when physical contact, including handholding, embracing and kissing was observed. Those women playing the masculine homosexual role were required to allow their hair to grow to a certain length. These specific instructions permitted more ready distinctions between deviant and legitimate behavior than had been the case earlier when "immorality" was not specifically defined. Reports of homosexuality as disciplinary infractions are thus affected by the degree to which the behavior to be sanctioned is explicitly defined. There is no evidence that there has been an actual increase in homosexuality at Frontera, but current rates reflect more precise definitions of homosexual behavior, the extension of prohibitions to previously uncovered areas, and a "drive" on the part of the staff to take action against this behavior.

For some inmates (both homosexual and non-homosexual), homosexuality does not connote a wide variety of behavioral expressions. They are concerned with reserving that term only for overt sexual behavior. Because some inmates hold hands, walk arm in arm, or embrace friends, they do not wish to have these actions construed as manifestations of homosexual involvement. But, as can be seen in Table 14–1, this view is not shared by all inmates. Forty-seven per cent of this sample of the inmate population view kissing and handholding as either having sexual connotations, or as symbolic of more explicit sexual behavior. The response of the staff to the same item indicates that overt displays of affection among non-homosexual inmates will likely raise the suspicion of many staff members.

Table 14-1

Staff and Inmate Replies to the Statement:
Handholding and kissing among inmates is usually
evidence of a sexual relationship

	Inmates	Staff
Agree	47%	52%
Disagree	53	48
Frequency	100%	100%
Frequency	280	61

No answer: Staff   5% (3)
Inmates 4% (13)

The difficulty here is that behavior that is permissible in the free world becomes problematic in prison. Once these actions have been defined as meaning more than friendship, they draw suspicious attention on all women. In the following statement the problems caused by acting spontaneously in the prison setting are described by a non-homosexual inmate:

It's tough to be *natural*. The thing that most of us are trying to accomplish here, we're trying to get our minds at a point to where we can handle whatever comes our way, to get our emotions balanced, to maybe straighten up our way of thinking. You know, it just makes it hard when you're trying to be a natural person—to react to things normally—when the staff won't let you be normal—when you do a normal thing that being a woman makes it normal, and then have them say no, you can't do that because if you do that's personal contact and that's homosexuality. So there's our mental hassle.

I know that when women are thrown together without men or without the companionship of men it makes it pretty rough on them—women being the emotional people that they are. They have to have a certain amount of affection and close companionship. You know, a woman, if she's with a man she'll put her hand on him or maybe she'll reach up and touch him. This is something that a woman does naturally without thinking, and so if a woman has a good friend here, or an affair, she does the same thing because this is her nature. The thing of it is—like I have a friend at the cottage—neither one of us have ever played. We're never gonna play. And if somebody tried to force us into it, we couldn't, wouldn't, or what have you. But being a woman and after being here for quite a while, we put our arms around each other, we don't think there's anything the matter with it, because there's nothing there—it's a friendship. We're walking down the hall, our records are both spotless, she's a council girl, I'm Minimum A [minimum custody classification]. I've never had anything on my record that was bad and my god, the supervisor comes out and says, "Now, now, girls, you know we don't allow that sort of thing here." And we look at her and say "What sort of thing?" "This personal contact." And yet this same supervisor, we saw her up at the corner putting her arm around another supervisor the very same way we were doing. So this is where part of our mental hassle comes in.

At issue here is the interpretation of certain behavior by staff and inmates. While there may be direct evidence of deviance, e.g., two women engaged in mutual masturbation or a woman whose hair is crewcut and whose dress and mannerisms are strongly masculine, problems arise over indirect evidence such as gossip, rumors and stories about an individual or couple. Such information then forms the basis for what Kitsuse calls "retrospective interpretation" of the behavior.[3] Staff and inmates review and reinterpret the behavior of the couple and find that handholding and walking arm-in-arm, which did not arouse suspicions in the past, may be viewed as evidence of a sexual relationship that has been going on all the while.

Kitsuse, in discussing the nature of evidence for judging one to be a homosexual, notes that there are fewer behavioral gestures and signs which indicate homosexuality on the part of females than males. The masculine appearance of women in the community, for example, is less likely to be linked to homosexual suspicions.[4] This is somewhat less the case in prison where staff and inmates are attuned to clues and symbols of female homosexuality and where differences are readily apparent to a one-sex group living in a small physical area. Thus, judgments about prison homosexuality are based on more than direct evidence of sexual activities.

Another reason for the differences in perception of homosexual behavior is that there are differences in the degree of homosexual involvement. Some women have affectional ties which can be objectively designated as homosexual, without actual intercourse having taken place. One interviewee, for example, reported that shortly after her arrival at Frontera she was asked by an "aggressive acting homosexual" if she *had people* (had a homosexual partner). She was questioned in the other girl's room and during their conversation two other inmates were engaged in homosexual activity on the bed. Our respondent said that in her opinion this was coincidental and was not meant as a demonstration for her benefit. She said, "My friend asked me if I wanted to go with her and I said 'no,' but it wasn't an emphatic 'no.' " She admitted that the "no" was meant and interpreted as "maybe." Her reason, she said, was that she was "curious" about homosexuality. She started seeing the girl frequently, waiting for her each day after work. The other girl soon became "very jealous and possessive" and was angered by the subject's close friendship with a third inmate. Our respondent was by now receiving love notes from her girlfriend which were ". . . pretty passionate, but I thought they were cute so I hid them in my closet where they were discovered in a shakedown. The notes said she wanted my warm body near her, she wanted to have me, etc." In describing this relationship the subject said, "We necked in each other's rooms and kissed and petted, but when she tried to draw me into sexual intercourse, I always stopped her, sometimes by pushing her away and sometimes by saying I heard a staff member coming. I would jump up and run off. . . . [The aggressive girl] was very frustrated and would want me to say why I would go no further, she'd call me cold and want to know why I would stiffen up." The subject claimed that she was "just teasing" and asserted that she "got nothing" emotionally or physically from the necking sessions. She reported that the other girl became so seriously involved with her that she tried to ease things off before the girl was released on parole. She said she did not become more deeply involved because she wanted to maintain her "self-respect" and not because she was afraid that reports of her affair would reach her parents or the parole board.

Clearly the subject derived satisfaction from the attention she received from her friend and a number of her statements suggested that this relationship was meaningful for her. Finally, in discussing homosexual versus platonic relationships, she remarked "maybe I got the wrong girl," implying that she might have been won by a girl who wooed her in a different manner.

While this inmate was regarded by the staff as being homosexually involved, she did not conceive herself to be homosexual. Her effort to maintain a heterosexual self-image took the form of distinguishing between homosexuality and what she called "playing around." This line beyond which she said she refused to go seems quite similar to the line drawn by women who permit necking, but refuse to "go all the way" to sexual intercourse with men. The subject employed her "rule of thumb" for differentiating homosexual couples from couples who were just friends. She said she would assume that two women are homosexually involved if they "go into a room [cell], close the door and stuff a towel in the wicket" [an eight-by-two-inch slit in each door]. During her "necking sessions," the door to her room was always open. She pointed out that while this action was ostensibly to prevent the arousal of staff and inmate suspicion, it really served to keep the amorous gestures of her suitor in check.

Regardless of her self-image, this inmate behaved in a manner which suggested homosexual involvement to staff and inmates. She embraced her girlfriend, walked hand in hand with her and violated prison rules by taking a shower in the same stall with her friend.

The distinction between sexual involvement and sexual restraint is as difficult to make regarding a definition of homosexuality as it is regarding heterosexual behavior in the outside community. The self-conception of our subject and other inmates like her who do not "go all the way" is heterosexual, regardless of what others think. These differences between objective and subjective evaluations of affectional behavior should be kept in mind in considering the estimates of the incidence of homosexuality made by staff and inmates.

The Prevalence of Homosexual Involvement Among Prison Inmates

Once having determined what is meant by homosexual behavior, it is still very difficult to determine accurately the amount of homosexual behavior at Frontera. Homosexuals, like others engaging in any kind of deviant behavior, have a variety of reasons for concealing their activities. Some inmates are fearful that prison staff members will inform their families of their affairs. Many inmates feel that staff knowledge of homosexual involvement hurts chances of early parole and draws extra staff surveillance. Such concerns are not groundless, for the label of homosexual by a staff member has important consequences for the inmate. The designation becomes a permanent part of her file information, available to all the staff. It may affect decisions about her housing and work assignments and other activities in prison, and as a violation of prison rules it calls for an appearance before the disciplinary committee. Being adjudged guilty means punishment and designation as a rule violator in addition to being labeled homosexual. Homosexuality, like other sexual behavior, is private behavior which takes place, for the most part, behind closed doors with only the participants knowing what actually transpires.

While some data on the incidence of female homosexuality in the larger community have been collected by Kinsey and his associates, the general neglect of the women's prison as an object of study is reflected in the fact that there is virtually no reliable information available on the incidence of homosexuality among adult female prison inmates. The one exhaustive study of characteristics and behavior of adult female prisoners (the Gluecks' *500 Delinquent Women*) does not mention homosexuality. Those estimates which are reported in the literature are impressionistic and generally made by prison staff members.

In our effort to judge the number of inmates who participate in homosexual affairs in prison, we distinguished inferences and allegations made by staff members from reports of clinicians, admissions by inmates, and actual observation of sexual activity. Although reports of clandestine behavior based on cases which come to official attention are always underestimates of the true prevalence, such data are worth examining to measure the degree to which official concern is actually implemented in actions taken against such behavior.

Homosexual behavior is indicated in inmate record files in the form of: (1) disciplinary reports; [5] (2) the reports of community investigations by probation officers; (3) case materials from other prisons; (4) reports by psychiatrists and psychologists; (5) admissions by inmates to custodial or social service personnel. These data for the Frontera population can be seen in Table 14–2, along with comparative data from the medium security prison for men.

In addition to data from the inmates' files, we included on our questionnaire to inmates and staff an item which asked respondents to estimate the number of women who have *sexual* affairs with other women while in prison. The question was so worded as to take into account the ambiguities in the definition of homosexuality, such as the distinction between handholding and explicit sexual activity. As can be seen in Table 14–3, staff and inmate estimates were higher than the nineteen per cent figure obtained from our examination of official records.

Estimates of the prevalence of homosexuality varied with the method of obtaining the data as well as with the source. In the interviews with forty-five inmates, estimates of the extent of homosexuality were never less than fifty per cent, with most respondents estimating sixty to seventy-five per cent. Individual conversations with staff members yielded similar high estimates. In these judgments, made in interview, the respondents knew specifically the kind of behavior in question and the basis on which their estimates were made could be questioned and evaluated.

Table 14-2
Official Prison Records of Extent of Homosexual Involvement for Male and Female Prisoners

Homosexual Involvement	Female	Male*
None Reported or Inferred	81%	89%
Reported in Prior Confinement Only	2	1
Reported on Outside Only	3	3
Reported in Prior Confinement and Outside, but Not Current Confinement	1	2
Reported Prior to and during Current Confinement	4	1
Observed, reliably reported, only in current confinement	4	–
Inferred, Alleged only in Current Confinement	3	1
Actual Homosexual Act Never Reported, but Homosexual Traits Ascribed to Subject	2	3
	100%	100%
Frequency	832	972

*Inmates of a California medium security prison.

Table 14-3

Estimates of Prevalence of Institutional Homosexuality

*Replies of women's prison staff and female and male inmates
to the statements "A rough estimate of the number of women
(men) who have sexual affairs at one time or another with
other women (men) in prison would be:"*

Estimate of Homosexuality	Women's Prison Staff	Female Inmates	Male Inmates
5 percent or less	12%	12%	29%
15 percent	31	12	25
30 percent	29	25	25
50 percent	14	22	12
70 percent	9	22	6
90 percent or more	5	7	3
	100%	100%	100%
Frequency	58*	263*	744*

*Six staff members, 30 female inmates, and 127 male inmates refused or
were unable to make an estimate.

While there was no major disparity between the estimates of homosexuals
and non-homosexuals, those who had been or were homosexually involved
may have tended to enlarge their estimates as they projected their own feelings and experiences. Staff concern with the problems created by homosexuality such as the frequent requests by inmates for job and housing changes,
the need to control and sanction overt displays of affection, and the distress
and anxiety of women unhappy in their affairs, perhaps accounts for the high
estimates made by top supervisory, administrative, case work and clinical
personnel.

Reconciling all estimates, including the grossly underreported official incidence of homosexuality and the overestimated reports of some of our interviewees, it appears that about *fifty percent of the inmates at Frontera are sexually
involved at least once during their term of imprisonment.*[6] (This figure
should not be construed to mean, however, that all of those involved were initiated into homosexuality at Frontera.) While about half of the inmate population comes to assume a homosexual role during their sentences, it should be
emphasized that *every* inmate at Frontera must come to terms with the homosexual adaptation. Those who reject homosexuality as an attempted solution
to their problems must learn to live in a society dominated by homosexual ideology and behavior. This point applies as well to the staff who must become
accustomed to working in a community where deviant sexual roles are an everyday fact of life.

The Techniques and the Locale of Prison Homosexuality

Data gathered in interview, such as the statement below, suggested that homosexual behavior at Frontera is characterized by the need to employ a variety of sexual techniques, including simulation of intercourse.[7]

Q. What form does the sexual behavior usually take—oral-genital, breast fondling, manual manipulation, or what?

A. Well, actually, you see, there is what we call *giving some head* [oral-genital contact]. Or what they call *dry fucking*—I don't know how to explain it. That's more or less a *bulldagger's* [a woman who plays the masculine homosexual role] kick, this dry fucking. You get in a position, one's on the top and one's on the bottom, and you more or less use your legs on their sensitive parts to get a rocking motion. Sometimes it's put into an act, at least part of it. Sometimes you combine all of these things together. But all women are different. Some women dig one thing, and some dig another. You have to kind of feel them out but usually, like in a heterosexual relationship, it usually follows a set pattern unless you get with a freak and they're usually freaky about only one or two things. But as a rule it's never a set pattern that's followed, and in a sexual act with a woman her moods and her emotional desires and her physical desires change so fast that you have to change the act five or six times in the course of one act to stay with her feelings, and it takes a while to learn a woman and even after you learn her it's a challenge each time you go to bed with her, to try to stay with her.

While public displays of affection such as handholding and embracing are subject to ambiguous interpretation, the intimate behavior described above makes clear the relationship between two women. Due to the fact that Frontera is a prison, one might wonder where and under what circumstances it is possible for inmates to engage in such intimate sexual activities. Staff surveillance and punitive sanctions are designed to discourage illicit meetings. Opportunities for intimacy are limited and usually require the cooperation and silence of fellow inmates, attributes not easily found in a population of snitches. These obstacles, however, do not seem to deter the meetings for several reasons: (1) inmates greatly outnumber staff, (2) lovers take the initiative in setting up meetings, (3) sanctions are viewed as illegitimate or worth risking to demonstrate affection, and (4) lovers can find one or two friends who will help them and keep quiet about their meeting.

The room of one of the lovers is the most frequent locale for sexual activity. It is especially convenient for women who reside in the same cottage, and particularly dangerous when it becomes necessary to rendezvous in the cottage of one's lover, where one of the partners is an obvious stranger in an all-too-familiar group cottage residents. Homosexual activity in one's room, as indicated earlier, usually calls for closing the door. This action may, however, alert the cottage supervisor whose glassed-in office is at the end of the corridor. Two corridors run at 45 degree and 80 degree angles from each side of the central dining and recreation areas and each set of corridors may be observed from the supervisor's office. Thus the usual practice is for the lovers to utilize a close friend or a trusted inmate to act as a lookout, referred to as *pinning*. This may involve making certain sounds if a staff member comes down the corridor or engaging the staff member in extended conversation in her office. The latter is often done under the guise of discussing an inmate's problems.

In addition to using rooms, some homosexuality takes place in the shower rooms.[8] Fondling and deep kissing may also occur in out-of-the way rooms in various service and industries buildings such as the library and the warehouse. At one time a large semi-trailer truck which brought laundry in and out of the institution, and which was left on the grounds between loads, was reputedly used as a trysting place.

In short, there are a variety of places where inmates may meet despite the rigorous efforts of staff to prevent them. There are not enough staff members to constantly supervise each inmate and until that custodial millennium is reached, lovers will find ways to be together.

NOTES

1. Alfred C. Kinsey, Wardell B. Pomeroy, Clyde E. Martin, Paul H. Gebhard, *Sexual Behavior in the Human Female* (Philadelphia: W. B. Saunders Company, 1953), pp. 452–453.

2. Howard S. Becker, *Outsiders*, p. 14.

3. John I. Kitsuse, "Societal Reactions to Deviant Behavior: Problems of Theory and Method," *Social Problems*, 9 (Winter, 1962), pp. 250–253. See a related article dealing with the designation of persons as mentally ill, by Thomas J. Scheff, "The Societal Reaction to Deviance: Ascriptive Elements in the Psychiatric Screening of Mental Patients in a Midwestern State," *Social Problems*, 11 (Spring, 1964), pp. 401–413.

4. Kitsuse, *ibid.*, p. 252.

5. For 476 files we tabulated the number of cases of homosexuality reported as violations of institution rules. Eight percent (thirty-eight cases) of this sample received such reports. There were fifty-three reports for "immorality": thirty-two offenders having a single report, four having from two to five reports, and two with more than six writeups. Disciplinary reports, like arrest records in the outside community, are clearly not the best source of data on which to base estimates of the incidence of illegal behavior.

6. It should also be pointed out that since we made public our estimate of homosexuality, not one member of the administrative staff, the professional treatment staff, or the inmate population, has agreed with it. All have indicated surprise and said they personally thought the incidence was higher than fifty percent.

7. For additional discussion of the techniques used in homosexual contacts, see Frank S. Caprio, *Female Homosexuality* (New York: Grove Press, Inc., 1954), pp. 19–22; Kinsey, Pomeroy, Martin, and Gebhard, *op. cit.*, pp. 466–468; and Bergher, *op. cit.*, p. 334.

8. Several interviewees made reference to a homosexual activity called the *daisy chain*, which calls for three or more persons to form a line and fondle the person in front of them. This activity allegedly took place in shower rooms where it would be possible for a number of women to be gathered in various stages of undress. Due to the hazard of being observed by the staff and other inmates and the fact that most homosexual behavior is private and personal, this activity is apparently infrequent.

Part II

EFFECTIVENESS
OF PUNISHMENT
AND TREATMENT

A

MEANING AND MEASUREMENT

15: Some Research Results and Problems / *R. G. Hood*

Nearly all inquiries have studied the effect of treatment from the point of view of its effect on the offender himself. They have been concerned with measuring the extent to which penal measures are ineffective in halting recidivism, and with assessing the reasons for this failure. Attention has therefore been paid only to measuring the effect of *one* of the objects of sentencing. There are no substantial research results that throw any light on the effectiveness of penalties in deterring potential offenders. Nor is there any research into the extent to which the courts successfully effect their broader social functions of reinforcing social values and allaying public fear of crime. There are two main reasons why research has been concentrated on the effect of treatment on the offender rather than on the other objectives. First, as the Streatfeild Committee emphasised, it is widely agreed that the principal objective in sentencing should be to stop the offender from offending again. Secondly, difficult though the task may be, the effects of sentences on convicted offenders are easier to measure than the effects of other objectives. But until such research is completed decisions will continue to be made without any knowledge of whether their objects are achieved. This chapter is concerned only with research on treatment effects on offenders. The problems of research into general deterrence of offenders have been recently provocatively discussed by both Lady Wootton [1] and Leslie Wilkins. [2]

There have been three different approaches to treatment research. The first two follow up offenders from the time of treatment for a specified period in order to study those who "succeed" and "fail" by various criteria. One of these approaches has been to concentrate on offenders who have undergone *one* particular treatment, the other attempts to compare results between different treatments. The third approach has been to study the content of the treatment as such and its impact on the attitudes, values and conduct of the offenders. These studies will be discussed in turn.

From R. G. Hood, "Research on the Effectiveness of Punishments and Treatments," in *Collected Studies in Criminological Research, I* (Strasbourg: Council of Europe, 1967), pp. 74–86, 89–102.

The Results of Research

Research on the effectiveness of treatments clearly shows that present knowledge amounts to a number of broad generalisations[5] which, while better than nothing, should be treated as the basis of judicial or administrative decisions only with the greatest care. The methods of research so far employed have been rudimentary and are consequently in need of much improvement. In the words of Wilkins, we are at a stage where "the nature of our ignorance is beginning to be revealed." And this, as he says, is encouraging.[3]

There are a number of methodological and practical issues which affect the confidence that can be placed in the results of any of the studies reported in this chapter. These include the difficulties associated with the choice of criteria by which "success" and "failure" should be assessed; the problems involved by the question of the extent to which research results remain valid over time. For the purposes of clarity it is intended to present the results of research first and to follow with a discussion of the methodological and practical problems they raise. In the discussion of results the criterion of "success" and "failure" used will be whether the offender has subsequently been reconvicted, as this criteria is used in all studies. Whether or not it is entirely satisfactory is a problem of methodology.

THE VALUE AND LIMITATIONS OF SINGLE TREATMENT STUDIES

A large number of follow-up studies have in the past been concerned with a single treatment only. In fact, the method of following up offenders after treatment and studying their records in order to find correlates of recidivism is the oldest and most unsophisticated method of attempting to evaluate treatment. To what extent is this method a useful way of studying treatment? What are its advantages and its limitations?

In reviewing the studies completed prior to the last war, Leon Radzinowicz [4] pointed out two major weaknesses. First, the studies only covered offenders who had been incarcerated and nothing was known about the after-conduct of those placed on probation or fined. Secondly, the studies were extremely crude. Radzinowicz drew attention to what he described as "inadequate methods of differentiation" in the way that offenders were classified: nearly all the studies simply divided offenders into age-groups and into first offenders and recidivists. Since the war both weaknesses have to some extent been remedied. New studies have been made of probation, probation with mental treatment, Borstal, short-term imprisonment, and of some of the new methods introduced in the Criminal Justice Act, 1948—attendance centres, detention centres and preventive detention.[5] All these studies (except the probation studies) have examined a wide number of penal and social factors in relation to recidivism. The Borstal, attendance centre and preventive detention studies have presented results in the form of prediction equations which show the maximum discrimination that can be made on the available data between those who are least and most likely to be reconvicted following treatment. It will be seen that no special after-conduct studies have so far been carried out on Approved School boys or on those fined or discharged by the courts.

What are the results of these studies? It is extremely difficult to compare the figures given by studies which present results in terms of the relationship between various characteristics of offenders (such as juvenile first offender) and reconviction, with those which give results in the form of prediction equations or relate a "typology" of offenders to reconviction. The first type of study shows in general that first offenders have the lowest reconviction rates in all treatments, that reconviction rates tend to increase as the number of previous convictions increases, that on the whole older offenders have lower reconviction rates than younger ones. These results confirm those reported by Radzinowicz for pre-war treatments. The studies of both attendance and detention centres show that juveniles with "adverse home backgrounds" do worse than those whose home conditions are described as good. For persistent offenders serving long-term imprisonment, Hammond and Chayen found that the likelihood of reconviction was related both to previous convictions and the length of the interval at liberty since the termination of their last sentence. The fewer previous convictions and the longer the interval of liberty the greater the chance of success.

Prediction studies for different treatments in England have shown that similar factors are highly related to reconviction. Offenders with a number of previous convictions, poor work records and poor or non-existent home backgrounds are bad risks for any treatment. A few studies have attempted to relate reconviction to a "typology of offenders" and those are difficult to compare because of the different typologies used. Ogden [6] and Rose [7] both developed typologies of Borstal boys: Ogden showed that after four years from release 89 per cent of the "egocentric type" were reconvicted, 43 per cent of the "emotionally unstable" and 69 per cent of the "physically and mentally abnormal." Rose found that after five years 89 per cent of the "apparently subnormal" were reconvicted compared with 12 per cent of the "well adjusted." Whether these figures represent real differences or are due to differences in the ways the types were defined it is not possible to say. Equally, the results could not be compared with Garrity's study of the predictive value of Schrag's typology of offenders in American prisons.[8]

Where do these results lead us? They show that offenders with certain characteristics do well after treatment and others do badly. The results are clearly helpful in defining those for whom a treatment is particularly *unsuccessful,* and prediction studies are especially helpful for this. These single-treatment studies may also be useful in generating hypotheses about the most appropriate ways of dealing with unsuccessful cases. For example, Hood [9] found that among homeless boys in Borstal there was a high correlation between lengthy institutional experience prior to Borstal and reconviction after Borstal. This would suggest that this type of "institutionalised" boy does not benefit from further institutional training and that perhaps results might be better if treatment aimed at combating the debilitating effects of institutionalisation. Andry's attempt to suggest alternative treatments for short-term prisoners is a further example.[10]

Do these studies help to assess how effective treatment is? A number of them suggest that for those not reconvicted the treatment has proved effective.[11] Yet without an assessment of what rate of reconviction could have been expected had the offenders had no treatment at all this is simply a statement of faith. Success could be due to any one of a large number of other factors such as the stigma and shame of conviction alone. One method of assessing effectiveness in these studies has therefore been to compare clinical prognoses of reconviction with the actual rates found. Grünhut, for example, compared clinical prognoses for probationers receiving mental treatment with their reconvictions. He found that a prognosis of success was by and large confirmed, while on the other hand a proportion of those predicted to fail in fact succeeded. He concluded that "these figures indicate that probation still has a chance in a proportion of cases for which medical experience sees no prospect of improving the offender's mental condition . . . there must . . . be a respectable minority of cases where the probation officer succeeded in keeping the probationer out of conflict with the law during and for some time after the period of supervision." [12] Such a conclusion raises a number of questions. Did the clinical prognosis rest on medical *experience* or medical *impressions?* A prognosis is a statement about probabilities; what probability of reconviction is signified by the term "bad prognosis"; was it greater or less than that found? Is not an equally acceptable hypothesis that the clinicians were wrong in their prognosis because they mis-classed an offender rather than because treatment helped him? Clearly such a method of assessing effectiveness is inadequate. It appears that follow-up studies of single treatment can tell us how *ineffective* the treatment is, but not how *effective*. If an offender is reconvicted then his treatment was *ipso facto* ineffective in stopping him from committing further crime.

Relative effectiveness, however, is measurable. To assess it we need to know what would have happened to an offender (or group of offenders with similar characteristics) if they had received one treatment rather than another. If two out of ten offenders were reconvicted after probation, but after six months' imprisonment four out of ten similar offenders were, we would know that imprisonment was ineffective for twice as many offenders as probation. At the other extreme another study may show that eight out of every ten offenders with certain characteristics are reconvicted following probation. One might simply assume that probation was ineffective for offenders of this type. But if a further inquiry showed that only five in every hundred among similar offenders imprisoned avoided reconviction, then we would have to regard probation as relatively effective. Clearly, only comparative studies can answer the vitally important question of the judge or penal administrator: *What treatment gives the best chance of an offender, with these characteristics, not again returning before the court?*

Are single-treatment studies of value for comparative purposes? To be useful these studies would have to differentiate adequately between reconviction figures for different types of offender. Two of the studies tell us, for example, that 64 per cent of male juvenile first offenders are not reconvicted after probation and 66 per cent are not after a detention centre order. Clearly the offenders could be very different in other respects affecting their likelihood of reconviction and therefore comparable. Prediction and typological research can, however, be used for comparative purposes and some of the findings using these methods are outlined below.

COMPARATIVE STUDIES OF TREATMENT RESULTS

If one wishes to compare the results of two or more treatments one must make allowance for any differences in the types of offender sentenced to each treatment. How can this be done? Broadly there are two methods:

(i) Offenders receiving one treatment can be "matched" with those receiving another. Matching may be either in terms of a number of separate variables thought to have a bearing on the likelihood of reconviction, or possibly on the basis of a typology.
(ii) Offenders can be matched on the statistical probabilities of their being reconvicted. The reconviction rates of offenders in the same "risk group" in a prediction equation may be compared. Or alternatively, as in the recent Home Office study, "expected" reconviction rates may be calculated for each treatment which take into account the characteristics of offenders sentenced to the treatment, and this "expected" rate compared with the "actual" rate.

Each of these methods has been used in comparing the effects of different treatments. They both pose a number of methodological and statistical problems which will be discussed later. Let us first consider the main conclusions:

(1) *There are indications that fines are more successful than probation or institutional treatment with both first offenders and those with previous conviction in all age groups*

The Home Office study published in *The Sentence of the Court* [13] is based on the treatment of all offenders convicted in April and May of 1957 in Metropolitan London and followed up for five years. By a system of comparing actual and expected reconviction rates (ii above) it shows that although probation is relatively more successful for those with previous convictions than first offenders it is actually for no age group any better than "expected."

(2) *Most studies show that lengthy institutional sentences are no more successful than shorter alternatives*

Sir George Benson applied the Mannheim-Wilkins prediction equation for Borstal boys to young persons aged 17–21 serving prison sentences.[14] He found that, although the average period of imprisonment was four months compared with eighteen months and over in Borstal, the results for the prisoners when matched in terms of "good or bad risks" were the same as for

Borstal boys. Sir George also stated that he carried out the same exercise on boys in detention centres for three months and again found no overall differences between treatments.

Mannheim and Wilkins [15] compared with the Borstal population those who had served over the average length of detention with those released earlier. Taking into account (as far as possible) the difference between boys released in the two periods they concluded "there was every reason to believe that long periods of detention (above average) may yield no better results than periods of, say, one year." They note however, that this result may be due to incomplete data.

In the United States, supportive evidence comes from Weeks' study of the Highfields experiment.[16] Highfields is an institution providing short-term treatment of up to four months combined with a form of group therapy called "guided group interaction" and a "permissive" regime. Furthermore, only a small number of boys were at the institution at any one time; they went to work daily outside Highfields to a mental institution and were allowed home leave. This form of treatment was compared with the large State reformatory at Annandale where treatment lasted about two years with an emphasis on vocational training and discipline. Using a prediction equation to match boys from each institution, Weeks found that slightly fewer white boys from Highfields were reconvicted than from Annandale (but the difference was not statistically different). For Negro boys Highfields was clearly superior. It is not possible to disentangle the separate effects of the various elements in the Highfields programme. But clearly the study proves that a short-term programme can be devised which is at least as effective as the longer training once thought essential for the reform of adolescents with poor backgrounds. Whether Highfields would have been less successful with some other short-term regime, say, disciplinary, it is impossible to know.

The only study on young offenders with evidence contrary to this general trend is the Home Office comparative study. That shows Borstal as having slightly better results than detention centres for offenders with a previous record.

Hammond and Chayen found that different treatments did not appear to affect the reconviction rate for adult persistent criminals. When those who had been given ordinary imprisonment of under four years were compared with preventive detainees serving between five and eight years, the results were remarkably similar. They also found that it made no difference to results whether offenders were given five, six or eight years' preventive detention, or whether they were released after two-thirds or five-sixths of their sentence.

The results of these studies, in general, show that nothing is achieved apart from extra expense (and longer protection of the public in the case of persistent offenders) in providing long rather than shorter periods of institutional treatment. None of the studies, however, give any indication of the optimum period for treatment. Nor do any suggest what particular type of regime is *most* likely to meet with success in the short run. It should be borne in mind, however, that this is a very general conclusion drawn from studies in which the methods of comparing offenders receiving different treatments have been rather rudimentary.

(3) *Open institutions, particularly for the "better type of offender," appear at least as effective as closed treatments*

The Highfields study showed that treatment in an open institution was as successful as at the closed Annandale. Whether the results at Highfields would have been worse had it been closed it is impossible to say as so many other factors differentiated the two institutions; but at least results were not worse. Mannheim and Wilkins compared boys who had been in open Borstals with those who had been in closed ones. After taking account of the fact that there were more worse risks in closed Borstals they found that the open institutions had only a marginally higher success rate for both good and bad risks. This is not very conclusive evidence, and perhaps in some sense disappointing to those who have believed that open institutions are inherently superior to closed ones for young offenders. Certainly there is a great need for more research on this aspect of treatment.

(4) A fourth conclusion rests on the evidence so far offered (especially by Benson, Weeks and Hammond and Chayen) and on a number of other studies: *That overall results are not much different as between different treatments*

The Home Office study, mentioned above, is the only one, to my knowledge, making general comparisons of treatments to give the opposite result: that different treatments do have different effects.

Wilkins compared the reconviction rates of offenders placed on probation by a court using probation in a large proportion of cases with offenders receiving a more normal distribution of punishments from another court.[17] He matched the age and criminal records of the probation cases with offenders dealt with at the other court who were imprisoned, sent to Borstal, fined, discharged or put on probation. He found that, overall, the proportion reconvicted at both courts was the same. "Why," he concluded, "did undoubtedly different treatment policies make little or no difference in subsequent criminal activity?" He suggested "that a larger proportion of offenders who are now sent to prison or borstal could be put on probation without any change in the reconviction rate as a whole, although with the selection of worse risks for probation the gross success rate for probation as a form of treatment might drop." In Israel, Shoham and Sandberg [18] compared the reconviction rates of offenders placed on a suspended sentence with a control group of other prisoners sentenced to other treatments, but excluded any dealt with by imprisonment of over a year. They were able to show which offenders were more likely to succeed on a suspended sentence, but in comparing them with the control group they concluded: "Since the general success rate in the research sample did not differ significantly from the general rate in the control group, we can only conclude that success and failure are more related to the offender's personality than to the type and severity of the sentence he receives." Age and previous criminal history were "the strongest determinants of success . . . *irrespective of the methods of punishment or treatment which were used"* (their italics).

Research in California by Joan Havel [19] has shown that those offenders who are shown by their prediction scores to be "good risks" for not violating parole did just as well when they were given minimum parole supervision as when similar offenders were given normal parole.

These results appear at first sight to be extremely negative, but they do have a positive side as far as treatment decisions are concerned. They show that there are offenders who can be judged as good risks whatever treatment they receive and this would point, as Shoham suggested, to using for them methods which do not involve either incarceration or careful supervision. The implication of both Shoham's and Havel's study is that some offenders can be dealt with in a manner that both avoids institutional contamination for the offender, offers equal protection to the public, saves the time of those engaged in treatment so that they can concentrate on more difficult cases, and saves public money. These offenders are, by and large, those who have little experience of crime and whose offences give no indication of professional criminal activity.

Nevertheless, as was pointed out at the beginning of this short survey of results, the evidence so far is of a very general nature. Although of more use to the penal administrator than no information at all, the studies do pose further questions rather than provide positive answers.

There seem to be three alternative hypotheses that could account for the evidence implying that all treatments give roughly the same results when differences in the offenders sent to them are taken into account. They are:

(i) That the methods of comparing offenders sent to different treatments are so crude that they fail adequately to take account of real differences in the types of offenders given different treatments;

(ii) That while *overall* results are the same, the treatments are each having successes and failures with different types of offenders so that the results balance out to look the same. For example, if treatment "A" gives very good results for offenders with characteristics "xyz" but bad ones for offenders "abc," while on the other hand treatment "B" gives moderate results for both "xyz" and "abc," the *overall* rate of success for each treatment could be the same. The particular appropriateness of treatment "A" for offenders "xyz" would be masked;

(iii) That at present treatments are more or less equally irrelevant. Those who are good risks succeed whatever one does to them, and those who are bad risks (usually with long criminal records) fail whatever is done.

The first hypothesis will be discussed in the methodological section below, but there is evidence to support both hypotheses (ii) and (iii).

(5) *Even if overall success rates for different treatments are much the same they have a different effect on different types of offenders*

Grant and Grant [20] have reported on an evaluation of an experiment in the treatment of naval delinquents in California. In this study there was no need to attempt to make an *ex post facto* matching of offenders given different treatments. The study set out to test a hypothesis that the offender with a high level of inter-personal maturity—that is, having an ability to visualise himself in the role of another person, being aware of the reasons for behaviour, being able to plan ahead and carry out plans, etc.—would respond best to a form of group therapy involving intensive group living. An experiment was set up by which inmates were given personality tests and classified on a scale of inter-personal maturity. They were then allocated to a number of intensive living groups in which they had no contact with other prisoners and where they were therefore forced to face the problems and anxieties of inter-personal relationships. Some groups had only high or low maturity members, in some the maturity levels were mixed. Some groups lasted for six weeks, some for nine. Finally the groups were divided into three types of supervision depending on the intensity of the treatment given—"T" predicted best supervision; "R" predicted next best; "S" predicted worst. Finally some groups were given mixed treatment—some of T, R and S in rotation.

Taking results overall after a short follow-up period (i.e., combining results from the nine and six weeks' courses, high and low maturity groups dealt with separately or mixed up) they show:

Percentage Not 'Reconvicted' Under Different Treatments

	T (Predicted best)	R (Predicted next best)	S (Predicted worst)	Total All Treatments
"High maturity" offenders	70	72	61	68
"Low maturity" offenders	41	55	60	53
All offenders	59	65	61	61

These figures clearly indicate an inter-action between the maturity of the offender and the type of treatment he receives. Overall, results are much the same for all treatments, but mature offenders do better with closed group intensive treatment, the immature with the least demanding S treatment. Wilkins has suggested that the results show that "optimum results would have been obtained by reserving the intensive group therapy for the 'socially mature', and subjecting the 'socially immature' to the simpler (and perhaps emotionally less threatening) retraining routines." [21] However, the inter-action between offender and treatment is highly complex and depended on the composition of the group undergoing treatment. Mature offenders in fact did best in a mixed group (i.e., also with immature); on the other hand, the immature did best when separated and dealt with under S treatment.

The offenders dealt with in this study were mainly men who had been absent without leave and, while the Grants claim they are similar to civilian offenders, the results are probably more valuable as an indication of the value of an experimental approach and of the extent to which overall comparisons between treatments (without looking at the inter-action between types of offender and treatment) can be misleading. This study demonstrates the obvious value of matching offenders to treatments relevant to their needs.

Similar conclusions have been reached by Adams in the PICO project in which a therapeutic programme was tested on "amenable" and "non-amenable" youths and results compared with control groups not receiving therapy. The "amenables" who received therapy had better results than their controls, the "non-amenables" did not—and it was suggested that such treatment may well have been unsuitable for them.[22]

Powers and Witmer also showed that one possible explanation of the lack of difference in the success rates of "treated" and "control" cases in the Cambridge-Somerville Youth Study was that the counselling "treatment" provided was not suitable for disturbed boys.[23] This study is, however, more properly in the field of research on prevention.

Miller's preliminary study of the results of special treatment for institutionalised Borstal boys during after-care provides similar evidence, although without the rigour of an experiment. He compared the reconviction rates of institutionalised homeless boys who had lived in a special small home providing psychiatric oversight and group therapy with those of offenders receiving normal supervision in the community. Evidence so far shows that fewer boys receiving special treatment have been reconvicted than a control group receiving normal after-care. These results are encouraging, for the treatment in the special home is based on a theoretical consideration of what institutionalised offenders need. A previous study by Hood had in fact shown how irrelevant present methods of after-care appear to be for institutionalised offenders. Hood's study attempted to assess, by the follow-up method, the effects of a hypothesised improvement in the after-care arrangements for homeless borstal boys. It had been considered that one of the factors making for a high reconviction rate for these offenders was the relatively poor plans made for their settlement in the community on discharge from borstal. Therefore a special unit was set up to plan for after-care arrangements, particularly in respect of finding a suitable home and work and commencing contact between the boy and his supervisor, before the boy was discharged. Two samples were matched by the prediction method—one not receiving this help, the other getting it. The results showed no improvement in success rates. Why? It was found that the factor most predictive of reconviction was whether a boy had spent over four and a half years in institutions prior to borstal. These boys besides being reconvicted had a dismal history during supervision indicative of social inadequacy. From these results it could be hypothesised that better pre-discharge planning for normal community-based supervision was irrelevant to their needs. The hostel experiment described by Miller does appear as a realistic attempt to help these boys learn to deal adequately with life in the open community.

Most of the research on treatment undoubtedly supports Shoham's generalisation from his study in Israel that "success rates are inversely proportional to the number of previous offences." Although the relationship may be more complicated than this, it nevertheless remains true that all studies show that every treatment is relatively unsuccessful with persistent offenders. One of the major roles that research can play is to study more intensively these "poor risks" in order to produce hypotheses about alternative and perhaps more appropriate treatments for the different types of offenders at present lumped together as the failures of the penal system. The work of Grant and Adams and of others like Andry, who have attempted to develop typologies and relate them to treatment, seems to be the right approach for research. In order to be useful for decision-making purposes typologies must be easily and reliably identified. Grant's methods are perhaps too expensive and Adams' too subjective—he reports that, after a change in personnel making the division into "amenables" and "non-amenables," the proportion put into the former category increased substantially. The use of typological research will depend in England on the willingness of penal authorities to experiment with treatment methods in order to test hypotheses. It may prove expensive but then so is continued crime.

Follow-up studies alone cannot help us understand what elements in treatment are conducive to success and which encourage (or fail to discourage) failure. In order to understand more fully the effects of treatment it is necessary to study the *content* of the treatment and its impact on the treated.

Methodological and Practical Problems

1. CRITERIA FOR ASSESSING THE EFFECTS OF TREATMENT

The first questions to be faced by research on effectiveness of treatment are: By what criteria should success and failure be assessed? Should the same criteria be used for different treatments? When should the judgment be made?

The problem of deciding on appropriate criteria has been much discussed in penological studies and it is intended here only to outline the main arguments.

(a) How Should Success Be Judged?

(i) Reconviction as the Criterion. All studies use reconviction as a criterion of failure whether or not they use additional criteria. There is, however, some

disagreement about *what* reconvictions should be counted. A simple criterion of reconviction tells us nothing of the type of offence, or the circumstances under which it was committed. There is clearly a great deal of difference between petty larceny and robbery with violence; between an offence committed under circumstances of exceptional deprivation and one carried out systematically as a professional activity; between one unfortunate lapse and a continued involvement in crime for gain. Some studies do not make clear whether misdemeanours or only indictable offences are included while others have purposefully not counted such offences as assaults and drunkenness. Yet others have made a return to prison the sole criterion—presumably because this signifies a major transgression. Rose attempted to classify offenders as either "occasional" or "habitual": offenders falling in the former category if they committed less than three offences within five years from leaving borstal and were never sent to prison for longer than six months. It is not at all obvious that such criteria would be accepted by other researchers, especially as the definitions are very elastic—Rose admitting that a more severe judgment would reduce his nonoffender category from 47 to 42 per cent. Other studies, in order to avoid the use of special criteria which made comparisons difficult, have used a single reconviction as the criterion but have elaborated results by giving figures showing the types of offences committed by the failures,[24] or distinguished those who have two or more convictions from the single offenders. McClintock, for example, gave figures in his robbery and crimes of violence studies for offenders who returned after treatment to the same sort of crime.[25] There are, of course, problems of using multiple convictions as a criterion. Two of the major difficulties are that offenders who receive a lengthy sentence for their first crime may not be "at risk" to commit a second, and success or failure after one conviction may be due to the sentence given on that occasion and not to the original treatment. Nevertheless, for offenders who are very poor risks for treatment, there is a case for describing as successful those who only collect one conviction (as long as it is not a major crime).

There remains the perennial problem that offenders may commit crimes but never be caught. In their study of robberies, McClintock and Gibson point out that the fact that the "professionals" have the lowest reconviction rate must be looked on with suspicion, for it suggests ability to avoid arrest.[26] The same fact may account for Garrity's finding that the "right guy" (the real professional) tended to have low reconviction rates after imprisonment.

(*ii*) *Criteria Other Than Reconviction*. It has been argued that treatments, especially those aimed at reforming the offender, are intended to do more than simply ensure avoidance of reconviction. They are, for example, supposed to provide trade training, develop constructive uses of leisure, improve attitudes towards authority, educate, improve personal relationships, make the inadequate more adequate. If research is to try to measure success in terms of these criteria is it possible to compare the effects of treatments which have different objectives? Offenders are placed on probation (theoretically) because they are considered to need supervision to help solve their personal problems, whereas fines are intended to have a punitive effect. By simply comparing reconviction rates are we not ignoring the main effect that probation was intended to achieve? The validity of this argument rests on the extent to which reconviction is correlated with these other measures. If success by other measures is highly correlated with success as measured by reconviction, a comparison of reconviction results will not be misleading.

Many studies have not found it possible to compare different criteria simply because without a period of supervision the data are not available. Hood, in his study of homeless Borstal boys, examined data on work habits, residential stability, leisure pursuits and response to supervision. Analysis showed that criteria of failure based on these factors were highly intercorrelated with each other and with reconviction. Measurement of failure by reconviction criteria would, by and large, identify the failures by other criteria. Rumney and Murphy in their interesting long-term follow-up of probation cases also found that criteria of deterioration and lack of adjustment were highly correlated with recidivism.[27] A recent study of parolees in California gave similar results.[28] This does not mean that attempts to measure the effectiveness of vocational training on work records or of training on attitudes to the after-care supervisor should not be investigated. There are areas of treatment which are intended to influence the offender: we do not know enough about whether they do so. Studies of Borstal boys, for example, indicate that few take up their trade on release and follow it for a continuous period of time.[29]

Grünhut has observed: "Reconvictions, though recorded as objective facts, have no conclusive relevance to an assessment of a former offender's career." Indeed it is perfectly true that a dichotomous criterion of success or failure does not allow any assessment to be made of the extent to which treatment has improved or deteriorated the offender's chances of reform. It may be a sign of success rather than failure that a man, although still liable to an occasional property offence, is no longer involved in violent or aggressive crime; or that the persistent thief is able to live for longer periods without stealing; or the inadequate who has been seeking the harbour of institutions is enabled to live for increasingly longer periods in the community without continuous support. It may be a sign of failure that the embezzling former bank clerk, although keeping out of the courts, finds himself drifting from one low-paid job to another after imprisonment. Clearly such criteria need to be developed. Rumney and Murphy made an interesting start in a relatively crude way that has not been followed, to my knowledge, elsewhere. Nor will it be while research is based on records of offenders—to develop such criteria will need intensive interviewing techniques.

Reconviction should, however, remain the main criterion—although be more refined in terms of the types of offences committed. Treatment is not given to make the offender a "better person" simply on the grounds of humanity but because it is considered that if he is a better person—in work habits, leisure pursuits and personal relations, etc.—he will be less likely to offend again. The acid test is his ability to "go straight."

A high correlation between other criteria of success and avoidance of reconviction should not be taken as proof of a causal relationship. Hood found that boys who stayed in their first job after Borstal, who stayed settled at one address and reported regularly to their supervisor usually also avoided reconviction, while those with the opposite behaviour did not. Does this mean that the job, home and reporting helped them to avoid reconviction? Or is success by these other criteria simply symptomatic of a desire to avoid getting into trouble again? Only research aimed at assessing the attitudes and reactions of the offender to treatment can provide answers to these alternative hypotheses.

(b) When Should Success Be Judged?

Should success be judged while treatment is still in progress or only after it has been terminated? There has been a tendency in considering results of institutional treatment to disregard that additional part of the treatment involving supervision (i.e., after-care) of the offender on his release from the institution. It has been traditional to regard offenders as failures if they have been reconvicted at any time after discharge from training, notwithstanding that supervision is considered an extension of the same treatment. While in the institution, no one has suggested that misbehaviour should be used as a criterion of failure: it would be asserted that the training process should be judged at its completion and that misbehaviour and the sanctions taken were but part of that process. At the moment, the effect of after-care is not being taken into account in the assessment of success simply because difficulties which occur under supervision in the community entail public, not institutional, law enforcement. This is not necessarily a sufficient reason for judging the whole process at a premature stage. There is a case for not making the assessment of success before supervision is completed. For example, those reconvicted during the period of the prob.. 'on order or attendance centre order who afterwards satisfactorily completed treatment were judged as "successes" in the Cambridge studies.

Finally, there is the important question of how long a follow-up period should be before results are assessed. Most studies take a two- or three-year period after treatment has ended; others regard five years as essential. A few studies have a variable follow-up period, sometimes with offenders being assessed after only a few months at liberty. This should be avoided since all offenders do not have an equal period at risk for reconviction, and analysis of results comparing successes and failures becomes suspect.

The work of Mannheim and Wilkins and McClintock indicates a possibility of estimating what proportion of offenders who will finally be reconvicted will actually receive their reconvictions during shorter follow-up periods. Mannheim and Wilkins show that "three or four years after release about 80 per cent of Borstal boys who will ever fail will have failed; that after one year only half the eventual failures will have failed; that nevertheless experience tables based on one year's follow-up yield results in all respects similar to those based on 80 per cent of the data." In other words, on the basis of reconviction figures collected one year after release it was possible to discriminate between those who would be successes and those who would be failures after three years, and that the actual results for three years' follow-up could be obtained simply by multiplying the failure rate for each risk group of boys by 1.7 times. McClintock's study of crimes of violence also shows that for offenders under 21 sent to all forms of treatment 77 per cent of those who would be reconvicted after five years had already been reconvicted after two.

Studies with short follow-up periods should only be compared with those having longer periods after a correction has been made to allow for the different intervals. For example, Grünhut compared the results of his study of probationers undergoing mental treatment with the results for ordinary probationers reported in the Cambridge study and found them to be about the same (about 12 per cent being reconvicted respectively). However, Grünhut's follow-up was one year and the Cambridge study three years. We might expect the comparison therefore to be invalid and the figure for mental cases after three years to be somewhere in the region of 20 per cent.

The fact that it appears possible to predict success after about one year is not (as Wilkins points out) without significance. When there is a need to try to keep the evidence from studies as up to date as possible there is certainly an advantage in knowing that results after one year can be used for comparative purposes.

2. METHODS OF COMPARING OFFENDERS
GIVEN DIFFERENT TREATMENTS

The major problem for studies which rely for data on recorded information is to provide a method for comparing offenders sentenced to different treatments. One wishes to be able to estimate what would have happened to an offender if he had received any other treatment than the one he actually received.

The most obvious method for dealing with this problem is the "matching" technique. But, as Wilkins has recently pointed out, it is of limited value in criminology—"the number of factors which might be matched is usually large, but it is necessary to select one or two whose validity is assumed rather than tested." The more powerful and efficient way of dealing with the problem is by using prediction methods which employ regression analysis. Prediction equations relate information about the offenders to their chances of being reconvicted. Some factors will be highly prognostic of success and some of failure. The regression analysis produces the best discrimination that is possible with the available data between those with a combination of factors that are related to success and those with factors highly prognostic of failure. Offenders are classed in terms of their relative chances or "risks" of reconviction following treatment. It should therefore be possible by using prediction equations to determine whether those sent to one treatment are worse risks than those sent to another. In fact, prediction equations have been used for comparative purposes in three ways:

(i) Offenders receiving one treatment have been classified on a prediction equation developed for another treatment. This is what Sir George Benson did in comparing young prisoners with Borstal inmates. Using this method he was, in effect, saying: imagine that those boys sent to prison had been sent to Borstal, what would their chances of success have been and how does it compare with their actual success rate? From this study it seems that the factors which predict different rates of success after Borstal predicted corresponding rates after imprisonment. It was, therefore, a reasonable inference that the treatments had similar effects. However, had Benson's study shown different rates of success for the young prisoners he could not have measured their relative success or failure in terms of the Borstal prediction equation. All that could reasonably have been inferred was that the effect of imprisonment was different from that of Borstal. To discover whether its results compared with Borstal were better or worse, a separate equation would have to be worked out for young prisoners. This is what the second method involves.

(ii) Separate prediction equations can be calculated for each treatment and the probabilities of reconviction for comparable offenders under different treatments contrasted. One might, for example, find that those who are good risks for treatment A do even better under treatment B, with reverse results for bad risks. With sufficient separate prediction equations this may prove a practical possibility. At the moment it is not, notwithstanding the tremendous efforts of the Gluecks in this direction.[30]

(iii) The method used by Mannheim and Wilkins and by Weeks in the Highfields study was to work out a combined prediction table for all boys undergoing treatment and to compare the results achieved by different treatments. This is the most developed method and the recent Home Office comparison between "expected" and "actual" reconviction rates for different treatments, although not a prediction study, uses the same logic (i.e., reconviction rates are calculated for all offenders of certain types (e.g., first offenders, male, aged 17–21), subject to *all* treatments. The *actual* (observed) reconviction rate for each treatment is then calculated and compared with the overall rate. The "observed" rate for each treatment would be the same as the overall rate ("expected" rate) if all treatments were equally successful.

The analysis by Mannheim and Wilkins in comparing results for boys trained in open and closed Borstals illustrates the method of prediction-matching, its value and possible limitations. The summarised results of this analysis are shown in the following table.

Wilkins came to the conclusion that, taking into account the fact that more of the good risks went to open Borstals, they still produced a success rate 8 per cent higher than closed Borstals. Two hypotheses were offered. Wilkins argued that the difference was probably due to treatment while Martin suggested that the results were better in open institutions because of the high proportion of good risk boys there having a good effect on each other.[31] But as Morrison,[32] among others, has pointed out, there is a third possibility. The boys in closed Borstals may have really been worse than those in open Borstals. If, for example, those sent to closed Borstals had more anti-authoritarian attitudes, were less amenable to persuasion, were more likely to abscond,

Comparison of Success Rates for Open
and Closed Borstals in Respect of
Offenders with Different Prognoses

Risk Category	Success Rate (%)		
	Open	Closed	Excess Success In Open Borstals
Good, A B	78	67	11
Average X	61	56	5
Poor C D	38	28	10
All cases	58	36	22

then there would be differences that one would hypothesise could both make closed confinement more necessary and make the cases more difficult to influence. Such a hypothesis is untestable because of lack of data.

There are two factors which suggest that prediction matching of this kind is a crude device which may obscure real differences in the effects of treatment on different types of offenders or lead to results little better than broad generalisations. These are: the inadequacy of the data available in records on offenders for sophisticated research, and the possibility that regression analysis is not the most appropriate statistical tool.

(a) The Adequacy of Records for Treatment Research

An almost universally reported finding of researchers who have used documents as research evidence is that certain information was missing in a considerable proportion of the files studied. Mannheim and Wilkins state, "we were faced with the problem that, for a large proportion of the cases, information which we had cause to believe might be valuable could not be found." [33] McClintock who has considerable research experience with records writes: "There is a paucity of information, especially for the post-war years, concerning the personal characteristics and social background of delinquents in general." [34] The Morrises in their study of Pentonville prison similarly found the records of very limited value.[35] Missing information causes particular problems of bias in analysis. For Borstal boys it was found that for those for whom information was not available reconviction rates were highest. Grünhut attempted to follow up 636 probationers undergoing mental treatment. He only found sufficient information to relate characteristics of offenders to reconviction in 393 cases. This kind of bias needs to be taken into account in interpreting results.

But not only are the data which are available haphazardly recorded; there is evidence to suggest that information on some topics is hardly available at all. In a recent (unpublished) study of the records of approved school boys Hood found that there was a great deal of bias in the records towards information about offences and family background. There were little data about the offender's involvement with his peers either in general or specifically in relation to his delinquency. Criminological theory suggests that these data could be of importance in relation to treatment results.

With such poor data available argument has centred around what sections of it are reliable enough for use. Wilkins has strongly taken Rose to task for making subjective and unrepeatable interpretations from case-work records. While this seems to be the correct position if research is to be validated and the relevant information precisely defined for the administrator, Morrison is surely also correct in pointing out that "so-called 'factual' data are often subject to various sources of contamination and are also, if to a lesser extent, unreliable." [36]

The results of comparative research recently published by the Home Office provide an example of the problems which poor records pose. The Home Office are careful to point out that the facts about the circumstances of offenders used to calculate the expected rates relate to the offenders' criminal history—there being little information available about their social circumstances. As they suggest, "The courts may have made allowance for factors not recorded in the documents available for research, and the possibility cannot be ignored that particular sentences may have been used more frequently for the 'worse' or for the 'better' offenders in any of the categories studied." In other words, the results should be treated with a great deal of caution. McClintock in *Crimes of Violence* [37] studied the reconviction rates of first offenders and recidivists sentenced to various penal measures and noted that the rates of reconviction for both first offenders and recidivists were lower for those fined and discharged than for those imprisoned or placed on probation. He concluded from a close study of the records that in fact those fined or discharged had mostly been convicted of an offence arising from loss of temper in a quarrel with a well-known acquaintance. The magistrates were therefore selecting for these punishments offenders who were less likely to be reconvicted despite the external similarity of their records in respect of type of offence, age and previous convictions. In his study of attendance centres McClintock compared results for those who were at the same time on probation with those serving only the attendance centre sentence. Even when an adjustment was made (by using a prediction table) for differences in the penal and social backgrounds of the two groups of offenders the failure rate for those on probation was still significantly higher than for those not on probation (48 per cent compared with 34 per cent). McClintock draws the following conclusion: "Two interpretations seem possible—either probation is *causing* the failure rate to increase or various factors other than those included in the investigation have influenced the magistrate in placing the boy on probation. The latter seems the more probable conclusion . . ." [38] As the Home Office study is based on less data than the Cambridge studies cited it would seem premature to suggest that the results are any better than preliminary indications of what *might* be done if sufficient data were available. Before comparative research on treatments that have already been imposed can provide more convincing data than that published in *The Sentence of the Court,* records must be improved. As Wilkins and Macnaughten-Smith point out, if relevant information is restricted, the estimations of success will lack power "since really distinct individuals will be lumped together if the information which should distinguish them is lacking." In their recent comparison of young prisoners and Borstal trainees they could find only 13 items of information common to the records of both groups.[39] If it is not possible to improve records, research designs making use of them might as well be abandoned.

(b) Methods of Statistical Analysis

Regression methods in prediction equations presume a homogeneous population. From what we know of the Borstal population, for example, it is far from homogeneous in any sense other than a basic similarity in criminal history as measured by numbers of previous convictions. Would one expect the aggressive psychopath to react to training in the same way as the socially inadequate or the socialised delinquent from a criminal area? If not, there is a need for techniques that both distinguish such "types" and are capable of showing the sort of interaction between types of offender and types of treatment.

The method of prediction equations has been to correlate factors which occur in the background of all delinquents undergoing the treatment with the criterion. If a factor added no power to the discrimination between success and failure it would be discarded. Gibbens, Pond and Stafford-Clark have shown that such a method can conceal correlations which exist between the factor and criterion for *some offenders only.*[40] In following up a group of criminal psychopaths they examined the prognostic value of the E.E.G. They found that, overall, abnormality of E.E.G. in psychopaths was not related to recidivism. However, when they distinguished between aggressive and inadequate psychopaths they found that abnormality in aggressive psychopaths was related to a bad prognosis while for inadequates to a good prognosis—the two opposing trends cancelling each other out in psychopaths as a whole. If this was true for a relatively homogeneous group such as these, would it not be even more true for the general populations of Borstal and other treatments?

There is evidence to suggest that the broad grouping of offenders in prediction equations contains a number of distinguishable groups of offenders each with a different risk of reconviction. Gibbens in a study of Borstal boys examined offenders who were in Mannheim-Wilkins prediction category C (66 per cent expected to be reconvicted). He found that when these offenders were classified further as "psychiatric," "problem" and "normal" the reconviction rates for each group within the prediction category were different,[41] and that predictions could be improved with the help of clinical evidence. In his study of homeless borstal boys Hood also applied the Mannheim-Wilkins equation. It was found that the equation did not discriminate between the successes and failures because these boys did worse than expected in each risk category. Clearly they made up a higher proportion of failures than some other types of offender falling within the same risk group. Within any one broad risk group established by studies of total treatment populations it should therefore be possible to identify a number of different types of offender each with a different probability of reconviction.

The prediction categories established regression techniques for all persons undergoing a treatment therefore obscures both the possibility that improved predictions can be made for different types of offenders and that they may react differently to different treatments. Benson's study and the comparison of open and closed Borstal results provide a good example of this. Benson showed that in the Mannheim-Wilkins group C, 66 per cent were reconvicted among both Borstal inmates and young prisoners. This is, as shown already, a crude comparison. Are the boys who fail in borstal the same as those who fail in prison? Or are there some boys who fail after prison who would succeed after Borstal and *vice-versa*—the compensating results giving a similar overall figure? And most important, are there ways of discovering who these offenders are and identifying them in a precise enough way?

New methods aimed at developing typologies of offenders and relating these to treatment outcome are likely to be more helpful. But as Wilkins has said, prediction methods have never claimed to be anything better than a crude tool—but better than no tool at all: "Prediction . . . when appropriately used, will help with *some* of the tasks, but every instrument of research is limited. The microscope is not a substitute for the thermometer; a stop watch will not measure blood pressure. Prediction methods are like thermometers, they tell us better than hand-on-brow techniques which offenders are 'hot.' " [42]

This analysis has made it clear that the key to progress in treatment research is the development of typologies, both of offenders and treatments. These typologies should be based in the first place on treatment theory. What kinds of people would respond best to discipline, counselling, therapy, fining, intensive case-work, limited supervision? And to what sort of discipline, how big a fine, and what length of treatment?

It has been shown that in recourse to records, studies are severely hampered by scarcity of data. Where data are now being collected purely for research purposes, such as in the Home Office probation project, it is interesting to see that one of the first priorities has been to study typologies of offenders and typologies of treatment. [43] Eclecticism in research is extremely wasteful and is bad scientific method. The choice of data must rest upon a hypothesis (or hypotheses) about their relevance to treatment. The value of such typologies that are constructed can then be empirically tested by their usefulness in distinguishing between the successes and failures of different treatment methods.

One other approach to the typology problem (especially where records have to be used) is to use statistical methods which will classify data into more homogeneous groups than regression methods do. The methods called "prognostic configuration analysis" by Glaser,[44] "predictive matching on the biological method" by Belson,[45] and "predictive attribute analysis" by Wilkins and Macnaughten-Smith [46] all have this in common. Briefly, the object of the method is to try to take into account the problem of a factor being correlated with recidivism for one group of offenders while the reverse is the case for another group, so that the factor does not appear as a predictor of recidivism for the whole population. The technique goes some way towards avoiding the pitfalls of lumping together offenders when they are *really* different. Among any population undergoing treatment these methods should discriminate more clearly between homogeneous groups of offenders than the current prediction techniques. As more data are included, these techniques should make prediction methods more powerful and allow more meaningful comparisons between treatments.

3. THE CONSTANCY OF RESULTS

To what extent can one rely on research carried out in the past? How valid are research results over time?

The Sentence of the Court states that the consistency of results achieved over a period of time between different studies "is encouraging." But there is alternative evidence which suggests that to take a sample from one year may give atypical results. McClintock showed that for offenders convicted of violence in 1950 and 1957 results were very different. Among first offenders under 21 sentenced in 1950, 16 per cent of those fined and 29 per cent of those placed on probation were reconvicted. Figures for comparable offenders sentenced in 1957 were 35 and 19 per cent respectively.[47]

One needs also to be aware that since some of the studies mentioned in this chapter were carried out there have been changes both in the nature of the treatments provided and in the types of offenders sent to them. For example, Grünhut's study of senior detention centre results concerned the offenders committed to the first centres opened. Since then the number of senior centres has increased from one to twelve and the sorts of boys sent to them have probably changed. At the time of his study 22 per cent had no previous convictions. In 1961 the proportion had fallen to 14 per cent, while 60 per cent had three or more previous convictions and a third had five or more (no equivalent figures are available for 1955). It is possible that developments in the system together with the intake of more difficult inmates could have invalidated his findings. The more recent applications to Borstal boys of the Mannheim-Wilkins prediction equation (based on data of boys sentenced in 1947 and a validation sample from 1948 cases) illustrate the same point. Gibbens found that it did not discriminate between the successes and failures among a sample of London boys sent to borstal in 1955.[48] The reason was either that London boys were different from a national sample of boys and/or that factors which were related to recidivism after borstal treatment in

1947/48 were not so related after treatment in 1955. Two recent prediction tables devised for boys at attendance centres and for men undergoing preventive detention were found not to discriminate between successes and failures in the same way when a validation study was carried out. Hammond and Chayen examined their results in detail and found that employment and psychological factors which had been related to recidivism in their first study were not so related in the validatory sample. By re-working the prediction they were able to restore the power of the prediction instrument.[49]

Despite the fact that prediction equations are classifying instruments they have been used in an attempt to assess the results of treatment over a time span. For example, a number of persons have attempted to understand the decline in the general success rate of the Borstal system by examining the prediction scores of new inmates. They have found two things. First, that there is a higher proportion of boys in the bad risk groups, secondly, all risk groups have a higher reconviction rate than in the original study. The interpretation is that boys are getting more difficult to train. Is it justified? Mannheim and Wilkins and Hammond and Chayen are at pains to point out that a prediction equation is not really a prediction, it is a forecast on the basis of past experience—the proof of the pudding is in the extent to which it gives the same predictions on a new sample. If it does not give the same predictions one cannot say that boys are getting worse or better, but simply that the factors formerly related to success after treatment are no longer so related. Alan Little has shown how the fact that drunkenness is no longer such a limited phenomenon among adolescents (and it has a very high correlation with failure in the original study) is one of the main reasons for more boys falling into the worse risk categories on the Mannheim-Wilkins equation.[50] It may also be that over time such factors as job instability could cease to be such effective predictors of failure. As social values change so may the variables predicting recidivism.[51] As treatment changes (and there have been some major changes in Borstal treatment since 1948) so the "experience" being predicted changes and new tables are called for. What is needed is the publication of the results of a continuous sequential prediction analysis if results are to be up-to-date.

Not only may the inmates change and the treatment change over time, but also the action of the courts in making decisions based on prediction studies may affect results. In the words of the Home Office booklet: "If the courts at present making relatively little use of the sentences which appear to be the most 'successful' were to use them more, it is unlikely that they would lose their effectiveness. On the other hand, if the courts now making most use of these sentences were to use them even more frequently, it is possible that they might not give such good results as at present. Such changes in sentencing practice would have to be checked by further research." [52]

If we wish to progress with treatment methods we must accept that research will be a continuous process of evaluation and re-evaluation. Constant results over time at this stage of treatment research will signify lack of such progress.

NOTES

1. B. Wootton (1963), *Crime and the Criminal Law*.
2. L. T. Wilkins (1962), "Criminology: An Operational Research Approach." In A. T. Welford (Ed.), *Society, Problems and Methods of Study*.
3. *Ibid.*, p. 320.
4. Leon Radzinowicz (1945), "After-Conduct of Convicted Offenders in England," in L. Radzinowicz and J. W. C. Turner (Eds.), *The Modern Approach to Criminal Law*.
5. Cambridge Studies in Criminal Science (1958), *The Results of Probation;* M. Grünhut (1963), *Probation and Mental Treatment;* H. Mannheim and L. T. Wilkins (1955), *Prediction Methods in Relation to Borstal Training;* A. G. Rose (1954), *Rive Hundred Borstal Boys;* T. C. N. Gibbens (1962), *Psychiatric Studies of Borstal Lads;* R. G. Andry (1963), *The Short-Term Prisoner;* F. H. McClintock (1961); *Attendance Centres;* M. Grünhut (1960), "After-Effects of Punitive Detention," *Brit. J. Delinq., X,* 178; W. H. Hammond and E. Chayen (1963), *Persistent Criminals*.
6. D. A. Ogden (1954), "A Borstal Typological Survey." *Brit. J. Delinq.* V. 99.
7. A. G. Rose, *op. cit.*, pp. 120–122.
8. D. Garrity (1961), "The Prison as a Rehabilitation Agency." In D. Cressey (Ed.), *The Prison*.
9. R. G. Hood (1968), *The Borstal System* (Unpublished University of Cambridge Ph.D. thesis to be published shortly).
10. R. G. Andry, *op. cit.*, pp. 103 ff.
11. For example this is implied in *The Results of Probation, op. cit.*
12. M. Grünhut, *Probation and Mental Treatment*, pp. 31–32 and 42–43.
13. Home Office (1964), *The Sentence of the Court*, pp. 40 ff.
14. Sir George Benson (1959), "Prediction Methods and Young Prisoners," *Brit. J. Delinq., IX,* 192.
15. *Prediction Methods and Borstal Training*, pp. 111–133.
16. H. A. Weeks (1958), *Youthful Offenders at Highfields*. See also L. W. McCorkle, et al. (1958), *The Highfields Story*.
17. L. T. Wilkins (1958), "A Small Comparative Study of the Results of Probation," *Brit. J. Delinq., VIII,* 201.
18. S. Shoham and M. Sandberg (1964), "Suspended Sentences in Israel," *Crime and Delinquency*, Jan. 1964, p. 74.
19. J. Havel (1961?), "The High Base Expectancy Study," SIPU 4. Research Division, Department of Corrections, State of California.
20. J. D. and M. Q. Grant (1959), "A Group Dynamics Approach to the Treatment of Nonconformists in the Navy," *Annals*, March 1959, 126. See also M. Q. Grant (1961), "Interaction between Kinds of Treatment and Kinds of Delinquents." In *Inquiries Concerning Kinds of Treatment for Kinds of Delinquents*, California Board of Corrections, Monograph No. 2.
21. In "Criminology: An Operational Research Approach," *op. cit.*, p. 319.
22. S. Adams (1961), "Interaction between Individual Interview Therapy and Treatment Amenability in Older Youth Authority Wards," in California Board of Corrections, Monograph No. 2, *op. cit.*
23. E. Powers and H. Witmer (1951), *An Experiment in the Prevention of Delinquency*.
24. For example, W. H. Hammond and E. Chayen, *op. cit.*; R. G. Hood, *op. cit.*
25. F. H. McClintock (1963), *Crimes of Violence*.
26. F. H. McClintock and E. Gibson (1961), *Robbery in London*.
27. J. Rumney and J. P. Murphy (1952), *Probation and Social Adjustment*.
28. R. B. Richardson (1961?), "A Pilot Investigation of Parole Follow-up Criteria," Research Report No. 9, Department of Corrections, California.
29. See Home Office (1962), *Work and Vocational Guidance in Borstal*, and R. G. Hood's figures for homeless cases, *op. cit.*

30. S. and E. Glueck (1959), *Predicting Delinquency and Crime*, especially Appendix B.

31. J. P. Martin (1955), Review in Case Conference.

32. R. L. Morrison (1955), "Predictive Research. A Critical Assessment of Its Practical Implications," *Brit. J. Delinq.*, VI, 99. Also, Symposium on Predictive Methods in the same issue.

33. *Op. cit.*, p. 58.

34. *Attendance Centres*, p. 63, fn. 1.

35. T. and P. Morris, *op. cit.*, p. 114.

36. R. L. Morrison, *op. cit.*, p. 107.

37. *Op. cit.*, p. 172.

38. *Op. cit.*, pp. 95–96.

39. L. T. Wilkins and P. Macnaughten-Smith (1964) "New Prediction and Classification Methods in Criminology," *J. Res. Cr. and Delinq.*, 1, 19.

40. T. C. N. Gibbens, D. A. Pond, and D. Stafford-Clark (1955), "A Follow-up Study of Criminal Psychopaths," *Brit. J. Delinq.*, VI, 126.

41. *Psychiatric Studies of Borstal Lads*, Appendix A.

42. See "Criminology: An Operational Research Approach," *op. cit.*, p. 318.

43. Comparisons of young offenders sent to detention centres, borstals and prisons are now being made on the basis of data collected by interview methods—with particular emphasis on psychological characteristics of offenders. See C. Banks (1964), "Reconviction of Young Offenders," *Current Legal Problems*.

44. D. Glaser (1961), "Parole Follow-up Studies in the Federal Correctional System." In *Research in Probation, Parole and Delinquency Prediction* (N.Y. School of Social Work). See also R. Metzner and G. Weil, "Predicting Recidivism: Base Rates for Massachusetts Correctional Institution Concord," *J. Crim. Law and Criminol.*, 54, 307.

45. W. A. Belson (1959), "Matching and Prediction on the Principles of Biological Classification," *Applied Statistics*, VIII, 65.

46. *Op. cit.*

47. *Op. cit.*, Table 94, p. 171.

48. *Psychiatric Studies of Borstal Lads*, Appendix A.

49. *Op. cit.*, pp. 171–176.

50. A. Little (1962), "Borstal Success and the Quality of Borstal Inmates," *Brit. J. Criminol.*, 2, 271.

51. See D. M. Gottfredson and J. A. Bonds (1961), "Systematic Study of Experience as an Aid to Decisions." Research Report No. 2. Department of Corrections, California.

52. *The Sentence of the Court*, para. 164.

16: Correctional Research: An Elusive Paradise / *Daniel Glaser*

Abandoned Utopias

From time to time in the past few decades, research offices have been established in correctional agencies and assigned the task of procuring facts for the

From Daniel Glaser, "Correctional Research: An Elusive Paradise," *Journal of Research in Crime and Delinquency* 2:1 (January 1965): 3; 5–8.

guidance of correctional decisions. Like other Utopian colonies, these offices either disappeared quickly or survived only by a metamorphosis in their goals and practices, through which they ceased to be a force for change. The research movement, however, is still with us, and there are signs that it may have a continuing impact on correction. A survey of its recent history can provide source material for new exhortations to mobilize research on the effective handling of criminals. It may also stimulate research on the integration of research with practice.

Terrors and Temptations

Are the new research establishments any more successful than the older ones at achieving the goal of scientifically guided correctional practice? Do they have any more influence on the treatment of criminals than did the sociologist-actuaries, or the correctional "head-count" statisticians?

To some extent, the developments which vitiated older endeavors have recurred in the new research efforts. One or more researchers in almost every one of the half-dozen correctional systems which conduct the most extensive evaluative research have, at one time or another in recent years, informed me of the suppression of their research reports. In some state correctional systems it is quite evident that research units have been largely coöpted into service of the *status quo,* for they have abandoned longitudinal evaluative statistics compilation in favor of "head counts" only.

The reasons for this are quite obvious. Correctional officials procure financial appropriations for their agency by convincing the legislature that their programs protect society, either by incapacitating criminals or by changing them into noncriminals. When research confirms these claims, the officials are happy to promulgate the findings. Frequently, however, research has indicated that added appropriations to make treatment more effective, by reducing caseloads, hiring more psychiatrists, etc., have made no difference in post-treatment criminality or may even have increased it. Time-study analysis of the average hours per week which presumed treatment personnel actually spend in what might be considered treatment activity almost invariably yields a figure which the public would find surprisingly low. These are types of research findings which agency heads are reluctant to release.

There have been two styles of research suppression in correctional agencies. One style not only prohibits release of the report, but cancels further research as dangerous to the agency's "public image," or as the British express it, "embarrassing to the Minister." The real problem usually is that some officials, just above the researchers in a staff hierarchy, feel threatened by negative findings; the Minister or his American equivalent never hears of the research.

A more constructive style of research suppression involves the insistence of higher officials that there be further research before any results are released. This may simply be an enlargement of the sample, often to cover a more recent time period, on the usually spurious assumption that the treatment services studied have been getting better all the time. Frequently it is a reanalysis, perhaps requiring additional data, to permit cross-tabulations, perhaps leading to inferences as to the conditions under which the treatment studied is ineffective and the conditions under which it is effective. Reanalysis of this sort often indicates, roughly speaking, that special treatment services succeed in reducing failure rates appreciably only for "middle risk" cases; the least criminal cases have a low failure rate with or without special services; the highly criminal or unstable cases often fool and exploit treatment personnel or get unrealistic expectations from special training, so their long-run failure rates are higher following some of the special measures than after traditional programs.[1]

In some projects, reanalysis of research has involved an alteration of the criterion by which a program is evaluated. For example, cases given special treatment often compare much more favorably with cases not receiving this treatment if the two groups are evaluated by "total *time* reconfined" during a given period after release, rather than by "*per cent of cases* reconfined." [2] The reason is that special programs often reduce the *speed* with which released offenders get into further difficulty with the law more markedly than they reduce the proportion who eventually get into difficulty.

Occasionally the release of research results is deferred long enough for the officials involved to realize that any results can be interpreted favorably if the program is given multiple goals, such as "treatment" and "control." Under these circumstances, a more rapid return of cases to incarceration is credited to "control," but a less rapid return would have been credited to "treatment." This "heads I win" and "tails you lose" arrangement achieves the gambler's dream, for the state does have this dual objective, although ideally it would achieve control by successful treatment.[3]

Some research reports from correctional agencies are not suppressed, but might as well be, for few officials—or even researchers—can understand them. Most notable among such reports are those which describe the use of various types of multiple correlation or multiple association statistical analysis of case data in administrative records to find guides for correctional operations. These reports are submitted to correctional officials who do not understand the statistical terminology and who feel no urgency to learn to understand it since the researchers share with the operations officials the impression that this statistical analysis has little or no practical value at present. Thus, these researchers operate in a separate world, inadequately linked either with the university social system, which seems to be their reference group, or with the leaders of the correctional system, which they are presumed to serve.

It is a statistical maxim, in most behavioral science problems, that with strong data you can use weak methods; the strong methods (e.g., factor analysis) are useful primarily to squeeze a suggestion of relationship out of weak data. Strong relationships can be demonstrated adequately with simple tables of percentages. Perhaps the high intelligence and dedicated effort invested in research into statistical methods would be more fruitful to the correctional system if they were employed not so much in seeking new methods of analysis for old types of data (that can be left to mathematical statisticians in the universities, who can be hired as consultants), but preferably in obtaining new types of data, derived from closer study and greater involvement in correctional operations. Furthermore, greater confidence in the reliability of correctional research results generally is gained by obtaining a redundancy of data, by procuring similar findings independently from several correctional situations, and by having several alternative indices of the key variables, than by mere statistical tests which assume the absence of bias in sampling or measurement.

Progress from Pitfalls

In the long run, I believe, the paradise lost is most likely to be regained by controlled experiments. In the past two decades we have had many evangelical movements, from Cambridge-Somerville to SIPU and beyond, vainly preaching salvation by experimentation. The earlier sects repeatedly assembled the faithful to await miracles—and then disappointed them. Many of the sins we have been ascribing to correctional research grew out of frustration from experimentation. Yet negative or inconclusive results are but trials by which these pilgrims to the shrines of science are tested. They still may progress toward grace if they recognize past sins and seek salvation through new research design.

The value of experiments, when comparing two ways of handling offenders, is that they reduce the prospect of statistically uncontrolled variables accounting for the findings obtained. As an extreme example, consider a comparison of prison and probation. The higher rate of return to crime following imprisonment may not mean that prison is a more criminalizing experience than release on probation would be, but that most offenders receiving imprisonment are more criminalized when sentenced than are most who receive probation. Even if we compare only prison and probation cases that are matched by every index considered relevant (number of previous arrests, age, employment record, marital status, and so forth), it is possible that within each category of classification by these variables the judges have differentially selected worse risk cases for prison and better risk cases for probation, employing some subjective indices or weights not taken into account by the researchers' categories. Sometimes researchers have reason for inferring that such judicial perspicacity does not prevail, an inference suggested by the superiority of statistical to case study prediction.[4] Nevertheless, judges and top correctional officials are not readily convinced by such indirect evidence. Only when they are willing to have an appreciable number of treatment decisions made by purely random selection can we sharply increase everyone's confidence that differences in the subsequent behavior of offenders are due to differences dependent on the correctional treatment to which they were assigned, rather than due to selection variables. But even this is not an easy path to knowledge.

The history of medicine is marked not only by major progress through experimentation, but also great resistance to such experimentation. People refuse to be in a control group if they know this means they are denied a treatment which they presume is helpful, or they refuse to be in an experimental group receiving a treatment whose worth still is unestablished. There are also confounding variables which render experimental results inconclusive. For example, the "placebo effect"—which sociologists know as the "Hawthorne effect"—arises from the fact that the special attention given any group just by their being studied can alter their lives in a more influential way than the treatment being investigated.

These familiar difficulties of medical research recur in correctional research, but often only the physician has checks against them. For example, medical researchers use the double-blind technique of randomly mixing medication with placebos, so that even the persons administering the drugs do not know which is which. In correctional research (as in such medical fields as psychiatry, surgery, and physical therapy), treatments cannot be readily masked. Furthermore, if several programs are provided at one location, both staff and subjects may have strong feelings about alleged reasons for differential treatment of control and experimental cases, and these feelings may have an impact on treatment results. If two programs are operated at different locations, there may be many other uncontrolled situational variables. Experimentation can nevertheless go on, but the prospect that confounding factors affect the results makes the repetition of experiments in many places highly desirable.

In addition to these parallels to problems in medical research, special research problems arise from the extent to which correctional treatment still is administered in a tradition of punishment and adjudication, and frequently in a setting of public hysteria over the crime problem, the latter leading to occasional searches for correctional whipping boys. All these influences have impinged upon the conduct of some experiments.

NOTES

1. *Cf.* J. Havel and E. Sulka, *Special Intensive Parole Unit, Phase Three* (*SIPU 3*), Research Report No. 3 (Sacramento, California Department of Corrections, March 1962).

2. *Cf.* S. Adams, "The PICO Project," *The Sociology of Punishment and Correction,* N. B. Johnston, *et al.,* eds. (New York, Wiley, 1962), pp. 213–214; and B. M. Johnson, *Parole Performance of the First Year's Releases, Parole Research Project: Evaluation of Reduced Caseloads,* Research Report No. 27 (Sacramento, California Youth Authority, Jan. 31, 1962).

3. *Cf.* W. R. Burkhardt and A. Sathmary, *Narcotic Treatment-Control Project, Phases I and II,* Research Report No. 19 (Sacramento, California Department of Corrections, May 1963).

4. *Cf.* H. G. Gough, "Clinical versus Statistical Prediction in Psychology," *Psychology in the Making,* L. J. Postman, ed. (New York, Knopf, 1962), ch. 9.

17: An Evaluation of One Hundred Reports / *Walter C. Bailey*

This article presents selected results of a content analysis of one hundred reports of empirical evaluations of correctional treatment. The reports, which are listed at the end of the article, were systematically selected primarily from those correctional outcome studies published between 1940 and 1960.[1] Within these broad limits, actual selection of reports was guided by three principles: (1) the report must have been based upon empirical data; (2) the treatment evaluated must have been dependent upon the manipulation of some form of interpersonal relations as the independent variable, and (3) the behavior to be corrected must have had a negative value in the sense of being actually or potentially subject to legal sanctions.

Five preliminary questions are explored: (1) What is the relative frequency of various types of correctional outcome reports in terms of research design? (2) What is the relative frequency of various forms of *group* treatment approaches as compared with *individual* forms such as *individual counseling, psychotherapy,* etc.? (3) What is the relative frequency of occurrence of study reports dealing with outcomes of treatment carried out in correctionally administered settings (forced treatment or "treatment at the point of a gun") as compared with treatment carried out in noncorrectional settings such as private practice, outpatient clinics, etc. (voluntary treatment)? (4) What kinds of persons, in terms of training and background, conduct correctional outcome research projects? and (5) What kinds of theories of causation of criminal behavior are implicit or explicit in the treatment programs evaluated? Finally, the main question is considered, namely, how effective is correctional treatment?

Frequency of Types of Study Reports

Of the 100 correctional outcome reports evaluated, 22% were classified as describing experimental study designs (those utilizing some form of control group design); 26% were classified as describing systematic-empirical study designs (those using control procedures but no control groups); and 52%

From Walter C. Bailey, "Correctional Outcome: An Evaluation of 100 Reports," *Journal of Criminal Law, Criminology and Police Science* 57:2 (1966): 153; 155–160.

were classified as describing nonsystematic empirical study designs (those based upon empirical observations but lacking control procedures). As expected, the more rigorous experimental type study report was the least frequently encountered and the least rigorous, least controlled type of study report, the most plentiful.

Effectiveness of Treatment

How corrective is correctional treatment? Of the total sample of correctional outcome reports evaluated, 10% described effects of the treatment as resulting in either "harm" or "no change" in behavior. Thirty-eight per cent of the studies reported "some improvement." Thirty-seven per cent reported a statistically significant difference in the direction of improvement for the group treated. Five per cent of the reported results were classified as "not relevant" to the outcome problem posed by the study.

Thus, roughly one-half of the outcome reports evaluated concluded considerable improvement in the treatment group. Almost one-fourth of the reports concluded either harmful results or "no change." These results, based upon the reported findings themselves, raise some serious questions regarding the efficacy of correctional treatment.

REPORTS DESCRIBING EXPERIMENTAL DESIGNS

Five of the 22 correctional outcome reports classified as experimental indicated either harmful results or "no change" in the treatment group. This amounts to roughly 23% of the sample of experimental studies. Four (17%) reported "some improvement"; four reported "marked improvement." Nine of these studies (43%) reported a "positive" statistically significant change in indices of the dependent variable applied to the treatment group.

Again, positive and negative findings are about equal. Roughly 60% ("marked improvement" plus statistically significant) may be classified as reporting successful outcomes. However, only 43% provided statistical evidence that the changes which occurred in the experimental group were not due to chance. On the other hand, roughly one-fourth of the experimental reports concluded that the treatment group either became worse, or there was no statistically significant change in the index of the dependent variable employed.

REPORTS DESCRIBING SYSTEMATIC-EMPIRICAL DESIGNS

Only 3 of the 26 systematic-empirical studies reported harmful results or "no change" (12%). Ten reported "some improvement" (38%). Eleven reported "marked improvement" (42%). Only one reported a statistically significant positive change in the treatment group (4%). Finally, one study finding was considered "not relevant."

REPORTS DESCRIBING NON-SYSTEMATIC EMPIRICAL DESIGNS

At the level of the least rigorously designed correctional outcome studies only 2 of the 52 studies evaluated reported harmful results or "no change" (4%). Twenty-four (46%) reported "some improvement" in the treatment group. Twenty-two (42%) reported "marked improvement." No studies in this category used tests of statistical significance. Finally, 4 (8%) cited findings considered to be irrelevant to the question posed.

Summary

A sample of 100 correctional outcome reports was subjected to a content analysis in an effort to obtain provisional answers to a number of questions relevant to an evaluation of the status of correctional treatment. Results of the analysis indicated that a slight majority of the correctional treatment programs evaluated in the reports was carried out in "forced treatment" settings (prison, parole or probation situations) as compared with correctional treatment programs carried out in "voluntary treatment" settings (private practice, private agencies, etc.). It was also found that psychologists and sociologists seem to have something of a monopoly on conducting this type of evaluative study. In addition, despite the fact that well over one-half of the reports were concerned with some form of group treatment, only a few described treatment procedures conceptually based upon the group relations premise. The most popular approach to explaining criminal or delinquent behavior and conceptualizing treatment goals and procedures involves some form of the sick premise regardless of whether the treatment deals with groups or individuals.

Over one-half of these reports described research designs of questionable rigor (classified as nonsystematic empirical). Roughly one-fourth of the reports dealt with more rigorous designs (systematic empirical). The remaining one-fourth of the reports described experimental designs. However, variations in research design seemed to have exerted little influence on frequency of reported successful treatment outcome. As the rigor of design increases, the frequency of reported treatment success increases (nonsystematic empirical—42%, systematic-empirical—46%, experimental—60%). Although the differences are not marked, the trend is in the unexpected direction. This is clarified somewhat when we note that as the rigor of design increases, the frequency of irrelevant conclusions markedly decreases; and that as the rigor of the design decreases, there is a marked decrease in the frequency of reported "harm" or "no change" in the treatment group (experimental—23%, systematic-empirical—12%, nonsystematic-empirical—4%). In this sample of reports apparently wishful thinking, when not subject to appropriate design controls, tends to be expressed in a resistance to negative results and indulgence in obscure generalities.

Since positive results were indicated in roughly one-half of the total sample of 100 reports analyzed, the problem of interpretation is not unrelated to that of determining "whether the cup is half empty or half full." But, when one recalls that these results, in terms of success or failure of the treatment used, are based upon the conclusions of the authors of the reports, themselves, then the implications of these findings regarding the effectiveness of correctional treatment become rather discouraging. A critical evaluation of the actual design and the specific research procedures described in each instance would substantially decrease the relative frequency of successful outcomes based upon reliably valid evidence. Therefore, it seems quite clear that, on the basis of this sample of outcome reports with all of its limitations, evidence supporting the efficacy of correctional treatment is slight, inconsistent, and of questionable reliability.

This negative conclusion regarding correctional treatment is in general agreement with those drawn from several reviews of the correctional outcome literature. For example, in 1952 Dalton reported his fairly pessimistic impression of the value of counseling techniques in probation work.[2] In 1954, Kirby reviewed the literature on the effects of treating criminals and delinquents and concluded that "most treatment programs are based on hope and perhaps informed speculation rather than on verified information."[3] Two years later, Witmer and Tufts reviewed the literature on the effectiveness of delinquency prevention programs and concluded that such programs had not been notably effective.[4]

On the positive side there is impressive evidence of an increasing concern with correctional outcome research and progressive improvement in the calibre of the scientific investigations conducted. This is shown in the increasing numbers of experimental and systematic-empirical investigations, the greater involvement of professionally trained researchers and the resulting increase in sophistication and rigor of research designs, and in the growing efforts to more explicitly relate treatment practice to behavioral science theory.

But how can we account for the apparent fact that although the operational means and resources of correctional outcome research have substantially improved, there has been no apparent progress in the actual demonstration of the validity of various types of correctional treatment? There probably could be no one answer to this question which, at least for a period, must remain unanswered. However, one or more of the following "explanations" may be suggestive: (1) there is the possibility that reformative treatment is "really" ineffectual either in its own right or as a consequence of the ambivalence of the "crime and punishment" setting in which it takes place; (2) one may hazard that much of the correctional treatment currently practiced is not corrective and that little of the rehabilitation work being done should be dignified by the term *treatment;* (3) it may be that some types of correctional treatment are "really" effective with some types of individuals under certain conditions, but so far we have been unable to describe operationally the independent variable (treatment), reliably identify in terms of treatment response the type of behavioral patterns being treated, adequately control the conditions under which such treatment takes place, or reliably delineate and measure relevant indices of the dependent variable; (4) perhaps much of the reformative treatment currently practiced is based upon the "wrong" theories of delinquent and criminal behavior.

List of the One Hundred Studies Reviewed

EXPERIMENTAL

Walter C. Bailey, *Differential Communication in the Supervision of Paroled Opiate Addicts* (Paper read at the 1958 Meeting of the American Sociological Society).

Bertram J. Black and Selma J. Glick, *Recidivism at the Hawthorne-Cedar Knolls School,* Research Monograph No. 2, New York: Jewish Board of Guardians (1952).

Paul Hoover Bowman, *Effects of Revised School Program on Potential Delinquents,* 332 Annals of the American Academy of Political and Social Science (1959).

Roscoe C. Brown, Jr., and Dan W. Dodson, *The Effectiveness of a Boys' Club in Reducing Delinquency,* 322 Annals of the American Academy of Political and Social Science (1959).

Vernon Fox, *Michigan's Experiment in Minimum Security Penology,* 41 Journal of Criminal Law and Criminology 150 (1950).

Vernon Fox, *The Effect of Counseling on Adjustment in Prison,* 3 Social Forces 285 (1954).

Charles Gersten, *Group Therapy with Institutionalized Delinquents,* 80 Journal of Genetic Psychology 35 (1952).

J. Douglas Grant and Marguerite Q. Grant, *A Group Dynamics Approach to the Treatment of Nonconformists in the Navy,* 322 Annals of the American Academy of Political and Social Science (1959).

Joan K. Jackson, *The Seattle Police Department Rehabilitation Project for Chronic Alcoholics,* 24 Federal Probation 36 (1958).

Isaac Joiles, *An Experiment in Group Therapy for Adult Offenders,* 9 Federal Probation 16 (1946).

Ruth Jacobs Levy, Reductions in Recidivism through Therapy (1941).

Herbert S. Lewin, *An Experiment in Non-Authoritative Treatment of Juvenile Delinquents,* 1 Journal of Child Psychiatry, 195 (1948).

Arthur Mann, *Group Therapy—Irradiation,* 46 Journal of Criminal Law, Criminology, and Police Science, 50 (1955).

Joan and William McCord, *A Follow-Up Report on the Cambridge-Somerville Youth Study,* 322 Annals of the American Academy of Political and Social Science, 89 (1959).

Edwin Powers and Helen Witmer, An Experiment in the Prevention of Delinquency (1951).

Ellery F. Reed, *How Effective Are Group-Work Agencies in Preventing Juvenile Delinquency?* 22 Social Service Review, 341 (1948).

Melvin Roman, Reaching Delinquents Through Reading (1957).

Alfred C. Schnur, *The Educational Treatment of Prisoners and Recidivism,* 54 American Journal of Sociology 143–147 (1948).

Harry M. Shulman, *Delinquency Treatment of the Controlled Activity Group,* 10 American Sociological Review 405 (1945).

Robert S. Wallerstein, *Comparative Study of Treatment Method for Chronic Alcoholism: The Alcoholism Research Project at Winter V.A. Hospital,* 113 American Journal of Psychiatry 228 (1956).

H. Ashley Weeks, Youthful Offenders at Highfields (1958).

Robert D. Wirt and James L. Jaconson, *Experimental Studies in Group Psychotherapy with Prisoners; Report N. L. Selected Groups*, Minnesota State Prison Department of Social Welfare (June, 1958) (mimeographed).

SYSTEMATIC-EMPIRICAL

Augusta F. Bronner, *Treatment and What Happened Afterward*, 14 AMERICAN JOURNAL OF ORTHOPSYCHIATRY 28 (1944).

Morris G. Caldwell, *Review of a New Type of Probation Study Made in Alabama*, 15 FEDERAL PROBATION 3 (1951).

James F. Chastin, *A Public School Offers Special Courses for Young Probationers*, 22 FEDERAL PROBATION 37 (1958).

Eric K. Clarke, *Group Therapy in Rehabilitation*, 16 FEDERAL PROBATION 28 (1952).

David Dressler, *Parole Results*, PROCEEDINGS OF THE AMERICAN PRISON ASSOCIATION (1941) 416–525.

Warren H. Dunham and Mary E. Knauer, *The Juvenile Court in Its Relationship to Adult Criminality*, 3 SOCIAL FORCES 290 (1954).

Warren H. Dunham and LeMay Adamson, *Clinical Treatment of Male Delinquents: A Case Study in Effort and Result*, 21 AMERICAN SOCIOLOGICAL REVIEW (1956).

Albert Ellis, *The Effectiveness of Psychotherapy with Individuals Who Have Severe Homosexual Problems*, 20 JOURNAL OF CONSULTING PSYCHOLOGY, 191 (1956).

Ralph England, *A Study of Post Probation Recidivism Among Federal Offenders*, 19 FEDERAL PROBATION 10 (1955).

Louisve V. Frishie, *The Treated Sex Offender*, 122 FEDERAL PROBATION 18 (1958).

John M. Gandy, *Preventive Work with Streetcorner Groups: Hyde Park Youth Project, Chicago*, 322 ANNALS OF THE AMERICAN ACADEMY OF POLITICAL AND SOCIAL SCIENCE 107 (1959).

Lester H. Gliedman, *et al.*, *Group Therapy with Alcoholics with Concurrent Group Meetings of Their Wives*, 17 QUARTERLY JOURNAL OF STUDIES ON ALCOHOL 655 (1956).

MAXWELL JONES, THE THERAPEUTIC COMMUNITY (1953).

Sidney Kosofsky, *Directive Therapy with Female Juvenile Delinquents*, 11 JOURNAL OF CLINICAL PSYCHOLOGY 357 (1955).

Gerald R. Ladhoff, *The Contribution of Physical Education in the Prevention of Potential Juvenile Delinquency* (unpublished Master's Thesis, University of California, Los Angeles, 1956).

R. Lessner, *Psychodrama in Prison*, 3 GROUP PSYCHOTHERAPY 77 (1950).

Tom McGee, *Changes in Adjustment During Detention*, ASSOCIATION NEWS (March, 1955) 7.

Walter B. Miller, *The Impact of a Community Group Work Program on Delinquent Corner Groups*, 31 SOCIAL SERVICE REVIEW 390 (1957).

Walter B. Miller, *Preventive Work with Streetcorner Groups: Boston Delinquency Project*, 322 ANNALS OF THE AMERICAN ACADEMY OF POLITICAL AND SOCIAL SCIENCE 97 (1959).

New York City Youth Board, *How They Were Reached: A Study of 310 Children and Their Families Known to Referral Units* (Youth Board Monograph, No. 2, New York: New York City Youth Board, 1954).

Florence Powdermaker, *Psychopathology and Treatment of Delinquent Girls*, 6 PASTORAL PSYCHOLOGY 33 (1955).

George J. Reed, *The Federal Youth Corrections Program*, 22 SOCIAL SERVICE REVIEW 340 (1956).

Vin Rosenthal and Edmund Shimberg, *The Program of Group Therapy with Incarcerated Narcotic Addicts*, 49 JOURNAL OF CRIMINAL LAW, CRIMINOLOGY AND POLICE SCIENCE 140 (1958).

Nathaniel Showstack, *Preliminary Report on the Psychiatric Treatment of Prisoners at the California Medical Facility, San Pedro, California*, a paper read at the annual meeting of the American Psychiatric Association, Atlantic City, New Jersey, May 12, 1955 (mimeographed).

Frederic M. Thrasher, *The Boys' Club and Juvenile Delinquency,* 42 American Journal of Sociology 66 (1936).

Lorranie O'Donnell Williams, *Short-Term Treatment of Women: An Experiment,* 21 Federal Probation 42 (1957).

NON-SYSTEMATIC EMPIRICAL

Joseph Andriola, *Success and Failure in the Treatment of Twenty-five Truants at a Child Guidance Clinic,* 13 American Journal of Orthopsychiatry 691 (1943).

Freed Bales, *Types of Social Structure as Factors in "Cures" for Alcohol Addiction,* 3 Applied Anthropology 1 (1942).

Ernest G. Beier, *Experimental Therapy with a Gang,* 30 Focus 97 (1951).

Howard Bennett, *Successful Treatment of a Sociopathic Personality, Anti-Social Type with Schizoid Trends,* 11 American Journal of Psychotherapy 111 (1957).

Benjamin Boshers, Lee G. Sewall and Mary Koga, *Management of the Narcotic Addict in an Outpatient Clinic,* 113 American Journal of Psychiatry 158 (1956).

Margaretta K. Bowers, M.D., *A Triangle of Treatment,* 30 Focus 161 (1951).

Harry J. Brevis, *Counseling Prison Inmates,* 7 Pastoral Psychology 35 (1956).

Martha Brunner-Orne and Martin T. Orne, *Alcoholics,* Slavson Fields of Group Psychotherapy, Ch. 5 (1956).

Martha Brunner-Orne, *The Utilization of Group Psychotherapy in Enforced Treatment Program for Alcoholics and Addicts,* 6 The International Journal of Group Psychotherapy 272 (1956).

Edward Cass, *Parole Can Be Successful,* 31 Journal of Criminal Law and Criminology 7 (1940).

F. C. Cesarman, *Religious Conversion of Sex Offenders During Psychotherapy: Two Cases,* 11 Journal of Pastoral Care 25 (1957).

Jack Chwast, *Casework Treatment in a Police Setting,* 18 Federal Probation 35 (1954).

J. H. Conn, *The Psychiatric Treatment of Certain Chronic Offenders,* 32 Journal of Criminal Law and Criminology 631 (1942).

Raymond J. Corsini, *Group Psychotherapy with a Hostile Group,* 6 Group Psychotherapy 168 (1954).

Marie Duffin, *Reaching Out to Prevent Delinquency,* 19 Federal Probation 27 (1955).

James R. Dumpson, *An Approach to Antisocial Street Gangs,* 13 Federal Probation 22 (1949).

Albert Eglash, *Adults Anonymous,* 49 Journal of Criminal Law, Criminology and Police Science 237 (1958).

Benjamin B. Ferencz, *Rehabilitation of Army Offenders,* 34 Journal of Criminal Law and Criminology 245 (1943).

Jay W. Fidler, Jr., M.D., *Possibilities of Group Therapy with Female Offenders,* 4 International Journal of Group Psychotherapy 330 (1951).

Maurice Flock, *Use of Fiction or Drama in Psychotherapy and Social Education,* Proceedings of 88th Congress of American Corrections Association 339 (1958).

John P. Fort, *The Psychodynamics of Drug Addiction and Group Psychotherapy,* 5 International Journal of Group Psychotherapy 150 (1955).

Adele Franklin, *The All-Day Neighborhood Schools,* 332 Annals of the American Academy of Political and Social Science, 62 (1959).

Antoinette Fried, *A Work Camp Program for Potential Delinquents,* 322 Annals of the American Academy of Political and Social Science 38 (1959).

James M. Hebron, *Study of Parole in Maryland* (Baltimore Criminal Justice Commission, 1935).

L. Wallace Hoffman, *Can You Trust Them?* 34 Journal of Criminal Law and Criminology 26 (1943).

Isaac Jolles, *An Experiment in Group Guidance,* 23 JOURNAL OF SOCIAL PSYCHOLOGY 55 (1946).

W. C. Jones, *Parole: A Five Year Study,* 31 JOURNAL OF CRIMINAL LAW and CRIMINOLOGY XXXI (May–June, 1940), 15–21.

Gisela Konopka, *Coordination of Services as a Means of Delinquency Prevention,* 322 ANNALS OF THE AMERICAN ACADEMY OF POLITICAL AND SOCIAL SCIENCE 30 (1959).

Solomon Korbin, *The Chicago Area Project—A 25 Year Assessment,* 322 ANNALS OF THE AMERICAN ACADEMY OF POLITICAL AND SOCIAL SCIENCE 19 (1959).

Arthur Lerner, *Self-Evaluation in Group Counseling with Male Alcoholic Inmates,* 5 INTERNATIONAL JOURNAL OF GROUP PSYCHOTHERAPY 286 (1955).

James V. Lowry, *Hospital Treatment of the Narcotic Addicts,* 20 FEDERAL PROBATION 42 (1956).

R. W. Newkirk, *Psychotherapy on Juvenile Delinquents,* 34 JOURNAL OF CRIMINAL LAW AND CRIMINOLOGY 100 (1943).

Clifford V. Oje, *The Air Force Corrections and Retraining Program,* 19 FEDERAL PROBATION 31 (1955).

J. W. Osberg and A. K. Berline, *The Developmental Stages in Group Psychotherapy with Hospitalized Narcotic Addicts,* 6 JOURNAL OF GROUP PSYCHOTHERAPY 35 (1956).

G. Lewis Penner, *An Experiment in Police and Social Agency Cooperation,* 322 ANNALS OF AMERICAN ACADEMY OF POLITICAL AND SOCIAL SCIENCE 79 (1959).

Ethel Perry, *The Treatment of Aggressive Juvenile Delinquents in "Family Group Therapy,"* 5 INTERNATIONAL JOURNAL OF GROUP PSYCHOTHERAPY 131 (1955).

Chester D. Poremba, *Group Probation: An Experiment,* 19 FEDERAL PROBATION 22 (1955).

Margaret G. Reilly and Robert A. Young, *Agency-Initiated Treatment of Potentially Delinquent Boys,* 16 AMERICAN JOURNAL OF ORTHOPSYCHIATRY 697 (1946).

Dietrich C. Reitzes, *The Effect of Social Environment upon Former Felons,* 46 JOURNAL OF CRIMINAL LAW, CRIMINOLOGY AND POLICE SCIENCE, 226 (1955).

Melitta Schmideberg, *Just Out of Prison,* FOCUS (January, 1951; taken from a reprint, no volume or number designation available).

Irving Schulman, *The Dynamics of Certain Reactions of Delinquents to Group Psychotherapy,* 2 INTERNATIONAL JOURNAL OF GROUP PSYCHOTHERAPY 334 (1952).

Leon N. Shapiro and Donald H. Russell, *Psychotherapeutic Investigation of Imprisoned Public Offenders* (part of report on meeting of March 9, 1956, of the Massachusetts Society for Research in Psychiatry), 123 JOURNAL OF NERVOUS AND MENTAL DISEASE 409 (1956).

E. Preston Sharp, *Group Counseling in a Short-Term Institution,* 23 FEDERAL PROBATION 7 (1959).

Bernard H. Shulman, *Group Psychotherapy in an Army Post Stockade,* 21 FEDERAL PROBATION 45 (1957).

Derrick Sington, *Redeeming the Murderer,* 184 NATION 117 (1957).

John C. Spencer and Tadeusz Grygier, *The Probation Hostel in England,* 6 FOCUS 165 (1952).

Marion Stranahan and Cecile Schwartzman, *An Experiment in Reaching Asocial Adolescents Through Group Therapy,* 322 ANNALS OF ACADEMY OF POLITICAL AND SOCIAL SCIENCE 117 (1959).

Leon Tec, *A Psychiatrist as a Participant Observer in a Group of "Delinquent" Boys,* 6 INTERNATIONAL JOURNAL OF GROUP PSYCHOTHERAPY 418 (1956).

Ruther S. Tefferteller, *Delinquency Prevention Through Revitalizing Parent-Child Relations,* 322 ANNALS OF AMERICAN ACADEMY OF POLITICAL AND SOCIAL SCIENCE 69 (1959).

James J. Thorpe and Bernard Smith, *Phases in Group Development in Treatment of Drug Addicts,* 3 INTERNATIONAL JOURNAL OF GROUP PSYCHOTHERAPY 66 (1953).

James J. Thorpe and Bernard Smith, *Operational Sequence in Group Therapy with Young Offenders,* 2 INTERNATIONAL JOURNAL OF GROUP PSYCHOTHERAPY 24 (1952).

George H. Weber, *The Boy Scout Program as a Group Approach in Institutional Delinquency Treatment*, 19 FEDERAL PROBATION 47 (1955).

NOTES

Professor Bailey's article is a modified version of a paper prepared for the California Study of Correctional Effectiveness under grant OM89R from the National Institutes of Health, Public Health Service, U. S. Department of Health, Education, and Welfare. He expresses his sincere appreciation to Dr. Daniel M. Wilner, Director of the California Study of Correctional Effectiveness, for his support and encouragement, and also to a number of assistants and assistant researchers for their help in collecting materials and annotating the research studies.

1. A few unpublished papers were included because of availability and some correctional outcome reports published prior to 1940 were included either because of their reputation as "classics" or because of some specific area of relevance. Selection of reports for this analysis was made on the basis of a systematic search through books and monographs, relevant journals, the American Prison Association Index, the International Index to Periodical Literature, the Public Affairs Index, and various government publications. The reports, listed below, comprise the sample upon which this analysis is based. Obviously, they constitute neither an exhaustive nor representative account of the literature. Also, a few represent evaluations of somewhat different aspects of the same general study projects. Nevertheless, the relatively large number of reports included and the selection methods employed suggest that this sample provides a reasonable basis for tentative judgments regarding the status of correctional outcome research in this country.

2. Dalton, *Value and Use of Counseling Techniques in the Work of Probation Officers*, 16 FEDERAL PROBATION 17 (1952).

3. Kirby, *Measuring Effects of Treatment of Criminals and Delinquents*, 38 SOCIOLOGY AND SOCIAL RESEARCH 374 (1954).

4. Witmer & Tufts, *The Effectiveness of Delinquency Prevention Programs*, Washington: U. S. Department of Health, Education, and Welfare, Government Printing Office, 1954.

18: Some Implications of Negative Findings / *David A. Ward*

Introduction

"Any correctional agency not using a prediction procedure to study the effectiveness of its decisions and operations is perpetrating a crime against the taxpayer." [1] This statement was made in 1962 by the, then, Chief of the Research Division of the California Department of Corrections, J. Douglas

From David A. Ward, "Evaluations of Correctional Treatment: Some Implications of Negative Findings," in *Law Enforcement, Science and Technology*, S. A. Yefsky, ed. (Washington, D.C.: Thompson Book Co., 1967), pp. 201, 204–208.

Grant. Mr. Grant contended that among other things experience was not a sufficient basis for decision-making, that correctional agencies were spending too much money collecting information which had little influence on decision-making, that research could develop useful prediction devices, and that current prison programs did not help many men who participated in them and were wasted on men who were good risks to begin with.[2]

It is not difficult to make a strong case for systematic assessment of organizational activities with a view toward increased efficiency, lower costs and more effective utilization of personnel and facilities.[3] Nor is it difficult to find departments of correction or prison officials who endorse the principle of evaluation. It is difficult, however, to find many prison systems where the principle has been implemented in terms of the establishment of research divisions which do more than actuarial data collection or so-called "human bookkeeping." Even smaller is the number of published studies of correctional program evaluations reported either by research divisions or by independent investigators. In fact, the majority of these studies have been conducted in just two prison systems: the Federal Bureau of Prisons and the California Department of Corrections.[4] In addition to developing most of the innovations in correctional treatment, most of what we now know of programs that do *not* work has come from studies undertaken in these two systems. In short, there seems to be general agreement among correctional officials in the United States that correctional program experimentation is needed and that there should be some evaluation of old and new programs. At the same time, there are actually only a limited number of new correctional programs being developed and little evaluation of existing programs.

It is the intention of this chapter to look at some evaluations of correctional programs to try to determine: (1) what such studies tell us about the success of efforts to reduce recidivism, and (2) what implications the findings of evaluative research have for personnel with a professional investment in the programs and for the organizations that encourage, support (or at least permit) evaluation. In the course of this discussion we shall try to shed some light on the question of why program evaluation is an exceptional practice rather than a standard procedure in most of the departments of correction in this country.

THE IMPLICATIONS OF NEGATIVE FINDINGS
FOR PUBLIC AGENCIES

The essential points in the argument that negative findings of treatment outcome may have political implications can be seen in the study of treatment effectiveness by Kassebaum, Ward and Wilner. From the beginning, the California Department of Corrections was supportive of this study, open in its dealings and cooperative at all levels. The Department agreed to every major condition required in the design, and it did not go back on its original commitment throughout the project's five-year period. The study was initiated largely because of the interest of the Department of Corrections itself in having an assessment made of group counseling—a program that was becoming a key part of the Department's treatment efforts. Thousands of inmates and hundreds of staff members were participating in this program at a substantial cost to the Department of Corrections in time, effort and money.

It is not possible here to describe the conduct of the study except to say that the inmates were tested and retested, interviewed and observed, data from their files were collected; the group counselors were queried, tested and observed in action; and parole agent reports, arrest records and parolee interviews were gathered.

Certain features of the research design were established to try to account for some of the defensive arguments that would be expected if findings did not support the efficacy of the program. These were:

1. The research was conducted in a prison system that is considered to be the most progressive in corrections, and in the most up-to-date prison in that system in terms of physical plant and staffing.
2. The inmates studied were neither the more intractable offenders confined in maximum security prisons, nor were they the good treatment potential men found in first term, minimum security institutions.
3. A sufficiently large study population was used to permit adequate statistical analysis.
4. Random assignment of subjects was made to the various treatment and control conditions.
5. Contamination of the sample groups was kept at a minimum due to the physical structure of the institution.
6. Also evaluated was a group counseling condition, especially included for this study, in which group leaders were given training beyond that which present resources of the Department of Corrections could afford.
7. Follow-up was extended for an unusually long period of time (two years) to take into consideration long-term effects of treatment.

Minimal criteria for inclusion in the follow-up sample were at least six months of participation in the treatment or control conditions and at least six months of parole supervision after release. Treatment varieties included voluntary group counseling, compulsory group counseling and a version of the therapeutic community approach called Community Living. The follow-up, involving about 1,000 men, was a more adequate measure of treatment outcome than had previously been obtained because we were able to take advantage of California's indeterminate sentencing laws and parole policy. Approximately 95 per cent of the men released from the prison left with at least six months of parole supervision ahead of them. This is a key factor in evaluating treatment outcome because no distinctions were made between good risks who get parole, and poor risks who are released at expiration of sentence, because the indeterminate sentence makes for longer periods of parole supervision, and because parole supervision guarantees collection of information about the post-release experiences of the samples. Another asset to the study was the availability of data obtained through the Research Division's well-ordered system for reporting status on parole at 6–12 and 24-month intervals after release. These conditions made it possible for us to follow-up 70 per cent of the sample for two years. (The remaining 30 per cent spent more than six months but less than 24 months on parole.)

Of the 24-month follow-up sample, the following results were obtained: No reported problems 26 per cent; minor problems (arrest or short-term jail confinement) 20 per cent; major problems (frequent arrests, longer jail terms) 11 per cent; returned to prison 43 per cent.

Contrary to the expectations of the treatment theory, there were no significant differences in outcome for those in the various treatment programs or between the treatment groups and the control group. Furthermore, contrary to sociological expectations, participation in group counseling and community living did not lessen even the limited endorsement of the inmate code, nor did it result in a demonstrable decrease in frequency of prison discipline problems.

Group counseling and Community Living have been made a part of the treatment program of every prison in the department; inmate participation in these programs is compulsory in some institutions; and participation in post-release group counseling is mandatory for every parolee in the state. With this array of evidence, what are the implications of the negative results of this study for the California Department of Corrections?

It would seem that in order for the Department of Corrections to continue to justify the widespread use of group counseling some new arguments must be advanced, such as, "participation in group counseling gives custodial officers a real part in the treatment program and seems to improve their morale," or "group sessions add a little variety to inmate life and take up time." Some of the arguments about the impact of this program on grounds other than reduction of prison disciplinary problems and recidivism may be entirely legitimate and are, by intention, beyond the scope of the present study. On the other hand, the Department may wish to alter the development of the group treatment program. The present Chief of the Research Division, John Conrad, has suggested such a course of action, perhaps in anticipation of a study such as ours.

> . . . the impact of group counseling on the correctional apparatus cannot be appraised until some models can be set up for test. The task now is not to prove that group counseling works. Eager advocates of research must be patient with an era of experimentation in group counseling. Nothing will be settled in any massive study which could conceivably be executed now. Dozens of small issues must be resolved before group counselors can be adequately trained. In the meantime, the gains which the correctional apparatus makes from the mere existence of this practice within its gates should sufficiently reward its tolerance.[5]

While the lack of evidence on the efficacy of group counseling certainly has not discouraged the expansion of this program, nevertheless there would seem to be problems for its supporters if they continue to assert that inmates behave better and parolees return less often for having participated in it.

Concerns of treatment specialists and penal administrators are based on realistic assessments of the exigencies of legislative appropriations. The problem begins in trying to justify expanded or experimental treatment programs solely on the grounds that more inmates will be rehabilitated by them. The substantial amounts of time, effort, and, most importantly, funds devoted to programs that do not achieve this express purpose are difficult to justify to legislative committees and budget analysts on grounds that staff morale is improved, that "one man was saved" or that inmates or parolees are happier or better able to relate to other people.

In short, correctional agencies face an inherent conflict between the pressures to develop new programs and empirically validate them and the requirement that these same agencies fulfill the public mandate to proceed efficiently and effectively with the business of rehabilitation. This conflict should provide a good part of the answer to the question of why correctional evaluation is a minority characteristic in American penology. Correctional administrators are aware of the fiscal and political implications latent in every research proposal that has to do with the assessment of correctional outcome. Limitations placed on the number of evaluative studies do not necessarily reflect a lack of appreciation for scientific studies of organizational effectiveness, but may represent an awareness of the vagaries of legislative appropriations and political realities.

THE IMPLICATIONS OF NEGATIVE FINDINGS
FOR FUTURE EVALUATIVE RESEARCH

It should be stressed that there is little clear evidence that a critical study or academic book or article has necessarily led to or influenced legislative cuts in funds, to say nothing of a public hue and cry. Furthermore, negative evaluations of correctional outcome do not inevitably spell the end of program evaluations, as they usually do not spell the end of the program. Legislative pressures were a major factor in the establishment of departmental research divisions to begin with, and these pressures are not likely to decrease with "crime in the streets" becoming an even more salient political issue.

There will be a variety of reactions to the current crop of correctional evaluations which report little or no impact of treatment.[6] One response may be to question the wisdom of encouraging program evaluations conducted by outside experts, evaluations that receive much public exposure through articles, books and papers read at professional meetings. Departmental administrators may feel that the same ends can be achieved in a different and less damaging way. If one's own staff members, particularly one's own research division, conduct these studies, then control could be exercised over how and to whom the findings would be disseminated. So-called "confidential department reports" with "restricted circulation" may be increasingly concerned with program evaluation as they are now concerned with investigations of *sensitive* areas such as prison discipline and homosexuality. Precedent already exists for not releasing reports of minor prison disturbances and the recidivism statistics for individual institutions because it is asserted that "the press and the public would not understand what is involved." There is no reason to think that this argument cannot be extended to reports of programs that do not reduce recidivism. An analogous situation exists for police officials in their reports of the number of crimes actually cleared by arrests. Clearance rates, like recidivism rates, can be interpreted to be tests of organizational efficiency.

Further, departments of corrections which have been most innovative in regard to correctional treatment and most supportive of research by outsiders, and who consequently get most of the bad reviews, are also the departments which have research divisions clearly capable of conducting their own program evaluations.

Serious problems are posed by this tactic, however, because research staff capability may not be enough to guarantee unrestricted program evaluation. Outside researchers are engaged for good reasons, notably: they have no personal investment in programs or the organization itself; they can insure the anonymity of respondents; they can examine conflicts and disagreements over treatment and custody and between administrators and the rank and file; and they are more likely to overcome traditional inmate suspicions and distrust of any representative of the correctional establishment. In addition, departmental control over findings would surely result in redundant studies, as well as the continuance of ineffective programs in departments of corrections which do not have their own research staffs.

But, there are courses of action open that do not involve battening down the hatches. Negative findings may give impetus to a wider variety of treatment approaches tried out on a more modest scale. Another response would be to change the tactics of presenting requests to legislatures for funding new programs by emphasizing the need for experimentation and innovation instead of arguing for new programs as if they had passed the test of empirical validation.

It is also possible that researchers, particularly university researchers, may have to extend their degree of responsibility from merely sending a copy of the report to the organization to standing up with agency heads and treatment specialists to argue for the principles of innovation, experimentation and evaluation. University investigators should find little comfort in the fact that while treatment evaluation results are not much to take to the legislature, the implications for the sociological and psychological theories underlying these programs are not much to take to their professional meetings. With the investment that all parties—prison and parole departments, treatment specialists and theoreticians—have in evaluations of correctional programs, there is no question that what would be helpful to all concerned, including the objects of treatment, would be the report of a prison treatment program that really worked.

NOTES

1. J. D. Grant
It's time to start counting
Crime and Delinquency 8 259 1962
  2. *Ibid.* pp. 259–264
  3. See for example
M. E. Wolfgang
Research in corrections
The Prison Journal 40 37–51 1960
L. T. Wilkins
Social deviance: social policy, action and research
Prentice-Hall, Inc. Englewood Cliffs, New Jersey 1964
D. R. Cressey
The nature and effectiveness of correctional techniques
Law and Contemporary Problems 23 754–771 1958
  4. R. H. Fosen and J. Campbell
Common sense and correctional science
The Journal of Research in Crime and Delinquency 2 73–81 1966
Fosen and Campbell report that a survey of forty-eight correctional systems in the United States indicated that only nineteen reported some kind of research operation. Of the total annual budget for adult correction in the United States, one-third of one per cent is devoted to self-study. Two systems, California and New York, account for over one-half of the total investment in research, p. 75
  5. J. P. Conrad
Crime and its correction
University of California Press Berkeley pp. 246–7 1965
  6. Another solution, already employed, is to establish a succession of programs, each of which is evaluated, found wanting and then immediately replaced by an "improved mode"
See the discussion of Scientific Newism by
J. W. Eaton
Stone walls not a prison make
Charles C. Thomas Publishers Springfield, Illinois pp. 35–41 1962

B

EX POST FACTO STUDIES

19: How Many Prisoners Return? /
Daniel Glaser

The Legend that Two-thirds Return to Prison

Diatribes against correctional practices frequently ascribe a specific high recidivism rate to American prisons. For example, one of our country's most
distinguished journalists of crime, John Bartlow Martin, confidently asserts:
". . . it is true that between 60 per cent and 70 per cent of the men who
leave prison come back for new crimes." [1] Martin's certainty probably is in-
spired by the fact that similar generalizations are uttered occasionally by police chiefs, judges, wardens, and professors of criminology. He could also
hear the same conclusions from inmate "politicians" in prison office jobs, or
from inmate contributors to prison publications, who assume the role of
spokesman for the society of convicts in transmitting complaints to journalists, sociologists, and other outsiders. They eagerly grasp statistics which justify their complaints. For example, an inmate magazine article comments:
"We must ask if our present penal systems have accomplished . . . [their]
purpose. One would hardly think so when we consider that our rate of recidivism is approximately 65 per cent. . . ." [2]

Where does this figure come from? Released prisoners in the United States
have not been regularly traced to determine the extent to which they return to
prison. As we shall show, the findings of those studies which have attempted
to follow releases do not justify this confidence in a two-thirds return figure.

It appears likely that this estimate of postrelease imprisonment stems from
knowledge of the prior prison records of men in certain penitentiaries. This
sort of reasoning is made explicit in the following publication by an ex-in-
mate:

In January of this year, in the prison where I served thirteen years of a life sentence, 20 per cent of the inmates had done a single previous jolt in that or another penitentiary, 16 per cent were three-time losers and 37 per cent had four or

From Daniel Glaser, *The Effectiveness of a Prison and Parole System* (Indianapolis:
The Bobbs-Merrill Co. Inc., 1964), pp. 13–15, 19–21, 24–27, 83–85. Copyright © 1964,
by The Bobbs-Merrill Company, Inc.; reprinted by permission of the publishers.

more prison commitments on their records. Only 27 per cent of the inmate body were first-timers, and of this group 6 per cent were twenty-one years of age or under and therefore hadn't yet had a fair chance to demonstrate their capacity for long-haul jousting with the law.

If these figures are typical of prisons throughout the land—and all available evidence says that the national record is actually even worse—then it's apparent that we taxpayers are pitching a great deal of money down an extremely deep rathole. If more than two-thirds of the inmates discharged from the nation's penal institutions are destined to pick up the pistol, the jimmy or the forger's pen again, then it's quite clear that prisons are thundering failures at the business of protecting society by reforming the criminal.[3]

Such predictions of future failures from the frequency of past failures of men in prison are misleading. Their most blatant error is neglect of the fact that offenders with prior imprisonment generally get longer sentences, and are much less readily paroled, than first imprisonment cases. Therefore, these "two- and three-time losers" accumulate in prison, so that they become higher as a percentage of men *in* the prison at any given time than as a percentage of men *received* or *released* by the prison in a given period. For example, in California prisons during 1960, 33 per cent of the men received had previously been imprisoned, but of the men imprisoned as of December 31, 1960, 48 per cent had served a previous prison term.[4]

A second source of error underlying this two-thirds return to prison estimate is generalization about an entire prison system from the few institutions in which offenders with prior imprisonment are unusually concentrated. Correctional systems operating more than one place of confinement usually separate inmates according to the extent of their previous incarceration, in addition to separating by age, length of sentence, and other considerations. In California, for example, on June 30, 1961, over half the state's prisoners had not previously served a prison term, but this proportion at different institutions varied from a low of 14 per cent at Folsom to a high of 82 per cent at Deuel.[5] In the quotation from an ex-prisoner that we used to illustrate the chain of reasoning leading to a two-thirds return conclusion, a prison was described in which only 27 per cent of the inmates had not served previous prison terms. Since about half the inmates of most prison *systems* have not previously served sentences in prison, this ex-prisoner's institution must have been part of a system which also included one or more prisons with well over half serving their first prison term.

A third reason has been advanced by Sol Rubin for questioning estimates of a reimprisonment rate such as this two-thirds figure. This reason, as he puts it, is that "the rate is impossible." In this contention, Rubin cites figures showing that the number confined in state and federal prisons in the United States is less than two and one-half times the number which the prisons release per year. Rubin then assumes, in his argument, that the average newly sentenced prisoner who is committed for his second or subsequent prison term is confined on his new term for at least four years. If two-thirds of the men released each year were returned to prison for an average period of four years, the number of men confined at any one time on their second or subsequent prison term would alone be over two and one-half times the total number of prisoners released per year.[6]

Data are not readily available on the validity of Rubin's four-year reimprisonment assumption. Nevertheless, a *National Prisoner Statistics* report in preparation by the U. S. Bureau of Prisons in 1963 indicated that as of December 31, 1960, for 149,617 inmates of the state prisons that compiled prior criminal record information, 51.2 per cent had no prior commitment. When one considers Rubin's argument in conjunction with the fact that about half the men confined in American prison systems are serving their first term in prison, one has strong logical grounds for dismissing the "two-thirds return to prison" speculation. But if this figure is spurious, what is the actual reimprisonment rate?

1956 FEDERAL PRISON RELEASEES

Our project began its statistical analysis of records of released offenders by drawing every tenth case from a list of adult males released from federal prisons during 1956. This yielded a sample of over one thousand. After F.B.I. fingerprint report sheets had been procured by the Bureau of Prisons in 1959 for 194 of these cases, a shortage of clerical assistance and pressure of other work in the F.B.I. prevented their supplying more of this special service to the Bureau of Prisons. Therefore we employed the following alternative checking procedure, which might usefully be copied by any state correctional agency desiring some follow-up of its releases even without current fingerprint reports.

During the summer of 1960, the cases in our sample for whom current F.B.I. reports had not been received were, first of all, checked in the U. S. Bureau of Prisons and Board of Parole files in Washington for records of reimprisonment in federal institutions, either for violation of parole or of conditional release or under new federal sentences. (A state correctional system would first check a list of releases of a past year in its own system's central files.) A list of the men who had no record of new federal imprisonment was sent by the Bureau of Prisons to the prisons from which they had been released and in which the complete institutional files of these men were kept. If, after the 1956 release, one of these men had been confined in a nonfederal prison, his file probably would contain a request from the new place of confinement for the behavior record and case analysis of the man during his federal confinement. (Most prisons today send such requests to every recidivist's institution of last confinement.) If no subsequent imprisonment had been recorded in the institution of last release, the Bureau of Prisons wrote to the U. S. Probation Office of the judicial district to which the man had been expected to go in 1956, asking whether this man had had any further difficulties with the law. (In a state system, such inquiry would be addressed to the local parole officer.) Generally, the probation office checked with local police in completing its reply to such a letter.

By the above process, of 1,015 cases constituting a random sample of adult male prisoners released from federal prisons in 1956, a total of about 31 per cent were found to have been reimprisoned:

26.6 per cent on new felony sentences;
1.7 per cent as parole or conditional release violators, when suspected of new felonies;
2.8 per cent as parole violators with no felonies alleged.

An additional 3.9 per cent received nonprison sentences for felony-like offenses (e.g., petty larceny, carrying concealed weapons). Including the latter, we arrived at what we call a total *"failure rate"* of 35 per cent. This consists of everyone returned to prison or convicted of a felony-type offense. The remaining 65 per cent were classified as "successes." They included:

52.2 per cent who had no further criminal record whatsoever;
2.4 per cent with one or more nonfelony arrests, but no convictions;
4.8 per cent with one or more arrests on felony charges, but no convictions;
4.5 per cent with one or more misdemeanor convictions, but no arrests on felony charges;
1.1 per cent with one or more misdemeanor convictions, and one or more arrests on felony charges, but no felony convictions.

It is clear that the last of the "success" categories above may include some marginal failures, while the nonfelony parole violators in the "failure" group may include some marginal successes. A line was drawn at what seemed to be the most reasonable boundary point, which would keep to a minimum the number of errors from classification of every case as either a "success" or a "failure." It is notable that few cases fell into the marginal categories.

HYPOTHESES OF RECIDIVISM

The evidence presented here from various follow-up studies is summarized in Table 19–1. The contrast of entries on the various lines of that table certainly highlights our lack of uniform information on the postprison consequences of efforts to rehabilitate men in prison. Nevertheless, if there is to be cumulative growth of a science of penology, we must attempt to express what seem, at present, to be the generalizations that our data make most tenable. Setting them forth in formal fashion should make it easier for future research to address itself to testing these generalizations, so as to lead either to their further confirmation or to their modification or replacement. For this purpose, the following statement is presented as the principal hypothesis for further testing suggested from the material summarized thus far in this chapter:

A1. In the first two to five years after their release, only about a third of all the men released from an entire prison system are returned to prison.

Table 19-1

Summary of Follow-Up Studies of Inmates Released from U.S. Prisons
Part 1, Total Systems

Prison System	Year of Release	Duration of Follow-Up	Releases Covered	Researchers	Sources of Follow-Up Information	Percent Returned to Prison	Percent Convicted or Accused of New Felony
Federal	1943-44	Approx. 5 yrs.	All releases (25% parolees)	U.S. Bureau of Prisons	F.B.I. fingerprint record	24	(not tabulated)
California	1946-49	3 yrs.	The 88% who were paroled	Calif. Bd. of Corrections (Beattie)	State parole and criminal identification records	44	28
Wisconsin	1952-56	2 yrs.	The approx. 85% who were paroled or conditionally released	Wisc. Dept. of Public Welfare (Mannering)	State parole and criminal identification records	31	14 (convicted)
New York	1956	Parole period or up to 5 yrs.	The 76% who were paroled	N.Y. Board of Parole (Stanton)	State parole records	44	7 (convicted)
Federal	1956	Approx. 4 yrs.	Every 10th adult male releasee (31% parolees)	U. of Ill. (Glaser)	Some F.B.I. fingerprint records; prison and probation office tracing	31	28
Washington	1957-59	½ to 2½ yrs.	99% of all releasees	Wash. Dept. of Institutions (Babst, Suver, Kusano, Little)	State parole records	20 (another 18% in "wanted" status)	13
Pennsylvania	1947-57	Parole period: Aver. 2½ yrs. Max. 5 yrs.	The approx. 70% who were paroled	Pa. Board of Parole (Jacks).	State parole records	31	17

Table 19-1 (continued)

Summary of Follow-Up Studies of Inmates Released from U.S. Prisons
Part 2, Youthful Offenders Only

Youth Prisons	Year of Release	Duration of Follow-Up	Releases Covered	Researchers	Sources of Follow-Up Information	Percent Returned to Prison	Percent Convicted or Accused of New Felony
Massachusetts Reformatory	1921	5 yrs. post-parole (8-10 yrs. post-release)	The 83% that could be traced (all parolees) of 510 total cases	Sheldon and Eleanor T. Glueck	Field inquiries; state and local records	31.5 (of those traced); 26.1 (of total)	36.1 during parole (of total); 43.8 post-parole (of those traced)
Minnesota Refomatory	1944 -45	Approx. 5 yrs.	All releasees (53% parolees)	Zuckerman, Barron, and Whittier	F.B.I. fingerprint and state parole records	38	23
Federal Youth Correction Act Cases	1955 -58	Parole period (2-4 yrs.)	Those committed 1954-55 (all parolees)	U.S. Board of Parole (Neagles)	Federal parole records	58	36 (includes some serious mis-demeanors)
Federal Youth Correction Act Cases	1955 -58	Parole period (2-4 yrs.)	All released 1955-58 (all parolees)	U. of Ill. (Glaser)	Federal parole records	49	34

The variation above or below one-third apparently may range as much as ten or fifteen percentage points. Highly limited evidence suggests the supplementary hypothesis:

A2. The proportion of releasees returned to prison tends to be higher:
  - a. where probation is used extensively, so that only the worst risks go to prison (although this use of probation may make the long-run recidivism of all felons lower;
  - b. where parole is used extensively, so that many poor-risk parolees are released on a trial basis;
  - c. where a large proportion of parolees are returned to prison when they have violated parole regulations but have not been charged with or convicted of new felonies;
  - d. where there is a high overall crime rate in the communities to which prisoners are released, so that there is high prospect of the releasee coming from and going to highly criminogenic circumstances.

Clearly, the second of the two formal propositions above is based on limited evidence.

The Relative Frequency of Postrelease Behavior Patterns

The careers of men are so infinitely diverse that we have to classify them into categories and types in order to comprehend patterns and relationships in their diversity. It should be remembered, when we do this, that the categories often have arbitrary boundaries, which create many borderline cases. Also, when types are based on several somewhat independent characteristics, an individual may be like one type in one respect and like another in some other respect. Thus, some of our releases who were unemployed extensively were difficult to classify as "clear reformation" rather than "economic retreatism," since one could not be certain how persistently they had sought work. Similarly, two or even all three of the retreatism patterns—economic, addictive, and juvenile—sometimes were manifested in a single case.

Perhaps a greater barrier to classification than the diversity of human behavior is its instability. People who behave in one way at any given time are likely to behave differently later. This is especially evident in the lives of those who have been involved in criminality. Almost all criminals have pursued noncriminal occupations at one time or another, and almost all will resume such pursuits at some time in the future. This is repeatedly indicated by our statistics and by our case studies. The classifications assigned to men in the compilation presented in this chapter were, in the success cases, those which seemed to fit them at the time they were interviewed by our staff; the classifications assigned the returned violators, who were interviewed in prison, were the patterns which seemed to describe their behavior at the time they were under the parole or mandatory-release supervision which they violated. If we had interviewed the success cases later, especially the "marginal" successes, doubtless some would be classified differently. This is evident from the fact that our follow-up in January 1962, on the 250 men interviewed in 1960 and 1961, revealed that in the post-interview interval twenty-three had violated. These included only 6 per cent of the clear-reformation cases, but 25 per cent of the marginal-reformation cases. It is also probable that some of the marginal-success cases had become "clear" successes during this period.

In addition to bearing the foregoing considerations in mind when assessing the relative frequency of the postrelease behavior patterns distinguished here, it should be noted that our sample of "success" cases is not a representative sample of non-recidivating federal releasees.

This sample was deliberately biased in two respects. First of all, by selecting only men under supervision for one year or more, it was limited to less than half of men released from federal prisons; to have over a year of postrelease supervision they had to be parolees with sentences of more than eighteen months or mandatory releasees with sentences of somewhat over five years (with a few exceptions of unusual early release dispensation). Secondly, the sample was deliberately selected to include men with as much or more prior criminality as the violators already interviewed; starting early in 1960, no one was added to this sample who did not have a record of felony behavior prior to the offense for which he was then successfully released. Therefore, the one-crime cases among federal successful releasees are grossly underrepresented in our sample.

A total of 250 successful releasees were interviewed, constituting over 90 per cent of men under federal supervision, in the areas of seven midwest states, who fit the selection specifications stated in the preceding paragraph. Of these 250 cases:

210, or 84 per cent, were classified as *clear reformation* cases, as follows:
Eighty, or 32 per cent of all the 250 successful releasees, were classified as *late reformation after criminal career;*
Thirty-seven, or 15 per cent, classified as *early reformation after criminal career;*
Three, or 1 per cent, classified as *crime-facilitated reformation;*
Forty-eight, or 19 per cent, classified as *reformation after crime interval;*
Twenty-six, or 10 per cent, classified as *reformation after only one felony;*
Sixteen, or 6 per cent, classified as *crime-interrupted noncriminal career.*

In addition, in these 250 successful releasees:

Forty, or 16 per cent, were classified as *marginal reformation* cases, as follows:
Twelve classified as *economic retreatism;*
Nine classified as *juvenile retreatism;*
Four classified as *addictive retreatism;*
Thirteen classified as *crime-contacting noncriminals;*
Two classified as *nonimprisoned criminals.*

The Returned Violator sample is believed to be fairly representative of all midwest returned federal-parole violators. The 308 cases in this sample consisted of every returned violator in four federal prisons who had been returned from one of fifteen federal judicial districts (in nine states) after parole or mandatory release from one of these four prisons, or from one other prison (Ashland) to which parole violators are not returned. Of these returned violators:

Ninety-three, or 30 per cent, were classified as *marginal failure cases,* including:
Nine, or 3 per cent, classified as *defective communication;*
Eighty-four, or 27 per cent, classified as *other nonfelony violations.*

In addition:

215, or 70 per cent, were classified as *clear recidivism* cases, including:
178, or 58 per cent, classified as *deferred recidivism;*
Thirty-seven, or 12 per cent, classified as *immediate recidivism.*

It should be noted that the above frequency distribution has very little relationship to the number of illustrative cases presented for each category. When the number of cases in each category in the 250 "successes" and 308 violators was counted, the low frequency of some types that impressed us during the data collection came as a surprise to us. It is my belief that this is illustrative of a common source of error in generalization from case study impressions. Cases are best remembered when they are outstanding illustrations of a type that one finds interesting to distinguish, and perhaps to argue with, to illustrate a point. After they are cited often, or are merely thought about much, one may acquire a grossly exaggerated impression of their frequency in the total population studied. This is an especially serious matter when major policy decisions are made on the basis of impressions from remembered cases, without relevant statistical information.

What becomes increasingly clear from all of the case studies and statistics on criminal careers presented thus far, or to be cited later, is that almost all criminals follow a zig-zag path. They go from noncrime to crime and to noncrime again. Sometimes this sequence is repeated many times, but sometimes they clearly go to crime only once; sometimes these shifts are for long duration or even permanent, and sometimes they are short lived.

NOTES

1. John Bartlow Martin, *Break Down the Walls* (New York, Ballantine Books, 1954), pp. 233–34.

2. Ross Crider, "Progressive Amelioration of Punishment," U. S. Penitentiary, Leavenworth, Kansas, *The New Era, 15,* no. 2 (1961), p. 154.

3. Hal Hollister, "I Say Prisons Are a Failure," *The Saturday Evening Post, 234,* no. 34 (August 26, 1961), p. 113.

4. California Department of Corrections, *California Prisoners 1960.* Table 9A, p. 22 and Table 20A, p. 42.

5. California Department of Corrections, *Characteristics of Resident Population of California State Prisons by Institution, June 30, 1962*, Research Div., Adm. Statistics Section. P. 2a and p. 2c.

6. Sol Rubin, "Recidivism and Recidivism Statistics," *National Probation and Parole Assoc. J., 4*, no. 3 (July 1958), p. 1236. Rubin is also assuming here that those who return to prison do so soon enough to be able to serve several four-year (or longer) terms before death.

20: The Effectiveness of Probation: A Review / R. F. Sparks

Virtually every study of the after-conduct of offenders placed on probation has found that the majority are not reconvicted within the chosen follow-up period. In England, the Cambridge study [1] published in 1958 found that no less than 79 per cent of the adults included in the research, and 73 per cent of the juveniles, successfully completed their periods of probation. Even when the offenders were followed up for a three-year period after the end of supervision, 70 per cent of the adults, and 58 per cent of the juveniles, could still be said to have succeeded. Similar results are reported from the United States. R. W. England [2] found that 82.3 per cent of a group of 490 offenders placed on probation in Pennsylvania were not reconvicted within a period of 6 to 12 years after completion of probation; and more recent figures for the U.S. Federal Probation system show success rates in terms of nonviolation while on probation, of about 88 per cent for 19 U.S. District Courts.

These figures are, of course, much higher than the overall success rates typically reported for institutional treatment. (For example, Glaser [3] found evidence that less than two-thirds of those discharged from U.S. prisons are "successes" in the sense that they are not reimprisoned.) But this crude comparison actually reveals nothing about the relative effectiveness of probation and imprisonment, since it takes no account of the differences in the offenders who are dealt with in each way, and their different liability to reconviction independent of the treatment they receive. Most of the surveys just cited have found that certain types of offender are more likely to be reconvicted during or after probation than others: the Cambridge study, for example, found higher reconviction rates among juveniles, males, and recidivists than among adults, females and first offenders. [4] The majority of the factors associated with reconviction on probation have also been found to be associated

From R. F. Sparks, "Research on the Use and Effectiveness of Probation, Parole and Measures of After-Care," in a Council of Europe report on *The Practical Organisation of Probation and After-Care Services* (Strasbourg: Council of Europe, 1968), pp. 4–7, 8–11 (unpublished).

with reconviction following other forms of treatment; and any differences in these respects between offenders placed on probation and offenders dealt with in other ways must be taken into account when comparing the success rates of probation and other forms of treatment.

The few studies which have done this strongly suggest that probation is in general at least as effective (in terms of reconviction rates) as imprisonment or other forms of custodial treatment. Wilkins [5] found no significant difference in the reconviction rates (in a three-year follow-up period) of a group of 31 offenders placed on probation at an English higher court, and a group of 31 individually matched controls dealt with in other ways (mostly prison and borstal). Babst and Mannering [6] followed up 5,274 adult male offenders in Wisconsin, and compared the reconviction rates (in a two-year period) of those placed on probation with those sent to prison and paroled. When type of current offence, criminal record and marital status (the factors most highly predictive of recidivism in this group) were held constant, it was found that the success rate of probation was about the same as that of imprisonment for recidivists, and was significantly better for first offenders. According to Martin [7] a similar result was found in a demonstration project carried out in Saginaw, Michigan. Finally, in a study carried out by the Home Office Research Unit,[8] Hammond found that the observed reconviction rates of offenders placed on probation in 1956 were broadly comparable with those of offenders given institutional treatment, in relation to expected reconviction rates computed from the characteristics of the offenders involved. In a re-assessment of the earlier Cambridge study of probation, Hammond suggested that it showed that when expected reconviction rates were taken into account, the effectiveness of probation was about the same as that of other treatments for first offenders, but slightly better than expected for recidivists; in his own sample, recidivists also did relatively better on probation than first offenders. (It should be noted, however, that the most significant finding of the Home Office study was that fines and discharges were relatively much more effective, overall, than either imprisonment or probation.)

Two recent studies of receptions into California penal institutions also support the view that probation might well be used more liberally instead of institutional treatment. In the first, Mueller [9] estimated that 20 per cent of all new adult male admissions to the California Department of Corrections could have been recommended for probation instead of imprisonment, since the risk of their being reconvicted (as determined by base expectancy tables regularly in use in California) under minimum supervision was relatively low. In the second, Roberts and Seckel [10] found evidence that about 40 per cent of California Youth Authority wards could be released immediately to the community without serious risk of reconviction, compared with the 16–17 per cent who are at present released immediately in this way.

The general conclusion that probation is at least as effective as institutional treatment also receives some support from a group of studies of experimental community treatment programmes carried out in the United States in recent years. These studies—the Provo project in Utah,[11] the Silverlake experiment in Los Angeles,[12] the Essexfields project in New Jersey [13] and the Community Treatment Project in Sacramento and Stockton, California [14]—all found that the reconviction rates of offenders placed on probation were markedly lower than those of control groups sent to penal institutions. However, it is probable that for present purposes not too much weight should be placed on these studies. None was specifically designed to evaluate probation; in two (the Community Treatment Project and Silverlake) the delinquents dealt with in the community did not receive regular probation, while three (the Community Treatment Project, Essexfields and Provo) suffer from methodological limitations concerning the matching of treatment and control groups and the supervision of each during the follow-up period.

It is important to bear in mind that the main conclusion to be drawn from the research discussed so far is really a negative one: namely, that institutional treatment is *not* more effective (in terms of preventing reconvictions) than treatment in the community. In the light of this conclusion, it would obviously be reasonable on grounds of cost alone to place on probation a proportion of those offenders now sent to prisons or other institutions. But it may also be that for some offenders who are now placed on probation, a nominal measure not involving supervision (for example, a fine or discharge) would be at least as effective as probation. This, as we have noted, is suggested by Hammond's study; and there is other evidence, to be discussed below, which points tentatively to the same conclusion.

The Effects of Case-Load Size and Supervision

The research discussed so far leaves unanswered a number of crucial questions about probation. How many offenders can a probation officer adequately supervise at any one time, and what is the optimum probation case-load? How much supervision do offenders on probation now receive, and how much do they need? What are the techniques of supervision now in use, and what effects have they on different types of probationers? What difference do the length of the probation order and the training of the probation officer make with different types of offender? Unfortunately, the answers to these and similar questions are now unclear, though there are two large research projects—being carried out by the Home Office in England [15] and by Lohman et al. in California [16]—which should produce important information on these points in the near future. These questions must be answered before we are in a position to say that it is the "treatment" given on probation—rather than, say, the harmfulness of imprisonment—which is responsible for the apparently high effectiveness of probation relative to institutional treatment.

The standard probation case-load of male probation officers in England is now between 50 and 60; but in many areas some officers must supervise much greater numbers.[17] In the United States, the position is much worse: according to the recent report of the President's Commission on Law Enforcement and the Administration of Criminal Justice,[18] no less than two-thirds of all adult felony offenders on probation in the United States in 1965 were in case-loads of over 100. In California, a recent survey [19] showed average case-loads of 140 adults per male officer, if allowance is made for pre-sentence inquiry work; in Virginia, a study carried out by the National Council on Crime and Delinquency [20] found average probation and parole case-loads of 74 per officer, plus pre-sentence inquiries. According to Pye, Shadoan and Snee,[21] in 1960 the average probation case-load in the U.S. Federal system (including an allowance for pre-sentence reports) was 84.

The number of probation cases under supervision at any one time is not, however, an accurate measure of the probation officer's *work-load,* since probation officers typically have many other duties to perform as well. The most important of these, in many jurisdictions, is to carry out pre-sentence investigations of offenders' social backgrounds, and submit reports to the courts. In terms of time spent one such inquiry is often equal to the supervision of several offenders on probation (estimates in the United States range from 5 cases per inquiry [22] up to 12.8,[23] though the figure in England is lower). Moreover, in many places (e.g., England [24]) it is this aspect of the probation officer's work which has increased most rapidly in recent years.[25] Moreover, the probation service is often responsible for a wide range of miscellaneous social-work services, both to offenders and non-offenders; in England, for instance, they carry out matrimonial conciliation, compulsory and voluntary after-care, parole, supervision of non-delinquent juveniles under court orders, and supervision of offenders who are fined, as well as a host of administrative duties. The result is that in many cases the supervision of offenders on probation occupies only a minority of the probation officer's time. (See, e.g., Wahl and Glaser; [26] Mandel et al.) [27] A probation officer with an active case-load of 50 may thus spend an average of only two hours or so per case per month; and in many cases the amount of contact between probationer and probation officer will be much less.

At first sight, it may seem surprising that anybody ever "succeeds" on probation at all. But this is to beg the question: what is the "right" amount of supervision for each individual offender on probation? As Carter [28] has pointed out, the often-quoted "ideal" case-load of 50 has no real empirical basis whatever. Some offenders need much more supervision than others; and it is certain that this is now taken into account, to some extent, by probation officers in practice.

Lohman et al.,[29] in their large-scale study of U.S. Federal probation and parole, found no significant differences in the success rates (no major violation) of offenders randomly allocated to "intensive," "ideal," "normal" and "minimum" supervision, though these ranged from case-loads of 25 and 6.71 contacts per month in the case of "intensive" supervision, to case-loads of 125 or more and .48 contacts per month in the case of "minimum" supervision. A questionnaire administered to a small number of those successfully completing supervision revealed that those who had received "intensive" and "ideal" supervision were somewhat more likely than the "normal" and "minimum" supervision groups to feel that their period on probation had been helpful to them. Nonetheless, not one of those given "intensive" supervision listed the probation officer as a significant factor in their success on probation; instead, like those given less supervision, they tended to attribute their success to their own (perceived) non-criminal orientation, and to assistance given by their families and friends.

In a study of juvenile probation in Los Angeles, Kawaguchi and Siff [30] found that intensive supervision—involving 2½ times as many contacts as normal juvenile probation in Los Angeles—produced a slight, though not statistically significant, increase in success rates; the intensive probation service was, however, slightly more expensive than the usual type. It is also relevant at this point to mention the series of studies carried out by the Special Intensive Parole Unit (SIPU) in California since 1953. Briefly, these studies suggest that *general* reduction in case-loads and a corresponding increase in contacts between the probationer or parolee and the supervisor are unlikely to have much effect on overall success rates; but that there is likely to be some improvement in the parole performance of certain types of offenders, viz. those with about an average risk of reconviction. In other words, the best risks and the worst risks are unlikely to show any marked improvement from supervision on a reduced case-load.[31] The SIPU project has also produced evidence that offenders who are good risks on parole do no worse, even if they only receive minimum supervision.[32]

From the research just summarized, it appears that two provisional conclusions may be drawn. The first is that a substantial proportion of offenders now placed on probation "succeed," even though they receive only nominal supervision and "treatment." It may well be that the majority of these offenders could be dealt with just as effectively by means of a fine, discharge or other nominal measure not involving supervision. Secondly, a general and undiscriminating reduction in case-loads is unlikely to make any significant difference to overall success rates of probationers. (As Pye et al.[33] have pointed out, no change in overall success rates took place in the U.S. Federal probation system during 1956–60, though workloads dropped during those years by 16 per cent.) Some offenders may be able to benefit from more intensive supervision, but the majority probably do not need it. In particular, offenders who are good risks (in the sense that they are unlikely to be reconvicted whatever is done to them) can just as well be dealt with by nominal supervision.

It is not possible at this stage to say what proportions or types of offenders placed on probation are likely to benefit from intensive supervision, and what proportions may be given minimum supervision. Lohman et al.[34] have suggested, on the basis of demographic data, that about 35 per cent of the offenders in their study in San Francisco could have been given "minimum" supervision without increased risk of reconviction; and that about 5 per cent appear to need "intensive" supervision. But the benefits of intensive supervision have not yet been clearly demonstrated for any group of offenders; and the proportions of offenders needing different types of supervision will be largely determined by the policies of the courts, and will probably thus vary from one jurisdiction to another.

NOTES

1. Cambridge Department of Criminal Science, *The Results of Probation* (London: Macmillan, 1958).

2. R. W. England, "A Study of Post-Probation Recidivism among 500 Federal Offenders," *Federal Probation* 19 (1955):10.

3. Daniel Glaser, *The Effectiveness of a Prison and Parole System* (Indianapolis: Bobbs-Merrill, 1964).

4. Cambridge Department of Criminal Science, *op. cit.*

5. Leslie T. Wilkins, "A Small Comparative Study of the Results of Probation," *British Journal of Delinquency* 8 (1958):201.

6. Dean V. Babst and John W. Mannering, "Probation versus Imprisonment for Similar Types of Offenders," *J. Res. Crime and Delinquency* 60 (1965).

7. John B. Martin, "The Saginaw Project," *Crime and Delinquency* 6 (1960): 357.

8. Home Office (United Kingdom), *The Sentence of the Court: A Handbook for Courts on the Treatment of Offenders* (London: Her Majesty's Stationery Office, 1964).

9. Paul F. C. Mueller, *The Development and Use of Parole Outcome Base Expectancies by the California Department of Corrections, 1958–1965* (California Department of Corrections, Crime Study Section, Research Division: January 1966).

10. California Board of Corrections, *The Board of Corrections Probation Study,* State of California Board of Corrections, Final Report (Sacramento, California: Board of Corrections, September 7, 1965), pp. 90–96.

11. L. T. Empey and Jerome Rabow, "The Provo Experiment in Delinquency Rehabilitation," *American Sociological Review* 26 (1961):679; L. T. Empey and Maynard L. Erickson, *The Provo Experiment in Delinquency Rehabilitation,* Fifth Annual Progress Report, 1963–64, Brigham Young University, Utah.

12. L. T. Empey, George E. Newland, Steven G. Lubeck, and Anthony J. Manocchio, *The Silverlake Experiment: A Community Study in Delinquency Rehabilitation,* Progress Report No. 3, Youth Studies Center of the University of Southern California, 1966.

13. Richard M. Stephenson and Frank R. Scarpitti, *The Rehabilitation of Delinquent Boys,* Final Report to the Ford Foundation (Rutgers: New Jersey, 1967).

14. Theodore B. Palmer and M. Q. Warren, *Community Treatment Project, Sixth Progress Report, Part I: The Sacramento and Stockton Experiments* (Sacramento, California, September 1967); M. Q. Warren, "An Experiment in Alternatives to Incarceration, etc.," in *Correction in the Community: Alternatives to Incarceration,* Monograph No. 4 (Sacramento, California, California Department of Corrections, 1964).

15. S. Folkard, K. Lyon, M. Carver, and E. O'Leary, *Probation Research: A Preliminary Report,* Home Office Research Unit Report No. 7 (London: Her Majesty's Stationery Office, 1966).

16. Lohman, Joseph D., Albert Wahl, and Robert M. Carter, *The San Francisco Project, Research Report No. 2: Three Hundred Presentence Report Recommendations* (Berkeley, California: University of California School of Criminology, June, 1965); *The San Francisco Project, Research Report No. 5: Presentence Report Recommendations and Demographic Data* (Berkeley, California: University of California School of Criminology, February, 1966); *The San Francisco Project, Research Report No. 6: Two Hundred Federal Parolees and Mandatory Releasees: Demographic Data* (Berkeley, California: University of California, School of Criminology, April 1966); *The San Fran-*

cisco Project, Research Report No. 8: The Minimum Supervision Caseload (Berkeley, California: 1966); *The San Francisco Project, Research Report No. 9: The Ideal Supervision Caseload* (Berkeley, California, 1966); *The San Francisco Project, Research Report No. 10: An Afterview of Supervision: The Research Design* (Berkeley, California, 1966); Joseph D. Lohman, Albert Wahl, Robert M. Carter, and Shirley P. Lewis, *The San Francisco Project, Research Report No. 11: The Intensive Supervision Caseload* (Berkeley, California: University of California School of Criminology, March 1967); Joseph D. Lohman, Albert Wahl, and Robert M. Carter, *The San Francisco Project, Research Report No. 12: Classification Criteria for Establishing Caseloads* (Berkeley, California: 1967); *The San Francisco Project, Research Report No. 13: The Impact of Supervision: Officer and Offender Assessment* (Berkeley, California, 1967).

17. Home Office (United Kingdom), *Probation Statistics, 1966*, Circular No. 3/1968 (London: Her Majesty's Stationery Office, January 5, 1968); Home Office (United Kingdom), *Report on the Work of the Probation and After-Care Department, 1962–1965*, Cmnd. 3107 (London: Her Majesty's Stationery Office, 1966).

18. United States, President's Commission on Law Enforcement and Administration of Justice, *Task Force Report: Corrections* (Washington, D. C., U. S. Government Printing Office, 1967).

19. R. E. Kelgord, Letter from National Council on Crime and Delinquency dated December 20, 1966, Re: 1963 Informal Survey of Probation Caseloads in California.

20. National Council on Crime and Delinquency, *Adult Probation and Parole in Virginia* (New York: June 22, 1965).

21. Kenneth A. Pye, George W. Shadoan and Joseph M. Snee, S.J., *A Preliminary Survey of the Federal Probation System* (Washington, D. C., Georgetown University Law Center, 1963).

22. *Kelgord*

23. Albert Wahl and Daniel Glaser, "Pilot Time Study of the Federal Probation Officer's Job," *Federal Probation* 27:3(1963):21.

24. *Report on the Work of the Probation and After-Care Department, 1962–1965.*

25. Parenthetically, the value of these pre-sentence inquiries may be doubted. Lohman *et al.* [*The San Francisco Project, Research Project No. 13: The Impact of Supervision: Officer and Offender Assessment*] have suggested that the pre-sentence interview with the offender may be helpful in establishing a relationship with the offender. But this will not be so, in cases in which the offender is not put on probation or is supervised (as often happens) by a different officer. The value to the court of the pre-sentence report is even more doubtful. Chandler and Wilkins [Leslie T. Wilkins and Ann Chandler, "Confidence and Competence in Decision-Making," *British Journal of Criminology* 5 (1965):22] and Carter [Robert M. Carter, "The Presentence Report and the Decision-Making Process," *J. Res. Crime and Delinquency* 4 (1967):203] have carried out experiments in decision-making by probation officers, which suggest that very little of the information included in the typical social inquiry report is used at all in deciding whether or not to recommend probation, and that there is little consensus among officers as to relevant information. Other research by Lohman *et al.* [*The San Francisco Project, Research Report No. 2: Three Hundred Presentence Report Recommendations*] suggests that this is probably also true for judges. Hood [Roger G. Hood, "A Study of the Effectiveness of Pre-Sentence Investigations in Reducing Recidivism," *British Journal of Criminology* 6 (1966):303] found that pre-sentence reports made no difference to recidivism at an English magistrates' court; a later study by Hood and Taylor [Roger G. Hood and Ian Taylor, "Second Report of the Study of the Effectiveness of Pre-Sentence Reports in Reducing Recidivism," *British Journal of Criminology* 8(1968)], however, has produced slightly more favorable results. On the limited utility of probation case records, see Miles [Arthur P. Miles, "The Utility of Case Records in Probation and Parole," *J. Crim. L., Crim. & P. S.* 56 (1965):285].

26. Wahl and Glaser.

27. Nathan G. Mandel, Hugh O. Krause, Joseph R. Rowan, and Robert L. Webb, *A Time and Function Study of the Division of Youth Corrections Parole and Probation Services Professional Staff* (Minnesota Department of Corrections, January 15, 1965).

28. Carter.

29. Lohman *et al.*, *The San Francisco Project, Research Report No. 11: The Intensive Supervision Caseload.*

30. Raym Kawaguchi and Leon M. Siff, *An Analysis of Intensive Probation Services—Phase II*, Research Report No. 29 (County of Los Angeles Probation Department, April 1967).

31. California Department of Corrections, *Special Intensive Parole Unit, Phase II: Thirty Man Caseload Study* (Sacramento, California: December 1958); California Adult Authority, *Special Intensive Parole Unit, Phase I: Fifteen Man Caseload Study* (Sacramento, California: November 1956); Joan Havel and Elaine Sulka, *Special Intensive Parole Unit, Phase III, Research Report No. 3* (California Department of Corrections, March 1962).

32. Joan Havel, *Special Intensive Parole Unit, Phase IV: The High Base Expectancy Study*, Research Report No. 10 (California Department of Corrections, June 1963).

33. Pye *et al.*

34. Lohman *et al.*, *The San Francisco Project, Research Report No. 12; Classification Criteria for Establishing Caseloads.*

21: Postprobation Recidivism /
Ralph W. England

This study reports some of the findings of an inquiry into rates of recidivism (that is, both misdemeanor and felony convictions) among a sample of 500 federal offenders placed on probation by United States judges in the Eastern District of Pennsylvania.[1] The universe from which the sample was drawn consisted of all offenders [2] whose probation terminated successfully between January 1, 1939, and December 31, 1944, who were not sentenced to imprisonment as part of their sentences or who were not otherwise incarcerated (except for detention purposes) at the time of sentencing, and who were supervised entirely under the jurisdiction of the Eastern District of Pennsylvania probation office. The total number of cases terminating in the district from 1939 to 1944 inclusive was 1,847; after eliminating those not satisfying the above conditions, the number totaled 1,238; a regular-interval sample of 500 was drawn from the latter group in a manner to assure that each of the six termination years was proportionately represented.

From Ralph W. England, "A Study of Postprobation Recidivism Among Five Hundred Federal Offenders," *Federal Probation* 19:3(1965):11, 14–16.

Purpose and Procedures

The basic questions this study sought to answer were: To what extent did the 500 ex-probationers remain law-abiding, and what variables were associated with subsequent lawful and lawless behavior, respectively? The general procedure followed in answering these questions was, first, to determine who the successes and failures were and, second, to learn the ways in which the resulting two groups differed in terms of factors presumably related to success and failure.

Criteria of Success and Failure.—Various criteria can be used to adjudge success and failure of persons subjected to penocorrectional treatment. Post-treatment histories of arrests, court appearances, convictions, commitments to mental hospitals, receiving public relief, etc., have been used singly or in combination in many criminological studies. Unfortunately, the criteria selected will usually reflect the interests and requirements of those conducting the studies, rather than representing the use of generally accepted standards against which success and failure can be measured. The single criterion used in the present study,[3] namely, subsequent misdemeanor and felony convictions, has the effect of reducing the number of failures to what approaches an absolute and somewhat unrealistic minimum, but has the decided virtue of being unequivocal. The most obvious rationale for the use of this criterion is that the ex-probationer again convicted is adjudged a malefactor by presumably competent public officials, including magistrates, judges, and jurymen, all of whom are assumed to be in possession of the facts in each case, and whose judgments, in the absence of successful appeals, are "correct." The acid test of penocorrectional efforts are recidivism rates as measured by convictions; any test less severe than this is assailable on the ground that, since public officials originally declare an individual guilty of a criminal act, and order him dealt with in ways designed to prevent further violations, only the findings of public officials should be used to decide whether or not the intent of the earlier dealings was fulfilled. Technically, at least, the administrators of the criminal law as applied to adults are concerned only with violations thereof, not with near violations, nor with types of personal or social adjustment which might conceivably lead to violations.[4]

The Major Findings

It will be recalled that the sample was drawn from persons released from probation during the years 1939 to 1944, inclusive. Because a minimum post-probation "testing" period of 5 years was stipulated in the original design of the study (i.e., every case must have been off probation at least 5 years before checkups were made), the followups were thus to have begun at the "dead-line" of January 1, 1950. Actually, however, effective followups did not begin until early in January 1951, which resulted in the adoption of a minimum post-probation period of 6 years instead of 5.

Excluded from success-failure analysis were 10 persons found to have died before they had been off probation for the minimum of 6 years; 8 others died prior to 1951 (but not prior to the expirations of their minimum periods)—5 in 1950 and 3 in 1949. These 8 were included in the analysis, along with an additional 3 who died after 1950. Analyses were based, therefore, on 490 cases rather than 500, with individual "test periods" of between 6 and 12 years.[5]

Eighty-seven (17.7 per cent) of the 490 ex-probationers surviving their minimum test periods were again reconvicted for either a felony or misdemeanor, or both, between the end of their probationary terms and December 31, 1950. Direct comparison of this failure rate of 17.7 per cent with those found in other postprobation studies is hazardous because of variations in important procedural details, particularly in the criteria of success-failure. Caldwell's study is (by design) the most comparable; he found a failure rate of 16.4 per cent in a sample differing markedly in socioeconomic characteristics when compared with those in the present writer's sample. The findings of other studies of adults vary from 12 per cent [6] to 45 per cent failures,[7] with a guessed mean of between 20 to 25 per cent. It might be stated with considerable caution that a postprobation failure rate of less than 20 per cent is relatively low.[8]

How were postprobation convictions related to the length of time elapsing after supervision ended? Referring to Table 21–1, it is seen that 27.6 per cent of the convictions occurred within the first year after release, and that the cumulative percentages increase to a point at which more than three-quarters (79.3 per cent) of the 87 recidivists are observed to have been convicted within 6 years after release.

Table 21-1

*Specific Year After End of Probation
within Which First Conviction Occurred*

Year	Number	Percent	Cumulative Per Cent
Total	87	100.0	—
1st	24	27.6	—
2nd	9	10.4	38.0
3rd	13	14.9	52.9
4th	5	5.8	58.7
5th	9	10.3	69.0
6th	9	10.3	79.3
7th	6	6.9	86.2
8th	5	5.8	92.0
9th	1	1.1	93.1
10th	4	4.6	97.7
11th	2	2.3	100.0
12th	0	0.0	—

Table 21-2

*Number of Persons Reconvicted
during Postprobation Period*

Number of Reconvictions	Total Persons Reconvicted	Per Cent of Total
Total	87	100.0
1	47	54.0
2	19	21.8
3	11	12.6
4	7	8.0
5	1	1.2
6	0	0.0
7	1	1.2
8	1	1.2

Table 21-3

*Offenses Which Led to Reconvictions
during Postprobation Period*

Offense	Number	Per Cent of Total
Total	166	100.0
Liquor	29	17.6
Gambling	20	12.0
Larceny	19	11.4
Disorderly Conduct and Related Offenses	19	11.4
Burglary	10	6.0
All others	69	41.6

The 87 failures experienced a total of 166 separate reconvictions, distributed as shown in Table 21–2. Over half the failures had only one subsequent reconviction, while nearly three-quarters experienced no more than two. The five most frequently charged offenses which led to reconvictions during the postprobation period were as shown in Table 21–3. Thus, nearly a third of the postprobation convictions involved liquor and gambling, with larceny and disorderly conduct accounting for an additional 20 per cent. Few of the convictions were for crimes commonly regarded as being serious threats to society; there were no cases of murder, rape, or arson; besides the 10 burglary convictions, there were 3 for aggravated assault and 4 for robbery. To get some idea of the relative frequency of felonies and misdemeanors, each offense was defined as if committed in Pennsylvania (or under federal jurisdiction, where applicable), with these results (10 offenses could not be classified):

Felonies	42	26.9%
Misdemeanors	114	73.1%
	156	100.0%

The charge sometimes made by its opponents that probation looses dangerous predators on society receives little support from these data.

FACTORS ASSOCIATED WITH RECIDIVISM

From a total of 30 categories of personal-social factors which could be tested in relation to recidivism,[9] 14 were found to be significantly associated with postprobation outcome.[10] Table 21–4 summarizes these findings.[11] They suggest that youthfulness, a history of previous trouble with the law, an urban background in socially and economically disadvantaged segments of society, and some element of personal *anomie* are related to postprobation recidivism. *Type of offense* (No. 11) and recidivism meet the theoretical expectation that white-collar offenders would have the lowest failure rates, but that draft-dodgers, rather than thieves or bootleggers, have the highest rate is somewhat unexpected since the popular conception of the evader of military service is that of one who is either a coward or is morally opposed to such service. However, most of the 29 men in the sample sentenced for draft-dodging had previous criminal histories, had been irregularly employed as low-grade workers, gave considerable trouble to their probation officers, and seemed, as a group, to be the toughest and least tractable of the five types of offenders. Categories 12, 13 and 14 indicate the close relationship between recidivism and previous criminal activity (although it should be noted that, except for those with nine or more arrests, less than half of such persons were subsequently reconvicted).

Summary

Using the criterion of *convictions,* a postprobation recidivism rate of 17.7 per cent was experienced by 490 federal offenders, 37.6 per cent of whom were already minor recidivists at the time of their instant probation.

Except for the first postprobation year, when 27.6 per cent of the initial postprobation convictions occurred, the first 6 years after release exhibited a more or less even accumulation of initial convictions, followed by a sharp decline in succeeding years (see Table 21–1). A process appears to operate wherein the most recidivist-prone are successively eliminated by the passage of time.

Most of the postprobation convictions (73.1 per cent) resulted from minor offenses involving mainly bootlegging, gambling, theft, and disorderly conduct.

Characteristics significantly a ssociated with recidivism appeared to be: previous criminal records, youthfulness, and personally unstable, lower-level urban socioeconomic backgrounds.

Table 21-4

Preprobation Characteristics and Recidivism Rates

Characteristic	Per Cent Recidivating	X^2	P
1. Negroes	29.2		
Whites	12.5	20.10	<.001
2. Males	19.0		
Females	8.6	3.76	.05
3. Reared in Broken Home	24.8		
Not so Reared	15.5	5.16	.02
4. Age at Probation:		12.67	<.02
15-24	28.8		
25-34	17.9		
35-44	19.0		
45-54	12.0		
55 and over	2.8		
5. Philadelphia and Vicinity	20.5		
Other Urban Places.	9.5	8.85	.02
Rural, Rural Nonfarm	5.7		
6. Laborers	24.0		
Others	15.5	4.36	.04
7. Unemployed	25.2		
Employed	15.8	5.34	.02
8. Married: No Children	27.4		
Married: Children	14.7	7.82	<.01
9. Dwelling: Room	27.3		
Apartment	28.6	9.03	.01
House	14.2		
10. No personal Insurance	21.0		
Had Insurance	12.2	5.90	<.02
11. Offense: Draft-Dodging	37.9		
"Other"	22.2		
Theft	18.5	12.40	.02
Liquor	16.4		
White Collar	10.6		
12. Previous Arrests	28.2	36.35	<.001
No Previous Arrests	7.8		
13. Number of Previous Arrests		16.10	<.01
1-2	20.9		
3-4	25.5		
5-6	47.8		
7-8	37.5		
9 and over	57.9		
14. Previous Convictions	32.6		
No Previous Convictions	11.8	8.52	<.01

NOTES

1. The present report is part of an evaluative research program instituted by the Administrative Office of the United States Courts. Morris G. Caldwell's "Preview of a New Type of Probation Study Made in Alabama," FEDERAL PROBATION, June 1951, is the first published result of that program, and this is the second. In an effort to assure a high degree of comparability between the two studies, the sampling procedures in both were virtually identical with Caldwell's as the paradigm.

2. Except for a few cases placed on probation under the Federal Juvenile Delinquency Act, all such cases were eliminated.

3. And in a few other probation researches, including the companion Alabama study.

4. Sociologically, of course, the criterion of subsequent convictions is unsatisfactory. An ex-probationer who has experienced frequent rearrests has no visible means of support, associates with criminals, bears a bad reputation, or manifests a high degree of social instability very possibly has not made a law-abiding adjustment—in which case the "real" intent of the administrators of justice has not been achieved.

5. To be rigidly scientific, uniform test periods should have been allowed for each probationer, since some "unfairness" is perpetrated against those with longer postprobation periods. An important circumstance made it advisable to follow a less strict procedure, however. The companion study in Alabama provided varying postprobation periods, with a minimum of 5 years, 6 months, and a maximum of 11 years, 7 months (Caldwell, op. cit., p. 10). It is felt, however, that the validity of the findings is not seriously affected thereby, because the mean number of years elasping between the several probation terminations and 1951 was 9.1, with 68 percent of the cases experiencing test periods of between 7.5 and 10.7 years. Furthermore, about 79 per cent of the (first) reconvictions occurred within six and 86 per cent within seven years after termination.

6. Halpern, op. cit., using convictions as criterion.

7. Report of the Commission on Probation on an Inquiry into the Permanent Results of Probation, op. cit., using "court records" as criterion.

8. Actually, so few comparable postprobation studies have been made that there exists no "average" success-failure rate to use as a standard. A reconviction rate of less than one-fifth or one-quarter might seem, using the admittedly vague standard of "reasonable expectation," to be an acceptable level of performance for a probation service.

9. Changes in presentence forms used by the federal probation system during 1939–1944, together with certain other limitations, made impracticable the analysis of more than 30 categories.

10. Using Chi-square and the .05 level of significance. In studies of this kind wherein the relatively small sample makes impracticable the use of partial correlation (or similar techniques), the possibility of spurious associations must be kept in mind. This shortcoming has been a serious deficiency in most followup studies to date.

11. Other categories tested were: nativity, number of siblings, birth order, education, religious faith, occupation, marital status, number of own children, home ownership, physical or mental disabilities, age at first arrest, and number of previous convictions. In general, the theoretical expectations with respect to these categories (that is, higher recidivism rates being associated with the "criminogenic" subcategories) were observed, but the associations were not statistically significant.

22: Probation Versus Imprisonment / Dean V. Babst and John W. Mannering

Even though the question of probation versus imprisonment is a major one, little research has been done to evaluate the impact of the two basic pro-

From Dean V. Babst and John W. Mannering, "Probation Versus Imprisonment for Similar Types of Offenders," Journal of Research in Crime and Delinquency 2 (July 1965):61–64, 66–69.

grams. A review of the literature revealed only two pilot studies [1] comparing these major programs in relationship to subsequent criminal activity. The reason for this lack of published research may be the size and complexity of the problem. The problem may be reduced, however, by specifying within the study design the factors to be considered; namely, the types of offenders for whom probation or imprisonment is most effective as measured by subsequent recurrence of criminality.

Situation in Wisconsin

Wisconsin has several advantages which combined to make a study of this type possible:

1. All adult correctional programs are under one administrative unit, the Division of Corrections of the State Department of Public Welfare. Probation and parole are handled by the same agents, and supervision and revocation procedures are standardized.

2. The high use of parole permits a comprehensive comparison between those placed on probation and those placed in prison and then on parole.

3. Wisconsin has developed the statistical reporting and data processing base necessary for comparative analysis. Since 1952 data have been collected on those admitted to probation and to correctional institutions. A follow-up system initiated at the same time records how each probation and parole case is terminated.

Data Restrictions

In order to make this study as comprehensive as possible, all cases of adult males placed on probation or released from state correctional institutions from 1954 through 1959 [2] were used, except for those intentionally and systematically excluded, to achieve maximum possible comparability between the types of cases committed to the two programs. All parole and mandatory releases were included; direct discharges were not included.[3]

The central problem in this type of study is to ascertain that differences in violation rates are due to differences in programs rather than in the types of offenders in the programs. This chapter presents what is essentially a pilot study, since with these data it is possible to control for only those factors making for comparability of offenders.

Another study will be described which should more completely control extraneous factors.

The postrelease record of each probationer and parolee (regular and mandatory release) was examined to determine whether he committed a new offense or violated the rules of supervision within two years. A parolee discharged from supervision before two years was followed for that length of time anyway to determine whether he was again committed to the Department while a probationer discharged in less than two years was not followed further. The probationers' violation rates were slightly lower, therefore, than if they had been followed up in the same manner as the parolees, but an earlier study [4] revealed that the violation rates increased less than one percentage point (0.6 per cent) when all probationers were followed for two years. Otherwise the two-year follow-up of probationers and parolees was the same.

In order to make the comparison between the two alternative programs as definitive as possible, we excluded from the parolee group those who had previously been placed on probation and were then sent to the prison or reformatory after probation had been revoked. Obviously, it would not be fair to include them, since judges had actually tried them on probation. Also, those offenders who had violated their parole, were returned to the institution, and were later paroled again were not included, since they had already been included in the study in terms of their first parole.

The offenders came from all Wisconsin counties except Milwaukee, which has its own adult probation system. Therefore, no Milwaukee probationers and no parolees committed to state correctional institutions from Milwaukee were included.

Certain offense categories contain such a wide variety of offenders that meaningful comparison of the two programs for such categories is very difficult to make; these were left out of the study. One such category was homicide, which includes cases varying from negligent homicide to first-degree murder. In the former instance men received mostly probation; in the latter, imprisonment. Another group excluded was sex offenders, about whom a series of special studies is currently being conducted.[5]

Most of the cases included in this study were property offenders—that is, men who committed larceny, embezzlement, burglary, fraud, or auto theft. Also included were offenders convicted of assault, robbery, or abandonment (nonsupport). All other types of offenders were left out of the study.

Base Expectancy Analysis

The base expectancy analysis used in England [6] and California [7] provides a method for statistically controlling violation risk variables. The central idea of the concept is to compare similar types of offenders exposed to different programs in order to evaluate the effects of the latter. Wisconsin has developed base expectancy tables for its adult male probationers and parolees; [8] these are based on probation and parole experience tables which have been tested for ability to predict violation rates for later groups. Of the items of information available to develop such tables, the following three were found to differentiate best between violators and nonviolators: the number of prior felony convictions, type of offense, and marital status at the time of commitment. Since those items predicted violation rates among subsequent groups, they were used to construct criminal classifications used in this study. This study constitutes the third use in Wisconsin of base expectancies to make preliminary assessment of program effectiveness.[9]

Of the various statistical methods for developing experience or base expectancy tables, Wisconsin used configural analysis.[10] That method has also been used to develop and refine probation or parole experience tables for the federal government, Los Angeles County (California), and Washington, Massachusetts and Florida.[11] One of the main reasons for the use of configural analysis is that it permits the development of a wide range of criminal classifications. This is important since it is very probable that two programs being compared would vary considerably in the classes of criminals they received.

Selection for Probation

Wisconsin judges use probation much more frequently than imprisonment when sentencing offenders. Table 22–1 shows that 72 per cent of the offenders in this study were given probation. As might be expected, the percentage of offenders given probation varied considerably depending upon the number of prior felonies: 79 per cent of the offenders with no prior felony convictions were placed on probation, compared with 63 per cent of those with one prior felony. The variation in the use of probation by county is provided in a separate Bureau of Research report.[12]

Evidence clearly indicates that Wisconsin judges consider the number of prior felonies, the type of offense, and marital status in assessing risk and imposing sentences. These were also the three factors found most markedly predictive of violation rates for probationers and parolees in Wisconsin.

Table 22-1

Wisconsin Adult Males Placed on Probation and Released from State Correctional Institutions, 1954-59

Number of Prior Felonies	Total	Number Placed on Probation	Per Cent Placed on Probation	First Releases* from Adult Institutions		
				Total	Parole	Mandatory Release
Total	7,554	5,406	71.6	2,148	1,785	363
None	5,274	4,184	79.3	1,090	1,009	81
One	1,340	846	63.1	494	411	83
Two or More	866	353	40.8	513	325	188
Unknowns**	74	23	–	51	40	11

*Offenders released by direct discharge, estimated at 60 cases, were not included in the study. Most of them (39) had one or more prior felonies.
**The prior felony or martial status of these 74 cases was unknown.

Violation Rates Compared

This study's main purpose is to compare probation and parole violation rates of similar types of Wisconsin offenders as a major first step toward learning which program is associated with the lower amount of subsequent criminal activity.

Any comparison of violation rates must be treated with caution, since there are always factors over which no statistical control is placed. Another cautionary note is that the smaller the number of cases in a classification, the greater the risk that chance variation will affect the violation rate. Previous research suggests that violation rates in expectancy classifications of twenty-five or more cases will probably remain about the same in future samples, while the violation rate for classification with fewer cases will be likely to vary owing to chance.

The parolees included those released by regular parole as well as those released by a special form of parole called mandatory release. Of all institutional releases, 81 per cent were by regular parole and 16 per cent by mandatory release. The remaining 3 per cent were released by direct discharge and were not included in this study. The overall violation rate (new offenses and rules violations) was 39 per cent for regular parolees and 41 per cent for mandatory releases. Most of the mandatory releases had one or more prior felonies.

The judges' estimates as to which types of offenders were most likely to violate appear to have been fairly good.

Judges tended to place offenders with low violation rates on probation and to imprison the high violator types. For example, offenders with no prior felonies demonstrated low violation rates; a higher proportion of these than of offenders with previous felony convictions were placed on probation. In nearly all criminal classifications, married offenders had lower violation rates than unmarried offenders; in all classifications higher proportions of married offenders than of unmarried offenders were placed on probation. The pattern by type of offense was similar but not quite so marked because gravity of offense appears to have affected sentencing. For example, assault and robbery cases, despite their generally lower violation rates, received probation less frequently than property offenders.

The offenders with no prior felonies, shown in Table 22–2, were the main concern in this study for two reasons. First, it is in this group that the choice of probation versus incarceration is most crucial; the more an offender repeats, the more difficult it is to justify probation. Second, offenders with no prior felonies constitute 70 per cent of the cases.

Among first offenders the violation rate for parolees was higher than for probationers in each of the six criminal classifications except abandonment (nonsupport). In four of the eleven comparisons, the parolees' violation rates were significantly higher.

Table 22-2

*Violation Experience of Wisconsin Adult Male Probationers and Parolees
with No Prior Felonies, 1954-59*

Criminal Classification	Number of Cases	Violators	
		Number	Per Cent
Total Probationers	4,184	1,043	25.0*
Total Parolees	1,090	359	32.9
Assault or Robbery			
Married			
Probation	165	29	17.6*
Parole	42	10	23.8
Not Married			
Probation	147	35	23.8
Parole	129	39	30.2
Larceny or Embezzlement			
Married			
Probation	294	29	9.9
Parole	43	8	18.6
Not Married			
Probation	687	127	18.5*
Parole	117	35	29.9
Abandonment (Nonsupport)			
Married			
Probation	589	167	28.4
Parole	61	17	27.9
Not Married			
Probation	554	164	29.6
Parole	77	20	26.0
Burglary			
Married			
Probation	163	27	16.6*
Parole	64	20	31.2
Not Married			
Probation	687	170	24.7*
Parole	325	113	34.8
Fraud			
Married			
Probation	335	90	26.8
Parole	45	14	31.1
Not Married			
Probation	305	123	40.3
Parole	84	35	41.7
Auto Theft			
Probation	258	82	31.8*
Parole	103	48	46.6

*Indicates that the difference between the violation rates was significant at the 5 per cent
level, according to the chi-square test.

The data show that offenders with one prior felony, whether on probation or parole, had about the same violation rate. Among repeated offenders the probationers' overall violation rate was higher than that of the parolees: 52 and 49 per cent, respectively. In six of the ten comparisons, the probationers had a higher violation rate.

NOTES

1. L. T. Wilkins, "A Small Comparative Study of the Results of Probation," *British Journal of Delinquency,* January 1958, pp. 201–09; and J. B. Martin, "The Saginaw Project," *Crime and Delinquency,* October 1960, pp. 357–64.

2. Those imprisoned were committed on the average about a year earlier than those placed on probation. Any difference between the two groups because of time of commitment, however, should be small, since the characteristics of those imprisoned each year are very similar. This similarity is shown by the Bureau of Research's annual reports on the characteristics of admissions and releases from Wisconsin's adult correctional institutions. Further, this study covers a six-year period during which most of the cases were committed. Data prior to 1954 were not used because the number of prior felonies for many of the institutional releases was not recorded. The present sample was terminated with the 1959 cases to provide for a two-year statistical follow-up period. Offenders placed on probation or released from correctional institutions but later transferred to other states were included; however, probationers or parolees from other states were not included. Also excluded were a few offenders who died while under supervision and juveniles placed on probation or transferred from correctional training schools to adult institutions.

3. An inmate receives a "mandatory release" from the institution before expiration of the sentence to the extent of "time off" earned for "good behavior"; the period of mandatory release supervision ends with expiration of the sentence. "Direct discharge" of an inmate occurs when parole supervision is not deemed to be in the public's best interest and the sentence has expired in the institution.

4. Bureau of Research, "How Many Criminal Offenders Succeed or Fail When Placed on Probation to Wisconsin Division of Corrections?" Research Bulletin C-1 (Madison, Wis., State Department of Public Welfare, February 1957).

5. L. M. Roberts and A. R. Pacht, "Termination of Inpatient Treatment for Sex Deviates: Psychiatric, Social, and Legal Factors," *American Journal of Psychiatry,* March 1965.

6. H. Mannheim and L. T. Wilkins, *Prediction Methods in Relation to Borstal Training* (London, Her Majesty's Stationery Office, 1955).

7. J. D. Grant, D. M. Gottfredson, and J. A. Bouds, "A Manual for Intake Base Expectancies Scoring" (Sacramento, Calif., Research Division, State Department of Corrections, April 1961).

8. Bureau of Research, "Wisconsin Base Expectancies for Adult Male Probationers," Progress Reports 1 and 3, and "Wisconsin Base Expectancies for Adult Male Parolees," Progress Reports 2 and 4 (Madison, Wis., State Department of Public Welfare, 1962–1963); S. B. Powers, "Standard Parole Prediction Methods—Views of a Correctional Administrator," *Crime and Delinquency,* July 1962, pp. 270–75; and J. W. Mannering, "Current Plans for Use of Parole Experience Tables in Wisconsin," *Proceedings,* American Correctional Association, Philadelphia, Pa., 1962.

9. Bureau of Research, "Preliminary Findings on the Relationship of Wisconsin State Reformatory Training and Work Programs to Later Parole Violation Experience. 1958 and 1959 Releases," Progress Report No. 5, and "Preliminary Findings on the Relationship of Training, Work, and Institutional Adjustment at Wisconsin State Prison to Later Parole Violation Experience, 1958 and 1959 Releases," Progress Report No. 6 (Madison, Wis., State Department of Public Welfare, 1964).

10. *Ibid.*

11. D. Glaser, *The Effectiveness of a Prison and Parole System* (Indianapolis, Bobbs-Merrill, 1961); E. Brooks, "Recidivism among Youthful Offenders Released to Urban Areas from Federal Institutions," unpublished master's thesis, George Washington University, 1963; S. Adams and M. Thompson, "Probationer Characteristics and Probation Performance," Research Report No. 10 (Los Angeles, Calif., Los Angeles County Probation Department, 1963); L. E. Hazelrigg, "Success and Failure among Persons Paroled in Florida in 1957–58 Using the Wisconsin Parole Expectancy Technique," master's thesis, Florida State University, 1964; R. Metzner and G. Weil, "Predicting Recidivism: Base-rates for Massachusetts Correctional Institution at Concord," *Journal of Criminal Law, Criminology, and Police Science,* September 1963, pp. 307–16; S. Wheeler, "Evaluation of Parole Prediction Techniques," unpublished master's thesis, Department of Sociology, University of Washington, 1956; and D. Strinden, "Parole Prediction Using Criminological Theory and Manifold-Classification Techniques," unpublished master's thesis, Department of Sociology, University of Washington, 1959.

12. Bureau of Research, "County of Residence of Adult Offenders Committed to Wisconsin Correctional Institutions and Placed on Probation, 1958 through 1962." Statistical Bulletin C-44 (Madison, Wis., State Department of Public Welfare, January 1965).

23: Results of Probation /
Frank R. Scarpitti and
Richard M. Stephenson

Of the twenty-two recommendations made by the President's Commission on Law Enforcement and Administration of Justice in the area of corrections, eight call for the expansion of community based treatment programs.[1] Prominent among the Commission's recommendations is a call for the expanded use of probation services for both juvenile and adult offenders. Citing the detrimental effects of institutionalization, especially on the young, the Commission's report concludes that placing an offender on probation allays these effects as well as increases his chances for a successful adjustment.[2] The negative consequences of institutionalization are well documented,[3] and obviously, keeping one out of the reformatory or prison will prevent his experiencing their debilitating effects. However, the effectiveness of probation as a rehabilitating program is not as well documented, and its crime or delinquency reducing impact upon offenders continues to be subject to many sceptical questions.

From Frank R. Scarpitti and Richard M. Stephenson: "A Study of Probation Effectiveness," *Journal of Criminal Law, Criminology and Police Science* 59:3(1968):361–369.

Conclusions regarding the effectiveness of probation are generally based upon the number of probationers who complete their supervision without revocation or the amount of post-release recidivism occurring among those who complete supervision. It can be seen that these are actually two different measures of success. In the former instance, many unknown and uncontrollable variables may influence the outcome of the probation experience: the philosophy of the probation department in revocation, the intensity of the officer's contacts with the probationer, the unknown offenses committed by the probationer while on probation, and the philosophy of the court in continuing or extending probation for known offenses. Nevertheless, England's review of eleven probation studies indicates that from 60 to 90 per cent succeed on probation.[4] A 1944 study of juvenile probationers showed that 35 per cent failed,[5] and a later study of 11,638 adult probationers revealed that only 29 per cent had their probation revoked.[6]

These success-failure rates are based upon official probation records and of course suffer from the deficiencies listed above. As such, they present a most favorable picture of probation success. Using more stringent, but perhaps unfair and unrealistic criteria of failure, the Gluecks have reported probation failure rates of 57.9 per cent for youthful offenders and 92.4 per cent for adult male offenders.[7]

Perhaps the second method of determining probation effectiveness, recidivism, is a better indicator of the true success or failure of probation as a rehabilitation mechanism. Again, England reports that of the eleven studies reviewed, eight fall within the 70 to 90 per cent range in terms of post-probation success. These include Diana's study of juvenile probationers (84 per cent success), and England's study of adult Federal probationers (82.3 per cent success).[8] In addition, other studies of post-release recidivism among both adult and juvenile offenders show success or nonrecidivism rates of 72, 79, 88 and 83 per cent.[9] These rates compare favorably with those reported for in-program success and appear to substantiate the call for increased probation usage.

Nevertheless, the high rates of probation and post-probation success are puzzling to those who are aware of the difficulties of resocialization and rehabilitation. Probation supervision and guidance have traditionally been only superficial, generally involving infrequent and ritualistic contacts between officer and offender.[10] At the same time, few if any special programs of more intensive treatment and worker-client contacts can approximate the probation success rates.[11] Such contradictory evidence causes one to ask questions that have not yet been or have only partially been answered. Are probationers the least likely of the offender population to become recidivists? Are probationers different from other adjudicated offenders? What differentiates the in-program successes from the failures? How does recidivism among ex-probationers compare with that of other offenders who have experienced alternative methods of treatment? This chapter will attempt to answer these and other questions pertaining to the effectiveness of probation as a treatment method.

The Present Study

Data presented in this chapter were collected as part of a larger comparative study of delinquency treatment facilities. From January, 1962, to January, 1965, some 1,210 adjudicated male delinquents between the ages of 16 and 18 from Essex County (Newark), New Jersey were admitted into the study.[12] Of these, 943 were committed to county probationary supervision, 100 to a non-residential guided group interaction center in the county, 67 to residential guided group interaction centers in the state, and 100 were sent to the State Reformatory at Annandale. All boys were followed up for recidivism until June, 1966.

The special admission criteria used by the court in committing boys to the group centers were also used to select participants in this study. Hence, all delinquents in this sample were male, 16 or 17 years of age, had no evidence of psychosis, severe neurosis or serious mental retardation, and had no prior commitment to a correctional institution. Assurance of reasonable comparability among cases, with respect to such differentiating factors as social background, psychological profiles, and delinquency history, presents a major problem in any comparative study. Ideally, it would be desirable to have boys assigned by the court to treatment facilities on a basis that would assure such comparability or, at least, on a random basis. In this study, as in others, this was not possible. However, it was felt that it would be possible to match boys across facilities on pertinent variables so as to control to some extent differences that might be found among the groups.

In order to obtain data upon which to match boys by treatment programs and to see how such data are related to progress in treatment and recidivism after release, the following information was obtained for each boy: first, social background data consisting of the usual demographic items relating to the boy and his family; second, delinquency history data consisting of the boy's entire court record (this information was up-dated during the post-treatment follow-up period); and third, a psychological profile determined by responses to questions on the Minnesota Multiphasic Personality Inventory.[13] The personality inventory was given whenever possible to each boy after his court appearance and before entrance into one of the treatment programs. Because of the large number of probationers relative to the other treatment groups, the MMPI was not administered to members of this group after January, 1964. In order to test for change during treatment, the study subjects were again given the inventory at the time of their release.[14]

Hence, it was not only possible to test the impact of the probation experience as measured by program completion, psychological change, and recidivism, but also to compare the results of probation with those of other programs available to the committing judge. The programs used for such comparison can be thought of as more "intense" and confining than probation. The nonresidential group center (Essexfields) program included a regimen of work and group interaction for approximately four months while the boys continued to live at home. The Group Centers program entailed the same elements for the same length of time, but boys resided in the Centers. At Annandale, the state reformatory, the program was restricted and irregular, and commitments averaged about nine months.

Characteristics of the Groups

The social background characteristics of each group are roughly associated with assignment to their treatment facility. Although the association is not always marked or consistent, Annandale tends to have a greater proportion of boys who are Negro, in the lower range of the socio-economic continuum, and more likely to terminate their education before high school graduation. Probationers, on the other hand, are equally divided racially and generally tend to be more positive on the socio-economic, family organization, and education variables. Between the extremes of Annandale and Probation are the other two treatment groups.

In addition, 37 per cent of the Probation group had completed the tenth grade or more compared with 24 per cent in the Group Centers, 18 per cent in Essexfields, and 14 per cent in Annandale. More of the Probation group also had some employment experience prior to their treatment assignment.

A fairly clear pattern of progression with respect to the association between delinquency history and treatment program is also evident. This pattern indicates that the extent of delinquency tends to increase from Probation through Essexfields and Group Centers to Annandale. This progression is most clearly indicated by the number of past court appearances. Nearly half of the Probationers had no prior court appearance, while only 7 per cent or less of the other boys fall into this category. Twenty per cent of the boys at Annandale, 15 per cent at Group Centers, 6 per cent at Essexfields, and 3 per cent on Probation had five or more appearances. Only 40 per cent of the Probationers, but over 90 per cent of the boys in the other groups had one or more prior petitions sustained by the court. Forty-one per cent of the Annandale boys had three or more petitions sustained, but only 5 per cent of the Probationers. Eighty per cent of the Probationers but only 19 per cent of the Annandale boys had never been on probation before. As a group, Probationers were older and Annandale boys younger at the time of the first court appearance. Almost two-thirds of the Probationers were 16 or 17 years of age at their first court appearance; less than a third of the boys in any other group were that old. Insofar as previous court history and age of first court appearance are associated with continued delinquency, the Probationers appear to be the best risks and Annandale boys the worst.

When the psychological characteristics of the four groups are examined, rather distinct differences can also be seen.[15] As with many of the social background and delinquency history characteristics, the Probation and Annandale groups are the most different, with the Essexfields and Group Centers groups falling between these two extremès. These results suggest that the Probation boys as a group are somewhat less anti-social, less delinquent (although exhibiting a distinctively delinquent personality pattern), and better emotionally adjusted than the boys in the other groups. They are also less anxious and less hostile, exhibit a slightly better attitude toward themselves, have a better work attitude, and score higher on the social responsibility dimension of the inventory.

From all indications, it would appear that Probation received the less delinquent and better socially and psychologically adjusted juvenile offender. In this sense, it becomes responsible for what might be termed "easier" cases, or boys for whom the probability of success is greater. The relationship between pre-treatment probability of success and actual success can be seen in terms of (1) program completion, (2) change during the program, and (3) post-treatment recidivism.

In-Program Success and Failure

"In-program failure" is used to refer to any boy who was sent back to the court during the course of the treatment program and who was not returned by the court to the same program. It refers to those boys returned to the court for committing a new delinquent offense, being incorrigible or unmanageable while in the program, or, in the case of Essexfields and Group Centers, being socially or emotionally unsuitable for the program. In essence, the in-program failures were those boys upon whom the various rehabilitation programs had the least immediate effect, not even providing them with an opportunity to experience the entire treatment process.

Aside from Annandale, a custodial institution where program completion is not a question, the in-program success and failure rates for the other facilities were strikingly similar. Although the failure rate for Probation, 28 per cent of the committed boys, is higher than that for Essexfields, 23 per cent, and the Group Centers, 27 per cent, these differences are not statistically significant. These rates do indicate, however, that the overwhelming majority of the boys in non-custodial programs complete their treatment experiences without becoming involved in further difficulty. Using only this criterion of success, probation fares no better than some others, and theoretically more meaningful, programs of treatment. In addition, some 219 Probationers appeared in court for a new offense during their probationary period, but were given dispositions of "Probation Extended" or "Probation Continued." Hence, they were not counted as in-program failures.

Examination of pertinent background, delinquency and personality variables shows interesting differences between Probation successes and failures. In Probation, whites have a lower failure rate and a higher success rate than Negroes. Failure is also more likely to occur for those boys who were out of school at the time of their admission. The same is true for those boys with a negative educational status score, a composite index which includes present school status, number of grades completed, and number of years retarded in school. The delinquency history score, another composite index consisting of age first known to court, number of delinquent offenses, and types of delinquent offenses, presents further evidence that the less delinquent and less delinquency-prone do better on probation than the more seriously delinquent. All of these differences are statistically significant at the .05 level or better. The same relationship, however, is not necessarily found between failures and successes in the other groups. Generally speaking, failures in the other groups are similar to Probation failures, but do not differ as markedly from the successes in their groups.

The MMPI data corroborate these findings. Again, the greatest differences are found between the Probation successes and failures. Nineteen of the 29 scales used in this study differentiate these two groups at the .05 level of significance or better. Among those tests which distinguish between the groups are the psychopathic deviancy, hypomania, schizophrenia, and F (indicating an attempt by the respondent to show himself in a bad light), as well as the delinquency, escapism, and social responsibility scales. As with the other tests which differentiate, the Probation successes score more positively than do the failures. The failures clearly have a more delinquent personality pattern, conforming closely to the classic pattern for delinquents.

All of the scores for the Probation successes indicate that they are not very disturbed and are fairly well adjusted. Probation failures, as indicated, are less so, but are similar to both the failures and successes in Essexfields and Group Centers. In these groups there are practically no significant differences between program successes and failures as determined by the MMPI tests. Failures in both programs, however, generally score more negatively than do successes on most scales. Although many of the success-failure differences in the Essexfields and Group Centers programs are in the same direction as those found in Probation, they are milder and less able to distinguish between the criterion groups.

These data seem to indicate that the Probation successes are less delinquent and better adjusted than all other boys in this study, successes or failures. In Essexfields and Group Centers the successes and failures are more similar to each other, as well as to the Probation failure group.

Changes During Treatment

The pre- to post-treatment MMPI changes made by boys while on Probation were relatively minimal. Of the basic MMPI scales, the significant changes were an increase on the depression and defensiveness scales and a decrease on the paranoia and social introversion scales. While this pattern of change is not readily meaningful, it becomes clearer upon examination of the remaining scales. Decreases occurred on the anxiety and neuroticism scales, although these changes tend to be inconsistent with the increase in depression. Other changes were an improvement in attitude toward others, in attitude toward self, in work attitude, in intelligence and in dominance.

These scores suggest that a definite though slight change did take place in the boys during their probationary term. However, the changes were not in the scores characteristic of delinquency (psychopathic deviancy, hypomania, and schizophrenia), but in a variety of other areas. Overall, the boys became a little less anxious, and more outgoing, secure, and intellectually efficient. Also, there was improvement in attitudes toward themselves, others, and work. The slight decrease in paranoia seems to have little meaning, since larger decreases were shown by all other groups.

Changes shown by the Essexfields and Group Centers boys were somewhat more marked than those shown in the Probation sample. Although the changes were not necessarily the type associated with delinquency reduction, they reflected general improvement in attitudes and ego-strength and a reduction of anxiety. Annandale boys, however, did not exhibit any of these positive changes and showed a greater tendency for change in a negative direction. Most noteworthy, perhaps, was an increase in the hostility score over the period of institutional confinement.

These findings indicate that the greatest positive changes, as measured by the MMPI, occurred in the group programs. Changes for the Probation group were slight, but in a positive direction. To account for Probation's more favorable initial group profile, groups within the four programs were matched on clinical scales regarded as predictive of delinquency. The changes for these matched groups were very similar to those of the unmatched groups. We might conclude then that Probation's effect in this respect is slight but positive. It is not as effective as either the nonresidential or residential group programs, but much more beneficial than the reformatory experience.

Recidivism

Perhaps the most crucial indicator of probation effectiveness is whether or not boys who complete the program continue to experience difficulty with the law. Objections to the use of recidivism as a criterion of "successful" treatment may be raised on several grounds. Recidivism indicates only one aspect of the effectiveness of a program of rehabilitation. Improvement in work habits, educational orientation, family adjustment, or personality characteristics are not necessarily indicated by the fact that a new offense is or is not committed. In addition, a person may commit numerous infractions of the law without arrest or conviction and still be regarded as a "success." Nevertheless, an avowed goal of corrections is to inhibit a return to crime and delinquency. Short of daily surveillance of individual cases or reliable community sources of informal information concerning them, the available evidence for estimating effectiveness in reaching this goal is the official record of court appearances and dispositions. This evaluation therefore seeks to answer one major question: to what extent do those released from a program of treatment become involved in delinquency or crime as indicated by court action?

Boys who completed treatment and had no court appearances from their date of release to June of 1966 are clearly non-recidivists. Those who had one or more court appearances after release are not so readily disposed of since a court appearance is not sufficient to regard a case as a recidivist. A wide range of alternative dispositions are available to the court that may indicate a minor offense or even none at all. Therefore, the following court dispositions were used as the basis for determining recidivism: fine, jail, probation, Essexfields, Group Centers, reformatory, and prison. A court appearance resulting in any other disposition [16] was regarded as non-recidivism, since the court obviously did not view the case as demanding intensive correctional treatment or punitive action.

Setting aside for the moment the fact that boys in different programs differ in social background and delinquency history, it can be seen from Table 23–1 that Annandale boys have the highest recidivism rate (55 per cent) and Probationers the lowest (15 per cent). Essexfields and Group Centers fall between these extremes, although recidivism is somewhat lower for Group Centers boys (41 per cent) than for Essexfields boys (48 per cent) and terminates earlier than that of any other program. It also is apparent that this general pattern is repeated when recidivism is calculated for each six month post-release period. The differences in rates of recidivism between Probation and each of the other three programs are statistically significant at a level greater than .001.

Among all recidivists, the highest percentage of recidivism was within the first six months, and nearly 75 per cent of the recidivism took place within a

Table 23-1

Number of Recidivists, Cumulative Recidivists and Cumulative Per cent of Releases Who Are Recidivists by Six Month Periods

Months	Probation (N = 671)			Essexfields (N = 77)			Group Centers (N = 49)			Annandale (N = 97)		
	R	CR	C%	R	CR	C%	R	CR	C%	R	CR	C%
6	50	50	7	12	12	16	8	8	8	20	20	21
12	37	87	13	9	21	27	5	13	27	16	36	38
18	9	96	14	8	29	38	5	18	37	9	45	46
24	5	101	15	6	35	45	2	20	41	6	51	53
30	1	102	15	1	36	47	–	–	–	1	52	54
36	–	–	–	1	37	48	–	–	–	1	53	55

N – Number of releases (completed treatment).
R – Number of recidivists.
CR – Cumulative recidivists.
C% – Cumulative per cent of releases.

year after release. Probation recidivists appear to have the highest rate of recidivism within the first year and decrease strikingly thereafter. Noting the early termination of recidivism among Group Centers boys, the other three programs appear to spread out recidivism over a longer time span.

Since boys in the four programs of treatment were found to differ with respect to social background and delinquency history, an attempt was made to match cases across programs. With the exception of Probation, the total number of boys in each program was relatively small. This meant that to match on more than two or three variables was not feasible. At the same time it was desirable to include as many of the relevant factors as possible. One way to handle this problem was to combine several related variables into one index. Three factors were selected for matching purposes: socio-economic status (index comprised of family income, education and occupation of family breadwinner), delinquency history (index described earlier), and race.

It was possible to match only 44 boys across all four programs on the three matching factors. After elimination of in-program failures, the following rates of recidivism were observed: Probation (N = 34), 21 per cent; Essexfields (N = 35), 49 per cent; Group Centers (N = 31), 45 per cent; and Annandale (N = 41), 56 per cent. The differences in rates between Probation and each of the other three programs are statistically significant at a level greater than .01. Probationers were then matched separately with Essexfields boys since these two programs were most similar. Ninety-nine boys were matched in each group and, after eliminating the in-program failures, recidivism rates of 19 per cent for Probation (N = 69) and 48 per cent for Essexfields (N = 76) were found. As these results from matched groups indicate, the relative proportion of recidivists for each program does not change greatly even when seemingly significant variables are controlled.

It appears that Probation is highly successful as a treatment device when compared with alternative methods of dealing with delinquent boys. Probationers who complete their treatment have lower rates of recidivism than those who complete other types of programs, even when matched on background and delinquency factors. A great difference can be observed, however, between the recidivism rates of Probationers who complete and those who fail to complete the program. This is a significant consideration because recidivism rates of in-program failures may bear upon the finding concerning recidivism among boys who successfully completed treatment.

The data suggest that boys who fail during treatment and are reassigned to another program are poor risks for rehabilitation. Although this is true for all programs in which in-program failure was possible, it is especially true for Probation. Not only do Probation failures have a much higher rate of recidivism than failures in other programs, but they also have a significantly higher (p > .001) rate than those who complete treatment. When program successes and failures are combined, that is, all boys originally assigned to Probation by the court, the recidivism rate for Probation more than doubles, although it still remains lower than that of the other programs.

Discussion

This chapter has presented data on the effectiveness of probation as a treatment program for 16 and 17 year old delinquent boys. Boys assigned to probationary supervision were compared with delinquents committed to group treatment programs and to the state reformatory. Pertinent data were collected for each group at the time of program assignment, during the programs, and after release from treatment.

As a group, boys assigned to Probation appear to be "better" or "easier" cases than those assigned to other treatment facilities. They appear to come from more stable family backgrounds, are less deprived, and have a more positive educational history. Their delinquency careers are shorter and involve fewer past offenses and official court actions. The MMPI scores suggest that Probation boys are less delinquent, less antisocial and better adjusted than boys in the other groups. Of the more than 1,200 delinquent boys selected for this study, it is clearly evident that the best "risks" were assigned to Probation. As others have indicated,[17] the bulk of Probationers are not seriously delinquent and probably not in need of intensive rehabilitative efforts.

Once assigned to Probation, some 72 per cent of the group complete the program and are successfully discharged. This is comparable to the percentage completing the group programs. More significantly, however, are the differences observed between the Probation successes and failures. On practically every count, the in-program failures are worse off than the successes. These differences are not seen between successes and failures in the other programs. Probation failures conform more to the profiles of all boys in the other groups than they do to the successes in Probation. Hence, it would appear that Probation rids itself during the course of treatment of those boys who are most delinquent and hardest to resocialize.

For those who complete probation, little change is reflected on the psychological and attitudinal dimensions of the MMPI. This is not surprising since the pre-tests did not indicate gross abnormalities among these youths and since the most disturbed, who had the greatest margin for improvement, were eliminated as in-program failures. It seems significant then that even modest positive changes were found in attitude, ego strength and anxiety. Although not as great as the changes made by boys in the group-oriented programs, they are certainly more favorable than those of the reformatory group.

In the last analysis, the crucial test of program effectiveness is recidivism, despite its many shortcomings. Again, boys assigned to Probation do much better in staying out of legal difficulty after release than their counterparts in other treatment programs. The Probation recidivism rate of 15 per cent is substantially below that of other programs. Although this low rate may result from Probationers' having the most favorable social backgrounds and delinquency histories, when boys were matched across programs, the relative rates of recidivism remained substantially unchanged.

The low rate of recidivism of the Probationers who complete treatment may partially be accounted for by the high rate of recidivism of in-program failures, on the grounds that Probation rids itself of high recidivism risks. By returning high risk boys to the court for further disposition, Probation may increase its chances of non-recidivism among boys who complete treatment. This is possible to a much lesser extent at Essexfields and Group Centers, and practically impossible at Annandale. This possibility must be considered as a strong conditioning factor in assessing the very low 15 per cent recidivism among Probationers who completed treatment.

On the basis of the criteria used in this study, Probation does appear to be an effective treatment agent, at least for certain types of boys. Those who are less delinquent and come from fairly stable backgrounds complete their treatment program and remain free of delinquency involvement. More severe cases, similar to those assigned to intensive or punitive programs, do not do as well on probation.

These findings lead us to a note of caution. It would appear that the good performance of probation is often misunderstood and thought to mean that all offenders can benefit from being placed under probationary supervision. This is clearly not the case. If probation is extended greatly, failure and recidivism rates will grow markedly, unless, of course, there is some monumental change in treatment techniques. Barring such change, a backlash effect is possible, with the public's reacting against probation, which they will assume to be ineffectual, and demanding more incarceration. The use of probation should be expanded, but its direction must be carefully guided and those assigned to it must be chosen with rigor.

NOTES

    The authors are indebted to the Ford Foundation whose research support made this study possible. This study was also supported in part by grants from the National Institute of Mental Health (MH 11945-01) and the Rutgers University Research Council. We are grateful for the assistance and helpful comments of Dr. John H. McGrath.

    1. THE CHALLENGE OF CRIME IN A FREE SOCIETY, a Report by the President's Commission on Law Enforcement and Administration of Justice, United States Government Printing Office, Washington, D.C., Chap. 6 (1967).
    2. Ibid., 165–171.
    3. Of the many studies that have attested to the anti-rehabilitation effects of total institutions such as prisons and reformatories, see, for example: Sykes, THE SOCIETY OF CAPTIVES (1958); Clemmer, THE PRISON COMMUNITY (1948); Cloward, Social Control in Prison, Chap. 2, Cloward, et al., THEORETICAL STUDIES IN SOCIAL ORGANIZATION OF THE PRISON (1960); Garrity, The Prison as a Rehabilitation Agency, Chap. 9, and Glaser and Stratton, Measuring Inmate Change in Prison, Chap. 10, Cressey, Ed., THE PRISON: STUDIES IN INSTITUTIONAL ORGANIZATION AND CHANGE (1961); Goffman, ASYLUMS (1961); Ward & Kassebaum, WOMEN'S PRISON (1965); Street, The Inmate Group in Custodial and Treatment Settings, 30 AMER. SOC. REV. 40–45 (1965); Berk, Organizational Goals and Inmate Organization, 71 AMER. J. SOC. 522–534 (1966); and Giallombardo, SOCIETY OF WOMEN: A STUDY OF A WOMEN'S PRISON (1966).
    4. England, Jr., What Is Responsible for Satisfactory Probation and Post-Probation Outcome?, 47 J. Crim. L. & C., 674 (1957).

5. Reiss, Jr., *Delinquency as the Failure of Personal and Social Control,* 16 Amer. Soc. Rev. 196–207 (1951).

6. THE CHALLENGE OF CRIME IN A FREE SOCIETY, *op. cit.,* p. 166.

7. GLUECK, S. & E. JUVENILE DELINQUENTS GROWN UP, 153 (1940) and CRIMINAL CAREERS IN RETROSPECT, 151 (1943).

8. England, *op. cit., supra* note 4, at pp. 667, 674.

9. Reported in SUTHERLAND & CRESSEY, PRINCIPLES OF CRIMINOLOGY 497 (7th ed. 1966).

10. England, *op. cit. supra* note 4; Diana, *Is Casework in Probation Necessary?,* 34 *Focus* 1–8 (1955).

11. See, for example, any or all of the following: WEEKS, YOUTHFUL OFFENDERS AT HIGHFIELDS (1958); *The Community Treatment Project After 5 Years,* California Youth Authority, no date; Empey and Erickson, *The Provo Experiment in Delinquency Rehabilitation,* Annual Progress Report for 1964, unpublished report to the Ford Foundation, 1965; Stephenson and Scarpitti, *The Rehabilitation of Delinquent Boys,* report to the Ford Foundation (mimeographed), 1967.

12. During this period nearly 15,000 children appeared before the Essex County Juvenile Court. Some 4,761 of these youths were boys sixteen or seventeen years of age.

13. Of the several psychological instruments available, the MMPI appeared to be most feasible for this purpose. Resources would not permit an exploration in depth, nor was it possible to design, test, validate and complete an instrument more suitable for this particular study. On the other hand, the MMPI has been widely used, is readily administered, and gives a reasonably broad psychological profile. Moreover, a number of studies have used the MMPI on both delinquent and non-delinquent populations. See: HATHAWAY & MONACHESI, ANALYZING AND PREDICTING JUVENILE DELINQUENCY WITH THE MMPI (1952); ADOLESCENT PERSONALITY AND BEHAVIOR (1963); DAHLSTROM & WELSH, AN MMPI HANDBOOK (1960); WELSH, BASIC READINGS ON THE MMPI IN PSYCHOLOGY AND EDUCATION (1956).

14. Since some of the boys were non-readers or failed to cooperate, it was impossible to test all in both pre- and post-treatment situations. Further attrition of cases was occasioned by changes in institutional personnel administering the tests, in-program failures, and a variety of administrative circumstances. When the inventories were scored and examined for validity, further losses were experienced. In all, there were 491 valid pre-treatment and 325 valid post-treatment MMPI inventories available.

15. In addition to the regular fourteen basic clinical and validity scales, fifteen other measures selected from Dahlstrom and Walsh (*op. cit.*) and other sources were used in the analysis of the MMPI's. For a detailed discussion, see Stephenson and Scarpitti, *The Rehabilitation of Delinquent Boys,* report to the Ford Foundation (1967) (mimeographed). The authors gratefully acknowledge the contribution of Dr. Richard Lanyon, Department of Psychology, Rutgers, The State University, in the analysis of these data.

16. Court dispositions not regarded as recidivism included dismissal, petition withdrawn, private placement, hospital placement, restitution ordered, counseled, adjustment to be reviewed, referred to parole (no further action taken), probation extended or continued (for Essexfields and Group Centers releasees), probation vacated, bench warrant issued and case pending.

17. Diana, *op. cit. supra* note 10; and England, *op. cit. supra* note 4.

24: The Use of Parole / *Report on Parole and Aftercare*

The test of the success of institutional corrections programs comes when offenders are released to the community. Whatever rehabilitation they have received, whatever deterrent effect their experience with incarceration has had, must upon release withstand the difficulties of readjustment to life in society and reintegration into employment, family, school, and the rest of community life. This is the time when most of the problems from which offenders were temporarily removed must be faced again and new problems arising from their status as ex-offenders must be confronted.

Many offenders are released outright into the community upon completion of their sentences, but a growing number—now more than 60 per cent of adult felons for the Nation as a whole—are released on parole prior to the expiration of the maximum term of their sentences. Parole supervision, which in general resembles probation in methods and purposes, is the basic way— and one of the oldest—of trying to continue in the community the correctional program begun in the institution and help offenders make the difficult adjustment to release without jeopardy to the community. Furloughs, halfway houses, and similar programs are important supplements to effective parole programs, as are prerelease guidance and other social services discussed later in this chapter.

Parole is generally granted by an administrative board or agency on the basis of such factors as an offender's prior history, his readiness for release, and his need for supervision and assistance in the community prior to the expiration of his sentence. The Federal system and those of a few States have a mandatory supervision procedure for offenders not released on parole. Under such a procedure, when an inmate is released for good behavior before serving his maximum term, he is supervised in the community for a period equivalent to his "good time credit."

From U.S., President's Commission on Law Enforcement and Administration of Justice, Report on "Parole and Aftercare," *Task Force on Corrections* (1967), pp. 60–61.

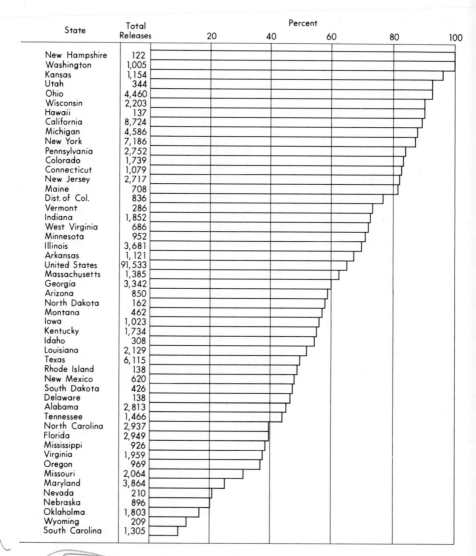

State	Total Releases	Percent
		20 · 40 · 60 · 80 · 100
New Hampshire	122	
Washington	1,005	
Kansas	1,154	
Utah	344	
Ohio	4,460	
Wisconsin	2,203	
Hawaii	137	
California	8,724	
Michigan	4,586	
New York	7,186	
Pennsylvania	2,752	
Colorado	1,739	
Connecticut	1,079	
New Jersey	2,717	
Maine	708	
Dist. of Col.	836	
Vermont	286	
Indiana	1,852	
West Virginia	686	
Minnesota	952	
Illinois	3,681	
Arkansas	1,121	
United States	91,533	
Massachusetts	1,385	
Georgia	3,342	
Arizona	850	
North Dakota	162	
Montana	462	
Iowa	1,023	
Kentucky	1,734	
Idaho	308	
Louisiana	2,129	
Texas	6,115	
Rhode Island	138	
New Mexico	620	
South Dakota	426	
Delaware	138	
Alabama	2,813	
Tennessee	1,466	
North Carolina	2,937	
Florida	2,949	
Mississippi	926	
Virginia	1,959	
Oregon	969	
Missouri	2,064	
Maryland	3,864	
Nevada	210	
Nebraska	896	
Oklahoma	1,803	
Wyoming	209	
South Carolina	1,305	

FIGURE 24–1. *Inmates Released on Parole as Percentage of All Persons Released from State Prisons, 1964.*

25: The Results of Parole / *Daniel Glaser* and *Vincent O'Leary*

Part I. Introduction

One of the principal roles of a parole board member is that of evaluator. He collects a large variety of information about an offender, and from this he must determine the risks in paroling that individual. What aspects of the case are favorable for parole outcome? What features are unfavorable? What other information is desirable? How can all the pros and cons best be combined into a single overall evaluation of each man?

When discussing the evaluation of a parolee's postrelease prospects, frequent references are made to statistics on the relative "success" or "failure" rates of various types of parolees. Since there are many objectives in parole, there can be numerous standards from which to assess parole "success." However, at this point we shall use somewhat broad criteria of parole outcome.

Parole is applied to persons who have committed crimes serious enough to justify the State's taking measures to confine them. Since parole is a conditional release from this confinement, the primary index of parole "success" used here will be negative, that the parolee's behavior does not provide State action to revoke his parole and again to confine him.

Statistics will be presented on the relationship of various characteristics of parolees to their post-release success. These statistics will be drawn from several different jurisdictions. However, it should be noted that overall parole success rates vary from one State to the next as a result of many characteristics of parole policy. For example, in States which parole only a small proportion of their prisoners, just the best risks may be paroled, so one expects that their violation rates will be lower than those of States which parole nearly all prisoners. Similarly, if the parole period is long or parole supervision is close, one expects that officials will know of more violations than would be reported under the opposite conditions.

In addition, there are many issues involved in the definition of parole violation. One agency might well return more parolees to institutions as violators than another, but because of a vigorous supervision program, proportionately

Reprinted from U.S. Dept. of Health, Education, and Welfare, Daniel Glaser and Vincent O'Leary, *Personal Characteristics and Parole Outcome* (Washington, D.C.: U.S. Government Printing Office, 1966), pp. 1–17.

fewer of those returned have committed new crimes. Differences between systems regarding the action taken in the cases of absconders or parolees given jail terms are also examples of variations in policy which can account for significant differences in "violation rates" when, in fact, the rates may be quite similar or even reversed.

Variations, like the above, should be borne in mind in examining the data presented here. Consequently, the statistics presented *cannot be employed to compare accurately overall violation rates between jurisdictions,* but only violation rate trends in different categories of parolees within the jurisdictions cited. For example, we can probe whether the younger parolees have higher violation rates than older ones or whether intelligence is related to parole violations citing data from several systems.

The following is a brief description of the principal sources of statistical data presented. Each is given below the title by which it will be cited:

1. *Wisconsin Parolees:* This information consists of separately tabulated data on 2,255 adult males, 206 adult females, 1,037 juvenile males, and 453 juvenile females who comprise all persons released on parole from Wisconsin's Division of Corrections from January 1, 1952, through December 31, 1954. The violation rate is based on every person whose parole was revoked, or who was again committed to a Wisconsin penal institution or placed on probation following discharge from parole, within 2 years of his release on parole. These tabulations were made available to us by the late John W. Mannering, Chief of the Bureau of Research of the Wisconsin Department of Public Welfare.

2. *New York Adult Parolees:* This information consists of separately tabulated data on 7,636 males and 738 females who comprise all parolees released on original parole by the New York Division of Parole in 1958 and 1959. The violation rate is based on those prisoners in this group who were declared "delinquent" on their parole during 1958, 1959, or 1960. These tabulations are published in the *Thirty-Second Annual Report of the Division of Parole of the Executive Department,* New York Legislative Department, 1962, No. 11, pp. 65–93.

3. *Minnesota Adult Male Parolees:* These data cover 525 men paroled from the Minnesota State Prison during 1957 and 1958. The violation rates are based on the number whose parole was rescinded within 1 year of release. These tabulations are reported in Robert Bergherr, James Brusseau, William McRae, and Richard Samelian, "Parole Success and Failure: A Study of the Influence of Selected Socio-Economic and Personal Factors and Their Effect on Parole Outcome," M.S.W. Thesis, University of Minnesota, 1962. This thesis was made available to us by Dr. Nathan G. Mandel, Director of Research, and Ira Phillips, Librarian, Minnesota Division of Correction.

4. *California Youth Authority Male Parolees:* These data cover 3,046 males released on parole during 1961 from their first admission to a California Youth Authority institution. The violation rate is based on all parole revocations occurring within 15 months of release, including both those returned to the institution, and those who were discharged from parole when under suspension, because they had committed either a parole rule violation or new offense. This tabulation was made available to us by Dr. Keith S. Griffiths, Chief of Research, California Youth Authority.

5. *Federal Adult Male Releasees:* These data cover 1,015 men who comprise a 10-per cent systematic sample of all adult males released from Federal prisons on a sentence of over 1 year during 1956. These include men released from prison by

expiration of sentence or by mandatory release, as well as parolees. "Failure" rates are based on all men returned to prison, for a new offense or for parole or mandatory release rule violation, as well as those men convicted of a felony-type offense or wanted for parole violation but not reimprisoned by summer of 1959. This study is reported in Daniel Glaser, *The Effectiveness of a Prison and Parole System,* Indianapolis: Bobbs-Merrill, 1963, primarily in chapters 2 and 3.

6. *Illinois Adult Parolees:* These data cover 955 men paroled from the Joliet-Stateville and Menard branches of the Illinois State Penitentiary during 1960. Violation rates are based on warrants issued through July 1, 1962. This study is reported in Illinois Department of Public Safety, Division of the Criminologist, *Bulletin of the Sociologist-Actuary,* No. 3, June 14, 1963.

7. *Illinois Youthful Male Parolees:* These data cover 2,693 men paroled from the Pontiac branch of the Illinois State Penitentiary in 1940–49. It excludes men paroled to the Armed Forces. This is an institution for "young and improvable" male offenders; these men had an average age of 24.1 years at parole. Violation rates are based on warrants issued through 1952. This study is reported fully in Daniel Glaser, "A Reformulation and Testing of Parole Prediction Factors," Ph.D. Thesis, University of Chicago, 1954, and more briefly in articles by the same author appearing in the *American Sociological Review* in 1954 and 1955.

8. *Washington Adult Parolees:* These data cover 1,731 persons who comprise all prisoners paroled from Washington State penal facilities from July 1957 through June 1959. Only 53 were women and data for this group were not tabulated separately. Violation rates are based on all persons whose parole was suspended for absconding, technical violation, or being in custody on a felony charge, between the date of their release and December 31, 1959. This study is reported in Washington State Board of Prison Terms and Paroles, *Adult Parolee Study,* August 1960.

Each table presented includes data from every one of the above studies which had information on the topic covered. However, the only topic on which every one of these studies had some information was the relationship between type of offense and postrelease violation, summarized in Table 25–4. Whenever there are no cases in a particular category of our tables from one of the studies, this is indicated by a line in the violation rate column; whenever there are some cases, but no violators (usually because there were very few cases), this is indicated by the entry "0%."

Part II. Gross Personal Characteristics and Parole Outcome

The first information available on prisoners is that which most immediately identifies them. These are facts which generally can be learned quickly, such as sex, race, age, offense, prior criminal record, intelligence, and body dimensions. Some of these attributes, for example, the offense and criminal record, may actually have intricate variations. However, we shall first consider them as broad categories into which inmates may be classified soon after they reach the prison. This chapter is concerned with the parole prognosis value of this gross information by which prisoners may be divided into the young and the old, the thieves and the murderers, the first offenders and the repeaters, and so forth.

AGE

One of the most firmly established pieces of statistical knowledge about criminals is that the older a man is when he is released from prison, the less likely he is to return to crime. By no means should it be inferred that all old prisoners are good risks or all youngsters poor risks. Nevertheless, as Table 25–1 shows, for all parolees taken collectively, the older they are at release the less likely they are to fail on parole.

Table 25–1 indicates that the parole violation rate predominantly de-

Table 25-1

Postrelease Violation Rates in Relation to Age at Release

Wisconsin Parolees					
	Juvenile			Adult	
Age at Release	Males	Females	Age at Release	Males	Females
	Per Cent	*Per Cent*		*Per Cent*	*Per Cent*
12 to 13	78	67	Under 20	31	40
14	54	58	20 to 24	37	26
15	58	40	25 to 29	41	13
16	50	33	30 to 34	40	23
17	44	40	35 to 39	34	29
18 and over	41	34	40 to 49	29	14
			50 to 59	28	50
			60 and over	21	—
Rates for All Cases	50	39		36	23
Number of Cases	1,037	453		2,255	206

New York Adult Parolees			Federal Adult Male Releases	
Age at Release	Males	Females	Age at Release	Failure Rate
	Per Cent	*Per Cent*		*Per Cent*
20 years or less	36	43	18 to 19	51
21 to 25	38	54	20 to 21	46
26 to 30	41	48	22 to 23	42
31 to 35	39	41	24 to 25	38
36 to 40	38	26	26 to 30	36
41 to 45	29	22	31 to 35	30
46 to 50	32	—	36 to 40	28
51 to 55	25	17	41 to 49	25
55 and over	18	9	50 and over	29
Rates for All Cases	37	43		35
Number of Cases	7,626	738		1,015

Note: The violation rates shown in this table, as in all other tables, are based on the number of "failures on parole" for all reasons. For example, the following are included in these rates: new commitments, serious violations of parole rules such as absconding, and preventive action on the part of parole authorities such as warrants issued for failure by individuals to abide by stipulated parole conditions.

creases as the age at parole increases, although there is some deviation from perfect consistency in this relationship. Such findings have been reported for many decades, and in numerous jurisdictions, both in the United States and abroad.[1] A related finding is that, as age at release increases, it is increasingly likely that if any further criminality occurs, it will be a misdemeanor rather than a felony.[2]

The easiest interpretation of this finding is that people become less criminal as they become more mature. Such an interpretation only has much validity if the word "mature" is used primarily in a nonbiological sense. Criminals generally are at least as well developed physically as the average person of their age. They can only be considered immature by defining normal maturation as change from delinquent youth to noncriminal adulthood.

It will suffice at this point to observe that the age group which has the highest crime rates in most industrialized societies is the vaguely defined one which is in transition between childhood and adulthood. These are the people we call "adolescents." For them to become adults, in the sense that others treat them as adults, requires not just physical maturation, but the acquisition of a self-sufficient position in the adult economic and social world. Prisoners tend to be persons who have failed in the past and may be handicapped in the future in achieving this transition, although most of them eventually do become self-sufficient in a legitimate adult life.

These data have two important general implications for parole policy in dealing with youthful offenders.

First is the emphasis on change. It is the consensus of both statistical analysis and personal impressions of experienced officials that youth are the least predictable of all prisoners. Although they have high rates of return to crime, this rate diminishes as they mature, and it is hard to predict when their criminal careers may end. They are in a period in which old associates and points of view may suddenly be dropped, and new ones gained. Innumerable cases can be cited where marriage, new employment, or other incidents marked a turning point which was followed by the complete metamorphosis of such offenders. Many individuals with long histories of juvenile crime, including acts of violence and drug addiction, are now leading respectable and law-abiding lives.[3]

The second implication is that youth are particularly in need of new paths to follow toward a secure and satisfying life. Frequently, they have only had gratification in delinquent pursuits, and have only felt at ease and important in a delinquent social world. Simply to release such a youth unconditionally, to give him "another chance" with no prospect that he will enter a new social and occupational world, is likely to be futile. Placing such a youth where he may have new and satisfying legitimate achievements which contribute to his self-sufficiency, and new types of contacts among his peers, is much preferable to merely "giving him a buck" by parole. A feasible school or work program, or a combination of the two, and a home in which the youth feels "at home," are ideal ingredients for rehabilitating a youthful criminal. While it is easy to state these desirable resources, their procurement is difficult. Frequently, relatives of youth make rash promises for parole placement which they do not intend to keep, or for which neither they nor the youth are adequately prepared. This includes both home and job arrangement.

Even where ideal placement seems to be guaranteed, success is never certain. Invariably, some youth will not perceive a work or school program as feasible for them, in comparison to illegal pursuits with which they are familiar, or about which they have illusions. Similarly, new homes which seem ideal to officials may be distinctly uncomfortable or even frightening to youth from another background who have had little gratifying personal experience in new relationships. For these reasons, testing parole placement in advance of complete release is particularly desirable for youth. Both for staff information and to aid the youth's adjustment, intensive counseling should be concomitant with the early placement experience. Minimal tests of a prospective parole home may be provided by furloughs from the institution in advance of parole. An optimum program involves transfer of the youth several months before parole to release guidance centers, in the community where parole will occur.

THE CRIMINAL RECORD

The extent to which a person has devoted himself to crime is not easily measured. We only know of the offenses for which he was apprehended, or which he will admit, and he may have been involved in considerable criminality not revealed to us. Nevertheless, that which can be learned about prior criminality often is the most valuable information that a parole board has about a prisoner.

At first inspection of a man's file, we usually learn only the events which appear on the FBI's list of his fingerprint reports. This is sometimes called his "rap sheet." It has a wealth of valuable information, but is often difficult to interpret. One problem in using these records is that a criminal commonly is fingerprinted several times on each major offense, and each fingerprinting leads to a new line on this report. First, the prisoner may be reported by the police who arrested him, then by the sheriff who operated the jail in which the prisoner was confined, then by each prison to which he may have been committed. Each of these separate lines on the FBI sheet should not be confused with those for a new offense. Of course, this problem will not confront a parole board if it receives a casework report which summarizes the criminal record in a simpler and clearer manner than that of the original record.

During the intervals in which he was free, between his major offenses, a prisoner often will have had numerous arrests not resulting in conviction. While a man must legally be presumed innocent of any charge for which he was not convicted, such arrests suggest that the person with whom we are dealing frequented places, had associates, or kept hours which got him into difficulties with the law. These could also interfere with his fulfillment of parole requirements. Minimally, these arrests may suggest that the prisoner's reputation with the police in his home community is not conducive to his parole success there. Even where there is a possibility that this was police harassment due to his earlier behavior, the prospect of its continuing should be taken into account.

Ideally, inquiry and investigation of gaps in the criminal record and of other matters should begin in the presentence study by the probation officer. Of course, such studies are not always made, or are not reported to the board. Remaining issues should be probed by the prison caseworker, by interview and by correspondence, so that adequate information is available when the parole board member confronts the prisoner. By directing appropriate questions to the caseworkers on gaps or errors in information available at the parole board hearing, the parole board may promote improvements in the material prepared for its case.

There are so many standpoints from which criminal records can be analyzed, that we cannot exhaust all of the possibilities here. Instead we shall focus on three principal types of information for which this record is our primary or our initial source. These are: the *duration* of the prisoner's prior involvement in crime, his *prior experience with government agencies dealing with crime* (police, courts, prisons, etc.), *and the types of offense* he has committed.

DURATION OF PRIOR CRIMINALITY

The duration of prior criminality can be estimated imperfectly from several types of evidence. For example, offenders can be differentiated according to the age at which they were first arrested, first adjudicated, first committed to a correctional institution, or first reported in any type of difficulty for delinquent activity. Presumably, among offenders of approximately the same age, the earlier they first have any of these experiences, the longer is the span of their prior involvement in crime, and the more likely they are to continue in crime. This is indicated by Table 25–2.

The foregoing conclusion has occasionally been challenged by a theory that all offenders have approximately the same period of delinquency and crime to go through, so that the earlier they start this period, the younger they will be when they conclude it. This is suggested by the finding that many older chronic offenders have no juvenile delinquency or youth crime record.[4]

Nevertheless, the predominance of evidence is against this conclusion. Despite some deviations, the overall generalization indicated by Table 25–2 is that at any age, the longer the span of prior criminality, the more likely it is that it will be extended in the future. Unfortunately, not many cross tabulations of violation rates are available which relate age at release to age of first arrest or other index of first criminality, as does Table 25–2.

The few rather persistent types of crime characteristically starting at a later age than the majority of offenses provide exceptions to the foregoing generalization that early onset means more persistence in crime. These late starting offenses consist of some crimes associated with alcoholism, especially check

Table 25-2

*Postrelease Failure Rates of Federal Adult Male Prisoners According to
Both Age at Release and Indices of Duration of Prior Criminality
[Number of cases is indicated in parentheses]*

Index of Duration of Prior Involvement in Crime		All Cases All Cases	Age at Release from Prison			
			18 to 21 18 to 21	22 to 25 22 to 25	26 to 35 26 to 35	30 and Over
Age at First Arrest:						
16 and under	Per cent	46	53	43	43	40
		(304)	(94)	(68)	(106)	(35)
17 to 20	Per cent	38	37	45	41	28
		(316)	(49)	(73)	(116)	(78)
21 and over	Per cent	24	—	24	(24)	24
		(395)	—	(37)	(184)	(174)
Number of Prior Sentences for Felony-Like Offenses:	Per cent					
None		25	44	31	21	11
		(423)	(78)	(98)	(151)	(96)
1	Per cent	37	82	46	34	25
		(221)	(31)	(37)	(105)	(48)
2	Per cent	44	57	52	45	28
		(154)	(23)	(27)	(64)	(40)
3 or more	Per cent	46	45	63	48	42
		(217)	(11)	(16)	(86)	(104)
All Cases	Per cent	35	48	40	34	27
		(1,015)	(143)	(178)	(406)	(288)

forgery, and some offenses that also seem to occur as an abnormal adjustment to senility. These include a petty theft and vagrancy combination, and certain sexual indecency offenses. The old and persistent criminals who do not have a criminal record which goes back to juvenile days, or have a long gap between youth and old age offenses, are not sufficiently numerous to contradict the overall generalization that the younger a person was when his crime began, the more likely he is to persist in it.

The number of prior felony convictions is only a rough indication of the duration of prior criminality. Of course, what we know about a man's criminal record generally is limited to that which was recorded by government agencies which dealt with him. Therefore, the duration past criminality often can be roughly estimated from many types of available records on a person's experience with agents of the law.

PRIOR POLICE, COURT, AND CORRECTIONAL EXPERIENCE

Since there are many ways of classifying a criminal's record of previous experience with government agencies, it is often difficult to compare statistical tabulations from different jurisdictions. A variety of ways of classifying the data are illustrated in Table 25–3.

These tabulations indicate, on the whole, that no matter how one counts the volume of previous experience with police, court, or correctional agencies, the overall trend is for the parole failure rate to increase as the magnitude of this prior experience increases. This trend, however, is offset by the influence of age: one or more commitments as a juvenile seems to be more unfavorable as a prognostic sign than the same number of commitments later. In general, the increase in violation rate with increasing number of prior commitments becomes progressively less, or halts completely, after a few terms of imprisonment, or even of successive felony convictions. However, Table 25–2 indicated quite clearly that this decrease in failure rate simply reflects the crime-diminishing effect of older age at release for those with three or more prior felony convictions. Possibly the reduced rate of return to crime with each successive commitment also reflects some rehabilitative or deterrent influence of imprisonment. It is clear, at any rate, that we cannot conclude with certainty that everyone in any category of prior criminal record will persist in crime indefinitely into the future.

The Wisconsin data in Table 25–3 show that prison commitments alone may not be as unfavorable for parole prognosis as combinations of prison and lesser commitments. This unfavorable prognosis is in terms of overall violation rate only; it ignores type of violation. Persons habitually in minor difficulty with the law, such as drunks and vagrants, may not be as serious a problem to parole boards as persons less likely to violate, but more likely to commit, serious new offenses if they do. This observation, of course, brings out the oversimplification we are employing in most of this discussion by not distinguishing different types of violation. Some correction of this deficiency will be made in considering offense as a factor in parole prognosis.

TYPES OF OFFENSE

Still another aspect of the vital information provided to parole boards by the criminal record is the type of offense for which a prisoner is currently committed, or in which he was previously involved. It is appropriate therefore to provide an overall view of the many types of offense, and to compare their significance in predicting continuation of criminality.

The most persistent types of common crime are those in which offenders obtain someone else's money without use of violence. These crimes can be divided into two major categories: illegal service and predatory crimes.

Illegal service crimes consist of economically motivated offenses in which there is no person who clearly considers himself a victim; instead, the persons with whom the criminals deal are his customers. Examples of such crimes are the sale of illicit alcoholic beverages ("moonshine"), narcotics and stolen goods, and the provision of illegal gambling and prostitution services. Only a minute proportion of these offenses lead to arrest and prosecution. Also, conviction on some of these charges, such as gambling and prostitution, seldom leads to imprisonment, so parole boards seldom confront such criminals. Because these criminal services are both more profitable and safer than most other offenses, one can reasonably speculate that they may be the most fre-

Table 25-3 (Part One)

Postrelease Violation Rates in Relation to Various
Classifications of Prior Contact with Agencies of the Law

California Youth Authority Male Parolees		New York Adult Parolees		
Prior Contacts	Violation Rate	Number of Prior Arrests	Violation Rate	
			Males	Females
	Per Cent		Per Cent	Per Cent
None	24	None	21	36
1 or 2 Contacts for Delinquency, No Commitment	37	1	27	45
3, 4, or 5 Contacts for Delinquency, No Commitment	44	2	35	50
		3	35	53
6 or More Contacts for Delinquency, No Commitment	44	4 or more	46	46
1 or 2 Contacts and One Commitment	49	Rates for All Cases	37	43
3, 4 or 5 Contacts and One Commitment	46	Number of Cases	7,636	738
6 or More Contacts and One Commitment	45			

California Youth Authority Male Parolees (cont.)		Washington Adult Parolees	
2 or More Prior Commitments	50	Prior Felony Conviction	Violation Rate
Violation Rate for All Cases	44		Per Cent
Number of Cases	3,046	None	23
		1	33
		2	40
		3 or More	50
		Rates for All Cases	38
		Number of Cases	1,731

quently committed clearly criminal acts, even though this is not confirmed by complaint or arrest statistics.

The crimes usually encountered by parole boards are predatory crimes. As indicated in Table 25–4, on the whole, these offenses usually fall into three main clusters, from the standpoint of violation rates. The offenses usually associated with the highest violation rates involve taking somebody else's property by stealth or by deceit. Notable here are the crimes of theft, burglary, and forgery.

Theft, which older criminal codes usually call "larceny," consists simply of taking somebody else's property. Both in the law and in statistical tabulations, the crime of auto theft usually is treated separately. Auto thieves have the highest rates of parole violation in most jurisdictions, possibly because they generally are the youngest parolees. Their crime usually is committed for the temporary enjoyment of transportation rather than for long-term economic gains. For this reason, in approximately 90 per cent of auto thefts the

Table 25-3 (Part Two)

Postrelease Violation Rates in Relation to Various
Classifications of Prior Contact with Agencies of the Law

Federal Adult Male Releases		Illinois Youthful Male Parolees	
Most Serious Prior Contact	Violation Rate	Most Serious Prior Contact	Violation Rate
	Per Cent		Per Cent
No Prior Contact	15	No Prior Contact	24
Arrests or Fines Only	25	Arrests or Fines Only	35
Jail and/or Probation	31	Jail and/or Probation	40
Training, Reform, or Industrial School	55	Training, Reform, or Industrial School	54
Reformatory or Prison	43	Reformatory or Prison	39
Rate for All Cases	35	Rate for All Cases	39
Number of Cases	1,015	Number of Cases	2,693

Wisconsin Parolees

	Juveniles		Adults	
Type of Prior Contacts	Males	Females	Males	Females
	Per Cent	Per Cent	Per Cent	Per Cent
Most Serious Prior Commitments:				
No Prior Commitment	46	40	27	13
Juvenile Detention, Jail, or Probation	61	41	42	26
1 Prison Only	—	—	45	50
Prison Plus Lesser Commitments	—	—	59	33
2 Prison Only	—	—	36	—
2 Prison Plus Lesser Commitments	—	—	53	—
3 Prison	—	—	50	—
4 or More Prison	—	—	70	—
Prior Releases on Present Commitment:				
None	48	38	34	23
1	58	41	51	25
2 or More	52	41	55	40
Rates for All Cases	50	39	36	23
Number of Cases	1,087	453	2,255	206

vehicle is recovered intact, even though the thieves usually are not caught. However, in some auto thefts the cars are stripped, and some older auto thieves are in gangs which falsify ownership papers and sell stolen cars.

Other types of theft include shoplifting, removing objects from parked cars, picking pockets, taking goods from places of employment, and many more varieties of "stealing." Most of the separate crimes are small, frequently

Table 25-4 (Part One)

Postrelease Violation Rates in Relation to Offense

Offense	Wisconsin Parolees				New York Adult Parolees	
	Juveniles[a]		Adults			
	Males	Females	Males	Females	Males	Females
	Per Cent	Per Cent	Per Cent	Per Cent	Per Cent	Per Cent
Highest Violations:						
Auto Theft	50	20	47	60	—	—
Other Theft	51	42	34	25	—	[a]27
Burglary	—	—	39	20	42	36
Forgery and Fraud	—	—	48	32	46	5
Intermediate and Inconsistent:						
Robbery	—	—	38	12	37	38
Narcotics	—	—	—	—	—	—
Lowest Violations:						
Rape and Assault to Rape	—	—	31	—	19	—
Other Sex Offenses	33	37	21	16	24	—
Felonious Assault	—	—	31	17	33	29
Homicide	—	—	16	20	19	28
All Others	44	41	35	25	38	19
Rates for All Cases	50	39	36	23	38	36
Number of Cases	1,037	453	2,255	206	[b]5,929	[b]329

[a] Offenses for juveniles were tabulated by Wilson officials separately for three major Offenses — theft, auto theft, and sex offenses — plus purely juvenile offenses like truancy, plus all combinations of these several categories. The above tabulations are based on all parolees charged with any of these three offenses, alone or in combination. The few multiple-major-offense cases are included under each of their offenses.

[b] Felonies only; excludes cases tabulated as "misdemeanors" and "youthful adjudications."

[c] Auto theft and all other thefts are compiled as one offense — grand larceny — in New York.

they are not immediately discovered by the victim, and probably a major portion is never reported to the police. Only a small proportion of theft reported to the police, other than auto theft, is solved by recovery of the stolen goods, or conviction of the offenders. Furthermore, the small value of the property taken in separate offenses frequently results in a convicted person receiving only a minor penalty, so that most of the time he never goes to prison or receives only a short sentence. Probably the persistence of these criminals is due in large part to the fact that they cannot readily be given certain or severe penalties.

Burglary consists of breaking and entering for the purpose of committing a felonious act, and it sometimes is designated in the law as "breaking" or "breaking and entering." Usually it is committed in conjunction with larceny at the place entered. However, burglary almost always causes a more severe penalty than larceny alone, so the offenders usually are prosecuted only for burglary. However, some State laws make "burglary and larceny" a single compound offense. A majority of persons arrested for burglary are under 19

Table 25-4 (Part Two)

Postrelease Violation Rates in Return to Offense

Offense	Minnesota Adult Male Parolees	California Youth Authority Parolees	Federal Adult Male Parolees	Illinois Adult Male Parolees	Illinois Youthful Male Parolees	Washington Adult Parolees
	Per Cent	*Per Cent*	*Per Cent*	*Per Cent*	*Per Cent*	*Per Cent*
Highest Violations:						
Auto Theft	58	49	47	—	50	52
Other Theft	57	54	38	36	39	40
Burglary	41	42	—	42	48	38
Forgery and Fraud	54	43	30	55	42	50
Intermediates and Inconsistent:						
Robbery	47	29	28	42	31	31
Narcotics	—	41	30	14	—	—
Lowest Violations:						
Rape and Assault to Rape	—	41	—	—	—	21
Other Sex Offenses	22	32	—	[a]14	[c]13	16
Felonious Assault	41	28	[a][b]18	—	—	36
Homicide	21	18	—	14	[d]20	21
All Others	38	48	25	44	35	34
Rates for All Cases	44	44	35	37	39	38
Number of Offenses	525	3,046	1,015	955	2,693	1,731

[a]Includes "rape."
[b]Includes "homicide."
[c]Includes "auto and stolen property."
[d]Includes "assault."

years of age, but an appreciable number of the burglars who are encountered in prison populations are older. These often include those for whom burglary has become a profession in which they work closely with dealers in stolen goods ("fences").

Another kind of recurrent economic offense not involving violence is the crime of forgery. Forgers differ from most criminals in the extent to which they commit their crimes alone, and in being relatively older. Petty or naïve forgery is notably associated with chronic alcoholism. Perhaps because cashing a fraudulent check requires a certain amount of facility at writing, and an appearance of success, forgers are also distinctive in generally having more education and less often coming from an impoverished home than most prisoners. Other types of fraud, often called "confidence games" or "bunko games," are less often associated with alcoholism than simple check forgery, and are more frequently persistent criminal professions. Embezzlement is a special kind of fraud, frequently involving violation of trust by a prominent and presumably trustworthy citizen, so that he is placed in a government or business position where he handles much money. These offenders generally are good risks as far as prospects for violation are concerned, but their parole poses special public relations problems.

The selling of narcotics has already been mentioned as an illegal service crime. Other narcotic offenses include illegal possession, use, and purchase of narcotic drugs. Evidence on the relative risk of these narcotic offenders, as parolees is inconsistent. There is some indication that they have very high violation rates when they are paroled to neighborhoods where narcotics usage is extensive, but that they have average or below average violation rates elsewhere.

Robbery is different from the economically motivated crimes described earlier, in that robbery involves the use or threat of violence in order to procure someone else's property. Like narcotics offenses, it is associated with diverse violation or recidivism rates in different jurisdictions, but robbers generally seem to have about the average violation rate for their age group. However, they are of concern to parole boards because of the serious injury or death which they may cause. Robbers vary tremendously in character. They include groups of adolescents in slum areas who "roll" drunks coming from taverns in the late hours of night, naïve individuals who make a foolhardy effort to solve economic crises by trying to hold up a large bank (often without a working weapon), and some highly dangerous individuals who have a psychological drive to hurt their victims.

The cluster of offenses associated with the lowest violation rates on parole are crimes which least often serve as vocations. These include homicide and rape. However, the strong public demand for punishment as an expression of revenge against such offenders, plus the extreme importance of preventing recurrence of these crimes, makes parole boards exceptionally cautious in paroling those who commit these offenses.

One of the least favorable crimes, from the standpoint of parole violation probability, is the crime of escape from prison. In some States, notably California, offenders sentenced for this offense have the highest violation rate of any offense category, even higher than auto thieves. However, escapees do not constitute a large proportion of prisoners.

Thus far, this discussion has dealt only with gross violation rates, although it has been noted that the nature of the probable parole violation may be a crucial consideration in parole decisions. The type of violation likely to be committed, if any, is a concern especially in the forefront of a parole board member's thoughts when he considers the type of offense for which a prisoner was last convicted. William L. Jacks, statistician of the Pennsylvania Board of Parole, has made one of the few studies of type of violation in relation to type of offense. This is summarized in Table 25–5.

Table 25–5 indicates, first, that in Pennsylvania the offenses fell into three main clusters in terms of prospects of committing a new crime on parole, and these three clusters were much like those for overall violation rates shown in table 25–4. However, larceny and narcotics offenses are ranked somewhat

Table 25-5

Type of Offense for Which Committed as a Factor in Type of Offense, if any, Committed on Parole (for Pennsylvania Only)

	All Parolees, 1946-1961[a]	
Offense for Which Imprisoned	*Per Cent* Committing New Crimes on Parole	*Per Cent* Repeating on Parole the Crime for Which Imprisoned
Auto Larceny[b]	—	—
Larceny	22.5	6.4
Burglary	23.4	11.1
Forgery	22.3	10.2
Robbery	19.5	5.1
Narcotics	15.9	10.1
Sex Offenders	8.8	2.9
Assault and Battery	12.3	3.6
Homicide	5.7	0.4
Other Offenses	10.2	3.1
Rates for All Cases	18.4	6.8
Number of Cases	29,346	29,346

[a]From Pennsylvania Board of Parole, "A Comparison of Releases and Recidivists from June 1, 1946, to May 31, 1961," Harrisburg: The Board, Dec. 20, 1961.
[b]Included in Larceny.

differently in these two compilations. Burglars, forgers, and narcotic drug offenders were most likely to commit the same offenses, while larceny and robbery were an intermediate cluster, followed by felonious assault and sex offenses. Homicides were lowest, only about 1 in 250 committed a homicide on parole after being imprisoned for homicide. The gravity of this offense, of course, still makes any repetition a crucial concern.

A California tabulation of adult male parolees returned to prison for a new offense in 1959, 1960, and 1961 concluded: 26 per cent are returned for a more serious offense than that on which they were paroled, 38 per cent are returned for an offense of similar seriousness to that on which they were paroled, and 37 per cent are returned for a less serious offense. Seriousness was measured by the length of the statutory maximum sentence for the offense in California, except that narcotics offenses were classified as more serious than property offenses with higher maximum sentences.

NOTES

1. Thorsten Sellin, "Recidivism and Maturation," *National Probation and Parole Association Journal*, Vol. 4, No. 3 (July 1958), pp. 241–250; Barbara Wooton, *Social Science and Social Pathology*, New York: Macmillan (1959), chapter 5.

2. California Director of Corrections and Adult Authority, *California Male Prisoners Released on Parole 1946–49*, p. 23 and p. 46 (tables 7 and 31). These tables indicate

felony and misdemeanor violations separately, for first paroles and for reparoles, by year of birth.

3. A variety of examples are illustrated by case histories in Daniel Glaser, *The Effectiveness of a Prison and Parole System,* Indianapolis: Bobbs-Merrill (1963), chapter 4.

4. Wooton, *op. cit.*

26: A Review of Reconviction Rates (England) / *The Sentence of the Courts*

152. The effectiveness of penal treatment can be considered from different points of view. Treatment may prevent the offender from offending again, either because he is deterred by the fear of further penalties or because he has become a reformed character, or for both these reasons. In addition, the penalty imposed upon one person may deter others from committing similar offences. Very little is so far known about the deterrent effect on the population as a whole of sentences passed on particular offenders. The Government Social Survey has recently begun research on this subject, but it will be some years before the results are of direct help to the courts. In the meantime, the only available information about the effect on offenders of different kinds of penal treatment consists of figures showing how many of them are convicted of another offence within certain periods. This information suffers from certain drawbacks which severely limit its usefulness to the courts:

(*a*) The reconviction rates are not based on standard criteria; for example, the offences which count for this purpose may differ, as may the length of the period during which reconvictions are noted.

(*b*) The different types of treatment are given to different (though usually overlapping) classes of offender, whose likelihood of success is *a priori* different.

(*c*) The information does not take account of the social background of offenders.

(*d*) The reconviction rates following discharges and fines have so far been studied very little, although over two-thirds of offenders are dealt with in these ways.

153. To be useful for the purpose of evaluating sentences, information must be comparative; that is, it should be based on offenders who may be

From United Kingdom (Home Office), *The Sentence of the Court: A Handbook for Courts on the Treatment of Offenders* (London: Her Majesty's Stationery Office, 1964), pp. 40–42, 44, 48–51.

given any one of a number of different sentences. The research results referred to in the following paragraph are based on this kind of information; in the remaining paragraphs the conclusions to be drawn from this comparative research are first discussed and are afterwards applied in an attempt to assess the reconviction results reported in several published and unpublished studies of particular forms of treatment.

Samples of Offenders Studied

154. Most of the information considered in this chapter comes from a study, now being carried out by the Home Office Research Unit, of all offenders convicted in the Metropolitan Police District during March and April 1957. The previous criminal histories of these offenders have been obtained from the Criminal Record Office, and they have also been followed up for five years from the time of the 1957 offence.

Factors Affecting the Likelihood of Reconviction

155. The initial object of these studies is to calculate the expectation of an offender being reconvicted within a stated period of his current conviction (or release from custody if a custodial sentence was imposed), having regard to factors in his criminal history. The reconviction rates following each type of treatment can then be compared with the expected rate. This should make it possible to compare the effectiveness, in preventing reconviction, of different types of treatment, and to assess whether a particular type has better results with one class of offender rather than another. The analyses that have so far been carried out show that the results obtained from the different samples mentioned in the last paragraph are fairly consistent, in spite of the differences in time and place. This gives good grounds for thinking that the factors used in calculating the expected reconviction rates are reliable.

156. Two of the most important factors are age and number of previous convictions. The chart which follows shows the five-year reconviction rates, according to these two factors, for the 1957 sample (see paragraph 154 above), excluding preventive detention, corrective training and prison sentences over four years. This table gives a clear indication of the differences in likelihood of reconviction within five years between one group of offenders and another. Two main conclusions can be drawn. First, the older the offender the less likely he is, generally speaking, to be reconvicted. Thus, over 50 per cent of offenders aged under 14 at their first offence were reconvicted within five years, compared with 30 per cent of first offenders aged 21–29 and only 9 per cent of first offenders aged 40 or over; similarly, all offenders aged 8–11 who had two previous offences were reconvicted, compared with only just over 40 per cent of such offenders aged 30 and over. Secondly, the

more offences an offender has already committed, the more likely he is to be reconvicted within a given period. The effect of the number of previous convictions on the proportion reconvicted differs somewhat according to the offender's age (see the chart), to his age at the time he was first found guilty and to the rate of committing the intervening offences. For juveniles, one previous conviction increases the five-year reconviction rate from about one out of two to two out of three offenders. But adult offenders with one previous conviction are about twice as likely to be reconvicted as first offenders of comparable age.

The result for the three age ranges which show most differentiation, namely juveniles, offenders aged 17 to under 30 and offenders aged 30 or over, is shown on the chart.

159. The next table attempts to compare the "effectiveness," in preventing reconviction, of different forms of treatment for certain classes of offender. The method of comparison is that referred to in paragraph 155 above. The

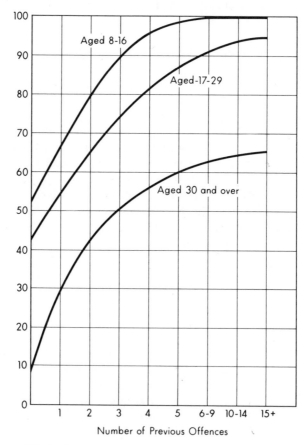

FIGURE 26–1. *Reconviction According to Offender's Age and Previous Convictions.* (*Percentage Reconvicted within 5 Years*)

expected number of reconvictions (within a certain period) for a particular class of offender—irrespective of the type of sentence—is calculated on the basis mainly of age, current offence and previous convictions. For the sake of simplicity the expected number is taken as 100. The figures shown in the table are the ratios of actual reconvictions (from the date of sentence or from the date of release from custody, whichever is later) to expected reconvictions and they are referred to as indices of effectiveness. Thus figures below 100 indicate fewer reconvictions than expected, while figures above 100 indicate more.

. . .

161. Table 26–1 assesses the "effectiveness," in preventing reconviction, of different types of treatment given to first and recidivist offenders from the 1957 sample. The expected reconviction rates for first offenders are calculated on the basis of the offender's age, the number of current charges (or offences

Table 26-1

First and Recidivist Offenders

Indices Showing Results of Sentences Compared with Expectation

(110 = Expected rate of reconviction within five years
except where otherwise stated)

	Under 17		17 to under 21		21 to under 30		30 and over	
	1st Offend- ers	Offend- ers with Previous Offences	1st Offend- ers	Offend- ers with Previous Offences	1st Offend- ers	Offend- ers with Previous Offences	1st Offend- ers	Offend- ers with Previous Offences
Discharge	89	100	89	98	109	90	133	104
Fine	75	83	75	94	63	99	84	65
Probation	118	101	122	101	153	115	(150)	121
Approved School	138	102	—	—	—	—	—	—
Borstal Training	—	101	—	95	—	—	—	—
Detention Centre	—	106	150	110	—	—	—	—
Attendance Centre	—	119	—	—	—	—	—	—
Imprison- ment	—	—	—	106*	146†	111*	(91†)	104*
Corrective Training	—	—	—	—	—	104*	—	—

*The calculation was based on a three year follow-up and it was necessary to exclude sentences of over three years.

†Excluding six sentences of three years or longer.

NOTES: (1) Round brackets indicate very small numbers of offenders.
(2) The number of juvenile first offenders committed to institutions other than approved schools was too small to provide a satisfactory result; similarly in the 17 to under 21 age group the results had to be combined into one figure for "institutional treatments". (Of the group, the Borstal result was the best, being about average in effectiveness.)

taken into consideration) and the type of offence. For recidivists account has been taken of the offender's age, type of current offence and number of previous convictions. The actual proportions reconvicted are expressed relative to the expected proportions as described in paragraph 159. The main points which emerge from this table are:

(a) Fines were followed by the fewest reconvictions compared with the expected numbers for both first offenders and recidivists of almost all age groups.

(b) Probation produced relatively better results (in comparison with the calculated expectation) when used for offenders with previous convictions than when used for first offenders, although at best the results were only about equal to expectation.

(c) Approved school results were also better for offenders with previous offences. (The poor result for first offenders may be accounted for by poor home backgrounds, since it is exceptional for first offenders to be given this treatment.)

(d) Detention centre results tended to be slightly inferior to Borstal results.

(e) Imprisonment results were better (compared with the expected results) for offenders with previous convictions than for first offenders, except among those aged 30 or over, but since the proportion of first offenders in this age-group who are reconvicted is, in any event, very small, too much reliance should not be placed on these figures.

162. When the sentences given to the recidivists in Table 26–1 were analysed according to the nature of the current offence the results tended to confirm the differences in "effectiveness" shown by the same sentences when used for first offenders, in the corresponding age groups, convicted of the same offences. Thus probation again appeared to be more successful for offenders convicted of breaking and entering than for those convicted of larceny, while fines were especially effective with the latter. The offences other than larceny or breaking committed by offenders between 17 and 21 mostly consisted of taking and driving away, and these offenders appeared to react better to Borstal training than to discharge, fines or other methods of treatment. Finally, fraud offenders, and particularly those put on probation, were among the least "successful" groups of adult offenders.

163. Some progress has been made towards evaluating sentences by means of comparative studies, and the consistency of the results is encouraging. To study reconviction rates is, of course, to assess the effectiveness of sentences from one point of view only; some kinds of sentence may have fewer disadvantages for society even though they do not give better relative reconviction rates. Moreover, until more information about offenders' social circumstances has been obtained for all kinds of offender, so that the assessment of expectation can be made more complete, the results of research should be treated with a good deal of reserve. Some significant points emerge from the figures discussed in the preceding paragraphs. Fines, particularly the heavier ones,

appear to be among the most "successful" penalties for almost all types of offender. Discharges, too, seem to have good results, particularly when used for juvenile offenders (for whom the fact of being caught and appearing before the court would often be a sufficient deterrent). Again, the relative "success" of probation for breaking and entering, as compared with other offences (see paragraphs 160 (*b*) and 162), is interesting.

164. The courts may have made allowance for factors not recorded in the documents available for research, and the possibility cannot be ignored that particular sentences may have been used more frequently for the "worse" or for the "better" offenders in any of the categories studied. The social circumstances of offenders have not, in any case, so far been specifically allowed for in the researches completed (though adverse environmental conditions have, of course, been covered to the extent that they are reflected in the offender's past criminal record). Inevitably the extent to which the various sentences are used differs from court to court. If the courts at present making relatively little use of the sentences which appear to be the most "successful" were to use them more, it is unlikely that they would lose their effectiveness. On the other hand, if the courts now making most use of these sentences were to use them even more frequently, it is possible that they might not give such good results as at present. Such changes in sentencing practice would have to be checked by further research.

C

EXPERIMENTAL STUDIES

27: The Provo Experiment: Theory and Design / *LaMar T. Empey* and *Jerome Rabow*

Major Assumptions for Treatment

In order to relate theoretical premises to the specific needs of treatment, the Provo Experiment adopted a series of major assumptions. They are as follows:

1. Delinquent behavior is primarily a group product and demands an approach to treatment far different from that which sees it as characteristic of a "sick," or "well-meaning" but "misguided," person.

2. An effective program must recognize the intrinsic nature of a delinquent's membership in a delinquent system and, therefore, must direct treatment to him as a part of that system.

3. Most habitual delinquents are affectively and ideologically dedicated to the delinquent system. Before they can be made amenable to change, they must be made anxious about the ultimate utility of that system for them.

4. Delinquents must be forced to deal with the conflicts which the demands of conventional and delinquent systems place upon them. The resolution of such conflicts, either for or against further law violations, must ultimately involve a community decision. For that reason, a treatment program, in order to force realistic decision-making, can be most effective if it permits continued participation in the community as well as in the treatment process.

5. Delinquent ambivalence for purposes of rehabilitation can only be utilized in a setting conducive to the free expression of feelings—both delinquent and conventional. This means that the protection and rewards provided by the treatment system for *candor* must exceed those provided either by delinquents for adherence to delinquent roles or by officials for adherence to

From LaMar T. Empey and Jerome Rabow, "The Provo Experiment in Delinquent Rehabilitation," *American Sociological Review* 26:5(October 1961):683–4, 685, 693–694.

custodial demands for "good behavior." Only in this way can delinquent individuals become aware of the extent to which other delinquents share conventional as well as delinquent aspirations and, only in this way, can they be encouraged to examine the ultimate utility of each.

6. An effective program must develop a unified and cohesive social system in which delinquents and authorities alike are devoted to one task—overcoming lawbreaking. In order to accomplish this the program must avoid two pitfalls: (a) it must avoid establishing authorities as "rejectors" and making inevitable the creation of two social systems within the program; and (b) it must avoid the institutionalization of means by which skilled offenders can evade norms and escape sanctions.[1] The occasional imposition of negative sanctions is as necessary in this system as in any other system.

7. A treatment system will be most effective if the delinquent peer group is used as the means of perpetuating the norms and imposing the sanctions of the system. The peer group should be seen by delinquents as the primary source of help and support. The traditional psychotherapeutic emphasis upon transference relationships is not viewed as the most vital factor in effecting change.

8. A program based on sociological theory may tend to exclude lectures, sermons, films, individual counseling, analytic psychotherapy, organized athletics, academic education, and vocational training as primary treatment techniques. It will have to concentrate, instead, on matters of another variety: changing reference group and normative orientations, utilizing ambivalent feelings resulting from the conflict of conventional and delinquent standards, and providing opportunities for recognition and achievement in conventional pursuits.

9. An effective treatment system must include rewards which are realistically meaningful to delinquents. They would include such things as peer acceptance for law-abiding behavior or the opportunity for gainful employment rather than badges, movies or furlough privileges which are designed primarily to facilitate institutional control. Rewards, therefore, must only be given for realistic and lasting changes, not for conformance to norms which concentrate upon effective custody as an end in itself.

10. Finally, in summary, a successful program must be viewed by delinquents as possessing four important characteristics: (a) a social climate in which delinquents are given the opportunity to examine and experience alternatives related to a realistic choice between delinquent or non-delinquent behavior; (b) the opportunity to declare publicly to peers and authorities a belief or disbelief that they can benefit from a change in values; (c) a type of social structure which will permit them to examine the role and legitimacy (for their purposes) of authorities in the treatment system; and (d) a type of treatment interaction which, because it places major responsibilities upon peer-group decision-making, grants status and recognition to individuals, not only for their own successful participation in the treatment interaction, but for their willingness to involve others.

The Treatment System [2]

The Provo Program, consistent with these basic assumptions, resides in the community and does not involve permanent incarceration. Boys live at home and spend only a part of each day at Pinehills (the program center). Otherwise they are free in the community.[3]

HISTORY AND LOCALE

The Provo Program was begun in 1956 as an "in-between" program designed specifically to help those habitual delinquents whose persistence made them candidates; in most cases, for a reformatory. It was instigated by a volunteer group of professional and lay people known as the *Citizens' Advisory Council to the Juvenile Court*. It has never had formal ties to government except through the Juvenile Court. This lack of ties has permitted considerable experimentation. Techniques have been modified to such a degree that the present program bears little resemblance to the original one. Legally, program officials are deputy probation officers appointed by the Juvenile Judge.

The cost of treatment is financed by county funds budgeted through the Juvenile Court. As near as we can estimate, the cost per boy is approximately one-tenth of what it would cost if he were incarcerated in a reformatory. Research operations are financed by the Ford Foundation. . . .

Despite the fact that Utah County is not a highly urbanized area when compared to large metropolitan centers, the concept of a "parent" delinquent subculture has real meaning for it. While there are no clear-cut gangs, *per se,* it is surprising to observe the extent to which delinquent boys from the entire county, who have never met, know each other by reputation, go with the same girls, use the same language, or can seek each other out when they change high schools. About half of them are permanently out of school, do not participate in any regular institutional activities, and are reliant almost entirely upon the delinquent system for social acceptance and participation.

ASSIGNEES

Only habitual offenders, 15–17 years, are assigned to the program. In the absence of public facilities, they are transported to and from home each day in automobiles driven by university students. Their offenses run the usual gamut, vandalism, trouble in school, shoplifting, car theft, burglary, forgery, and so forth. Highly disturbed and psychotic boys are not assigned. The presentence investigation is used to exclude these people. They constitute an extremely small minority.

NUMBER IN ATTENDANCE

No more than twenty boys are assigned to the program at any one time. A large number would make difficult any attempts to establish and maintain a unified, cohesive system. This group of twenty is broken into two smaller groups, each of which operates as a separate discussion unit. When an older boy is released from one of these units, a new boy is added. This is an important feature because it serves as the means by which the culture of the system is perpetuated.

LENGTH OF ATTENDANCE

No length of stay is specified. It is intimately tied to the group and its processes because a boy's release depends not only upon his own behavior, but upon the maturation processes through which his group goes. Release usually comes somewhere between four and seven months.

NATURE OF PROGRAM

The program does not utilize any testing, gathering of case histories, or clinical diagnosis. One of its key tools, peer group interaction, is believed to provide a considerably richer source of information about boys and delinquency than do clinical methods.

The program, *per se,* is divided into two phases. Phase I is an intensive group program, utilizing work and the delinquent peer group as the principal instruments for change. During the winter, boys attend this phase three hours a day, five days a week, and all day on Saturdays. Activities include daily group discussions, hard work, and some unstructured activities in which boys are left entirely on their own. During the summer they attend an all-day program which involves work and group discussions. However, there are no practices without exceptions. For example, if a boy has a full-time job, he may be allowed to continue the job in lieu of working in the program. Other innovations occur repeatedly.

Phase II is designed to aid a boy after release from intensive treatment in Phase I. It involves two things: (1) an attempt to maintain some reference group support for a boy; and (2) community action to help him find employment.

It should be remembered that, in terms familiar to delinquents, every effort is made at Pinehills to include as many positive experiences as possible. The following are some which seem to function:

1. Peers examine problems which are common to all.

2. There is a recurring opportunity for each individual to be the focal point of attention among peers in which his behavior and problems become the most important concern of the moment.

3. Delinquent peers articulate in front of conventional adults without constraint with regard to topic, language, or feeling.

4. Delinquents have the opportunity, for the first time in an institutional setting, to make crucial decisions about their own lives. This in itself is a change in the opportunity structure and is a means of obligating them to the treatment system. In a reformatory a boy cannot help but see the official system as doing things to him in which he has no say: locking him up, testing

him, feeding him, making his decisions. Why should he feel obligated? But when some important decision-making is turned over to him, he no longer has so many grounds for rejecting the system. Rejection in a reformatory might be functional in relating him to his peers, but in this system it is not so functional.

5. Delinquents participate in a treatment system that grants status in three ways: (a) for age and experience in the treatment process—old boys have the responsibility of teaching new boys the norms of the system; (b) for the exhibition of law-abiding behavior, not only in a minimal sense, but for actual qualitative changes in specific role behavior at Pinehills, home or with friends; and (c) for the willingness to confront other boys, in a group setting, with their delinquent behavior. (In a reformatory where he has to contend with the inmate system a boy can gain little and lose much for his willingness to be candid in front of adults about peers, but at Pinehills it is a primary source of prestige.) The ability to confront others often reflects more about the *confronter* than it does about the *confronted*. It is an indication of the extent to which he has accepted the reformation process and identified himself with it.[4]

6. Boys can find encouragement in a program which poses the possibility of relatively short restriction and the avoidance of incarceration.

7. The peer group is a potential source of reference group support for law-abiding behavior. Boys commonly refer to the fact that their group knows more about them than any other persons: parents or friends.

Research Design

An integral part of the Provo Experiment is an evaluation of treatment extending over a five-year period. It includes means by which offenders who receive treatment are compared to two control groups: (1) a similar group of offenders who at time of sentence are placed on probation and left in the community; and (2) a similar group who at time of sentence are incarcerated in the Utah State Industrial School. Since it is virtually impossible to match all three groups, random selection is used to minimize the effect of sample bias. All three groups are drawn from a population of habitual delinquents who reside in Utah County, Utah, and who come before the Juvenile Court. Actual selection is as follows:

The Judge of the Court has in his possession two series of numbered envelopes—one series for selecting individuals to be placed in the *probation* treatment and control groups and one series for selecting the *reformatory* treatment and control groups. These series of envelopes are supplied by the research team and contain randomly selected slips of paper on which are written either *Control Group* or *Treatment Group*.

In making an assignment to one of these groups the Judge takes the following steps: (1) After hearing a case he decides whether he would ordinarily place the offender on probation or in the reformatory. He makes this decision as though Pinehills did not exist. Then, (2) he brings the practice of random placement into play. He does so by opening an envelope from one of the two series supplied him (see figure 27–1 below). For example, if he decides initially that he would ordinarily send the boy to the reformatory, he would select an envelope from the *reformatory* series and depend upon the designation therein as to whether the boy would actually go to the reformatory, and become a member of the *control* group, or be sent to Pinehills as a member of the *treatment* group.

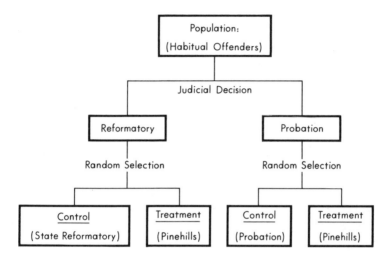

FIGURE 27–1. *Selection of Treatment and Control Groups.*

This technique does not interfere with the judicial decision regarding the alternatives previously available to the Judge, but it does intercede, after the decision, by posing another alternative. The Judge is willing to permit the use of this alternative on the premise that, in the long run, his contributions to research will enable judicial decisions to be based ultimately on a more realistic evaluation of treatment programs available.

In order to make the comparison of treatment and control groups more meaningful, additional research is being conducted on the treatment process. Efforts are made to examine the problems involved in relating causation theory to intervention strategy, the role of the therapist in Guided Group Interaction, and the types of group interaction that seem most beneficial. Finally, a detailed examination is being made of the ways in which boys handle "critical incidents"[5] after release from treatment as compared to the way they handled them prior to treatment.

NOTES

1. McCorkle and Korn, "Resocialization within Walls," *The Annals of the American Academy of Political and Social Science,* 293 (May, 1954), pp. 88–91.
2. Except for the community aspects, the above assumptions and the treatment sys-

tem are similar to those pioneered at Highfields. See McCorkle, Elias, and Bixby, *The Highfields Story: A Unique Experiment in the Treatment of Juvenile Delinquency.* New York:'Henry Holt & Co., 1958. The Provo Program is especially indebted to Albert Elias, the present director of Highfields, not only for his knowledge about treatment techniques, but for his criticisms of the Provo Experiment.

3. The idea of a community program is not new. The Boston Citizenship Training Group, Inc., a non-residential program, was begun in 1934–36. However, it is for younger boys and utilizes a different approach. A similar program, initiated by Professor Ray R. Canning, in Provo, was a forerunner to this experiment. See "A New Treatment Program for Juvenile Delinquents," *Journal of Criminal Law and Criminology,* 31 (March–April, 1941), pp. 712–719.

4. Support for this idea can be found in a recently developed matrix designed to measure the impact of group interaction. See William and Ida Hill, *Interaction Matrix for Group Psychotherapy,* mimeographed manuscript, Utah State Mental Hospital, Provo, Utah, 1960. This matrix has been many years in development.

5. John C. Flanagan, "The Critical Incident Technique," *Psychological Bulletin,* 51 (July, 1954), pp. 327–358.

28: The Provo Experiment: Research and Findings / *LaMar T. Empey**

It was felt that in order to test the theoretical postulates of the study and to determine something about its effectiveness, research would have to be concerned with three things: program *input,* describing the characteristics of the offenders assigned to the program; program *process,* a study of whether the theory of treatment had actually been implemented; and program *impact,* some measurement of program influence on clients, staff and community.

Examination of Input

The reason for collecting *input* data on offender characteristics is to determine wherein the basic assumptions of the study may be correct or incorrect. Such a collection of data is necessary because, if the basic assumptions about offenders have no basis in fact, then theoretically the treatment program would be relatively ineffective. It would be oriented to changing characteristics which in reality are unimportant.

From LaMar T. Empey, "The Provo Experiment: Research and Findings," in *Combatting Social Problems: Techniques of Intervention,* ed. by Harry Gold and Frank R. Scarpitti (New York: Holt, Rinehart and Winston, Inc., 1967), pp. 395–404. Copyright © 1967 by Holt, Rinehart and Winston, Inc.; reproduced by permission of Holt, Rinehart and Winston, Inc.

* In collaboration with Maynard Erickson, Max Scott, and Jerome Rabow.

Data which will reflect on basic causation assumptions have been gathered, not only from the experimental and control groups but from nondelinquents as well. In order to test postulates it is equally, or more, important to study differences between nondelinquents and delinquents. The reason is that the factors which distinguish delinquents from nondelinquents are those which are most crucial. It is those on which change should occur. At the same time such differences can also be used for testing the comparability of experimental and control groups. If they do not differ this is one method of assuring that samples are comparable, that the same types of people have been included in experimental and control groups.

Preliminary analyses on such variables as family adjustment, class level, school behavior, future aspirations, delinquent history and friendship patterns have been made. Two papers describing the delinquent history of four delinquent and nondelinquent subsamples have been published.[1]

They present some striking findings. First, they indicate that the persistent offenders assigned to this study, as experimental and control groups, are far more delinquent than non- and one-time offenders. The selection process appears, therefore, to be valid.

Second, they indicate that the same kinds of differences do not exist between offenders from different status levels. Instead, boys on one status level seem to be no more nor no less delinquent than boys on another. There are instead rather distinctive patterns of delinquent behavior distinguishing different status groups.

Such findings are but a part of those that will be presented in the final report on the Experiment. They will indicate possible weaknesses in the basic assumptions and indicate ways in which they might be modified. Furthermore, they will provide information which will be useful in evaluating the impact of the treatment process. For example, changes in family and school adjustment, diminution of delinquent behavior and changes in friendship patterns will be useful indices in assessing outcome.

Examination of Process

GROUP DEVELOPMENT

During the whole course of the Experiment a taped recording and a research description of each group meeting were made. These materials were gathered in order to test experimental treatment assumptions, especially to relate the theory regarding the use of groups to what actually occurred.

The task of measuring group interaction is a monumental one. Very little empirical measurement has been carried out. Adequate tools have not been available. Because of these complex problems, the tape recordings and other research data were utilized primarily to provide a descriptive rather than evaluative analysis.

During the past year, the taped recordings and the research analysis have been examined in order to make a systematic analysis of the processual development and structure of the total treatment system and groups within it.

Although the analysis has not been completed, an examination of the process suggests that the group development goes through a series of stages, from one in which involvement is minimal to one in which boys carry increasingly heavy responsibilities. Some groups develop more effectively than others. In those which do, the evolutionary process seems to be both threatening and rewarding, not only to boys but to staff.

On one hand, in order for boys to increase their capacity to take responsibility, power has to be granted to them by staff. Staff has to honor youthful participation in decision-making and other processes. It has to pay heed to differential perceptions and seek ways to change staff as well as delinquents if the two are to be successful in collaborating. It is not always easy for a staff to be willing to share power and responsibility.

On the other hand, problems face delinquent members of the group. They must decide whether they have more to lose than to gain if they do change. But, in addition, once having made an attempt to change, a group is still faced with community resistance. The question is not whether boys can assume responsibility, but whether the community is willing to *let* them assume it. Adults are often hypocritical. On one hand, they are critical because delinquents are not responsible citizens. Yet, on the other, they are afraid of efforts which permit adolescents to make decisions, solve problems, or exercise control over one of their members. Nevertheless, the evidence seems to indicate that the capacity of a group of delinquents to find new solutions or to deal with complex issues may exceed the willingness of authorities to let them exercise it.

The capacity to deal with such problems varied somewhat from group to group. In general, however, the evidence seemed to be that most groups reached a stage in which the group as a whole became adept in isolating basic problems, in judging the performance of group members and in making decisions about individual members. The process departed so far from traditional concepts of group therapy that it was these kinds of functions that encountered resistance from professional and community officials.

WORK PROGRAM

The work program at the Provo Experiment involved a variety of activities: work at the city cemetery, the building of a flood-control canal, minor construction on city streets or work at the city sewage disposal plant. Such work activities are generally seen by lay and professional people as having some inherent therapeutic quality. Ranches, institutions, farms and youth camps utilize work programs on the premise that hard work will change delinquent characteristics. Perhaps it was because of this orientation that our community work program was reluctantly, but nevertheless eventually, accepted and supported by local and state funds. Two interesting consequences resulted.

On one hand, our experiences during the first two years of the Experiment caused us to question the rationale expressed, above. We wondered whether, by having delinquent boys work together, we were perpetuating rather than changing delinquent behavior. There was continual friction between the boys and the adult supervisors who were hired to direct them. These supervisors tended either to take an unbending authoritarian stance with the boys, or to be seduced by them, succumbing in the last case to manipulations in an apparent desire to be accepted by the boys. The result was that the responsibility for work failures and delinquent acts on the job were shifted from the boys and their supervisors to the group leaders at the Experiment. It fell to them to try to maintain control and prevent outbursts. Consequently, rather than work becoming a productive and positive experience, it became a thorn in the side.

These circumstances served primarily to reinforce rather than diminish delinquent perceptions. Any difficulties were blamed by boys upon adults. The gap between offenders and adults remained as wide as ever. There was no mechanism by which to bridge this gap and to share responsibility for that which occurred. This led, in the third year of the Experiment, to a rather drastic change.

In an attempt to locate responsibility for difficulties on the job, adult work supervisors were fired and members of the work crews themselves were appointed as supervisors.

Initially, the change resulted in anxiety and confusion. Boy supervisors now found themselves in the role of adults attempting to exercise control over their peers. Such conditions provided an insightful experience. Boys began to recognize for the first time some of the pressures that they had put previously upon those who had attempted to control them.

Fortunately, the work activities did not degenerate but tended to improve. A different attitude began to develop among the work crews. When mistakes were made, the boys, rather than adults, had to bear the responsibility. There was no adult present upon which to levy blame. It was much easier in the group meetings, therefore, to examine realistically what the problems were on the job: who the poor workers were, what kind of delinquent manipulations were taking place, what it meant to be an adult rather than a child. The change seemed to provide an opportunity for boys to experiment realistically with new adult roles. Furthermore, the work output increased.

The second major observation relative to the work program has to do with the kinds of problems that were generated in providing work opportunities for the delinquent boys. A city government or a private business is not always organized to employ young people, even if they have a contribution to make. Child labor laws often create difficulties and young people competing for jobs may even be seen as a threat to the job security of older people.

Thus, although there seemed to be considerable work that needed to be done in Provo, and, although wages paid to the delinquent work crews were small, it was not always possible to have work projects outlined in advance.

In addition, it was difficult for city foremen to accept the notion that the boys in the work crews could become supervisors. Not only were foremen concerned about legal responsibility, but the age, mode of dress, and mode of speaking of many of these offenders. It was difficult to have the work crews accepted as a part of the daily operation.

It seems unlikely that such problems can be overcome on a permanent basis. Instead, they must be dealt with on a day-to-day basis. In order to do this, a mechanism must be set up and nourished which will permit differences to come into the open. Only after they are made explicit and examined is it possible to work out an accommodation which will result in the perpetuation of adolescent work programs. There was some evidence that this finally developed in Provo.

The role of work crews at the Experiment gradually became that of trouble shooter; that is the crews were used in a variety of places wherever the need was greatest. One summer they built a flood-control ditch in a particularly dangerous area. During the winter they worked to maintain a city skating rink. In the spring they worked at the cemetery and other places, cleaning them up after the winter's debris. They were able to perform a useful and productive function.

As some evidence of this, Provo City eventually expanded its work program to include adolescents other than those at the Experiment. In so doing, they sought the assistance of the staff at the Provo Experiment in terms of the best means for obtaining insurance coverage, determining pay scale and procedures, controlling adolescent workers and the best means for selecting and employing supervisors. The most unique thing of all was the fact that the City hired former delinquents from the Experiment as supervisors for both the delinquent and nondelinquent work crews. These adolescent supervisors were carefully selected and seemed to be able to deal well with the problems which they encountered. This use of former delinquents seems very important in light of contemporary efforts to find work opportunities for out-of-school youth. Not all graduates of the Experiment could perform the functions but several could.

COURT RELATIONS

The Judge of the Juvenile Court, Monroe J. Paxman, played a vital and indispensable role in the Experiment. Without his active and consistent support, it could not have occurred. Yet, a number of problems were generated which should be considered in any future experimentation.

The first has to do with the Court staff itself. They could not escape its impact. One very obvious reason is that the Experiment design put them in competition, in one sense, with the Experiment. The boys who were members of the probation control group were members of probation officer case loads. Consequently, it was impossible for the Chief Probation Officer and his deputies to ignore the possibility that those for whom they were responsible might do more poorly than boys who attended the experimental program. No amount of discussion regarding the scientific need to try different methods or to recognize that the treatment approaches were vastly different could do away with a sense of competition.

A second problem had to do with differences in treatment philosophy. For example, the intervention strategy of the Experiment called for intense efforts to promote anxiety and to pose alternatives clearly for delinquents. If boys who were assigned to the program failed to attend or continued to get into trouble, requests were sometimes made to the Court that they be placed in detention. The effort was then made to use their position in detention as a means of involving them more effectively in group discussions. The idea was to use negative sanctions more effectively, to utilize them as means for change rather than as means for punishment. Such practices and philosophy differed, of course, from the practices and philosophy of many professionals and organizations now in the field.

But there are not many happy alternatives to the use of occasional short-term detentions for the serious offender. Unless short-term detention along with other activities in the community can be utilized to change these offenders, then the only alternative is to incarcerate them permanently. This paradox was discussed on several occasions with opponents. It was never resolved.

Another problem seems in retrospect to be that of a failure on the part of the Experimental staff to devote long periods of time with the Court staff in discussing philosophy and experimental findings. One problem was that research takes many years to accomplish. Its results cannot be made immediately available. Nevertheless, greater efforts should have been made.

All of these problems placed the Judge of the Juvenile Court in a difficult position. Efforts to bridge the gap on his part may have only served to broaden the rift. The Judge found himself in a difficult position of trying to support both his own staff and the Experiment as well. His position was made even more difficult because of the publicity accorded the Experiment, both locally and nationally.

On a local level the Experiment gained considerable attention because of the efforts of the Experiment staff to gain the support of political, citizen and bureaucratic officials. Court staff could not but feel left out because of all the attention the Experiment was getting.

On a national level, the Judge found himself in a position of explaining and supporting the Experiment's theoretical design, methodology and techniques. But while doing so, he again may have appeared to be ignoring the efforts of his own staff. Regardless of what probation officers did, it may have been perceived by them as being insignificant in the eyes of the Judge when compared to what the Experiment was doing.

When these problems were added to the feeling of the Court staff that their own work was being evaluated and researched, a situation was created which was not easily resolved. However, there are some fascinating findings which may have resulted from these tensions. They will be explained in the statistics on recidivism.

The problems with the Court, especially the Chief Probation Officer, had direct influence on the treatment program during the last few months of operation, particularly, in terms of the availability of detention facilities. Eventually the pressure became so great that all use of detention facilities was discontinued. This seriously hampered efforts to control boys who were continuing to get in trouble, and although new methods were devised to cope with the problem, it placed considerably more demands upon the treatment staff in terms of time and energy. In our opinion, these other methods were not so successful as the use of detention. It remains, however, for the research analysis to indicate whether or not this was in fact the case.

THE SCHOOLS

In the initial phases of the Provo Experiment, it was felt that some delinquent boys who had had a long history of school failure might better be encouraged to leave school. We felt that, given some support to find jobs, a job might diminish some of the tensions felt by the boys. However, as the discussion groups began to develop it was with some surprise that we discovered that most of the boys in the groups did not share this opinion. They seemed to feel that despite all problems, the best place for adolescents to be was in school. Consequently, the emphasis changed. Considerable effort was made by the groups to help boys remain in school.

School problems became a matter of great importance in group meetings; school progress was used by group members as a criterion for judging progress and release; and a more effective liaison between experimental staff and school officials was established. A system for exchanging progress reports in both agencies was developed. In addition, a tutorial program was added to the Experiment.

The result was the development of an exceptionally cooperative relationship between the Experiment staff and school officials. We are not sure yet as to the basic reasons for the success of this relationship. Some boys who otherwise would have dropped from school have remained in. However, until research analyses are made, we are not sure that their staying in school was because of a better academic performance on their part or because their attitude and behavior had changed markedly.

We suspect that part of the reason they seemed to get along better in school was because they became much less a conduct problem. School officials were delighted because boys who previously had caused a great deal of trouble were now much less trouble. School principals, counselors and teachers, therefore, expressed considerable concern that the treatment program would end once the original experimental period was over. They were among those who most actively supported the notion that the program should become a community fixture.

COMMUNITY RELATIONSHIPS

Support by the community for the Experiment was mixed. On one hand, the support of citizens and organized groups in developing the Experiment was indispensable. There was virtually no opposition to having a special program for delinquents in the community. Local groups vigorously supported the use of County funds by which to run the program.

On the other hand, it was extremely difficult to obtain the support of key County and State officials. During the early years of the program, before it was formalized as an Experiment, Utah County provided a small amount annually with which to run it. When a research grant was obtained, County funds, approximately $12,000 per year for treatment purposes, was matched by funds from the Ford Foundation. (In addition, Ford funds financed the research operation.) But, when, in the elections of 1960, political control of the County Commission changed hands, strong opposition was raised to any further County financing.

During that year, and for two subsequent years, County funds were budgeted only after a running battle between the County Commission and supportive citizens' groups. County officials contended, and with some justification, that since both the Juvenile Court and probation systems in Utah are state systems, the State, not the County, should finance the program. State officials, on the other hand, demurred, arguing that since the program was started on a local level it should be financed on the local level.

The Speaker of the Utah House of Representatives attempted to intercede, feeling that the State had some investment in seeing the Experiment completed since it was much less expensive than total incarceration and might be equally or more successful. On one occasion he arranged a meeting involving the Utah County Commission, the Utah State Welfare Commission and legislative representatives from Utah County. The goal was to see if the State and County could not cooperate in providing the small amount of funds needed for the experimental program. His suggested solution was a matching of State and local funds but state officials were unwilling to support the suggestion, even though funds would have come from a separate bill which would not have endangered their regular appropriation. The irony, of course, was that the amount needed per year was very small. The program was being run in an ordinary home, required only two full-time staff members, a secretary and incidental expenses.

Insofar as the program staff was concerned, the struggle to obtain local financing grew so great that the treatment and research aspects of the Experiment were being slighted. After careful study, it was determined that the original design of the 6 year Experiment could be carried out if funds were carefully expended and, therefore, that the political and bureaucratic battles would not be waged any longer. If the program were to continue after Experimental funds were exhausted, new solutions would have to be found.

Several articles appeared in the newspapers indicating that the program would close unless local funds could be found. The result was that numerous meetings were held with citizens' committees and the program's budgetary needs made public. The Utah County Mental Health Association offered $10,000 if this money would insure continuation of the program. This offer was especially meritorious because the Mental Health Association itself was under considerable financial stress and its own future was uncertain. But because the amount would not have been adequate for a single year's operation, the treatment staff of the Experiment could not be expected to stay on so uncertain a future. Therefore, after the fifth year of the Experiment, treatment was ended and the remaining time devoted to research matters.

The fact that the program has discontinued is a lesson in community and organizational failure. As will be seen from subsequent findings, the Experiment did seem to provide a marked increase in success with delinquents. It was a pioneer effort in the search for alternatives to incarceration. Yet, it failed for precisely the same reason that correctional and mental health programs have had such difficulty in the past: key decision-makers in the community would not commit themselves to experimentation and innovation.

There is no doubt that those who operated the Experiment contributed to some of its problems. The most glaring fault was the lack of effort at the very outset to involve State officials. So much attention was devoted initially to the difficult tasks of conceptualizing and implementing the Experiment, that the necessary organizational steps were not taken. Perhaps if State officials had been involved, they would have supported the Experiment and incorporated the better parts of it in the State system or have been willing to try it out further. But this is speculation without empirical evidence as to just what strategy should be adopted in attempts at innovation. It may well be that bureaucratic resistance at the outset would have prevented the Experiment's ever beginning. Certainly, strong early resistance, coupled with other problems, could have spelled the end of the effort without any program ever having been developed. The Experiment departed sufficiently far from tradition that continuing differences over them could, and eventually did, block an extended testing of them.

Research on Outcome

It will be recalled that, in order to evaluate *impact* on offenders, an experimental design was created in which delinquents assigned to the program could be compared to two control groups: one group which was left in the community on probation and a second which was incarcerated in the Utah State Industrial School.

The initial experimental design was set up with the idea that all three groups could be drawn randomly from a common population of persistent offenders residing solely in Utah County. However, some modifications had to be made. The reasons were these:

The population of persistent offenders to be included in the Experiment was restricted to only 15 per cent of all cases coming before the local juvenile court. This small proportion was not always adequate to fill one experimental and two control groups. But, in addition, Judge Paxman has always been disinclined to commit boys to a state institution. Consequently, the *reformatory* control group was not adequately filled. Too few boys, in Judge Paxman's mind, seemed to warrant institutionalization. Consequently, it became necessary to select a similar rather than a random sample from the Utah State Industrial School and to determine if, and on what characteristics, it might differ from the experimental control groups from Utah County.

Statistical comparisons among the three groups on a large number of variables—offense history official and undetected amount and type of undetected delinquency, family characteristics, education, and future aspirations—have not revealed many significant differences. It was felt, therefore, that some confidence might be placed in comparisons. Nevertheless, the comparison between the experimental program and the incarcerated group will be affected by the change.

SIX MONTHS' SUCCESS RATES

A very stringent measure of recidivism was used, namely, the filing of an arrest report on a boy. This measure was used in an attempt to avoid all of the formal and informal decisions that are made once an offense is detected; that is, to handle the offense informally without court hearing, to return the arrestee to court or even to revoke probation or parole. Once these factors enter the picture it is almost impossible to establish any consistent criterion of success or failure unless the same procedure and persons are used in all cases—a condition which rarely, if ever, exists.

Prior to the introduction of the Experiment in Provo, only about 55 per cent of the kinds of persistent offenders who were eventually assigned to it were succeeding on probation. In order to see if improvement could be made for this hard-core group, the Experiment was introduced and treatment and control groups were selected. The evidence is strong that improvement did occur.

Six months after release, 73 per cent of those who were assigned to, and 84 per cent of those who completed, the experimental program had not been arrested. The remainder had been arrested only once and none had been incarcerated. But this possibly was not the most impressive finding.

During the same period, the success rate for the control group under regular probation had gone up almost as precipitously. From its original success rate of 55 per cent the Probation Department developed a success rate of 73 per cent for those assigned to regular probation and 77 per cent for those who completed it.

Apparently the introduction of the Experiment and the research which accompanied it had some influence on the Probation Department itself. Improved efforts, perhaps a sense of competition with the Experiment, and some alteration in techniques seem to have resulted. In addition, the community struggled with and helped to provide a daily work program and other facilities as aids both to the Experiment and to the Probation Department.

On the other hand, the second control group, made up of incarcerated offenders, was not nearly so successful as the experimental and probation control groups. Six months after release, only 42 per cent of the incarcerated offenders had remained unarrested. Of the remaining 58 per cent, half had been arrested two or more times.

This finding, of course, must be tempered by the fact that random selection from a common population broke down and thus the incarcerated, comparison group had to be selected on another basis. Yet, if the differences are due to factors other than treatment, our research cannot indicate what they are. As mentioned above, a statistical comparison of the incarcerated group with the experimental and community central groups, over a long list of variables, did not isolate any differences. Other than differences in recidivism rates, the three groups did not seem to differ. If there is any validity to the figures, therefore, the community programs not only resulted in significantly less recidivism but they cost only a fraction of the money. However, the followup is continuing and final figures may change somewhat.

COMPARATIVE COSTS OF DIFFERENT TREATMENTS INVOLVED

The experimental program was considerably cheaper than different kinds of residential programs. For example, a California State Youth Authority School at Whittier, California, had an annual expenditure per boy which was approximately 4 times as great as that of the Experiment, the Federal youth institution at Inglewood, Colorado, an expenditure which was 3 times as high and the Utah State Industrial School an expenditure which was over twice as high.

The cost for the probation control group was lower than any of the above. Some estimates run as low as $200 per boy but these are inexact figures because this is an average cost which overlooks the extra time usually spent on persistent offenders. We do not at this time have an exact figure on the matter.

Another cost estimate was based on the cost of treating one boy at the Experiment and at the Utah State Industrial School. The average stay at the Utah State Industrial School in 1962 was 9½ months and cost approximately $2,015. The average stay at the Provo Experiment was approximately 7 months (although it will be recalled that a boy continued to live at home) and cost about $609 per boy. This would mean roughly a saving of $1,406 per boy plus 2½ months of his time.

In addition to basic recidivism figures other *outcome* analyses are being conducted: before-and-after psychological changes, school performance, work behavior, changes in peer relations, and predictions of success and failure by both boys and staff members.

NOTE

1. Maynard L. Erickson and LaMar T. Empey, "Court Records, Undetected Delinquency and Decision-Making," *The Journal of Criminal Law, Criminology and Police Science,* 54 (Dec., 1963), pp. 456–469; Maynard L. Erickson and LaMar T. Empey,

"Class Position, Peers and Delinquency," *Sociology and Social Research,* 49 (April, 1965), pp. 268–282; and LaMar T. Empey and Maynard L. Erickson, "Hidden Delinquency and Social Status," *Social Forces,* forthcoming.

29: The Highfields Study / *H. A. Weeks*

The Highfields Project for the Short-Term Treatment of Youthful Offenders inaugurated in New Jersey has been in operation since July 5, 1950. This report is an attempt to measure and evaluate various aspects of the Highfields Project for the first several years of its life.

The Short-Term Treatment of Youthful Offenders Program evolved from the need felt by many New Jersey judges for a new law to permit them to make definite sentences of not more than three months to the existing New Jersey facilities such as the reformatories and training schools. These judges believed that such a law would act as a deterrent to many boys—it would demonstrate to delinquent boys that commitment and incarceration for a much longer period would be their lot if they did not mend their ways. The judges felt that many delinquent boys were not yet serious enough offenders to warrant their being sent to The New Jersey State Home for Boys at Jamesburg or to one of the state's reformatories for an indeterminate period of confinement. Such boys had demonstrated that their misbehavior was serious enough to raise doubts in the minds of the judges as to whether they could be placed or continued on probation with safety to the community and protection to themselves. Juvenile court judges are frequently loath to commit a boy to an institution which he is not likely to leave short of a year. They feel, with justification, that a boy often becomes worse when he is kept too long in an institution.

The Proposed Program

The New Jersey program for the short-term treatment of youthful offenders originally included these points:

Boys, while still officially on probation, would live, work, and play together in a unit which would house only a few boys at any one time.

Small groups of boys—not more than ten in any one group—would meet each day with the director, a trained guided group interactionist, in sessions designed to uncover their problems and help them begin to solve them.

From H. Ashley Weeks, *Youthful Offenders at Highfields* (Ann Arbor: University of Michigan Press, 1958), pp. 1–2; 3–5; 7–10; 6–20; 21–24; 41–46; 50–54; 59–62; 118–128. Copyright by University of Michigan Press.

The boys would live as nearly normal lives as possible. There would be no outward symbols of incarceration, force, or even control. There would be no officers or guards. The personnel would consist only of the director, who would be responsible for establishing and maintaining a therapeutic climate, a man and his wife to supervise housekeeping and to assume the role of house-parents, and a handyman or jack-of-all-trades to assist the boys in developing their hobbies and in making themselves useful around the place.

There would be no formal educational program, but boys would listen to the radio and read newspapers and magazines and other material. This material would be thoroughly discussed and would give the residents a chance to evaluate and interpret together the information and opinions with which these mass media continually bombard us all.

The boys would work on some constructive project, not for vocational training but to gain work experience, and they would be paid a small wage for this work.

There would be hobby and craft projects in which all would participate. Each boy would be expected to select and finish one such project during his residency, whether it be "writing a short story, building a radio cabinet, over-hauling a gasoline engine, or almost anything else that the individual feels he would like to do."

The boys would be allowed to go to local villages, accompanied by an adult, to shop, attend the movies, have a soda, or indulge in other approved activities of interest to them. On Sundays, religious activities and experiences would be available in the nearby community churches. There would be many opportunities to maintain community contacts. Periodically, during their short stay, they would be granted furloughs home. These would be in the nature of test situations and would also furnish experiences that could be discussed in the group sessions.

As actually established, the project embodies some changes in the original plan as proposed by Dr. Bixby. The guided group interaction sessions are not held every night, but only five nights during each week. Usually, there are no sessions Thursday and Saturday nights. So far as is known, there is no specific discussion session in which the boys evaluate and interpret the information they have received from the mass media. Of course, certain attitudes and expressions received from their reading or listening are often brought forward in the sessions and aired and analyzed there, but this as observed by the writer is more by happenstance than design. Nor is there any hobby or craft program in which all participate. Boys can and do carry on projects, but again it is because of an individual interest and not by design. With these exceptions the program is very similar to the one Dr. Bixby originally conceived.

Certain criteria for the kind of residents were set up. In the first place, it was decided to limit the project to delinquent boys sixteen and seventeen years of age. Boys under this age would have to have school facilities provided for them in accordance with the state law, and those over seventeen are beyond the age when they may be handled as juveniles by the courts of the state. It was also decided to limit the project to first commitment boys, that is, boys who had not formerly been committed to a state industrial school or other place of confinement. It was reasoned that boys who had had former institutional experience might be so conditioned in their behavioral reactions that it would be difficult for them to participate wholeheartedly and freely in the guided group interaction sessions. The kind of resident to be sent to Highfields was further limited by the exclusion of known sexual perverts and feebleminded and/or psychotic boys.

Before Highfields began to accept boys, discussions were held with the judges of the four large northeastern counties which have separate juvenile courts. It was explained to them that Highfields was not necessarily a substitute for either probation or incarceration, but a third choice. Whenever a judge had a boy before him who was sixteen or seventeen years of age and met the other criteria, the judge could consider whether the short-term treatment afforded at Highfields might be preferable to commitment or regular probation. A specialized facility such as Highfields would be helpful when he was in doubt. He could still place a boy on probation provided the boy would agree to spend a relatively short term (up to four months) under the treatment program.[1] If he decided a boy was suitable for Highfields, he could ascertain whether a bed was available there, and if it was he could see whether a boy would volunteer to go to Highfields. If a bed was not available, the former choice was still possible—incarceration or probation.

Original Research Design

In order to secure the information needed to evaluate the program proposed by Dr. Bixby, it appeared that there were three basic questions which should be answered:

1. Do delinquents participating in the short-term treatment program show a higher, the same, or a lower recidivist rate than boys participating in other kinds of treatment programs?

2. Do delinquents participating in the short-term treatment program change their expressed attitudes, values, and opinions toward their families, law and order, and their own outlook on life?

3. Do delinquents participating in the short-term treatment program change their basic personality structures or at least the overt manifestations of their personalities?

These questions were based on certain theoretical considerations. It is generally assumed that correctional training, whether punitive or therapeutically oriented, changes and improves the overt behavior of the person undergoing the training. The lay public as well as the professionals at work in the field hope that the experiences persons have in correctional facilities will be reflected in an improvement in the behavior they exhibit after they are released.

As Dr. Bixby has written: "The objective of all correctional procedures is the permanent protection of society through the rehabilitation of the greatest possible number of convicted offenders." [2] Recidivist rates, then, should be a general measure of the effectiveness of a correctional program.

But recidivism is not the sole measure of effectiveness. Persons who have experienced correctional training may be favorably affected by the treatment only to have the good effects discounted by the fact that they are returned to the same family, the same neighborhood, and the same detrimental social groupings and influences which contributed to their anti-social behavior in the first place. But whether or not they subsequently get into further trouble with the law, the treatment they receive, if effective, should alter their attitudes, values, and opinions, and this alteration should be observable at the time they leave the treatment facility. We felt that the short-term treatment program should especially bring about changes in values, attitudes, and opinions. Guided group interaction sessions, we believed, should encourage the participants to recognize their problems in terms of their behavior, attitudes, and values and allow them to explore alternative solutions to their problems. . . .

In order to insure meaningful answers to the questions we were asking, an experimental design was called for. Therefore, we advocated securing pre- and post-information on each boy sent to the short-term treatment project and like information on boys who were handled in other ways. These other ways might include release with no further action by the court, probation, committal to a training school or reformatory, or even to a jail or other local place of incarceration. Theoretically, at least, samples of boys similar in every way to those sent to the short-term treatment facility could be drawn from those handled in each of these other ways, and comparisons made between them and the boys experiencing the short-term treatment program.

New Jersey has an excellent Diagnostic Center at Menlo Park, and it was suggested that all boys be screened at the Center and complete diagnostic workups on each boy be obtained when he first came to the attention of the court and again when he was discharged from whatever treatment he had been undergoing. Comparisons could then be made in terms of the changes revealed between the two workups and the particular treatment accorded the various groups of boys.

As the research plan was discussed with the judges of the four separate juvenile courts, it appeared that the great majority of boys would probably be committed to Annandale Farms, the New Jersey State Reformatory for Males, if there were no room for them at Highfields. It could be assumed that if Highfields did not exist almost all of the more serious delinquents as old as sixteen or seventeen would be sent to the reformatory at Annandale. Thus, it was decided for research purposes to use as a control group boys of the same ages as those eligible for Highfields who were committed to this reformatory. The control group would, of course, be selected according to the other criteria established for Highfields eligibility: it would be composed of boys who had not previously been in a state correctional institution, who did not appear to be feebleminded or psychotic and who were not known sexual perverts.

Highfields

The type of group therapy carried on at Highfields is called Guided Group Interaction for a number of reasons. The name was selected to differentiate this kind of group therapy from the more common group psychotherapy and, as Dr. Bixby and Dr. McCorkle write, to indicate their belief that not all prisoners are mentally abnormal or sick; that the leader, especially in initial sessions, assumes an active role as contrasted to his more passive one in other types of group therapy; that this type of group activity is distinguished from the more exhaustive type of analysis characteristic of group psychotherapy; and that modification takes place in the application of group therapy principles when applied to the unique environment of the penal and correctional institution.[3]

During the first few months of the project Dr. McCorkle often sat in on court hearings, and from listening to what a boy had to say there and in talking with him personally, he learned something about the boy's problems and whether the Highfields program could help him. At this time no one could say, although all connected with the project had great faith and hope, whether the aims and goals of Highfields could be carried out. No one knew whether the answers to the following questions would be affirmative or negative:

1. Would it be possible to organize and operate a short-term residential center for the treatment of delinquent boys on a noncustodial basis?
2. Would boys take part in the sessions of guided group interaction?
3. Would boys be successful in analyzing the factors in their delinquent behavior and careers?
4. If Highfields achieved its objectives, would the success be attributed to the unique personality and wide experience of the director or could his methods be successfully applied by other persons?

We now have answers to each of these questions. The first three can be answered affirmatively. It has been possible to organize and operate the Highfields Project in a noncustodial way; boys participate wholeheartedly in the sessions; and they are able cogently and sometimes in great detail to analyze the complex relationships involved in their lives and delinquent behavior. We also know that the methods of the original director can be successfully applied by other persons. The success of organizing and carrying on a project such as Highfields is not contingent on the personality or wide experience of a single individual. The techniques of conducting the guided group interaction sessions can be transmitted from one person to another.

Highfields has been in operation over five years, continually receiving seriously delinquent boys from the courts and, for the most part, sending them back to their communities after their treatment period of four months was completed. It seems to those of us that got in on some of the sessions that they are vital, revealing experiences for the boys, who participate freely and often with much insight. Dubious at first and careful of what they might reveal, boys soon learn to trust the therapist and the other boys and as a result discuss together their most intimate problems. No one who has had the opportunity to sit in on the sessions can doubt that the boys are capable of analyzing the factors in their delinquent behavior. Many of them can also give shrewd appraisals of one another's conduct and in most instances in a way that makes it obvious that they have a sincere desire to help. It has been demonstrated that another director trained by Dr. McCorkle could take over and carry on successfully the sessions and other duties and responsibilities connected with the administration of the project. Dr. McCorkle was asked to become warden of the New Jersey State Prison in Trenton after he had been the director of Highfields for the first twenty months of its operation, and Mr. Albert Elias took over at Highfields. Earlier, Mr. Elias had come to Highfields from Illinois to interne at the project. After returning to Illinois and starting guided group interaction sessions at Sheridan, one of the Illinois reformatories, he was asked to return to Highfields and assume the directorship. Highfields has been under Mr. Elias' direction since June 1952.

Highfields operates with a very small staff. Besides the director, a man and his wife serve as a cottage supervisor and cook, and a general handyman acts as caretaker. Recently, a secretary to the director and a work supervisor have been employed. These six adults comprise the total staff. From time to time throughout the project there has been an interne or trainee at the project learning the techniques of conducting the sessions.

The Research

Administrative procedures and routines would not permit the processing of all the boys through the Diagnostic Center, as called for in the original design. There was not available at the time nor was it possible to procure the psychological and psychiatric staff to do the job. Because of this the research design had to be altered, and much of the psychological and psychiatric information we had planned to use had to be foregone. Fortunately, some psychological information could be collected. The late Dr. J. Quinter Holsopple, a member of the Scientific Advisory Committee, together with Dr. Florence Miale, had developed a sentence completion test which could be used to provide psychological data.

During the first six months of the project, before the actual research operation began,[4] a series of tests were developed in hopes that they would provide answers to some of the questions raised in our original design. These tests were devised to tap attitudinal and opinion areas which we thought the guided group interaction sessions as well as the total Highfields program might stress. In addition, a schedule for securing social background information on each boy was prepared. . . .

During the spring of 1951 the following policy, initiated with the co-operation of the juvenile courts and parole offices, became the standard operating procedure carried on for the remainder of the study. Each time a judge decided to send a boy to either Highfields or Annandale, his office notified the research division at New York University and one of the staff traveled to the probation office or parental school of the respective court, where the tests were administered. Each time a boy was released from Highfields the director notified the research office and a member of the staff went to the respective probation office and administered the same tests as were given before. When a boy in the control group was released from Annandale the institution parole officer notified the district parole officer that the boy was in the control sample. This officer in turn notified the research office and arrangements were made to meet with the parolee and administer the tests. In this way almost all of the boys were tested just before they went to their respective facilities and just after they were released.[5]

In addition to the testing, we have, through co-operation of the probation and parole offices, kept in touch with each boy over the length of the study. Periodically, we received reports from the respective offices on each boy's adjustment. If he got into further trouble and was returned to the court and recommitted to any correctional facility we were immediately notified.

For the purposes of this study the following definition of a recidivist, or failure, was adopted. A recidivist is one who, for any reason, was returned to court and/or violated probation or parole and as a result was committed to an institution. When we speak of failures or recidivists, we mean only boys who, subsequent to their first stay in either Highfields or Annandale, have been committed a second time. This commitment may be in Annandale, as is the case with most of the boys in our sample who have failed, or in a jail for a period of thirty days or longer, or penal institution in another state. Boys who have been called in to the probation or parole office or even brought before the court and admonished or warned but were not recommitted but continued on probation or parole are not failures by this definition. . . .

No boys committed to Annandale were pre-tested after February 1954, and no boys sent to Highfields after April of this same year. It was necessary to cut off the Annandale cases earlier than the Highfields ones because of the longer commitment period of the reformatory boys. Few boys, unless recalled by the committing judge, are released from Annandale earlier than twelve months. Therefore, boys committed through February 1954 would not leave Annandale before the end of January 1955; and because we wished to allow at least a six-month period after release to ascertain whether or not a boy made good, none could be included who would not be out of the institution for at least six months by the end of August 1955. The same reasoning was applied to the Highfields cases. Boys at Highfields stay as long as four months. All of the boys admitted to Highfields through April 1954, therefore, would normally be released by the last of August and would have been on probation in their communities for at least six months by the end of February 1955. The main reason for the earlier six-month cut-off date for the Highfields boys was that many more Highfields than Annandale boys had to be processed. It was also felt that numerically enough boys were in the Highfields sample and nothing would be gained by extending the time. Both groups of boys were finally followed up until October 1955.

From February 1951, when the first boys were tested, to the last of April 1954, two hundred and thirty-three boys were sent to Highfields by the courts, an average of about sixty-one boys a year.

From this beginning date to the end of January 1954, the same courts committed 122 boys to Annandale. Nearly three-quarters of the boys sent to Highfields came almost equally from two of the most populous counties. One of these counties committed very few boys to Annandale—only three— whereas the second county committed almost two-thirds of the Annandale sample. This discrepancy in commitment rates was an indication that the Highfields and Annandale samples might not be exactly comparable. We shall compare the two samples in order to convey just how they differ.[6]

Success Rates for Highfields and Annandale

One test of whether delinquents have been rehabilitated is whether they get into further difficulty after their release from treatment, whatever the treatment program may be. Of course, many persons argue that no matter how good a given treatment program may be, it may not permanently rehabilitate if delinquents are sent back into the same environment which brought on their trouble in the first place. This argument is a strong one, yet it can be maintained that if a delinquent is fundamentally changed, or realizes what his problems have been and attempts to do something about those problems, he does not approach his past environment with the same reference as he did prior to his treatment. In this sense the environment to which a delinquent returns is not the same environment he left. But this depends on how thoroughly his personality or way of looking at himself and others has altered.

OUTCOME FOR ALL BOYS SENT TO
THE RESPECTIVE FACILITIES

We shall first present the findings for all the boys sent to Highfields or Annandale. There can be no question that Highfields rehabilitates more boys than does Annandale. Of the 229 boys sent to Highfields, 145, or 63 per cent, completed their treatment and have been in no further difficulty great enough to send them to another custodial facility after having been released for at least a year. In contrast, of the 116 boys sent to Annandale only 55, or 47 per cent, completed their treatment program and have been in no further difficulty severe enough to send them back to Annandale or to another custodial facility after having been released for at least *eight months or more.*[7] In other words, Highfields appears to succeed with sixteen more boys in every hundred than does Annandale.

Let us look further into these figures. When we compare only white boys sent to the two facilities we find that there is no statistical difference in the relative number who need no further custodial care. Of every hundred white boys, 64 Highfields and 59 Annandale boys completed their treatment and needed no further institutional care. The situation is quite different for the Negro boys: 59 of every hundred Highfields Negroes completed their treatment and got into no further difficulty severe enough to reinstitutionalize them, whereas this is true for only 33 of every hundred Annandale Negroes. Figure 29–1 shows the relative differences in the success rates for boys sent to Highfields and Annandale.

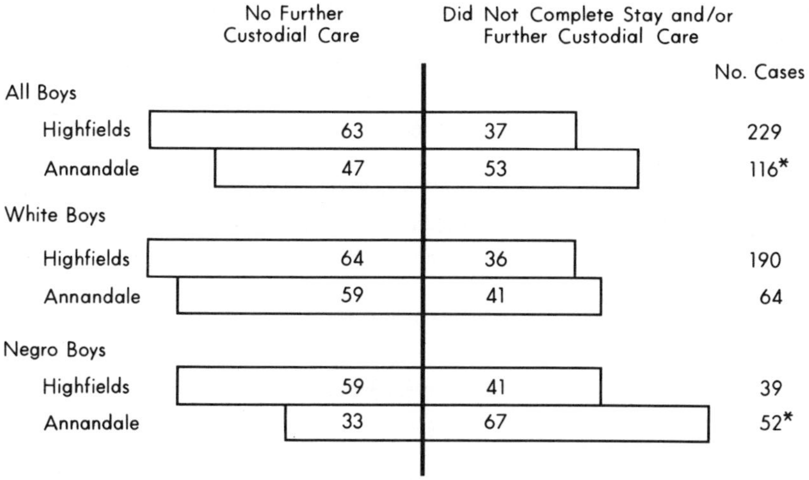

FIGURE 29–1. *Relative Distributions of Boys Sent to Highfields and Annandale Who Completed Their Stay and Have Had No Further Custodial Care, and Who Have Not Completed Their Stay and / or Have Had Further Custodial Care.*

Thus, the over-all differences in the success rates are almost wholly due to the large discrepancy between the rate for Negroes sent to Highfields and that for Negroes sent to Annandale.

The majority of Negroes sent to Highfields (three-quarters) came from Essex County. We shall therefore use Essex County for a comparison of the rates of white and Negro boys sent to Highfields and Annandale. . . .

It can be seen from a study of Table 29–1 that the difference between the percentage distributions of the totals for Highfields and Annandale boys results from the extreme difference between the distributions for Negro boys in the two facilities. Of the Negroes sent to Highfields, six in every ten completed their stay and got into no further trouble severe enough to warrant custodial care; but of the Negroes sent to Annandale not even half this proportion—less than three in ten—had no further custodial care. This is a striking finding.

But what about Negro boys sent to the respective facilities? Is there reason to believe that the Negroes sent to Annandale from Essex County differ from those sent to Highfields from this county? Can the fact that these Negroes have different social backgrounds explain the difference in the proportion in the two facilities who need no further custodial care? There is no question that the Negroes sent to Annandale by Essex County differ from those sent to Highfields in a number of ways. As is the case with white boys, the Negroes sent to Highfields tend to be younger and better educated than those sent to Annandale. In addition, Highfields Negroes appear to differ from Annandale Negroes in the number of jobs they have held, the degree of mobility from state to state, from city to city and within the city where they live at present, the occupation of their mothers, broken homes, father's occupation, size of family, number of prior delinquencies, and number of associates in the delinquency which sent them to their respective facility.[8] However, none of these background variables is related to outcome. For example, when we hold age constant, the Highfields Negro is still much more likely to be successful than the Annandale Negro. And the success rate is a good deal higher for Highfields Negroes than it is for Annandale Negroes regardless of the educational level of the boys.

From this analysis it would seem that differences in the total programs at

Table 29-1

Comparison of Essex County Boys sent to Highfields and Annandale Who Completed Their Stay and Have Had No Further Custodial Care and Boys Who Did Not Complete Their Stay and/or Have Had Further Custodial Care

	Highfields						Annandale					
	Total		White		Negro		Total		White		Negro	
	No.	Per Cent	No.	Per Cent	No.	Per Cent	No.	Per Cent	No.	Per Cent	No.	Per Cent
No further custodial care*	52	59	34	58	18	62	29	39	19	54	10	26
Did not complete stay and/or further custo-dial care	36	41	25	42	11	38	45	61	16	46	29	74
Total	88	100	59	100	29	100	74	100	35	100	39	100

*The differences between these percentages for the total cases would occur by chance only about once in one hundred times. There is no statistically significant difference between the white boys, but the difference between the percentages for Negro boys in Highfields and Annandale would occur by change hardly more than once in 1000 times.

the two facilities must account for the large difference between the proportions of Negroes at the respective facilities who complete their residence and do not get into further trouble.

Whatever accounts for the difference between the rates for Negroes in the two facilities, this difference explains the over-all difference in outcome between *all* Highfields and Annandale boys.

Outcome for Boys Who Complete Treatment at the Respective Facilities

When only the boys who have completed their treatment program at Highfields are compared with those who have been released from Annandale (Figure 29–2), the relative success rate for Highfields becomes much greater: 77

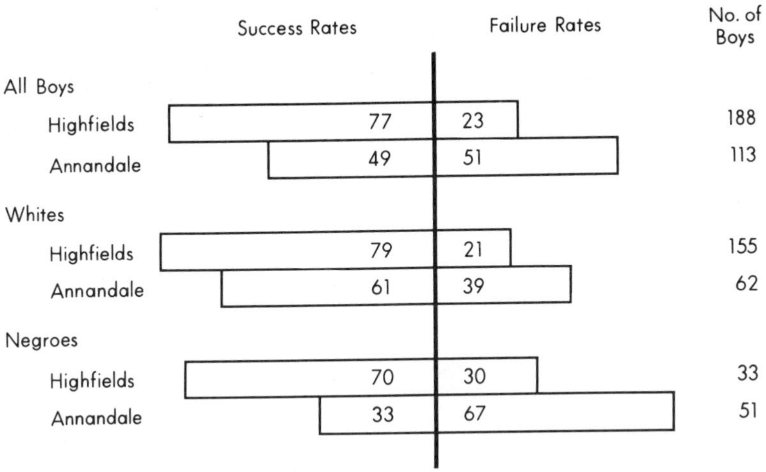

	Success Rates	Failure Rates	No. of Boys
All Boys			
Highfields	77	23	188
Annandale	49	51	113
Whites			
Highfields	79	21	155
Annandale	61	39	62
Negroes			
Highfields	70	30	33
Annandale	33	67	51

FIGURE 29–2. *Comparison of the Success and Failure Rates for All Highfields and Annandale Boys Who Completed Their Treatment by County and Race.*

per cent for Highfields as contrasted with 49 per cent for Annandale. When we look at the white and Negro rates separately, we find that again the Negroes account for the largest share of the differences observed; the success rate for Highfields Negroes is more than twice as high as that for Annandale Negroes: 70 per cent as against 33 per cent. The major differences between both the white and the Negro rates are found in Essex County. Among the Highfields boys, the over-all success rates by county are surprisingly similar. The Negro and white success rates for Highfields boys from Essex County do not differ appreciably; whereas there is a striking difference between the Negro and white success rates for Annandale boys from this county.

Because, as Figure 29–2 illustrates, the major difference between the success rates for Highfields and Annandale is found in Essex County, we should ascertain whether there are background factors which can account for the differential in the success rates for boys from this county.

The following lists show the background variables which differentiate white and Negro Highfields boys from white and Negro Annandale boys sent to each facility from Essex County.

ESSEX COUNTY	ESSEX COUNTY
Highfields white boys are more likely than Annandale white boys	Highfields Negro boys are more likely than Annandale Negro boys
To be younger	To be younger
To be better educated	To be better educated
To have had no jobs	To have had only one job
To have moved from state to state and from city to city	Not to have moved from state to state or from city to city, but to have moved within the city
To be from broken homes	Not to be from broken homes
To have fathers who are white-collar workers	To have fathers who are non-skilled workers and mothers who are housewives
To have committed few delin-quencies	To have committed few delin-quencies
To have committed their present delinquency alone	To have committed their present delinquency with one or two others
	To be from large families

None of these differences between Highfields and Annandale boys is statistically significant because of the small number of boys in the samples, but the lists show that the backgrounds of Highfields boys differ somewhat from those of Annandale boys.

Analysis of the relationships which prevail between these variables and outcome shows that when each of these variables is held constant the large discrepancy between outcome of Annandale Negroes and Highfields Negroes cannot be explained by such variables. The differences in the experiences which Negro boys have as the result of being sent to the respective facilities must account for the differential in the rates. It may well be that the guided group interaction sessions decidedly help the Negroes sent to Highfields, and/or that Negroes sent to Annandale become even more antisocial than they were because of their experience there. There may be a difference between probation treatment after these boys leave Highfields and parole treatment after Negro boys leave Annandale.

It is likely that Negroes at Highfields learn, possibly for the first time, that they have problems no different from those of white boys. One night we sat in one of the guided group interaction sessions where a Negro boy became aware of this fact. A rather small Negro lad appeared to pay no attention to what was going on. He sat slouched in his chair with his cap pulled down over his eyes, pretending to be asleep or at least totally uninterested. A white boy was explaining his problem to the group. Suddenly this boy shoved up the visor of his cap. He listened intently to what was being said. His eyes grew wider and wider. He sat up straight in his chair and finally blurted out, "Why, that's the same problem I've got." It was rather obvious that this boy had not imagined that a white boy could feel the same as he did. Later, he discussed his problem in some detail, and from that time on he participated in the sessions and began to work on the solution to his difficulty.

It is very possible that the problems of many Negroes are not so deep-seated as those of whites. Once they begin to see what their problems are and to realize that their problems are basically no different from those of other boys, they have a better chance to resolve them. Undoubtedly, differential association is a factor in this awareness. Whatever the reason, it is rather amazing that the success rate for both white and Negro boys sent to Highfields from Essex County is virtually the same, whereas the success rate for Negroes sent to Annandale from this county is less than half (46 per cent) that for white boys. Moreover, although Essex County has sent ten more Negroes to Annandale than it has to Highfields, seven more Highfields than Annandale Negroes have needed no further custodial care after release. If this ratio holds, it means that of every hundred Negroes sent to Highfields from Essex County, sixty-two would need no further custodial care after release, whereas of every hundred Negroes from Essex County sent to Annandale, only twenty-eight would be so fortunate.

NOTES

1. Judges are loath to institutionalize a delinquent if they can possibly avoid it. This can be seen from the fact that boys often have long histories of delinquency and court appearances without commitment. They frequently are placed in probation again and again, or continued on probation. The ordinary delinquent has three or more official prior delinquencies before he is committed to a State institution. This is true not only in New Jersey but elsewhere.

2. "A Plan for the Short-Term Treatment of Youthful Offenders" (mimeographed), p. 1.

3. F. Lovell Bixby and Lloyd W. McCorkle, "Guided Group Interaction in Correctional Work," *American Sociological Review*, 16 (August 1951): 55–56. For those interested in the communication which takes place in the session, this article will reward careful study. See also James Finan, "Inside the Prison," *Reader's Digest*, 56 (May 1950): 61–72; and F. L. Bixby and L. W. McCorkle, "A Recorded Presentation of a Program of Guided Group Interaction in New Jersey's Correctional Institutions," *Boston Proceedings of the 78th Annual Congress of Correction of American Prison Association* (Boston, 1948).

4. Before the activation of Highfields, it was decided at the 1950 spring meeting of the Scientific Advisory Committee to postpone the research for a period of time. It was felt that Dr. McCorkle needed a shakedown period to get the guided group interaction sessions well established and to discover some of the problems which might need to be taken into consideration. In hindsight, it might have been better to postpone the research even longer. There should have been time for the researchers to observe the reactions of the boys in the guided group interaction sessions and to study some of the

behavior problems the boys showed at Highfields. If this had been done, more concrete questions might have been devised to reveal changes in the boys' attitudes.

5. Without the co-operation, interest, and awareness on the part of the judges of the juvenile court or the probation and parole officers, and the superintendent of the reformatory of the necessity for this procedure the research staff would have had much more difficulty than it encountered. We recognize that the procedure added to their already heavy burdens and we are exceedingly grateful.

6. When we began the Highfields research, fifteen boys had already been there and were released at the end of their treatment or sent back to the court as unsuitable for residence at Highfields. These boys are not, of course, included in our analysis. It should be pointed out, however, that the results would not be altered in any significant way if they were.

7. The difference between the periods is due to the fact that Annandale boys spend so much longer in the facility. A few of the Annandale boys had been out only eight months when we had to cut off in order to process the data. The rates would be essentially no different if we had taken only Annandale boys who had been released for a year or more.

8. Although there are large differences between the percentages in most of these categories, none proves to be statistically significant on the basis of the number of cases involved except the difference in the percentage of Highfields and Annandale Negroes by educational level. A much higher proportion of Annandale than Highfields Negroes report a grade school education or less. The percentages are 57 and 27, respectively.

30: The Community Treatment Project: History and Prospects /
Marguerite Q. Warren

Introduction

The California Youth Authority is a state department whose primary responsibility is the operation of a program for the custody, treatment and retraining of juveniles committed by the courts of the 58 counties of California. The department is an integral part of the total process for dealing with juvenile offenders—a process which involves a number of community and state agencies. The process begins with an arrest of a youth by a law enforcement officer and continues, in the more serious cases, with a referral to the juvenile court for youths under the age of 18. The youth may be made a ward of the court and a program of treatment be prescribed. Depending upon the re-

From Marguerite Q. Warren, "The Community Treatment Project: History and Prospects," in *Law Enforcement, Science and Technology,* S. A. Yefsky, ed. (Washington, D.C.: Thompson Book Co., 1967), pp. 191–200.

sources available and the needs of the youth, treatment may take the form of county-supervised probation, placement in a foster home, confinement in a private or county camp, or commitment to the California Youth Authority. The decision to commit to the Youth Authority is ordinarily made when local resources are deemed to be ineffective or inappropriate to control the offender's antisocial behavior and is thus apt to involve the most serious or habitual delinquents. Actually, only 5 per cent of delinquency referrals to probation departments lead to Youth Authority commitment.

Upon commitment to the Youth Authority, the juvenile ward is sent to one of the department's two reception centers. Here the ward is studied, a treatment program is developed, and he is ordinarily assigned to one of the institutional programs operated by the department. Following the incarceration period, the youth is released to the community and to the Youth Authority's parole supervision program. The after-care program continues for a minimum of 18 months.

The Problem

During the early 1960s there were several factors which suggested the desirability of developing a new approach to the rehabilitation of many juvenile offenders who were being committed to the Youth Authority. One major factor related to the high rates of recidivism which, while no greater than comparable programs in other states, still testified to the lack of knowledge of appropriate methods for turning delinquents into nondelinquents. An even more pressing concern in California derived from the tremendous population growth which, even with non-increasing delinquency *rates,* still led to overflow *numbers* in existing institutions and to projected needs for double the institutional bed-space within a 10-year period. To meet the population problem by building new institutions was viewed as extremely costly and as ignoring serious doubts about institutions' rehabilitative potential for all delinquents.

The Community Treatment Project

In 1961, as a result of the above considerations, the California Youth Authority initiated a research experiment with an intensive treatment-control program in the community as a substitute for traditional types of institutionalization.[1] This program, now five and a half years old, is jointly financed by the State of California and the National Institute of Mental Health. Phase 1 of the Project has been conducted in the cities of Sacramento and Stockton. The program is known as the Community Treatment Project, although its official title is "Comparative Assessment of Institutional and Community Treatment for Comparable Groups of Youth Authority Wards." Although the Project also has a Phase 2, which will be briefly described later, the results to be reported in this chapter involve only the Phase 1 experiment.

Phase 1 of the Community Treatment Project has included two major goals. The first involves a comparison of the effectiveness of a period of intensive treatment in the community with a period of incarceration for similar groups of habitual delinquents. The second goal involves the development of optimum treatment control plans for defined types of delinquents, as an answer to the crucial question: What kinds of treatment programs, in what kinds of settings, are most effective with what kinds of juvenile delinquents?

In accordance with the research design, cases have been randomly assigned to the community program (Experimental group) and to the Youth Authority's regular program (Control group) from an eligible pool of boys and girls undergoing their first commitment from the juvenile courts. This experimental design is shown in Figure 30–1. Seriously assaultive cases and cases to

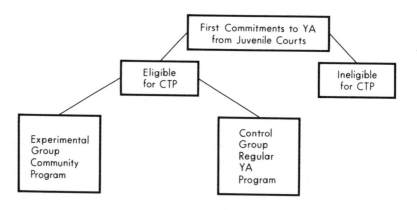

FIGURE 30–1. *Experimental Design of Phase 1, Community Treatment Project.*

which there is a community objection are excluded from the eligible pool. To date, 90 per cent of the girls and 73 per cent of the boys having first commitments have been found eligible. Their average age at intake into the Project is 16, with a range of from 9 to 19 years. The eligible group is comparable on most recorded factors to juvenile court commitments statewide. By February 1967, 286 Experimental cases had entered the Phase 1 community program and 361 comparable Control subjects had been assigned to the traditional Youth Authority program.

Underlying Assumptions

To treat delinquents in the community who have been adjudged by county officials as unsuitable for further handling in the existing county probation programs is obviously a serious undertaking. None of the Community Treatment Project's program elements are, in themselves, new concepts. Probation and parole departments everywhere use some br all of the treatment methods. Some experiments have even used highly intensive, low caseload programs without improved success rates. Because intensive treatment, by competent personnel, does not of itself guarantee results that differ significantly from those of routine, non-intensive programs, it was assumed that the Project must include something more than skilled workers, small caseloads, and even good intentions. Therefore, the Project has been organized around a typological approach growing out of a theory of delinquency and providing a method of classification which prescribes effective treatment.

One of the few agreed-upon "facts" in the field of corrections is that offenders are not all alike. That is, they differ from each other, not only in the form of their offense, but also in the reasons for and the meaning of their crime. Some individuals violate the law because the peer group on which they are dependent for approval prescribed criminal behavior as the price of acceptance, or because the values which they have internalized are those of a deviant subculture. Other individuals break laws because of insufficient socialization, which has left them at the mercy of any except the most protected of environments. Still others are delinquently acting out internal conflicts, identity struggles or family crises. This list is of course illustrative, not exhaustive.

Much of the literature in the field is still written as if all offenders are alike. Many causal theories, purporting to explain "delinquency," have described only one segment of the total offender population and have concluded, for example, that "delinquency is a peer group phenomenon." Differential association theories,[2] social disorganization theories,[3] role theories,[4] psychogenic theories [5]—all appear to have some validity when applied to some segment of the offender population, but none of these theories alone is sufficiently complex to account for the total observable range of causal factors.[6]

Program prescriptions as well have tended to be made in an "across-the-board" fashion, with increased staff-offender ratios, improved job opportunities or insight therapy recommended for all. Although some action programs have been aimed at specific segments of the heterogeneous offender population (for example, psychiatric treatment for the emotionally disturbed delinquent), few programs indeed have based their goals for intervention and their treatment and management prescriptions on a specified rationale for handling differentially the varieties of offender problems which appear in a correctional setting.

A comment should perhaps be made with regard to an extreme opposite position taken by some treatment-oriented people who have emphasized the great differences among offenders and have resisted any schematization on the basis of loss of meaningful information about individuals. This position does guard against the mistake of administering the same kind of treatment to all offenders, but at the cost of requiring an infinite variety of treatments to fit the uniqueness of each case. This position almost precludes conceptualizing the delinquency problem, developing intervention theories and practices, and instigating research investigations. As such, the position must be rejected.

Theoreticians, practitioners and researchers increasingly seek some classification system—some meaningful grouping of offenders into categories— which offers (1) a step in the direction of explanatory theory with the resulting aid to prediction which follows from understanding, (2) implications for efficient management and effective treatment decisions, and (3) greater precision for maximally effective research.

Following from this rationale, two important theoretical assumptions underlie the Community Treatment Project approach to treatment and control of delinquents: (1) delinquents are not all alike, and (2) delinquents can be subdivided into types which have clear-cut implications for the kinds of treatment required.

The typology used in the Community Treatment Project is called the "Interpersonal Maturity Level Classification: Juvenile." [7] The classification of a delinquent youth is made in two steps. The individual is first diagnosed according to level of perceptual differentiation or degree of complexity in his view of himself and others. This step identifies the individual's Interpersonal Maturity Level (also called Integration Level or I-Level). In the second classification step, individuals within each Maturity Level are further diagnosed according to *response set* or way of responding to their perceptions of the world. There are two major ways in which the Integration Level 2 (I_2) individual responds to his perceptual frame of reference. Similarly, there are three typical response sets among delinquent I_3s, and four typical response sets among delinquent I_4s. In this manner, nine delinquent subtypes have been identified.* These subtypes have been described by lists of item definitions which characterize the manner in which the members of each group perceive the world, respond to the world, and are perceived by others. The descriptions of the subtypes, with predicted-most-effective intervention or treatment plans, combine to make up the Differential Treatment Model used in the Experimental program of the Project.

Brief descriptions of the three Maturity Levels and the nine subtypes are given below:

MATURITY LEVEL 2 (I_2)

The individual whose interpersonal understanding and behavior are integrated at this level is primarily involved with demands that the world take care of him. He sees others primarily as "givers" or "withholders" and has no conception of interpersonal refinement beyond this. He has poor capacity to explain, understand, or predict the behavior or reactions of others. He is not interested in things outside himself except as a source of supply. He be-

---

* One of the nine subtypes—I_2 Aa (Asocial, Aggressive)—has so rarely been found eligible for the Project that their characteristics have not been separately defined, nor has a treatment strategy been developed for them. The Aa subtype represents less than 1 per cent of the eligible group.

haves impulsively, unaware of anything except the grossest effects of his behavior on others.

Subtypes (1) *Asocial, Aggressive* (Aa) responds with active demands and open hostility when frustrated. (2) *Asocial, Passive* (Ap) responds with whining, complaining and withdrawal when frustrated.

MATURITY LEVEL 3 (I_3)

The individual who is functioning at this level, although somewhat more differentiated than the I_2, still has social perceptual deficiencies which lead to an underestimation of the differences among others and between himself and others. More than the I_2, he does understand that his own behavior has something to do with whether or not he gets what he wants. He makes an effort to manipulate his environment to bring about "giving" rather than "denying" response. He does not operate from an internalized value system but rather seeks external structure in terms of rules and formulas for operation. His understanding of formulas is indiscriminate and oversimplified. He perceives the world and his part in it on a power dimension. Although he can learn to play a few stereotyped roles, he cannot understand many of the needs, feelings and motives of another person who is different from himself. He is unmotivated to achieve in a long-range sense, or to plan for the future. Many of these features contribute to his inability to predict accurately the response of others to him.

Subtypes (3) *Immature Conformist* (Cfm) responds with immediate compliance to whoever seems to have the power at the moment. (4) *Cultural Conformist* (Cfc) responds with conformity to specific reference group, delinquent peers. (5) *Manipulator* (Mp) operates by attempting to undermine the power of authority figures and/or usurp the power role for himself.

MATURITY LEVEL 4 (I_4)

An individual whose understanding and behavior are integrated at this level has internalized a set of standards by which he judges his and others' behavior. He can perceive a level of interpersonal interaction in which individuals have expectations of each other and can influence each other. He shows some ability to understand reasons for behavior, some ability to relate to people emotionally and on a long-term basis. He is concerned about status and respect and is strongly influenced by people he admires.

Subtypes (6) *Neurotic, Acting-out* (Na) responds to underlying guilt with attempts to "outrun" conscious anxiety and condemnation of self. (7) *Neurotic, Anxious* (Nx) responds with symptoms of emotional disturbance to conflict produced by feelings of inadequacy and guilt. (8) *Situational Emotional Reaction* (Se) responds to immediate family or personal crisis by acting-out. (9) *Cultural Identifier* (Ci) responds to identification with a deviant value system by living out his delinquent beliefs.

The delinquent subtypes, along with their code names, may be summarized as follows:

Code Name	Delinquent Subtype
I_2 Aa	Asocial, Aggressive
Ap	Asocial, Passive
I_3 Cfm	Conformist, Immature
Cfc	Conformist, Cultural
Mp	Manipulator
I_4 Na	Neurotic, Acting-out
Nx	Neurotic, Anxious
Se	Situational Emotional Reaction
Ci	Cultural Identifier

The Experimental Treatment Program

The treatment program for Experimental wards can be described adequately only in terms of the differential treatment plans for each subtype. However, certain common treatment elements for all the subtypes within a Maturity Level can be identified.

The essence of the treatment plan with I_2s is to place the youth in a supportive environment (usually foster home) and attempt to meet some of his unmet dependency needs while helping him learn to perceive more accurately and respond more appropriately to the demands of society and its institutions.[8] The treatment strategies for all I_3 subtypes involve an adult (the Community Agent) expressing *concern* for the youth by *controlling* his behavior. Group treatment is also used, taking advantage of the I_3's dependence on peers, in order to control behavior, change delinquent attitudes, and increase social perceptiveness. Treatment for the I_4 subtypes works toward reducing internal conflicts and increasing insight into personal and family dynamics which play a part in the acting-out behavior. These goals may be reached through family group therapy, individual psychotherapy, or group therapy. These treatment descriptions are much oversimplified, since treatment goals and methods vary considerably among subtypes within Maturity Levels. Detailed descriptions of the subtypes and corollary treatment strategies are available from the Project office in Sacramento.

The Experimental action staff which is carrying out Phase 1 in Sacramento and Stockton consists of one Treatment Supervisor, six male Community Agents and one female Community Agent in each unit, and an Administrative Supervisor responsible for both units. A few of the Agents have Masters' degrees; most have simply a B.S. in one of the social sciences. Three Research Analysts are involved in the Phase I study.

Each Community Agent carries a caseload of 12. Only one or two subtypes of delinquents are assigned to a particular Agent, so that treatment style and skill of the Agent can be matched with the needs of the youth.[9] The personality characteristics of the Agent and his treatment stance are more related to assignment to a particular subtype than his academic or work experience. During the intensive stage of treatment in the community, the youth is seen by the Agent two to five times weekly either individually or in group or family meetings. Partial or full-day programming may be involved. Most of the Experimental wards reside in their own homes. However, if it appears that a youth cannot live in his own home and remain nondelinquent, he or she is placed in a foster or group home. Twenty to 30 per cent of cases are in out-of-home placement at any one time. Average length of the Experimental treatment program until good discharge is comparable to that for Control cases in the regular Youth Authority program—about two years.[10]

Comparative Effectiveness of the Experimental and Control Programs

Of the several kinds of data relative to comparative effectiveness which have been collected in the Project, two will be reported here—those data having to do with parole success, and measures of personal and attitudinal change as reflected in test scores.[11] These two major sources of data have been used to help answer the questions: For what kinds of delinquents is a community alternative to institutionalization feasible and preferable? What kinds of delinquents require or benefit from a period of incarceration?

Although the emphasis has been on the differential impact of the two alternatives (community and institution) on *various kinds of delinquents,* it is worth asking whether or not there are any advantages to one program over the other for *all cases combined.* The evidence is clear with respect to both parole success criteria and test score changes that, for all subjects combined, the advantage lies with the Experimental program.

PAROLE CRITERIA

The failure rates (including all revocations of parole, recommitments from the courts and unfavorable discharges) for *Control* cases are 52 per cent (51 per cent for boys, 57 per cent for girls) after 15 months of community exposure time and 61 per cent after 24 months of community exposure time. These rates are comparable to statewide failure rates. In contrast, the failure rates for the *Experimental* cases are 28 per cent (30 per cent for boys, 13 per cent for girls) at 15 months and 38 per cent at 24 months. These Experimental-Control differences are highly significant statistically.

It should be noted that part of the differences in failure rates can be explained by differences in decision-making with regard to parole restoral following an offense. Experimental cases tend more often to be restored to parole by the Youth Authority Board following a suspension of parole than do Control cases. Several factors enter into this difference. Although Experimentals have their parole *suspended* more frequently than do Controls, the Experimental suspensions are much more often for minor misbehavior; 46 per cent of Experimental suspensions and only 26 per cent of Control suspensions were based on *technical violations* of parole. Experimental cases are rarely *revoked* for minor offenses, while Control cases are fairly often revoked for such offenses as placement failure, poor home or school adjustment, truancy or runaway. Even when a more serious offense is involved, Experimental Agents more often request the youth's restoral to parole if some growth has been shown. These differences in restoral request and decision are to some extent a function of caseload size and treatment planning, with the Experimental Agents being able to increase contact and surveillance or to develop a new treatment plan for the offender. The intensive work with the Experimental cases may also make more visible to the decision-makers the growth or improvement in a youth (e.g., school and job performance, attitudes to authority figures) even when the change has not been sufficient to eliminate all delinquent behavior. While these differences in restoration practice may account for some revocation-rate differences, it is very unlikely that it explains away all Experimental-Control failure rate differences. This becomes more apparent when the delinquent subtypes are viewed separately and when the test score data are added to the picture.

Suspension of parole is used somewhat differently in the regular parole program than in the Experimental program. Suspension, followed by temporary confinement, is often used as a treatment technique by the Experimental Agents, e.g., the youth is arrested and his parole suspended in order to demonstrate that the Community Agent is *concerned* about the youth and is willing to punish minor misbehavior (missing a group meeting, "sassing" a teacher), or parole is suspended in order to remove a youth from his home when a family crisis threatens. The differences in the use of suspension in the Experimental and Control programs are reflected in (1) the much higher proportion of arrests made by the Youth Authority Agent than by other law enforcement agencies in the case of Experimental cases as opposed to Control cases, and (2) as previously mentioned, the much higher proportion of arrests of the "low-severity" type in the Experimental as opposed to the Control group.

Five per cent of all Experimental offenses and 6 per cent of all Control offenses were classified as felonies. Six per cent of Experimental and 10 per cent of Control offenses involved violence.

TEST SCORE COMPARISONS

Psychological tests (California Psychological Inventory and Jesness Inventory) are given to all eligible cases, both Experimental and Control, at intake into the Youth Authority (the pre-test). The Control cases are again tested following discharge from an institution, and the Experimental cases are again tested after the intensive stage of treatment in the community (the post-test). Findings for the overall Experimental and Control groups (all delinquent subtypes combined) indicate that, although both groups showed improvement from pre-test to post-test, the Experimental cases showed considerably *more positive change* than the Control cases, together with a *higher level of personal and social adjustment* at post-test when compared with Controls.

Comparative Effectiveness of the Two Programs
for the Various Delinquent Subtypes

Figure 30–2 shows comparative parole violation and unfavorable discharge rates by delinquent subtypes for Experimental and Control groups followed for 15 months in the community. The subtypes showing the largest differences in failure rates, in favor of the Experimental group, are the Acting-out Neurotic (Na), the Immature Conformist (Cfm), the Cultural Conformist (Cfc) and the Asocial, Passive (Ap). Only the Cultural Identifier (Ci) group shows a failure rate difference in favor of the Control program.

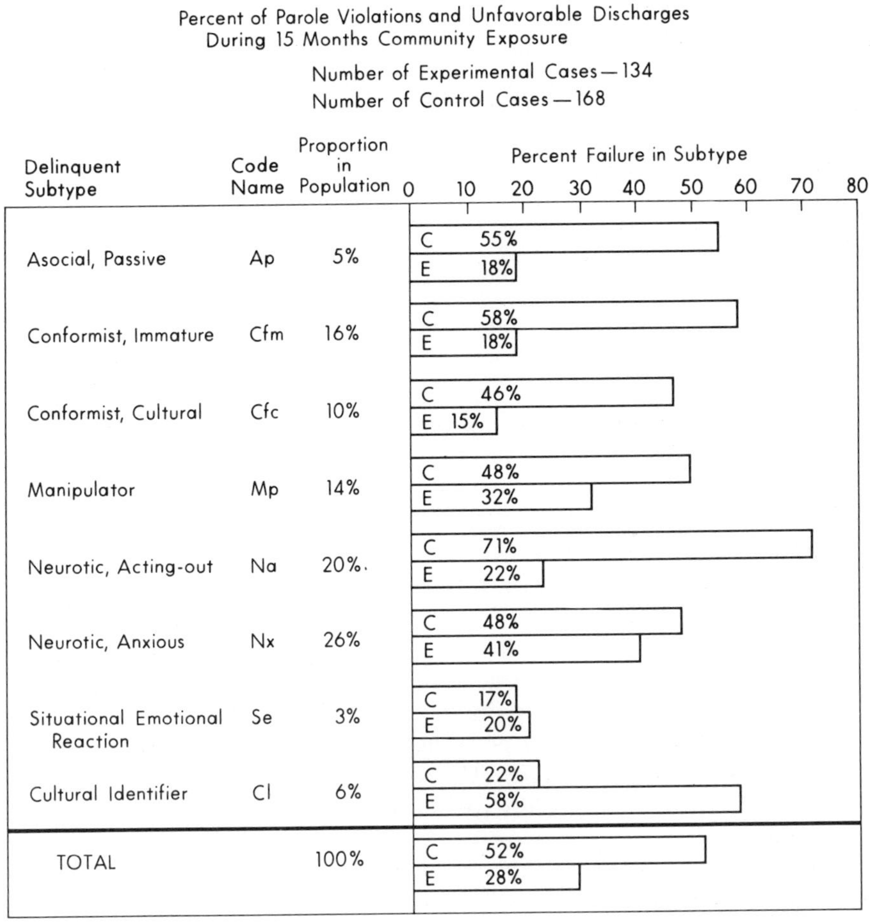

Percent of Parole Violations and Unfavorable Discharges
During 15 Months Community Exposure

Number of Experimental Cases — 134
Number of Control Cases — 168

Delinquent Subtype	Code Name	Proportion in Population	Percent Failure in Subtype
Asocial, Passive	Ap	5%	C 55% / E 18%
Conformist, Immature	Cfm	16%	C 58% / E 18%
Conformist, Cultural	Cfc	10%	C 46% / E 15%
Manipulator	Mp	14%	C 48% / E 32%
Neurotic, Acting-out	Na	20%.	C 71% / E 22%
Neurotic, Anxious	Nx	26%	C 48% / E 41%
Situational Emotional Reaction	Se	3%	C 17% / E 20%
Cultural Identifier	CI	6%	C 22% / E 58%
TOTAL		100%	C 52% / E 28%

FIGURE 30–2. *Parole Performance of Experimental and Control Groups.*

Table 30–1 shows those subtypes in either the Experimental or the Control group whose test score changes indicated greater improvement than their counterparts in either the Experimental or Control program.

Table 30-1

*Test Score Changes Experimental
and Control Groups*

	Amount of Positive Change	
Delinquent Subtype	Experimental Test Scores Ahead	Control Test Scores Ahead
Asocial, Passive		+++
Conformist, Immature	+	
Conformist, Cultural	++	
Manipulator	++	
Neurotic, Acting-out	+++	
Neurotic, Anxious		++
Situational Emotional Reaction	+++	
Cultural Identifier	+	

+Group slightly ahead
++Group ahead
+++Group far ahead

The following summary statements may be made with respect to the comparative effectiveness of the Experimental and Control programs for each of the delinquent subtypes, using the above recidivism and test score data, as well as other data when relevant.

NEUROTIC, ACTING-OUT (NA)

Of all subtypes, the Na (which includes 20 per cent of the eligible population) shows the greatest advantages of the community program over the regular Youth Authority program. Recidivism rates and test score changes both reflect this larger difference. In addition, the Experimental Na group represents a higher-than-expected proportion of the early favorable discharges from the Youth Authority (30 per cent of the favorable discharges); this is not the case in the Control group. The rate of occurrence of felony offenses is also low in this subtype of the Experimental group compared with the Control group.

Two possible factors in the success of the community program with the Na subject are (1) the continuous close relationship between the youth and the Community Agent permitted by low caseloads, and (2) the Experimental treatment strategy emphasis on dealing with the youth's feelings and inner conflicts which lead to acting-out behavior.

IMMATURE CONFORMIST (CFM)

For this subtype (involving 16 per cent of the population) also, the Experimental program shows considerable advantage over the regular program, with very large failure rate differences and with test score changes slightly in favor of the Experimental group. The rate of felony offenses is lower for Experimental than Control Cfms. Both Experimental and Control Cfms show a low rate of offenses involving violence, compared with other delinquent subtypes.

As indicated earlier, the Cfm youth is especially responsive to his immediate environment. The large recidivism rate differences testify to the possibility of building a nondelinquent and supportive environment for the Cfm in the community. Research evidence also indicates the tendency of Cfms in institutions to become more delinquently oriented.

CULTURAL CONFORMIST (CFC)

Again this subtype (10 per cent of the population) shows large failure rate differences and test score differences in favor of the Experimental group. Compared with other subtypes, the Cfcs in both the Experimental and Control groups have high rates of felony and violence offenses. This finding is consistent with the fact that, in the regular Youth Authority program, a large proportion of the Cfcs receive one-year continuances in institutions because of the seriousness of their offenses.

The greater success with this subtype in the Experimental program is probably based on the same factors as those described for the Cfms, as well as the additional factor of emphasis on close control by the Community Agent.

ASOCIAL, PASSIVE (AP)

For this subtype, which includes only a small proportion (5 per cent) of the population, recidivism rates and test score results appear inconsistent. The Control Aps look much improved at post-testing but fail on parole at a much higher rate than the Experimental Aps. Rates of felonies and violent offenses are lower for the Control than the Experimental group of Aps.

The Asocial delinquents are difficult cases to deal with under any conditions but especially so in a community setting and on a large caseload. They are in tremendous need of supportive structure (which their own homes usually do not offer) and of a large amount of time and attention from a Parole Agent. The Community Agent in the Experimental program can afford to spend a large amount of time developing a supportive living arrangement for the youth and does not need to handle "nuisance" behavior with revocation of parole. The structure available in an institutional setting does appear to help the Control Aps settle down; they appear to be in much better psychological health when leaving the institution than when they arrived. It is possible that return to the same nonsupportive community environment cancels the gains which were made in the institution, or that the gains made in the institution, while great, were not sufficient to bring about and/or support needed behavioral changes.

MANIPULATOR (MP)

Recidivism rates for this subtype (14 per cent of the population) still favor the Experimental group, although differences are not as great as in the subtypes previously described. Test score changes also favor the Experimental group, this result being accounted for primarily by the negative changes in the tests of Control subjects during the regular program. For the Mps, the felony and violence rates are low and the early good discharge rates high in the Control group. Thus the results for this subtype are inconsistent, with the Experimental group looking better on some criteria and the Control group looking better on others.

The Mp subtype represents one of the most difficult treatment problems in the field of corrections. Of the I-Level subtypes, it is the one closest to the classical definitions of the "psychopath." The aim in the Experimental program has *not* been to teach the Mps more skillful or "socially acceptable" ways of manipulating, but rather it has been to bring about important *inner* changes in them—changes which permit the youths alternatives to survival by "conning" or "using" others. In this effort the program has had some success with some Mps who have been in the community unit for several years—a success which involves an increase in capacity to relate honestly and responsibly, and a reduction in hostility toward authority figures.

NEUROTIC, ANXIOUS (NX)

For this subtype (26 per cent of the population), there is little difference between the Experimental and Control groups in recidivism rates. With respect to test scores, the Control group showed more positive change than did the Experimental group, although both groups changed in a positive direction. Neither group shows an advantage in rate of felonies nor offenses involving violence.

A sizable proportion of the Nx youths are seriously disturbed emotionally, having tensions which are difficult to manage in a community setting. *Compared with other subtypes,* the Experimental program does not have a good record with these youths. It is possible that the more seriously disturbed of the Nx group should be given intensive treatment in the protection of a residential setting.

SITUATIONAL EMOTIONAL REACTION (SE)

This subtype includes only a very small proportion of the eligible population (3 per cent), and most of the data suggest that they do well behaviorally both in the Experimental and Control programs. Both groups have low recidivism rates, commit neither felony nor violent offenses while on parole, and represent a higher-than-expected proportion of the early good discharge group. The only evidence in favor of either program comes from test score results, with the post-tests of the Control subjects showing marked negative change and those of the Experimentals showing neither positive nor negative change.

CULTURAL IDENTIFIER (CI)

This group, which includes a small proportion of the eligible population (6 per cent), is the only subtype which shows a large recidivism rate difference in favor of the Controls. Findings on other criteria are inconsistent, with Control Cis committing a lower rate of felonies and with Experimentals committing a much lower rate of violent offenses and showing somewhat more positive change than Controls on post-testing.

Cis are viewed as "normal" youths who need to learn that crime does not pay. Project results suggest that perhaps the more efficient way of teaching this may be to deprive the Ci of something which is very important to him —his freedom—by a short stay in an institution.

In summary of the comparative effectiveness data, the most clear-cut of the Project's findings suggest that the intensive community program is more effective than the regular Youth Authority program with the subtypes identified as: Acting-out Neurotic (Na), Immature Conformist (Cfm) and Cultural Conformist (Cfc). The Situational Emotional Reaction subtype (Se) can be added to this list if the question to be asked is which kinds of delinquents can be handled successfully in an intensive community program. These four subtypes combined represent about 50 per cent of the eligible population. Evidence to date suggests that the Cultural Identifier (Ci) may be more effectively handled in a program involving institutionalization. This subtype includes 6 per cent of the population. For the three remaining subtypes, the data do not, at this time, point to a clear advantage for either program. If recidivism rate is considered the most important of the criteria, then two of these three subtypes—Asocial, Passive (Ap) and Manipulator (Mp)—would have an advantage in the Experimental program.

Implications of the Community Treatment Project

Since the feasibility of substituting intensive community programs for incarceration of many juvenile delinquents has been demonstrated, the Youth Authority has moved toward the development of a series of such programs. It is the Agency's hope that in doing this, the effectiveness of the Youth Authority's rehabilitation program will be increased and, in addition, that the tremendous cost of institution-building will be decreased.

The average monthly costs of the Community Treatment program are considerably lower than institutional costs: boys' institutions—$318; girls' institutions—$461; CTP—$161. However, when the monthly costs of CTP are compared with costs for regular parole, CTP is much higher. Since CTP cases tend to remain in intensive treatment longer than Control cases spend in institutions, CTP is *not* less expensive in the *short* run. Since CTP shows fewer failures and thus fewer returns to institutions, however, career costs for the Experimental program are apt to be less than for the regular program. In addition, when delinquent youths are kept in the community, capital outlay costs for new institutions are reduced. This, although it is impossible to say at this time that the community alternative is less costly, preliminary indications (lower recidivism and fewer institutions needed) are that the community program is a more economical method of handling delinquent youths.

At the beginning of the Project, law enforcement agencies and other community groups expressed skepticism about the way confirmed delinquents would respond to a program that appeared to be giving them "one more break." However, a recent survey indicated that community agencies are aware that tight controls are exerted over Experimental cases during intensive treatment and that serious attempts are made to bring about permanent changes in both the youths and their families. The survey indicated that nearly all official community agencies accept in principle the idea of treatment in the community. Satisfaction with the caliber and dedication of the Project staff was also expressed. Differences of opinion between Project staff and local agency personnel do arise from time to time, however—typically in connection with the handling of individual cases.

Experimentation in the areas of community programs continues. The Phase 1 study is on-going in Sacramento and Stockton. Phase 2 of the Community Treatment Project began in San Francisco in late 1965.[12] In this study, boys and girls who are first commitments from the juvenile court and who have been found eligible for the Project are assigned randomly to one of three programs—E_1—a community unit using the Differential Treatment Model developed in Phase 1; E_2—a community unit following the Guided Group Interaction Model of Empey's Provo Experiment; or C—the traditional Youth Authority program. This experimental design is shown in Figure 30–3. Phase 2, also jointly sponsored by the State and NIMH, will run until late 1969. The goals of Phase 2 involve continued attempts to determine the most effective programs for the various subtypes of delinquents, as well as

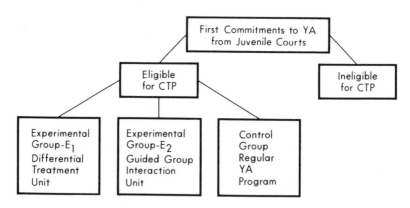

FIGURE 30–3. *Experimental Design of Phase 2, Community Treatment Project.*

the attempt to replicate the Differential Treatment program in another community.

Although the feasibility of treating serious delinquents in a community setting is an important finding, perhaps the development of a treatment model which prescribes differentially for various kinds of delinquents has even more far-reaching implications. There is nothing which suggests that differential treatment—using a Community Treatment Project definition or any other method of assuring intervention appropriate to the nature of the problem—is relevant only to community programs. In fact, a number of Youth Authority institution programs are now assigning wards to living units on the basis of their subtype diagnosis and are developing treatment programs specific to the needs of that subtype.[13] Early reports are enthusiastic about the advantages of such grouping for both management and treatment purposes.

REFERENCES

1. S. Adams and M. Q. Grant
   A demonstration project: an evaluation of community-located treatment for delinquents
   California Youth Authority publication   1961
2. E. H. Sutherland and D. R. Cressey
   Principles of criminology
   Lippincott   Philadelphia   1960
3. C. R. Shaw and H. D. McKay
   Juvenile delinquency and urban areas
   University of Chicago Press   Chicago   1942
   R. K. Merton
   Social theory and social structure
   The Free Press   Glencoe   1957
   R. A. Cloward and L. E. Ohlin
   Delinquency and opportunity: a theory of delinquent gangs
   The Free Press   Glencoe   1960
4. H. G. Gough and D. R. Peterson
   The identification and measurement of predispositional factors in crime and delinquency
   J. Consult. Psych.   16   207–212   1952
   T. R. Sarbin
   A preface to a psychological analysis of the self
   Psych. Rev.   59   11–23   1952
   T. Parsons
   The social system
   The Free Press   Glencoe   1951
   A. H. Cohen
   The sociology of the deviant act: anomie theory and beyond
   Amer. Soc. Rev.   30   5–14   1965
5. K. Friedlander
   Formation of the antisocial character
   Psychoanalytic Study of the Child   1945   vol. 1
   W. Healy and A. F. Bronner
   New light on delinquency and its treatment
   Yale University Press   1936

F. Redl
H. L. Witmer and R. Kotinsky (Eds)
New perspectives for research on juvenile delinquency
Children's Bureau Publication no. 356   1956
E. H. Erikson
Childhood and society
Norton   New York   1950
6. M. Q. Warren
    The community treatment project: an integration of theories of causation and correctional practice
    Annual Conference of the Illinois Academy of Criminology Chicago   1965
    M. Q. Warren
    Classification of offenders as an aid to efficient management and effective treatment
    Prepared for the President's Commission on Law Enforcement and Administration of Justice   1966
7. C. E. Sullivan   M. Q. Grant and J. D. Grant
    The development of interpersonal maturity: applications to delinquency
    Psychiatry 20   373–385   1957
    M. Q. Grant
    Interpersonal maturity level classification: juvenile
    1961
    M. Q. Warren
    and CTP staff
    Interpersonal maturity level classification: juvenile
    1966
8. J. E. Riggs   W. Underwood and M. Q. Warren
    Interpersonal maturity level classification: juvenile, 1. diagnosis and treatment of low maturity delinquents
    CTP Research Report no. 4   1964
9. T. B. Palmer
    Types of treaters and types of juvenile offenders
    California Youth Authority Quarterly   18   14–23   1965
10. CTP Staff
    First year report of action and evaluation
    CTP Research Report no. 2   1963
    M. Q. Grant   M. Warren and J. Turner
    Community treatment project
    CTP Research Report no. 3   1963
    M. Q. Grant
    A differential treatment approach to the delinquent and his family
    Presented   at   the   California   Conference   for   Health   and   Welfare   Los Angeles   1963
11. M. Q. Warren and T. B. Palmer
    CTP research reports 5, 6 and 7
    1964   1965   1966
12. M. Q. Warren   T. B. Palmer and J. Turner
    A demonstration project: an evaluation of community-located treatment for delinquents, proposal for phase 2
    CTP Report   1964
13. C. F. Jesness
    The Preston typology study: application of a treatment typology to delinquents
    First Progress Report to NIMH   1966

31: Preventing Delinquency /
Walter B. Miller

THE MIDCITY PROJECT: METHODS AND CLIENT POPULATION

The Midcity Project conducted a delinquency control program in a lower-class district of Boston between the years 1954 and 1957. A major objective of the Project was to inhibit or reduce the amount of illegal activity engaged in by resident adolescents. Project methods derived from a "total community" philosophy which has become increasingly popular in recent years, and currently forms the basis of several large-scale delinquency control programs.[1] On the assumption that delinquent behavior by urban lower-class adolescents, whatever their personality characteristics, is in some significant degree facilitated by or actualized through certain structural features of the community, the Project executed "action" programs directed at three of the societal units seem to figure importantly in the genesis and perpetuation of delinquent behavior—the community, the family, and the gang.

The community program involved two major efforts: 1) the development and strengthening of local citizens' groups so as to enable them to take direct action in regard to local problems, including delinquency, and 2) an attempt to secure cooperation between those professional agencies whose operations in the community in some way involved adolescents (e.g., settlement houses, churches, schools, psychiatric and medical clinics, police, courts and probation departments, corrections and parole departments). A major short-term objective was to increase the possibility of concerted action both among the professional agencies themselves and between the professionals and the citizens' groups. The ultimate objective of these organizational efforts was to focus a variety of diffuse and uncoordinated efforts on problems of youth and delinquency in a single community so as to bring about more effective processes of prevention and control.[2]

Work with families was conducted within the framework of a "chronic-problem-family" approach; a group of families with histories of repeated and long-term utilization of public welfare services were located and subjected to a special and intensive program of psychiatrically-oriented casework.[3]

Work with gangs, the major effort of the Project, was based on the detached worker or area worker approach utilized by the New York Youth

From Walter B. Miller, "The Impact of a 'Total-Community' Delinquency Control Project," *Social Problems* 10:2 (1962); 168–191.

Board and similar projects.[4] An adult worker is assigned to an area, group, or groups with a mandate to contact, establish relations with, and attempt to change resident gangs. The application of this method by the Midcity Project incorporated three features not generally included in earlier programs: 1) all workers were professionally trained, with degrees in case work, group work, or both; 2) each worker but one devoted primary attention to a single group, maintaining recurrent and intensive contact with group members over an extended time period; 3) psychiatric consultation was made available on a regular basis, so that workers were in a position to utilize methods and perspectives of psychodynamic psychiatry in addition to the group dynamics and recreational approaches in which they had been trained.

Between June 1954 and May 1957, seven project field workers (five men, two women) maintained contact with approximately 400 youngsters between the ages of 12 and 21, comprising the membership of some 21 corner gangs. Seven of these, totaling 205 members, were subjected to intensive attention. Workers contacted their groups on an average of 3.5 times a week; contact periods averaged about 5 or 6 hours; total duration of contact ranged from 10 to 34 months. Four of the intensive service groups were white males (Catholic, largely Irish, some Italians and Canadian French); one was Negro male, one white female, and one Negro female. All groups "hung out" in contiguous neighborhoods of a single district of Midcity—a fairly typical lower-class "inner-city" community.[5]

The average size of male groups was 30, and of female 9. All intensive service groups, as well as most of the other known groups, were "locality-based" rather than "emergent" or "situationally organized" groups.[6] This meant that the groups were indigenous, self-formed, and inheritors of a gang tradition which in some cases extended back for fifty years or more. This kind of gang system in important respects resembled certain African age-class systems in that a new "class" or corner-group unit was formed every two or three years, recruiting from like-aged boys residing in the vicinity of the central "hanging" locale.[7] Thus the total corner aggregate in relatively stable residential areas generally consisted of three to five age-graded male groups, each maintaining a sense of allegiance to their corner and/or traditional gang name, and at the same time maintaining a clear sense of identity as a particular age-graded unit within the larger grouping.

Girls' groups, for the most part, achieved their identity primarily through their relations with specific boys' units, which were both larger and more solidary. Each locality aggregate thus included several female groups, generally bearing a feminized version of the male group name (Bandits-Bandettes; Kings-Queens).

Action Methods with Corner Gangs

The methods used by Project workers encompassed a wide range of techniques and entailed work on many levels with many kinds of groups, agencies and organizations.[8] Workers conceptualized the process of working with the groups as a series of sequential phases, on the model of individual psychotherapy. Three major phases were delineated—roughly, relationship establishment, behavior modification, and termination. In practice workers found it difficult to conduct operations according to the planned "phase" sequence, and techniques seen as primarily appropriate to one phase were often used during another. There was, however, sufficiently close adherence to the phase concept as to make it possible to consider specific techniques as primarily associated with a given phase.

Phase I: Contact and Relationship Establishment. During this phase workers sought out and located resident corner gangs and established an acceptable role-identity. Neither the location of the groups nor the establishment of a viable basis for a continued relationship entailed particular difficulties.[9] This phase included considerable "testing" of the workers; the youngsters put on display a wide range of their customary behaviors, with particular stress on violative forms—watching the worker closely to see whether his reactions and evaluative responses fell within an acceptable range. The workers, for their part, had to evince sufficient familiarity with and control over the basic subcultural system of lower-class adolescents and its component skills as to merit the respect of the groups, and the right to continued association.

A major objective in gaining entree to the groups was to establish what workers called a "relationship." Influenced in part by concepts derived from individual psychotherapy, Project staff felt that the establishment of close and meaningful relationships with group members was a major device for effecting behavior change, and was in fact a necessary precondition of all other direct service methods. The workers' conception of a "good" relationship was complex, but can be described briefly as a situation in which both worker and group defined themselves as contained within a common orbit whose major conditions were mutual trust, mutual affection, and maintenance of reciprocal obligations. The workers in fact succeeded in establishing and maintaining relationships of just this type. Considering the fact that these alliances had to bridge both age (adult-adolescent) and social status (lower class-middle class) differences, they were achieved and maintained with a surprising degree of success.[10]

Phase II: Behavior Modification via Mutual Activity Involvement. The behavior modification phase made the greatest demands on the skills, resourcefulness, and energy of the workers. Workers engaged in a wide variety of activities with and in behalf of their groups. The bulk of these activities, however, centered around three major kinds of effort: 1) organizing groups and using these as the basis of involvement in organized activities; 2) serving as intermediary between group members and adult institutions; 3) utilizing techniques of direct influence.

The workers devoted considerable effort to changing group relational systems from the informal type of the street gang to the formal type of the club or athletic team, and involving the groups so reorganized in a range of activities such as club meetings, athletic contests, dances, and fund-raising dinners. In most cases this effort was highly successful. Clubs formed from the corner groups met regularly, adopted constitutions, carried out extensive and effective club activities. Athletic teams moved from cellar positions to championships in city athletic leagues. One group grossed close to a thousand dollars at a fund-raising dance.

Project use of the "organized group and planned activities" method was buttressed by rationale which included at least five premises. 1) The experience of learning to operate in the "rule-governed" atmosphere of the formal club would, it was felt, increase the group members' ability to conduct collective activities in an orderly and law-abiding fashion. 2) The influence of the more lawfully-oriented leaders would be increased, since authority roles in clubs or teams would be allocated on different bases from those in the corner gang. 3) The need for the clubs to rely heavily on the adult worker for advice and facilitation would place him in a strategic position to influence group behavior. 4) The need for clubs to maintain harmonious relations with local adults such as settlement house personnel and dance hall owners in order to carry out their activity program, as well as the increasing visibility of the organized group, would put a premium on maintaining a public reputation as non-troublesome, and thus inhibit behavior which would jeopardize this objective. Active and extensive involvement in lawful and adult-approved recreational activities would, it was felt, substantially curtail both time and energy potentially available for unlawful activity. This devil-finds-work premise was taken as self-evidently valid, and was reinforced by the idleness-boredom explanation frequently forwarded by group members themselves—"We get in trouble because there's nuthin to do around here." On these grounds as well as others, the use of this method appeared amply justified.[11]

In performing the role of intermediary, workers proceeded on the premise that gang members were essentially isolated within their own adolescent slum world and were either denied, or lacked the ability to seek out, "access" to major adult institutions. This blocked access, it was felt, prevented the youngsters from seeking prestige through "legitimate" channels, forcing them instead to resort to "illegitimate" forms of achievement such as thievery, fighting, and prostitution. On this assumption, the Project aimed deliberately to open up channels of access to adult institutions—particularly in the areas of education and employment.

In the world of work, Project workers arranged appointments with employment agencies, drove group members to job interviews, counseled them as to proper demeanor as job applicants and as employees, urged wavering workers not to quit their jobs. Workers also contacted business firms and urged them to hire group members. In the area of education, workers attempted to solid-ify the often tenuous bonds between group members and the schools. They visited teachers, acted to discourage truancy, and worked assiduously—through means ranging from subtle persuasion to vigorous argument—to dis-courage the practice of dropping out of school at or before the legally-per-missible age. Workers arranged meetings with school personnel and attempted to acquaint teachers and other school staff with the special prob-lems of corner youngsters. Every effort was made to arrange scholarships (generally athletic) for those group members for whom college seemed a pos-sibility.

Workers also acted as go-between for their youngsters and a variety of other institutions. They arranged for lawyers in the event of court appear-ances, and interceded with judges, probation officers, correctional officials and parole personnel. They obtained the use of the recreational facilities and meeting places in settlement houses and gyms which would not have consid-ered admitting the rough and troublesome gang members in the absence of a responsible adult sponsor. They persuaded local storekeepers and business-men to aid the groups in their money-raising efforts. They arranged for the use or rental of dance halls, and solicited radio stations to provide locally fa-mous disc jockeys to conduct record hops. They organized meetings between gang members and local policemen during which both sides were given the opportunity to air their mutual grievances.

During later stages of the Project, workers brought together the clubs of the corner gangs and the adult organizations formed by the Project's Commu-nity Organization program, and gang members and community adults served together on joint committees working in the area of community improvement. One such committee exerted sufficient pressure on municipal authorities to obtain a $60,000 allocation for the improvement of a local ball field; another committee instituted an annual "Sports Night" during which most of the com-munity's gangs—some of whom were active gang-fighting enemies—attended a large banquet in which city officials and well-known sports figures made speeches and presented awards for meritorious athletic achievement.

Thus, as a consequence of the workers' activities, gang members gained ac-cess to a wide variety of legitimate adult institutions and organizations—schools, business establishments, settlement houses, municipal athletic leagues, public recreational facilities, guidance services, health facilities, municipal governmental agencies, citizens' groups, and others. It could no longer be said that the groups were isolated, in any practical sense, from the world of legiti-mate opportunity.[12]

While Project methods placed major stress on changing environmental con-ditions through organization, activity involvement, and opening channels of access, workers were also committed to the use of methods designed to in-duce personality change. The training of most workers had involved exposure to the principles of, and some practice in the techniques of, psychodynamic psychotherapy, and serious consideration was given to the possibility of attempting some form of direct application of psychotherapeutic principles, or techniques based on "insight" therapy. After much discussion workers decided that the use of techniques appropriate to the controlled therapist-patient situation would not be practicable in the open and multi-cliented arena of the corner gang world, and arrangements were made to utilize this approach through indirect rather than direct means.

Psychodynamic methods and individual treatment approaches were utilized in two ways. First, a contract was made with a well-known child-psychiatry clinic, and workers consulted with psychodynamically trained psychiatrists on a regular basis. During these sessions the psychiatrists analyzed individual cases on the basis of detailed case summaries, and recommended procedures for the workers to execute. In this way the actual operating policies of the workers were directly influenced by the diagnostic concepts and therapeutic procedures of psychodynamic psychiatry. Second, in cases where the workers or the psychiatric consultants felt that more direct or intensive therapy for group members or their families was indicated, arrangements were made to refer these cases either to the psychiatric clinic or to local casework or family-service agencies.

Another type of direct influence technique utilized by the workers was "group-dynamics"—a method which combined approaches of both psychodynamic and small-group theory. As adult advisors during club meetings, during informal bull sessions, and in some instances during specially-arranged group-therapy sessions, workers employed the specific techniques of persuasion and influence developed out of the group-dynamics approach (indirect suggestion, non-directive leadership, permissive group guidance, collective reinforcement). Sessions based on the group-therapy model were generally geared to specific emergent situations—such as an episode of sexual misbehavior among the girls or an upsurge of racial sentiment among the boys.[13]

The direct-influence technique which operated most consistently, however, was simply the continued presence with the group of a law-abiding, middle-class-oriented adult who provided active support for a particular value position. This value stance was communicated to the youngsters through two principal devices—advice and exemplification. The worker served as counsellor, advisor, mentor in a wide range of specific issues, problems and areas of behavioral choice as these emerged in the course of daily life. Should I continue school or drop out? Can we refrain from retaliatory attack and still maintain our honor? How does one approach girls? How does one handle an overly-romantic boy? Should I start a pimping operation? In all these issues and many more—sometimes broached by the worker, more frequently by the youngsters—the workers put their support—often subtle but nonetheless consistent—behind the law-abiding versus the law-violating choice, and, to a lesser extent, the middle-class-oriented over the lower-call-oriented course of action in regard to long-term issues such as education, occupation, and family life.[14]

But the continued association of worker and group engaged a mechanism of influence which proved in many ways more potent than advice and counsel. The fact of constant association, and the fact that workers became increasingly accepted and admired, meant that they were in a particularly strategic position to serve as a "role model," or object of emulation. A strong case can be made for the influencive potency of this device. Adolescents, as they move towards adult status, are often pictured as highly sensitive to, and in search of, models of estimable adult behavior, and to be particularly susceptible to emulation of an adult who plays an important role in their lives, and whom they respect and admire. It appeared, in fact, that gang members were considerably more impressed by what the workers *were* than by what they said or did. The youngsters were particularly aware that the workers were college people, that they were responsible spouses and parents in stable mother-father families, that they were conscientious workers under circumstances which afforded maximum opportunities for goofing-off. The workers' statuses as college people, "good" family people, and responsible workers constituted an implicit endorsement of these statuses, and the course of action they implied.

In some instances the admiration of group members for their worker approached hero-worship. One group set up a kind of shrine to their worker after his departure; on a shelf in the corner store where they hung out they placed his photograph, the athletic trophies they had won under his aegis, and a scrap-book containing accounts of the many activities they had shared together. Visitors who knew the worker were importuned to relay to him a vital message—"Tell him we're keepin' our noses clean. . . ."

Phase III: Termination. Since the Project was set up on a three-year "demonstration" basis, the date of final contact was known well in advance. Due largely to the influence of psychodynamic concepts, workers were very much concerned about the possibly harmful effects of "termination," and formulated careful and extensive plans for effecting disengagement from their groups. During the termination phase the workers' efforts centered around three major areas: scheduling a gradual reduction in the frequency of contact and "services" so as to avoid an abrupt cut-off; preparing the groups emotionally for the idea of termination by probing for and discussing feelings of "desertion" anger and loss; and arranging for community agencies to assume as many as possible of the services workers had provided for the groups (e.g., recreational involvement, counseling, meeting places for the clubs).

Despite some difficult moments for both workers and group members (one worker's car was stolen during the tearful farewell banquet tendered him by his group the night before he was to leave for a new job in another city; group members explained this as a symbolic way of saying "Don't leave Midcity!"), termination was effected quite successfully; workers moved off to other involvements and the groups reassumed their workerless position within the community.

In sum, then, the methods used in the Project's attempt to inhibit delinquent behavior were based on a sophisticated rationale, utilized both socio-cultural and psychological concepts and methods, encompassed an unusually wide range of practice techniques, and were executed with care, diligence and energy by competent and professionally trained workers. It was impossible, of course, to execute all planned programs and methods as fully or as exten-sively as might have been desired, but in overall perspective the execution of the Project showed an unusually close degree of adherence to its ambitious and comprehensive plan of operation.[15] What, then, was the impact of these efforts on delinquent behavior?

The Impact of Project Efforts

The Midcity Project was originally instituted in response to a community per-ception that uncontrolled gang violence was rampant in Midcity. Once the furor attending its inception had abated, the Project was reconceptualized as a "demonstration" project in community delinquency control.[16] This meant that in addition to setting up methods for effecting changes in its client popu-lation, the Project also assumed responsibility for testing the efficacy of these methods. The task of evaluating project effectiveness was assigned to a social science research staff which operated in conjunction with the action pro-gram.[17] Since the major effort of the Project was its work with gangs, the evaluative aspect of the research design focused on the gang program, and took as a major concern the impact of group-directed methods on the behav-ior of target gangs. However, since the focal "client" population of the group-work program (gang members) was a subpopulation of the larger client population of the overall project ("trouble"-prone Midcity adolescents), measures of change in the gangs also constituted a test of the totality of con-trol measures utilized by the Project, including its community organization and family-service programs.

The broad question—"Did the Project have any impact on the behavior of the groups it worked with?"—has, in effect, already been answered. The above description of Project methods shows that workers became actively and intensively involved in the lives and activities of the groups. It is hardly con-ceivable that relatively small groups of adolescents could experience daily as-sociation with an adult—especially an adult committed to the task of changing their behavior—without undergoing some substantial modification. But the fundamental *raison d'être* of the Project was not that of demonstrating the possibility of establishing close relationships with gangs, or of organizing them into clubs, or of increasing their involvement in recreational activities, or of providing them with access to occupational or educational opportuni-ties, or of forming citizens' organizations, or of increasing inter-agency coop-eration. These objectives, estimable as they might be, were pursued not as ends in themselves but as means to a further and more fundamental end—the inhibition and control of criminal behavior. The substantial effects of the

Project on nonviolent forms of behavior will be reported elsewhere; this chapter addresses itself to a central and critical measure—the impact of the Project on specifically violative behavior.[18]

The principal question of the evaluative research was phrased as follows: *Was there a significant measurable inhibition of law-violating or morally-disapproved behavior as a consequence of Project efforts?* For purposes of research procedure this question was broken down into two component questions: 1) to what extent was there a measurable reduction in the actual or expected frequency of violative behavior by Project group members during or after the period of Project contact? and 2) to what extent could observed changes in violative behavior be attributed to Project activity rather than to other possible "causative" factors such as maturation or police activity? [19] Firm affirmative answers to the first question would necessarily have to precede attempts to answer further questions such as "Which methods were most effective?"; the value of describing what the workers did in order to reduce delinquency would evidently depend on whether it could be shown that delinquency had in fact been reduced.

Following sections will report three separate measures of change in patterns of violative behavior. These are: 1) disapproved forms of customary behavior; 2) illegal behavior; 3) court appearance rates. These three sets of measures represent different methods of analysis, different orders of specificity, and were derived from different sources. The implications of this for achieved results will be discussed later.

TRENDS IN DISAPPROVED BEHAVIOR

A central form of "violative" behavior is that which violates specific legal statutes (e.g., theft, armed assault). Also important, however, is behavior which violates "moral" norms or ethical standards. Concern with such behavior is of interest in its own right (Was there a reduction in morally-violative behavior?) as well as in relation to illegal behavior (Were developments in the areas of illegal and immoral behavior related or independent?). The relationship between immoral and illegal behavior is highly complex; most behavior which violates legal norms also violates moral norms (overtime parking is one example of an exception), but much immoral behavior seldom results in legal action (homosexual intimacy between women; failure to attempt to rescue a drowning stranger).

Designating specific forms of behavior as "illegal" presents a relatively simple task, since detailed and fairly explicit criminal codes are available; designating behavior as "immoral" is far more difficult, both because of the multiplicity of moral codes in American society, and because many important moral norms are not explicitly codified.[20] In addressing the question—"Did the Project bring about a decrease in morally-violative behavior?", at least four sets of moral codes are of relevance—those of middle-class adults, of middle-class adolescents, of lower-class adults, and of lower-class adolescents.[21] While there are large areas of concordance among these sets, there are also important areas of noncorrespondence. The method employed in this area was as follows:

A major source of data for Project research was a large population of "behavior sequences" engaged in by group members during the study period. These were derived from a variety of sources, the principal source being the detailed descriptive daily field reports of the workers.[22] All recorded behavioral events involving group members were extracted from the records and typed on separate data cards. These cards were coded, and filed in chronological order under 65 separate categories of behavior such as drinking behavior, sexual behavior, and theft. A total of 100,000 behavior sequences was recorded, coded, and filed.

Fourteen of the 65 behavior categories were selected for the purpose of analyzing trends in immoral behavior.[23] These were: theft, assault, drinking, sex, mating, work, education, religion, and involvement with courts, police, corrections, social welfare, family, and other gangs. Seventy-five thousand behavioral sequences were included under these fourteen categories.

A separate set of evaluative standards, based primarily on the workers' own values, was developed for each of the fourteen areas. The workers as individuals were essentially oriented to the value system of middle-class adults, but due largely to their training in social work, they espoused an "easier" or more permissive version of these standards. In addition, as a result of their experiences in the lower-class community, their standards had been further modified to accommodate in some degree those of the adolescent gangs. The workers' standards thus comprised an easier baseline against which to measure change since they were considerably less rigid than those which would be applied by most middle-class adults.

Listings were drawn up for each of the fourteen areas which designated as "approved" or "disapproved" about 25 specific forms of behavior per area. A distinction was made between "actions" (behavioral events observed to occur) and "sentiments" (attitudes or intentions).[24] Designations were based on three kinds of information: evaluative statements made by the workers concerning particular areas of behavior; attitudes or actions workers had supported or opposed in actual situations, and an attitude questionnaire administered to each worker. Preliminary listings were submitted to the workers to see if the items did in fact reflect the evaluative standards they felt themselves to espouse; there was high agreement with the listings; in a few instances of disagreement modifications were made.

A total of 14,471 actions and sentiments were categorized as "approved," "disapproved," or "evaluatively-neutral." While these data made possible detailed and extensive analysis of differential patterns of behavior change in various areas and on different levels, the primary question for the most general purposes of impact measurement was phrased as—"Was there a significant reduction in the relative frequency of *disapproved actions* during the period of worker contact?" With some qualifications, the answer was "No."

Each worker's term of contact was divided into three equal phases, and the relative frequency of disapproved actions during the first and third phase was compared.[25] During the full study period, the 205 members of the seven intensive analysis groups engaged in 4,518 approved or disapproved actions. During the initial phase, 785 of 1,604 actions (48.9%) were disapproved; during the final phase, 613 of 1,364 (44.9%)—a reduction of only 4%.

Of the fourteen behavior areas, only one ("school-oriented behavior") showed a statistically significant reduction in disapproved actions. Of the remaining 13, ten showed decreases in disapproved actions, one no change, and two (church- and social-agency-oriented behavior) showed increases. Of the seven analysis groups, only one (white, male, younger, higher social status) showed a statistically significant reduction. Of the remaining six, five showed decreases in disapproved actions, one no change, and one (white, male, older, lower social status) an increase.[26]

The unexpected degree of stability over time in the ratio of approved to disapproved actions is all the more noteworthy in view of the fact that one might have expected the area of moral behavior to have felt the most direct impact of the workers' presence. One clue to the stability of the change figures lies in the fact that there was a good correspondence between the degree of change in disapproved actions and the social status of the group; in general, the lower the group's social status, the smaller the reduction in disapproved actions.[27]

TRENDS IN ILLEGAL ACTS

The central question to be asked of a delinquency control program is— "Does it control delinquency?" One direct way of approaching this question is to focus on that "target" population most directly exposed to program action methods and ask "Was there a decrease in the frequency of crimes committed by the target population during the period of the program?" Under most circumstances this is difficult to answer, owing to the necessity of relying on records collected by police, courts, or other "official" agencies. The drawbacks of utilizing official incidence statistics as a measure of the actual occurrence of criminal behavior have frequently been pointed out; among these is the very complex process of selectivity which governs the conversion of committed crimes into official statistics; many crimes are never officially detected; many of those detected do not result in an official arrest; many arrests do not eventuate in court action, and so on. At each stage of the conversion process, there is a multiplicity of factors relatively independent of the commission of the crime itself which determines whether or not a crime will be officially recorded, and in what form.

The Midcity Project was able to a large extent to overcome this difficulty by the nature of its base data. Because of their intimate daily association with gang members, workers were in a position both to observe crimes directly and to receive reports of crimes shortly after they occurred. The great majority of these never appeared in official records.[28]

The research question in the area of illegal behavior was phrased: "Was there a significant decrease in the frequency of statute violations committed by Project group members during the period of worker contract?" As in the case of disapproved actions, the answer was, with some qualifications, "No." Methods and results were as follows.

Every statute-violating act committed by a Project group member during the course of the contact period was recorded on an individual record form. While the bulk of recorded acts were derived from the workers' field reports, information was obtained from all available sources, including official records. Very few of the crimes recorded by official agencies were not also recorded by the Project; many of the crimes recorded by the Project did not appear in official records. During the course of the Project, a total of 1,005 legally violative acts was recorded for members of the seven intensive analysis groups. Eighty-three per cent of the 205 Project group members had committed at least one illegal act; 90% of the 150 males had been so involved. These figures alone show that the Project did not prevent crime, and there had been no expectation that it would. But did it "control" or "inhibit" crime?

Offenses were classified under ten categories: theft, assault, alcohol violations, sex offenses, trespassing, disorderly conduct, truancy, vandalism, gambling violations, and "other" (e.g., strewing tacks on street, killing cats).[29] Each worker's term of contact was divided into three equal phases, and the frequency of offenses during the initial and final phase was compared.

Seven hundred and fifty-two of the 1,005 offenses were committed during the initial and final phases. Of these, 394 occurred during the initial phase, and 358 during the final—a reduction of 9.1%. Considering males only, however, 614 male crimes accounting for 81.6% of all offenses showed an *increase* of 1.3% between initial and final phases. In order to localize areas of greater and lesser change, a distinction was made between "major" and "minor" types of offense, in which theft, assault, and alcohol offenses, accounting for 70.5% of all male offenses, were categorized as "major." On these major offenses the male groups showed an increase of 11.2%—the older male groups showing an increase of 4.7%, and the younger an increase of 21.8%.

In sum, then, it could not be said that there was any significant reduction in the frequency of known crimes during the course of the Project. The modest decrease shown by the total sample was accounted for largely by the girls and by minor offenses; major offenses by boys, in contrast, increased in frequency during the course of the Project, and major offenses by younger boys increased most of all.[30]

TRENDS IN COURT APPEARANCES

The third major index to Project impact was based on court-appearance statistics. The principal research question in this area was phrased: "Did the Project effect any decrease in the frequency with which Project group members appeared in court in connection with crimes?"[31] The use of court-appearance data made it possible to amplify and strengthen the measurement of impact in three major ways. 1) It permitted a considerable time-extension. Previous sections describe trends which occurred during the actual period of worker contact. Sound determination of impact makes it necessary to know how these "during" trends related to trends both preceding and following the contact period. Post-contact trends become particularly important in light of the "negligible change" findings of the "during-contact" period, which raise the possibility that the real impact of the Project may have occurred following the workers' departure, as a kind of delayed reaction response. 2) The data were compiled by agencies which were essentially independent of the Project. Although the Project made every attempt to recognize, accommodate to, and correct for the possibility of in-project bias,[32] exclusive reliance on data collected primarily by those in the employ of the Project would admit the possibility that the objectives or values of Project staff would in some way prejudice results. Despite some contact between Project and court personnel, the operations of the courts were essentially independent of those of the Project, and the likelihood that the various courts in which group members appeared would be influenced in any consistent way by Project values or objectives was extremely small. 3) It made possible the application of time-trend measures to groups other than those taken by the Project as objects of change. The inclusion of a control population as part of the basic evaluative design was of vital importance. Despite the detail obtainable through the continued and intimate contact of group and worker, it would have been difficult to know, without a control population, the extent to which the experience of Project group members during the contact period was a response to worker influence rather than a variety of other possible influencing factors.

Court-appearance data were processed in three different ways. The first made these data directly comparable with the other "during-contact" measures by asking—"Was there a significant decrease in the frequency with which Project group members appeared in court in connection with crimes during the contact period?" The second exploited the time-extension potentialities of the data by asking—"How did the frequency of court appearance during the contact period compare with frequency preceding and following this period?" The third utilized a control population and asked—"Did the court-appearance experience of gang members worked with by a delinquency control project for various periods between the ages of 14 and 19 differ significantly from the experience of similar gang members not so worked with?"

Contact Period Trends. Names of the 205 members of the Project's intensive contact groups were submitted to the state's central criminal records division. Court appearance records were returned for all group members with court experience. These records contained full court appearance and correctional commitment data for the 16 year period from 1945 to 1961—at which time older group members averaged 23 years of age, and younger, 21. It was thus possible to process the full sample as an age cohort in regard to court experience between the ages of 7 and 23, and including the period of Project contact. Each appearance in court on a new count for all male group members was tabulated.[33] "During-contact" appearance trends were analyzed in the same fashion as disapproved and illegal actions. The contact term for each group was divided into three equal phases, and the frequency of appearances during the initial and final phase was compared.

Trends in court-appearance offenses were essentially the same as trends in illegal actions. Group members appeared in court in connection with 144 offenses during the contact period. Fifty-one appearances occurred during the initial period and 48 during the final—a decrease of 5.8%. However, categorizing offenses as "major" and "minor" as was done in the case of illegal actions showed that for major offenses (theft, assault, alcohol), 31 appearances occurred during the initial phase and 35 during the final—an increase of 12.9%.[34] There was, therefore, no significant decrease in the frequency with which group members appeared in court during the term of worker contact. Neither the slight decrease in all-offense trends nor the increase in major offense trends proved statistically significant. The fact that these "during-contact" court appearance trends, involving 155 offenses, closely paralleled illegal act trends, involving 1,005 offenses, served to corroborate both sets of trends and to reinforce the finding of "negligible change" in legally-violative behavior for the period of worker contact.

Before-During-After Trends: Project Groups. In order to place the "during-contact" offense trends in a broader time-perspective, it was necessary to compare them to rates preceding and following the contact period. Since group members were of different ages during the contact period, data were processed so as to make it possible to compare the court experience of the several groups at equivalent age periods. The average age of each group was determined, and the number of court appearances per group for each six month period between the ages of 7 and 23 was tabulated. One set of results is shown in Figure 31–1. The frequency curve of yearly court appearances resembled a normal distribution curve, skewed to the right. Appearance frequency increased gradually between the ages of 7 and 16, maintained a high level between 16 and 20, and dropped off quite rapidly after 20.

The period of maximum frequency of court appearances coincided, in general, with the period of worker contact. Although no single group remained in contact with a worker during the full period between ages 16 and 20, each of the groups experienced contact for periods ranging from one to two and a half years during this period. It could not be said, then, that frequency of court appearance during the contact period was appreciably lower than during the pre-contact period; on the contrary, groups achieved a peak of appearance frequency during the period of Project service efforts.

Another way of describing these trends is by examining appearance frequency by six month periods. During the six months preceding contact there were 21 appearances; during the first six months of contact there were 29, and during the last, 27. In the six months following termination appearances rose to 39, dropped to 20 for the next six months, and rose to 39 for the

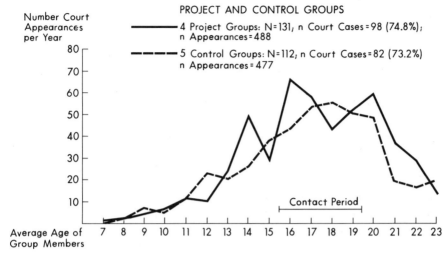

FIGURE 31–1. *Number of Court Appearances Per Year* *:
Ages 7–23

next. Thus, 18 months after Project termination, appearance frequency was at
its highest point for the total adolescent period.

The yearly appearance curve (Figure 31–1) does, however, show two
rather prominent dips—one at age 15, the other at 18. The dip at 15 could
not have been related to the Project, since contact had not yet begun. The dip
at 18, however, occurred at a time when each of the three older groups was
in contact with workers, and thus admits the possibility of worker influence.[35]
It is also possible that the post-twenty decline may have represented a de-
layed-action effect. Thus, looking at the period of worker contact as one
phase within the overall period of adolescence, it would appear that the presence of the workers did not inhibit the frequency of court appearances, but
that a dip in appearance frequency at age 18 and a drop in frequency after
age 20 may have been related to the workers' efforts.

COMPARISON OF PROJECT AND CONTROL GROUP TRENDS

Extending the examination of offense trends from the during-contact period to "before" and "after" periods, while furnishing important additional
information, also raised additional questions. Was it just coincidental that the
16 to 19 peak in court appearances occurred during the contact period—or
could the presence of the workers have been in some way responsible? Was
the sharp decline in frequency of appearances after age 20 a delayed action
result of worker effort? To clarify these questions it was necessary to examine the court appearance experience of a control population—a set of corner
gangs as similar as possible to Project gangs, but who had *not* been worked
with by the Project. The indexes reported so far have provided information

as to whether significant change occurred, but have been inconclusive as to the all-important question of cause-and-effect (to what extent were observed trends related to the workers' efforts?). The use of a control population entailed certain risks—primarily the possibility that service and control populations might not be adequately matched in some respects—but the unique potency of the control method as a device for furnishing evidence in the vital area of "cause" outweighed these risks.

Each of the Project's seven intensive service groups was matched with a somewhat smaller number of members of similarly organized corner gangs of similar age, sex, ethnic status, and social status. Most of these groups hung out in the same district as did Project groups, and their existence and membership had been ascertained during the course of the Project. Since the total membership of the Control groups was not known as fully as that of Project groups, it was necessary in some instances to match one Project group with two Control groups of similar status characteristics. By this process, a population comprising 172 members of 11 corner gangs was selected to serve as a control population for the 205 members of the seven Project gangs. Court appearance data on Control groups were obtained, and the groups were processed as an age cohort in the same manner as Project groups.

The court appearance frequency curves for Project and Control groups are very similar (see Figure 31–1). If the two dips in the Project curve are eliminated by joining the peaks at 14, 16 and 20, the shape of the two curves becomes almost identical. Both curves show a gradual rise from ages 7 to 16 or 17, maintain a high level to age 20, and drop rapidly between 20 and 23. Figure 31–2 compares Project and Control groups according to the number of *individuals* per year per group to appear in court, rather than according to

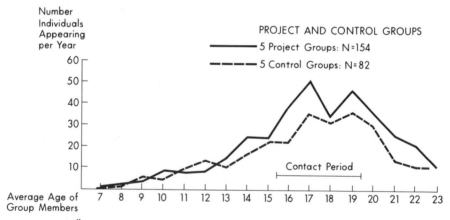

*At least once, on new charges, all offenses.

FIGURE 31–2. *Number of Individuals Appearing in Court Per Year *: Ages 7–23*

the number of *appearances* per year per group. On this basis, the similarity between Project and Control curves becomes even more marked. The dip at age 14 in the Project appearance curve (Figure 31–1) flattens out, and both Project and Control groups show a dip at age 18, making the Project and Control curves virtually identical.[36]

The unusual degree of similarity between the court appearance curves of Project and Control groups constitutes the single most powerful piece of evidence on Project impact obtained by the research. The fact that a group of similar gangs not worked with by the Project showed an almost identical decrease in court appearance frequency between ages 20 and 23 removes any reasonable basis for attributing the post-20 decline of Project groups to worker efforts. Indeed, the high degree of overall similarity in court appearance experience between "served" and "unserved" groups makes it most difficult to claim that anything done by the Project had any significant influence on the likelihood of court appearance.

Project and Control groups show equally striking similarities in regard to three additional measures—the proportion of individuals who had appeared in court by age 23, the proportion who had re-appeared, and the number of appearances per individual. Of 131 members of four male Project groups, 98, or 74.9%, had appeared in court at least once by age 23. The fact that 75% of the members of gangs worked with by social workers had nevertheless appeared in court by age 23 would in itself appear to indicate very limited Project impact. This finding, however, still admits the possibility that appearance frequency might have been even higher in the absence of the workers, or conversely, that the high figure was in some way a consequence of the workers' efforts. Both of these possibilities are weakened by the Control cohort figures. Of 112 members of five male groups *not* worked with by the Project, 82, or 73.2%, had appeared in court by age 23—almost exactly the same percentage shown by Project groups.[37]

The possibility still remains that Project group members, once having appeared in court, would be less likely than Control members to *reappear*. This was not the case. Of 98 members of Project groups who appeared in court at least once, 72, or 73.5%, appeared at least once again; of 82 Control group members who appeared at least once, 61, or 74.3%, appeared at least once more. A further possibility exists that while similar proportions of *individuals* might have appeared in court, Project group members might have made fewer *appearances* per individual. However, Project and Control groups were also similar in this respect. Ninety-eight Project members who appeared in court between the ages of 7 and 23 appeared 488 times, or 5.0 appearances per individual. Eighty-two Control males appeared 447 times, or 5.4 appearances per individual. These figures, while not as close to identity as the outcome figures, fail to show a statistically significant difference. The unusual degree of closeness in all these court appearance measures for male Project and Control groups provides a firm basis for concluding that Project impact on the likelihood of court appearance was negligible.

SUMMARY OF "IMPACT" FINDINGS

It is now possible to provide a definite answer to the principal evaluative research question—"Was there a significant measurable inhibition of law-violating or morally-disapproved behavior as a consequence of Project efforts?" The answer, with little necessary qualification, is "No." All major measures of violative behavior—disapproved actions, illegal actions, during-contact court appearances, before-during-after appearances, and Project-Control group appearances—provide consistent support for a finding of "negligible impact."

There was a modest decrease, during the period of worker contact, in the frequency of disapproved actions in 14 areas of behavior—but much of this reduction was due to a decrease in a single area—school oriented behavior. The overall change in the other 13 areas was only -2.3%.[38] The total number of illegal actions engaged in by group members also decreased slightly, though not significantly, during the course of the Project. Most of this reduction, however, was accounted for by minor offenses; major offenses showed a slight increase. Similarly, while there was a small decrease in the frequency of all categories of court-appeared offenses, major offenses showed an increase. Examining the group members' court-appearance trends between the ages 7 and 23 showed that court appearances were most frequent during the age period when Project workers were with the groups. The possibility that a pronounced decrease in court-appearance frequency after age 20 represented a delayed response to the Project was weakened by the fact that a similar decline occurred in the case of a set of similar gangs not worked with by the Project, and which, in fact, showed extremely similar court appearance trends both before, during, and after the age period during which Project groups were in contact with workers.

The fact that the various measures of impact are mutually consistent increases confidence in the overall "negligible impact" finding. Not only do the several indexes delineate similar trends in regard to the direction and magnitude of change (e.g., "during-period" change in disapproved actions, -4.0%; in illegal actions, -9.1%; in court appearance frequency, -5.8%), but also show a high degree of internal consistency in other respects. For example, the rank position of the five male groups in the degree of reduction in violative behavior shown by the three major indexes was very similar.[39]

Two previous papers reporting impact findings of the Midcity Project conveyed the impression of a limited but definite reduction in delinquency.[40] Why does the present report support a different conclusion? In the first place, present findings are based on new data not available in 1957 and '59, as well as on more extensive analysis of data then available. Both previous papers stated that reported results were preliminary, and cited the possibility of modification by future analysis.[41] Second, present data focus more directly on the specific experience of a specific target population; some of the previous impact findings were based on less focused indexes of general community trends, in which the behavior of the Project's target groups was not as directly distinguishable. Third, the "before" and "after" time extension made possible by the use of court data show some previously reported trends to have been relatively temporary fluctuations. Fourth, the use of a control population made it possible to anchor results more firmly by showing that important observed trends were common to both Project and non-Project groups, thus making possible a better determination of the extent to which "during" Project variation was in fact related to the workers' efforts.

The Efficacy of Project Control Methods

Which of the Project's methods were "tested" by the "negligible impact" findings? This complex question can be addressed only briefly here. It is evident that it was those methods which were most extensively employed or successfully executed which were shown most directly to have been least effective in inhibiting delinquency. Fifteen separate methods or techniques were cited earlier in connection with the three major programs (Community Organization, Family Service, Gang Work) of the Midcity Project. Of these, seven could be designated as extensively employed or successfully executed: establishment of district citizens' council; locating and contracting adolescent corner gangs; establishing relationships with gang members; effecting formal organization and involvement in organized recreational activity; provision of access to adult institutions; provision of adult role model. It is to these seven methods that the "negligible impact" finding applies most directly. Of these, "recreation" is already recognized quite widely to be of limited effectiveness as an exclusive method; "relationship" is still seen in many quarters as quite effective; "adult role model" was also found, by the Cambridge-Somerville Project, to have had little effect. Of two aspects of "access provision"— enabling youngsters to avail themselves of existing opportunities, and altering larger societal institutions so as to create new opportunities—the Project achieved the former but exerted limited systematic effort in regard to the latter, so that this aspect of access provision was only minimally tested.

Six methods could be characterized as less extensively employed or implemented with only moderate success: formation of citizens' groups; coordination of efforts of youth groups and adult citizens' groups; coordination of family-service agencies; treatment of "chronic problem" families; psychodynamic counseling and therapy; group dynamics. Some of these programs continued beyond the Project's three year demonstration period, but there is as yet no evidence available that any of these have had an impact on delinquency substantially different from that of the "best-tested" methods.

Two final methods—effecting concerted effort between citizens' groups and professional agencies, and coordinating the varied efforts of professional agencies themselves—were implemented only minimally. It is to these methods, then, that the "negligible impact" finding has least applicability. However, this failure of effectuation, especially in the area of inter-agency cooperation, was achieved only after extensive expenditure of effort, which might suggest that the cost of implementing this type of method, whose potential impact on delinquency is as yet undetermined, might not be commensurate with the degree of delinquency-reduction it could perhaps produce.

In addition, granting that some of the Project's methods were tested less fully than others, the fact that all 15 (and others) were applied concurrently and in concert also constituted a test of the "synergism" concept—that the simultaneous and concerted application of multiple and diverse programs on different levels will produce an impact greater than the summed impact of the component programs. Thus the total-community-multiple-programs approach, as executed by the Midcity Project, also fell within the category of methods best tested by the finding of "negligible impact."

In evaluating the significance of these "negligible impact" findings three considerations should be borne in mind. The first concerns the scope and nature of the question to which "negligible impact" is an answer, the second the level on which the answer is presented, and the third the value of the Project to delinquency control as a larger enterprise.

The phrasing of the principal evaluative research question tests the effectiveness of the Project against a single and central criterion—the measurable inhibition of explicitly violative behavior of a designated target population. The Project had considerable impact in other areas. To cite only two of these: the establishment of the control project and the spread of knowledge as to its existence had a calming effect on the adult community. Pre-Project gang activities in Midcity had activated a sense of fear among many adults and a feeling of helplessness in the face of actual and potential violence. Simple knowledge of the existence of the Project served to alleviate the community's sense of threat, in that there was now an established locus of responsibility for gang crime. The fact that *something* was being done was in itself important quite independent of the possible effectiveness of what was being done.

The Project was also instrumental in establishing new delinquency-control organizations, and left the community a legacy of organizations and programs which it had either brought into being or taken primary responsibility for. Among these were the District Community Council organized by Project staff, the project for providing direct service to "chronic problem" famillies, an annual sports award dinner for the youth of the community, and a permanent program of area work administered by the municipal government. The organizational plan of this latter enterprise was drawn up before Project termination, so that the municipal delinquency control bureau, once established, was able to extend the general approach of the Project to the entire municipal area.[42] While the value of these organized enterprises must also be measured against the same "impact on delinquency" criterion which was applied to the Project, it is clear that their existence was one tangible product of the Project.

A second consideration concerns the "level" of the reported findings. Data presented in connection with each of the major indexes to impact are at the most gross analytical level—that is, they neither specify nor analyze systematically the internal variation of the reported trends in three important respects—variations among the several groups, variations among the several behavior areas, and finer fluctuations over time. The finding of "negligible impact" encompasses, most accurately, *all* analyzed forms of behavior of *all* analyzed groups for extended periods. Internal analyses not reported here show that some groups showed considerable change in some areas, and that some areas showed considerable change for some groups. Further, while initial and final levels of violative behavior in many instances showed little difference, a good deal of turbulence or fluctuation characterized intervening periods. The flat "negligible impact" statement, then, by concealing a considerable degree of internal variability, obscures the fact that there was differential vulnerability to change in different areas and for different groups. Fuller analyses of these variations, along with the methods associated with greater and lesser vulnerability, will furnish specific policy guides to more and less strategic points of intervention.

A final consideration concerns the "value" of the Project in the face of its "negligible inhibition of delinquent behavior" outcome. There can be an important distinction, obscured by the term "evaluation," between the "effect" of an enterprise and its "value." The Midcity Project was established to test the possible effectiveness of its several approaches. These were in fact tested, and the Project was thus successful in the achievement of its "demonstration" objective. The evaluation model used here, based on multiple indexes to change, and using the "behavioral event" as a primary unit of analysis, can be applied in other instances where the impact of a specific change enterprise is at issue. Even more important, perhaps, is the fact that the process of gathering and analyzing the great bulk of data necessary to furnish a sound answer to the question of impact also produced a large volume of information of direct relevance to basic theoretical questions as to the origins of gangs and of gang delinquency. These findings also bear directly on a further question of considerable importance—"Why did the Project have so little impact on delinquency?"—a question to be addressed in some detail in future reports.[43]

NOTES

1. The principal current example is the extensive "Mobilization for Youth" project now underway in the Lower East Side of Manhattan. Present plans call for over 30 separate "action" programs in four major areas of work, education, community, and group service. The project is reported in detail in "A Proposal for the Prevention and Control of Delinquency by Expanding Opportunities," New York City: Mobilization for Youth, Inc. (December, 1961), and in brief in "Report on Juvenile Delinquency," Washington: Hearings of the Subcommittee on Appropriations, 1960, pp. 113–116.

2. See Lester Houston and Lena DiCicco, "Community Development in a Boston District," on file United Community Services of Boston, 1956.

3. See David M. Austin, "The Special Youth Program Approach to Chronic Problem Families," Community Organization Papers, New York City: Columbia University Press, 1958. Also, Joan Zilbach, "Work with Chronic Problem Families: A Five Year Appraisal," Boston: on file Judge Baker Guidance Center, 1962.

4. A brief description of the background of this method appears on p. 406 of Walter B. Miller, "The Impact of a Community Group Work Program on Delinquent Corner Groups," The Social Service Review, 31 (December, 1957), pp. 390–406.

5. The term "lower class" is used in this paper to refer to that sector of the population in the lowest education and occupational categories. For the purposes of Project statistical analyses, those census tracts in Midcity were designated as "lower class" in which 50% or more of the adult residents had failed to finish high school, and 60% or more of resident males pursued occupations in the bottom five occupational categories delineated by the 1950 United States Census. Nineteen of the 21 census tracts in Midcity were designated "lower class" by these criteria. Within lower class, three levels were distinguished. "Lower-class 3" included census tracts with 80% or more of adult males in the bottom five occupational categories and 70% or more of the adults in the "high-school non-completion" category; "Lower-class 2" included tracts with 70–80% males in low occupations and 60–70% adults not having completed high school; "Lower-class 1," 60–70% low occupation males, 50–60% high school non-completion. Of the 6,500 adolescents in Midcity, 17.5% lived in Lower-class 3 tracts; 53.1% in Lower-class 2, and 20.4% in Lower-class 1. The remaining 8.8% were designated "middle class." Project gangs derived primarily from Lower-class 2 and 3 areas; studied gangs comprised approximately 16% of the adolescent (13–19) Lower-class 2 and 3 population of the study area—roughly 30% of the males and 4% of the females.

6. Beyond this crude distinction between "locality-based" gangs and "other" types, a more systematic typology of Midcity gangs cannot be presented here. Karl Holton also distinguishes a locality-based gang ("area gang") as one type in Los Angeles County, and includes a classic brief description which applies without modification to the Midcity type. Karl Holton, "Juvenile Gangs in the Los Angeles Area," in Hearings of the Subcommittee on Juvenile Delinquency, 86th Congress, Part 5, Washington, D.C. (November, 1960), pp. 886–888. The importance of the "locality-based" typological distinction in this context is to emphasize the fact that Project gangs were not "emergent" groups organized in response to some common activity interest such as athletics, or formed around a single influential "magnetic" youngster, or organized under the influence of recreational or social work personnel. The gang structure pre-existed the Project, was coordinate with and systematically related to the kinship structure, and was "multi-functional" and "versatile" in that it served as a staging base for a wide range of activities and served a wide range of functions, both practical and psychological, for its members.

7. The age-class system of Midcity closely resembles that of the Otoro of Central Sudan as described by Asmarom Legesse, "[Some East African Age-] Class Systems," Special Paper, Graduate School of Education, Harvard University, May 1961 and S. F. Nadel, The Nuba, London: Oxford University Press, 1947, pp. 132–146. The Otoro age-class system, "one of the simplest . . . in eastern Africa" is in operation between the ages of 11 and 26 (in contrast to other systems which operate during the total life span), and comprises five classes formed at three-year intervals (Class I, 11–14; II, 14–17; III, 17–20; IV, 20–23; V, 23–26). The Midcity system, while less formalized, operates roughly between the ages of 12 and 23, and generally comprises four classes with new classes forming every two to four years, depending on the size of the available recruitment pool, density of population, and other factors. (Class I [Midgets] 12–14; II [Juniors] 14–16; III [Intermediates] 16–19; IV [Seniors] 19–22.) Otoro age classes, like Midcity's, are "multi-functional" in that they form the basis of athletic teams, work groups, and other types of associational unit.

8. Project "action" methods have been described briefly in several published papers:

David M. Austin, "Goals for Gang Workers," *Social Work*, 2 (October 1957), pp. 43–50; Ethel Ackley and Beverly Fliegel, "A Social Work Approach to Street-Corner Girls," *Social Work*, 5 (October 1960), pp. 27–36; Walter B. Miller, "The Impact of a Community Group Work Program on Delinquent Corner Groups," *op. cit.*, and "Preventive Work with Street-Corner Groups: Boston Delinquency Project," *The Annals of the American Academy of Political and Social Science*, 322 (March 1959), pp. 97–106, and in detail in one unpublished report, David Kantor and Lester Houston, *Methods of Working with Street Corner Youth*, 1959, mimeo., 227 pp., on file Harvard Student Volunteers Project.

9. Extensive discussion of the specific techniques of contact, role-identity establishment and relationship maintenance is included in Kantor and Houston, *ibid.*

10. Research methods for categorizing worker-group relationships according to intensity and intimacy will be cited in future reports.

11. Further elaboration of the rationale behind the "group-organization-and-activity" method, as well as some additional detail on its operation, is contained in David Austin, "Goals for Gang Workers," *op. cit.*, p. 49, and Walter B. Miller, *"The Place of the Organized Club in Corner-Group Work Method*, Boston: on file Special Youth Program, mimeo., 7 pp. (November 1956).

12. Project research data made it possible to determine the relative amount of worker effort devoted to various types of activity. The frequency of 12 different kinds of activity engaged in by workers toward or in behalf of group members ("worker functions") was tabulated for all 7 workers. Of 9,958 recorded worker functions, 3,878 were executed in connection with 22 organizations or agencies. Of these "institutionally-oriented" functions, workers acted in the capacity of "intermediary" for group members 768 times (19.8%), making "intermediation" the second most frequent type of "institutionally-oriented" worker function. The most frequent function was the exercise of "direct influence" (28.7%). Thus about one-half of all institutionally-oriented worker activity involved two functions—acting as intermediary and engaging in direct influence efforts. Of the 768 intermediary functions, 466 (60.7%) were exercised in connection with 6 kinds of organizations or groups—business organizations, schools, social welfare agencies, families, and other gangs.

13. A description of the use of group-dynamics techniques by Project workers is included in A. Paul Hare, "Group Dynamics as a Technique for Reducing Inter-group Tensions," Cambridge: Harvard University, unpublished paper, 1957, pp. 14–22.

14. For the frequency of use of "direct influence" techniques, see footnote 12.

15. A previous report, "Preventive Work with Street-Corner Groups: Boston Delinquency Project," *op. cit.*, p. 106, cited certain factors which made it difficult to execute some Project methods as fully as might have been desired. With greater perspective, derived both from the passage of time and increased knowledge of the experience of other projects, it would now appear that the Midcity Project was relatively less impeded in this regard than many similar projects, especially in regard to difficulties with police, courts, and schools, and that from a comparative viewpoint the Project was able to proceed relatively freely to effect most of its major methods.

16. Events attending the inception of the Midcity Project are cited in "The Impact of a Community Group Work Program on Delinquent Corner Groups," *op. cit.*, and in Walter B. Miller, "Inter-Institutional Conflict as a Major Impediment to Delinquency Prevention," *Human Organization*, 17 (Fall 1958), pp. 20–23.

17. Research methods were complex, utilizing a wide range of techniques and approaches. A major distinction was made between "evaluative" (measurement of impact) and "informational" (ethnographic description and analysis) research. No detailed account of research methods has been published, but brief descriptions appear in "The Impact of a Community Group Work Program on Delinquent Corner Groups," *op. cit.*, pp. 392–396, and "Preventive Work with Street-Corner Groups: Boston Delinquency Project," *op. cit.*, pp. 99–100, *passim*. A somewhat more detailed description of one

kind of content analysis method used in an earlier pilot study, and modified for use in the larger study, appears in Walter B. Miller, Hildred Geertz and Henry S. G. Cutter, "Aggression in a Boys' Street-Corner Group," *Psychiatry,* 24 (November 1961), pp. 284–285.

18. Detailed analyses of changes in "non-violative" forms of behavior (e.g., frequency of recreational activities, trends in "evaluatively neutral" behaviors) as well as more generalized "change-process" analyses (e.g., "structural" changes in groups—factions, leadership; overall patterning of change and relations between changes in violative and non-violative patterns) will appear in Walter B. Miller, *City Gangs: An Experiment in Changing Gang Behavior,* John Wiley and Sons, in preparation.

19. The "study population" toward which these questions were directed was the 205 members of the seven corner gangs subjected to "intensive service" by workers. Unless otherwise specified, the term "Project Groups" will be used to refer to this population.

20. A brief discussion of the complexities of the "multiple-moral-norm" system of the United States is contained in William C. Kvaraceus, Walter B. Miller *et al. Delinquent Behavior: Culture and the Individual,* Washington: National Education Association of the United States, 1959, pp. 46–49.

21. This four-type distinction is very gross; a range of subsystems could be delineated within each of the four cited "systems."

22. 8,870 pages of typescript records were subjected to coding. Of these, 6,600 pages were self-recorded field reports by workers; 690 pages were worker reports to the Project Director; 640 were field reports and interviews by research staff; 150 were tape-recorded transcriptions of group interaction. A brief description of the principles of the data-coding system, based on the concept of the "object-oriented-behavior-sequence," is included in Ernest Lilienstein, James Short *et al.,* "Procedural Notes for the Coding of Detached Worker Interviews," Chicago: University of Chicago Youth Studies Program (February 1962), pp. 2–7.

23. These 14 were selected because they included the largest numbers of recorded events, and because they represented a range of behaviors along the dimension "high violative potential" (theft, assault) through "low violative potential" (church, family-oriented behavior).

24. Examples of approved and disapproved actions and sentiments in the area of drinking are as follows: *Approved action;* "refusal to buy or accept liquor": *disapproved action;* "getting drunk, going on a drinking spree"; *approved sentiment;* "stated intention to discontinue or reduce frequency of drinking": *disapproved sentiment;* "bragging of one's drinking prowess."

25. Selected findings in regard only to disapproved actions are reported here. Future reports will present and analyze trends in both actions and sentiments, and in approved, disapproved and evaluatively-neutral forms, and the relations among these.

26. Chi-square was used to test significance. For all 14 behavior areas for all seven groups, chi-square was 4.57 (one d.f.), which was significant between the .02 and .05 level. However, almost all the "change" variance was accounted for by the single area which showed a significant reduction (chi-square for "school" was 14.32, significant beyond the .01 level). The other 13 behavior areas, accounting for 91.6% of the evaluated actions, showed a reduction of only 2.3%. Chi-square was 1.52 (one d.f.) which fails of significance. Chi-square for the one significant change group (Junior Outlaws) was 9.21, significant at the .01 level. However, omitting the one "significant change" behavior area (school) from consideration, chi-square for the remaining 90% of Junior Outlaws behavior areas was 3.19—which fails of significance at the .05 level.

27. Rank-difference correlation between "reduction in disapproved actions" and "lower social status" was −.82. The fact that this kind of association (the lower the social status the less change) appeared frequently in analyses of specific forms of behavior attests to the strength of the influence of group social status on patterns of delinquency and vulnerability to change efforts.

28. The availability to the Project of both official and unofficial statistics on crime frequency made it possible to derive "conversion ratios" showing the proportion of crimes recorded by official agencies to those recorded by the Project. These ratios will be reported in greater detail in *City Gangs, op. cit.*; in brief, ratios of "Project-recorded" to "court-appeared" offenses were as follows. For all categories of offense for both sexes, 15% of known crimes resulted in court action. For males only this ratio was 16%; fewer than 1% of recorded female crimes were court processed. The highest ratio was in the case of theft-type offenses by males; about 25% were court processed. About 10% of male drinking and assaultive offenses resulted in court appearance.

29. Determination of illegality was based on the offense classifications of the Massachusetts Penal Code. The complexities of definition of the various offense categories cannot be detailed here, but most categories represent higher level generality definitions than those of the code. For example, the category "theft" is used here to include all forms of unlawful appropriation of property, thus subsuming the more than 30 distinctions of the Penal code, e.g., robbery, armed, unarmed; larceny, grand, petty; burglary, etc. Non-theft auto violations are included under "other" since so few were recorded; similarly, narcotics violations, a major form of crime from a "seriousness" point of view, are included under "other" since virtually no instances were recorded.

30. None of these changes proved significant on the basis of chi-square. Chi-square for the largest change, the increase of 21.8% for the younger males, was 3.32, which is just below the .05 level. More detailed analyses of these trends, broken down according to type of offense, sex, age, etc., will be presented in *City Gangs, op. cit.*

31. Phrasing the question in this way was one of the devices used to accommodate the difficulties in using statistics cornpiled by official agencies. This phrasing takes the court appearance itself as an essentially independent index of impact; it does not assume any systematic connection between frequency of court appearance and frequency of criminal behavior. Having separate measures of Project-recorded and court-processed crimes (see footnote 28) makes possible separate computations of these ratios. Further, since court-appeared crime rather than committed crime can be seen, from one perspective, as the more serious social problem, Project impact on the likelihood of appearance itself can be taken as one relatively independent measure of effectiveness.

32. The technical and methodological devices for accommodating to or correcting for the possibility of in-project bias will be detailed in future reporting.

33. Out of 145 "during-contact" court appearances, only one involved a girl. Since 155 illegal acts involved females, this supports the frequently reported finding that females are far less likely to be subjected to official processing for crimes than males. All following figures, therefore, refer to males only.

34. Neither of these changes was statistically significant, testing with chi-square and Fisher's Exact Test. The three "major" offenses showed differing trends—with "theft" showing some decrease (23 to 19), "assault" remaining about the same (5 to 6) and "alcohol" showing a considerable increase (3 to 10). "Minor" crimes decreased from 20 to 13. These trends will be reported and analyzed more fully in future reports.

35. This "dip" phenomenon—a lowering of the frequency of violative behavior during the "middle" phase of worker contact—was also noted in connection with a somewhat different kind of processing of illegal acts reported in "Preventive Work with Street-Corner Groups: Boston Delinquency Project," *op. cit.*, p. 100. Currently available data make it possible to amplify and modify the interpretation presented in the earlier paper.

36. The implications of these court-appearance frequency trends transcend their utility as a technique for "controlling" for worker influence. One implication will be cited in footnote 43; more detailed interpretation and analysis, with special attention to the relative influence of worker activity and subcultural forces on the shape of the curves will be included in *City Gangs, op. cit.* Also included will be greater detail on the process of locating, selecting, matching and processing the control population.

37. The finding of negligible difference in court appearance frequency between Project and Control groups parallels the findings of the Cambridge-Somerville Youth Study —one of the few delinquency control projects to report findings of careful evaluative research (Edwin Powers and Helen Witmer, *An Experiment in the Prevention of Delinquency,* New York: Columbia University Press, 1951). It was found that 29.5% of a 325 boy treatment group had appeared in court by the time the oldest boys were 21, as compared with 28.3% of a 325 boy control group (p. 326). Despite differences in methods (Cambridge-Somerville used primarily individually-focused counseling) and client populations (Cambridge-Somerville boys were less delinquent), the degree of similarity between the two projects in treatment and control outcomes is striking.

38. It is possible that the decrease in disapproved school-oriented actions was due largely to a decrease in the frequency of truancy brought about by the fact that many of the earlier period truants had, by Project termination, passed the age at which school attendance was compulsory, thus ending their truancy. This possibility will be tested as part of a detailed analysis of change trends in each behavior area.

39. Rank-difference correlation coefficients were as follows: disapproved acts and illegal acts $+.80$; disapproved acts and court appearances $+.87$; illegal acts and court appearances $+.97$. Even with the small N of 5, the good correspondence between disapproved acts and court appearances is impressive, since the data for the two rank series were derived from completely independent sources.

40. "The Impact of a Community Group Work Program on Delinquent Corner Groups," *op. cit.,* pp. 390–406, and "Preventive Work with Street-Corner Groups: Boston Delinquency Project," *op. cit.,* pp 97–106.

41. It is similarly possible that some of the results cited here will be modified in the final Project report, especially in areas where more extensive internal analysis will enable fuller interpretations of reported trends.

42. See D. Austin, "Recommendations for a Municipal Program of Delinquency Prevention," mimeo., 7 pp., United Community Services of Boston, 1957.

43. Factors accounting for the limited impact of Project efforts will be treated in detail in *City Gangs, op. cit.* The explanatory analysis will forward the thesis that culturally-derived incentives for engaging in violative behavior were far stronger than any counterpressures the Project could bring to bear. This explanation will derive from a general theory of gang delinquency whose central proposition, to be expanded at length, will be that patterned involvement in violative behavior by gangs of the Midcity type occurs where four cultural "conditions" exist concurrently—*maleness, adolescence, urban residence,* and *low-skill laboring class status.* Each of these conditions is conceptualized as a particular type of subcultural system—each of whose "demanded" sets of behavior, taken separately, contribute some element of the motivation for engagement in gang delinquency, and whose concerted operation produces a subcultural milieu which furnishes strong and consistent support for customary involvement in criminal behavior. Data on "impact" presented here document the influence of two of these conditions—age status and social status. Court-appearance frequency trends (Figures 31–1 and 31–2) would appear to indicate that the single most important determinant of the frequency of that order of criminal behavior which eventuated in court appearance for Midcity male gangs was *age,* or, more specifically, movement through a series of age-based subcultural stages. Commission of criminal acts of given types and frequency appeared as a required concomitant of passing through the successive age-stages of adolescence and a prerequisite to the assumption of adult status. The influence of these age-class demands, on the basis of this and other evidence, would appear to exceed that of other factors—including conditions of the family, school, neighborhood or job world; police arrest policies, sentencing, confinement, probation and parole policies, and others. Data on *social status* (e.g., footnote 27, passim), along with much additional data not reported here, indicate a systematic relationship between social status *within* the lower class, and delinquency. 1. Within the 21 gang sample of the Midcity study, crime was both

more prevalent and more serious among those whose social status, measured by occupational and educational indexes, was lowest. 2. Relatively small differences in status were associated with relatively large differences in patterned behavior; as lower-status levels were approached, delinquency incidence increased exponentially rather than linearly; this indicates the necessity of making refined intra-class distinctions when analyzing the social "location" of criminal behavior. 3. Groups of lower social status showed the least reduction in violative forms of behavior; this lower vulnerability to change efforts would indicate that violative behavior was more entrenched, and thus more central to the subcultural system.

Part III

IDENTIFYING AND PREDICTING OFFENDERS

32: Assessment of Methods /
Don M. Gottfredson

Prediction, a traditional aim of science, is a requisite to any effective crime and delinquency prevention or control program. If we seek to control delinquent and criminal behavior, then first we will need to be able to predict it.

William James warned that we cannot hope to write biographies in advance. He asserted also, however, that we *can* establish general expectations. "We live forwards, but we understand backwards," he said, pointing out that any prediction method provides merely a way of summarizing previous experience in the hope of finding a useful guide to future decisions (87).

The problems of prediction in delinquency and related areas have interested many people. This has led to an extensive literature and a variety of techniques for developing and evaluating predictions. The resulting prediction methods have brought about arguments concerning the research methods used and inferences drawn, suggestions for practical uses, and complaints concerning misuses. This work has suggested avenues for further research and possibilities for more effective practice in the entire field of crime and delinquency, including delinquency prevention; and where prevention fails, each step in the process of the administration of criminal justice, from arrest to final discharge.

The nature of the prediction problem in this field is the same in many others.* A large body of literature is available concerning attempts to predict behavior in many sectors of social life. Examples are found in the prediction of social adjustment (79), of academic achievement (24, 59, 99), of vocational interest and performance (2, 133, 134, 136), and of the outcomes of marriage (16, 17).

Along with prediction studies in various social problem areas, the literature addressing theoretical and technical issues in prediction has grown. It includes studies of the logic prediction (116), of the role of prediction in the study of personality (62, 80, 84, 96, 100, 101, 102, 103, 123), of psychometric problems (5, 6, 21, 26, 27, 55, 66, 83), and of the role of prediction methods in evaluating studies of different treatments (50, 57, 67, 98, 152).

From U.S. President's Commission on Law Enforcement and Administration of Justice, "Assessment and Prediction Methods in Crime and Delinquency" by Don M. Gottfredson, in *Task Force Report: Juvenile Delinquency*, (Washington, D.C.: U.S. Government Printing Office, 1967), Appendix K, pp. 171–187.

* This review of prediction problems has been adapted largely from the excellent summary given by Bechtoldt and it has been aided considerably by the summary of much of the pertinent literature provided by Gough.

The objective in this chapter will be to summarize some of this extensive work in order to identify the major general problems, limitations, and potentials of methods for prediction of delinquency or crime. The general nature of the prediction problem will be reviewed. The steps followed in prediction research, some simplifying assumptions that commonly are made, and some requirements of useful prediction methods will be identified. Some basic concepts underlying prediction efforts and a number of general problems commonly found will be discussed. Some factors which influence the utility of prediction methods will be identified. This will help in evaluation of the "state of the art." Finally, various applications, in both research and practice, will be reviewed. This will suggest further research needs and point up some implications concerning appropriate roles for prediction methods in crime and delinquency treatment and control programs.

The scope of this chapter will be limited to some problems of prediction for individuals. More global prediction problems (e.g., estimations of population trends, or predictions of the number of offenses or offenders to be expected in a given place at a given time) may be very useful in correctional planning, or in testing hypotheses derived from social theories (94, 150), but they will be excluded. A vast literature concerning personality assessment generally, and evaluation of offenders specifically, is relevant to the prediction problem. No attempt will be made to review comprehensively, or even to list, the many delinquency prediction devices which have been proposed, discussed, and argued about. A number of bibliographies are available (9, 57, 62, 98, 124). No attempt will be made to discuss the methods and problems of the standardization of tests, or the preparation of norms, or to review even generally the large number of methods available and in widespread use in the clinical assessment of personality (26).

Some statistical problems will be discussed briefly; but no attempt will be made to present a full discussion of assumptions underlying the use of various techniques. The basic concepts of probability and statistical inference will not be discussed, even though they are basic to any prediction.

The Nature of the Prediction Problem

The common goal of the assessment methods to be discussed is the prediction of an individual's performance, that is, an assessment of his *expected* behavior, at some future time. The criterion of performance, of course, must be defined in terms of attributes or characteristics other than those used in whatever operations are performed in arriving at the prediction. The prediction problem, viewed in this way, involves two independent assessments of persons; the two assessments are separated in time. On the basis of one assessment, "predictor categories" are established (by various means). These are items of information believed to be helpful in prediction; they are the "predictors." The second assessment establishes "criterion categories"; these are the classifications of performance to be predicted. The predictions represent estimates of the expected values for the criterion categories, and these estimates are determined from earlier empirical investigations of the relations between the two sets of categories. On the basis of previously observed relationships between the predictor and criterion categories, an attempt is made to determine, for each category of persons, the most probable outcomes in terms of the criterion.

Predictions are sometimes qualified by making them conditional upon the occurrence of some later specific event, and then they are said to be conditional predictions (79). The determination of specific conditional factors which are relevant to the criterion classifications is a crucial problem, not only for prediction; it is a critical problem also in the evaluation of the effectiveness of treatment and control programs. The goals of delinquency prevention and correctional programs may be defined in terms of changing the probabilities of delinquent and criminal behavior.

A predictor category may represent any attribute or measure describing the individual. It may be defined by his own report, or by observations or judgments of others; it may be defined by what he can do or by how he perceives the world. It may be a measure of what he has done, and in this case it may include any of his past achievements or difficulties. It might be defined by exposure to specific treatment programs.

The criterion classification is based upon performance. In the area of crime and delinquency, the measurement of the performance criterion has special features which are critical but often overlooked.

The Criterion Problem

Requirements of reliability and validity must be met for the criterion classifications, as for the predictors. These requirements usually are discussed with reference to predictor variables; measures of differences among individuals which are believed to be predictive must meet certain basic requirements if we are to have confidence in them. Often it is forgotten that these same requirements apply equally to the things we wish to predict. A criterion of delinquency, of criminal behavior, or of probation or parole violation, is itself a measure of individual differences. It may be accurate, explicit, and clear in meaning, or inaccurate, vague, and ambiguous. A number of factors reduce the reliability and validity of the performance criteria commonly used in this field. To the extent that this occurs the validity of predictions will be reduced.

The need for improvement of reliability and validity of measures of criminal and delinquent behavior is a much neglected field, and it is only beginning to receive careful attention as a measurement problem (128). Criteria of delinquency, criminal behavior, and of parole or probation violations are ordinarily quite crude. For example, a common criterion of delinquency is a definition in terms of confinement. If among the confined population some are wrongly convicted, while the nonconfined group contains any individuals who are in fact engaged in delinquent behavior, the validity of the criterion is reduced to that extent. Criteria may not depend solely on the behavior of the person about whom the prediction is made, but they also may depend upon the behavior of others. In the above example, the classification may depend upon the behavior of the police and the courts as well as the accused. Commonly used parole violation criteria, when a designation as a "parole violator" is made on the basis not only of the parolee's behavior, but also on the response of the parole agent or the paroling authority provide another example. In this situation, an increase in "parole violations" may reflect increased offending behavior by parolees, increased surveillance by parole agents, or changes in policy of the paroling authority. The argument may be carried a step further, since the behavior of a victim might be an important component in determining the "delinquency" or "parole violation." The reliability and validity of criterion categories often are related closely to the efficiency of law enforcement and the administration of criminal justice. They may be affected by policy changes in the relevant social agencies and by changes in the categories of behavior which, in a changing social context, become defined as socially acceptable or unacceptable. The need for development of more adequate assessments of delinquent and criminal behavior, in order to provide criterion measures which are not artificially tied to social agency responses to that behavior, is apparent.

An acceptable criterion of delinquency is critical to any prediction effort since it provides the standard for identification of relevant predictor variables. It constitutes the basis for determining the validity of the prediction method, and it thereby determines whether or not the prediction method will be useful for any specific practical applications.

The reliability and discrimination of criterion measures must be evaluated in terms of consistencies over periods of time and over samples of situations. If this is not done, we can have little confidence that the prediction method will "work" when later applied to new samples. A ruler made of rubber, stretching variably each time a wooden table is measured, cannot be depended upon to provide a reliable measure; similarly, a wooden ruler will be inadequate if the table continuously expands and contracts.

No procedure can predict consistently a criterion which has no reliability; but while high reliability in the criterion is desirable, it does not follow that it is completely necessary. Low reliability introduces random variation which decreases the strength of relations between the predictors and the criterion; but it does not introduce systematic irrelevant variables (137). One consequence of this is that useful prediction methods may be developed despite relatively crude criteria; another is that improvement of the criterion measures may provide one avenue to improved prediction.

The Steps Followed in Prediction Studies

Five steps must be followed in any prediction study; the list below is modified from the steps identified by Horst (80), by Sarbin (123), and by Bechtoldt (7).

First, the criterion categories of "favorable" performance or of "delinquency" must be established. This involves the definitions of the behavior to be predicted and the development of procedures for classification of persons on the basis of their performance.

Second, the attributes or characteristics on which the predictions are to be based must be selected and defined. These predictor candidates are those that are expected to have significant relationships with the criterion classifications. Critics of prediction methods sometimes argue that the procedures ignore individual differences among persons. Actually, individual differences, often assuméd to be a source of error in other problems, provide the basis for any prediction effort. If the persons studied are alike with respect to the predictor candidates, no differential prediction can be made. If they are alike with respect to the criterion categories, there is no prediction problem.

Third, the relationships between the criterion categories and the predictor candidates must be determined, in a sample representative of the population for which inferences are to be drawn.

Fourth, the relationship determined on the basis of the original sample must be verified by application of the prediction procedures to a new sample (or new samples) of the population. This verification, commonly called cross-validation, is a crucial step; but it is often omitted. Without it, there can be little confidence in the utility of a prediction method for any practical application; nevertheless applications are often suggested. Those who argue for applications of prediction methods while ignoring this critical step properly should be excluded from the argument until they learn what the first question is. There may be good reasons for not using demonstrably valid prediction methods in any specific application, but there can be no justification for confident use of these methods in the absence of cross-validation studies.

Fifth, the prediction methods may be applied in situations for which they were developed, provided that the stability of predictions has been supported in the cross-validation step and appropriate samples have been used.

Simplifying Assumptions

In prediction studies certain assumptions commonly are made· in order to simplify operational procedures. As a result, statistical procedures which are not justified on the basis of logical implications of assumptions underlying measurement in science nevertheless are followed. For example, numerals are used to represent differences in attributes, since this serves a practical purpose. Qualitative dichotomous attributes may be assigned numbers such as zero and one, with various statistics then computed. Qualitative variables with multiple categories may be scaled in various ways with numerical scores assigned. These practices, of ignoring a number of measurement problems pertinent to the use of various statistical procedures (130), undoubtedly will continue since the results are useful. It would not seem wise to ignore these problems, however, since the improved measurement of individual differences with hypothesized relationships to later delinquency behavior offers another means for the eventual improvement of prediction.

A second example of a simplifying assumption, common in prediction studies, is that the criterion magnitudes are linear functions of the predictor variables. A number of authors have pointed out that increased accuracy of prediction may require the use of non-linear relations (80, 67, 98, 143, 149). In response it may be argued that a linear equation may provide a useful first approximation (7) or turn out to be entirely adequate (26). It may be argued also that nonlinearity of relationships may not be critical, since linearity might be secured by modifying the measuring devices or by a transformation of scales or scores. Furthermore, as pointed out by Bechtoldt, "empirical evidence indicates that sampling fluctuations of regression parameters are of such magnitude that very large representative samples would be required to provide accurate estimates of nonlinearity (7, 35)."

An additional example of a simplifying assumption, usually implicit in the procedures for developing prediction methods, is that the relations among predictor candidates, and between predictor candidates and the criterion, hold for subgroups of a heterogeneous population. The prediction methods are ordinarily based upon a study of a total sample of offenders, or of combined delinquent and non-delinquent populations, with no attempt to establish any relatively homogeneous subgroupings within the larger population (53, 55). This suggests a third approach toward improvement of prediction; predictive efficiency might be improved through separate study of various subgroups of persons.

Requirements of Predictor Classifications

Two requirements for any predictor candidate, aside from the relationship with the criterion, are *discrimination* and *reliability*. *Discrimination* is reflected in the number of categories to which significant proportions of persons are assigned. A classification which assigns all individuals to one class does not discriminate. An index of discrimination has been developed (33), and it may be shown that the best procedure is one which provides a rectangular distribution of categorizations for the sample. For a dichotomous item, the most discriminating item is one that has 50 per cent of the cases in each of the two categories (1). However, when two or more items are used the maximum number of discriminations made by the total prediction instrument may or may not be obtained with items at this fifty percent level; the intercorrelations of items and their reliabilities must be considered (13, 19, 34, 69, 120).

One consequence of the requirement of discrimination is that the predictor items found useful in one jurisdiction may not be helpful in another. For example, in parole prediction studies in California, where 15 to 20 per cent of the parolee population has a history of opiate drug use, this item has been found useful in parole prediction studies (56). However, in the State of Washington, where fewer than one percent of adult parolees have histories of drug use, the item would not be expected to be a helpful predictor.* The requirement of discrimination points to the need for cross-validation studies in various jurisdictions and points up one hazard in untested acceptance of prediction measures developed from study elsewhere in a single jurisdiction. (Considerations of sampling and of the concept of validity, discussed below, result in the same conclusion.) A classification procedure may discriminate but not be valid for a given criterion, and there seems to be no reason that the extent of discrimination would provide an effective weighting of the item in arriving at a prediction device.

Reliability refers to the consistency or stability of repeated observations, scores, or other classifications. If a procedure is reliable, then repetitions of the procedure lead to similar classifications. The topic of reliability of measurement is a large one indeed, and it has been discussed by many writers (25, 73, 74, 82).

Valid prediction is not possible with completely unreliable measures, but all measurement is relatively unreliable. This means that some variation is always expected. It also means that if valid prediction is demonstrated, then the predictor attributes may not be completely unreliable. The main interest in a prediction method is how well the method works; so more importance is attached to the question of validity than of reliability. This does not mean the issue of reliability is unimportant; the improvement of reliability of predictor variables provides another means for the possible improvement of prediction and therefore deserves much study. Unfortunately, analyses of the reliability of individual predictor items (or of a total prediction instrument) frequently are not reported in delinquency prediction studies.

Probability and Validity

No estimate of future behavior, arrived at by any means, can be made with certainty; a statement of degree of probability is a more appropriate prediction. Individual prediction, with which this chapter is concerned, is actually a misnomer. Predictions properly are applied not to individuals but to groups of persons, similar with respect to some set of characteristics (123). In any prediction problem individuals are assigned to classes, and then statements

* Thompson, J., Washington State Probation and Parole Board. *personal communication.*

are made about the expected performance of members of the classes. The expected performance outcomes, for specific classifications of persons, ought to be those which provide the most probable values for the population as a whole (12, 72).

The validity of a prediction method refers to the degree to which earlier assessments are related to later criterion classifications. The question of validity asks how well the prediction method "works." Any prediction instrument or method, however, may be thought of as having and lacking not one but many validities of varying degrees. For example, an intelligence test might provide a valid prediction of high school grades. It might provide a much less valid, but still useful, measure of expected social adjustment, and it might have no validity for prediction of delinquency. The validity of prediction refers to the relationship between a specific criterion measure and some earlier assessment, and it is dependent upon the particular criterion used. A prediction method has as many validities as there are criterion measures to be predicted.

Evidence of validity with respect to the specific criterion of interest obviously is necessary before any practical application of the method. Nevertheless, "prediction" studies in the field of crime and delinquency frequently are reported in which the verification, or "cross-validation" step has been omitted.

The concept of validity of prediction is "the tie that binds" all prediction efforts together (101). This is the case whether they are considered clinical or statistical, and regardless of the specific procedures used in developing the method. The "proof of the pudding" in any prediction study is the degree to which the method is valid with respect to specific criterion classifications.

Predictors

The predictor items, on which expectations are based, may be obtained from the self-report of the subjects concerned, reports of observers or judges, records of past performance, or by direct observation by the individual making the prediction. Thus, predictor items may include psychological test scores, measures of attitudes or interests, biographical items, ratings, or indeed any information about the subject.

The objective in most prediction studies has been the formulation of empirical rules based upon observed relationships between individual attributes and the criteria of interest. Those engaged in these studies have tended to consider their problems in these strict empirical terms. The focus of interest has been in the empirical relationships between the predictors and the criterion. If the resulting prediction procedures work, they are accepted as useful.

Some writers have asked whether a theoretically blind prediction technique can provide the basis for effective interventions in the crime and delinquency field (140); this suggests that criminological theory can be helpful in development of more useful prediction instruments. It may be suggested also that the development of prediction methods provides opportunities for the hypothesis testing necessary for development of theory. Prediction methods do not require that hypotheses be derived from a single, consistent theoretical framework; any hypotheses (and conflicting ones) may provide a source of predictor candidates. They do require that these hypotheses be tested as the prediction methods are developed. The strictly empirical, atheoretical approach of many prediction studies has, as Toby points out, led to neglected opportunities for improvement of both prediction and criminological theory.

The Evaluation of Prediction

A number of measures have been developed for the assessment of predictive efficiency. Traditionally, for a qualitative criterion such as "Delinquent vs. Non-Delinquent," the efficiency of prediction has been expressed in terms of the proportion of individuals correctly assigned to these criterion categories (72). For quantitative predictions, efficiency is usually expressed as some function of the correlation between the predictor and criterion measures. Some measures provide interpretations of a validity coefficient with special reference to the accuracy of prediction of individual scores. They include the coefficient of alienation (75) and the index of forecasting efficiency (80). Efficiency of prediction may be assessed also by the relative number of correct predictions in terms of exceeding some critical value of the criterion (81). Sometimes the correlation coefficient is regarded as a direct index to the efficiency of prediction (13); the square of the correlation coefficient, called the coefficient of determination, measures the proportion of variance in the criterion classifications which is "accounted for" by the items included in the prediction method. Another means of evaluating the efficiency of prediction is in terms of the increase in accuracy of prediction when the prediction method is used, as compared with selecting cases at random (88).

Ohlin and Duncan proposed an index of predictive efficiency defined by the percentage change in errors of prediction by the prediction method rather than the "base rate," i.e., the proportion of persons in the criterion category to be predicted (108). Their later method (31) was modified by Duncan and Duncan and called the "mean cost rating" (32), a procedure which reflects the degree to which a classification method accurately assigns persons to a dichotomous criterion classification.

Evaluations of predictive efficiency by means of these and other available measures can provide useful comparisons of the predictive accuracy of various prediction approaches, and they provide general statements concerning the efficiency of prediction. Such comparisons of efficiency of predictions, when the expectancies are arrived at by various methods, are needed but are quite rare in the crime and delinquency field.

It should be noted that (depending upon the purpose to which the prediction method is to be put) prediction methods with even quite low validity may be useful (27). On the other hand, prediction methods with high validity in one sample may be of little use in an application which concerns a sample from another population, or the degree of validity required may depend upon other components of the problem. A number of factors influence the utility of prediction methods and bear upon issues of practical applications.

Factors Influencing the Utility of Prediction

Predictive efficiency and the utility of prediction methods both are affected by various factors other than the relationship between the predictor items and the criterion. Besides the reliability of predictor candidates, these factors may include the "selection ratio," the "base rate," the method of combining predictor variables, the representativeness of the sample on which the prediction method has been based, and the number of predictor variables. Each of these should be discussed briefly as a basis for consideration of existing prediction methods.

THE SELECTION RATIO

In any selection problem, such as placement on probation or parole, some individuals are chosen and some are rejected. The ratio of the number who are chosen to the total number available is called the selection ratio (7). The usefulness of a selection procedure depends not only upon the validity of the prediction method but depends also upon this ratio. If the selection ratio is low, as for example when only a few individuals are to be accepted for parole, fairly low validity coefficients in a prediction device may prove useful. If only a few individuals are to be rejected, then a much higher validity would be required for the same degree of effectiveness as an aid in selection.

THE BASE RATE

The "base rate" refers to the proportion of individuals in some populations who fall into a category which is to be predicted. Fortunately for society, but unfortunately for those who aspire to predict delinquency, delinquency is a rather uncommon state of affairs (76). Even more fortunate for society at large is that shocking crimes against persons are relatively infrequent in proportion to the population as a whole; but at the same time that we wish most to predict these relatively rare occurrences, the predictive task is made more difficult by the base rate. The base rate affects both our ability to discover predictors which differentiate criterion categories and the accuracy of prediction when methods are applied to new samples.

This means that for relatively rare occurrences we may expect greater difficulty in finding predictive information. At the same time, a prediction method (in order to be useful) must be a more efficient one if the event to be predicted is relatively rare.

The first problem is that if there are relatively few "failures" or "delinquents" in a population we'll be hard put to find items which discriminate between the successes and the failures.* It will be more difficult to find useful predictors, because the variation in the criterion is reduced, and it is this variation which must be analyzed in the search for predictors.

The effect of base rates on the accuracy of prediction has been discussed by Meehl and Rosen (104), by Cureton (28), and with illustrations in the field of delinquency by Gough (62), Hanley (76), Grygier (67), and Walters (145).

In order for a prediction method to be useful, it must provide more information than that given by the base rate alone. For example, if 90 percent of the children in the population can be expected to be nondelinquent in any event, then there is little value in a method unless the proportion of non-delinquent individuals among those expected to be non-delinquent can be significantly increased over the 90 percent value (141). Frequently, however, a prediction method is devised on the basis of study of a sample containing equal (or about equal) numbers of delinquents and non-delinquents. Then it is applied to the general population where the proportion who actually become delinquent is considerably lower. This procedure can be expected to result in a serious overestimation of the practical effectiveness of the prediction device. In order to evaluate the utility of the prediction method, it is necessary to know not only how well it discriminates between the future delinquents and non-delinquents, but how common is delinquency in the general population.

It is important to know also the relative costs and utilities of forestalling delinquency in a predicted delinquent in relation to the possible costs of misclassifying an individual who will not become delinquent (27). Similarly, in probation or parole selection applications it is important to know not only the probable outcomes of probation or parole and the associated costs but the expected outcomes and costs of denial of these alternatives to confinement.

METHODS OF COMBINING PREDICTORS

If a number of predictor items are to be used in establishing a single prediction, then the items may be combined in various ways. Either the predictors all may be used without weighting them, or some procedure for weighting the various predictor items may be used, or some type of "configural" method may be employed.

The most widely used method of combining predictors has been the assignment of unit weights; many predictive characteristics are used without a weighting system. Each item found to be related to the criterion is assigned one point regardless of the strength of its association; and the sum of the points thus assigned provides a measure of the probability of delinquency,

---

* It can be shown also that as a sample proportion of failures (or of successes) becomes smaller, larger samples are needed in order to reduce error in estimating the numbers of success and failures in the total population.

parole violation, or some other criterion classification. This has been a popular procedure (15, 36, 63, 109, 110, 117, 118, 119, 138, 139, 147, 126). As pointed out by Grygier, it is democratic as well as popular, considering all predictors equally; however, it may be inefficient (67). This procedure ignores intercorrelations among the predictors, but if a large number of items is used there is nevertheless a good argument for it. It may be assumed that as the number of positively correlated variables increases, the correlation between any two sets of weighted scores approaches one and the effect of differential weighting of the various items tends to disappear. If the number of measures to be added together is not large, however, the dispersions and intercorrelations of the measures may influence significantly the weights expected on theoretical grounds to increase predictive efficiency.

The second method (really a set of methods) employs a smaller number of predictive characteristics and some weighting system. Items with the highest correlations with the criterion are generally selected and various methods of weighting are applied.

The best known of these is found in the series of prediction studies by the Gluecks (38, 39, 40, 41, 42, 43, 44, 45, 46, 47, 48). Contingency coefficients are found, in order to measure the association of the initial assessments with the criterion classification, and to select significant predictors. Each item is weighted in scoring by assigning it the percent figure for the criterion among persons characterized by the predictor attribute. As in the case of assignment of unit weights, correlations among predictors are ignored, and there is no reason to suppose that an "optimal" weighting procedure would result. The weighting is based upon discrimination in the criterion classification and ignores overlapping of items. In two studies, the method was not found superior to assignment of unit weights (106, 144).

Two theoretically better models are provided by multiple linear regression and by linear discriminant function. These methods take account of the intercorrelations of the predictor variables as well as the correlations with the criterion. In multiple regression, the linear equation is found such that weights are assigned in order to minimize the squared deviations of observed and expected criterion values. If Fisher's discriminant function is used, the weights in the linear equation are found such that the criterion classification groups are maximally separated (in terms of the mean values for the prediction scores, in relation to their pooled standard deviations).

These methods have been used in a number of studies. Multiple regression was used by Mannheim and Wilkins (98), in their English Borstal prediction study, and they reported that more efficient prediction was thereby achieved than that found with assignment of unit weights. The method was employed in parole prediction by Kirby (90), and it has been the method used in a number of California Parole Prediction Studies (51, 52, 56). The discriminant function has been employed for prediction in various areas, including problems in classification of students (3), of farmers (11), of air force radio operators (146), of aviation cadets (93), and military delinquents (70).

A series of studies conducted for the United States Naval Retraining Command represents one of the most careful and sophisticated studies in delinquency prediction but is perhaps less well known than others (5, 70, 66, 85, 71). Discriminant functions were developed, from study of an initial sample of 20,000 naval recruits, and from study of the proportion defined as offenders from various follow-up sources (1,339 persons). Among other results, the study demonstrated clearly that a pencil and paper Delinquency Potential Scale (developed in the same study) made a unique contribution to the separation of the offender and non-offender groups.

Regression analyses have many advantages. One is the theoretically optimal weighting of predictors (in terms of the linear assumption). Another is the special utility of the method for selection of predictors, since they may be selected after determining the proportionate reduction of unaccounted-for variance in the criterion by inclusion of each item; that is, the gain in prediction by adding the item may be determined readily as an increase in the coefficient of determination.

The method has some shortcomings. One may be the assumption of linearity already discussed. Another is that the weights are derived from the correlation matrix (for all predictor candidates and the criterion) for the total sample of subjects. It is therefore assumed implicitly that these correlations are adequate estimates of comparable coefficients for subsamples, that is, for subgroups of persons, within the larger sample. This assumption may be demonstrably false (53).

Configural prediction methods also have been used in delinquency prediction, again with variations of method. In other areas, they generally have not been found to provide increases in predictive efficiency over linear models (26). One method, described by MacNaughten-Smith (95), has been called "predictive attribute analysis." This approach also has been used in parole predictions by Wilkins (153), by Grygier (67), and by Ballard (6). A closely related procedure is the "configural analysis" method of Glaser (37), also used in parole prediction studies by Mannering and Babst in Wisconsin (97). When both linear regression and the configural analysis methods were applied to the same set of Wisconsin data, results of these methods gave similar predictive efficiency (54). A shortcoming of the general approach is that the successive partitioning of the sample into subgroups may involve a capitalization on sampling error (55).

The basis for the method proposed by MacNaughten-Smith is a successive partitioning of a sample into subgroups on the basis of the single item found in each subgroup to have the closest association with the criterion. That is, first the single most predictive item is found and the total sample is divided on this attribute. Each of the two resulting subsamples is studied further, in order to identify, within each, the single best predictor. Then the two subsamples are further subdivided and the process repeated until no further items significantly associated with the criterion are found.

Another configural approach is given by the method called association analysis. The method, developed by Williams and Lambert for studies in plant ecology (154), has been employed in delinquency prediction by Wilkins and MacNaughten-Smith (152), and by Gottfredson, Ballard and Lane (53). The method provides an empirical means for subdividing a heterogeneous population into subgroups which are relatively homogeneous with respect to the attributes studied. It is more properly called a classification method; unlike other prediction methods, the criterion classifications are ignored in establishing the subgrouping. The establishment of the classifications is not dependent upon the relationships of predictor candidates to the criterion; the classification may provide, nevertheless, a valid prediction method.

A combination of association analysis and regression methods has been suggested. Association analysis would be used in order to define relatively homogeneous subgroups of persons. Then regression methods would provide the means for development of prediction devices for each subgroup so identified. This or similar procedures providing for separate prediction studies for meaningful subgroups of offenders may provide an avenue to improved prediction.

Despite the variety of methods which have been used for combining predictors, empirical comparisons of resulting predictive efficiency are rare; and they are needed (62).

SAMPLING

A shortcoming of many delinquency prediction studies is the use of samples, studied for development of the prediction method, which are not representative of the populations to which generalizations are to be made. If systematic biases are introduced by the sampling procedure, then the validity in new samples will be decreased. General application of prediction methods based upon study of non-representative samples, as in a study completed in a high delinquency area, is very questionable; the same is true of application of probation or parole prediction procedures in jurisdictions other than those studied in developing the measures. In any such intended application, further cross-validation is necessary, attention to the base rate problem is imperative, and continued assessment of the stability of predictive validity over time is essential.

NUMBER OF PREDICTOR VARIABLES

When multiple regression is used as the method of combining predictor variables, the stability of predictions for new samples tends to decrease with an increase in the number of items included in the equation. Adding items to the original set of predictors will not reduce the accuracy of prediction in the original sample, however (80, 115). If only the original sample is studied, the investigator risks being misled by an accumulation of errors; his only safeguard is found in study of new samples. This emphasizes again the need for cross-validation studies.

For stable predictive validity a small number of items which are not only predictive but relatively independent of one another is sought. In this situation, each item makes a unique contribution to the prediction.

Predictive Information

In the Glueck studies, already mentioned, attempts have been made to identify potential delinquents at a very early age. Various prediction tables have been developed. One of these, called "Social Factors," has been evaluated intensively over a long term. The tables rest on the determination of predictive items in a study comparing 500 delinquents and 500 non-delinquents.

In a ten year validation study, with retention of a three factor scale including "supervision of the boy by his father," "supervision of the boy by his mother," and "family cohesiveness," as well as a two factor scale including "supervision of the boy by his mother" and "family cohesiveness," the investigators concluded:

The Glueck Social Prediction Table, after nine years of study and experimentation, is showing evidence of being a good differentiator between potential delinquents (serious and persisting) and non-delinquents.

They asserted also that:

The Three-Factor Table yielded approximately a 70 percent accuracy in predicting delinquents and an 85 percent accuracy in predicting non-delinquents (22, 23).

The procedures used by the Gluecks in developing their methods and the conclusions reached on the basis of their study have been strongly supported and severely criticized. A 1951 symposium of reviews in the *Journal of Criminal Law and Criminology* was generally highly favorable. The most incisive criticisms have been addressed to the sampling methods used and the base rate problem. It has been argued that a non-representative sample was studied, the research having been carried out in a high delinquency area in New York City (122, 92). The criticisms of Rubin and of Shaplin and Tiedman (129) discuss the sampling problem and the point that delinquents were not studied in their youth (extrapolations having been made from data obtained after the boys had been institutionalized in adolescence).

Similar strong objections by Reiss (119), by Gough (62), by Grygier (66), and by Hanley (76) emphasize the implications of the base rate problem and demonstrate its importance for applications in delinquency prediction. The reported accuracy of the Glueck Tables is based on the situation with equal numbers of delinquents and controls. When the base rate is set at a more realistic figure in terms of the incidence of delinquency generally, the tables turn out to be far less discriminating than claimed. The criticism is also made by Walters (145), who demonstrates that a base rate of between two and four percent makes prediction from the tables quite inaccurate. It is clear that if the base rate problem is ignored, the practical effectiveness of the Glueck Tables will be greatly overestimated.

A sequential procedure for identifying potential delinquents has been offered by Stott (132). Based upon the incidence of symptoms of non-delinquent behavior disturbances among probationers and controls, the *Bristol Social Adjustment Guide* was developed. A preliminary screening is completed by teachers on the basis of six yes-no items concerning behavior disturbances found to be associated with delinquency. If a boy is rated adversely on one or more items, then the full *Guide* is used in assessment. Evidence from a Glasgow survey suggests these procedures as promising, but they have not been validated in the United States.

Of various prediction measures developed by Kvaraceus, the non-verbal KD Proneness Scale has undergone the most extensive validation (91). Sixty-two circles each include four pictures based on concepts concerning reported differences between delinquents and non-delinquents. The subject indicates the item he likes most and the one he likes least. Validation data are available from a careful three year follow-up study of 1,594 junior high school students (and for a small sample of retarded children in special classes). While some evidence of validity was reported, inconsistencies in the results of the validation study led the author to urge caution in the employment of this tool for prediction on a routine or perfunctory basis. Reported as the most significant result was that teacher nominations (based on pupil behavior) were found equally effective and sometimes more effective as predictors of future delinquency.

A procedure reported by Bower as a method for identification of children most vulnerable to or handicapped by emotional disorders also makes use of teacher ratings in a sequential screening process (10). The usefulness of the screening process has been extensively studied. Results indicate that it is a practical approach for identification of emotionally disturbed children not otherwise recognized in the school situation; further validation studies again are needed.

A number of additional prediction methods, aimed at the identification of future delinquents, give evidence of promise; all need further validation, and all require validation in specific jurisdictions before application (131, 112, 148, 114).

The Minnesota Multiphasic Personality Inventory is a widely used empirically derived set of personality scales which may be used in group administration (77). The validity of this instrument in delinquency prediction has been investigated in a sample of 4,048 ninth grade boys and girls in Minneapolis (78). Two years after administration of the test, county and city records were checked and it was found that 591 (about 22 percent of the boys and 8 percent of the girls) had been brought before the courts or the police. The criterion of delinquency employed was a broad one, including three levels of seriousness of offenses.

Two subscales of the test, namely the "Psychopathic Deviancy" subscale and the "Hypomanic" subscale, were found predictive of delinquency. Considerable attention was given to the contribution of profiles of the *MMPI* as an aid to understanding the dynamics of delinquent behavior. Also, 33 *MMPI* items discriminating pre-delinquent from normal boys later were identified (79); further validation of these items as a separate scale is needed.

The *MMPI* was originally prepared for adult use, and it has been noted that it contains a large number of emotionally charged items to which parents and teachers frequently raise objections (92). The predictive utility of the *MMPI* in the prediction of delinquency among prisoners (in terms of misbehavior during confinement) has been investigated by Paton (111), and by Jacobson and Wirt (86).

There are many other psychological assessment procedures which may help in development of improved prediction methods. As recently as 1950, a review of the literature concerning comparisons of delinquents and non-delinquents on personality measures led to the conclusion that no consistent significant differences between these two groups were to be found (127). More recent studies, using more recently available instruments, demonstrate that a number of these do discriminate between delinquents and non-delinquents. Already mentioned is the Psychopathic Deviate scale of the *MMPI* which has been found in a number of studies consistently to differentiate delinquents and non-delinquents (107, 78). Another discriminator is the Socialization scale of the *California Personality Inventory* (58, 61); another is the already mentioned *Delinquency Potential Scale*. These studies themselves demonstrate that there are measurable personality differences between delinquents and non-delinquents.

In a 1961 review, Argyle points to a large number of reported differences between delinquents and non-delinquents on personality measures (4). These are enumerated under categories of tests of cheating and of moral values; measures of extra-punitiveness; of attitude toward parents, toward authority, and toward peer groups; measures of level of aspiration, of motor control, time span, compulsiveness, and emotional maturity; measures of cruelty and aggressiveness, and of skill and social perception; and measures of neuroticism.

Still other personality measures have identified variables discriminating delinquent and non-delinquent subjects. Differences in ability between delinquent and non-delinquent boys were described by Zakolski (156). Another study demonstrated that institutionalized delinquent boys obtained lower scores than controls on a "perceptual-completion" measure (89). Differences in measured levels of aspiration were described in yet another study (20), and differences in Porteus Maze Test performance have been identified in still another (30). Differences were reported in Rorschach responses by delinquent and normal adolescents in the Glueck study; the same study reports a high degree of discrimination between delinquent and normal Rorschach records when these are made by skilled clinical workers (126).

There are promising results, though they do not hold forth much hope of immediate applicability. Often the data describe differences between delinquent and control samples which may not be assumed to be representative of the general population, and the problem of the base rate is ignored. This does not mean they are unimportant in pointing the way to improvement of predictive efficiency. The utility of discriminators such as these in a prediction study which includes adequate investigation of the validity problem, and investigates the consequences of application of realistic base rates, can only be settled by the empirical study which is needed.

In a lengthy history of parole prediction studies, a number of consistently reported differentiators of parole performance criteria have been found. The most useful guides to prediction of parole violation behavior are indices of past criminal behavior. This result, discouraging in terms of treatment concerns, finds support in most parole prediction studies (56, 38, 138, 15, 18, 37, 126, 142, 109, 98).

Offenders against persons have been found at least since 1923 to be generally better risks, so far as parole violations are concerned, than are offenders against property (147). Glaser includes an excellent review of evidence, from a variety of jurisdictions, that leaves little room for doubt as to the predictive nature of offense classifications (37).

In general, the probability of parole violation decreases with age (45, 41, 18, 122, 155). The contention that offenders who are older at release are less likely to return to crime is supported by parolee data from the states of Wisconsin, New York, California, and the United States Federal System. Similar results have been found, as Glaser notes, for many decades, and in numerous jurisdictions, both in the United States and abroad.

Histories of opiate drug use or of alcoholic difficulties are unfavorable prognostic signs for parole performance; this has been found for both male and female parolees (49, 52, 56). Burgess and Tibbetts found a "drunkard" classification to yield an unfavorable sign, as did Ohlin. Similarly, Schiedt considered alcohol use important. The social types from earlier work were redefined by Glaser into seven general categories, "toward which the subjects seemed to be developing prior to their offenses," taking account of alcoholic difficulties.*

The use of aliases has been found, in California studies, to be predictive of unfavorable parole performance among both male and female adult prisoners. When the offender's history reflects a criminal record for others in the person's immediate family, this too is an unfavorable prognostic sign.

Recent studies indicate that a combination of life history information, which provides the main basis for prediction in most studies, when combined with data from personality testing may result in a superior prediction of parole violations (64, 57). Measures of "social maturity," have been found helpful in prediction in a number of studies. "Social Maturity" has been defined variously, but in each case has had its roots particularly in studies by Gough (60), by Gough and Peterson (63), and by Grant (65).

* A review of literature concerning the predictive utility of age, offense, prior record, race, intelligence, and body build is given by Glaser.

Clinical Assessment as an Avenue
to Improvement of Prediction

Comparisons of empirically derived and "subjective experience" derived behavior predictions, along with the extensive literature dealing with this topic, have been well reviewed by Meehl (100) and by Gough (62). When statistical prediction devices are pitted against clinical judgment and the accuracy of prediction compared, statistical prediction has generally fared better. A less competitive, more collaborative, attack on prediction problems is needed.

As indicated twenty-five years ago by Horst, "The statistician and the case study investigator can make mutual gains if they'll quit quarreling with each other and begin borrowing from each other (80)." In the same vein, DeGroot has argued there is more to be gained through efforts to improve statistical prediction by way of clinical prediction than through continuation of arguments or comparisons of the predictive accuracy of the two approaches (29). This suggests that the clinician be given the best available statistical prediction device, and that he then attempt to improve, by any means, upon the accuracy of predictions which may be made through its use. When it can be demonstrated that he can do so, then the attempt should be made to define adequately the information used in establishing the expectancy. If this can be done, then a reliable measure can be developed; and ultimately it can be included in the statistical prediction device.

Prediction devices, developed by any method, can do no more than summarize experience. They can do this quite objectively and efficiently; and therefore they can provide an adequate means of summarizing that which is known about the prediction of delinquency or crime. Possible predictors which are as yet only vaguely felt or ill-defined may be refined into more adequate hypotheses which then may be tested for possible inclusion in the prediction device. In this way, a means is provided not only for the summarization of knowledge but for its extension.

Clinical Assessment and Delinquency Prediction

Personality assessment techniques of a different variety are in widespread use in schools, in private clinical practice, in evaluations prepared for courts, and diagnostic studies in detention. They are used in making decisions about individuals, often on the basis of assumptions concerning predictive validity with respect to future delinquency, criminal behavior, or probation or parole violation. A whole literature of clinical psychology, psychiatry, and social work is relevant to the problem of predictions based upon interviews, projective tests, or other samples of the person's behavior. How can the utility of this vast array of assessment methods be considered briefly?

Cronbach and Gleser have suggested an important, useful distinction between two general types of assessment methods (27, 26). Their discussion is based upon a model from information theory in which two aspects of any communication system are distinguished: bandwidth and fidelity.

Some procedures, like the interview, the psychologist's report from projective testing, written evaluations prepared by clinical or custodial institution staff, or a social history report, provide a wide variety of information. Each of the "wide band" procedures is characteristically found to be unsatisfactory, by any usual standards of reliability and validity, for prediction of specific behavior. This does not mean they are useless; it means that the wider coverage is purchased at the price of low dependability (fidelity). What purposes, then, do these procedures fulfill?

Evidence that interviews, for example, are useful in prediction, is preponderantly negative; repeatedly, comparisons have shown statistical prediction devices to be more valid. But, as Cronbach and Gleser point out, even the most forceful advocates of statistical prediction insist on an interview when *they* must make a decision. Since interviewer judgments disagree notoriously with one another and have little relationship to outcomes, we must ask why we persist in interviewing.

The interviewer can address any aspect of the other person's personality, character and life situation. His delinquency history, employment record, relations with his family, group identifications, feelings about authority, his disappointments and expectations are some frequent topics. The interview may reveal something of his abilities and interests, his sexual attitudes, his major conflicts, defenses against anxiety, his values and his plans. It is a sequential process which can turn in any direction to follow leads, unexpected but judged important during the interview, that any structured objective test or prediction procedure cannot. This flexibility and potential scope are its virtue, because by covering a broad range of information it may shed light on *many different decisions*. It is clear that the interview may not bear only on a single problem or relate to a single criterion classification we wish to predict. It may suggest a further treatment plan, particular areas of weakness to be guarded against, and special potentials for favorable adjustment in certain situations.

The "wide band" methods are exhaustive but undependable; that is, they cover more of the ground we wish to know about—but any one prediction from this wide range of information cannot be depended upon to be valid. The narrow range procedures may give more accurate information with respect to *one* decision outcome when adequate validation data are available; but they give no guidance at all with respect to *other* decision outcomes.

What about "narrow band" procedures? These include any objective psychological test with established validity for prediction of a single behavioral criterion, parole or probation violation prediction devices, some delinquency prediction scales, certain college aptitude tests, and the like. Their virtue is dependability (high fidelity)—compared with the interview and other broad scope methods. Their limitation is that they cover relatively little ground; that is, they bear only on that part of the decision which is concerned with the specific question they help answer.

The narrow scope (and therefore both the potential power and limited utility) of such a prediction device is apparent. Though it gives a more dependable prediction of outcome than generally obtained by broad band methods, it is relevant only to the *specific* criterion defined for the purpose of study. Unless it has been shown valid also for predicting other specific outcomes of interest to the decision maker, it provides no guidance for decisions based on expected behavior in other areas. It may tell nothing about appropriate treatment placement.

In general, a narrow range procedure such as an objective test, delinquency scale, or parole prediction device is more reliable (that is, different people will tend to agree on the scores for various others). It is more valid (that is, it predicts better). But it covers only a limited sector of all behavior in which there is interest. In short, it has limited range but high fidelity; if the narrow scope is unrecognized, the procedure may provide a good answer to the wrong question.

How can these two types of information be profitably used together? We wish to utilize the best features of each, recognizing the limitations of both, in order to make optimal decisions on the basis of available knowledge.

The optimal use of both, however, will depend upon the nature of the decision problem. It will depend upon the resources available, the alternative courses of action, and the goals of crime and delinquency programs. This suggests that optimal procedures for one agency might not be the best for others with differing resources, alternatives, or goals. Recently developed methods in applied statistical decision theory are pertinent to this problem; and development of applications of these methods to delinquency and crime prevention, treatment, and control problems offers one of the most promising available routes to increased effectiveness of the social agencies concerned.

Applications of Prediction Methods

Despite the painstaking studies, item analyses, and validation studies implied by the preceding pages, all currently available prediction methods still have only relatively low predictive power. In most instances the problem of any application is confounded by the base rate problem and by inadequate cross-validation in samples from populations in which practical applications might be proposed.

The routine use of any available instruments in programs for early identification and treatment of delinquency has been regarded by many as somewhat dangerous on one or more of three grounds. First, the available validity data are questionable. Second, there is the base rate problem; and finally, there is apprehension concerning the "self-fulfilling prophecy." The latter concern is with the possible negative effects of a classification procedure itself upon the persons classified, through labeling them undesirable. Toby asks:

How can early identification and intensive treatment programs avoid "self-fulfilling prophecies?"

If the treatment program concentrates its efforts on youngsters who are especially vulnerable to delinquency, how can it justify its discriminatory policy except by stigmatizing pre-delinquents? And may not the delinquency-producing effects of the stigmatizing equal or exceed the delinquency-preventing benefits of the treatment? (140)

In any proposed application, the question of validity of prediction is only one component of the decision problem. The objective of the decision should be to minimize errors and to make them less costly.

In the absence of a perfection which is not expected, any prediction (made by any procedure) is uncertain; the result will be errors of two kinds. Some persons will be expected to be delinquents who will not be identified later as delinquent. Some will be expected to be non-delinquent but later will be found to be delinquent. The concept of the "self-fulfilling prophecy" calls attention to the probability that the two types of error may not have equal consequences. It suggests that it may be much more damaging to treat as delinquents those persons misclassified as expected delinquents than to treat pre-delinquents as if they were not expected to be delinquent.

The application of statistical decision theory methods as a means of minimizing errors in placement or selection decisions will require the assignment of values to the outcomes, i.e., to the consequences, of the decision alternatives; the positive and negative values of outcomes of both correct and incorrect decisions must be considered. This points again to the need for attention to problems of measurement of the consequences of decisions, that is, to the criterion problem. It will require careful and explicit statement of the objectives of any given decision, but this may be a healthy exercise for the decision makers concerned.

Programs of early identification and prevention of delinquency have been recently reviewed by Kvaraceus (92). Pointing to the low predictive power of available instruments, he indicates that "as yet, no simple, practical, and valid tests for delinquency prediction can be found on the test market." He notes also a growing conviction that separate techniques or tests must be developed for middle-class youngsters and for lower-class children and that it may be easier to predict certain types of delinquents compared with others.

Related suggestions are made by Toby. Along with demonstrating that in both the Cambridge-Somerville Youth Study (113) and the New York City Youth Board Prediction Study (135) attention to the social context can improve the accuracy of predictions, he discusses the needs for integration of prediction efforts within a consistent theoretical framework.

The entire July 1962 issue of the journal of *Crime and Delinquency* was given to discussion of parole prediction devices. Most of this discussion relates to the applicability of parole prediction methods to individual selection for parole. Before discussing this role, however, it should be noted that parole prediction methods have demonstrated utility (in one practical situation) in broad screening programs and for parole supervision caseload assignments (50).

In the first application, as an aid to a program intended to reduce confinement costs, a large prison population was screened, first by the parole prediction device, then by further clinical criteria. The result was a small group of men referred for parole consideration at a date earlier than originally scheduled, with substantial monetary savings and no increase in parole violations, as a result. In the second application, the parole prediction measure aided the establishment of minimal supervision caseloads for both male and female parolees. Persons classed as having a high probability of successful parole completion received minimal supervision (experience having demonstrated that these cases may be given less supervision with no increase in the parole violation rate) with the result that parole workers might be assigned to spend their effort in areas where help is more needed. Again, a substantial saving of money was reported.

When applications to parole selection are considered, in the light of the "band width-fidelity" concept discussed above, it appears that the best use of prediction methods will depend upon not only the established validity of the prediction method but also upon the goals of a particular decision in a specific social agency. Ultimately, the contribution of any prediction method to a particular decision process should be assessed in reference to available decision alternatives and in terms of costs and utilities (27).

The most useful role, and at any rate the most immediately feasible application, for prediction methods may be found not in selection or placement applications but in treatment evaluation research (98, 51, 52, 50, 57). Studies of effectiveness of any treatment or control program may be conducted according to experimental or statistical designs. Experimental designs provide the most rigorous approach. In the field of crime and delinquency, however, this approach often is beset with problems or is simply not feasible. When this is the case, statistical means of control must be substituted for the lacking experimental controls. The prediction method can provide a measure of the expected performance for any group of subjects. Then the expected and actual outcomes, for a specific criterion classification, may be compared. One such approach may be described as follows:

Prediction devices, to estimate the likelihood of agency program outcomes, first must be developed and tested. These represent experience with various groups of people, summarized by appropriate statistical methods; they provide a way of quantifying expectations based upon past experience. They are needed for application to each person *before* assignment to treatment. When persons are assigned to specific kinds of treatments, then we may ask whether the actual outcome is more or less favorable than *expected* (from past experience with other, similar groups). Since we wish to find treatments that improve the chances of success, we will be pleased if the prediction device is made invalid by helpful treatment.

If the outcome following treatment can be predicted not only before treatment but *regardless* of treatment, then it is very hard to argue that this treatment makes any difference with respect to the specific outcome studied.

However, persons assigned to a given treatment may "succeed" (or "fail") significantly more often than expected from their risk classifications. If the validity of the prediction device has been established on other groups, then the observed differences in outcomes must be due to treatment, or to factors associated with treatment, or to both.

Further research, using experimental designs, might then be developed in order to test hypotheses about the source of the difference. Meanwhile, decision makers at least can be made aware of the relationship—positive, negative, or none—between the program and the outcomes. The most useful role for prediction methods, therefore, will be found when their development and validation are studied continuously as one component of an agency-wide information system for assessment of the effectiveness of programs.

Implications

In each social agency responsible for crime and delinquency treatment and control programs, a systematic study of "natural variation" is needed. Improvement of predictive efficiency and evaluations of differing treatment alternatives are closely related problems; in a concerted effort they can be attacked together. The main requirements are:

1. Systematic collection of reliable data for "predictor candidates" at critical decision points within the total system.
2. Repeated studies of the relations between predictor categories and criterion categories defined in terms of agency goals.
3. Repeated validation of any prediction methods devised.
4. Periodic determination, on the basis of prediction methods, of expected outcomes of various programs within the agency.
5. Comparisons of criterion outcomes expected (by the prediction method) and observed (in actual practice).
6. Development of experimental programs to identify the sources of discrepancies between expected and observed results, when such differences are found.
7. Periodic provision, to decision makers of the agency, of information concerning the probable criterion outcomes of program decision alternatives.

In any agency, a continuous cycle of development of prediction methods, repeated validation, comparisons of program outcomes, modification of practice, research, and practice is needed. This requires systematic collection of information over the total system and repeated study of relationships to correctional goals. Prediction methods should occupy a prominent place in this cycle, primarily because they are needed as tools for the assessment of programs.

The next need will be for collaborative studies by agencies in various jurisdictions and by agencies whose responsibilities focus at different points in the continuum of correctional services from arrest to discharge. Examples of areas in which careful development of prediction methods, and extensive validation studies, are needed may be found throughout this continuum. Applications may be envisioned, but not yet proposed, as aids in selection or placement and the research applications of prediction methods can be immediately helpful.

Potential applications may be found at each stage of the process of the administration of justice. Problems of early identification of delinquency have been reviewed briefly. Immediately upon arrest of an alleged offender, other prediction problems arise. The general problem of "release on recognizance" includes at least the prediction question of appearance for trial. This problem demands (in fairness to the courts and to the accused) much more empirical study than ever has been attempted. Prediction of probation outcomes has received little study, despite the needs for assessment of variations in criterion outcomes associated with probation supervision alternatives. Prediction methods, with adequate validation, are needed for evaluation studies of a variety of community treatment programs. They are needed equally as tools for assessment of the wide variety of programs conducted in confinement, in detention, in jails, or in prisons. They are needed as aids in determining probable outcomes of alternative programs after institutional release.

This review shows that work is needed particularly in a number of areas:

1. Improvement of measures of the criteria of delinquency or crime to be predicted is required. This includes the development of more reliable measures, more specifically related to the behavior of offenders, and the assessment of reliability over time. There is a broader question, however, of explicit identification of the goals of social agencies concerned with delinquency and its correction. This general problem has led Wilkins to remark that one of the most important problems is not *how* to predict but *what* to predict (151).

2. Cross-validation studies of available measures in order to test their applicability in various jurisdictions are needed, and repeated assessment of validity along with social change will be in order.

3. Development of prediction measures for specific subgroups, rather than for samples of total populations of children or of offenders is apparently a promising route to improved prediction.

4. Empirical comparisons of various methods in use for combining predictors are needed.

5. Leads from studies demonstrating a variety of discriminators of delinquent and non-delinquent samples should be followed up systematically to improve current prediction methods.

6. Attempts to improve statistical prediction methods by testing hypotheses from clinical practice represent another avenue to improved prediction.

7. Studies of specific decision functions, utilizing recently developed tools in applied decision theory, are needed at various points in the correctional

process, wherever decisions are made about offenders. These will require assessment of the social and monetary costs and values associated with errors and successes along the correctional continuum.

8. Prediction methods should be built into the information system of each social agency responsible for custody, treatment, or release of offenders. This can permit necessary, repeated validation studies, or necessary modifications, of available prediction tools. It can permit programs for systematic feedback to decision makers concerning the predictive relevance of information used in arriving at individual decisions. It can provide helpful tools for evaluations of programs, thereby enabling administrators to assess the probable consequences of program decisions.

There is much to be learned about the prediction of delinquency and crime, and with presently available instruments caution is ordinarily required when applications are proposed. Yet much has been learned; methods are available for improvement of these instruments, and we should use them. The resulting prediction methods can summarize that which is known. More important, they can provide very useful tools for discovery of that which is not yet known concerning effective interventions to prevent delinquency and crime.

REFERENCES

1. Adkins, B. C., *Construction and Analysis of Achievement Tests*, Washington, D.C.: Superintendent of Documents, 1947.

2. Adkins, B. C., "Selecting Public Employees," *Pub. Personnel Rev.*, 1956, 17, 259–267.

3. Ahman, J. S., "An Application of Fisher's Discriminant Function in the Classification of Students," *J. Educ. Psychol.*, 1955, 46, 184–188.

4. Argyle, M., "A New Approach to the Classification of Delinquents with Implications for Treatment," in *Enquiries Concerning Kinds of Treatment for Kinds of Delinquents*, Monograph No. 2, Sacramento, California: Board of Corrections, July 1961, 15–26.

5. Ballard, K. B. Jr., Bobinski, C. A., Grant, J. D., *A Pilot Study of Factors in Retraining Which Change Delinquency Attitudes*, Third Technical Report, Rehabilitation Research, U.S. Naval Retraining Command, Camp Elliott, San Diego, California, Jan. 1956.

6. Ballard K. B. Jr., and Gottfredson, D. M., *Predictive Attribute Analysis and Prediction of Parole Performance*, Vacaville, California: Institute for the Study of Crime and Delinquency, Dec. 1963.

7. Bechtoldt, H. P., "Selection," in Stevens, S. S., *Handbook of Experimental Psychology*, New York: Wiley, 1951, pp. 1237–1266.

8. Black, B. J., and Glick, S. J., *Recidivism at the Hawthorne Cedar Knolls School: Predicted vs. Actual Outcome for Delinquent Boys*, Hawthorne-Cedars, Research Monograph No. 2, New York: Jewish Board of Guardians, 1952.

9. Blum, R. N., "Predicting Criminal Behavior: An Annotated Bibliography," *J. of Corr. Psychol.*, Monograph No. 1, 1957.

10. Bower, *The Education of Emotionally Handicapped Children*, a report to the California Legislature prepared pursuant to Sec. 1, of Chap. 2385, Statutes of 1957, Sacramento, California: State Dept. of Education, March 1961.

11. Brandon, G. E., and Potter, A. K., "An Application of the Linear Discriminant Function," *Rural Sociol.*, 1953, 18, 321–326.

12. Bridgman, P. W., *The Logic of Modern Physics*, New York: Macmillan, 1932.

13. Brogden, H. E., "On the Interpretation of the Correlation Coefficient as a Measure of Predictive Efficiency," *J. of Educ. Psychol.*, 1946, 37, 65–76.

14. Brogden, H. E., "Variation in Test Validity with Variation in the Distribution of Item Difficulties, Number of Items, and Degree of Their Intercorrelation," *Psychometrika*, 1946, 11, 197–214.

15. Burgess, E. W., in Bruce, Burgess and Harno, *The Working of the Indeterminate Sentence Law and the Parole System in Illinois*, Springfield: Illinois State Board of Parole, 1928, 205–249.

16. Burgess, E. W., and Cottrell, L. S. Jr., *Predicting Success or Failure in Marriage*, New York: Prentice-Hall, 1939.

17. Burgess, E. W., and Wallin, T., *Engagement and Marriage*, Philadelphia: Lippincott, 1953.

18. Caldwell, N. G., "Preview of a New Type of Probation Study Made in Alabama," *Federal Probation*, June 1951.

19. Carroll, J. B., "The Effect of Difficulty and Chance Success on Correlations between Items or between Tests," *Psychometrika*, 1945, 10, 1–19.

20. Cassell, R. N., and Van Vorst, R., "Level of Aspiration as a Means for Discerning Between 'In Prison' and 'Out of Prison' Groups of Individuals," *J. Soc. Psychol.*, 1954, 40, 121–135.

21. Cattell, R. B., "Measurement vs. Intuition in Applied Psychology," *Charact. and Personal.*, 1937, 6, 114–131.

22. Craig, M. M., and Glick, S. J., "Ten Years' Experience with the Glueck Social Prediction Table," *Crime and Delinquency*, July 1963, 249–261.

23. Craig, M. M., and Glick, S. J., *A Manual of Procedures for the Application of the Glueck Prediction Table*, New York: New York City Youth Board, Office of the Mayor, 1964.

24. Crawford, A. B., and Burnham, B. S., *Forecasting College Achievement*, New Haven: Yale University Press, 1946.

25. Cronbach, L. J., "Test Reliability: Its Meaning and Determination," *Psychometrika*, 1947, 12, 1–16.

26. Cronbach, L. J., *Essentials of Psychological Testing, 2nd Ed.*, New York: Harper, 1960.

27. Cronbach, L. J., and Gleser, G. C., *Psychological Tests and Personnel Decisions*, Urbana: University of Illinois Press, 1957.

28. Cureton, E. E., "Recipe for a Cookbook," *Psychol. Bull.*, 1957, 54, 494–497.

29. De Groot, A. D., *Via Clinical to Statistical Prediction*, invited address, Western Psychological Association, San Jose, April 1960.

30. Doctor, R. S., and Winder, C. L., "Delinquent vs. Non-Delinquent Performance on the Porteus Qualitative Maze Test," *J. Consult. Psychol.*, 1954, 18, 71–73.

31. Duncan, O. D., Ohlin, L. E., Reiss, A. J., and Stanton, H. R., "Formal Devices for Making Selection Decisions," *Amer. J. Sociol.*, 1953, 48, 573–584.

32. Duncan, O. D., and Duncan, B., "A Methodological Analysis of Segregation Indexes," *Amer. Sociol. Rev.*, 1955, 20, 210–217.

33. Ferguson, G. A., "On the Theory of Test Discrimination," *Psychometrika*, 1949, 14, 61–68.

34. Flanagan, J. C., "General Considerations in the Selections of Test Items and a Short Method of Estimating the Product Moment Coefficient from the Data at the Tails of the Distribution," *J. Educ. Psychol.*, 1939, 30, 674–680.

35. Flanagan, J. C., "The Aviation Psychology Program in the Army Air Forces," *Army Aviation Psychology Research Program Report 1*, Washington, D.C.: U.S. Government Printing Office, 1948.

36. Gillin, J. L., "Predicting Outcome of Adult Probationers in Wisconsin," *Amer. Sociol. Rev.*, 1950, 15, 550–553.

37. Glaser, D., *The Effectiveness of a Prison and Parole System*, New York: Bobbs-Merrill, 1964, Chapter 3.

38. Glueck, S., and Glueck, E. T., *500 Criminal Careers*, New York: Knopf, 1930.

39. Glueck, S., and Glueck, E. T., *Five Hundred Delinquent Women*, New York: Knopf, 1934.

40. Glueck, S., and Glueck, E. T., *One Thousand Juvenile Delinquents*, Cambridge: Harvard University Press, 1934.

41. Glueck, S., and Glueck, E. T., *Juvenile Delinquents Grown Up*. New York: The Commonwealth Fund, 1940.

42. Glueck, S., and Glueck, E. T., *Criminal Careers in Retrospect*, New York: The Commonwealth Fund, 1943.

43. Glueck, S., and Glueck, E. T., *Unravelling Juvenile Delinquency*, New York: The Commonwealth Fund, 1950.

44. Glueck, S., "Pre-Sentence Examination of Offenders to Aid In Choosing a Method of Treatment," *J. Crim. Law Criminol.*, 1951, 41, 717–731.

45. Glueck, S., and Glueck, E. T., *Later Criminal Careers*, New York: The Commonwealth Fund, 1957.

46. Glueck, S., and Glueck, E. T., *Predicting Delinquency and Crime*, Cambridge: Harvard University Press, 1959.

47. Glueck, E. T., "Efforts to Identify Delinquents," *Federal Probation*, 24, June, 1960, 49–56.

48. Glueck, E. T., "Toward Improving the Identification of Delinquents," *J. Crim. Law Criminol.*, 1962, 53, 164–170.

49. Gottfredson, D. M., *A Shorthand Formula for Base Expectancies*, Sacramento, California: California Department of Corrections, Dec., 1962.

50. Gottfredson, D. M., "The Practical Application of Research," *Canadian J. Corr.*, 5, 4, Oct., 1963, 212–228.

51. Gottfredson, D. M., and Bonds, J. A., *A Manual for Intake Base Expectancy Scoring (Form CDC BE61A)*, Sacramento, California: California Department of Corrections, April, 1961.

52. Gottfredson, D. M., Ballard, K. B., Jr., and Bonds, J. A., *Base Expectancy: California Institution for Women*, Sacramento, California: Institute for the Study of Crime and Delinquency and California Department of Corrections, Sept., 1962.

53. Gottfredson, D. M., Ballard, K. B., Jr., and Lane, L., *Association Analysis in a Prison Sample and Prediction of Parole Performance*, Vacaville, California: Institute for the Study of Crime and Delinquency, Nov., 1963.

54. Gottfredson, D. M., Ballard, K. B., Jr., Mannering, J. W., and Babst, D. V., *Wisconsin Base Expectancies for Reformatories and Prisons*, Vacaville, California: Institute for the Study of Crime and Delinquency, June, 1965.

55. Gottfredson, D. M., and Ballard, K. B., Jr., *Association Analysis, Predictive Attribute Analysis, and Parole Behavior*, paper presented at the Western Psychological Association meetings, Portland, Oregon, April, 1964.

56. Gottfredson, D. M., and Ballard, K. B., Jr., *The Validity of Two Parole Prediction Scales: An 8 Year Follow Up Study*, Vacaville, California, 1965.

57. Gottfredson, D. M., and Ballard, K. B., Jr., *Testing Prison and Parole Decisions*, unpublished manuscript, July, 1966.

58. Gough, H. G., "A Sociological Theory of Psychopathy," *Amer. Sociol. Rev.*, 1948, 53, 359–366.

59. Gough, H. G., "What Determines the Academic Achievement of High School Students?," *J. Educ. Res.*, 1953, 321–331.

60. Gough, H. G., *Systematic Validation of a Test for Delinquency*, paper presented at

the American Psychological Association meeting, New York, New York, September, 1954.

61. Gough, H. G., "Theory and Measurement of Socialization," *J. Consult. Psychol.*, 1960, 24, 23–30.

62. Gough, H. G., "Clinical vs. Statistical Prediction in Psychology," Chapter 9, in Postman, L., Ed., *Psychology in the Making*, New York: Knopf, 1962, 526–584.

63. Gough, H. G., and Peterson, D. R., "The Identification and Measurement of Predispositional Factors in Crime and Delinquency," *J. of Consult. Psychol.*, 1952, 26, 207–212.

64. Gough, H. G., Wenk, E. A., and Rosynko, V. V., "Parole Outcome as Predicted from the CPI, the MMPI, and a Base Expectancy Table," *J. Abnorm. Psych.*, 70, 6, December, 1965.

65. Grant, J. D., *The Navy's Attack on the Problems of Delinquency*, Rehabilitation Research, U.S. Naval Retraining Command, Camp Elliott, San Diego, California, (Mimeo.), April 6, 1955.

66. Grant, J. D., Bobinski, C. A., and Ballard, K. B., Jr., *Factors in Retraining Which Affect Delinquency Proneness*, Fifth Technical Report, Rehabilitation Research, U.S. Naval Retraining Command, Camp Elliott, San Diego, California, January, 1956.

67. Grygier, T., *Treatment Variables in Non-linear Prediction*, paper presented to the Joint Annual Meeting of the American Society of Criminology and the American Association for the Advancement of Science, Montreal, December, 1964.

68. Guilford, J. P., *Personality*, New York: McGraw-Hill, 1959.

69. Gulliksen, H., "The Relation of Item Difficulty and Inter-Item Correlation to Test Variance and Reliability," *Psychometrika*, 1945, 10, 79–91.

70. Gunderson, E. K., Grant, J. D., and Ballard, K. B., Jr., *The Prediction of Military Delinquency*, San Diego, California: U.S. Naval Retraining Command (Mimeo.) 1956.

71. Gunderson, E. K., and Ballard, K. B., Jr., *Discriminant Analysis of Variables Related to Nonconformity in Naval Recruits*, Eleventh Technical Report, Rehabilitation Research, U.S. Naval Retraining Command, Camp Elliott, San Diego, California (Mimeo.), August, 1959.

72. Guttman, Louis, "Mathematical and Tabulation Techniques. Supplemental Study B," in Horst, P., *The Prediction of Personal Adjustment*, New York: Social Science Research Council, 1941, 253–364.

73. Guttman, L., "A Basis for Analyzing Test-Retest Reliability," *Psychometrika*, 1945, 10, 255–282.

74. Guttman, L., "Test-Retest Reliability of Qualitative Data," *Psychometrika*, 1946, 9, 81–95.

75. Hall, C. L., *Aptitude Testing*, New York: World, 1928.

76. Hanley, C., "The Gauging of Criminal Predispositions," in Toch, H., *Legal and Criminal Psychology*, New York: Holt, Rinehart and Winston, 1961, 213–242.

77. Hathaway, S. R., and McKinley, J. C., *The Minnesota Multiphasic Personality Inventory Manual* (Revised), New York: The Psychological Corp., 1951.

78. Hathaway, S. R., and Monachesi, E. D., *Analyzing and Predicting Juvenile Delinquency with the MMPI*, New York: The Psychological Corp., 1954.

79. Hathaway, S. R., and Monachesi, E. D., "The Personalities of Pre-Delinquent Boys," *J. Crim. Law Criminol.*, 1957, 48, 149–163.

80. Horst, P., *The Prediction of Personal Adjustment*, New York: Social Science Research Council Bulletin No. 48, 1941.

81. Horst, P., "Mathematical Contributions. Supplemental Study E," *The Prediction of Personal Adjustment*, Social Science Research Council, New York: 194, 407–447.

82. Horst, P., "A Generalized Expression for the Reliability of Measures," *Psychometrika*, 1949, 14, 21–32.
83. Hunt, H. F., "Clinical Methods: Psychodiagnostics," in Stone, C. B., and Taylor, V. W., Eds., *Annual Review of Psychology*, Vol. 1, Stanford: Annual Reviews, Inc., 1950, 207–220.
84. Hunt, W. A., "An Actuarial Approach to Clinical Judgment," in Bass, B. N., and Berg, I. A., *Objective Approaches to Personality Study*, Princeton: Van Nostrand, 1959, 169–191.
85. Ives, V., Grant, M. Q., and Ballard, K. B., Jr., *Interpersonal Variables Related to Recidivism in Military Delinquency*, Eighth Technical Report, Rehabilitation Research, U.S. Naval Retraining Command, Camp Elliott, San Diego, California, (Mimeo.), December, 1957.
86. Jacobson, J. L., and Wirt, R. D., *Studies in Psychological and Sociological Variables in State Prison Inmates, Section No. 1, 18 Variable Profile*, Minneapolis: University of Minnesota, December, 1961.
87. James, W., "Pragmatism. A New Name for Some Old Ways of Thinking," 1907, reprinted as "Pragmatism's Conception of Truth," in *Essays in Pragmatism*, New York, Hafner, 1955.
88. Jarrett, R. F., "Percent Increase in Output of Selected Personnel as an Index to Test Efficiency," *J. Appl. Psychol.*, 1948, 32, 135–145.
89. Jones, D. S., Livson, N. H., and Sarbin, T., "Perceptual Completion Behavior in Juvenile Delinquents," *Percept. Mot. Skills*, 1955, 5, 141–146.
90. Kirby, B. C., "Parole Prediction Using Multiple Correlation," *Amer. J. Sociol.*, 1953–4, 59, 539–550.
91. Kvaraceus, W. C., "Forecasting Juvenile Delinquency: A Three Year Experiment," *Exceptional Children*, XVIII, April, 1961, 429–435.
92. Kvaraceus, W. C., "Programs of Early Identification and Prevention of Delinquency," *Social Deviancy Among Youth*, 65th *Yearbook of the National Society for the Study of Education*, Chicago: National Society for the Study of Education, 1966, 189–220.
93. Lackman, R., *The Predictive Use of the Linear Discriminant Function in Naval Aviation Cadet Selection*, U.S. Naval Sch. Aviat. Med. Res. Rep. 1953, Rep. II N.M. 001057.16.02–11p.
94. Lunden, W. A., "Forecast for 1955: Predicting Prison Population," *The Presidio*, 1952, 19, No. 2.
95. MacNaughten-Smith, P., "The Classification of Individuals by the Possession of Attributes Associated with a Criterion," *Biometrics*, June, 1963.
96. McArthur, C., "Analyzing the Clinical Process," *J. Counsel. Psychol.*, 1954, 1, 203–207.
97. Mannering, J. W., and Babst, D. V., *Wisconsin Base Expectancies for Adult Male Parolees*, Progress Report No. 4, Wisconsin State Department of Public Welfare, Bureau of Research and Division of Corrections, April, 1963.
98. Mannheim, H., and Wilkins, L. T., *Prediction Methods in Relation to Borstal Training*, London: Her Majesty's Stationery Office, 1955.
99. May, M. A., "Predicting Academic Success," *J. Educ. Psychol.*, 1923, 14, 429–440.
100. Meehl, P. E., *Clinical vs. Statistical Prediction*, Minneapolis: University of Minnesota Press, 1954.
101. Meehl, P. E., "Clinical vs. Actuarial Prediction," in *Proceedings, 1955 Invitational Conference on Testing Problems*, Princeton: Educational Testing Service, 1956, 136–141.
102. Meehl, P. E., "When Should We Use Our Heads Instead of the Formula?" *J. Counsel. Psychol.*, 1957, 4, 268–273.
103. Meehl, P. E., "A Comparison of Conditions with Five Statistical Methods of Identifying MMPI Profiles," *J. Counsel. Psychol.*, 1959, 6, 102–109.
104. Meehl, P. E., and Rosen, A., "Antecedent Probability and the Efficiency of Psy-

chometric Signs, Patterns, or Cutting Scores," *Psychol. Bull.*, 1955, 52, 194–215.
105. Meehl, P. E., "The Tie That Binds," *J. Counsel. Psychol.*, 1956, 3, 163–164, 171, 173.
106. Monachesi, E. D., *Prediction Factors in Probation*, Hanover, N. H.: The Sociological Press, 1932.
107. Monachesi, E. D., "Personality Characteristics and Socio-Economic Status of Delinquents and Non-Delinquents," *J. Crim. Law Criminol.*, 1950, 40, 570–583.
108. Ohlin, L. E., and Duncan, O. D., "The Efficiency of Prediction in Criminology," *Amer. J. Sociol.*, 1949, 54, 441–451.
109. Ohlin, L. E., *Selection for Parole: A Manual of Parole Prediction*, New York: Russell Sage Foundation, 1951.
110. Ohlin, L. E., *Some Parole Prediction Problems in the United States*, paper presented at the Third International Congress of Criminology, London, September, 1955.
111. Paton, J. H., "Predicting Prison Adjustment with the Minnesota Multiphasic Personality Inventory," *J. Clin. Psychol.*, 1958, 14, 213–308.
112. Porteus, S. D., *Qualitative Performance in the Maze Test*, The Psychological Corp.
113. Powers, E., and Witmer, H., *An Experiment in the Prevention of Delinquency: The Cambridge-Summerville Youth Study*, New York: Columbia University Press, 1951.
114. Quay, H., and Peterson, D. R., "A Brief Scale for Juvenile Delinquency," *J. Clin. Psychol.*, 14, April, 1958, 139–142.
115. Reed, R. R., "An Empirical Study in the Reduction of the Number of Variables Used in Prediction. Supplementary Study C" in Horst, P., *The Prediction of Social Adjustment*, New York: Social Science Research Council, 1941.
116. Reichenbach, M., *Experience and Prediction*, Chicago: University of Chicago Press, 1938.
117. Reiss, A. J., Jr., "The Accuracy, Efficiency, and Validity of a Prediction Instrument," unpublished Ph. D. dissertation, Dept. of Sociology, University of Chicago, 1949.
118. Reiss, A. J., Jr., "Delinquency as a Failure of Personal and Social Control," *Amer. Sociol. Rev.*, 1951, 16, 196–207.
119. Reiss, A. J., Jr., "Unravelling Juvenile Delinquency: II, An Appraisal of the Research Methods," *Amer. J. Sociol.*, 1951, 57, 115–121.
120. Richardson, M. W., "The Combination of Measures. Supplemental Study D," in Horst, P., *The Prediction of Personal Adjustment*, New York: Social Science Research Council, 1941, 379–401.
121. Rubin, S., "Unravelling Juvenile Delinquency: I. Illusions in a Research Project Using Match Pairs," *Amer. J. Sociol.*, 1951, 57, 107–114.
122. Saline T., "Recidivism and Maturation," *National Probation and Parole Association Journal*, 4, 3, July, 1958, 241–250.
123. Sarbin, T. R., "The Logic of Prediction in Psychology," *Psychol. Rev.*, 1944, 51, 210–228.
124. Savitz, L. D., "Prediction Studies in Criminology," *International Bibliography on Crime and Delinquency*, New York: National Council on Crime and Delinquency, 1965.
125. Schactel, E. G., "Notes on the Use of the Rorschach Test," in Glueck, S., and Glueck, E. T., *Unravelling Juvenile Delinquency*, New York: The Commonwealth Fund, 1950.
126. Schiedt, R., *Ein Beitrag Zum Problem der Ruckfallsprognose*, Munchen, 1936.
127. Schuessler, K. F., and Cressey, D. R., "Personality Characteristics of Criminals," *Amer. J. Sociol.*, 1950, 55, 483–484.
128. Sellin, T., and Wolfgang, M. E., *The Measurement of Delinquency*, New York: Wiley, 1964.
129. Shaplin, J. T., and Tiedman, D. V., "Comment on the Juvenile Prediction Tables

in the Gluecks' *Unravelling Juvenile Delinquency*," *Amer. Sociol. Rev.*, 1951, 16, 544–548.

130. Stevens, S. S., "Mathematics, Measurement, and Psychophysics," in Stevens, S. S., *Handbook of Experimental Psychology*, New York: John Wiley and Sons, 1957, 1–49.

131. Stogtill, M., *Behavior Cards: A Test-Interview for Delinquent Children*, The Psychological Corp.

132. Stott, D. H., "A New Delinquency Prediction Instrument Using Behavioral Indications," *International Journal of Social Psychiatry*, VI, 1960, 195–205.

133. Strong, E. K., Jr., *Vocational Interests of Men and Women*, Stanford University Press, 1943.

134. Strong, E. K., Jr., *Vocational Interests Eighteen Years After College*, Minneapolis: University of Minnesota Press, 1955.

135. Taylor, D. W., "An Analysis of Delinquency Based on Case Studies," *J. Abnorm. Soc. Psychol.*, 42, January, 1947.

136. Thorndike, E. L., *et al. Prediction of Vocational Success*, New York: The Commonwealth Fund, 1934.

137. Thorndike, E. L., *Personnel Selection*, New York: Wiley, 1949.

138. Tibbitts, C., "Success and Failure on Parole Can Be Predicted," *J. Crim. Law Criminol.*, 1931, 22, 11–50.

139. Tibbitts, C. "The Reliability of Factors Used in Predicting Success or Failure on Parole," *J. Crim. Law Criminol.*, 1932, 22, 844–853.

140. Toby, J., "An Evaluation of Early Identification and Intensive Treatment Programs for Pre-Delinquents," *Social Problems*, 13, 2, 1965.

141. Toops, H. A., "Philosophy and Practice of Personnel Selection," *Educ. Psychol. Measmt.*, 1945, 5, 95–124.

142. Trunk, H., *Sociale Prognosen Strafgefangenen*, 28 Monatsschift fur Kriminolobiologie und Strafrechtsreform, 1937.

143. Vernone, P. E., "The Assessment of Children: Recent Studies in Mental Measurement and Statistical Analysis," *Studies in Education No. 7*, London: University of London Institute of Education and Evans Bros. Ltd., 1955, 189–215.

144. Vold, G. B., "Prediction Methods Applied to Problems of Classification within Institutions," *J. Crim. Law and Criminol.*, 1936, 26, 202–209.

145. Walters, A. A., "A Note on Statistical Methods of Predicting Delinquency," *Brit. J. Delinquency*, 1956, 6, 297–302.

146. Ward, J. H., Jr., *An Application of Linear and Curvilinear Joint Functional Regression in Psychological Prediction*, U.S.A.F. Pers. Train. Res. Cent., Res. Bul., 1954, No. AFPTRC-TR54-86, W29p.

147. Warner, S. B., "Factors Determining Parole from the Massachusetts Reformatory," *J. Crim. Law Criminol.*, 1923, 14, 172–207.

148. Washburne, J. W., *The Washburne Social Adjustment Inventory*, Harcourt, Brace & World.

149. Wilkins, L. T., *Classification and Contamination*, a memorandum from the Research Unit, Home Office, London, December, 1955.

150. Wilkins, L. T., *Delinquent Generations: A Home Office Research Unit Report*, London: Her Majesty's Stationery Office, 1960.

151. Wilkins, L. T., "Who Does What with What and to Whom?" Sacramento, California, Department of Corrections, *The Research Newsletter*, 1, March, 1959.

152. Wilkins, L. T., "What Is Prediction and Is It Necessary in Evaluating Treatment?" in *Research and Potential Application of Research in Probation, Parole, and Delinquency Prediction*, New York: Citizens' Committee for Children of New York, Research Center, New York School of Social Work, Columbia University, July, 1961.

153. Wilkins, L. T., and MacNaughten-Smith, P., "New Prediction and Classification

Methods in Criminology," *The Journal of Research in Crime and Delinquency,* 1954, 1, 19–32.

154. Williams, W. T., and Lambert, J. M., "Multivariate Methods in Plant Ecology: Parts I, II, and III," *J. Ecol.,* 1959, 47, 83–101; 1960, 48, 680–710; 1961, 49, 717–729.

155. Wooton, B., *Social Science and Social Pathology,* New York: Macmillan, 1959, Chapter 5.

156. Zakilski, F. C., "Studies in Delinquency: II. Personality Structure of Delinquent Boys," *J. Genet. Psychol.,* 1949, 74, 109–117.

33: The Case for Prediction /
Leslie T. Wilkins

6.2.17.   It is remarkable that despite a tradition in behavioural research for all test materials to be validated upon different samples from those used in the construction of any test set, the prediction tables derived by almost all criminologists lacked this safeguard. Where validation has been claimed, it has most frequently been only partial validation, and such partial validation may be more unsatisfactory than none. It must be noted that in any "prediction" there will be two classes of error:

(a) some offenders will be "predicted" as non-recidivists (or delinquents) who will, in fact, subsequently not become delinquent or recidivist;

(b) some offenders will be "predicted" as non-recidivists (or non-delinquents) who will, in fact, subsequently become delinquent or recidivist.

6.2.18.   In any assessment of the validity of the "prediction" both kinds of error must be considered. It is not sufficient to show that of "recidivists" (or delinquents) a high percentage could have been "predicted without also showing that among non-recidivists (or non-delinquents) what percentage would also have been correctly classified. Moreover, the sample upon which the "prediction tables" are based should not be an "artificial" or "biased" one, unless appropriate corrections are made by weighting to the proportions in the population to which the decisions may be relevant.

6.2.19.   In any reasonable decision-making situation it is unlikely that the two types of error will have identical and equal effect. It may be a far more serious consideration to treat a person who is not in fact later a recidivist as though he were expected to be one, than to treat a recidivist as though he were not likely to be one. Exactly in what ways the errors of the first and sec-

From Leslie T. Wilkins, "Prediction Methods: A Survey of the Field from the Standpoint of Facts and Figures," in European Committee on Crime Problems, *The Effectiveness of Punishments and Other Methods of Treatment,* Strasbourg: Council of Europe (1967), pp. 60–69.

ond kind differ in their consequences does not seem to have been discussed either by those who propose or those who oppose "prediction methods."

6.2.20.   It is, of course, possible to consider a "penalty" for every wrong decision made, and to weight the different types of wrong decisions differently according to some concept of a generally desired good. There has been no discussion of these problems in criminological literature, although the problem is well known in regard to business decisions and is specifically solved for "consumer risk" and "producer risk" in quality control of products by statistical sampling methods. Of course, the decisions which are made about offenders are more complex, but the type and nature of the questions which seem relevant have similarities. No matter how decisions are made, no matter how experienced the decision maker, or how effective the methods upon which reliance is placed, some decisions will be made incorrectly.

6.2.21.   This is a factor in human decision-making which does not seem to have received attention to the extent that it deserves. If it is accepted that wrong decisions will, at times, be made, then it seems desirable to go on to consider what types of wrong decisions are likely to be made, and which types of wrong decisions should receive the more attention, because, in terms of some further considerations, these errors are less acceptable than others.

6.4.   *Criticism of Estimation Methods*

6.4.1.   It is often claimed that any methods for estimation of pre-sentence or pre-release probabilities of reconviction are deterministic and imply a fixed sequence of cause and effect. It is suggested that the methods should be rejected because in human affairs, indeterminacy and uncertainty outweigh any "prediction" that might be possible. At the extreme of metaphysical objection is the claim that such methods of estimation deny the existence of "free will."

6.4.2.   The claim that methods of estimation are deterministic reveals a total lack of understanding regarding the basic statistical methods which are used in the calculation of probabilities. The concept of uncertainty is basic to the statistical approach. The only difference is that by statistical methods uncertainty can be dealt with. There is a calculus of probabilities (uncertainties) of much the same order as any other calculus. The argument against determinism is an argument for the use of statistical methods, not against them. Knowledge is expected to be partial. No statements are made about "truth," but only estimates; no statements are made about certainty, but only degrees of uncertainty; no statements are made in terms of absolutes, but only of relative differences. The amount of uncertainty is dependent upon the amount of "information" which can be used to constitute the "experience" used as the basis for the systems of estimation. As knowledge advances the degrees of uncertainty may diminish, but there is no need to assume that the size of the "error" will ever reach zero (determinacy).

6.4.3.   Estimation depends upon the philosophy of "as though." Volumes have been written on this concept, but it is sufficient here to indicate the nature of the argument quite simply by example. Suppose that an employer were about to engage an employee. His decision is a simple dichotomous one, to engage or not to engage. Suppose that, within the area with which this discussion is concerned, he was aware that the applicant had served a sentence in Borstal, but had only this single piece of information. The employer will be making the best decision in these circumstances if he acts "as though" the probability of the applicant returning to crime was equal to the proportion of failures in the whole Borstal system.

6.4.4.   In this particular case this would mean that the employer would be best advised to act "as though" the applicant has about equal chances of making good or being reconvicted. (What acting "as though" the applicant had about equal chances of returning to crime might mean in terms of other decisions could be dealt with similarly, but would render the example highly complex and involve points outside the scope of the special point now being considered.)

6.4.5.   But let it now be supposed that the employer was able to obtain more information—say, that the applicant had a total of six previous offences. His action would be likely to be different from that where his information did not include this item. His action, if it is to be rational, should be based on the two items of information. In this particular case, he should act "as though" the applicant had about one chance in three of avoiding further convictions. Similarly each additional piece of information may modify the concept of rational decision.

6.4.6.   The amount and power of the available information determine the nature of the rational decision. But complete information is not to be found, and accordingly it is not possible to discuss certainty or determinism, but only probabilities as estimated in the light of limited information. The more powerful and relevant the information, the better, in theory at least, is the estimate of the probability likely to be and the smaller the error component in the decision process. The term "error" may be a misleading one. Errors are usually things which it is possible to avoid, but in this use of the term, error indicates the short-fall from determinism, and thus will persist.

6.4.7.   As has been noted, there are two types of error. Both types of error may be estimated. By use of certain prediction tables constructed for Borstal inmates it has been possible to describe a class of youth who, subjected to Borstal training, has an estimated probability of success (non-reconviction within three years) of 87%. It has been pointed out by critics of the "estimation" method that this means that, in 13 cases out of a 100, decisions which regard these youths as successes are likely to be wrong. Or, that in fact, some of the youths do not have a 0.13 chance of failure, but just will not fail. The fact that, say, 13 of this class of risk are "wrongly classified as successes" proves that the estimate for the class is correct. If there were more or less successes, the estimate of the probability would need adjustment. It is the philosophy which argues when presented with this situation that "prediction is wrong" for 13% of the cases that are deterministic. Does the criticism claim that other methods would show less "errors"? If so, do they claim that other methods would not reveal a 13% "error" but be correct every time? If so, then *these* methods are deterministic, but they are unknown, and likely to remain so! It may be possible to derive more efficient estimates, but all such estimation will have some "error," and the only methods known to assess whether other methods are or are not "better" are the same methods as are subject to criticism.

6.4.8.   Another objection relies upon the claim that such methods utilise background factors to provide estimates for future behaviour. That it follows that the methods are "static" and unable to take account of changes in the social or personal conditions of the offenders.

6.4.9.   Background factors are, of course, employed in arriving at estimates by use of statistical methods. But in subjective assessments background factors are also used. It may be that the objection really rests upon the assumption that the human decision maker can assess background factors more efficiently than can be done with symbolic manipulation of logical or mathematical models. This assumption has not been substantiated by any research which has attempted to test it. But perhaps the objection is better informed than that. Perhaps it is the claim that the quality and nature of experience of trained observers are different from the quality of information used in mathematical models.

6.4.10.   Human experience is continuous, and action may be geared to any experience obtained at any time up to the time of making the decision. Experience gained for strictly reproducible models has to be gained over a fixed period of time according to that fixed by the design. This objection would have had more point twenty years ago—before the development of sequential statistical procedures which allow of information to be processed continuously, in a way closely resembling the human system, but under control. Rather than representing a strength of the human processing of information, the continuous "dynamic" system may be a disadvantage for purposes of valid inference. Information gained, in fact, after a certain experience, may be regarded as though it were gained earlier. It is too much to expect the human mind, not only to remember the information but to recall precisely the time and sequence in which the information was received. If, however, it is the claim that "experience" gathered unsystematically, though continuously, and processed by subjective means provides a superior estimate of probabilities than the "static" (or, better, controlled) models, this claim is unsubstantiated.

6.4.11.   But there may be cases where a static model is more appropriate than a "dynamic" one. The type of model to be preferred, or even valid, depends upon the type of problem which is posed and the nature of the solutions sought. If by a "static model" we define a model for which information is obtained over a specified period regarding the position at a certain definite time, or over a definite time, or including events up to a certain time, then this may be more appropriate than continuous experience or continuous information processing. For example, it may be desirable to know exactly what might be said about likely outcomes of treatments before the treatment decision was made by the judge or other person concerned. In such cases information which is obtainable only during the period of training is not relevant and should be excluded. If, on the other hand, the decisions concern parole, it may be appropriate to include also information available up to the time of appearance before the parole authority. The type of information and the time at which it is available or could be available are clearly an essential element in the design of a "model."

6.4.12. The human mind cannot ignore information it has received after any critical period. The statistical model can. The "static model" affords a means of development for further research tools. Moreover, different "static models" may be constructed and related together. The nature of the objection to the use of statistical models as "static" is not clear without specification of the exact nature of the problem for which the instrument is believed to be inappropriate. A model of any kind may be appropriate for some purpose, and it is not possible to object to a model in principle, but only with specific reference to the situation or problem for which it is claimed that it is unsuitable.

6.4.13. In the usual case where objections of this kind are made to the use of statistical models, and of "prediction methods" in particular, it is pointed out that conditions may change and render the "prediction tables" invalid. It may be that the human mind can make all necessary adjustments under conditions of change, but it would appear that, if this objection can be sustained for the statistical utilisation of experience, then it must also hold for the subjective utilisation of experience by means of personal assessments. The problem of what happens under conditions of change is, however, a real problem, whether considered with respect to decisions based on statistics or otherwise. The statistical approach makes it possible to say something about what happens under conditions of certain types of change. Little is known of how the human assessors react but it seems highly probable that different assessors react differently to different types of changes of situation.

6.4.14. There are only limited cases where situations may change so as to render an efficiently constructed "prediction table" (estimates of, say, pre-sentence probabilities of recidivism) no longer efficient as a "prediction" instrument. These conditions can be stated. But let it be supposed that the limitations do not apply for the purpose of a first examination of the problem of change.

6.4.15. It will, of course, be necessary to have means for knowing when the "prediction tables" cease to "predict," or more correctly when the estimates of the probability of recidivism based on information at the time of sentence fail to hold true. It might seem reasonable to suggest that the effectiveness of "treatment" or "training" is measured by its capacity to change the "pre-sentence probabilities" of recidivism. What else can measure the effectiveness of treatment? Or again, if two forms of treatment are given to offenders of the same levels of "pre-sentence probability" of recidivism, and one treatment seems to reduce the level of expectation of failure, then a provisional conclusion might be that that treatment was more effective. This conclusion would, however, be a superficial one, but clearly any instrument which did not have the capacity to reveal change would be worthless. The charge that the instrument may show different readings under different conditions is no more than a charge that the instrument is working! Everything depends, not upon the fact that the instrument shows change, but the relation of the change to the situation and the nature of the inference about the changes and the situations concerned. Let us consider one specific type of change which might be regarded as providing some guidance for action, and suggest a possibility of action by use of an instrument measuring pre-sentence probabilities of recidivism.

6.4.16.　At present it is always possible for probation officers and others concerned with, say, the after-care of offenders to claim that their "success rates" are lower than for other officers because they have "worse" material upon which to work. This may indeed be true. Pre-sentence probabilities provide a check, and indicate a line of action. It is possible to identify, say, after-care officers who have a higher success rate than would be expected in view of the probabilities of recidivism estimated from the equations in respect of their case-load. That is to say, the equations were "untrue" for their cases. It becomes possible then to ask what are the characteristics and methods of those officers who are more successful than expected, and how do these differ from those who are not so successful?

6.4.17.　It might be possible to pass on to those who were not so successful some of the methods which their colleagues had developed. If this training becomes possible and works in practice, then the equations which were first derived will cease to hold true and become generally invalid by just that amount by which after-care has changed the pre-sentence expectation of success or failure.

6.4.18.　This type of argument is used only to indicate the nature of the equations. The application of valid inference is, however, more complex than the simple models suggested in the preceding paragraphs. The problem is that in the treatment situation we are not dealing with a simple cause-effect situation but with interactional situations and possibly cybernetic systems. Nonetheless, the type of instrument which may be used and the nature of the instrument in the simple case are indicated by the type of action which might, under certain conditions, seem reasonable. The defence of the "model" or instrument is as valid as the objection, but neither is adequate explanation of the problem as it is now known. The "static" nature of the equations is not to be confused with situations developing during treatment or after-care. Because only one problem can be answered at any one time, the "static" nature of models is essential when they are applied to postulates which are themselves basically "static" theories. More complex theories need more complex models.

6.4.19.   There are other factors of change which are of a different order and which are more concerned with the types of "prediction equations" which may be used. The objection of the "static" nature of probability estimates may refer to the fact that different weights are attached to items of information known at the time of sentencing, or some other time, as applicable to the types of estimation. It may be claimed that the appropriate weight to be given to a factor in the background of the offender may itself change with time. For example, heavy drinking may be prognostic of failure, but if drinking habits change, the weight to be given to the factor will also need to be changed. This is true, but since social changes and changes of patterns of living take place slowly this may not be a serious objection. The problem of possible changing weights is recognised by research workers in their search for "stable correlates." Factors such as "overcrowding," "bad housing" (however assessed or measured), and economic circumstances may change quickly for any one individual but not for large aggregates of individuals. In building up estimates it is usually possible to find several items of information which may substitute for each other. Social factors are patterned, and it is only the unique contribution of any item that is of significance in estimation. Thus items of information which may change rapidly may be rejected and replaced by more stable correlates.

6.4.20.   In practical research situations several forms of estimation will be attempted. It may, for example, be useful to explain as much variation as possible using information relating to the earliest periods for which it can be reliably obtained; alternatively, an explanation may be sought in terms of social factors, or psychological factors, or in terms of factors which may be changed by administrative action. All these estimations are likely to overlap, and all of them will need to be compared with an estimate of maximum efficiency.

6.4.21.   In cases where "prediction" systems have been used, the instruments have shown themselves to be remarkably stable. The Mannheim-Wilkins Borstal Training Prediction equations completed in 1954 in respect of training in 1948 were still holding true in 1960 with only some minor differences which might have been due to changes in recording of "drunkenness." In fact, it proved very useful that the tables had been prepared. The Borstal success rate dropped very considerably in the period after the tables were constructed, and it was suggested that Borstal training was not being as effective as it had been in the past. In opposition, it was argued that since Detention Centres had been started, many youths who were not such "bad risks" were sent to Detention Centres rather than committed to Borstal, and that the quality of the Borstal inmates had deteriorated and that this explained the fall in success rate. Without the prediction tables there could have been no resolution of this debate. But, in fact, the tables showed that the drop in success rates was almost exactly what would be expected in view of the change in the risk being allocated to Borstal training. In these circumstances the tables were useful because they were "static" and had remained a powerful "prediction" instrument over the years. It is interesting to speculate what interpretation would have been possible if the success rate had remained constant although the "input" had either improved or deteriorated. But the complexity of the question must be matched with the complexity of the information used to provide an answer.

6.4.22.   The methodological soundness of "prediction systems" has varied from the totally unacceptable to the satisfactory. The inferences made have ranged from the ridiculous to the reasonable. The utility of the work has, however, always been in doubt. The prediction phase has provided a stepping-stone on which some have merely stubbed their toes and fallen into worse errors, while others are using it as the way forward. Of course some are just standing on it seeming only to block the path!

34: The Outcome of Parole According to Base Expectancy Rates /
Don M. Gottfredson, K. B. Ballard, John W. Mannering and *Dean V. Babst*

Base Expectancy measures are especially useful in studies of effectiveness of differing treatment programs. Experience tables previously developed for Wisconsin parolees use a configural method for classification of offenders, basing the classification upon inmate characteristics known to be related to parole performance. The method used in the present study was multiple linear regression. This report describes only the development and testing of devices by the latter method. . . .

Three prediction measures were devised. One is based upon the combined prison and reformatory samples studied. A second is based only on prison inmates, while the third is based only upon reformatory subjects. Only the first is presented here as illustrative of the method.

The prediction devices were tested using two separate samples additional to the sample studied to develop the methods. In each case, it was found that persons with higher scores were more often found to be non-violators. Also, the expected number of parole violators for a given Base Expectancy classification was found, in general, to be stable over the two time periods studied.

From Don M. Gottfredson, K. B. Ballard, John W. Mannering and Dean V. Babst, *Wisconsin Base Expectancies for Reformatories and Prisons* (Vacaville, Calif.: Institute for the Study of Crime and Delinquency, June 1965), pp. i; 2–9; 12; 16; 19; 23.

Subjects

Construction Sample. A study sample made up of all men with an odd digit as the last number of the case number was selected from all 3,693 Wisconsin parolees released to parole supervision between January 1, 1954, and December 31, 1957. There were 1,846 such subjects, selected by this procedure, which was assumed to approximate random selection.

Validation Sample No. 1. All men released between January 1, 1954, and December 31, 1957, not selected as above were included for the sample designated as Validation Sample No. 1. There were 1,847 subjects.

Validation Sample No. 2. All men released to parole supervision in Wisconsin between January 1, 1958, and December 31, 1959, were included in the sample designated Validation Sample No. 2. There were 2,112 men in this group.

Inmate Characteristics Considered

The study was limited to information available on punch cards and coded consistently since 1954. Analysis of each available item, considered separately in relation to the parole violation criterion with all study sample subjects, resulted in selection of the items indicated below. Further definition of the items may be found in previous publications of the Bureau of Research, Wisconsin State Department of Public Welfare.*

Item 1—Assaultive Offense. The following offenses were classified as "Assaultive": murder, manslaughter, negligent homicide, aggravated assault, other assault, rape, incest, sex offense against children, other sex offenses, and armed robbery. Presence of "Assaultive Offense" was scored as one; absence was scored as zero.

Item 2—Favorable Offense. Offenses classed as "favorable" (in the sense that previous studies have suggested a relatively favorable proportion of non-violators from these groups) included all offenses classed above as assaultive, plus abandonment and non-support, embezzlement, and all others except unarmed robbery, burglary, fraud, auto theft, and narcotics law violation. Offenses classed as "favorable" were assigned a score of one; all others were given a score of zero.

Item 3—Homicide or Assault. Offenses included here were murder, manslaughter and negligent homicide, aggravated assault, and other assaults. These offenses were assigned a score of one, and all other offenses were given a score of zero.

---

* "Instructions for Form RS–15; Report on Offenders Admitted to State Correctional Institutions," State of Wisconsin: State Department of Public Welfare, Bureau of Research and Statistics, July 1, 1953, and "Instructions for Report of Offenders Admitted to Wisconsin Adult Correctional Institutions (Form RS–27)," State of Wisconsin: State Department of Public Welfare, Bureau of Research, January 1, 1958.

Item 4—Sex Offense. This included rape, incest, sex offense against children, and other sex offenses. If the offense was classed as "sex offense," then a score of one was assigned, otherwise a score of zero was given.

Item 5—Auto Theft. If the offense was auto theft, then a score of zero was assigned, otherwise a score of one was given.

Item 6—Milwaukee Auto Theft. If the offense was auto theft and subject was committed from Milwaukee, then a score of zero was assigned, while the remainder of subjects were assigned a score of one.

Item 7—Priors. A score equal to the number of prior felony convictions in the case history of the individual was assigned except that a score of three was assigned to indicate three or more prior felony convictions.

Item 8—Age at Release. Age at release was plotted for the two criterion groups (i.e., violators and non-violators of the total study sample) against the cumulative percent of subjects. This suggested the following procedure:

> Men between the ages of 25 and 34, inclusive, were assigned a score of zero.
> Men under 20 years up to and including 24 years of age were assigned a score of one.
> Men 35 years of age and over were assigned a score of two.

Item 9—Marital Status. Subject was assigned a score of zero if not married and a score of one if married.

Item 10—Indian. A score of zero was assigned when subject was classified as American or Mexican Indian; he was assigned a score of one if classified as not Indian.

Item 11—Re-paroled. Subject was assigned a score of zero if the current release to parole supervision followed a previous return to prison as a parole violator; he was assigned a score of one if not classed as a parole violator re-released.

Parole Violation Criterion. A subject was classed as a "violator" if parole was revoked as a consequence of rules violation or conviction for a new offense after discharge from parole. This includes absconding and revocation for a new offense. Otherwise, the subject was classed as a "non-violator." All subjects were followed for 24 months after parole release.

Statistical Method

A multiple linear regression analysis was completed with respect to the combined prison and reformatory study samples (1,846 subjects), the prison study sample (1,053 subjects) and the reformatory study sample (793 subjects). A major advantage of this method is that assignment of weights to individual predictor items is based not only on the degree of relationship to the parole violation criterion but upon the interrelationships (i.e. "overlap") among predictor items. . . .

Results   Prison / Reformatory Base Expectancy

The raw score for the Base Expectancy calculated on the basis of combined prison and reformatory samples may be calculated as shown in Table 34–1. It should be mentioned . . . that the main contribution to prediction by means of this equation is based upon "assault or sex offense," "number of priors," and "auto theft." All correlations with the criterion are quite small and the largest single partial correlation coefficient (− .12) describes the relationship of "number of priors" to the criterion. . . .

Application of Prediction Devices to Validation Samples 1 and 2. The Base Expectancy measures described above were applied to the first validation sample, which was comprised of all 1954 and 1957 Wisconsin parolees not included in the sample for construction of the devices. Results are shown

Table 34-1

Calculation of Prison/Reformatory Base Expectancy

If	Add
A. Assault or Sex	3
Not Auto Theft	17
Married	8
Not Indian	20
Not Reparoled	12
B. Add 13 for all cases	13
Sum	

C. Age at Release:		
24 or under	Add 6	
25 to 34	Add 0	
35 and over	Add 12	+

D. Add B plus C

E. Multiply number of priors by − 10   −

F. Subtract (D − E)   Raw Score:

Assault or Sex Includes:

    Murder
    Manslaughter and Negligent
      Homicide
    Aggravated Assault
    Other Assault
    Rape
    Incest
    Sex Offense Against Children
    Other Sex Offenses
    Armed Robbery

Married means:

    "Living with spouse"
    (disregard previous
    divorce)

Indian Includes:

    American Indian and
    Mexican Indian

Table 34-2

*Prison/Reformatory Base Expectancy
Scores and Number of Violators and Non-Violators;
Validation Sample Number 1
(1954-1957 Parolees)*

Base Expectancy		Number		Percent	
Score	Group	Violators	Non-Violators	Non-Violators	Total
81-85	A	18	64	78	82
74-80	B	52	155	75	207
67-73	C	124	294	70	418
59-66	D	116	222	66	338
52-58	E	143	175	55	318
45-51	F	94	85	48	179
38-44	G	90	75	45	165
0-37	H	88	52	37	140
TOTAL		725	1122	61	1847

	Base Expectancy	
	Mean	Standard Deviation
Violators	55.0	14.7
Non-Violators	62.3	13.3
TOTAL	59.4	14.3

Biserial Correlation Coefficient = .32

Point Biserial Correlation Coefficient = .25

in Table 34–2. In each case, the proportion of men classed as non-violators decreases with decreasing Base Expectancy scores. The prediction devices were applied also to the second test sample of 1958–1959 parolees. Results are shown in Table 34–3. . . . For score groups based on Prison / Reformatory Base Expectancy scores, results in each case support the null hypothesis at the five percent level of confidence; observed differences in proportions may be reasonably attributed to random sampling.

It may be concluded that the relationship observed in the construction

Table 34-3

*Base Expectancy Scores and Number of Violators and
Non-Violators; Validation Sample Number 2
(1959-1959 Parolees)*

Base Expectancy		Number		Percent	
Score	Group	Violators	Non-Violators	Non-Violators	Total
80-85	A	20	70	78	90
73-79	B	60	176	75	236
66-72	C	167	328	66	495
58-65	D	160	252	61	412
51-57	E	138	177	56	315
44-50	F	101	87	46	188
36-43	G	106	96	48	202
0-35	H	107	67	38	174
TOTAL		859	1253	59	2112

	Base Expectancy	
	Mean	Standard Deviation
Violators	55.0	14.7
Non-Violators	62.3	13.3
TOTAL	59.4	14.3

Biserial Correlation Coefficient	=	.32
Point Biserial Correlation Coefficient	=	.25

sample and tested in Validation Sample No. 1 was in general confirmed in Validation Sample No. 2. . . .

The Base Expectancy measures developed provide tools which, it is hoped, may be helpful in studying effects of differing treatment programs. Some validity of these measures . . . has been demonstrated; the purpose stated at the outset will be fulfilled if we can now identify programs which make these measures *invalid* by treatment helpful to inmates, assuring increased proportions of non-violators.

35: Glueck Method of Constructing Prediction Tables / *Sheldon and Eleanor Glueck*

Two basic methods for the construction of prediction tables have been developed in the United States—that of Ernest W. Burgess,[1] and that of the authors of the present work.[2] The Burgess method gives equal weight to numerous factors found to be differentially related to success or failure on parole; the Glueck method employs in a prediction table only those few factors (usually five) that have been demonstrated through follow-up studies to bear a high relationship to subsequent behavior. By the Glueck method, each case is scored on the basis of the actual violation rate (variously referred to as maladaptation, recidivism, or delinquency rate) of the particular subclass of each predictive factor to which the individual belongs. His total score on the group of five factors yields his chance of success or failure during the particular period for which a prediction of behavior is desired.

There have been modifications of these basic methods in the United States and England. As adequate documentation exists on other methods of prediction, we leave to the reader an exploration of them without any further reference to them here.[3]

Although, as an introduction to the prediction tables themselves, it is well to give the reader a conception of how these tables are constructed, it is not our purpose to enter into great detail. The preparation of prediction tables by our method is a long process based on intensive follow-up studies, and although there may be many who would wish to use such devices, there are few who will want to construct them.

It needs, first, to be emphasized that unless the raw materials entering into the construction of a predictive instrument have been carefully defined, competently gathered, and thoroughly verified, and the follow-up of conduct (be it during or after treatment) has been equally adequate, the resultant prediction table will be at best a useless and even deceptive, albeit interesting, exercise in mathematics. Obviously, no mathematical procedure, however refined and sophisticated, can erase the inadequacy of raw data.[4]

From Sheldon and Eleanor Glueck, *Predicting Delinquency and Crime* (Cambridge, Mass.: Harvard University Press, 1959), pp. 23–32; *Delinquents and Nondelinquents in Perspective* (Cambridge, Mass.: Harvard University Press, 1968), pp. 190–192. Copyright 1959 and 1968, respectively, by the President and Fellows of Harvard College.

It should also be pointed out that until a prediction table is applied to samples of cases other than the one on which it was constructed, it is more accurate to regard it as an "experience" table; for at this stage it records merely an existing situation with reference to the particular example from which it is derived. Testing for validity by applying an experience table to other samples of cases is clearly necessary to determine whether the interconnection of factors and behavior is quite general.

Turning now to the method of constructing our prediction tables, the first step is to relate each factor encompassed in the particular inquiry to the behavior of the offenders during or following that form of peno-correctional treatment for which a prediction device is desired. Obviously, the greater the difference in the incidence of a subclass of a particular factor between those who do and those who do not behave acceptably during (or following) a particular form of treatment, the more potent is that factor as a predictor.

From among the completed correlations, those factors are selected for possible use in the prediction table which are found to bear the highest relationship to behavior during or following the particular form of correction for which a table is to be constructed.[5] Experience has shown, however, that it is not indispensable to utilize the five factors bearing the very highest association with behavior; even the cumulative effect of small differences can result in a competent predictive device. It is essential, however, that the factors selected make, when combined, a workable prognostic device; and this is best determined by testing it on other samples of cases.

There are other considerations in choosing the five factors out of a range of possibilities. We find it advisable, for example, to consider whether the factors chosen are mutually exclusive and, if possible, to select from among all the possibilities those that are relatively independent of one another. However, a small amount of overlap is not necessarily objectionable.

Also, the practical question has to be considered, whether peno-correctional authorities who might use such tables would have the needed data readily available. Great expertness in the gathering of data by probation officers is not likely to be generally found; hence data that are more, rather than less, easily obtained by those who staff peno-correctional systems are preferable when selecting the factors to be included in the prediction instrument. In a number of our tables we have sometimes through early inexperience, and at other times because of the limited number of the factors from among which choices could be made, included items that should be avoided, such as, for example, *Intelligence of Offender* or *Mental Condition of Offender*. Obviously, the ascertainment of these requires expert skills not possessed by peno-correctional staffs and is dependent on the availability of psychological and psychiatric services that are still rarely at hand.

In brief, given a sufficiently wide choice of factors of fairly equal prognostic power, it is best to select from among them the ones that are least difficult to assemble in the day-to-day practice of courts and associated agencies.

After the selection of the factors, the next step in the construction of prediction tables by our method is to set down the percentage of offenders actually misbehaving within each subclass of a factor. For example, in Table 35–1 are presented the five factors selected as the basis for a table predicting the behavior of juvenile delinquents on parole, with their subcategories and the percentage incidence (within each of these subcategories) of those who actually had shown clear evidences of antisocial behavior during parole.[6]

The next step is to determine what are the highest and the lowest violation scores it is possible for an offender to obtain on the five factors involved. (It should be clear to the reader by now that the scores represent the actual percentage of offenders [in each subclass of a factor and in the sample from which the table is being constructed] who failed to respond satisfactorily during parole.) By adding the smallest percentages in the subcategories of the five factors, the *lowest possible parole violation score* is obtained; by summating the five largest percentages of the subcategories of the five factors, the *highest possible parole violation score* is determined. For example, Table 35–1 shows that summation of the lowest scores—64.3, 66.9, 40.3, 50.0, and 55.2—provides one extreme of the range of scores, namely, 276.7; sum-

Table 35-1

Factors Predictive of Behavior of Juvenile Offenders during Parole

Predictive Factors and Subcategories*	Percentage Incidence of Parole Violators
Birthplace of Father	
Foreign Countries other than Ireland	64.3
United States	77.9
Ireland	89.7
Birthplace of Mother	
United States, Poland, Russia, Lithuania, Italy	66.9
Foreign Countries other than Poland, Russia, Lithuania,	
Italy, Ireland	72.7
Ireland	86.7
Discipline by Father	
Firm but Kindly	40.3
Erratic	63.9
Overstrict or Lax	74.1
Discipline by Mother	
Firm but Kindly	50.0
Erratic	61.7
Overstrict or Lax	73.8
School Misconduct	
None	55.2
Some	72.2

*Whatever contractions have been made of the original, more detailed, subcategories of the factors are based on an examination of the raw tables, from which it could readily be determined which subcategories to combine.

mation of the highest possible scores—89.7, 86.7, 74.1, 73.8, and 72.2— gives us the other, namely, 396.5. Between these minimal and maximal limits, score classes are first established in narrow, equidistant intervals. Within this tabular framework, each offender in the group is placed according to his total score on the five predictive factors.

Another illustration might be helpful. This one deals with the prediction table constructed in *Unraveling Juvenile Delinquency* which was designed to identify potential delinquents at the time of school entrance and is known as the Glueck Social Prediction Table.

In 35–2 are presented the five factors selected as the basis for a table for predicting who, among young school children, are potential delinquents, with the subcategories of the factors and the percentage incidence (within each of these subcategories) of those who actually became delinquents.[7]

Table 35-2
Social Factors Identifying Potential Juvenile Delinquents

Predictive Factors and Subcategories	Percentage Incidence of Delinquents
Discipline of Boy by Father	
Firm but Kindly	9.3
Lax	59.8
Overstrict or Erratic	72.5
Supervision of Boy by Mother	
Suitable	9.9
Fair	57.5
Unsuitable	83.2
Affection of Father for Boy	
Warm (including overprotective)	33.8
Indifferent or Hostile	75.9
Affection of Mother for Boy	
Warm (including overprotective)	43.1
Indifferent or Hostile	86.2
Cohesiveness of Family	
Marked	20.6
Some	61.3
None	96.9

Note: Those who wish to apply the table are asked to note that the determination of the particular category into which a case falls is based on the situation generally prevailing in a child's life up to the point at which the prediction is made. In cases in which one or another parent has left or been removed from the home before a child was three years old, and there is no parent surrogate (stepparent, foster parent,) discipline of the missing parent is graded as "lax," affection as "indifferent," and supervision as "unsuitable." But if there has been a substitute parent, at least since the child was three years old, the discipline, affection, and supervision of the parent substitute is rated.

Again, by adding the smallest percentages in the subcategories of the five factors, the *lowest potential delinquency score* was obtained; by summating the five largest percentages of the subcategories of the five factors, the *highest potential delinquency score* was determined. For example, from the series of factors just presented, summation of the lowest scores—9.3, 9.9, 33.8, 43.1, and 20.6—provides one extreme of the range of scores, namely, 116.7; summation of the highest possible scores—72.5, 83.2, 75.9, 86.2, and 96.9—gives us the other, namely, 414.7. Between these minimal and maximal limits, score classes were first established in narrow, equidistant intervals. Within this tabular framework, each individual in the group was placed according to his total score on the five predictive factors, on the one hand, and in respect to whether he was a delinquent or a non-delinquent, on the other.

An illustration of such a distribution of cases within class intervals is given in this prediction table which, as already stated, is designed to identify at an early age those children who are likely to become delinquents unless suitable intervention occurs. To review, the factors involved are: *Discipline of Boy by Father, Supervision of Boy by Mother, Affection of Father for Boy, Affection of Mother for Boy,* and *Cohesiveness of Family;* and the resulting distribution of the 890 cases from among the original 1,000 (500 delinquents and 500 non-delinquents) who could be categorized on all five factors is seen in 35–3.[8]

Inspection of the percentages shows that the first two groupings might well be combined, and also the last three, resulting in a four score-class table.[9]

To summarize the Glueck method of constructing prediction tables:

(1) From among the highly differentiating factors, five are selected, taking into consideration whether or not these factors are mutually exclusive. If possible, those are selected that are relatively independent of one another. The practical matter of the ease or difficulty of gathering the data by those who would be charged with the task is also considered in making the selection.

(2) The percentages of subclass incidence of violation, or maladaptation, or recidivism, or delinquency, as the case may be, are next set down for each of the five selected factors.

(3) The next step is to determine the lowest and the highest possible scores by adding all the smallest percentages of the subcategories of the five factors, on the one hand, and all the largest percentages of the subcategories of the five factors, on the other.

(4) Next, score classes are established in equidistant intervals between the minimum and maximum score limits.

(5) Then, each case in the group is scored on the five factors and placed in the appropriate score class and appropriate behavior category, the number falling into each score class being converted into percentages.

(6) The resulting distribution of percentages is the basis for the predictive instrument.

(7) Finally, the distribution of the percentages is examined to determine what combinations of the score classes provide the sharpest predictive instrumentality.[10]

Table 35-3

Detailed Prediction Table from Five Factors of Social Background

Weighted Failure Score Class	Number of Delinquents	% of Delinquents within Respective Score Classes	Number of Non-Delinquents	% of Non-Delinquents within Respective Score Classes
Less than 150	5	2.9%	167	97.1%
150-199	19	15.7	102	84.3
200-249	40	37.0	68	63.0
250-299	122	63.5	70	36.5
300-349	141	86.0	23	14.0
350-399	73	90.1	8	9.9
400 or Over	51	98.1	1	1.9
Total	451		439	

Table 35-4

Four-Class Prediction Table from Five Factors of Social Background

Weighted Failure Score Class	Delinquency Rate	Non-Delinquency Rate
Less than 200	8.2%	91.8%
200-249	37.0	63.0
250-299	63.5	36.5
300 or Over	89.2	10.8

Illustrative Interpretation of a Prediction Table

To understand how to interpret a prediction table, the reader is asked to examine the following table designed to predict the behavior of juvenile offenders on probation. This shows that an offender scoring less than 240 on the five factors involved has 36/100 chances of violating probation; while if he scores between 240–270 his chances of violation rise to 67/100; and if he scores more than this his chances are 86/100.

Score Class*	Probation Violation Rate	Probation Non-Violation Rate
Less than 240	36.0%	64.0%
240-270	66.7	33.3
270 or Over	85.6	14.4

*The factors involved, together with their subcategories and definitions and the "violation score" for each subcategory of a factor are also in Appendix B.

The use of prediction tables as aids in the administration of criminal justice does not carry with it any commitment to a new form of "mechanical jurisprudence." It must be borne in mind that we are dealing here with an instrument in aid, not in replacement, of the judgmental process. An authority in the practical application of predictive devices has put the matter very clearly as regards parole, and this is equally applicable to all forms of peno-correctional treatment:

An evaluation of the risk of violation involved in the decision to grant parole is helpful to the parole board. Whether or not the risk should be taken in an individual case remains a matter of judgment on the part of the board since there are many other considerations which may be of equal or even of greater importance. Thus the fear that use of an experience table may lead to the automatic granting of parole is unfounded. The table covers only a portion of the factors entering into the parole decision, and affords a statement of violation risk useful only in conjunction with these other considerations.[11]

Whether the relevant factors derive from psychiatric examinations, personality tests, or assessments of parent-child relationships, the resultant predictive instrument is not to be used mechanically, any more than the case history is to be blindly followed by the judge or parole board. What we said a quarter of a century ago is still true today:

The wise judge does not surrender the judging process to the specialist in psychiatry, psychology, sociology, or education. It is his domain to pass their contributions through the alembic of his mind and distil them into a workable program that takes account of legal demands and social limitations, as well as clinical findings.[12]

Probably one reason why the social prediction table has been found to have considerable potency in classifying youngsters into such categories is because the family factors involved are interrelated with many other factors and traits in parents and children that have been shown to increase or lower the chances of subsequent delinquency. The social prediction table demonstrates that maladaptive acts and antisocial influences involved in delinquency, though extremely numerous and complexly interrelated, can be potently represented by a handful of indices. This does not of course mean that only a small number of criminogenic influences are actually involved in the development of an antisocial character and career; it means, simply, that just a few factors, proven markedly to differentiate a large sample of true delinquents from a control sample of true nondelinquents, are enough for the purposes of prediction, though not sufficient for adequate understanding and therapy.

More recently, other predictive devices have been developed to take account of "the prejudice against this approach . . . among those who fear not only that the civil rights of children and parents may be infringed, but that the children erroneously identified as delinquents would be unnecessarily stigmatized." [13] These tables—one based on four behavioral manifestations in school, the other on five activities reflecting adventuresome interests—have not yet been tested on other samples. However, judging by the wide divergence between the delinquents and nondelinquents in respect to the data involved in the original table, and the fact that there is a high correlation of the placement of the delinquents and nondelinquents between the more recent tables and the earlier one, it can reasonably be expected that these later devices, if tested on other samples of cases, would also show great discriminative power in prediction.

In the meantime it may be observed that if we were to accept as sound the argument of those who oppose identification techniques to disclose the children who are especially vulnerable,[14] we should logically close all child guidance clinics, dismiss school counselors and visiting teachers, and sit back complacently (as, unfortunately, we too often have been doing) until the child has developed into a true persistent delinquent or gang member and then bring him into court with the usual far-from-satisfactory results illustrated by follow-up data.

The choice presented to a community is whether its citizens prefer to let potentially delinquent children ripen into persistent offenders or to intervene preventively, in specific instances shown to involve high risk of delinquency, at a stage in development which gives the promise of changing their dangerous attitudes and behavior. This can be done through aiding the parents of such children to modify their damaging and nonaffectionate (or sometimes morbidly overprotective) attitudes and practices which have been demonstrated in many prior instances to be potent influences toward maladapted conduct. The follow-ups of the subjects of the present study, as well as our previous follow-up studies, have consistently shown the tragic role of *deep-rootedness* in rendering antisocial behavior impervious to the usual methods of "treatment" thus far provided by society.[15]

NOTES

1. E. W. Burgess, "Factors Determining Success or Failure on Parole," in *The Workings of the Indeterminate-Sentence Law and the Parole System in Illinois,* by Bruce, Harno, Burgess, and Landesco, Illinois State Board of Parole, Springfield, 1928, Chapter XXX.

2. "Predictability in the Administration of Criminal Justice," 42 *Harvard Law Review* (1929), pp. 297–329; reprinted in 13 *Mental Hygiene* (1929), pp. 678 *et seq.;* this article is the substance of Chapter XVIII of *500 Criminal Careers* (a five-year post-sentence follow-up study of 500 Massachusetts Reformatory inmates). See, also: Chapter XII of *Later Criminal Careers* (a ten-year follow-up study); Chapters XIV, XV, and XVI of *Criminal Careers in Retrospect* (a fifteen-year follow-up study of these same cases); Chapter XI of *One Thousand Juvenile Delinquents* (a follow-up of delinquents during a five-year period); Chapter XIX of *Juvenile Delinquents Grown Up,* covering these same delinquents during a fifteen-year follow-up; Chapter XVII of *Five Hundred Delinquent Women* (a five-year follow-up of 500 inmates of the Massachusetts Reformatory for Women); Chapter VI of *After-Conduct of Discharged Offenders,* Macmillan Company, London, 1945 (summary of the various findings of these studies of recidivism). In *Unraveling Juvenile Delinquency,* Chapter XX, prediction tables are presented, designed to forecast delinquency on the part of children, these being based on the traits and factors found to differentiate most markedly between a sample of 500 delinquents and 500 non-delinquents.

3. See "Historical Survey of Prediction Studies in the Field of Criminology," from *Prediction Methods in Relation to Borstal Training,* by Dr. Hermann Mannheim and Leslie T. Wilkins, London, H. M. Stationery Office, 1955. Here will be found detailed reference to the Burgess and the Glueck methods and to all the other predictive techniques so far developed.

In addition we call attention to excellent papers prepared by Lloyd E. Ohlin and Elio D. Monachesi for the Third International Congress of Criminology, London, 1955 (thus far these have not appeared in print). See, also: 7 *British Journal of Delinquency* (1956); and S. Glueck, *Prognosis of Recidivism,* General Report Section IV, Third International Congress of Criminology, London, 1955.

4. See Lloyd E. Ohlin, book review of "Prediction Methods in Relation to Borstal Training," by Hermann Mannheim and Leslie T. Wilkins, 70 *Harvard Law Review* (1956), pp. 398–400.

5. In our earliest studies we relied on the Pearsonian coefficient of mean-square contingency ("C") to determine the degree of relationship between a factor and behavior during or after treatment. "The greatest possible value of the coefficient" (Karl Pearson's "mean-square contingency coefficient") "is . . . only unity if the number of classes be infinitely great; for any finite number of classes the limiting value of C is the smaller, the smaller the number of classes," quoted by G. Udny Yule, *An Introduction to the Theory of Statistics,* 1922, p. 65. In a twofold table, C cannot exceed 0.71; in a threefold, 0.82; in a fourfold, 0.87; etc. (*ibid.,* p. 66). The coefficient used is a mathematical device for indicating the associations shown in tables by means of a single convenient figure. For the mathematical process involved in ascertaining this coefficient, see Yule, pp. 66–67; *500 Criminal Careers,* pp. 239–240.

In *Five Hundred Delinquent Women* (p. 286), we resorted to a simpler, less time-consuming computation suggested by the late Professor Ernest A. Hooton of Harvard University. This consisted in establishing the degree of association between any particular factor and behavior by the simple determination of the maximum percentage difference between any subclass of a particular factor and the expectancy of recidivism for the entire group of cases involved. By comparing the total degree of relationship to recidivism by this method with that yielded by the more elaborate computation in the use of the mean-square contingency coefficient, the following scale was established (see *Five Hundred Delinquent Women,* p. 287:

Maximum Difference in Percentages between Category of a Factor and Expectancy of Recidivism	Degree of Relationship Indicated between the Factor and Recidivism
Less than 4	None
4–7	Slight
7–15	Appreciable
15–26	Considerable
26 or Over	High

Reference to this table of values facilitated the selection of the predictive factors.

Considerably later in our work, i.e., when we came to preparing the prediction tables in *Unraveling Juvenile Delinquency* (see Chapter XX of that volume), we pursued an even simpler method. We inspected those factors in which significant differences (P<0.01 as determined by the computation of the chi-square) occurred between the delinquents and their matched non-delinquents; and from among these, we selected as predictive factors those showing the *widest range of differences* between the delinquents and non-delinquents in the subclasses of each factor. For example, although there is statistical significance in the differences between the delinquents ("failures") and non-delinquents ("successes") in their ordinal rank among their brothers and sisters (see *Unraveling Juvenile Delinquency,* Table XI–5, p. 120), the actual differences are not nearly so great as the differences between the delinquents and non-delinquents as to *Affection of Father for Boy* (see *Unraveling Juvenile Delinquency*, Table XI–13, p. 125). The latter factor became one of a cluster of five factors in a table designed to differentiate at an early age—at school entrance—between those youngsters who are likely to become delinquents and those who are not.

6. *Juvenile Delinquents Grown Up*, Table 73, p. 206.

7. *Unraveling Juvenile Delinquency*, p. 261.

8. *Ibid.*, Table XX–2.

9. *Ibid.*, p. 262, Table XX–3.

10. For the reader who would profit from a more detailed illustration of the selection of factors and the construction of prediction tables than is given, see E. T. Glueck, "Identifying Juvenile Delinquents and Neurotics," 40 *Mental Hygiene* (1956), pp. 24–43.

11. Ohlin, pp. 68–69.

12. *One Thousand Juvenile Delinquents*, p. 114.

13. E. T. Glueck, "Distinguishing Delinquents from Pseudodelinquents," *Harvard Educational Review*, 36:119–130 (Spring 1966). For answers to such criticisms, see S. Glueck, "Ten Years of Unraveling Juvenile Delinquency," *The Journal of Criminal Law, Criminology and Police Science*, 5:283 and 306 (September–October 1960).

14. *The Challenge of Crime in a Free Society*, p. 59.

15. In S. and E. Glueck, *Predicting Delinquency and Crime* (Cambridge, Mass.: Harvard University Press, 1960), pp. 44, 81–82, it is shown that in 18 out of 30 prediction tables dealing with adult offenders and 3 out of 10 concerned with juvenile delinquents during all forms of sentence and treatment and for 15 years thereafter, the factor of *age at onset of antisocial behavior* had to be included as a differentiative indicator because of its strong predictive involvement as between successes and failures under correctional treatment. In all but four of the tables dealing with adult offenders, *the earlier the onset* of the delinquency, the higher the failure score under one or another form of peno-correctional treatment and during a significant test period thereafter; or, to state it differently, the deeper the roots of childhood maladjustment, the smaller the chance of adult law-abiding adjustment. In this connection, it will be recalled that the mean age at onset of misbehavior among the delinquents of *Unraveling Juvenile Delinquency*, whose careers are traced well into adulthood in the present work, was 8.35 years (S. D. ± 2.39), and that 87.6% were 10 years or younger (48.4%, 7 years or younger) at the onset of definitive acts of misconduct (*Unraveling*, p. 28). The antisocial acts involved so early in life include stealing, truancy, destructive mischief, running away from home, stealing rides, stealing junk, sex affairs, tantrums, disobedience, stubbornness.

36: Ten Years' Experience with the Glueck Social Prediction Table / *Maude M. Craig* and *Selma J. Glick*

In 1952 the Youth Board embarked upon the first prospective study to test the validity of the Glueck Social Prediction Table. In 1957 it published its first progress report, which described the terms, methodology, behavioral categories employed, and the limitations of the project as then seen and which gave a preliminary evaluation of the prediction table's usefulness in selecting potential delinquents.[1]

In this article we shall summarize the results of this experiment, indicating briefly some of the thinking that entered into the various modifications and changes that have taken place since the study was initiated. The findings reported here are based on 244 boys (out of a total of 303) who have been followed up for ten years. The remaining 59 boys in the sample have not yet reached their seventeenth birthday and therefore require another two years of study.

The table which the Youth Board set out to validate in 1952 was the Glueck five-factor table. During the ten years of the study, however, refinements were made, various abbreviated combinations of factors were tested, and ultimately the table was reduced to three factors.[2] This latter table, based on discipline of boy by mother, supervision by mother, and family cohesiveness, is the one we are presently using.

Selection of the Sample

Two criteria were established for selecting a sample of boys to whom the table would be applied for purposes of testing its validity: (1) boys had to be from 5½ to 6½ years old; and (2) boys had to live in high-delinquency areas (thereby making it possible to select a maximum sample of potential delinquents).

Since the age range selected coincided with the age at which children enter school, the Youth Board decided to use for the sample *all* the boys from the incoming classes of two elementary schools in comparable high-delinquency

From Maude M. Craig and Selma J. Glick, "Ten Years' Experience with the Glueck Social Prediction Table," *Crime and Delinquency* 9:3 (July 1963): 251–261.

areas.[3] There were 224 boys ranging from 5½ to 6½ years old. All lived near the school. Of these, 131 were Negroes, 40 were Puerto Ricans, and 53 were white (43 per cent of whom were of Jewish descent). This contrasted with the Glueck sample of 1,000 white boys who were mainly of Irish, Italian, Lithuanian, and English descent. Although we realized that cultural differences between the Glueck sample and ours might well affect the results of the experiment, we believed that if this table was to have general usefulness, it must be applicable to as heterogeneous a population as one might find in any metropolitan city. Nevertheless, a major question arose concerning the wisdom of applying the Glueck Table to boys so different in racial and ethnic backgrounds. To make the Youth Board sample more comparable to the Glueck sample, we asked the cooperating schools to submit, in the next two years, the names of entering first graders who were white but not Puerto Rican. In this way 79 boys were added, for a grand total of 303 to be followed up. In view of the age difference between the 224 boys in the first sample and the 79 more recent additions to the study, and in view of the problems which would necessarily ensue in data analysis, the total sample was not increased beyond equating the Negro and white groups. Table 36–1

Table 36-1

Number and Percent of Boys by Ethnic Groupings

Ethnic Groups	Total Sample—303		Sample Reported—244	
	No.	%	No.	%
White	130	42.9	73	29.9
Negro	131	43.2	131	53.6
Puerto Rican*	42	13.9	40	16.5

*Children of Puerto Rican descent were classified separately to permit study of this cultural group. (Two boys referred to as white in the second sample were later found to be Puerto Rican.)

shows the final distribution by ethnic origin for the total sample of 303 boys as well as for the 244 boys currently reported on because they are seventeen years old.

Gathering Data

After a number of orientation sessions more than thirty trained caseworkers from Youth Board Referral Units, the Research Department, and a school clinic served as home interviewers. Although no manual of procedures was yet available during the training period, we relied heavily upon the definitions found in *Unraveling Juvenile Delinquency*, stressing the fact that all data to be used for case ratings had to be factual and observed rather than impressionistic or diagnostic.

The interviewers, who interviewed the mothers—and in a few cases both the mothers and fathers—of the boys, used a structured form for recording information on family background. All cases were cleared through the Social Service Exchange and information was secured from all social agencies that had served these families. This clearance proved to be an important supplement to the family picture and, when available, was used to corroborate information provided by the family to the Youth Board interviewers.

The research design called for a comprehensive follow-up of all boys in the study to their seventeenth birthday. Each year, the caseworkers interviewed teachers, principals, and guidance counselors to assess each boy's school adjustment.[4] Recognizing that in this kind of evaluation some teachers would have individual biases, the interviewers asked for concrete examples of the problems presented by the boys. School personnel were unaware of the boys' delinquency prediction score. In addition, cases were cleared annually with the Social Service Exchange and the Police Department.

In the ten-year follow-up, only 4 of the total sample of 303 boys have been lost, even though families have moved to twenty-nine states, Puerto Rico, South America, and Malta. For those boys living outside New York City, the Youth Board received an annual written report from the schools they were attending.

Behavior Classification

Because the research design presented an opportunity to study not only delinquent behavior but also other forms of behavioral deviation, a classification system was devised for evaluating the behavior of each boy each year. Cases were submitted at staff meetings and a consensus was required before a behavior rating could be assigned. The behavioral classifications were as follows:

Category 1—Boys range from the very well adjusted to those showing mild behavior deviations. They are well ordered and cooperative and present no serious behavior problems. Some may show evidence of assertive and mild acting-out, annoying behavior, but within acceptable limits. Example:

Teacher described boy as fully dependable although he was inclined to be aggressive at times, shoving his classmates playfully and hiding their pencils. Since the teacher spoke to him there has been a diminution of the problem.

He is not one to let others "step all over him" and he will be quick to defend himself in a fight. He will not, however, start a fight unless provoked by the other boys.

He is of average intelligence and is working up to capacity.

Category 2—Children are disruptive and essentially troublesome in school. Among them are the highly energetic, hyperactive, noncomforming, attention-getting, mischievous pupils. This classification we have termed our "suspended judgment" category in anticipation that some of these children may develop increasingly aggressive patterns, whereas others will manage to stay out of serious difficulty. Example:

A hyperactive boy, who is scrappy, quarrelsome, and antagonistic toward his peers. He is apt to be restless and disruptive and a source of annoyance to his teacher. He leaves the room frequently and wanders about the corridors. He has been inattentive and has poor working habits.

Category 3—This group, called the predelinquent group, includes those children with severe behavior disorders and those who have come into conflict with the school society. Essentially hostile and severely assaultive behavior prevails, although they have not committed any serious delinquent acts. In this group, too, are the serious attendance problems—those who persistently come to school late or associate with the predelinquent ringleaders in school. Example:

A boy who provokes, fights, is defiant, aggressive, and determined to do exactly as he pleases. He has taken many of his classmates' school belongings and thus is known as a "stealer." The teacher has a hard time containing him in the classroom and is considering transferring him to a school for problem boys.

In his eight years in school, his class placement was frequently shifted to provide a reprieve for the teacher.

Category 4—Unofficial Delinquents. Children in this group have committed a specific act equivalent to an official delinquent act, but have not received any official handling by the juvenile courts. Also included in this classification are those children whose persistently destructive or overaggressive behavior would warrant their suspension from school even though it might not warrant court action. Example:

Boy started his destructive school career at a rather early age. He could not follow school routines and was constantly in conflict with the school society. He is being transferred to a school for children with behavior problems, for no teacher will put up with him.

He has threatened to "knock the teacher's brains out" if she reported his theft of $2 from her desk. He is known to have been truant from school and on one occasion he was brought back by the police. Later in the year, he was picked up as a fare-beat.

This boy is reported to be a war counselor in an antisocial gang, which has engaged in rumbles in recent months.

Category 5—Official Delinquents. Children adjudicated delinquent by the court for misbehavior of a serious nature or persistent delinquency that involved several police or court contacts. Example:

A problem from the time he entered school, he cannot get along with other children. He disrupts the class, singing and whistling when the class is working and using any method at his disposal to get attention.

He is not able to keep up with his classmates, even though he has an above average I.Q. He has been truant for 26 days and is known to the Bureau of Attendance. He has had several encounters with the police for fighting and stealing.

He and his mother violently disagree as to where he can go and when he should return. During one of these disagreements, he beat his mother severely. She, in turn, took him to court on a petition of delinquency. He was charged with incorrigibility and as being beyond the control of his parents. He was then classified as a delinquent.

For the purposes of this study, the Youth Board adopted the definition of delinquency presented by the Gluecks in *Unraveling Juvenile Delinquency:*

Delinquency refers to repeated acts of a kind which when committed by persons beyond the statutory juvenile court age of sixteen are punishable as crimes (either felonies or misdemeanors)—except for a few instances of persistent stubbornness, truancy, running away, associating with immoral persons, and the like. Children who once or twice during the period of growing up in an excitingly attractive milieu steal a toy in a ten-cent store, sneak into a subway or motion picture theater, play hooky, and the like and soon outgrow such peccadilloes are not true delinquents even though they have violated the law.[5]

Boys whom the Youth Board includes in the delinquency category are serious offenders or persistent minor delinquents.

Rating the Cases

Two raters scored each case; one was a caseworker and the other a psychologist and statistical analyst who was not then a Youth Board staff member but who had had some experience with the social prediction table. Only after scoring each case independently could the raters discuss them.[6] After scoring a group of cases, they met with the research director. If the raters agreed on the total score classification, it was accepted; if they disagreed, a third and sometimes a fourth rater was used. The prediction scores were not disclosed to teachers, principals, or parents but were placed in a confidential file. Only the raters knew them.

From the total score, the boys were classified in groups according to their probability of becoming delinquent.

Problems

Throughout the study various problems emerged.[7] One of the major difficulties which confronted the raters at the very outset was how to score boys who came from one-parent families where there was no father or mother substitute. In the majority of these cases, the father was usually never in the home at all, was absent for the major portion of the boy's life, or was present only on occasion. The Gluecks had supplied no definitions to account for these situations. Thus, the factor of *cohesiveness of the family* caused a good deal of concern, since, by our original definition, a home could not be markedly cohesive unless there were two parents residing in it—a decision based not on experience but on an automatic judgment. Accordingly, one-parent families were at best rated as having "some elements of cohesion." Further analysis of our data, however, led us to the conclusion that a home can be cohesive even though there is an absent parent.

After cases were initially scored (see Table 36–2), we agreed that the number of boys rated potentially delinquent was out of proportion to the total number of delinquents in the population of the areas from which the boys emanated. We therefore decided to study those boys whose fathers were away from home for the major portion of the boy's life or who were in and out of the home erratically. We also re-evaluated those families that had been automatically rated as having some elements of cohesion (61.3 per cent) even though one of the parents was not part of the family group.

The new definitions and concepts that emerged from this appraisal resulted in a change of rating for 16 boys. In 11 of the 16 cases, the boys were classified as nondelinquent rather than delinquent.

After the obvious corrections had been made, Table 36–3 indicated that 126 boys were identified by the five-factor table as having a very low chance of becoming delinquent, while at the other extreme 17 boys were identified as having a very high chance. Between these two extremes was a group of 57 boys found to have a little less than an even chance of becoming delinquent and 40 boys to have a little more than an even chance. Regarding the actual outcomes based on the use of the original five-factor table, 119 (94 per cent) of the 126 predicted as having very little chance of delinquency are still, at

Table 36-2

Classification of Boys According to Probability of Delinquency Five-Factor Table

Weighted Failure Score	Probability of Delinquency	Original Rating	
		No.	%
Under 200	8.2	125	51.2
200 to 249	37.0	51	20.9
250 to 299	63.5	49	20.0
300 and over	89.2	19	7.9
Total		244	100.0

Table 36-3

Results of the Five-Factor Table

Score and Delinquency Probability	Total	Behavior		Lost
		Delinquent	Nondelinquent	
Total	244	40	200	4
8.2 (low)	126	7	119	—
37.0 (less than even)	57	9	48	—
63.5 (more than even)	40	10	30	—
89.2 (high)	17	14	3	—
Lost	4	—	—	4

the end of ten years, nondelinquent. At the other extreme, 14 (82 per cent) of the 17 are serious or persistent offenders. At both extremes, therefore, the five-factor table was good, but for the 97 boys in the middle group—that is, those having a little less or a little more than an even chance of becoming delinquent—the table did not predict well; in fact, it *overpredicted*. The five-factor table as a predictor of potential delinquency was accurate in about two-fifths of the cases. In those situations where behavior contradicted the prediction score, the prediction scores were found to cluster around the borderline. For example, a weighted failure score of 249 would place the boy in a nondelinquent category in which he would have 37 chances out of 100 of becoming delinquent whereas a score of 250 would make him a delinquent (or 63.5 chances out of 100).[8] The majority of the boys whose behavior was incorrectly predicted were found to have scores of 247 to 255, hovering around the borderline. In light of these findings, the Youth Board had to secure new weighted failure scores from the Gluecks based on their original data.

Reliability of Raters on Five-factor Table

Meanwhile, a statistical consultant who was not in any way connected with the project [9] made a study of reliability among raters on the five-factor table. The rate of reliability on the factors of affection proved to be extremely low, but the other three factors yielded a very high rate of agreement. People from different disciplines were inclined to assign different ratings to the former. For example, a caseworker might tend to rate affection on the basis of psychoanalytic concepts whereas a research worker might rate on the basis of surface manifestations.[10] In view of the Gluecks' finding that the coefficient of correlation between the scores on the five-factor table and the scores on the three factors (omitting affection of mother for boy and affection of father for boy) was .961, these two factors were eliminated. The remaining three factors—discipline by father, supervision by mother, and family cohesiveness —constituted the three-factor table. For these three factors, rating was based on more objective criteria which were well defined and did not cause difficulty to the raters.

Three-factor Table

After the study had been in progress five years, the Youth Board began experimenting with the three-factor table. For this table to be applicable, however, the raters' agreement had to be on a factor-by-factor basis rather than on a total score. Thus, every case in which raters disagreed on any one of the three factors had to be reexamined. There were 22 such cases. These were submitted to the principal raters for rescoring, using only the original data on which the initial scores were based. In only 3 out of the 22 rescored cases were scores changed from a delinquent to a nondelinquent category.

The three-factor table yielded approximately a 70 per cent accuracy in predicting delinquents and an 85 per cent accuracy in predicting nondelinquents. Thus it was not accomplishing its purpose. Further examination revealed that because of the father's absence in a large number of instances (30 cases) and the resulting difficulty in rating his discipline of the boy, a substitution would have to be made for this factor. Furthermore, the mother's role during the first six years of a child's life seemed to assume greater significance than we had thought and perhaps should be weighted more heavily.

Thus, once again we shared our experiences with the Gluecks who then constructed another three-factor table, using two of the original factors—supervision of the boy by his mother and cohesiveness of the family unit—and substituting discipline of boy by his mother for discipline of the boy by his father. The Gluecks could have made the same substitution, since discipline of the boy by his mother differentiates delinquents from nondelinquents just as markedly as does discipline by father. The Gluecks supplied the Youth Board with a new set of weighted failure scores for the new three-factor table (Table 36–4).[11]

Note that Table 36–5 on the revised prediction table shows three score classes rather than four: low chance of delinquency (8.6), high chance (89.0), and a class indicating an even chance of becoming delinquent or remaining nondelinquent (58.2). By using this instead of the original five-factor table, the number of ambiguous or borderline cases (that is, not classifiable as having either a very low or a very high chance of delinquency) was reduced from

Table 36-4

Predictive Factors	Delinquency Probability
Supervision of Boy by Mother	
Suitable	9.9
Fair	57.5
Unsuitable	83.2
Discipline of Boy by Mother	
Firm but kindly	6.1
Erratic	62.3
Overstrict	73.3
Lax	82.9
Cohesiveness of Family	
Marked	20.6
Some	61.3
None	96.9

Score Class	Chances for Delinquency
Less than 140	8.6%
140-200	58.2%
200 or over	89.0%

Table 36-5

Findings on Revised Three-factor Table

Probability of Delinquency	Total Group	Behavior		Lost
		Delinquent	Non delinquent	
Total	244	40	200	4
8.6 (low)	193	7	186	—
58.2 (almost even chance)	19	9	10	—
89.0 (high)	27	23	4	—
Unable to rate[a]	1	1	—	—
Lost	4	—	—	4

[a]Record data on the factor of mother's discipline were insufficient so that this case could not be rated.

97 to 19—the other cases clearly falling into the low or the high chance of delinquency groups. The original Youth Board raters scored all cases on the new factor, using only the original interview material.[12]

Results of applying the new table indicate that of the 27 boys predicted as delinquent, 23 are serious or persistent delinquents—an 85.1 per cent accuracy in predicting delinquency. Of the 193 cases predicted nondelinquents, 186 (or 96.4 per cent) are, in fact, nondelinquents. Of the 19 boys who were predicted as having an almost even chance of becoming delinquent or remaining nondelinquent, almost half are delinquent and the other half nondelinquent. This revised three-factor table has yielded the highest rate of accuracy in predicting delinquents of any of the tables we have tested to date for all ethnic groups. Since 59 boys have not as yet reached their seventeenth birthday, an analysis of the findings by ethnic groups will be presented in a later publication.

These results obtained by the Youth Board are similar to the findings of the Maximum Benefits Project in Washington, D.C., in which the Social Prediction Table was applied to 179 children from high-delinquency areas.[13]

Other Findings

Nondelinquents. Of the 186 boys who were predicted nondelinquent and are, in fact, nondelinquent, not all are free of problems. Approximately 20 per cent of them exhibited problem behavior in school each year. They are the youngsters usually described as pesty, annoying, attention seeking. However, they have not committed delinquent acts and are less likely than the delinquents to be sullen, aggressive, or defiant.

Delinquent Boys. A study of the 40 boys who became delinquent indicated that 30 had been adjudicated delinquent by the court; 34 boys had manifested serious problems in school during their first three years; and 10 had been persistent delinquents before they reached their tenth birthday. Fourteen boys became delinquent between the ages of 12 and 14 and 16 boys were included in the delinquent category before they reached their sixteenth birthday. Of the 40 delinquents, 4 were reported to be members of organized antisocial gangs. The delinquent careers of this group began at an early age and a large proportion of the boys have proven to be recidivists.

Pathology in the Boys' Families. The Youth Board found that in 21 families of the boys who became delinquent one or more members had a criminal record. Problems of alcoholism, promiscuity, severe marital discord, and physical and emotional neglect were frequent in these homes. In only 7 homes was discipline considered good; in the remaining 33, discipline was rated as lacking, unsound, or erratic. Only 3 boys were noted as coming from cohesive homes; 9 boys scored well on mother's supervision. Over 30 of the families were known to one or more social agencies, testifying to their difficulties and need for assistance.

Reliability of the Raters

The scores of each rater using the original three-factor table were submitted for analysis to the statistical consultant. His results contradicted the findings of Dr. Charles S. Prigmore, whose study indicated a low rate of reliability.[14] Nevertheless, one may question whether the court records on the child's first six years of life, used by Dr. Prigmore's raters for various tests of reliability, were sufficiently detailed and objective to enable them to apply the Glueck Social Prediction Table.

A statement by Dr. Angoff, the statistical consultant, sums up the results of the Youth Board's testing:

A reliability analysis has been made of the degree to which raters, operating independently, have reached agreement in the assessment of the home conditions described by the sums of the factors (1, 2 and 5). These reliabilities—in the low .90's for judgments of conditions in white and Puerto Rican homes, and in the low .80's for judgments of conditions in Negro homes—may be considered quite high, particularly in consideration of the fact that they necessarily derive from subjective judgments. The figures indicate that rigorously objective criteria must have been used in the formation of these judgments.

The Glueck Prediction Table has undergone many changes since its original construction, all aimed at refining it and making it a better method of examining the family backgrounds of boys, and for sensitizing us to certain specific factors in family life which, if allowed to persist, will tend to produce delinquency.

The revised three-factor table appears to be an important guide in highlighting those factors. We do not regard it as a substitute for sound clinical judgment but as an additional tool to aid in the diagnostic process.

Six years' exposure to deleterious home situations does not necessarily predestine a youngster to delinquency. The findings of this study show the justification and need for eradicating the family pathology and enriching family life as a primary step in the prevention of juvenile delinquency.

NOTES

1. Research Department, New York City Youth Board, *Delinquency Prediction—A Progress Report, 1952–1956,* July 1957.

2. The evolution of this three-factor table has been described in the following series of papers by Eleanor T. Glueck: "Spotting Potential Delinquents: Can It Be Done?" *Federal Probation,* Sept. 1956; "Efforts to Identify Delinquents," *Federal Probation,* June 1960; "Toward Improving the Identification of Delinquents," *Journal of Criminal Law, Criminology and Police Science,* June 1962; "Toward Further Improving the Identification of Delinquents," *Journal of Criminal Law, Criminology and Police Science,* June 1963.

3. A study of these areas was presented in an unpublished manuscript by the Research Department, New York City Youth Board, Dec. 1953.

4. This study would not have been possible without the cooperation of the teachers and principals of the schools.

5. Glueck, *op. cit.* note 1, p. 13.

6. From continued discussion of problems encountered in rating were evolved more objective criteria which may have influenced the high rate of reliability.

7. We should emphasize the fact that the original study which the Gluecks conducted and on whose findings the prediction table was based was for all practical purposes a *retrospective study* of boys ranging from eleven to seventeen years old. The Gluecks had much more data than the Youth Board on which to base judgments. Many of the difficulties the Youth Board encountered in carrying on a study of very young children were not encountered by the Gluecks. If the Gluecks did not have sufficiently clear information on any one of the factors, they omitted the case from their Prediction Table (thus, their Prediction Table was based on 890 and not on 1,000 cases). Then, too, the cultural differences in the Youth Board's sample as contrasted with the Gluecks' sample also presented rating problems.

8. For a full description of the way in which weighted failure scores were derived see Glueck, *op. cit,* note 1.

9. Dr. William Angoff, Assistant Director of Statistical Analyses, Educational Testing Service, Princeton, N.J.

10. Eleanor T. Glueck discussed this in "Efforts to Identify Delinquents," *Federal Probation,* June 1960, in a section entitled "Resolution of Difficulties in Applying the Table," pp. 55–56.

11. Eleanor T. Glueck, "Toward Further Improving the Identification of Potential Delinquents," *Journal of Criminal Law, Criminology and Police Science,* June 1963.

12. Ten years had elapsed since the original rating so that raters could not be influenced by their previous scores.

13. Communication from Mrs. Nina Trevvett, Executive Director, Commissioners' Youth Council, Washington, D.C., April 1963.

14. Charles S. Prigmore, "An Analysis of Rater Reliability on the Glueck Scale for the Prediction of Juvenile Delinquency," *Journal of Criminal Law, Criminology and Police Science,* March 1963. The Youth Board plans to test the reliability of the table still further by using raters from different disciplines and regions for scoring cases.

37: Making Proper Inferences /
Travis Hirschi and *Hanan C. Selvin*

In *Unraveling* the Gluecks construct prediction instruments using "factors that clearly differentiate the delinquents and nondelinquents in this research." The technique for constructing these tables is as follows: Because 83.2 percent of those who are unsuitably supervised are delinquents, any boy who is unsuitably supervised is given a "failure score" on this item of 83.2; likewise, since 9.9 percent of those who are suitably supervised are delinquents, suitably supervised boys are given a failure score on supervision of 9.9. This procedure is repeated for each of the items used (the number of items never exceeds five), and each boy receives a total failure score. The percentage of delinquents within each failure-score category is then considered to be the chances of delinquency for boys with the score in question (Table 37–1).

Table 37-1
*Detailed Prediction Table from Five Factors of Social Background**

Weighted Failure	Number of Delinquents	Chances of Delinquency (per Hundred)	Number of Nondelinquents	Chances of Non delinquency (per Hundred)
Under 150	5	2.9	167	97.1
150-199	19	15.7	102	84.3
200-249	40	37.0	68	63.0
250-299	122	63.5	70	36.5
300-349	141	86.0	23	14.0
350-399	73	90.1	8	9.9
400 and over	51	98.1	1	1.9
	451		439	

*Sheldon and Eleanor Glueck, *Unraveling*, p. 261.

By assigning to each delinquent and non-delinquent, concerning whom information was available on all five factors, his score on each, summating the scores, and distributing the cases into the appropriate score class, we arrive at the detailed prediction table . . . after translating the number of cases in each subclass into a per cent of the total number in each score class. These then became the chances out of a hundred of potential delinquency and nondelinquency.[1]

From Travis Hirschi and Hanan C. Selvin, *Delinquency Research* (New York: The Free Press, 1967), Chapter 14, pp. 235–252; 255–256.

Table 37-2

*Prediction Table for Five Factors of Social Background**

(1) Weighted Failure Score (Gluecks)	(2) Number of Delinquents (Gluecks)	(3) Number of Nondelinquents (Gluecks)	(4) Number of Nondelinquents (Rate Delinquency Estimated at 10 Percent)	(5) Chances of Delinquency (Gluecks)	(6) Chances of Delinquency (Rate Estimated at 10 Percent)	(7) Expected Errors (Rate Estimated at 10 Percent)**
Under 150	5	167	1,503	2.9	0.3	5
150-199	19	102	918	15.7	2.0	19
200-249	40	68	612	37.0	6.2	40
250-299	122	70	630	63.5	16.2	122
300-349	141	23	207	86.0	40.5	141
350-399	73	8	72	90.1	50.3	72
400 and over	51	1	9	98.1	85.0	9
Missing cases	49	61	549	44.5	8.2	49
Total	500	500	4,500	50.0	10.0	457

*Reiss, *op. cit.*, p. 119. We have added the column numbers.
**The percentage reduction in the error of prediction is 8.6 percent.

The Gluecks assume that boys with failure scores between, say, 350 and 399 will become delinquents 90.1 per cent of the time. In an early review of the Gluecks' book, Reiss argued that "unless this [sampling rate of 50 per cent delinquents] is the actual rate in a similar population for which the predictions are made, the tables will yield very poor prediction."[2] Reiss then shows how the predictive power of the instrument would be affected by its use in a population in which only one boy in ten was delinquent.[3]

The first three columns of Table 37–2 are taken from the Gluecks' table. In the fourth column Reiss calculates the number of nondelinquents that would occur in each row if there were 4,500 nondelinquents instead of 500 (thus making the delinquents 10 percent of the population) and if these 4,500 nondelinquents distributed themselves in the same proportions as the 500 nondelinquents in the third column (1,503 is the same proportion of 4,500 as 167 is of 500). Column 6 is derived from columns 2 and 4 in the same way that column 5 was derived from columns 2 and 3: $5/(5+167)=2.9$ percent; $5'/(5+1,503)=0.3$ percent.

The two "Chances of Delinquency" columns, 5 and 6, are the basis for prediction. Whenever the chances are 50 percent or more, the best prediction that can be made is that all of the boys in that category are delinquent. When the chances are less than 50 percent, the best prediction is that all are nondelinquent. Column 7 shows how many errors would be made by following these rules of prediction in the 10 percent delinquent population. In the first row, all 172 cases would be predicted nondelinquent, but 0.3 percent, or 5 cases, would actually be delinquent. The same reasoning applies to all but the last two rows, where all cases would be predicted delinquent by both methods. Finally, Reiss computes an overall measure of the value of the revised prediction: the reduction in the proportion of errors made by taking into account the failure scores, as compared with the best prediction that could be made without them. It is a disappointing 8.6 per cent.[4]

Despite the attacks by Reiss and others on the Gluecks' predictive instrument, the issue is not as clear as it may appear at first glance. Thus the Gluecks' reply to their critics:

Reiss and similar critics have not clearly explained just why the adjustment to a supposed actual proportion of 9:1 is necessary; or why differences in the incidence of delinquents and non-delinquents in any population should and would have a serious distorting influence on the distribution of scores of the predictive factors as presented in our 50–50.[5]

However, as further passages from the Gluecks' reply indicate, the Gluecks and their critics sometimes appear to be talking about two different things:

The use of equal numbers in the samples originally compared is not only legitimate but important for the accurate determination of the incidence of the factors under comparison. It is, for example, a frequent technique in medical research. . . . Assuming that the sample of delinquents and the sample of nondelinquents are fairly representative of the populations from which the cases were derived, the fact that the total group of nondelinquents in the general population is nine times as numerous as the total group of delinquents can have little to do with the outcome when comparing the two samples; and it should, equally, have little to do with the outcome when applying the table to new populations.[6]

As we have already shown, it is possible to use the Gluecks' tables to describe their delinquent and nondelinquent populations—for example, to predict the proportion of delinquents who attend church regularly. Insofar as such predictions are concerned, the Gluecks are correct: The use of equal numbers of delinquents and nondelinquents is perfectly legitimate.

The critics, however, are not arguing that the incidence of the factors cannot be predicted accurately; they are arguing that delinquency cannot be predicted accurately. And this is a separate question. The difference becomes clearer in still another quotation from Sheldon Glueck's defense:

If one were making a study comparing the incidence of blood pressure [sic], pulse [sic], certain chemicals in the blood and urine, etc. of persons with a malignant disease, with their incidence among healthy persons, would it make any difference whether the *general* incidence of such diseased persons in the particular community amounted to 10 per cent or 50 per cent? And, assuming that in the city in which the original experiment was done the population proportions of the well and the ill were 50–50, would this fact interfere with the predictive capacity of a table of indications and symptoms when applied to a city in which the proportions were 90:10? [7]

Again, two different questions are being asked. The answer to the first one is No, it wouldn't make any difference if one wanted to predict the incidence of (high) blood pressure, (rapid) pulse, certain chemicals in the blood and urine, and so on, from knowledge of the presence or absence of malignant disease. One simply follows the rule of percentaging in the representative direction.

The answer to the second question, however, is clearly Yes, it certainly would.[8] The accuracy of predictions of disease from a set of symptoms depends on the proportion having the disease for the same reason that the efficiency of the Gluecks' predictive instrument depends upon the percentage of delinquents in the population on which it is used.

This argument may be more compelling with an extreme example. Suppose that five hundred persons with stomach cancer are compared with five hundred healthy persons on the variables suggested by the Gluecks and that the following results were obtained.

	Stomach Cancer Patients	Healthy Persons
With high blood pressure, rapid pulse, and chemical X in blood and urine	450	50
Without high blood pressure, rapid pulse, or chemical X in blood and urine	50	450

	Stomach Cancer Patients	Healthy Persons
With high blood pressure, rapid pulse, and chemical X in Blood and urine	450	4,950
Without high blood pressure, rapid pulse, or chemical X in blood and urine	50	44,550

Following the Gluecks' logic, there is a 90 per cent chance that a person with high blood pressure, rapid pulse, and chemical X in his blood and urine is suffering from stomach cancer. This seems sufficient to justify an exploratory operation. Suppose, however, that the proportion of persons in the population with stomach cancer is only 1 per cent. The above table would be obtained from a representative sample of this population (assuming the same proportions as in the table above). It turns out, then, that the chance that a person with the described symptoms has stomach cancer is only 8.3 per cent (450/5,400). (The chance that a person with stomach cancer has the described symptoms is, of course, unchanged.) Let us all hope that this "frequent technique in medical research" is used only to predict symptoms once the presence of the disease is known and that it is not the basis upon which surgeons decide to operate.[9]

The Gluecks' prediction tables thus illustrate an important methodological point: If an investigator wishes to make statements about the population from which his sample was drawn, he must percentage within categories representative of that population.[10] The Gluecks can (perhaps) make accurate statements about the distributions of their independent variables within the delinquent and nondelinquent populations; they cannot make accurate statements about the distributions of delinquency within categories of their independent variables for some larger population.

Sheldon Glueck suggests that this is an empirical question: ". . . one should not dogmatize at the outset that the influence of differences in proportions will seriously affect the outcome; one must await the proof of the pudding." [11] It is, on the contrary, strictly a logical question. The Gluecks' predictions for populations with different distributions of the dependent variable cannot be correct unless the data upon which the original predictive device was based were in error. How, then, is one to account for the many validation studies that purport to show the accuracy of the Gluecks' predictive device?

It should be pointed out that the tables reflecting the experience in these checkups resemble *not* the adjusted tables of Reiss and others, but the original Glueck table.[12]

Most of these studies examine the distribution of delinquency prediction scores within samples of delinquents or nondelinquents.[13] Again, this is not the issue. The prediction device was designed to predict delinquency from individual characteristics, not vice versa.

The New York City Youth Board study, which followed a sample of 301 boys from the time they entered school until they were seventeen, got results much like the original Glueck table.[14] Since only about one boy in seven in this sample was eventually classified as delinquent, it may appear that the rocks in the pudding had no effect on its quality. However, what this study really shows is that purely logical truths are unaffected by empirical investigation.

In the Youth Board study, only 5 of 257 nondelinquents had scores on the prediction scale indicating that they were very likely to become delinquent, while 28 of the 44 delinquents had such scores, for an 85 percent (28/33) success rate. This success rate compares favorably with the 89 percent success rate expected on the basis of the *Unraveling* sample. Now, in order to do almost as well in a sample in which one of seven boys is delinquent as one did in a sample in which one of two boys is delinquent, something has to give: In this case, of course, it is the distribution of scores on the items used to predict delinquency. Only about one-fourth as many nondelinquents are incorrectly predicted delinquent as one would expect by comparing the composition of the *Unraveling* and the Youth Board samples. To compensate, there are only about one-fourth as many nondelinquents with high scores on the predictive instrument as one would expect from their relative distribution in the *Unraveling* sample. There is abundant evidence that vagaries of sampling alone do not account for the unexpected dearth of nondelinquents with high scores:

After cases were initially scored . . . , we agreed that *the number of boys rated potentially delinquent was out of proportion to the total number of delinquents in the population of the areas from which the boys emanated.* We therefore [!] decided to study those boys whose fathers were away from home for the major portion of the boy's life. . . .[15]

This "back to the drawing board" or "if at first you don't succeed" approach to validation of a predictive instrument was not counted upon by the critics.[16] They assumed they were giving the Gluecks the benefit of a very serious doubt by simply extending the relation found in *Unraveling* to populations differing in the ratio of delinquents to nondelinquents. They did not suspect that the Gluecks' data-dredging procedures had produced a predictive instrument more strongly related to delinquency in samples other than the one suggesting it. For that matter, how did the Gluecks know that their *Unraveling* data were consistently underestimating the relations between their independent variables and delinquency?

NOTES

1. Sheldon and Eleanor Glueck, *Unraveling Juvenile Delinquency.* Cambridge: Harvard University Press, 1950, p. 261.

2. Albert J. Reiss, *"Unraveling Juvenile Delinquency, II. An appraisal of the research methods,"* American Journal of Sociology, 57, 1951, pp. 115–120.

3. This seems to be a reasonable figure for illustrative purposes: ". . . even in the most marked 'delinquency areas' or delinquency subcultures of our cities, not more than

a small fraction of the boys (say 10 or 15 percent) become delinquent." Sheldon Glueck, *"Ten Years of Unraveling Juvenile Delinquency," Journal of Criminal Law, Criminology and Police Science,* 51, 1960, p. 300.

4. Had nothing been known about the boys, the best prediction would have been that each boy was nondelinquent; this would have resulted in five hundred errors. Using the revised prediction table yields 457 errors, a reduction of 43 errors, or a proportionate reduction of 43 / 500 (8.6 per cent).

5. Sheldon Glueck, *"Ten Years of Unraveling Juvenile Delinquency,"* p. 302.

6. *Ibid.,* p. 303.

7. *Ibid.*

8. We are assuming that the medical researchers have samples of equal size of persons with malignant disease and of healthy persons and that they wish to be able to predict disease from an examination of symptoms. That is, we are assuming that the case is analogous to the Gluecks' case.

9. The logic of our example is exactly the same as that used by Reiss and the other critics of the Gluecks' predictive instrument.

10. Unless, of course, population distributions are known; it would then be possible to weight the results appropriately.

11. Sheldon Glueck, *"Ten Years of Unraveling Juvenile Delinquency,"* p. 303.

12. *Ibid.,* pp. 305.

13. Many of the validation studies are briefly summarized in Sheldon Glueck, *ibid.,* pp. 303–307. See also Sheldon and Eleanor Glueck, *Predicting Delinquency and Crime.* Cambridge: Harvard University Press, 1959, and their *Ventures in Criminology.* Cambridge: Harvard University Press, 1964, Part II.

14. Maude M. Craig and Selma J. Glick, "Ten Years' Experience with the Glueck Social Prediction Table," *Crime and Delinquency,* 9, 1963, pp. 249–261. See also *A Manual of Procedures for Application of the Glueck Prediction Table.* New York City Youth Board, 1964.

15. Craig and Glick, *op. cit.,* p. 256. (Authors' italics.)

16. Alfred J. Kahn ("The Case of the Premature Claims: Public Policy and Delinquency Prediction," *Crime and Delinquency,* 11, 1965, pp. 217–228) notes several adjustments that transformed this attempt to validate the Gluecks' prediction device into an exploratory study. The issues raised by the "success" of the Youth Board study are more serious than our discussion of sampling error and the direction of percentaging suggests. See also Kenneth Keniston, "Entangling Juvenile Delinquency," *Commentary,* June, 1960, pp. 486–491.

38: Public Policy and Delinquency Prediction / *Alfred J. Kahn*

The claims are specific and sweeping and the agencies affected are told that a new tool is ready for use:

"The Glueck Social Prediction Table, which the New York City Youth Board set out to test in 1952, has been validated . . . ," report Craig and

From Alfred J. Kahn, "The Case of the Premature Claims," *Crime and Delinquency* 11:3 (July 1965): 218–228.

Glick.[1] Moreover, they add, "It has yielded a sufficient degree of accuracy to warrant its use by those agencies interested in delinquency prevention and control."[2]

In this they repeat the claim of their executive director, whose introduction to *A Manual of Procedures for Application of the Glueck Prediction Table,* published some five months before the research article cited above, announced: "We are glad to note that this prediction table is a valid instrument."[3]

At the same time another major project involving prospective testing of the table announced: "The D.C. Commissioner's Youth Council will immediately begin applying it—to identify, from among the hordes of children who pass our way, those who are most in need of our protective services."[4]

Professor Sheldon Glueck has summed up these evaluations by stating that "the evidence of the various follow-up studies on a wide variety of samples, and especially the evidence of the New York and Washington investigations, constitutes proof beyond a reasonable doubt."[5]

It is easy to understand why the local and national press picks up these claims with headlines such as "Are You Raising a Delinquent? Two Criminologists Can Tell." Small wonder, too, that school board members and influential citizens ask why this instrument is not at work assisting with their local delinquency problems.

Why, then, all of the expressions of doubt and public criticism from criminologists and sociologists—and the urging, in agency publications, that the user beware?[6] Fully analyzed, the controversy revolves around issues of research standards and public policy. The potential user of the Glueck tables in their current variations will want to explore both of these dimensions.

In brief, the critics are almost unanimous in the following views:

1. Neither the New York City Youth Board nor the Commissioner's Youth Council has validated the scale which they set out to test.

2. Neither of the two studies reported has shown that delinquency prediction helps the children affected—and there is reason to believe that it may harm them.

3. Even if one accepts the framework of the reported studies, the statistical interpretation of the predictive efficiency of the findings is exaggerated, to say the least.

4. There are significant reasons, from both theoretical and public policy perspectives, to doubt whether one should ever think of the Glueck tables as potential operational tools.

Validation

Researchers make a fundamental distinction between an *exploratory study* and an *experiment*. The former is tentative in its conceptualizations, flexible in its methods. It seeks leads and hypotheses. Its intent is to generate findings of sufficient significance to justify moving toward experimental work. The experiment, on the other hand, has tighter rules. Something is to be proven or disproven, shown to have or not to have a specified relationship—in this case, demonstrated as capable or not capable of predicting delinquency. Standards of reliability, validity, precision, and statistical significance must be adhered to. *The rules of the game may not be changed en route.*

Both of the projects analyzed here were obviously intended to be "experimental" from the very beginning. They are, as already indicated, the main bases for the claims by the Gluecks that their tables have been validated.[7]

When the Youth Board project began in 1952 the objectives were clear. Sheldon and Eleanor Glueck had produced a five-factor prediction table based on analysis of the differences between delinquents and nondelinquents in Massachusetts. It was derived from retrospective analysis of known institutionalized delinquents and nondelinquents and it involved rating the children's familial relationships and environment.[8]

The Glueck tables were constructed by isolating factors found to distinguish known delinquents from nondelinquents in their study. The percentage of those characterized by a factor who were delinquent is used in developing a score for that factor. (Thus, if of the boys whose fathers' discipline could be described as "overstrict or erratic," 71.8 per cent were found to be delinquent in the original group studied, the presence of an "overstrict or erratic" father would add 71.8 points to the "weighted failure score" for any boy in a new group for which predictions are being made.) Five factors were initially employed and a child's score was the sum of the weighted scores reflecting his classification on each of these factors.

The five initial factors employed in the Youth Board scale were (1) discipline of boy by father (overstrict or erratic, lax, firm but kindly), (2) supervision of boy by mother (unsuitable, fair, close or suitable), (3) affection of father for boy (indifferent or hostile, warm [including overprotective]), (4) affection of mother for boy (indifferent or hostile, warm [including overprotective]), and (5) cohesiveness of family (unintegrated, some elements of cohesion, cohesive).

When a total score is obtained in the manner described, it is compared to the table developed by the Gluecks giving the percentage of boys in their Massachusetts sample with the given score who were delinquent and the percentage who were nondelinquent. These percentages are then used as delinquency "probabilities" for the entire class of boys with the score. A prediction, in other words, is thus made relative to the *group* rate for boys with a given score.

From the very beginning various questions were raised about *Unraveling Juvenile Delinquency* which are not directly relevant here; but it was agreed, too, that testing of the Glueck tables could contribute to theory development. Special caution was expressed about the predictive instrument as an operational tool since it had been developed on the basis of a particular Massachusetts population, had not yet been validated on a new group, had not been tested in actual use with young children for whom predictions could be made, and had left unanswered the question of whether it would not, on the level of service, be more valuable to locate children "in need of help" rather than "potential delinquents." [9]

During the next several years the authors of *Unraveling* were encouraged by the results of a series of retrospective applications of their tables.[10] Where children were adjudicated delinquents (particularly where they were already institutionalized) the table was applied to ask: Would these children have been predicted as likely delinquents if the table had been used when they were younger? The answers were overwhelmingly affirmative. But by the very nature of these studies the results could not tell how many delinquents would have been missed and how many nondelinquents inappropriately labeled. Nor could an answer be given to the objection raised about *Unraveling*— contamination of the evaluations of early childhood experience and relationships by the evaluator's knowledge that certain children had actually become delinquent. Clearly, *prospective* studies were needed. Could the Glueck table predict in advance?

The New York City Youth Board in 1952 and the D.C. Maximum Benefits Project in 1954 launched such *prospective* studies. In each instance, provision was made for services to be given to a subsample of those predicted delinquent to see whether the prediction could be reversed. It is because these were prospective studies which tried to test the social usefulness of the Glueck tools that they have been given so much attention. For this same reason it is urgent to stress that the studies have not yet attained either objective: validation of the table, or successful intervention with predicted delinquents.

The Youth Board undertook testing the table to find out whether, at age five or six, the likely delinquent could be differentiated from the nondelinquent. Children would be followed up for ten years. Of those predicted as likely to become delinquent, some would be sent to a school child-guidance clinic for treatment to determine whether a method existed for making use of (and thus counteracting) a delinquency prediction.

The first Youth Board progress report, covering the 1952–56 period, was published in 1957.[11] It could not be a final report, since the children were still young, but it seemed to point to the likelihood of an overprediction of delinquency. It also indicated "high attrition" in the group predicted as probable delinquents and assigned for child guidance treatment because several had already moved away. There has been no subsequent published treatment report, but informal information suggests that treatment results were not promising after four years (nor has the D.C. project been able as yet to report success with a treatment group from among predicted delinquents). One cannot know, therefore, from current Youth Board reports whether children predicted as delinquent and served in a clinic (or elsewhere, for that matter) actually can be helped or whether the community can be protected.

Thus, at best—even if all serious questions about the research status of the scale are put aside—what has been produced is a prediction instrument of *potential* worth in identifying children who need help and for testing the Gluecks' causation theories. There is still no èvidence that the prediction actually helps schools, communities, or families in any way since no test has been reported and successfully completed involving use of the predictions to help children. On the other hand, a good deal of social-psychological theory suggests—as pointed out below—that the prediction may harm rather than help if it results in application of a negative label to the child.

In 1960 the director of the Youth Board issued a press release (rather than a research report) announcing that the work had attained the status of "relatively exact science" and recommending that "the prediction scale be applied broadly through selected schools throughout the city." The Citizens' Committee for Children of New York, the New York Society for the Psychological Study of Social Issues, and others questioned the research status of the scale and its suitability, at that time, for widespread use. They noted that the scale obviously overpredicted delinquency and that the Youth Board used definitions of delinquency which were different from those generally accepted and which included antisocial behavior, mental illness, unofficial delinquency, and delinquent traits—in addition to official delinquency. The reliability and validity of the scales were still undetermined. The Citizens' Committee's report also noted:

This specialized scale poses an additional problem. Delinquency is a stigma-bearing legal adjudication, not a specific disease or diagnosis. A child labeled as a potential delinquent may well suffer consequences in teacher attitude, school program, and his own self-respect which will contribute to maladjustment and delinquency. To label a child as a "future bad boy" (*New York Times* report of press conference) may help make him one. The Youth Board announcement did not clarify how the device would be given to the schools while labeling was to be avoided. For a delinquency instrument would be practicable for use in the schools only if it could be administered by teachers or other school-based personnel. The Youth Board experiment involves ratings and judgments by trained personnel on the basis of data assembled by a special staff from three sources: home interviews with parents, interviews with teachers, collateral information from social agencies. Thus far, there has been no public report of what has been done to convert this research tool into a practical instrument or to test what occurs in the course of such conversion. This, too, would make it premature to plan for its use in the schools even if the scale were validated.

Responding to these questions, the Youth Board announced that more time was needed and that as the boys moved into the delinquency ages, the accuracy of the scale would probably increase. The test was to continue for another three years at least. In addition, the Youth Board announced: "For the past two years simplified methods for this purpose (i.e., to convert this research tool into a practical instrument) have been under study . . . and a full report is currently in preparation."

The statement was welcomed—as was the decision not to move into the schools with this unproved instrument in 1960.

Despite the 1960 announcement, however, a 1963 research article from the

Youth Board,[12] the 1964 *Manual,* and the April 1965 article [13] do not cope with the question of converting the scale into a practical instrument. All the results are based on judgments by highly trained social workers and psychologists—so that there is no way to know whether the *Manual* or scale turned over to anyone else could achieve the same results. In fact, even if one were to grant all the claims of research findings in the Craig and Glick papers of 1963 and 1965, we would know only that a highly skilled staff with a high level of foundation financing and infinite time to rate cases and reconcile differences can presumably train itself in reliable and valid use of a scale. There is no way to tell whether this would help school personnel—or any agency unable to plan for home visits, social service exchange clearance, record analysis, and highly qualified, specially trained staff!

Nor is there any indication that school personnel, given such a scale, can use the results objectively without its use affecting the way a child is seen and dealt with. In the one published reference to the matter we are told that the teachers and guidance staff are not to have the material. Who then is to have it? The *Manual* does not deal with these matters. A new experiment with the scale, announced by the Youth Board almost three weeks after the initial story and apparently the basis of a request it has made for funding, may address these issues. If so, the need for the experiment only serves to confirm that the *Manual* was far from ready for release. A manual should be an operational tool.

From Experiment to Exploration

As indicated, the very first published report (1957) revealed problems in scoring which contributed to mispredictions. The 1960 public critiques noted that a greater degree of statistical accuracy could be obtained by simply predicting that no one would be delinquent than by using the Glueck scale. The public discussion and a conference of experts which confirmed the public criticism [14] were followed by an intensive period of work within the Youth Board.

As reported in the Youth Board's 1963 article, the research staff gradually came to realize that the differences between the New York City population and the population with which the Gluecks had worked in Massachusetts, particularly in the number of fatherless families, demanded a change in the scale if the predictive accuracy was to improve and overprediction of delinquency was to be kept down (just as the D.C. project confronted the fact that a considerable portion of its sample was Negro). Over a long period, "experimentation with various factors and combinations of factors led to the three-factor table." The Youth Board turned to the Gluecks for "new weighted failure scores" and dropped those factors showing low levels of agreement among raters. A three-factor table (retaining judgments about the father) was in use by the fifth year but was too inaccurate. Then the Gluecks produced another three-factor table, *using only two of the five factors with which the Youth Board had begun in 1952* and making some minor changes in one of these. (The prediction scale or table as now offered requires rating of the "discipline of boy by mother," "supervision of boy by mother," and "cohesiveness of family." It deals only with boys. (The subcategories under "cohesiveness of the family unit" are reworded a bit.) Or, to put it differently, the Youth Board has gradually, and through a series of applications and modifications, had a prediction model designed that fits its group. Even the score weights were changed to give three prediction score classes ("low chance of delinquency," "high chance," "even chance") in place of its original (and too inaccurate) four classes.

A similar process has been followed in the D.C. undertaking. After a series of interim measures instituted because of the inapplicability of the original five-factor table to the population involved, the 179 cases were rescored in 1962. We are told that only the original rating material was used, but we are not told of the degree to which knowledge of subsequent events may have "contaminated" the ratings—and we are not told of the extent to which such knowledge entered into the process of developing a three-factor table that would fit. Here, too, the Youth Board report of July 1963 is vague but there is considerable evidence that what finally emerged was a table fitted to the population under study and able to account for it, not a predictive table based *independently* on the Glueck work alone and thus *prospectively* tested by this new research.

Given the extensive "fitting" process, the new tables, as might be expected, fit the data reasonably well (although, as indicated below, the degree of misprediction may still cause concern or raise questions as to whether the investment and side effects are worth it). But the constant shifting and redesigning have changed this from a prediction *experiment* to a new *exploratory study*. The results do not tell us whether the Youth Board scale actually predicts. It may be able to identify delinquents retrospectively, with a population of New York boys. The Youth Board is now at the same stage with New York data as the Gluecks were in offering a possible device for Boston in 1952. Its own July 1963 report states, "The Glueck Prediction Table has undergone many changes. . . ."

The Youth Board and the D.C. Maximum Benefits Project should now try to predict forward with a new group and not change the rules of the game en route. Until this is done, no one can claim a validated prediction scale. Nobody knows whether the scale offered in the *Manual* will or will not predict delinquency among New York boys rated while in elementary school. Of, if successful predictions are made with boys from one socio-economic or ethnic or racial grouping, it is certainly not known whether the scale would work elsewhere in the city, in other cities, or in the suburbs. Only some years of true prospective research *with a scale not tampered with during the study* and with several different populations will tell.

Interpreting the Statistics

Even the results thus far obtained should not be exaggerated. The crucial table in the Youth Board *Manual* is summarized in the table below, with the headings rephrased to increase clarity. The Youth Board describes this as 95.6 per cent accuracy (correct predictions in 236 cases of nondelinquency and in 28 cases of delinquency, or 264 of 276 if one ignores "even chance" predictions). Since the real issue is the delinquency prediction (classification in the "high" group), the accuracy may better be seen as 28 of 33, or 84.8 per cent.

Probability of Delinquency	Cases in Total Sample	Classification at Follow-up	
		Delinquent	Nondelinquent
Total	301	44	257
Low Chance	243	7	236
Even Chance	25	9	16
High Chance	33	28	5

Most of the predictions are inevitably predictions of nondelinquency. If the issue is not the percentage of accuracy in predicting delinquency plus nondelinquency, or the percentage of accuracy where delinquency is predicted, but rather the *efficiency* of the scale as a finder of potential delinquents, then the relevant rate is 63.6 per cent. The scale places in the "high" category (children predicted to be delinquent) 28 of the 44 actually classified eventually as delinquents.

The same general point may be made with reference to the April 1965 Craig and Glick article, which states that "in predicting delinquency, the table chose 7 of the 8 white boys who became delinquent (87.5%), 16 of the 20 Negro boys (80%), and all of the 5 Puerto Rican boys (100%)."

However, the authors dismiss as irrelevant the fact that, in addition, 13 Negro boys whom the Youth Board researchers had not placed in the "delinquency predicted" category did become delinquent. A scale which predicts 16 out of 29 cases accurately has an efficiency of 55 per cent—a more realistic figure than the 80 per cent advertised. In these terms the Puerto Rican percentage was not 100 per cent but 71 per cent (5 correct predictions in 7 cases of delinquency).

In apparently acknowledging in a footnote [15] this issue of how to read the percentages, the authors state that they are answering the following question only: "Of that group selected as potential delinquents, how many became delinquent?" They are "not concerned," they go on to say, "with the total delinquent population." Obviously a public to which a scale is offered *is* concerned.

The Trevvett article in the same issue of *Crime and Delinquency* presents a similarly debatable pattern of interpretation in all tables.[16] To select only one for illustration: Table 1 is said to show that the five-factor scale originally used predicts nondelinquency at a 79 per cent rate of accuracy. This is derived from the finding that 15 of the 19 children predicted to be nondelinquent were, in fact, nondelinquent. However, there were, in fact, 52 nondelinquents, of whom 37 had been predicted as likely delinquents! A more reasonable statement would be that the efficiency in predicting nondelinquency was 29 per cent (15 out of 52!).

The approach to analysis adopted by the authors "rewards" extreme caution in predicting "sure things" and does not take account of all the cases that are missed. The public, of course, wants efficient instruments that do not miss cases. At the very least, the authors owe it to the nonstatistician public—the judges, probation officers, and newspaper reporters—to record their "scores" in the two separate senses of predictive accuracy.

The Citizens' Committee for Children statement of January 1965 made the point that "all prediction is actuarial (deals with rates within groups), not individual." The Youth Board research staff concurred in a summary prepared the following month for the Legislation Information Bureau of the State Charities Aid Association. However, the difference between actuarial and individual prediction carries policy implications not reflected in Youth Board publicity and writing. It also serves to introduce a variety of relevant public policy questions.

Problems of Policy and Practice

At the time of the 1960 public debate on the Youth Board's plan to use the scale, the Council of the Society for the Psychological Study of Social Issues noted in a public statement:

Unless the utmost caution and care are taken, children who are "identified" and labeled as probable future delinquents are likely to be treated and isolated as "bad" children by teachers and others who are now subjected to the virtually hysterical climate of opinion concerning juvenile delinquency. Such treatment is likely to increase the child's sense of social alienation and, thereby, increase the probability of his becoming delinquent or of developing other forms of psychological maladjustment.

To this the Legislation Information Bureau responded: "This last objection seems as frail as a claim that no tuberculin tests should be given because a positive finding might stigmatize the individual." Unfortunately, they miss the point that delinquency is not a disease but rather an administrative category which joins together many behaviors, circumstances, and statuses and which reflects certain societal assessments and strategies for coping with deviance.[17] Social definition and self-identification are apparently large elements in the etiology of some delinquencies.[18] Unlike the case of a recognized disease entity, identification as a delinquent carries negative consequences far more often than it leads to assured help. Those who would help delinquents have yet to assert and sustain their purposes in most public institutional contexts. That is why we continue to interpose due process between the individual and the adjudicatory label. Public definitions and self-image are crucial in this domain, and the question of whether the status of "predicted delinquent" is helpful or harmful (or whether it is helpful in some ways and harmful in others, depending on how and with whom the information is shared) remains a legitimate research issue which cannot be ignored by proponents of delinquency prediction scales.

The need for caution is heightened by the fact that the prediction *is* actuarial: it may tell us that a boy is in a group whose members have an 85 per cent chance of being delinquent. *His* chances do not thereby become 85 out of 100, since special things may operate for him.

The Craig and Glick article of July 1963 tells us that "school personnel were unaware of the boys' delinquency prediction score." (But some *were* sent for treatment!) We are not told, however, what the case would be if and when the research ended and the system became operative. What is to be done by the many individuals and agencies now receiving the published *Manual?* What should be done with a positive prediction? Could it be used to help a child without labeling him in the teacher's eyes—once the research is over? If a prediction is not to go to a teacher, to whom will it go? Who, in fact, will rate the case? Will such ratings be as reliable and valid as those of special research staff?

Another operational issue requiring considerable research has not yet been dealt with in the reports. The results thus far are based on judgments by highly trained and specially employed social workers and psychologists with considerable time for home interviews. The *Manual* is offered to school or social agency personnel who are provided with several pages of written guidance.

Those who would develop an instrument for prediction are under obligation to deal with such issues before it is offered for general use. Otherwise they become involved in the equivalent of encouraging front-page news coverage of the "discovery" of a new drug before they have undertaken research into side effects and checked out the degree of medical supervision essential in its usage. The recent public announcement of a request for funds for planned operational research, repeating announcements of intention in 1960, does not change the scientific status of what is now offered or diminish the validity of the policy questions raised.

The scholar who approaches these matters without commitment to any particular instrument, or the tax-oriented citizen, may in fact choose to focus on the fact that, of the nondelinquent boys in the Youth Board sample, "approximately 22 per cent of the group each year were reported as problems to the school personnel." A considerable body of research literature has reported that, in this respect, teachers are excellent "case finders." [19] Shouldn't one build systems of help around this fact? Many people have contended that all children in need of help should be identified as early as possible—and that the pursuit of a delinquency-identification scale as an *operational* tool is questionable.

If one wants to go beyond the teacher's perceptions and develop a formal instrument, why not perfect one of many quite successful devices now available for identification of those children who may need help, rather than concentrating on the technically more complex job of differentiation by the type of trouble likely to emerge? Such approaches may be less costly, may be more readily used in a school system laboring under limitations of time and personnel, and may also decrease the risk of negative consequences for a child.

Theory and Prediction

The behavioral science theorist may comment at this point that prediction studies are necessary to test causal theories: a full test of a theory of causation demands in effect a predictive effort. True; consequently, one would not wish to discourage predictive efforts. But this is something quite different from producing manuals for translation of predictive devices into operational tools.

The very considerable technical problems of the Glueck research in relation to etiological theory have been thoroughly discussed in the academic literature and are not relevant here—except to note that the groups studied have similar environmental deprivation, thus eliminating this factor as a possible research finding. (Their delinquents and nondelinquents are picked from similar social backgrounds.)

Furthermore, individual delinquency prediction, while it has merits, gives up another possibility, that of identifying neighborhoods or areas which produce high rates of deviance and mobilizing services and resources in such areas, along the lines of the activities sponsored by the President's Committee on Delinquency and Youth Crime and the Office of Economic Opportunity. In addition, new services for youth (education, recreation, job counseling) may be more effective if addressed to "young people" than if shaped for (and stigmatized by reference to) those considered "predelinquent."

Other Issues

The reader may wonder about a critique as long as or longer than some of the individual articles which generated it. The truth is that the Youth Board and D.C. reports are not long enough. A ten-year study in a major policy area is under obligation to publish complete reports. These should provide details which answer questions, such as the following, of concern to researchers and policy makers:

1. Exactly what were the results of the treatment experiments?

2. What do the brief references to reliability statistics mean? Do the researchers know whether their *Manual* instructions would produce comparable ratings by different raters to whom the instrument is offered?

3. How are discrepancies between home interviews and records reconciled in judgments? What of discrepancies among records? How are corrections made for cultural differences?

4. How are the home visits justified when, at the time of rating, none of the children is delinquent? How do people respond to them? On what basis does the *Manual* recommend "the unplanned interview [as] more fruitful?" [20] Is the application of delinquency prediction devices also an excuse for invasion of privacy?

5. Exactly what was done, step by step, in fitting the new three-factor scales to the groups now studied?

What, finally, is the criterion here for the predicted delinquency? The 1957 Youth Board report combined under "delinquency traits" such diverse items as antisocial behavior, mental illness, and unofficial delinquency, as well as delinquent traits and official delinquency. The more recent reports score as correct predictions of delinquency only cases which meet the definition formulated by the Gluecks: "Delinquency refers to repeated acts of a kind which when committed by persons beyond the statutory juvenile court age are punishable as crimes (either felonies or misdemeanors). . . ." However, "Youth Board categorizing of boys as delinquent did not depend on their being so adjudicated by the court." [21]

Trevvett reports: "We define as delinquent any child whose actual offenses are serious or persistent, whether or not he has been formally adjudicated delinquent" (because the local court is understaffed and has a backlog). In fact, "Of the 110 children counted as delinquent, 68 have been thus far so adjudicated." [22]

Those to whom the tables are now offered should obviously have access to much more data about this entire evaluative process. What was *done* by all the children in the Youth Board and D.C. samples classified as delinquent, and how well is this known? Present partial reporting raises more questions than it answers. The evaluators decided, on follow-up, that certain children not in contact with the law were to be classified as delinquents. Did they make "blind" judgments, or did they know the child's prediction?

Conclusion

The issue is not the importance of the home environment or the parent-child relationship. The issue is not the validity of prediction research to test causal hypotheses about delinquency. The issue is the status of efforts to validate the Glueck scale and to determine whether delinquency prediction can be used to help children. A review of the recently published reports discussed above does not permit the expansive conclusions apparently being encouraged.

NOTES

1. M. M. Craig and S. J. Glick, "Application of the Glueck Social Prediction Table on an Ethnic Basis," *Crime and Delinquency*, April 1965, p. 175.

2. *Ibid.*

3. M. M. Craig and S. J. Glick, *A Manual of Procedures for Application of the Glueck Prediction Table* (New York: New York City Youth Board, 1964), p. 3.

4. N. B. Trevvett, "Identifying Delinquency-Prone Children," *Crime and Delinquency*, April 1965, p. 191.

5. S. Glueck, "Some 'Unfinished Business' in the Management of Juvenile Delinquency," *Syracuse Law Review*, Summer 1964, p. 650.

6. See E. Herzog, *Identifying Potential Delinquents*, Children's Bureau Facts and Facets, No. 5 (Washington, D.C.: Government Printing Office, 1960); J. Toby, "Early Identification and Intensive Treatment of Pre-Delinquents," *Social Work*, July 1961; Citizens' Committee for Children of New York and Columbia University School of Social Work Research Center, *Research and Potential Application of Research in Probation, Parole, Delinquency Prediction* (New York: 1961); *Newsday*, Jan. 29, 1965, for statements by Dr. Frank Hartung (Wayne University), Prof. Harwin Voss (San Diego State College), Sol Rubin (NCCD), and Citizens' Committee for Children of New York, "The Status of the New York City Youth Board's Delinquency Prediction" (New York: January 1965, mimeo.).

7. To simplify communication and analysis, we concentrate mainly on the New York City Youth Board research, which has published somewhat more extensively, has been carried out more intensively, and has in some ways guided the D.C. undertaking.

8. Sheldon and Eleanor Glueck, *Unraveling Juvenile Delinquency* (Cambridge, Mass.: Harvard University Press, 1950). Subsequent reports by the Gluecks of their thinking about prediction and their assessment of progress appear in a number of places. The reader may wish to consult footnotes to the Craig and Glick articles cited *supra* note 1 and *infra* note 12, and the Gluecks' Foreword to the Youth Board *Manual, supra* note 3, as well as E. T. Glueck, "Toward Improving the Identification of Delinquents" and "Toward Further Improving the Identification of Delinquents," *Journal of Criminal Law, Criminology, and Police Science*, June 1962 and June 1963, respectively. Also see Sheldon and Eleanor Glueck, *Predicting Delinquency and Crime* (Cambridge, Mass.: Harvard University Press, 1959).

9. For a sampling, see S. Rubin, "Illusions in a Research Study—Unraveling Juvenile Delinquency," *Crime and Juvenile Delinquency* (New York: Oceana Publications, 1958), pp. 219–234. Also see A. J. Kahn, "Analysis of Methodology of Unraveling Juvenile Delinquency," *An Approach to Measuring Results in Social Work*, D. G. French, ed. (New York: Columbia University Press, 1952), pp. 161–172.

10. Cited in the several items in *supra* note 8.

11. New York City Youth Board, *An Experiment in the Validation of the Glueck Prediction Scale* (New York: 1957).

12. M. M. Craig and S. J. Glick, "Ten Years' Experience with the Glueck Social Prediction Table," *Crime and Delinquency*, July 1963, pp. 249–261.

13. Craig and Glick, *supra* note 1.

14. Citizens' Committee for Children of New York and Columbia University School of Social Work Research Center, *Research and Potential Application of Research in Probation, Parole, Delinquency Prediction* (New York: 1961).

15. Craig and Glick, *supra* note 1, p. 178, note 7.

16. Trevvett, *supra* note 4.

17. For a discussion see A. J. Kahn, "Social Work and the Control of Delinquency," *Social Work*, July 1965, and *Planning Community Services for Children in Trouble* (New York: Columbia University Press, 1963).

18. See A. Cohen, *Delinquency Boys: The Culture of the Gang* (New York: The Free

Press of Glencoe, 1955), and R. A. Cloward and L. E. Ohlin, *Delinquency and Opportunity* (New York: The Free Press of Glencoe, 1960).

19. B. B. Khleif, "Teachers as Predictors of Juvenile Delinquency and Psychiatric Disturbance," *Social Problems,* Winter 1964, pp. 270–282. Major studies are listed under footnote 1 of the Khleif article.

20. Craig and Glick, *supra* note 3, p. 19.

21. Craig and Glick, *supra* note 1, p. 177.

22. Trevvett, *supra* note 4, p. 188.

39: Validating Prediction Scales /
P. G. Ward

In recent articles much discussion has taken place concerning the validation and efficiency of prediction scales. There is a marked tendency for the arguments put forward by both sides to be led off into side issues because of the confounding of the concept of validity with several other concepts which are more strictly related to variations between populations. The technique of validation commonly used at present is critically examined in this article and it is shown that this technique can lead to the rejection of valid prediction scales as invalid because the criterion used in this technique is not simply dependent upon validity but on the simultaneous satisfaction of other conditions. The problems of the efficiency and practical use of prediction scales are also considered.

In a recent article, entitled "The Case of the Premature Claims," Professor Kahn (1965) has severely criticised the efforts of the New York City Youth Board to validate the Glueck Social Prediction Scale. While much of Kahn's criticism is well founded, the basic assumptions which both he and Craig and Glick (1965, 1963) make about the technique used to validate a prediction scale could well be subjected to critical analysis.

A particularly well-known technique of validating a prediction scale has become traditional in the field of criminology. This technique consists of using data from sample (A) of known delinquents and non-delinquents to obtain a prediction scale which separates the sample into sub-groups containing high, medium, and low proportions of delinquents. A second sample is then taken in which each subject's status as delinquent or non-delinquent is unknown. The sample (B) is later separated into the same sub-groups as sample (A) and the proportion of delinquents found in each sub-group of (B) is

From P. G. Ward, "Validating Prediction Scales—The Case of the False Technique," *British Journal of Criminology* 7:1 (1967): 36–42; 43–44.

compared with the proportion originally found in the corresponding sub-group of (A). This technique does not merely test validity. For the criteria imposed by this technique to be satisfied, it is not sufficient that the scale be valid but also that the following three conditions be met:

(a) The original and validation samples must be samples of the same population.
(b) Social conditions must remain stable over the period of time covering the original test and the validation.
(c) The original sample and the validation sample must *both* be representative of the population.

These conditions are independent of validity, and unless evidence is available that the conditions have been met it is improper to reject a scale as invalid simply because it fails to meet the criteria imposed by the traditional technique. Examples will later be given of cases where a valid scale would fail to meet the criteria because of failure to comply with the conditions outlined above.

What Is Validity?

One can distinguish several types of validity but that with which criminologists are most concerned is what is called empirical validity. "Essentially such validity refers to the relation between test scores and a criterion, the latter being an independent and direct measure of that which the test is designed to predict" (Anastasi, 1957, pp. 127–131). The word "test" used in the previous quotation refers to psychological tests used to predict success in academic courses. A score on such a test is, of course, simply a prediction scale score.

Craig and Glick (1963) applied the Gluecks' Five Factor Scale (1950) to a sample of young children from a high delinquency area of New York. Subsequently, their result showed that the scale separated the sample into subgroups of significantly different probabilities of delinquency. This Five Factor Scale is therefore empirically valid, and the fact that the scale "over-predicts" when compared with the results obtained on a sample of Bostonians is immaterial. Craig and Glick (1965), however, have rejected the Five Factor Scale and attempted to substitute a new scale, which has been rightly criticised by Kahn as not validated because it was prepared when results were available to indicate the differences between the results of New York and Boston, and the new scale was chosen to minimise these differences.

The failure of the two sets of results to compare could be the result of any or all of the conditions outlined above. To illustrate how failure to observe each of these conditions can affect the proportion of cases in a given subgroup, even when the scale used is valid, examples of each case will now be given.

Samples from Different Populations

Consider an I.Q. test used as a predictor of later university success. It is generally conceded that such tests are valid without being 100 per cent accurate. Suppose an experimenter applies the validation technique described above, using for sample (A) pre-university youths from families where the father is professionally employed, and for sample (B) youths from families where the father is an unskilled worker. In both samples, the experimenter would almost certainly find that the group with I.Q. 130 + would have a higher proportion of university graduates than the group with I.Q. 120–129. However, it is also almost certain that the proportion of graduates in a sub-group of sample (B) would be significantly smaller in the proportion in the corresponding sub-group of (A).

This is explicable in terms of the different expectations of, and the relative difference of, the financial burden to the families of the two samples. Hence it can be seen that, before a difference in the proportions meeting the criterion in samples (A) and (B) (in corresponding sub-groups) can be ascribed to a failure in validity, it must be shown that (A) and (B) are samples of the same population. In the New York study differences in the ethnic composition of the sample compared with the original Boston sample show that this condition was not met.

Different Social Conditions

Consider the same I.Q. test as in the previous example, with sample (A) the same sample as before and sample (B) from the same population some years later. Suppose during this period coaching in answering items similar to those used in the test has become generally available, so that on the average the scores that the population obtained on the test have increased by five points. The I.Q. test will still be valid but the proportion of graduates in any sub-group will have dropped slightly when compared with the original sample. This illustrates the necessity of stable social conditions.

Samples Not Representative of Population

The best example of this is to consider two hypothetical experiments using the same prediction scale in the same district. The first experimenter takes a random sample of 250 known delinquents and 250 non-delinquents from the population and finds the following results set out in Table 39–1 below.

The second experimenter, knowing the delinquency rate in the population is 20 per cent, decides to take a sample which will be representative of the population and therefore takes 100 delinquents and 400 non-delinquents. As-

Table 39-1

	Delinquent	Non-Delinquent
High Risk	160	10
Medium Risk	80	80
Low Risk	10	160
Total	250	250

Table 39-2

	Delinquent	Non-Delinquent
High Risk	64	16
Medium Risk	32	128
Low Risk	4	256
Total	100	400

Table 39-3

	Experimenter I	Experimenter II
High Risk	94.1%	80.0%
Medium Risk	50.0%	20.0%
Low Risk	5.9%	1.5%

suming sampling fluctuations cancel out in these two experiments, the second experimenter will find only 40 per cent as many delinquents and 60 per cent more non-delinquents in each risk category compared with the results of the first experimenter. His expected results will therefore be as shown in Table 39–2.

Table 39–3 compares the probability of delinquency calculated by each experimenter for each risk group.

This example shows that the proportion of delinquents taken in the sample will markedly affect the calculated probability of delinquency. When the above examples are considered, it can be seen that it is very unlikely that the results of a sample in New York should match those of a sample from Boston, with a population of different ethnic composition, probably subject to different social conditions, and with a significantly higher proportion of delinquents in the sample.

A similar version of this argument has been put forward by Reiss (1951) but rejected by Professor Glueck (1959, pp. 1006–1007), who considers that the following argument shows the essential fallacy in this kind of reasoning: "Suppose a public health official were testing the bacterial and chemical content of two samples of water drawn from two lakes and suppose that Lake No. 1 was only one-tenth the size of Lake No. 2. Now assume he found Lake

No. 1 shows the water to be non-drinkable but in Lake No. 2 it is safely drinkable, while a mixture of the two is potable or not depending upon the proportion of water from each of the samples mixed together. Would the fact that one lake is much smaller than the other make any serious difference in his ability to predict whether subsequent samples of water drawn from each of these lakes or various combinations thereof would be drinkable or not?"

Professor Glueck obviously means this situation to be an analogue of the delinquency prediction situation, but it is difficult to ascertain exactly what is supposed to be directly analogous to what. Apparently Lake 1 represents delinquents and Lake 2 non-delinquents, while differences in potability represent prediction score, in so far as it is possible to predict what percentage of a sample came from Lake 1 and what from Lake 2 by analysis of potability. This immediately shows up the falseness of the analogy, as a sample from Lake 1 split into 500 parts gives 500 equally unpotable units, whereas a sample of 500 delinquents gives 500 widely differing prediction scores. Glueck's analogy is only applicable to the case where all the delinquents have a different prediction score from that of the non-delinquents.

To make the two-lake model analogous to the delinquency prediction situation, consider Lake 1 to have a large number of salt springs scattered randomly throughout its area and Lake 2 to have a small number similarly scattered in it. An experimenter is randomly taking measurements on samples from both lakes. If he takes "x" measurements from Lake 1 and "y" measurements from Lake 2 and if the chance of finding a measurement greater than 10 mg. of salt/litre is 50 per cent in Lake 1 and 20 per cent in Lake 2, then the percentage coming from Lake 1 of all the samples with a salt content greater than 10 mg. of salt/litre will be on the average:

$$\text{Per cent from Lake 1} = \frac{50x}{50x + 20y}$$

This percentage is obviously not independent of x and y but this is precisely analogous to the procedure carried out in determining the probability of delinquency in scaling studies. It follows, therefore, that if a prediction scale showing probabilities of delinquency for various category groups is required to predict a given population, then the original sample on which the prediction scale is based must be a stratified random sample of that population. This requirement is all too frequently ignored.

It must be stressed again that, subject to some reservations due to the lack of objectivity of the definition of delinquency used by Craig and Glick (1963), the Five Factor Scale of the Gluecks validly predicted delinquency in New York. Considering the length of time over which the study lasted, the efficiency of prediction appears very good. To achieve this efficiency, however, it may be necessary, as Kahn (1965) points out, to use only highly trained personnel to make the ratings on which the scale is based.

As well as critically examining the New York study, Kahn has levelled criticisms at some aspects of prediction scaling in general. These are:

(a) The efficiency of prediction scales is overrated.
(b) Prediction scales tend to "label" children and thus tend to force them into delinquent roles.
(c) Prediction scaling research is diverting money from projects more likely to reduce delinquency.

What Is the Efficiency of Prediction Scales?

It is possible to calculate the efficiency of prediction scales in a variety of ways. Apart from the natural tendency of the supporters of these devices to use the method giving the highest figures and of their critics to use the method giving the lowest, there exist at least two criteria which should be considered when selecting an appropriate measure of efficiency: (a) The purpose for which the scale is devised. (b) The relative efficiency of the scale compared with other methods of prediction.

If the principal of an institution, who has to select candidates for a certain course and who needs at least a certain number of graduates from the course each year, uses a predictive test, the appropriate measure of the efficiency of the test is the smallest number of candidates who can be selected with confidence that the required number of successful candidates will be obtained.

In the field of delinquency prediction, on the other hand, one is usually more interested in the comparative efficiency of the scale and some other method of predicting such as the judgments of trained persons. Mannheim and Wilkins (1955) have given an extensive discussion of this problem and provided a rational method of calculating relative efficiency. It is strongly suggested that this measure of efficiency be generally adopted.

Do Prediction Scales Label Children?

While Kahn's (1965) criticism that prediction scaling techniques may tend to force children into delinquent roles by giving them a bad name has a great deal of common-sense appeal, it would be wise to consider whether there is any real evidence of this effect in the Craig and Glick (1965) study. These workers state that they readjusted their initial ratings so that the number of boys rated potentially delinquent was in proportion to the number of delinquents in the neighbourhood. Assuming they thought that the probability of delinquency given for the Boston sample was going to apply in New York (which appears plain from their rejection of the Five Factor Scale) then obviously they expect $(126 \text{x} \cdot 082 + 57 \text{x} \cdot 37 + \ldots)$ or approximately seventy-two delinquents. Actually, their sample was found to contain only 40 delinquents, some of these not even officially adjudged delinquent. Three possibilities arise: (a) Craig and Glick's estimate was wrong. (b) There was a marked drop in delinquency in the area sampled. (c) There was a marked drop in delinquency in the sample relative to the average delinquency of the area. Whatever the explanation, there is no evidence that the labelling of the children caused any increase in delinquency in the sample.

REFERENCES

ANASTASI, A. (1957). *Psychological Testing.* New York: Macmillan.

CRAIG, M. M. and GLICK, S. J. (1963). "Ten Years Experience with the Glueck Social Prediction Table." *Crime and Delinquency, 9,* 244–261.

CRAIG, M. M. and GLICK, S. J. (1965). "Application of the Glueck Table on an Ethnic Basis." *Crime and Delinquency, 11,* 137–161.

GLUECK, S. and GLUECK, E. (1950). *Unraveling Juvenile Delinquency.* Cambridge, Mass.: Harvard Univ. Press.

GLUECK, S. (ed.) (1959). *The Problem of Delinquency.* Boston: Houghton Mifflin.

KAHN, A. J. (1965). "The Case of the Premature Claims." *Crime and Delinquency, 11,* 217–228.

MANNHEIM, H. and WILKINS, L. T. (1955). *Prediction Methods in Relation to Borstal Training.* London: H.M.S.O.

POWERS, E. and WITMER, H. L. (1950). *An Experiment in the Prevention of Delinquency.* New York: Columb. U.P.

REISS, A. (1951). "*Unraveling Juvenile Delinquency.* II. An Appraisal of the Research Methods." *American Journal of Sociology, 57,* 115–120.

Index

435